IMAGE DATA COMPRESSION

BLOCK TRUNCATION CODING

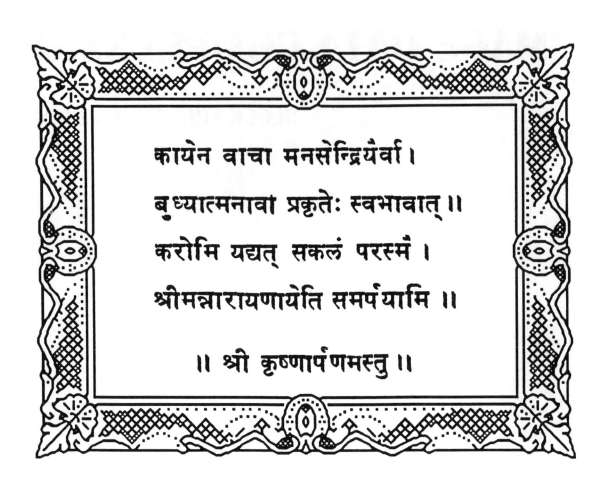

कायेन वाचा मनसेन्द्रियैर्वा ।
बुध्यात्मनावा प्रकृतेः स्वभावात् ॥
करोमि यद्यत् सकलं परस्मैं ।
श्रीमन्नारायणायेति समर्पयामि ॥

॥ श्री कृष्णार्पणमस्तु ॥

IMAGE DATA COMPRESSION

BLOCK TRUNCATION CODING

BELUR V. DASARATHY

IEEE Computer Society Press
Los Alamitos, California

Washington • Brussels • Tokyo

Library of Congress Cataloging-in-Publication Data

Image data compression: block truncation coding / [compiled by] Belur V. Dasarathy.
      p.   cm
  Includes bibliographical references (p.).
  ISBN 0-8186-6847-4
    1. Image processing—Digital techniques.   2. Image compression–Data processing.
    3. Coding theory.   I. Dasarathy, Belur V.
TA1637.I423   1995
621.36 ' 7—dc20
                                   94-45993
                                      CIP

Published by the
IEEE Computer Society Press
10662 Los Vaqueros Circle
P.O. Box 3014
Los Alamitos, CA 90720-1264

IEEE Computer Society Press Order Number BP06847
IEEE Catalog Number EH0414-3
Library of Congress Number 94-45993
ISBN 0-8186-6847-4

Additional copies can be ordered from

IEEE Computer Society Press Customer Service Center 10662 Los Vaqueros Circle P.O. Box 3014 Los Alamitos, CA 90720-1264 Tel: (714) 821-8380 Fax: (714) 821-4641 Email: cs.books@computer.org	IEEE Service Center 445 Hoes Lane P.O. Box 1331 Piscataway, NJ 08855-1331 Tel: (908) 981-1393 Fax: (908) 981-9667 mis.custserv@computer.org	IEEE Computer Society 13, avenue de l'Aquilon B-1200 Brussels BELGIUM Tel: +32-2-770-2198 Fax: +32-2-770-8505 euro.ofc@computer.org	IEEE Computer Society Ooshima Building 2-19-1 Minami-Aoyama Minato-ku, Tokyo 107 JAPAN Tel: +81-3-3408-3118 Fax: +81-3-3408-3553 tokyo.ofc@computer.org

Technical Editor: A.R.K. Sastry
Production Editor: Lisa O'Conner
Cover Artist: Alex Torres

Printed in the United States of America by Braun-Brumfield, Inc.
99 98 97 96   4 3 2 1

The Institute of Electrical and Electronics Engineers, Inc.

CONTENTS

PREFACE

A preface is traditionally an author's opportunity for rationalizing the destruction of trees necessitated by the publication of a book. Expressed in these lofty terms, it may be difficult to justify most publications, including this one. At a more mundane level, however, providing the warrant for a book on block truncation coding (BTC) techniques is not much of a challenge—especially in view of the recent resurgence of interest in the area of data compression. The reasons for choosing this topic were many and, for the most part, objective. While the conceptual elegance of BTC was largely responsible for the initial attraction, other technical aspects, such as quality of performance relative to its computational requirements and flexibility in combining with other methods to form effective hybrid schemes, confirmed the desirability of the venture.

The book is divided into two parts. Part A, consisting of three chapters, begins with an introduction to the data compression field, mainly to provide a backdrop to the BTC area and show how BTC fits into the overall picture. This introduction includes a bibliography of nearly eight hundred references, the majority of which are recent publications covering different facets of data compression. The bibliography is meant to be representative only; an exhaustive list would span more than a few thousand entries, a number outside the scope of this effort. The second chapter delves into the developments in BTC and chronologically lays out the evolution of this technique over the past sixteen years. This chapter reflects the renewed attention BTC has received in recent years, thereby confirming the timeliness of this publication. Chapter 3 is devoted to experimental experience with BTC, offering additional insights into both the conceptual and computational aspects of the methodology. The presentation in Part A ends with a glossary of all the acronyms encountered in this tutorial. Acronyms, which are, in effect, but one form of data compression, are a common phenomenon in the data compression literature; hence the inclusion of this glossary to serve as a codebook for their decompression and understanding.

Part B, which starts with an overview, is divided into five chapters. Chapters 4 through 7, entitled "Core Contributions," "Appreciable Advances," "Innovative Implementations," and "Harmonious Hybrids," provide a brief introduction to the corresponding studies included as reprints therein. Chapter 8, "Desirable Developments," offers a road map to the future of BTC, with a brief discussion on promising avenues of investigation.

As newer studies continue to appear in the BTC area, it has been difficult to wrap up the marathon effort and mail the manuscript off to the publisher. (Additions have been made right up to the time of going to press.) On the one hand there is an unavoidable sense of incompleteness about it; on the other hand there is the satisfaction that the topic is of current interest and hence propitious. The book is therefore being brought out in the hope that, despite its shortfalls, it will add impetus to further developments in the BTC area.

Acknowledgments

The prospect of failing to recognize those who helped or supported this marathon effort in some fashion makes this task particularly arduous. However, I hope any such failures will be attributed appropriately to a penchant for data compression rather than to carelessness or disregard.

The continued patience and understanding of my wife, Harini (who, incidentally, shared the hardly pleasant task of proofreading), and our sons, Raghava (who did his bit in working out the numerical examples) and Keshava (who escaped these chores by going away to college just in time), in putting up with my constant, almost worn-out, excuse of "I don't have time for that; I have to work on my books!" deserve the top billing. I also acknowledge my first teacher, my mother, Andal, whose continued interest in her son's accomplishments has been a motivating factor. My sister, Sheela, who has her own accomplishments in the area of data compression, has also indirectly influenced this effort.

The support provided by my employers, Tom Baumbach, Executive Vice-President, and Marc Bendickson, President, of Dynetics, Inc. is sincerely appreciated. I express my gratitude to Dr. A.R.K. Sastry, Technical Editor, IEEE Computer Society, for ably navigating the book through the turbulent waters of the long-drawn-out review process. Thanks are also due to the anonymous reviewers (including, I suspect from the wording of the reviews, one of the originators of the block truncation coding concept) for their detailed and valuable comments that improved the manuscript considerably. Finally, I also acknowledge the efforts of the many members of the production staff at IEEE Computer Society Press who worked on the book.

Chapter 1
Data Compression:
An Overview

The main objective of this book is to present a comprehensive tutorial on *block truncation coding* (BTC) techniques—a specialized area within the data compression domain. The choice of this area as the topic for a book was driven by several factors, including the conceptual simplicity and elegance of BTC. However, its qualitative performance relative to its computational requirements justified the subsequent detailed study and relative assessment. Admittedly, computational complexity is not the critical issue it was when BTC was first conceived, thanks largely to the phenomenal progress achieved in computational hardware over the past decade. The renewed interest in BTC in recent years is, however, evidence enough of the timeliness of the topic. This case is further strengthened by BTC's capacity to be combined with other recently popular data compression techniques, such as vector quantization and subband coding, to yield highly effective hybrid data compression tools.

In order to lay a proper foundation for this study, it is desirable to present an overview of data compression as a whole to demonstrate how BTC techniques fit into the overall field. The field of data compression—the concepts, tools, and techniques employed in achieving compaction in the volume of data with little or no loss of information—is indeed vast; accordingly, no attempt is made here to provide an exhaustive review. This overview does include a bibliography with nearly 800 entries, but this bibliography is representative rather than exhaustive. It is heavily weighted toward recent publications, not only because they represent the state of the art, but also because earlier work has been included in previous survey papers listed here and thus is indirectly cited in the bibliography. As a prerequisite to the presentation of such an overview, it is appropriate to define the related terminology and delineate the criteria for comparing performance of different techniques. The objectives of data compression are well known and include reduced memory requirements for data storage and more efficient data transmission. An excellent compilation of data compression algorithms is offered by Nelson in his comprehensive 1991 book [D255][1] on data compression.

---

[1] The numbers in parentheses starting with the letter D refer to the citations listed under the general bibliography on data compression presented at the end of this chapter.

COMPARISON CRITERIA

A review of the data compression literature shows that there are generally three accepted criteria for relative evaluation of different data compression techniques:

- Compression ratio (or, inversely, bits/pixel)
- Output-image fidelity (or, inversely, an error measure)
- Computational costs (or, inversely, computational ease)

Thus, compression techniques are best evaluated in a relative sense in a three-dimensional space, as shown in **Figure 1-1**. While one technique, T1, may have a high compression ratio with low image fidelity and another technique, T2, may have a low compression ratio with high image fidelity, a third technique, T3, may have a moderate compression ratio and medium fidelity. Moreover, each of these techniques will have its own level of computational costs associated with it.

Compression ratio is the fundamental measure of performance of a data compression process; it defines the main goal of the process and offers a quantitative assessment of its effectiveness. A direct quantitative measure of the actual data compaction achieved by the coding method, the compression ratio is the ratio of the bits/pixel in the original image to the bits/pixel in the compressed image. In the context of many, if not most, imagery applications, 8 bits/pixel is common for the input image. Hence, instead of the actual compression ratio, the bits/pixel of the compressed image itself is often viewed,

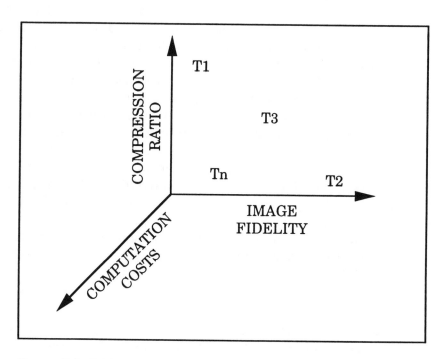

Figure 1-1. Data compression techniques evaluation space.

inversely, as the measure of compression; that is, the lower the number of bits/pixel required to describe the image, the higher the compression ratio. While the two are thus equivalent measures, the hardware community tends to prefer bits/pixel since it offers a measure of the system requirements in terms of memory, processing speed, and the like. On the other hand, compression ratio is more descriptive of the compression process. Usage of one measure or the other is a matter of personal choice rather than one based on scientific reasoning.

Image fidelity, a qualitative description of the compression process, is the next important criterion. It is worthy of note, however, that the two criteria are highly coupled. Evaluation of different schemes requires a good measure of distortion or loss of information caused by data compression. An obvious measure would be one that evaluates the differences in image intensity values between the original image and the reconstructed image across the whole scene. The different measures commonly specified for this purpose are:

- MSE—mean square error
- RMS—root mean square error
- NMSE—normalized MSE
- NRMS—normalized RMS error

Note that the mean square error and its variants are not, by themselves, enough to perform the qualitative assessment. Although subjective, visual comparisons are considered desirable, if not essential, when the image is a picture designed for human visual consumption, as in picture phones. We can also define other special-purpose performance measures that are suited for specific classes of techniques only, as does the 1972 study by Pearl, Andrews, and Pratt [D11], which presents measures designed for evaluation of transform coding techniques. When images are to be subsequently processed through statistical procedures, the best measure may be the fidelity of the statistics of the image regions rather than the individual pixel intensities. There is, in fact, no single unique measure to assess the image fidelity that will be useful across applications.

The next criterion of significance is the computational cost of accomplishing data compaction. The two facets of this criterion are the cost of compression and the cost of decompression (the process of retrieving the original image from the compressed version). In the context of data compression for minimal storage applications, the cost of compression can be viewed as a one-time cost and hence as relatively less significant than the cost of decompression, which must be incurred every time an image is to be retrieved from storage. In the context of compression designed for fast data transmission applications, the relative costs of compression at one end and decompression at the other may be equally significant.

Accordingly, there are three trade-off factors to be considered in a relative assessment of different compression schemes: compression ratio, image fidelity, and computational costs. In general, the image fidelity decreases with increases in the compression ratio. Conversely, an increase in image fidelity is almost always accompanied by a corresponding increase in the total computational costs. The trade-off thus represents a problem in a three-dimensional space, with image fidelity being a function dependent on the total computational (compression and decompression) costs incurred as well as the compression ratio achieved. In fact, there is both the need and scope to develop formal relative assessment procedures for comparing different compression techniques jointly on the basis of all of the different viewpoints discussed above. While research along these lines is currently under way in-house, a discussion thereof is beyond the scope of this book. Accordingly, with these basic definitions in place, we now proceed to a review of some of the well-known categories of data compression techniques.

OVERVIEW

A large literature (possibly in excess of a few thousand publications) currently exists in the field of data compression techniques. Over the past three decades a multitude of surveys, reviews, and bibliographic papers [D5, D13, D32, D44, D45, D49, D50, D72, D226] have been written covering different segments of developments in this area, each citing hundreds of studies. For example, the 1967 paper by Andrews, Davies, and Schwarz [D5] groups the numerous adaptive data compression techniques into four categories and reviews the progress made in each category. The 1974 survey by Habibi and Robinson [D13] covers similar ground but offers more detail in certain aspects by providing some experimental results. A subsequent survey by Habibi [D32] in 1977 stresses the adaptive aspects of these techniques.

The 1980 review by Netravali and Limb [D44] covers a much broader range of topics under the label of picture encoding. Data compression, although representing only one aspect of concern, is covered therein in great detail. It has a bibliography of more than two hundred articles. The later review by Jain [D49], published in 1981, concentrates fully on the data compression aspects of image coding and provides a good summary of most of the different techniques reported up to about 1980. However, an important class of techniques referred to as BTC schemes (first reported in 1979 [D42]) is not covered by this review. The review concludes in favor of transform and hybrid techniques over differential pulse code modulation (DPCM) techniques for intraframe data compression. Jain's review also has more than two hundred references listed, with a fair overlap with the references listed in the previous survey [D44]. Although significant overlaps exist among these different bibliographic listings, an exhaustive compilation covering all aspects of the data compression field would span several thousand citations.

Although it is beyond the scope of this introductory overview to cover all the developments in image compression exhaustively, some key contributions that initiated whole new avenues of research are included, such as the now classic 1952 paper by Huffman [D2], which put forth what has since come to be known as Huffman coding. The objective here is to show how BTC techniques relate to the other areas in the data compression field. Accordingly, this overview primarily touches upon the techniques that deal with the main domain of application of BTC techniques—namely, the compression aspects of image data. Not addressed are effects of channel errors and other noise considerations that arise in the context of transmission of images. While not exhaustive, the coverage here is comprehensive enough to acknowledge all the different classes of techniques. Accordingly, the developments in the field can be broadly classified as detailed below.

CONCEPTUAL CATEGORIES

Different authors have different perspectives for categorizing data compression techniques. For example, in 1967, Andrews, Davies, and Schwarz [D5] categorized them into four groups: direct data compression, transformation compression, parameter extraction compression, and selective monitoring compression. However, from the most basic perspective, the compression area can be categorized into two groups:

- Distortionless, or error-free, data compaction
- Error-prone, or lossy, data compression

Error-free data compaction permits a reconstruction resulting in an exact reproduction of the original image. These techniques are also variously referred to in the literature as lossless, information-preserving, or reversible methods of data compression. The constraint of error-free recovery automatically restricts the freedom of action; hence, relatively less work has been reported in this category under image data compression. However, in the classic (one-dimensional) data compression arena, for example, as in the compression of information in the form of data or character strings, considerable work has been reported in the computer science and communications literature. A survey of these studies is, however, outside the purview of this study.

Under the category of error-prone data compression, the cost of the compression achieved includes not only the cost of the process of compression and decompression, but also a cost in terms of some (presumably tolerable) distortion of the original image. These classes of compression schemes are referred to variously as lossy, non–information-preserving, or irreversible methods.

Most of the reported work in the field of data compression falls loosely under the second category, which can be further grouped into transform coding and spatial coding techniques. Some of the non–error-free methods proposed recently represent a hybrid of these two subclasses. The ensuing presentation will first cover briefly the error-free encoding and then review the rest according to the conceptual underpinnings of the approach.

ERROR-FREE OR LOSSLESS ENCODING

Encoding schemes, such as run-length encoding, Huffman coding [D2—a pioneering study first reported in 1952; see also D38, D64, D122, D212, D296, D303, D510, D612, D643, D738], and arithmetic coding [D51, D69, D118, D139, D142–143, D166, D168, D243, D275, D296, D314, D352, D416–D417, D423–424, D443, D445–446, D487, D491, D514, D534, D580, D610, D661–662, D706], fall into this error-free category, in which information is essentially compacted or packed for storage and/or transmission through redundancy reduction and optimal coding. Some additional examples of developments in arithmetic coding are the significant works of Langdon and Rissanen [D51] in 1981 and more recently that of Howard and Vitter [D423–424] in 1992. Under these schemes, the images can be retrieved essentially intact when needed. The only costs involved in these methods are the costs of encoding and decoding. A good example of this class of compression tools is the widely available UNIX-based compression utility CLIX, which is based on a modified version of the Lempel–Ziv algorithm [D29] discussed in the paper by Welch [D59] in 1984. Experience with this utility has shown that a compression ratio in the range of 1.2–4 or better is achievable in remotely sensed data sets. Most of these schemes are truly effective only for images with large homogeneous areas, that is, those with slowly changing values (which makes differences small), or those having common substring patterns, in which long substrings may be replaced by short codes. Until recently, this algorithm and variants thereof were available only in software. However, during the past year special-purpose hardware, a silicon engine, implementing a variant of this algorithm, namely adaptive lossless data compression, has been introduced by IBM and very recently versions approaching a throughput of 40 Mbytes/sec have been announced.

Also falling under this category are the schemes in which successive values are estimated a priori (based on interpolation or extrapolation of other known values) and only the differences between the estimated and actual values are stored. Presumably, fewer bits/pixel are needed to store these differences than are required for storing the actual values themselves. In theory, these deterministically predictive schemes (which should be clearly distinguished from such probabilistic prediction schemes as DPCM) are fully reversible and can retrieve the original image (except for the errors caused by computational round-off errors and quantization-caused errors). A variation to these is the bit-plane encoding technique discussed in 1966 by Schwartz and Barker [D4] wherein the N-bit gray-scale image is broken up into N binary images, each coded and stored independently with its own optimal coding. Also, these techniques are generally applied in the spatial domain, although Huffman-like codes can be applied elsewhere as well. A 1988 report on these noise-free or lossless coding techniques can be found in a paper by Blumer in the proceedings of a workshop on scientific data compression [D76] sponsored by NASA.

TRANSFORM TECHNIQUES

Transform techniques, which were first discussed in detail by Wintz [D12] in 1972, are frequency domain approaches. They involve reversible linear transformations leading to decorrelated coefficients representing the image in the transformed space. Both one- and two-dimensional transforms can be visualized. In the former case, the one-dimensional transform can be reapplied for the second dimension or another restructuring of the data can be visualized to permit viewing the data as a one-dimensional data set. Alternatively, another technique such as DPCM can be used for the second dimension to derive a hybrid approach. However, in every case, transform techniques necessarily result in some image distortion on retrieval because some of the frequency domain coefficients must be dropped to achieve the required data compression. A variety of such transform techniques have been proposed in the literature over the years. Some prominent transform techniques (which in their implementation are usually fast discrete versions applied to subimage blocks rather than to the image as a whole) are

- Karhunen–Loeve (KL) transforms [D26]
- Fourier transforms [D61]
- Hadamard transforms [D6, D28]
- Cosine transforms [D14, D30, D53, D104, D114, D117, D216–217, D232, D288, D331, D395, D399, D429, D451–452, D520, D557, D569, D575, D578, D604, D623, D672–673, D681, D732, D759, D767]
- Haar transforms [D61]
- Walsh transforms [D12]
- Walsh–Hadamard transforms [D12]
- Hadamard–Haar transforms [D22]
- Slant transforms [D20]
- Singular value decomposition (SVD) transforms [D24, D358]
- Wavelet transforms [D106, D121, D131, D158–159, D252, D264–265, D285–286, D366, D370–371, D373, D394, D4043–404, D406, D455–457, D505, D519, D539, D555–556, D558–562, D573, D592, D605, D616, D670–671, D691, D694–695, D701, D705, D750, D761, D775]

KL Transforms

Of these different transform techniques, the Karhunen–Loeve (KL) transform represents the theoretically optimal approach; but it is considered computationally expensive, requiring inversion of a matrix of size $D \times D$, where $D = N*N$ and N is the size of the subimage block being transformed. Admittedly, this optimality is based on the minimal mean square error criterion and as such does not take into account visual fidelity. The compression achieved and the resulting image distortions are functions of the number of coefficients retained and the number of quantization levels used in storing these coefficients. For example, if only half the coefficients are retained and only 4 bits (16 levels) are used for storing these coefficients, only 2 bits/pixel are required to store the image; that is, a compression ratio of 4 is achieved for an input image of 8 bits/pixel. Various nonuniform quantization strategies can be construed to further improve the compression ratio gained under the approach without additional degradation of the image fidelity. However, variable-length output codes have their own inherent disadvantages in terms of possible interpretation problems.

Fourier Transforms

Comparatively, Fourier transforms, the best known of these transforms, are suboptimal in the sense that the coefficients derived by the transform are not uncorrelated. But as the sample size increases, the Fourier transform asymptotically becomes equivalent to the KL transform. As before, the number of coefficients retained and the quantization levels, as well as quantization strategies, dictate the results in terms of image fidelity and compression ratios.

Hadamard Transforms

Hadamard transforms are computationally the most efficient, as the Hadamard matrix is composed solely of +1s and −1s only. Computation of the Hadamard transform does not require multiplications. As in Fourier transforms, the coefficients are not completely uncorrelated, but still less correlated than the input-image pixels. As earlier, normalization and quantization strategies dictate the quality of results.

Discrete Cosine Transforms

Discrete cosine transforms (DCT) are a more recent example of transform methods that are gaining popularity. The DCT approach avoids some of the artifacts induced by the Fourier transform method, and it comes closest to the KL transform in its optimality of performance. The DCT can be implemented as a double-sized fast Fourier transform (FFT) by zero padding the data to double its size. A faster and more direct DCT approach was reported by Chen, Smith, and Fralick in 1977 [D30]; this approach is claimed to be six times more efficient in terms of computational complexity. Given the large number of algorithmic and computational-aspects–oriented studies that have been reported on the subject of DCT, a separate review of this topic is justified. Indeed, DCT is the key component of the baseline system [D114, D190, D195, D227, D241, D482, D557, D607] developed over the past several years by the Joint Photographic Experts Group (JPEG). It has also been found to have potential for use in conjunction with BTC techniques as discussed in Chapters 2 and 7.

Haar, Walsh, and Walsh–Hadamard Transforms

Other transforms that have found application in the field of data compression include the Haar transform [D61], the Walsh transform [D12], and the Walsh–Hadamard transform [D12].

Slant Transforms

Slant transforms represent another variation in the transform domain, although they are not as well known or as well studied as others. In 1974, the authors of this approach, Pratt, Welch, and Chen [D20], claimed a lower mean square error for moderate-sized image blocks as compared to other unitary transforms. The advantages of slant transforms over other methods have not been established clearly enough to accept the claims of superior performance.

SVD Transforms

The 1976 study by Andrews and Patterson [D24] on singular value decomposition (SVD)-based image coding offers yet another alternative approach to application of the transform concept to data compression. It provides a comparative table of most of the alternatives (other than the Hadamard transform) and hence is likely to be of use in any simulation studies that may be undertaken as a consequence of this review. The SVD method is claimed to be a deterministically optimum orthogonal transform, while the KL transform is optimal only in a statistical sense. But, once again, SVD coding is computationally very complex.

Wavelet Transforms

Wavelet transforms represent the latest development in the field of transform coding and have become the topic of active research, as evidenced by a spate of publications dealing with their use in data compression [D106, D121, D131, D158–159, D252, D264–265, D285–286, D366, D370–371, D373, D394, D403–404, D406, D455–457, D505, D519, D539, D555–556, D558–562, D573, D592, D605, D616, D670–671, D691, D694–695, D701, D705, D750, D761, D775]. Although as of this writing, no study suggesting the use of wavelet transforms in conjunction with BTC has appeared, such a combination is distinctly feasible. As such, wavelet transforms are of potential interest to those looking for ways to enhance the BTC approach. Indeed, the author of this book is currently exploring this potential, and the findings thereof will be reported in due course in an appropriate forum.

In summation, block quantization and other adaptive techniques [D7, D32] can be employed to improve the performance of linear transforms in a quantitative sense. Typical strategies include adaptations of the transform, bit allocation, and the quantizer levels to suit the statistics of each block. Fourier, Hadamard, and KL transforms were compared under a block quantization scheme by Habibi and Wintz [D7] in 1971, with KL transforms showing the most promise. The literature on these quantization schemes is abundant. Block quantization generally involves a change of tactics for each block and consequent overhead to keep track of the method used for each block. The smaller the block size, the higher the cost of this overhead. This tends to make larger block sizes more efficient. However, larger block sizes make the linear transforms more expensive and thus create another cost-versus-efficiency trade-off scenario that requires experimental resolution.

PREDICTIVE PROCEDURES

Most predictive compression techniques fall under lossy techniques and are viewed as nonorthonormal transformations which generally operate in the spatial domain. Differential pulse code modulation (DPCM) is a prime example. It was first invented and patented in 1952 by Cutler [D1]. A host of variations of this basic approach have been reported since then [D8, D19, D31, D34, D112, D307, D353, D568]. In the basic version of the DPCM coder, a prediction of the current pixel is based upon the previously processed pixels. The difference between this predicted value and the actual value of the pixel is then quantized and coded. The efficiency of the coder is a function of the prediction algorithm and the quantization scheme. A number of variations of both these aspects have been developed over the years [D9, D36].

With the spectrum of options reported, it is difficult to pick a specific candidate without relative evaluation through an actual implementation and simulation of several different options. However, the attraction of this class of approaches is that predictive coding can be integrated with other techniques to make them more adaptive and to permit derivation of hybrid techniques that improve the overall performance in terms of higher compression ratios. Also, DPCM coding techniques were extensively compared with linear transform techniques by Habibi [D8] in 1971. He concluded that DPCM techniques of the type studied tend to perform better than some of the transforms included in the study. Notably DCT is not included in Habibi's comparative analysis [D8]. Also, DPCM techniques are far more sensitive to changes in the nature of the image; that is, they perform less predictably when not optimized to a specific class of images.

MISCELLANEOUS METHODS

Projection Schemes

An interesting alternative to the preceding techniques is the projection approach [D10, D17, D23, D25] wherein the projections of the image at different angles are determined and stored and the image is reconstructed from these projections. If, for example, only two (say, horizontal and vertical) projections are used, we will have $2N$ terms instead of $N*N$ terms representing the image. For $N > 2$, this represents a meaningful compression ratio of $N/2$ with the interpolation during image reconstruction posing an underdetermined algebraic problem. Obviously, this problem lacks a unique solution and hence is subject to distortion. However, many techniques have been proposed in the literature to minimize the degradation of the reconstruction process. The basic projection ideas presented by Herman [D10] in 1972 and the fast Fourier transform (FFT) methods were combined by Wee and Hsieh in 1976 to derive a projection transform approach [D25]. In effect, this may be looked upon as a hybrid technique. It should be possible to conceive a similar hybrid formulation using the DCT instead of the FFT, although no such efforts seem to have been reported.

Block Truncation Coding

Another interesting scheme, first published in the literature around 1978–79, is block truncation coding (BTC) [D42], which is the main topic of this book. Here, the image is segmented into small blocks (of, say, 4 × 4 or 8 × 8) and a binary representation of the block is created by applying a threshold to the intensity values within the block. The threshold, the quantization levels (above and below the threshold), and/or the number of pixels above and below the threshold are determined to ensure the preservation of the moments (first, second, and in some approaches the third also) of the image.

Under the basic version of BTC [D42], the two quantization levels (which correspond to the two states of the binary encoded output) are determined by solving the two simultaneous linear equations set up to ensure that the first two moments (average value and variance) remain unaltered under the encoding transformation. The threshold for the dichotomy of the data set is determined as the average value of the pixel intensities within the block being encoded. Instead of this simplistic approach, one can treat the threshold as a third unknown parameter to be determined by another equation designed to preserve the third-order moment of the data in addition to the first two moments which were being preserved under the previous approach.

Several algorithmic and conceptual modifications to the BTC have been reported by the authors who originated the scheme as well as by others since then, and these are discussed in great detail in Chapter 2. Some examples of variations of this approach include generalized block truncation coding (GBTC) and block-separated component progressive coding (BSCPC) [D83–85], wherein up to 2 bits (instead of 1 bit) per pixel can be used when necessary to handle blocks with relatively larger ranges. The progressive coding scheme (PCS), based on subsampling and predictive coding, is applied to increase the final compression ratios further. These tools were part of the candidate set chosen for evaluation by the International Standards Organization (ISO) committee. The developments in this class of techniques are discussed in more detail separately in subsequent chapters.

Laplacian Pyramid

The Laplacian pyramid method, reported in 1983 by Burt and Adelson [D58], is the first of the since widely used pyramidal schemes [D66–68, D86, D92–93, D101–102, D108, D234, D262, D525, D580, D617, D708] employed for progressive coding and transmission. The method combines the features of predictive and transform approaches in that it is noncausal as in transform methods, but computations are simple and local as under predictive methods. The differences in the pixel intensities between the image and its low-pass filtered version are determined to derive a relatively uncorrelated image describable effectively by fewer numbers of bits. The low-pass filtered image is recursively processed as before. A pyramid of such difference images (sampled each time at a lower spatial resolution) is built and stored along with the final low-pass filtered image of a spatially much reduced size. The method is significantly different from other approaches and is perhaps worthy

11

of consideration based on the results reported. While loss-free, this procedure does not have as much compression as the previous method. However, it may be of interest whenever no error can be tolerated.

Adaptive Binary Arithmetic Coding

Adaptive binary arithmetic coding (ABAC) also has a pyramidal structure and employs the concept of determining and storing the difference between the image and its low-pass filtered and down-sampled (to lower resolution) image. Adaptive binary arithmetic coding has a progressive build-up potential that can be used to reach reversibility; that is, an exact replica can be obtained (albeit with more cost and less compression). This approach was the third of the three methods selected by the ISO committee [D83–85] for final detailed evaluation. It is to be noted that the objective of this ISO-committee evaluation effort was tailored more specifically to the communication applications and hence does not necessarily represent the image compression objectives with which BTC and its variants have been developed.

Vector Quantization Approaches

Vector quantization (VQ) is a relatively recent development but has gathered considerable steam in a fairly short period. A comprehensive review of this area by Nasrabadi and King [D72] appeared in 1988, and the reader is referred to this excellent article for details of the VQ approach as applied to data compression. A host of other studies [D82, D101, D103, D112, D121, D126, D150–151, D153–155, D175, D180, D203, D205, D223, D225, D234, D245, D251, D266–268, D278–279, D281, D284, D298, D300, D309, D320, D324, D330, D336–337, D347, D350, D365, D382, D391, D397, D406, D410–416, D418–419, D421, D429–430, D433–434, D436–437, D456, D461, D464, D472, D475, D481–482, D504, D516, D518, D523, D529, D536, D541, D545–546, D548, D556, D569, D601-602, D624, D635-637, D639, D654, D656, D663, D666, D675–678, D681, D692, D707–708, D711, D721–723, D726, D728, D731, D736, D741, D748, D752, D754] have also appeared since the publication of this initial review [D72]. It would therefore seem that the time is almost ripe for an update on the review of VQ methods as applied to data compression. However, for the purposes of this book, it is sufficient to note that VQ has been extensively used in conjunction with other techniques to form potentially powerful hybrids. It has been one of the favorite tools for developing hybrid approaches in conjunction with BTC, and this aspect is discussed in detail in Chapters 2 and 7.

Fractal Approaches

In addition to the approaches reviewed above, fractals—a very recent development—deserve a passing mention because of the significantly large compression ratios (up to 10,000:1) claimed for it [D75, D157, D206, D219, D246, D257, D292, D325, D457–459, D497, D553, D589, D713, D757]. Computationally, as per the reported figures, the approach is not yet very practical, especially in the encoding phase; but it has been recently reported that customized hardware can speed up the decoding effort to a reasonable level. There is, however, little mention of the scope for achieving practicality in the encoding phase. Irrespective of the exact status of practicality of this approach, little formal connection to the domain of BTC techniques has been developed, and as such no further discussion of this approach is deemed necessary here.

HYBRID TECHNIQUES

Many hybrid techniques have been proposed [D18, D92, D103, D109, D240, D285, D289, D511, D521, D548, D556, D569, D658] that combine the attractive features of several different schemes. Hybrid techniques tend to be more adaptive and efficient than any of their individual components. In 1974, Habibi [D18] presented two hybrid coding schemes that utilize such unitary transforms as Hadamard, Fourier, cosine, slant, and KL in cascade with a bank of DPCM encoders to encode the transformed data. The first of these schemes employs a one-dimensional transform and the second employs a two-dimensional transform. The second scheme is essentially equivalent to the classic two-dimensional transform with the coding efficiency improved by the DPCM scheme that utilizes the interblock correlation effectively. In contrast, the first hybrid scheme uses the one-dimensional transform approach to decorrelate the data in one spatial direction, whereas the decorrelation in the other is attained by the DPCM scheme. This makes it insensitive to block size and allows efficient parallel implementation. The results are shown to be superior to both the DPCM and the two-dimensional transform approaches applied independently. Block truncation coding itself has been adapted into several hybrid schemes which are discussed at length in Chapters 2 and 7.

Another approach that may be regarded either as an entry under miscellaneous methods or under hybrid techniques is that of neural networks [D100, D124, D175, D233, D245, D267, D377–382, D385, D387–390, D412, D419, D454, D508, D546, D655, D722, D729, D769]. Neural nets have been employed in image compression in a variety of ways, both directly and indirectly as a means of implementing other data compression concepts such as BTC and VQ.

No discussion on data compression in general, and hybrid techniques in particular, could be considered comprehensive without at least a mention of the yeoman services of the Joint Photographic Experts Group (JPEG) whose standards have evolved and matured over the years. The JPEG evolved as a collaborative effort between the International Committee on Telegraph and Telephone (CCITT) and ISO. Discrete cosine transform methods play a key role in the JPEG standard. It would be difficult to do justice to this important topic within this brief review, and therefore readers are referred to one of a number of excellent review articles and books that discuss the subject at great length, as does the April 1991 issue of the *Communications of the ACM* [D227], for example. A series of articles published in the literature on JPEG [D113, D190, D195, D227, D241, D283, D334, D482, D500, D511, D521, D557, D607, D613, D615–616, D650–651, D742] offers an interesting historical perspective on its evolution and development. In this context, it is worth noting that, while BTC is not a component of the final JPEG standard as it stands now, it was indeed one of the finalists considered for the JPEG Still Image Data Compression Standards as described in the recent book by Pennebaker and Mitchell [D607]. The Moving Picture Experts Group (MPEG), an outgrowth of JPEG, concerns itself with more than just video compression aspects; it also includes compression of the associated audio and issues of synchronization of audio-visual information. The impact of MPEG [D476, D565, D600, D631, D650, D716] and other video compression techniques on digital television and other related aspects are discussed in detail in a recent review article on the topic by Anastassiou [D770]. These details are, however, well beyond the scope of this book. The developments in the field of hardware dedicated to data compression have also been impressive, especially with the emphasis on "multimedia" and the "information superhighway," which are the recent popular buzzwords. A brief review of the status of video compression by Ang et al. [D247] appeared in an *IEEE Spectrum* article in late 1991.

Data compression has also been recently combined with another equally laudable objective—pattern classification, using vector quantization—by Oehler and Gray [D776]. This, however, is an example of a hybrid objective rather than a hybrid approach.

CLOSING COMMENTS

Among the transform techniques listed and briefly discussed above, the KL transform has been accepted in the literature as the best approach when image fidelity is assessed in terms of mean square error. (It should be noted in this context that this view does not take into account the human visual fidelity requirements.) The DCT technique has an edge in terms of implementation complexity with relatively small loss in image fidelity, and that, too, only at large block sizes. At small practical block sizes, this loss is negligible. Hadamard transforms are the simplest of these from a computational viewpoint, but the error rates are significantly larger than those of DCT.

The BTC method is computationally much simpler than any of the transform methods. Tests show that the decompressed image fidelity with BTC is within the range of experience reported for the transform methods, although the reported performance of ADCT seems to be qualitatively superior.

The ADCT method seems to be the most promising of the approaches purely from the viewpoint of fidelity of the image, based on the experience reported in many of the independent relative evaluation studies. The adaptive scheme includes elements of the DPCM and, in essence, represents a hybrid scheme. Even within this class of techniques many variations have been reported. However, these are outside the scope of this review. On the other hand, the BTC scheme (or one of its variants) is very easy to implement both in software and in hardware, as reported in the literature. If BTC-derived fidelity and compression are determined to be acceptable for a given application and related environment constraints (in terms of mass storage availability), then its simplicity would dictate it as the best choice. Otherwise, ADCT-like approaches, which pose an order of magnitude or more in computational complexity, may have to be adapted.

The objective of this review, as stated at the outset, has been mainly to delineate the role of BTC within the overall field of data compression and to identify the key techniques that have potential for use in conjunction with BTC in developing effective hybrid approaches. This review has therefore not covered techniques handling channel errors (the effect of noise in transmission and storage), computational round-off errors, sampling effects, and the like. More attention was paid to conclusions reported in recent studies as compared to those of earlier reports, with the expectation that these were already taken into consideration by the more recent work. However, the earlier studies have also been reviewed, albeit briefly, to ensure that no important alternatives were overlooked.

Among the many candidate compression techniques identified as significant in this review, the BTC approach has been considered as a prime choice in many instances because it is the simplest to implement and is quite satisfactory from the viewpoint of resulting fidelity and compression ratios. In addition to the ease of implementation and other factors mentioned earlier, the BTC class of techniques, as will be made clear by the material presented in the succeeding chapters, have the following additional advantages:

- Large computer memory is not required since, under the block-oriented BTC, one can incrementally process the data; hence the computational load on the system is less from this viewpoint.

- Repeated compression and decompression cycles do not deteriorate the data beyond that occurring in the very first cycle.

- BTC design permits the user to meet desired specifications within an easily selectable range of compression and fidelity specifications just by the choice of two parameters: a block size and a threshold on the standard deviation of the block.

- Since the statistics of the blocks (which have a standard deviation greater than the user-specified threshold) are maintained, future processing, which involves the statistics of the data (rather than subjective visual fidelity—a significant factor in digital picture transmission types of applications), remains unaffected; hence the effective fidelity of the image is higher than that portrayed by the common measures. In essence, BTC preserves edge information over sample decimation.

- The cost of the decompression phase is significantly lower than the cost of the compression phase; that is, BTC is asymmetric relative to compression and decompression phases of operation. Accordingly, in applications environments wherein one-time compression and multiple-decompression operations are likely (for example, in broadcast or information retrieval), this method is highly attractive compared to transform techniques in which the cost of decompression is also equally significant.

The major countervailing disadvantage of BTC is that the compression ratios achieved may not be high enough if the fidelity requirements are too rigorous under the contemplated applications.

With this introduction to the field of data compression and the role of BTC techniques within it, we now proceed to the detailed presentations of the various facets of BTC. Chapter 2 offers a critique of all of the reported developments in BTC in chronological order. Experimental investigations are reported in Chapter 3 as insights to illustrate the various trade-offs involved in implementing BTC in any application. Part B, Chapters 4 through 7, presents in reprint form some key contributions, categorized for convenience into four broad groups: core contributions, appreciable advances, innovative implementations, and harmonious hybrids. Chapter 8, "Desirable Developments," closes with some thoughts on the future directions of research in this area.

BIBLIOGRAPHY

In the interest of avoiding duplication and conserving publication space, this bibliography does not include studies in the area of block truncation coding (except for a single reference to the initial work of Delp and Mitchell), which are covered separately in Chapter 2.

[D1]   C.C. Cutler, "Differential PCM," US Patent 2 605 361, July 29, 1952.

[D2]   D.A. Huffman, "A Method for the Construction of Minimum Redundancy Codes," *Proc. IEEE*, Vol. 40, No. 10, pp. 1098–1101, Sept. 1952.

[D3]   J. Max, "Quantizing for Minimum Distortion," *IRE Trans. Information Theory*, Vol. IT-6, pp. 7–12, Mar. 1960.

[D4]   J.W. Schwartz and R.C. Barker, "Bit Plane Encoding: A Technique for Source Encoding," *IEEE Trans. Aerospace Electronic Systems*, Vol. AES-2, No. 3, pp. 385–392, July 1966.

[D5]   C.A. Andrews, J.M. Davies, and C.R. Schwarz, "Adaptive Data Compression," *Proc. IEEE*, Vol. 55, No. 3, pp. 267–277, Mar. 1967.

[D6]   W.K. Pratt, J. Kane, and H.C. Andrews, "Hadamard Transform Image Coding," *Proc. IEEE*, Vol. 57, No. 1, pp. 58–68, Jan. 1969.

[D7]   A. Habibi and P.A. Wintz, "Image Coding by Linear Transformation and Block Quantization," *IEEE Trans. Comm. Technology*, Vol. COM-19, No. 1, pp. 50–62, Feb. 1971.

[D8]   A. Habibi, "Comparison of Nth Order DPCM Encoder with Linear Transformations and Block Quantization Techniques," *IEEE Trans. Comm. Technology*, Vol. COM-19, No. 6, pp. 948–956, Dec. 1971.

[D9]   M. Tasto and P.A. Wintz, "Image Coding by Adaptive Block Quantization," *IEEE Trans. Comm. Technology*, Vol. COM-19, No. 12, pp. 957–972, Dec. 1971.

[D10]   G.T. Herman, "Two Direct Methods for Reconstructing Pictures from Their Projections: A Comparative Study," *Computer Graphics and Image Processing*, Vol. 1, pp. 123–144, 1972.

[D11]   J. Pearl, H.C. Andrews, and W.K. Pratt, "Performance Measures for Transform Data Coding," *IEEE Trans. Comm.*, Vol. COM-20, No. 3, pp. 411–415, June 1972.

[D12]   P.A. Wintz, "Transform Picture Coding," *Proc. IEEE*, Vol. 60, No. 7, pp. 809–820, July 1972.

[D13] A. Habibi and G.S. Robinson, "A Survey of Digital Coding," *Computer*, Vol. 7, No. 5, pp. 22–34, May 1974.

[D14] N. Ahmed, T. Natarajan, and K.R. Rao, "Discrete Cosine Transform," *IEEE Trans. Computers*, Vol. C-23, No. 1, pp. 90–93, Jan. 1974.

[D15] C.K. Chow, B.L. Deekshatulu, and L.S. Loh, "Some Computer Experiments in Picture Processing for Data Compaction," *Computer Graphics and Image Processing*, Vol. 3, pp. 203–214, 1974.

[D16] T. Pavlidis, "Techniques for Optimal Compaction of Pictures and Maps," *Computer Graphics and Image Processing*, Vol. 3, pp. 215–224, 1974.

[D17] E.V. Krishna Murthy et al., "Reconstruction of Objects from Their Projections Using Generalized Inverses," *Computer Graphics and Image Processing*, Vol. 3, pp. 336–345, 1974.

[D18] A. Habibi, "Hybrid Coding of Pictorial Data," *IEEE Trans. Comm.*, Vol. COM-22, No. 5, pp. 614–621, May 1974.

[D19] A. Habibi and R.S. Hershel, "A Unified Representation of Differential Pulse-Code Modulation (DPCM) and Transform Coding Systems," *IEEE Trans. Comm.*, Vol. COM-22, No. 5, pp. 693–696, May 1974.

[D20] W.K Pratt, L.R. Welch, and W. Chen, "Slant Transform for Image Coding," *IEEE Trans. Comm.*, Vol. COM-22, No. 8, pp. 1075–1093, Aug. 1974.

[D21] A.K. Jain, "Image Coding via a Nearest Neighbors Image Model," *IEEE Trans. Comm.*, Vol. COM-23, No. 3, pp. 318–331, Mar. 1975.

[D22] K.R. Rao, M.A. Narasimhan, and K. Revulure, "Image Data Processing by Hadamard–Haar Transforms," *IEEE Trans. Computers*, Vol. C-24, No. 9, pp. 888–896, Sept. 1975.

[D23] R.L. Kashyap and M.C. Mittal, "Picture Reconstruction from Projections," *IEEE Trans. Computers*, Vol. C-24, No. 9, pp. 915–923, Sept. 1975.

[D24] H.C. Andrews and C.L. Patterson, "Singular Value Decomposition (SVD) Image Coding," *IEEE Trans. Comm.*, Vol. COM-24, No. 4, pp. 425–432, Apr. 1976.

[D25] W.G. Wee and T.T. Hsieh, "An Application of the Projection Transform Technique in Image Transmission," *IEEE Trans. Systems, Man and Cybernetics*, Vol. SMC-6, No. 7, pp. 486–493, July 1976.

[D26] A.K. Jain, "A Fast Karhunen–Loeve Transform for a Class of Random Processes," *Comm. ACM*, Vol. 19, No. 11, pp. 617–623, Nov. 1976.

[D27] F. Rubin, "Experiments in Text File Compression," *Comm. ACM*, Vol. 19, No. 11, pp. 617–623, Nov. 1976.

[D28] F.W. Mounts, A.N. Netravali, and B. Prasada, "Design of Quantizer for Real-Time Hadamard Transform Coding of Pictures," *Bell System Technical J.*, Vol. 56, No. 1, pp. 21–48, Jan. 1977.

[D29] J. Ziv and A. Lempel, "A Universal Algorithm for Sequential Data Compression," *IEEE Trans. Information Theory*, Vol. IT-23, No. 3, pp. 337–343, May 1977.

[D30] W. Chen, C.H. Smith, and S. Fralick, "A Fast Computational Algorithm for the Discrete Cosine Transform," *IEEE Trans. Comm.*, Vol. COM-25, No. 9, pp. 1004–1009, Sept. 1977.

[D31] D.K. Sharma and A.N. Netravali, "Design of Quantizers for DPCM Coding of Picture Signals," *IEEE Trans. Comm.*, Vol. COM-25, No. 11, pp. 1267–1274, Nov. 1977.

[D32] A. Habibi, "Survey of Adaptive Image Coding Techniques," *IEEE Trans. Comm.*, Vol. COM-25, No. 11, pp. 1275–1284, Nov. 1977.

[D33] W. Chen and C.H. Smith, "Adaptive Coding of Monochrome and Color Images," *IEEE Trans. Comm.*, Vol. COM-25, No. 11, pp. 1285–1291, Nov. 1977.

[D34] W. Zschunke, "DPCM Picture Coding with Adaptive Prediction," *IEEE Trans. Comm.*, Vol. COM-25, No. 11, pp. 1295–1301, Nov. 1977.

[D35] T.S. Huang, "Coding of Two-Tone Images," *IEEE Trans. Comm.*, Vol. COM-25, No. 11, pp. 1406–1424, Nov. 1977.

[D36] S.A. Kassam, "Quantization Based on the Mean-Absolute-Error Criterion," *IEEE Trans. Comm.*, Vol. COM-26, pp. 267–270, Feb. 1978.

[D37] J. Ziv and A. Lempel, "Compression of Individual Sequences via Variable Rate Coding," *IEEE Trans. Information Theory*, Vol. IT-24, No. 5, pp. 530–536, Sept. 1978.

[D38] R.G. Gallager, "Variations on a Theme by Huffman," *IEEE Trans. Information Theory*, Vol. IT-24, No. 6, pp. 668–674, Nov. 1978.

[D39] E.J. Delp, R.L. Kashyap, and O.R. Mitchell, "Image Data Compression Using Autoregressive Time Series Models," *Pattern Recognition*, Vol. 11, pp. 313–323, 1979.

[D40] A.N. Netravali and J.D. Robbins, "Motion-Compensated Television Coding: Part I," *Bell System Technical J.*, Vol. 58, No. 3, pp. 631–670, Mar. 1979.

[D41] A.N. Netravali and J.A. Stuller, "Motion-Compensated Transform Coding," *Bell System Technical J.*, Vol. 58, No. 9, pp. 1703–1718, Sept. 1979.

[D42] E.J. Delp and O.R. Mitchell, "Image Compression Using Block Truncation Coding," *IEEE Trans. Comm.*, Vol. COM-27, No. 9, pp. 1335–1342, Sept. 1979.

[D43] A.G. Tescher, "Transform Image Coding," *Image Transmission Techniques*, Academic Press, New York, 1979.

[D44] A.N. Netravali and J.O. Limb, "Picture Coding: A Review," *Proc. IEEE*, Vol. 68, No. 3, pp. 366–406, Mar. 1980. (Cites 210 references.)

[D45] R.B. Arps, "Bibliography on Binary Image Compression," *Proc. IEEE*, Vol. 68, No. 7, pp. 922–924, July 1980. (Cites 100 references.)

[D46] J.W. Mark and T.D. Todd, "A Nonuniform Sampling Approach to Data Compression," *IEEE Trans. Comm.*, Vol. COM-29, No. 1, pp. 24–32, Jan. 1981.

[D47] T.W. Goeddel and S.C. Bass, "A Two-Dimensional Quantizer for Coding of Digital Imagery," *IEEE Trans. Comm.*, Vol. COM-29, No. 1, pp. 60–67, Jan. 1981.

[D48] M. Rodeh, V.R. Pratt, and S. Even, "Linear Algorithm for Data Compression via String Matching," *J. ACM*, Vol. 28, No. 1, pp. 16–24, Jan. 1981.

[D49] A. K Jain, "Image Data Compression—A Review," *Proc. IEEE*, Vol. 69, No. 3, pp. 349–389, Mar. 1981. (Cites 223 references.)

[D50] H.K. Reghbati, "An Overview of Data Compression Techniques," *Computer*, Vol. 14, No. 4, pp. 71–76, Apr. 1981.

[D51] G.G. Langdon and J. Rissanen, "Arithmetic Coding," *IEEE Trans. Comm.*, Vol. COM-29, No. 6, pp. 858–867, June 1981.

[D52] J.W. Modestino and V. Bhaskaran, "Robust Two-Dimensional Tree Encoding of Images," *IEEE Trans. Comm.*, Vol. COM-29, No. 11, pp. 1786–1798, Dec. 1981.

[D53] F.A. Kamangar and K.R. Rao, "Fast Algorithms for 2-D Discrete Cosine Transform," *IEEE Trans. Computers*, Vol. C-31, No. 9, pp. 899–906, Sept. 1982.

[D54] M. Pechura, "File Archival Techniques Using Data Compression," *Comm. ACM*, Vol. 25, No. 9, pp. 605–609, Sept. 1982.

[D55] J.A. Storer and T.G. Szymanki, "Data Compression via Textual Substitution," *J. ACM*, Vol. 29, No. 4, pp. 928–951, Oct. 1982.

[D56] D.R. Halverson, "On the Implementation of a Block Truncation Coding Algorithm," *IEEE Trans. Comm.*, Vol. COM-30, No. 11, pp. 2482–2484, Nov. 1982.

[D57] R. Wilson, H.E. Knutsson, and G.H. Granlund, "Anisotropic Nonstationary Image Estimation and Its Applications: Part II—Predictive Image Coding," *IEEE Trans. Comm.*, Vol. COM-31, No. 3, pp. 398–404, Mar. 1983.

[D58] P.J. Burt and E.H. Adelson, "The Laplacian Pyramid as a Compact Image Code," *IEEE Trans. Comm.*, Vol. COM-31, No. 4, pp. 532–540, Apr. 1983.

[D59] T.A. Welch, "A Technique for High Performance Data Compression," *Computer*, Vol. 17, No. 6, pp. 8–19, June 1984.

[D60] D.R. McIntyre and M.A. Pechura, "Data Compression Using Static Huffman Code-Decode Tables," *Comm. ACM*, Vol. 28, No. 6, pp. 612–616, June 1985.

[D61] A. Rosenfeld and A.C. Kak, "Compression," in *Digital Picture Processing*, Academic Press, New York, pp. 116–208, 1985.

[D62] A. Habibi, "Image Coding," in *Handbook of Pattern Recognition and Image Processing*, Academic Press, New York, 1986.

[D63] J.A. Saghri and A.G. Tescher, "Adaptive Transform Coding Based on Chain Coding Concepts," *IEEE Trans. Comm.*, Vol. COM-34, No. 2, pp. 112–117, Feb. 1986.

[D64] J. Amsterdam, "Data Compression with Huffman Coding," *Byte*, Vol. 11, No. 5, pp. 99–108, May 1986.

[D65] A.G. Tescher and J.A. Saghri, "Adaptive Transform Coding and Image Quality," *Optical Eng.*, Vol. 25, No. 8, pp. 979–983, Aug. 1986.

[D66] P.J. Burt, "The Pyramid as a Structure for Efficient Computation," in *Multiresolution Image Processing and Analysis*, A. Rosenfeld, ed., Springer-Verlag, Berlin, pp. 6–35, 1986.

[D67] V. Cantoni and S. Levialdi, eds., *Pyramidal Systems for Computer Vision*, Springer-Verlag, Berlin, 1986.

[D68] D.J. Vaisey and A. Gersho, "Variable Block-Size Image Coding," *Proc. IEEE Int'l Conf. Acoustics, Speech, and Signal Processing*, IEEE Press, Piscataway, N.J., pp. 1051–1054, 1987.

[D69] I. Witten, R. Neal, and J. Cleary, "Arithmetic Coding for Data Compression," *Comm. ACM*, Vol. 30, No. 4, pp. 520–540, June 1987.

[D70] L.J.C. Woolliscroft, M.P. Gough, and A. Sumner, "On-Board Data Compression of Geophysical Data," *Proc. IEE Colloquium on 'Satellite Instrumentation,'* IEE Press, Stevenage, Hertfordshire, UK, pp. 10/1–4, 1988.

[D71] M.F. Barnsley and A.D. Sloan, "A Better Way to Compress Images," *Byte*, pp. 215–223, Jan. 1988.

[D72] N.M. Nasrabadi and R.A. King, "Image Coding Using Vector Quantization: A Review," *IEEE Trans. Comm.*, Vol. COM-36, No. 3, pp. 957–971, Mar. 1988.

[D73] S.A. Rajala, M.R. Civanlar, and W.M. Lee, "Video Data Compression Using Three-Dimensional Segmentation Based on HVS Properties," *Proc. 1988 Int'l Conf. Acoustics, Speech, and Signal Processing (ICASSP 88)*, Vol. 2, pp. 1092–1095, 1988.

[D74] G.S. Plattel and K. Bowyer, "Dynamically Differenced Rectangles for Reversible Image Data Compression," *Proc. SPIE: Hybrid Image and Signal Processing*, Vol. 939, SPIE Press, Bellingham, Wash., pp. 79–84, 1988.

[D75] M.F. Barnsley and A.D. Sloan, "Fractal Image Compression," *Proc. Scientific Data Compression Workshop*, NASA Conf. Publication 3025, pp. 351–365, 1988.

[D76] H.K. Ramapriyan, ed., *Proc. Scientific Data Compression Workshop*, NASA Conf. Publication 3025, 1988.

[D77] V.S. Miller and M.N. Wegman, "Variations on a Theme by Ziv and Lempel (Data Compression)," *Proc. IEEE Int'l Conf. Comm. '88: Digital Technology—Spanning the Universe*, Vol. 1, IEEE Press, Piscataway, N.J., pp. 390–394, 1988.

[D78] C. Lamberti and P. Coccia, "ECG Data Compression for Ambulatory Device," *Proc. Conf. Computers in Cardiology 1988*, pp. 171–174, 1988.

[D79] P.-W. Hsia, "Electrocardiographic Data Compression Using Preceding Consecutive QRS Information," *Proc. Conf. Computers in Cardiology '88*, CS Press, Los Alamitos, Calif., pp. 465–468, 1989.

[D80] J.A. Saghri and A.G. Tescher, "Feature Based Image Bandwidth Compression," *Optical Eng.*, Vol. 27, No. 10, pp. 854–860, Oct. 1988.

[D81] V.-E. Neagoe, "Predictive Ordering and Linear Approximation for Image Data Compression," *IEEE Trans. Comm.*, Vol. 36, No. 9, pp. 1151–1156, Sept. 1988.

[D82] L.D. Cohen, "A New Approach of Vector Quantization for Image Data Compression and Texture Detection," *Proc. 9th Int'l Conf. Pattern Recognition*, Vol. 2, CS Press, Los Alamitos, Calif., pp. 1250–1254, 1988.

[D83] G.P. Hudson, H. Yasuda, and I. Sebestyen, "The International Standardisation of a Still Picture Compression Technique," *Proc. IEEE Global Telecommunications Conf. (Globcom '88)*, IEEE Press, Piscataway, N.J., pp. 1016–1021, 1988.

[D84] G. Wallace, R. Vivian, and H. Poulsen, "Subjective Testing Results for Still Picture Compression Algorithms for International Standardisation," *Proc. IEEE Global Telecommunications Conf. (Globcom '88)*, IEEE Press, Piscataway, N.J., pp. 1022–1027, 1988.

[D85]   A. Leger, J.L. Mitchell, and Y. Yamazaki, "Still Picture Compression Algorithms Evaluated For International Standardisation," *Proc. IEEE Global Telecommunications Conf. (Globcom '88)*, IEEE Press, Piscataway, N.J., pp. 1028–1032, 1988.

[D86]   G. Eichmann et al., "Pyramidal Image Processing Using Morphology," *Proc. SPIE: Applications of Digital Image Processing Conf. XI*, Vol. 974, SPIE Press, Bellingham, Wash., pp. 30–37, 1988.

[D87]   J.A. Copeland, "Data Compression Technique for PC Communications," *IEEE J. Selected Areas in Comm.*, Vol. 7, No. 2, pp. 246–248, Feb. 1989.

[D88]   R.A. Fowell and D.D. McNeil, "Faster Plots by Fan Data Compression," *IEEE Computer Graphics and Applications*, Vol. 9, No. 2, pp. 58–66, Mar. 1989.

[D89]   I. Heller and P. Lucas, "Use of Data Compression Techniques in Digital Fault Recorder," *Proc. 4th Int'l Conf. Development in Power Protection*, pp. 18–22, 1989.

[D90]   M.Y. Jaisimha et al., "Data Compression Techniques for Maps," *Proc. Conf. Energy and Information Technologies in the Southeast (SOUTHEASTCON '89)*, Vol. 2, pp. 878–883, 1989.

[D91]   M. Todd and R. Wilson, "An Anisotropic Multi-Resolution Image Data Compression Algorithm," *ICASSP-89: Proc. 1989 Int'l Conf. Acoustics, Speech and Signal Processing*, Vol. 3, IEEE Press, Piscataway, N.J., pp. 1969–1972, 1989.

[D92]   S.-C. Pei and I.-I. Yang, "Hybrid Pyramid Image Coding and Data Compression," *Proc. 1989 IEEE Int'l Symp. Circuits and Systems*, Vol. 2, IEEE Press, Piscataway, N.J., pp. 1358–1361, 1989.

[D93]   A. Toet, "A Morphological Pyramidal Image Decomposition," *Pattern Recognition Letters*, Vol. 9, No. 1, pp. 255–261, May 1989.

[D94]   Y. Bar-Ness and C. Peckham, "Word Based Data Compression Schemes," *Proc. 1989 IEEE Int'l Symp. Circuits and Systems*, Vol. 1, IEEE Press, Piscataway, N.J., pp. 300–303, 1989.

[D95]   J.P. Noonan and P.M. Semeter, "Data Compression of a +1, −1 and 0 Representation," *Proc. 1989 IEEE Int'l Symp. Circuits and Systems*, Vol. 1, IEEE Press, Piscataway, N.J., pp. 304–305, 1989.

[D96]   H.C. Kotze and G.J. Kuhn, "An Evaluation of the Lempel–Ziv–Welch Data Compression Algorithm," *Proc. Southern African Conf. Comm. and Signal Processing (COMSIG 1989)*, pp. 65–69, 1989.

[D97]   A.J. Redfern and E.L. Hines, "Medical Image Data Compression Techniques," *Proc. 3rd Int'l Conf. Image Processing and its Applications*, pp. 558–562, 1989.

[D98]   K. Mehta and B.D. Russell, "Data Compression for Digital Data from Power Systems Disturbances: Requirements and Technique Evaluation," *IEEE Trans. Power Delivery*, Vol. 4, No. 3, pp. 1683–1688, July 1989.

[D99]   A. Mobin et al., "A Novel Technique of Data Compression for Spoken Word Recognition Systems," *Proc. 4th IEEE Region 10 Int'l Conf. (TENCON '89). 'Information Technologies for the 90's' E/sup 2/C/sup 2/; Energy, Electronics, Computers, and Communications*, IEEE Press, Piscataway, N.J., pp. 756–759, 1989.

[D100] D. Anthony et al., "A Study of Data Compression Using Neural Networks and Principal Component Analysis (of Pulmonary Scintigrams)," *Proc. IEE Colloquium on Biomedical Applications of Digital Signal Processing*, IEE Press, Stevenage, Hertfordshire, UK, pp. 2/1–5, 1989.

[D101] Y. Ho and A. Gersho, "A Pyramidal Image Coder with Contour-Based Interpolative Vector Quantization," *Proc. SPIE: Visual Communications Image Processing Conf.*, Vol. 1199, SPIE Press, Bellingham, Wash., pp. 733–740, 1989.

[D102] F. Sun and P. Maragos, "Experiments on Image Compression Using Morphological Pyramids," *Proc. SPIE: Visual Communications and Image Processing Conf.*, Vol. 1199, SPIE Press, Bellingham, Wash., pp. 1303–1312, Nov. 1989.

[D103] L.D. Thede and S.C. Kwatra, "A Hybrid Data Compression Scheme Using Quaternary Decomposition and Selective Multistage Vector Quantization," *Proc. IEEE Global Telecommunications Conf. and Exhibition (GLOBECOM '89), Comm. Technology for the 1990s and Beyond*, Vol. 3, IEEE Press, Piscataway, N.J., pp. 1901–1905, 1989.

[D104] E. Feig, "Fast Scaled DCT Algorithm," *Proc. SPIE: Image Processing Algorithms and Techniques*, Vol. 1244, SPIE Press, Bellingham, Wash., pp. 2–13, 1990.

[D105] M.C. Tzannes, A.P. Tzannes, and N.C. Tzannes, "Cascade Coding for Sub-Bit Image Compression," *Proc. SPIE: Image Processing Algorithms and Techniques*, Vol. 1244, SPIE Press, Bellingham, Wash., pp. 14–25, 1990.

[D106] W.R. Zettler, J. Huffman, and D.C.P. Linden, "Application of Compactly Supported Wavelets to Image Compression," *Proc. SPIE: Image Processing Algorithms and Techniques*, Vol. 1244, SPIE Press, Bellingham, Wash., pp. 150–160, 1990.

[D107] T. Yu and S.K. Mitra, "Simple Image Analysis/Synthesis Technique and Its Application in Image Coding," *Proc. SPIE: Image Processing Algorithms and Techniques*, Vol. 1244, SPIE Press, Bellingham, Wash., pp. 161–170, 1990.

[D108] L. Wang and M. Goldberg, "Reduced-Difference Pyramid: A Data Structure for Progressive Image Transmission," *Proc. SPIE: Image Processing Algorithms and Techniques*, Vol. 1244, SPIE Press, Bellingham, Wash., pp. 171–181, 1990.

[D109] H.G. Lewis and W.B. Forsyth, "Hybrid LZW Compression," *Proc. SPIE: Image Processing Algorithms and Techniques*, Vol. 1244, SPIE Press, Bellingham, Wash., pp. 182–189, 1990.

[D110] H.Q. Nguyen and E. Dubois, "Two-Dimensional Code Excited Linear Prediction Image Coding System," *Proc. SPIE: Image Processing Algorithms and Techniques*, Vol. 1244, SPIE Press, Bellingham, Wash., pp. 190–198, 1990.

[D111] D.G. Daut and D. Zhao, "Improved DPCM Algorithm for Image Data Compression," *Proc. SPIE: Image Processing Algorithms and Techniques*, Vol. 1244, SPIE Press, Bellingham, Wash., pp. 199–210, 1990.

[D112] R. Ju et al., "Stationary Vector Quantization Approach for Image Coding," *Proc. SPIE: Image Processing Algorithms and Techniques*, Vol. 1244, SPIE Press, Bellingham, Wash., pp. 211–219, 1990.

[D113] G.K. Wallace, "Overview of the JPEG (ISO/CCITT) Still Image Compression Standard," *Proc. SPIE: Image Processing Algorithms and Techniques*, Vol. 1244, SPIE Press, Bellingham, Wash., pp. 220–233, 1990.

[D114] M. Watanabe et al., "Bit-Rate-Controlled DCT Compression Algorithm for Digital Still Camera," *Proc. SPIE: Image Processing Algorithms and Techniques*, Vol. 1244, SPIE Press, Bellingham, Wash., pp. 234–239, 1990.

[D115] N. Farvardin and N. Tanabe, "Subband Image Coding Using Entropy-Coded Quantization," *Proc. SPIE: Image Processing Algorithms and Techniques*, Vol. 1244, SPIE Press, Bellingham, Wash., pp. 240–254, 1990.

[D116] P.W. Melnychuck, M.J. Barry, and M.S. Mathieu, "Effect of Noise and MTF on the Compressibility of High-Resolution Color Images," *Proc. SPIE: Image Processing Algorithms and Techniques*, Vol. 1244, SPIE Press, Bellingham, Wash., pp. 255–262, 1990.

[D117] C.A. Gonzales, K.L. Anderson, and W.B. Pennebaker, "DCT-Based Video Compression Using Arithmetic Coding," *Proc. SPIE: Image Processing Algorithms and Techniques*, Vol. 1244, SPIE Press, Bellingham, Wash., pp. 305–311, 1990.

[D118] M.R. Haghiri and P. Denoyelle, "Motion Adaptive Spatiotemporal Subsampling and Its Application in Full Motion Image Coding," *Proc. SPIE: Image Processing Algorithms and Techniques*, Vol. 1244, SPIE Press, Bellingham, Wash., pp. 312–324, 1990.

[D119] S.B. Jonsson and A.S. Spanias, "Seismic Data Compression," *Proc. 9th Ann. Int'l Phoenix Conf. Computers and Communications*, CS Press, Los Alamitos, Calif., pp. 276–279, 1990.

[D120] S.M.S. Jalaleddine et al., "ECG Data Compression Techniques—A Unified Approach," *IEEE Trans. Biomedical Eng.*, Vol. 37, No. 4, pp. 329–343, Apr. 1990.

[D121] M. Antonini et al., "Image Coding Using Vector Quantization in the Wavelet Transform Domain," *Proc. 1990 IEEE Int'l Conf. Acoustics, Speech, and Signal Processing*, IEEE Press, Piscataway, N.J., pp. 2297–2300, 1990.

[D122] F. Saeed, H. Lu, and G.E. Hedrick, "Data Compression with Huffman Coding; an Efficient Dynamic Implementation Using File Partitioning," *Proc. 1990 Symp. Applied Computing*, CS Press, Los Alamitos, Calif., pp. 348–354, 1990.

[D123] A.S. Spanias, S.B. Jonsson, and S.D. Stearns, "Transform Coding Algorithms for Seismic Data Compression," *Proc. 1990 IEEE Int'l Symp. Circuits and Systems*, Vol. 2, IEEE Press, Piscataway, N.J., pp. 1573–1576, 1990.

[D124] M. Arozullah and A. Namphol, "A Data Compression System Using Neural Network Based Architecture," *Proc. Int'l Joint Conf. Neural Networks (IJCNN)*, Vol. 1, IEEE Press, Piscataway, N.J., pp. 531–536, 1990.

[D125] T.M.E. Frost and C.J. Theaker, "Real-Time Video Data Compression System," *IEE Proc. E [Computers and Digital Techniques]*, Vol. 137, No. 5, IEE Press, Stevenage, Hertfordshire, UK, pp. 337–342, 1990.

[D126] E.A. Riskin et al., "Variable Rate Vector Quantization for Medical Image Compression," *IEEE Trans. Medical Imaging*, Vol. 9, No. 3, pp. 290–298, Sept. 1990.

[D127] C. Lamberti et al., "Evaluation of Algorithms for Real-Time ECG Data Compression," *Proc. Conf. Computers in Cardiology 1990*, CS Press, Los Alamitos, Calif., pp. 399–402, 1990.

[D128] R. Bedini et al., "Performance Evaluation and Choice Criteria of Data Compression Algorithms by Extensive Test on CSE Database," *Proc. Conf. Computers in Cardiology 1990*, CS Press, Los Alamitos, Calif., pp. 403–406, 1990.

[D129] D.W. Sharp and D.S. Roth, "Adaptive Data Compression for VLF Communication System," *Proc. 1990 IEEE Military Comm. Conf. (MILCOM 90)—A New Era*, Vol. 3, IEEE Press, Piscataway, N.J., pp. 1030–1035, 1990.

[D130] B. Moghaddam, K.J. Hintz, and C.V. Stewart, "Fractal Image Compression and Texture Analysis," *Proc. SPIE—Image Understanding in the 90's: Building Systems That Work*, Vol. 1406, SPIE Press, Bellingham, Wash., pp. 42–57, 1990.

[D131] J.A. Storer and J.H. Reif, "A Parallel Architecture for High Speed Data Compression," *Proc. 3rd Symp. Frontiers of Massively Parallel Computation*, CS Press, Los Alamitos, Calif., pp. 238–243, 1990.

[D132] R.A. Strelitz and Y. Keshet, "Integral Transforms, Data Compressions, and Automatic Analysis of Seismic Sections," *IEEE Trans. Geoscience and Remote Sensing*, Vol. 28, No. 6, pp. 982–991, Nov., 1990.

[D133] S. Henriques and N. Ranganathan, "A Parallel Architecture for Data Compression," *Proc. 2nd IEEE Symp. Parallel and Distributed Processing 1990*, CS Press, Los Alamitos, Calif., pp. 260–266, 1990.

[D134] Y.-Q. Zhang, R.L. Pickholtz, and M.H. Loew, "A Combined-Transform Coding (CTC) Scheme for Image Data Compression," *Proc. IEEE Global Telecommunications Conf. and Exhibition (GLOBECOM '90)—Communications: Connecting the Future*, Vol. 2, IEEE Press, Piscataway, N.J., pp. 972–977, 1990.

[D135] N. Ranganathan and S. Henriques, "A Systolic Chip for LZ Based Data Compression," *Proc. 4th Int'l Symp. VLSI Design*, CS Press, Los Alamitos, Calif., pp. 310–311, 1991.

[D136] M.C. Aydin, A.E. Cetin, and H. Koymen, "ECG Data Compression by Sub-Band Coding," *Electronic Letters*, Vol. 27, No. 4, pp. 359–360, 14 Feb. 1991.

[D137] L. Huang and A. Bijaoui, "An Efficient Image Compression Algorithm without Distortion," *Pattern Recognition*, Vol. 12, No. 2, pp. 69–72, Feb. 1991.

[D138] T. Stern, "An Algorithm for the Construction of a Critical Clustered Exponential Code for Use in Image Data Compression," *Proc. 10th Ann. Int'l Phoenix Conf. Computers and Comm.*, CS Press, Los Alamitos, Calif., pp. 747–753, 1991.

[D139] P.G. Howard and J.S. Vitter, "Analysis of Arithmetic Coding for Data Compression," *Proc. Data Compression Conf. (DCC '91)*, CS Press, Los Alamitos, Calif., pp. 3–12, 1991.

[D140] G.G. Langdon, Jr., "Probabilistic and Q-Coder Algorithms for Binary Source Adaptation," *Proc. Data Compression Conf. (DCC '91)*, CS Press, Los Alamitos, Calif., pp. 13–22, 1991.

[D141] I.H. Witten, T.C. Bell and C.G. Nevill, "Models for Compression in Full-Text Retrieval Systems," *Proc. Data Compression Conf. (DCC '91)*, CS Press, Los Alamitos, Calif., pp. 23–32, 1991.

[D142] J. Teuhola and T. Raita, "Piecewise Arithmetic Coding," *Proc. Data Compression Conf. (DCC '91)*, CS Press, Los Alamitos, Calif., pp. 33–42, 1991.

[D143] D. Chevion, E.D. Karnin, and E. Walach, "High Efficiency, Multiplication Free Approximation of Arithmetic Coding," *Proc. Data Compression Conf. (DCC '91)*, CS Press, Los Alamitos, Calif., pp. 43–52, 1991.

[D144] M. Malak and J. Baker, "An Image Database for Low Bandwidth Communication Links," *Proc. Data Compression Conf. (DCC '91)*, CS Press, Los Alamitos, Calif., pp. 53–62, 1991.

[D145] J. Lin, J.A. Storer, and M. Cohn, "On the Complexity of Optimal Tree Pruning for Source Coding," *Proc. Data Compression Conf. (DCC '91)*, CS Press, Los Alamitos, Calif., pp. 63–72, 1991.

[D146] X. Wu and C. Yao, "Image Coding by Adaptive Tree-Structured Segmentation," *Proc. Data Compression Conf. (DCC '91)*, CS Press, Los Alamitos, Calif., pp. 73–82, 1991.

[D147] N.D. Memon, S.S. Magliveras, and K. Sayood, "Prediction Trees and Lossless Image Compression: An Extended Abstract," *Proc. Data Compression Conf. (DCC '91)*, CS Press, Los Alamitos, Calif., pp. 83–92, 1991.

[D148] T. Markas and J. Reif, "Image Compression Methods with Distortion Controlled Capabilities," *Proc. Data Compression Conf. (DCC '91)*, CS Press, Los Alamitos, Calif., pp. 93–102, 1991.

[D149] T.R. Fischer and M. Wang, "Entropy-Constrained Trellis Coded Quantization," *Proc. Data Compression Conf. (DCC '91)*, CS Press, Los Alamitos, Calif., pp. 103–112, 1991.

[D150] P.C. Cosman, E.A. Riskin, and R.M. Gray, "Combining Vector Quantization and Histogram Equalization," *Proc. Data Compression Conf. (DCC '91)*, CS Press, Los Alamitos, Calif., pp. 113–118, 1991.

[D151] H. Nguyen and J.W. Mark, "Concentric-Shell Partition Vector Quantization with Application to Image Coding," *Proc. Data Compression Conf. (DCC '91)*, CS Press, Los Alamitos, Calif., pp. 119–128, 1991.

[D152] R.L. Frost, C.F. Barnes, and F. Xu, "Design and Performance of Residual Quantizers," *Proc. Data Compression Conf. (DCC '91)*, CS Press, Los Alamitos, Calif., pp. 129–138, 1991.

[D153] K. Xue and J.M. Crissey, "An Iteratively Interpolative Vector Quantization Algorithm for Image Data Compression," *Proc. Data Compression Conf. (DCC '91)*, CS Press, Los Alamitos, Calif., pp. 139–148, 1991.

[D154] P.P. Polit and N.M. Nasrabadi, "A New Transform Domain Vector Quantization Technique for Image Data Compression in an Asynchronous Transfer Mode Network," *Proc. Data Compression Conf. (DCC '91)*, CS Press, Los Alamitos, Calif., pp. 149–158, 1991.

[D155] R. Lindsay and D.E. Abercrombie, "Restricted Boundary Vector Quantization," *Proc. Data Compression Conf. (DCC '91)*, CS Press, Los Alamitos, Calif., pp. 159–165, 1991.

[D156] Y. Liu and H. Ma, "W-Orbit Finite Automata for Data Compression," *Proc. Data Compression Conf. (DCC '91)*, CS Press, Los Alamitos, Calif., pp. 166–175, 1991.

[D157] A. Pentland and B. Horowitz, "A Practical Approach to Fractal-Based Image Compression," *Proc. Data Compression Conf. (DCC '91)*, CS Press, Los Alamitos, Calif., pp. 176–185, 1991.

[D158] R.A. Devore, B. Jawerth, and B.J. Lucier, "Data Compression Using Wavelets: Error, Smoothness, and Quantization," *Proc. Data Compression Conf. (DCC '91)*, CS Press, Los Alamitos, Calif., pp. 186–195, 1991.

[D159] A.S. Lewis and G. Knowles, "A 64 Kb/s Video Codec Using the 2-D Wavelet Transform," *Proc. Data Compression Conf. (DCC '91)*, CS Press, Los Alamitos, Calif., pp. 196–201, 1991.

[D160] A.D. Wyner and J. Ziv, "Fixed Data Base Version of the Lempel–Ziv Data Compression Algorithm," *Proc. Data Compression Conf. (DCC '91)*, CS Press, Los Alamitos, Calif., pp. 202–207, 1991.

[D161] G H. Freernan, "Asymptotic Convergence of Dual-Tree Entropy Codes," *Proc. Data Compression Conf. (DCC '91)*, CS Press, Los Alamitos, Calif., pp. 208–217, 1991.

[D162] D. Sheinwald, A. Lempel, and J. Ziv, "On Compression with Two-Way Head Machines," *Proc. Data Compression Conf. (DCC '91)*, CS Press, Los Alamitos, Calif., pp. 218–227, 1991.

[D163] L. Gerencser, "Asymptotics of Predictive Stochastic Complexity," *Proc. Data Compression Conf. (DCC '91)*, CS Press, Los Alamitos, Calif., pp. 228–238, 1991.

[D164] M. Weinberger, J. Ziv, and A. Lempel, "On the Optimal Asymptotic Performance of Universal Ordering and Discrimination of Individual Sequences," *Proc. Data Compression Conf. (DCC '91)*, CS Press, Los Alamitos, Calif., pp. 239–246, 1991.

[D165] W. Szpankowski, "A Typical Behaviour of Some Data Compression Schemes," *Proc. Data Compression Conf. (DCC '91)*, CS Press, Los Alamitos, Calif., pp. 247–256, 1991.

[D166] P. Howard and J.S. Vitter, "New Methods for Lossless Image Compression Using Arithmetic Coding," *Proc. Data Compression Conf. (DCC '91)*, CS Press, Los Alamitos, Calif., pp. 257–266, 1991.

[D167] W.H. Leung and S. Skiena, "Inducing Codes from Examples," *Proc. Data Compression Conf. (DCC '91)*, CS Press, Los Alamitos, Calif., pp. 267–276, 1991.

[D168] Y. Perl, V. Maram, and N. Kadakuntla, "The Cascading of the LZW Compression Algorithm with Arithmetic Coding," *Proc. Data Compression Conf. (DCC '91)*, CS Press, Los Alamitos, Calif., pp. 277–286, 1991.

[D169] H. Bodlaender, T. Gonzales, and T. Kloks, "Complexity Aspects of Map Compression," *Proc. Data Compression Conf. (DCC '91)*, CS Press, Los Alamitos, Calif., pp. 287–296, 1991.

[D170] A. De Santis and G. Persiano, "An Optimal Algorithm for the Construction of Optimal Prefix Codes with Given Fringe," *Proc. Data Compression Conf. (DCC '91)*, CS Press, Los Alamitos, Calif., pp. 297–306, 1991.

[D171] J.A. Robinson, "Compression of Natural Images Using Thread-Like Visual Primitives," *Proc. Data Compression Conf. (DCC '91)*, CS Press, Los Alamitos, Calif., pp. 307–312, 1991.

[D172] D.A. Lelewer and D.S. Hirschberg, "Streamlining Context Models for Data Compression," *Proc. Data Compression Conf. (DCC '91)*, CS Press, Los Alamitos, Calif., pp. 313–322, 1991.

[D173] G. Promhouse and M. Bennett, "Semantic Data Compression," *Proc. Data Compression Conf. (DCC '91)*, CS Press, Los Alamitos, Calif., pp. 323–331, 1991.

[D174] R.N. Horspool, "Improving LZW," *Proc. Data Compression Conf. (DCC '91)*, CS Press, Los Alamitos, Calif., pp. 332–341, 1991.

[D175] W. Fang, B. Sheu, and O.T. Chen, "A Neural Network Based VLSI Vector Quantizer for Real-Time Image Compression," *Proc. Data Compression Conf. (DCC '91)*, CS Press, Los Alamitos, Calif., pp. 342–351, 1991.

[D176] A. Mukherjee et al., "Multibit Decoding/Encoding of Binary Codes Using Memory Based Architecture," *Proc. Data Compression Conf. (DCC '91)*, CS Press, Los Alamitos, Calif., pp. 352–361, 1991.

[D177] R.N. Williams, "An Extremely Fast ZIV–Lempel Data Compression Algorithm," *Proc. Data Compression Conf. (DCC '91)*, CS Press, Los Alamitos, Calif., pp. 362–372, 1991.

[D178] D.W. Jones, "Practical Evaluation of a Data Compression Algorithm," *Proc. Data Compression Conf. (DCC '91)*, CS Press, Los Alamitos, Calif., pp. 372–381, 1991.

[D179] A. Moffat, "Two-Level Context Based Compression of Binary Images," *Proc. Data Compression Conf. (DCC '91)*, CS Press, Los Alamitos, Calif., pp. 382–391, 1991.

[D180] X. Wu and K. Zhang, "A Better Tree-Structured Vector Quantizer," *Proc. Data Compression Conf. (DCC '91)*, CS Press, Los Alamitos, Calif., pp. 392–401, 1991.

[D181] A. Bookstein and S.T. Klein, "Flexible Compression for Bitmap Sets," *Proc. Data Compression Conf. (DCC '91)*, CS Press, Los Alamitos, Calif., pp. 402–410, 1991.

[D182] J.C. Tilton, D. Han, and M. Manohar, "Compression Experiments with AVHRR Data," *Proc. Data Compression Conf. (DCC '91)*, CS Press, Los Alamitos, Calif., pp. 411–422, 1991.

[D183] C.C. Lu and N. Choong, "Adaptive Source Modeling Using Conditioning Tree," *Proc. Data Compression Conf. (DCC '91)*, CS Press, Los Alamitos, Calif., p. 423, 1991.

[D184] K. Van Houton and P.W. Oman, "An Algorithm for Tree Structure Compression," *Proc. Data Compression Conf. (DCC '91)*, CS Press, Los Alamitos, Calif., p. 424, 1991.

[D185] E. Salari and W.A. Whyte, Jr., "Compression of Stereoscopic Image Data," *Proc. Data Compression Conf. (DCC '91)*, CS Press, Los Alamitos, Calif., p. 425, 1991.

[D186] J.A. Elliott, P.M. Grant, and G.G. Sexton, "Concurrent Techniques for Developing Motion Video Compression Algorithms," *Proc. Data Compression Conf. (DCC '91)*, CS Press, Los Alamitos, Calif., p. 426, 1991.

[D187] E. Koch and M. Sommer, "Data Compression in View of Data Sealing," *Proc. Data Compression Conf. (DCC '91)*, CS Press, Los Alamitos, Calif., p. 427, 1991.

[D188] M. Zipstein, "Data Compression with Factor Automata," *Proc. Data Compression Conf. (DCC '91)*, CS Press, Los Alamitos, Calif., p. 428, 1991.

[D189] R. Blitstein, "A Design to Increase Media-Independent Data Integrity and Availability Through the Use of Robotic Media Management Systems," *Proc. Data Compression Conf. (DCC '91)*, CS Press, Los Alamitos, Calif., p. 429, 1991.

[D190] M. Chang and G.G. Langdon, "Effects of Coefficient Coding on JPEG Baseline Image Compression," *Proc. Data Compression Conf. (DCC '91)*, CS Press, Los Alamitos, Calif., p. 430, 1991.

[D191] D.K. Chang, "Exact Data Compression Using Hierarchical Dictionaries," *Proc. Data Compression Conf. (DCC '91)*, CS Press, Los Alamitos, Calif., p. 431, 1991.

[D192] M.R. Lagana, G. Turrini, and G. Zanchi, "Experiments on the Compression of Dictionary Entries," *Proc. Data Compression Conf. (DCC '91)*, CS Press, Los Alamitos, Calif., p. 432, 1991.

[D193] M. Bassiouni, A. Mukherjee, and N. Tzannes, "Experiments on Improving the Compression of Special Data Types," *Proc. Data Compression Conf. (DCC '91)*, CS Press, Los Alamitos, Calif., p. 433, 1991.

[D194] L. Gertner and Y.Y. Zeevi, "Generalized Scanning and Multiresolution Image Compression," *Proc. Data Compression Conf. (DCC '91)*, CS Press, Los Alamitos, Calif., p. 434, 1991.

[D195] A. Omodeo, M. Pugassi, and N. Scarabottolo, "Implementing JPEG Algorithm on INMOS Transputer Equipped Machines," *Proc. Data Compression Conf. (DCC '91)*, CS Press, Los Alamitos, Calif., p. 435, 1991.

[D196] K. Chen and T.V. Ramabadran, "An Improved Hierarchical Interpolation (HINT) Method for the Reversible Compression of Gray Scale Images," *Proc. Data Compression Conf. (DCC '91)*, CS Press, Los Alamitos, Calif., p. 436, 1991.

[D197] R.P. Millett and E.L. Ivie, "Index Compression Method with Compressed Mode Boolean Operators," *Proc. Data Compression Conf. (DCC '91)*, CS Press, Los Alamitos, Calif., p. 437, 1991.

[D198] T. Masui, "Keyword Dictionary Compression Using Efficient Tree Implementation," *Proc. Data Compression Conf. (DCC '91)*, CS Press, Los Alamitos, Calif., p. 438, 1991.

[D199] G.S. Yovanof and J.R. Sullivan, "Lossless Coding Techniques for Color Graphical Images," *Proc. Data Compression Conf. (DCC '91)*, CS Press, Los Alamitos, Calif., p. 439, 1991.

[D200] C.W. Wong, "Motion-Compensated Video Image Compression Using Luminance and Chrominance Components for Motion Estimation," *Proc. Data Compression Conf. (DCC '91)*, CS Press, Los Alamitos, Calif., p. 440, 1991.

[D201] W.K. Chau et al., "On the Selection of Color Basis for Image Compression," *Proc. Data Compression Conf. (DCC '91)*, CS Press, Los Alamitos, Calif., p. 441, 1991.

[D202] S. Minami and A. Zakhor, "An Optimization Approach for Removing Blocking Effects in Transform Coding," *Proc. Data Compression Conf. (DCC '91)*, CS Press, Los Alamitos, Calif., p. 442, 1991.

[D203] A. Desoky and Y. You, "Performance Analysis of a Vector Quantization Algorithm of Image Data," *Proc. Data Compression Conf. (DCC '91)*, CS Press, Los Alamitos, Calif., p. 443, 1991.

[D204] E.T. Lee, "Pictorial Data Compression Using Array Grammars," *Proc. Data Compression Conf. (DCC '91)*, CS Press, Los Alamitos, Calif., p. 444, 1991.

[D205] K.M. Liang, S.E. Budge, and R.W. Harris, "Rate Distortion Performance of VQ and PVQ Compression Algorithms," *Proc. Data Compression Conf. (DCC '91)*, CS Press, Los Alamitos, Calif., p. 445, 1991.

[D206] D. Indjic, "Reduction in Power System Load Data Training Sets Size Using Fractal Approximation Theory," *Proc. Data Compression Conf. (DCC '91)*, CS Press, Los Alamitos, Calif., p. 446, 1991.

[D207] K. Nickels and C. Thacker, "Satellite Data Archives Algorithm, *Proc. Data Compression Conf. (DCC '91)*, CS Press, Los Alamitos, Calif., p. 447, 1991.

[D208] Y.T. Tsai, "Signal Processing and Compression for Image Capturing System Using a Single-Chip Sensor," *Proc. Data Compression Conf. (DCC '91)*, CS Press, Los Alamitos, Calif., p. 448, 1991.

[D209] T.V. Ramabadran, "Some Results on Adaptive Statistics Estimation for the Reversible Compression of Sequences," *Proc. Data Compression Conf. (DCC '91)*, CS Press, Los Alamitos, Calif., p. 449, 1991.

[D210] N. Ranganathan and S. Henriques, "A Systolic Architecture for LZ Based Decompression," *Proc. Data Compression Conf. (DCC '91)*, CS Press, Los Alamitos, Calif., p. 450, 1991.

[D211] E.L. Ivie, "Techniques for Index Compression," *Proc. Data Compression Conf. (DCC '91)*, CS Press, Los Alamitos, Calif., p. 451, 1991.

[D212] D. Bas, "Text Compression Using Several Huffman Trees," *Proc. Data Compression Conf. (DCC '91)*, CS Press, Los Alamitos, Calif., p. 452, 1991.

[D213] H. Lee et al., "3-D Image Compression for X-Ray CT Images Using Displacement Estimation," *Proc. Data Compression Conf. (DCC '91)*, CS Press, Los Alamitos, Calif., p. 453, 1991.

[D214] K.L. Tong and M.-W. Marcellin, "Transform Coding of Monochrome and Color Images Using Trellis Coded Quantization," *Proc. Data Compression Conf. (DCC '91)*, CS Press, Los Alamitos, Calif., p. 454, 1991.

[D215] P. Mermelstein, "Trends in Audio and Speech Compression for Storage and Real-Time Communication," *Proc. Data Compression Conf. (DCC '91)*, CS Press, Los Alamitos, Calif., p. 455, 1991.

[D216] C. Ko and W. Chung, "2-D Discrete Cosine Transform Array Processor Using Non-Planar Connections," *Proc. Data Compression Conf. (DCC '91)*, CS Press, Los Alamitos, Calif., p. 456, 1991.

[D217] W.K. Chou and D.Y. Yun, "A Uniform Model for Parallel Fast Fourier Transform (FFT) and Fast Discrete Cosine Transform (FDCT)," *Proc. Data Compression Conf. (DCC '91)*, CS Press, Los Alamitos, Calif., p. 457, 1991.

[D218] S.Y. Chang and J.J. Metzner, "Universal Data Compression Algorithms by Using Full Tree Models," *Proc. Data Compression Conf. (DCC '91)*, CS Press, Los Alamitos, Calif., p. 458, 1991.

[D219] K. Culik and S. Dube, "Using Fractal Geometry for Image Compression," *Proc. Data Compression Conf. (DCC '91)*, CS Press, Los Alamitos, Calif., p. 459, 1991.

[D220] C. Thomborson, "V.42bis and Other Ziv–Lempel Variants," *Proc. Data Compression Conf. (DCC '91)*, CS Press, Los Alamitos, Calif., p. 460, 1991.

[D221] J. Venbrux and N. Li, "A Very High Speed Lossless Compression/Decompression Chip Set," *Proc. Data Compression Conf. (DCC '91)*, CS Press, Los Alamitos, Calif., p. 461, 1991.

[D222] R. Anderson et al., "A Very High Speed Noiseless Data Compression Chip for Space Imaging Applications," *Proc. Data Compression Conf. (DCC '91)*, CS Press, Los Alamitos, Calif., p. 462, 1991.

[D223] P. Israelsen, "VLSI Implementation of a Vector Quantization Processor," *Proc. Data Compression Conf. (DCC '91)*, CS Press, Los Alamitos, Calif., p. 463, 1991.

[D224] S.D. Stearns, "Waveform Data Compression with Exact Recovery," *Proc. Data Compression Conf. (DCC '91)*, CS Press, Los Alamitos, Calif., p. 464, 1991.

[D225] J. Foster and C. Trowell, "Distortionless Data Compression of NMR Images Using Vector Quantization," *IEEE Proc. SOUTHEASTCON '91*, Vol. 1, IEEE Press, Piscataway, N.J., pp. 487–489, 1991.

[D226] W. Carlson, "A Survey of Computer Graphics Image Encoding and Storage Formats," *Computer Graphics*, Vol. 25, No. 2, Apr. 1991.

[D227] G.K. Wallace, "The JPEG Still Picture Compression Standard," *Comm. ACM*, Vol. 34, No. 4, pp. 30–44, Apr. 1991.

[D228] E.H. Feria, "Analog Data Compression of Images Via Predictive Transform Coding," *Proc. 1991 Int'l Conf. Acoustics, Speech and Signal Processing (ICASSP 91)*, Vol. 4, IEEE Press, Piscataway, N.J., pp. 2893–2896, 1991.

[D229] W. Kinsner and R.H. Greenfield, "The Lempel–Ziv–Welch (LZW) Data Compression Algorithm for Packet Radio," *Proc. IEEE Western Canada Conf. Computer, Power and Communications Systems in a Rural Environment (Wescanex '91)*, IEEE Press, Piscataway, N.J., pp. 225–229, 1991.

[D230] A.S. Spanias, S.B. Jonsson, and S.D. Stearns, "Transform Methods for Seismic Data Compression," *IEEE Trans. Geoscience and Remote Sensing*, Vol. 29, No. 3, pp. 407–416, May 1991.

[D231] N. Ranganathan and S. Henriques, "A High Speed VLSI Chip for Data Compression," *Proc. 9th Biennial University/Government/Industry Microelectronics Symp.*, pp. 190–194, 1991.

[D232] Y.-H. Chan and W.-C. Siu, "Symmetric Realization of DCT for Multi-Dimensional Data Compression," *Proc. 1991 Int'l Conf. Circuits and Systems*, Vol. 1, IEEE Press, Piscataway, N.J., pp. 309–312, 1991.

[D233] A. Namphol, M. Arozullah, and S. Chin, "Higher Order Data Compression with Neural Networks," *Proc. Int'l Joint Conf. Neural Networks (IJCNN-91)*, Vol. 1, IEEE Press, Piscataway, N.J., pp. 55–59, 1991.

[D234] R.P. Rao and W.A. Pearlman, "Alphabet and Entropy-Constrained Vector Quantization of Image Pyramids," *Optical Eng.*, Vol. 30, No. 7, pp. 865–872, July 1991.

[D235] T. Ebrahimi and M. Kunt, "Image Compression by Gabor Expansion," *Optical Eng.*, Vol. 30, No. 7, pp. 873–880, July 1991.

[D236] J.H. Husoy, "Low Complexity Subband Coding of Still Images and Video," *Optical Eng.*, Vol. 30, No. 7, pp. 904–911, July 1991.

[D237] A.N. Akansu and Y. Liu, "On-Signal Decomposition Techniques," *Optical Eng.*, Vol. 30, No. 7, pp. 912–920, July 1991.

[D238] S.-C. Pei and F.-C. Chen, "Subband Decomposition of Monochrome and Color Images by Mathematical Morphology," *Optical Eng.*, Vol. 30, No. 7, pp. 921–933, July 1991.

[D239] J.A. Saghri and A.G. Tescher, "Near-Lossless Bandwidth Compression for Radiometric Data," *Optical Eng.*, Vol. 30, No. 7, pp. 934–939, July 1991.

[D240] K.N. Ngan, H.C. Koh, and W.C. Wong, "Hybrid Image Coding Scheme Incorporating Human Visual System Characteristics," *Optical Eng.*, Vol. 30, No. 7, pp. 940–946, July 1991.

[D241] A. Leger, T. Omachi, and G.K. Wallace, "JPEG Still Picture Compression Algorithm," *Optical Eng.*, Vol. 30, No. 7, pp. 947–954, July 1991.

[D242] T.A. York et al., "Design and VLSI Implementation of Mod-127 Multiplier Using Cellular Automaton-Based Data Compression Techniques," *IEE Proc. E [Computers and Digital Techniques]*, Vol. 138, No. 5, IEE Press, Stevenage, Hertfordshire, UK, pp. 351–356, Sept. 1991.

[D243] G. Passariello et al., "Arithmetic Coding for ECG Data Compression," *Proc. Conf. Computers in Cardiology*, CS Press, Los Alamitos, Calif., pp. 593–596, 1991.

[D244] Y. Mano and Y. Sato, "A Data Compression Scheme Which Achieves Good Compression for Practical Use," *Proc. 15th Ann. Int'l Computer Software and Applications Conf.*, CS Press, Los Alamitos, Calif., pp. 442–449, 1991.

[D245] C. Lu and Y. Shin, "Image Compression Using Vector Quantization and Artificial Neural Networks," *Proc. IEEE Int'l Conf. Systems, Man, and Cybernetics*, IEEE Press, Piscataway, N.J., 1991.

[D246] L. Anson and M. Barnsley, "Graphics Compression Technology: A New Method for Image Reproduction Using the Fractal Transform Process," *Sun World*, Vol. 4, No. 10, pp. 43–52, Oct. 1991.

[D247] P.H. Ang, P.A. Ruetz, and D. Auld, "Video Compression Makes Big Gains," *IEEE Spectrum*, Vol. 28, No. 10, pp. 16–19, Oct. 1991.

[D248] J.S. Vitter and P. Krishnan, "Optimal Prefetching via Data Compression," *Proc. 32nd Ann. Symp. Foundations of Computer Science*, CS Press, Los Alamitos, Calif., pp. 121–130, 1991.

[D249] C.S. Chen and K.-S. Huo, "Karhunen–Loeve Method for Data Compression and Speech Synthesis," *IEE Proc. (Communications, Speech and Vision)*, Vol. 138, No. 5, IEE Press, Stevenage, Hertfordshire, UK, pp. 377–380, Oct. 1991.

[D250] B.J. Cooke et al., "Superconducting Super Collider Data Compression and Driver/Modulator Architecture," *Conf. Record 1991 IEEE Nuclear Science Symp. and Medical Imaging Conf.*, Vol. 2, IEEE Press, Piscataway, N.J., pp. 799–802, 1991.

[D251] Y. Hussain and N. Farvardin, "Adaptive Block Transform Coding of Speech Based on LPC Vector Quantization," *IEEE Trans. Signal Processing*, Vol. 39, No. 12, pp. 2611–2620, Dec. 1991.

[D252] G. Beylkin, R. Coifman, and V. Rokhlin, "Fast Wavelet Transforms and Numerical Algorithms I," *Comm. Pure and Applied Math.*, Vol. XLIV, pp. 141–183, 1991.

[D253] M. Rabbani and P.W. Jones, *Digital Image Compression Techniques*, SPIE Press Tutorial Texts Series, SPIE Press, Bellingham, Wash., 1991.

[D254] G. Held, *Data Compression*, Wiley, New York, 1991.

[D255] M. Nelson, *The Data Compression Book*, M&T Books, Redwood City, Calif., 1991.

[D256] H. Yokoo, "Improved Variations Relating the Ziv–Lempel and Welch-Type Algorithms for Sequential Data Compression," *IEEE Trans. Information Theory*, Vol. 38, No, 1, pp. 73–81, Jan. 1992.

[D257] A.E. Jacquin, "Image Coding Based on a Fractal Theory of Iterated Contractive Image Transformations," *IEEE Trans. Image Processing*, Vol. 1, No. 1, pp. 18–30, Jan. 1992.

[D258] Y.H. Kim and J.W. Modestino, "Adaptive Entropy Coded Subband Coding of Images," *IEEE Trans. Image Processing*, Vol. 1, No. 1, pp. 31–48, Jan. 1992.

[D259] K. Sayood and K. Anderson, "A Differential Lossless Image Compression Scheme," *IEEE Trans. Signal Processing*, Vol. 40, No. 1, pp. 236–241, Jan. 1992.

[D260] P.H.N. de With, M. Breeuwer, and P.A.M. van Grinsven, "Data Compression Systems for Home-Use Digital Video Recording," *IEEE J. Selected Areas in Communications*, Vol. 10, No. 1, pp. 97–121, Jan. 1992.

[D261] R.H. Ju, I.C. Jou, and M.K. Tsay, "Global Study on Data Compression Techniques for Digital Chinese Character Patterns," *IEE Proc. E (Computers and Digital Techniques)*, Vol. 139, No. 1, IEE Press, Stevenage, Hertfordshire, UK, pp. 1–8, Jan. 1992.

[D262] L.A. Overturf, M.L. Comer, and E.J. Delp, "Color Image Coding Using Morphological Pyramid Decomposition," *Proc. SPIE Conf. Human Vision, Visual Processing, and Digital Display III*, Vol. 1666, SPIE Press, Bellingham, Wash., pp. 265–275, 1992.

[D263] V.-E.I. Neagoe, "Predictive Ordering Technique and Feedback Transform Coding for Data Compression of Still Pictures," *IEEE Trans. Comm.*, Vol. 40, No. 2, pp. 385–396, Feb. 1992.

[D264] R.A. DeVore, B. Jawerth, and B.L. Lucier, "Image Compression through Wavelet Transform Coding," *IEEE Trans. Information Theory*, Vol. 38, No. 2, pp. 719–746, Mar. 1992.

[D265] O. Rioul and P. Duhamel, "Fast Algorithms for Discrete and Continuous Wavelet Transforms," *IEEE Trans. Information Theory*, Vol. 38, No. 2, pp. 569–586, Mar. 1992.

[D266] O.S. Haddadin, V.J. Mathews, and T.G. Stockham, Jr., "Subband Vector Quantization of Images Using Hexagonal Filter Bands," *Proc. Data Compression Conf. (DCC '92)*, CS Press, Los Alamitos, Calif., pp. 2–11, 1992.

[D267] J. Buhmann and H. Kuhnel, "Complexity Optimized Vector Quantization: A Neural Network Approach," *Proc. Data Compression Conf. (DCC '92)*, CS Press, Los Alamitos, Calif., pp. 12–21, 1992.

[D268] J.-H. Lin and J.S. Vitter, "Nearly Optimal Vector Quantization via Linear Programming," *Proc. Data Compression Conf. (DCC '92)*, CS Press, Los Alamitos, Calif., pp. 22–31, 1992.

[D269] J.H. Reif and A. Yoshida, "Optical Techniques for Image Compression," *Proc. Data Compression Conf. (DCC '92)*, CS Press, Los Alamitos, Calif., pp. 32–40, 1992.

[D270] I.H. Witten et al., "Textual Image Compression," *Proc. Data Compression Conf. (DCC '92)*, CS Press, Los Alamitos, Calif., pp. 42–51, 1992.

[D271] S. De Agostino and J.A. Storer, "Parallel Algorithm for Optimal Compression Using Dictionaries with the Prefix Property," *Proc. Data Compression Conf. (DCC '92)*, CS Press, Los Alamitos, Calif., pp. 52–61, 1992.

[D272] R.N. Horspool and G.V. Cormack, "Constructing Word-Based Text Compression Algorithms," *Proc. Data Compression Conf. (DCC '92)*, CS Press, Los Alamitos, Calif., pp. 62–71, 1992.

[D273] A. Moffat and J. Zobel, "Coding for Compression in Full-Text Retrieval Systems," *Proc. Data Compression Conf. (DCC '92)*, CS Press, Los Alamitos, Calif., pp. 72–81, 1992.

[D274] A. Bookstein, S.T. Klein, and T. Raita, "Model Based Concordance Compression," *Proc. Data Compression Conf. (DCC '92)*, CS Press, Los Alamitos, Calif., pp. 82–91, 1992.

[D275] S.A. Savari and R.G. Gallager, "Arithmetic Coding for Memoryless Cost Channels," *Proc. Data Compression Conf. (DCC '92)*, CS Press, Los Alamitos, Calif., pp. 92–101, 1992.

[D276] M.J. Weinberger, A. Lempel, and J. Ziv, "On the Coding Delay of a General Coder," *Proc. Data Compression Conf. (DCC '92)*, CS Press, Los Alamitos, Calif., pp. 102–111, 1992.

[D277] D. Sheinwald, "On Binary Alphabetical Codes," *Proc. Data Compression Conf. (DCC '92)*, CS Press, Los Alamitos, Calif., pp. 112–121, 1992.

[D278] R.F. Sproull and I.E. Sutherland, "A Comparison of Codebook Generation Techniques for Vector Quantization," *Proc. Data Compression Conf. (DCC '92)*, CS Press, Los Alamitos, Calif., pp. 122–131, 1992.

[D279] X. Wu, "Vector Quantizer Design by Constrained Global," *Proc. Data Compression Conf. (DCC '92)*, CS Press, Los Alamitos, Calif., pp. 132–141, 1992.

[D280] T.R. Reed et al., "Perceptually Based Coding of Monochrome and Color Still Images," *Proc. Data Compression Conf. (DCC '92)*, CS Press, Los Alamitos, Calif., pp. 142–151, 1992.

[D281] A. Madisetti, R. Jain, and R.L. Baker, "Real Time Implementation of Pruned Tree Search Vector Quantization," *Proc. Data Compression Conf. (DCC '92)*, CS Press, Los Alamitos, Calif., pp. 152–161, 1992.

[D282] L.M. Stauffer and D.S. Hirschberg, "Transpose Coding on the Systolic Array," *Proc. Data Compression Conf. (DCC '92)*, CS Press, Los Alamitos, Calif., pp. 162–171, 1992.

[D283] G. Langdon, A. Gulati, and E. Seiler, "On the JPEG Model for Lossless Image Compression," *Proc. Data Compression Conf. (DCC '92)*, CS Press, Los Alamitos, Calif., pp. 172–180, 1992.

[D284] M. Manohar and J.C. Tilton, "Progressive Vector Quantization of Multispectral Image Data Using a Massively Parallel SIMD Machine," *Proc. Data Compression Conf. (DCC '92)*, CS Press, Los Alamitos, Calif., pp. 181–190, 1992.

[D285] M. Rollins and F. Carden, "Possible Harmonic-Wavelet Hybrids in Image Compression," *Proc. Data Compression Conf. (DCC '92)*, CS Press, Los Alamitos, Calif., pp. 191–199, 1992.

[D286] B.R. Epstein et al., "Multispectral KLT-Wavelet Data Compression for Landsat Thematic Mapper Images," *Proc. Data Compression Conf. (DCC '92)*, CS Press, Los Alamitos, Calif., pp. 200–208, 1992.

[D287] M.R.K. Khansari, I. Widjaja, and A. Leon-Garcia, "Convolutional Interpolative Coding Algorithms," *Proc. Data Compression Conf. (DCC '92)*, CS Press, Los Alamitos, Calif., pp. 209–218, 1992.

[D288] L. McMillan and L. Westover, "A Forward-Mapping Realization of the Inverse Discrete Cosine Transform," *Proc. Data Compression Conf. (DCC '92)*, CS Press, Los Alamitos, Calif., pp. 219–228, 1992.

[D289] Q.-F. Zhu, Y. Wang, and L. Shaw, "Image Reconstruction for Hybrid Video Coding Systems," *Proc. Data Compression Conf. (DCC '92)*, CS Press, Los Alamitos, Calif., pp. 229–238, 1992.

[D290] B. Carpentieri and J.A. Storer, "A Split-Merge Parallel Block-Matching Algorithm for Video Displacement Estimation," *Proc. Data Compression Conf. (DCC '92)*, CS Press, Los Alamitos, Calif., pp. 239–248, 1992.

[D291] X. Wu and Y. Fang, "Lossless Interframe Compression of Medical Images," *Proc. Data Compression Conf. (DCC '92)*, CS Press, Los Alamitos, Calif., pp. 249–258, 1992.

[D292] M. Ali, C. Papadopoulos, and T. Clarkson, "The Use of Fractal Theory in Video Compression System," *Proc. Data Compression Conf. (DCC '92)*, CS Press, Los Alamitos, Calif., pp. 259–268, 1992.

[D293] P.G. Howard and J.S. Vitter, "Error Modeling for Hierarchical Lossless Image Compression," *Proc. Data Compression Conf. (DCC '92)*, CS Press, Los Alamitos, Calif., pp. 269–278, 1992.

[D294] A. Amir and C. Benson, "Efficient Two-Dimensional Compressed Matching," *Proc. Data Compression Conf. (DCC '92)*, CS Press, Los Alamitos, Calif., pp. 279–288, 1992.

[D295] Y. Wang and J.-M. Wu., "Vector Run-Length Coding of Bilevel Images," *Proc. Data Compression Conf. (DCC '92)*, CS Press, Los Alamitos, Calif., pp. 289–298, 1992.

[D296] P.G. Howard and J.S. Vitter, "Parallel Lossless Image Compression Using Huffman and Arithmetic Coding," *Proc. Data Compression Conf. (DCC '92)*, CS Press, Los Alamitos, Calif., pp. 299–308, 1992.

[D297] T. Hopper and F. Preston, "Compression of Gray-Scale Fingerprint Images," *Proc. Data Compression Conf. (DCC '92)*, CS Press, Los Alamitos, Calif., pp. 309–318, 1992.

[D298] R. Dionysian and M.D. Ercegovac, "Variable Precision Representation for Efficient VQ Codebook Storage," *Proc. Data Compression Conf. (DCC '92)*, CS Press, Los Alamitos, Calif., pp. 319–328, 1992.

[D299] R. Zamir and M. Feder, "Universal Coding of Band-Limited Sources and Dithered Quantization," *Proc. Data Compression Conf. (DCC '92)*, CS Press, Los Alamitos, Calif., pp. 329–338, 1992.

[D300] J. Lin and J.A. Storer, "Improving Search for Tree-Structured Vector Quantization," *Proc. Data Compression Conf. (DCC '92)*, CS Press, Los Alamitos, Calif., pp. 339–348, 1992.

[D301] O.T.-C. Chen, Z. Zhang, and B.J. Sheu, "An Adaptive High-Speed Lossy Data Compression," *Proc. Data Compression Conf. (DCC '92)*, CS Press, Los Alamitos, Calif., pp. 349–358, 1992.

[D302] A. Gammerman and A. Bellotti, "Experiments Using Minimal-Length Encoding to Solve Machine Learning Problems," *Proc. Data Compression Conf. (DCC '92)*, CS Press, Los Alamitos, Calif., pp. 359–367, 1992.

[D303] G. Jacobson, "Random Access in Huffman-Coded Files," *Proc. Data Compression Conf. (DCC '92)*, CS Press, Los Alamitos, Calif., pp. 368–379, 1992.

[D304] D.A. Novik and J.C. Tilton, "Adjustable Lossless Image Compression Based on a Natural Splitting of an Image into Drawing, Shading, and Fine Grained Components," *Proc. Data Compression Conf. (DCC '92)*, CS Press, Los Alamitos, Calif., p. 380, 1992.

[D305] C. Fenimore and B.F. Field, "An Analysis of Frame Interpolation in Video Compression and Standards Conversion," *Proc. Data Compression Conf. (DCC '92)*, CS Press, Los Alamitos, Calif., p. 381, 1992.

[D306] A. Zandi and G.G. Langdon, Jr., "Bayesian Approach to a Family of Fast Attack Priors for Binary Adaptive Compression," *Proc. Data Compression Conf. (DCC '92)*, CS Press, Los Alamitos, Calif., p. 382, 1992.

[D307] R.K. Guha and A.J. Roy, "Cascading Modified DPCM with LZW for Lossless Image Compression," *Proc. Data Compression Conf. (DCC '92)*, CS Press, Los Alamitos, Calif., p. 383, 1992.

[D308] G. Davis, "Collision String Repopulation of Hash Tables," *Proc. Data Compression Conf. (DCC '92)*, CS Press, Los Alamitos, Calif., p. 384, 1992.

[D309] C.W. Wong, "Color Video Compression Using Motion-Compensated Vector Quantization," *Proc. Data Compression Conf. (DCC '92)*, CS Press, Los Alamitos, Calif., p. 385, 1992.

[D310] J.J. Bloomer, "Compression for Medical Digital Fluoroscopy," *Proc. Data Compression Conf. (DCC '92)*, CS Press, Los Alamitos, Calif., p. 386, 1992.

[D311] J.R. Schiess and K. Stacy, "Compression of Object Boundaries in Digital Imagery by Using Fractional Brownian Motion," *Proc. Data Compression Conf. (DCC '92)*, CS Press, Los Alamitos, Calif., p. 387, 1992.

[D312] K. Miettinen, "Compression of Spectral Meterological Imagery," *Proc. Data Compression Conf. (DCC '92)*, CS Press, Los Alamitos, Calif., p. 388, 1992.

[D313] G.A. King, "Data Compression Using Pattern Matching, Substitution, and Morse Coding," *Proc. Data Compression Conf. (DCC '92)*, CS Press, Los Alamitos, Calif., p. 389, 1992.

[D314] H.A. Bergen and J.M. Hogan, "Data Security in Arithmetic Coding Compression Algorithms," *Proc. Data Compression Conf. (DCC '92)*, CS Press, Los Alamitos, Calif., p. 390, 1992.

[D315] E. Koch and M. Sommer, "Design and Analysis of Self-Synchronising Codeword Sets Using Various Models," *Proc. Data Compression Conf. (DCC '92)*, CS Press, Los Alamitos, Calif., p. 391, 1992.

[D316] I. Sadeh, "On Digital Data Compression—The Asymptotic Large Deviations Approach," *Proc. Data Compression Conf. (DCC '92)*, CS Press, Los Alamitos, Calif., p. 392, 1992.

[D317] W.M. Anderson, "A Dynamic Dictionary Compression Method with Genetic Algorithm Optimization," *Proc. Data Compression Conf. (DCC '92)*, CS Press, Los Alamitos, Calif., p. 393, 1992.

[D318] D. Revuz and M. Zipstein, "DZ: A Universal Compression Algorithm Specialized in Text," *Proc. Data Compression Conf. (DCC '92)*, CS Press, Los Alamitos, Calif., p. 394, 1992.

[D319] R.F. Haines and S.L. Chuang, "The Effects of Video Compression on Acceptability of Images for Monitoring Life Sciences Experiments," *Proc. Data Compression Conf. (DCC '92)*, CS Press, Los Alamitos, Calif., p. 395, 1992.

[D320] V.S. Sitaram and C.M. Huang, "Efficient Codebooks for Vector Quantization Image Compression," *Proc. Data Compression Conf. (DCC '92)*, CS Press, Los Alamitos, Calif., p. 396, 1992.

[D321] Z.M. Yin et al., "Efficient Data Coding and Algorithms for Volume Compression," *Proc. Data Compression Conf. (DCC '92)*, CS Press, Los Alamitos, Calif., p. 397, 1992.

[D322] M.J. Turner, "Entropy Reduction via Simplified Image Contourization," *Proc. Data Compression Conf. (DCC '92)*, CS Press, Los Alamitos, Calif., p. 398, 1992.

[D323] O.S. Schoepke, "Executing Compressed Code: A New Approach," *Proc. Data Compression Conf. (DCC '92)*, CS Press, Los Alamitos, Calif., p. 399, 1992.

[D324] S.S. Huang, J.-S. Wang, and W.-T. Chen, "FASVQ: The Filtering and Seeking Vector Quantization," *Proc. Data Compression Conf. (DCC '92)*, CS Press, Los Alamitos, Calif., p. 400, 1992.

[D325] A.D. Sloan, "Fractal Image Compression: A Resolution Independent Representation for Imagery," *Proc. Data Compression Conf. (DCC '92)*, CS Press, Los Alamitos, Calif., p. 401, 1992.

[D326] T.L. Yu and K.W. Yu, "Further Study of the DMC Data Compression Scheme," *Proc. Data Compression Conf. (DCC '92)*, CS Press, Los Alamitos, Calif., p. 402, 1992.

[D327] R.L. White, "High-Performance Data Compression of Astronomical Images," *Proc. Data Compression Conf. (DCC '92)*, CS Press, Los Alamitos, Calif., p. 403, 1992.

[D328] X. Li and B. Woo, "A High Performance Data Compression Coprocessor with Fully Programmable ISA Interface," *Proc. Data Compression Conf. (DCC '92)*, CS Press, Los Alamitos, Calif., p. 404, 1992.

[D329] S.-C. Cheng and W.-H. Tsai, "Image Compression by Moment Preserving Edge Detection," *Proc. Data Compression Conf. (DCC '92)*, CS Press, Los Alamitos, Calif., p. 405, 1992.

[D330] W. Li, "Image Data Compression Using Vector Transformation and Vector Quantization," *Proc. Data Compression Conf. (DCC '92)*, CS Press, Los Alamitos, Calif., p. 406, 1992.

[D331] V.S. Srinivasan and L. Chandrasekhar, "Image Data Compression with Adaptive Discrete Cosine Transform," *Proc. Data Compression Conf. (DCC '92)*, CS Press, Los Alamitos, Calif., p. 407, 1992.

[D332] I. Sadeh and A. Averbuch, "Image Encoding by Polynomial Approximation," *Proc. Data Compression Conf. (DCC '92)*, CS Press, Los Alamitos, Calif., p. 408, 1992.

[D333] S.C. Jones and R.J. Moorhead, "Image-Sequence Compression of Computational Fluid Dynamic Animations," *Proc. Data Compression Conf. (DCC '92)*, CS Press, Los Alamitos, Calif., p. 409, 1992.

[D334] S. Daly, "Incorporation of Imaging System and Visual Parameters into JPEG Quantization Tables," *Proc. Data Compression Conf. (DCC '92)*, CS Press, Los Alamitos, Calif., p. 410, 1992.

[D335] J. Jeuring, "Incremental Data Compression," *Proc. Data Compression Conf. (DCC '92)*, CS Press, Los Alamitos, Calif., p. 411, 1992.

[D336] H. Nguyen and J.W. Mark, "Interframe Coding Using Quadtree Composition and Concentric-Shell Partition Vector Quantization," *Proc. Data Compression Conf. (DCC '92)*, CS Press, Los Alamitos, Calif., p. 412, 1992.

[D337] C.-M. Huang and R.W. Harris, "Large Vector Quantization Codebook Generation Problems and Solutions," *Proc. Data Compression Conf. (DCC '92)*, CS Press, Los Alamitos, Calif., p. 413, 1992.

[D338] N.D. Memon and K. Sayood, "Lossless Image Compression Using a Codebook of Prediction Trees," *Proc. Data Compression Conf. (DCC '92)*, CS Press, Los Alamitos, Calif., p. 414, 1992.

[D339] N. Coppisetti, S.C. Kwatra, and A.K. Al-Asmari, "Low Complexity Subband Encoding for HDTV Images," *Proc. Data Compression Conf. (DCC '92)*, CS Press, Los Alamitos, Calif., p. 415, 1992.

[D340] A. Mukherjee, J. Flieder, and N. Ranganathan, "MARVLE: A VLSI Chip of a Memory-Based Architecture for Variable-Length Encoding and Decoding," *Proc. Data Compression Conf. (DCC '92)*, CS Press, Los Alamitos, Calif., p. 416, 1992.

[D341] L.K. Barrett and R.K. Boyd, "Minimization of Expected Distortion through Simulated Annealing of Codebook Vectors," *Proc. Data Compression Conf. (DCC '92)*, CS Press, Los Alamitos, Calif., p. 417, 1992.

[D342] C.-L. Yu and J.-L. Wu, "Modeling Adaptive Multilevel-Dictionary Coding Scheme by Cache Memory Management Policy," *Proc. Data Compression Conf. (DCC '92)*, CS Press, Los Alamitos, Calif., p. 418, 1992.

[D343] K. Salem, "MR-CDF: Managing Multi-Resolution Scientific Data," *Proc. Data Compression Conf. (DCC '92)*, CS Press, Los Alamitos, Calif., p. 419, 1992.

[D344] J.-S. Shiau, J.C. Tseng, and W.-P. Yang, "A New Compression-Based Signature Extraction Method," *Proc. Data Compression Conf. (DCC '92)*, CS Press, Los Alamitos, Calif., p. 420, 1992.

[D345] H.K. Chang and S.-H. Chen, "A New, Locally Adaptive Data Compression Scheme Using Multilist Structure," *Proc. Data Compression Conf. (DCC '92)*, CS Press, Los Alamitos, Calif., p. 421, 1992.

[D346] A. Razavi, "A New VLSl Image Coder for Digital Still Video Camera Applications," *Proc. Data Compression Conf. (DCC '92)*, CS Press, Los Alamitos, Calif., p. 422, 1992.

[D347] Y. Cheng and P. Fortier, "A Parallel Algorithm for Vector Quantizer Design," *Proc. Data Compression Conf. (DCC '92)*, CS Press, Los Alamitos, Calif., p. 423, 1992.

[D348] W.-J. Duh and J.-L. Wu, "Parallel Image and Video Coding Schemes in Multi-Computers," *Proc. Data Compression Conf. (DCC '92)*, CS Press, Los Alamitos, Calif., p. 424, 1992.

[D349] T. Markas, J. Reif, and J.A. Storer, "On Parallel Implementations and Experimentations of Lossless Data Compression Algorithms," *Proc. Data Compression Conf. (DCC '92)*, CS Press, Los Alamitos, Calif., p. 425, 1992.

[D350] A. Narayan and T.V. Ramabadran, "Predictive Vector Quantization of Gray Scale Images," *Proc. Data Compression Conf. (DCC '92)*, CS Press, Los Alamitos, Calif., p. 426, 1992.

[D351] W.D. Maurer, "Proving the Correctness of a Data Compression Program," *Proc. Data Compression Conf. (DCC '92)*, CS Press, Los Alamitos, Calif., p. 427, 1992.

[D352] J.-M. Cheng and G. Langdon, "QM-AYA Adaptive Arithmetic Coder," *Proc. Data Compression Conf. (DCC '92)*, CS Press, Los Alamitos, Calif., p. 428, 1992.

[D353] T.P. Bizon, W.A. Whyte, and V.R. Marcopoli, "Real Time Demonstration Hardware for Enhanced DPCM Video Compression Algorithm," *Proc. Data Compression Conf. (DCC '92)*, CS Press, Los Alamitos, Calif., p. 429, 1992.

[D354] H. Rosche, "Reducing Information Loss during Spatial Compression of Digital Map Image Data," *Proc. Data Compression Conf. (DCC '92)*, CS Press, Los Alamitos, Calif., p. 430, 1992.

[D355] C.-C. Wang and H.-S. Don, "Robust Measures for Fuzzy Entropy and Fuzzy Conditioning," *Proc. Data Compression Conf. (DCC '92)*, CS Press, Los Alamitos, Calif., p. 431, 1992.

[D356] K. Keeler and J. Westbrook, "Short Encodings of Planar Graphs and Maps," *Proc. Data Compression Conf. (DCC '92)*, CS Press, Los Alamitos, Calif., p. 432, 1992.

[D357] D. Tran, B.W. Wei, and M. Desai, "A Single-Chip Data Compression/Decompression Processor," *Proc. Data Compression Conf. (DCC '92)*, CS Press, Los Alamitos, Calif., p. 433, 1992.

[D358] C.-C. Chen and J.-H. Hsieh, "Singular Value Decomposition for Texture Compression," *Proc. Data Compression Conf. (DCC '92)*, CS Press, Los Alamitos, Calif., p. 434, 1992.

[D359] J.A. Greszczuk and M. Deshon, " A Study of Methods for Reducing Blocking Artifacts Caused by Block Transform Coding," *Proc. Data Compression Conf. (DCC '92)*, CS Press, Los Alamitos, Calif., p. 435, 1992.

[D360] D. Glover and S.C. Kwatra, "Subband Coding for Image Data Archiving," *Proc. Data Compression Conf. (DCC '92)*, CS Press, Los Alamitos, Calif., p. 436, 1992.

[D361] L.H. Croft and J.A. Robinson, "Subband Image Coding Using Watershed and Watercourse Lines," *Proc. Data Compression Conf. (DCC '92)*, CS Press, Los Alamitos, Calif., p. 437, 1992.

[D362] M. Cohn and C. Kozhukhin, "Symmetric-Context Coding Schemes," *Proc. Data Compression Conf. (DCC '92)*, CS Press, Los Alamitos, Calif., p. 438, 1992.

[D363] E. Antonidakis and D.A. Perreault, "Time-Space Compression Method Using Simultaneous Program Execution," *Proc. Data Compression Conf. (DCC '92)*, CS Press, Los Alamitos, Calif., p. 439, 1992.

[D364] A.K. Huber, S.E. Budge, and R.W. Harris, "Variable-Rate, Real Time Image Compression for Images Dominated by Point Sources," *Proc. Data Compression Conf. (DCC '92)*, CS Press, Los Alamitos, Calif., p. 440, 1992.

[D365] H. Park, V.K. Prasanna, and C.-L. Wang, "VLSI Architectures for Vector Quantization Based on Clustering," *Proc. Data Compression Conf. (DCC '92)*, CS Press, Los Alamitos, Calif., p. 441, 1992.

[D366] O. Kiselyov and P. Fisher, "Wavelet Compression with Feature Preservation and Derivative Definition," *Proc. Data Compression Conf. (DCC '92)*, CS Press, Los Alamitos, Calif., p. 442, 1992.

[D367] U. Kondrragunta and D.A. Lelewer, "Word Position as a Context," *Proc. Data Compression Conf. (DCC '92)*, CS Press, Los Alamitos, Calif., p. 443, 1992.

[D368] C.A. Papadopoulos and T.G. Clarkson, "Data Compression of Moving Images Using Geometric Transformations," *Proc. Int'l Conf. Image Processing and Its Applications*, pp. 101–104, 1992.

[D369] S. Nanda and W.A. Pearlman, "Tree Coding of Image Subbands," *IEEE Trans. Image Processing*, Vol. 1, No. 2, pp. 133–147, Apr. 1992.

[D370] M. Antonini et al., "Image Coding Using Wavelet Transform," *IEEE Trans. Image Processing*, Vol. 1, No. 2, pp. 205–220, Apr. 1992.

[D371] A.S. Lewis and G. Knowles, "Image Compression Using 2-D Wavelet Transform," *IEEE Trans. Image Processing*, Vol. 1, No. 2, pp. 244–250, Apr. 1992.

[D372] M.C. Rost and K. Sayood, "An Edge Preserving Differential Image Coding Scheme," *IEEE Trans. Image Processing*, Vol. 1, No. 2, pp. 250–256, Apr. 1992.

[D373] M.A. Cody, "The Fast Wavelet Transform," *Dr. Dobb's J.*, pp. 16–28, Apr. 1992.

[D374] D. Chen and A.C. Bovik, "Hierarchical Visual Pattern Image Coding," *IEEE Trans. Comm.*, Vol. 40, No. 4, pp. 671–675, Apr. 1992.

[D375] M. Rabbani, ed., *Selected Papers on Image Coding and Compression*, Milestone Series No. 48, SPIE Press, Bellingham, Wash., 1992.

[D376] L.G. Allred and G.E. Kelly, "A Lossless Image Compression Technique for Infrared Thermal Images," *Proc. SPIE: Hybrid Image and Signal Processing III*, Vol. 1702, SPIE Press, Bellingham, Wash., pp. 230–237, 1992.

[D377] S. Panchanathan, T.H. Yeap, and B. Pilache, "Neural Network for Image Compression," *Proc. SPIE: Applications of Artificial Neural Networks III*, Vol. 1709, SPIE Press, Bellingham, Wash., pp. 376–385, 1992.

[D378] K. Min and H.L. Min, "Neural-Network-Based Image Compression Using AMT DAP 610," *Proc. SPIE: Applications of Artificial Neural Networks III*, Vol. 1709, SPIE Press, Bellingham, Wash., pp. 386–393, 1992.

[D379] S.K. Kenue, "Modified Backpropagation Neural Network with Applications to Image Compression," *Proc. SPIE: Applications of Artificial Neural Networks III*, Vol. 1709, SPIE Press, Bellingham, Wash., pp. 394–407, 1992.

[D380] H. Liu and D.Y. Yun, "Competitive Learning Algorithms for Image Coding," *Proc. SPIE: Applications of Artificial Neural Networks III*, Vol. 1709, SPIE Press, Bellingham, Wash., pp. 408–417, 1992.

[D381] M.L. Hambaba, B.P. Coffey, and N.R. Khemlani, "Image Coding Using a Knowledge-Based Recognition System," *Proc. SPIE: Applications of Artificial Neural Networks III*, Vol. 1709, SPIE Press, Bellingham, Wash., pp. 418–421, 1992.

[D382] M.R. Carbonara, J.E. Fowler, and S.C. Ahalt, "Compression of Digital Video Data Using Artificial Neural Network Differential Vector Quantization," *Proc. SPIE: Applications of Artificial Neural Networks III*, Vol. 1709, SPIE Press, Bellingham, Wash., pp. 376–385, 1992.

[D383] M.G. Perkins, "Data Compression of Stereopairs," *IEEE Trans. Comm.*, Vol. 40, No. 4, pp. 684–696, 1992.

[D384] W. Philips and G. De Jonghe, "Data Compression of ECG's by High-Degree Polynomial Approximation," *IEEE Trans. Biomedical Eng.*, Vol. 39, No. 4, pp. 330–337, Apr. 1992.

[D385] W.-C. Fang et al., "A VLSI Neural Processor for Image Data Compression Using Self-Organization Networks," *IEEE Trans. Neural Networks*, Vol. 3, No. 3, pp. 506–518, May 1992.

[D386] B.Y. Kavalerchick, "A New Technique for High-Performance Computer Data Compression," *Proc. SUPERCOMM/ICC '92 Discovering a New World of Communications*, Vol. 3, pp. 1423–1425, 1992.

[D387] J. Liu and D. Wang, "Data Compression for Image Recognition Using Neural Network," *Proc. Int'l Joint Conf. Neural Networks (IJCNN)*, Vol. 4, IEEE Press, Piscataway, N.J., pp. 333–338, 1992.

[D388] J. Liu and D. Wang, "Image Compression Using Neural Network," *Proc. SPIE: Neural and Stochastic Methods in Image and Signal Processing*, Vol. 1766, SPIE Press, Bellingham, Wash., pp. 639–644, 1992.

[D389] D. Cai and M. Zhou, "Adaptive Image Compression Based on Backpropogation Networks," *Proc. SPIE: Neural and Stochastic Methods in Image and Signal Processing*, Vol. 1766, SPIE Press, Bellingham, Wash., pp. 678–683, 1992.

[D390] D. Cai, W. Wang, and F. Wan, "Unsupervised Neural Network Algorithm for Image Compression," *Proc. SPIE: Neural and Stochastic Methods in Image and Signal Processing*, Vol. 1766, SPIE Press, Bellingham, Wash., pp. 720–725, 1992.

[D391] C.-M. Huang et al., "Fast Full Search Equivalent Encoding Algorithms for Image Compression Using Vector Quantization," *IEEE Trans. Image Processing*, Vol. 1, No. 3, pp. 413–416, July 1992.

[D392] M. Evin and M. Korurek, "A New Data Compression Technique for Electrocardiograms," *Proc. 1992 Int'l Biomedical Eng. Days*, pp. 61–63, 1992.

[D393] A. Bijaoui and L. Huang, "Image Data Compression without Distortion by Minimizing Entropy," *Proc. 11th IAPR Conf. Pattern Recognition—Conf. D: Architectures for Vision and Pattern Recognition*, Vol. IV, CS Press, Los Alamitos, Calif., pp. 22–24, 1992.

[D394] M.G. Albanesi and M. Ferreti, "An Architecture for Image Compression through Wavelet Transform," *Proc. 11th IAPR Conf. Pattern Recognition—Conf. D: Architectures for Vision and Pattern Recognition*, Vol. IV, CS Press, Los Alamitos, Calif., pp. 155–159, 1992.

[D395] Y. Huang, H.M. Driezen, and N.P. Galatsanos, "Prioritized DCT for Compression and Progressive Transmission of Images," *IEEE Trans. Image Processing*, Vol. 1, No. 4, pp. 477–487, Oct. 1992.

[D396] B.Y. Kavalerchik, "Generalized Block Coding of Black and White Images," *IEEE Trans. Image Processing*, Vol. 1, No. 4, pp. 518–520, Oct. 1992.

[D397] T. Senoo and B. Girod, "Vector Quantization for Entropy Coding of Image Subbands," *IEEE Trans. Image Processing*, Vol. 1, No. 4, pp. 526–533, Oct. 1992.

[D398] F. Pinciroli et al., "Effective Data Compression of Angiocardiographic Static Images with PABCEL Method," *Proc. Computers in Cardiology '92*, CS Press, Los Alamitos, Calif., pp. 267–270, 1992.

[D399] V.A. Allen and J. Belina, "ECG Data Compression Using the Discrete Cosine Transform (DCT)," *Proc. Computers in Cardiology*, CS Press, Los Alamitos, Calif., pp. 687–690, 1992.

[D400] M. Barbero and M. Stroppiana, "Data Compression for HDTV Transmission and Distribution," *Proc. IEE Colloquium on Applications of Video Compression in Broadcasting*, IEE Press, Stevenage, Hertfordshire, UK, pp. 10/1–5, 1992.

[D401] J.H. Husoy and S.O. Aase, "Image Subband Coding with Adaptive Filter Banks," *Proc. SPIE: Visual Communications and Image Processing '92*, Vol. 1818, SPIE Press, Bellingham, Wash., pp. 2–11, 1992.

[D402] X. Li et al., "Hierarchical Image Coding with Diamond Shaped Subbands," *Proc. SPIE: Visual Communications and Image Processing '92*, Vol. 1818, SPIE Press, Bellingham, Wash., pp. 42–48, 1992.

[D403] M.R. Banham, J.C. Brailean, and A.K. Katsaggelos, "Wavelet Transform Image Sequence Coder Using Nonstationary Displacement Estimation," *Proc. SPIE: Visual Communications and Image Processing '92*, Vol. 1818, SPIE Press, Bellingham, Wash., pp. 210–221, 1992.

[D404] T. Ebrahimi and M. Kunt, "Image Sequence Coding Using a Three-Dimensional Wavelet Packet and Adaptive Selection," *Proc. SPIE: Visual Communications and Image Processing '92,* Vol. 1818, SPIE Press, Bellingham, Wash., pp. 222–232, 1992.

[D405] Y. Zhang and W. Li, "Study of Nonseparable Subband Filters for Video Coding," *Proc. SPIE: Visual Communications and Image Processing '92,* Vol. 1818, SPIE Press, Bellingham, Wash., pp. 233–240, 1992.

[D406] T. Gaidon, M. Barlaud, and P. Mathieu, "Image Sequence Coding Using Quincunx Wavelet Transform, Motion Compensation, and Lattice Vector Quantization," *Proc. SPIE: Visual Communications and Image Processing '92,* Vol. 1818, SPIE Press, Bellingham, Wash., pp. 241–252, 1992.

[D407] H. Paek, R.C. Kim, and S.U. Lee, "Motion-Compensated Transform Coding Technique Employing Subband Decomposition," *Proc. SPIE: Visual Communications and Image Processing '92,* Vol. 1818, SPIE Press, Bellingham, Wash., pp. 253–264, 1992.

[D408] M. Breeuwer, "Motion-Adaptive Subband Coding of Interlaced Video," *Proc. SPIE: Visual Communications and Image Processing '92,* Vol. 1818, SPIE Press, Bellingham, Wash., pp. 265–275, 1992.

[D409] R.W. Young and N.G. Kingsbury, "Video Compression Using Lapped Transforms for Motion Estimation/Compensation and Coding," *Proc. SPIE: Visual Communications and Image Processing '92,* Vol. 1818, SPIE Press, Bellingham, Wash., pp. 276–287, 1992.

[D410] I. Moccagatta and M. Kunt, "Lattice Vector Quantization Approach to Image Coding," *Proc. SPIE: Visual Comunications. and Image Processing '92,* Vol. 1818, SPIE Press, Bellingham, Wash., pp. 430–440, 1992.

[D411] M. Antonini, M. Barlaud, and T. Gaidon, "Adaptive Entropy-Constrained Lattice Vector Quantization for Multiresolution Image Coding," *Proc. SPIE: Visual Communications and Image Processing '92,* Vol. 1818, SPIE Press, Bellingham, Wash., pp. 441–457, 1992.

[D412] N. Mohsenian and M.M. Nasrabadi, "A Neural Net Approach to Predictive Vector Quantization," *Proc. SPIE: Visual Communications and Image Processing '92,* Vol. 1818, SPIE Press, Bellingham, Wash., pp. 476–487, 1992.

[D413] S.W. Wu and A. Gersho, "Lapped Block Decoding for Vector Quantization of Images," *Proc. SPIE: Visual Communications and Image Processing '92,* Vol. 1818, SPIE Press, Bellingham, Wash., pp. 488–499, 1992.

[D414] S. Venkatraman, J.Y. Nam, and K.R. Rao, "Image Coding Based on Classified Lapped Orthogonal Transform Vector Quantization," *Proc. SPIE: Visual Communications and Image Processing '92,* Vol. 1818, SPIE Press, Bellingham, Wash., pp. 500–511, 1992.

[D415] C. Wang and L. Chang, "Color Image Coding Using Variable Blocksize Vector Quantization in (R,G,B) Domains," *Proc. SPIE: Visual Communications and Image Processing '92,* Vol. 1818, SPIE Press, Bellingham, Wash., pp. 512–523, 1992.

[D416] A. Nicoulin and M. Mattavelli, "Statistic Model for Coding Subband Images Using VQ and Arithmetic Coding," *Proc. SPIE: Visual Communications and Image Processing '92,* Vol. 1818, SPIE Press, Bellingham, Wash., pp. 700–710, 1992.

[D417] G.H. Ong, "A Multi-Block Data Compression Method Based on Arithmetic Coding for a Library Database," *ICCS/ISITA '92: Communications on the Move,* Vol. 3, pp. 1067–1071, 1992.

[D418] P.C. Cosman, E.A. Riskin, and R.M. Gray, "Combining Vector Quantization with Histogram Equalization," *Information Processing and Management,* Vol. 28, No. 6, pp. 681–686, Nov./Dec. 1992.

[D419] O.T.-C. Chen, B.J. Sheu, and W.-C. Fang, "Image Compression on a VLSI Neural-Based Vector Quantizer," *Information Processing and Management,* Vol. 28, No. 6, pp. 687–706, Nov./Dec. 1992.

[D420] T. Markas and J. Reif, "Quad Tree Structures for Image Compression Applications," *Information Processing and Management,* Vol. 28, No. 6, pp. 707–721, Nov./Dec. 1992.

[D421] J. Lin, J.A. Storer, and M. Cohn, "Optimal Pruning for Tree-Structured Vector Quantization," *Information Processing and Management*, Vol. 28, No. 6, pp. 723–733, Nov./Dec. 1992.

[D422] A. Bookstein and S.T. Klein, "Models of Bitmap Generation: A Systematic Approach to Bitmap Compression," *Information Processing and Management*, Vol. 28, No. 6, pp. 735–748, Nov./Dec. 1992.

[D423] P.G. Howard and J.S. Vitter, "Analysis of Arithmetic Coding for Data Compression," *Information Processing and Management*, Vol. 28, No. 6, pp. 749–764, Nov./Dec. 1992.

[D424] P.G. Howard and J.S. Vitter, "New Methods for Lossless Image Compression Using Arithmetic Coding," *Information Processing and Management*, Vol. 28, No. 6, pp. 765–779, Nov./Dec. 1992.

[D425] C. Nevill and T. Bell, "Compression of Parallel Texts," *Information Processing and Management*, Vol. 28, No. 6, pp. 781–793, Nov./Dec. 1992.

[D426] A. Bookstein, S.T. Klein, and D.A. Ziff, "A Systematic Approach to Compressing a Full-Text Retrieval System," *Information Processing and Management*, Vol. 28, No. 6, pp. 795–806, Nov./Dec. 1992.

[D427] E.D. Chesmore and A.H. Khalil, "Knowledge-Based Approach to Adaptive Compression of Telemetered Data," *Electronic Letters*, Vol. 28, No. 25, pp. 2325–2326, Dec. 1992.

[D428] J. Venbrux, P.-S. Yeh, and M.N. Liu, "A VLSI Chip Set for High-Speed Lossless Data Compression," *IEEE Trans. Circuits and Systems for Video Technology*, Vol. 2, No. 4, pp. 381–391, Dec. 1992.

[D429] C.-H. Hsieh, "DCT-Based Codebook Design for Vector Quantization of Images," *IEEE Trans. Circuits and Systems for Video Technology*, Vol. 2, No. 4, pp. 401–409, Dec. 1992.

[D430] A. Gersho, *Vector Quantization and Signal Compression*, Kluwer Academic Publishers, Dordrecht, The Netherlands, 1992.

[D431] N. Ranganathan and S. Henriques, "High-Speed VLSI Designs for Lempel–Ziv-Based Data Compression," *IEEE Trans. Circuits and Systems II: Analog and Digital Signal Processing,* Vol. 40, No. 2, pp. 98–106, Feb. 1993.

[D432] I.M. Bockstein, "A Method of Lossless Image Compression," *Pattern Recognition and Image Analysis*, Vol. 3, No. 2, pp. 92–98, Feb. 1993.

[D433] K.L. Oehler and R.M. Gray, "Combining Image Classification and Image Compression Using Vector Quantization," *Proc. Data Compression Conf. (DCC '93)*, CS Press, Los Alamitos, Calif., pp. 2–11, 1993.

[D434] D. Miller and K. Rose, "An Improved Sequential Search Multistage Vector Quantizer," *Proc. Data Compression Conf. (DCC '93)*, CS Press, Los Alamitos, Calif., pp. 12–21, Apr. 1993.

[D435] X. Wu, "Globally Optimal Bit Allocation," *Proc. Data Compression Conf. (DCC '93)*, CS Press, Los Alamitos, Calif., pp. 22–31, 1993.

[D436] C. Constantinescu and J.A. Storer, "On-Line Adaptive Vector Quantization with Variable Size Codebook Entries," *Proc. Data Compression Conf. (DCC '93)*, CS Press, Los Alamitos, Calif., pp. 32–41, 1993.

[D437] W-Y. Chan, A. Gersho, and S.W. Soong, "Joint Codebook Design for Summation Product-Coed Vector Quantizers," *Proc. Data Compression Conf. (DCC '93)*, CS Press, Los Alamitos, Calif., pp. 42–51, 1993.

[D438] J. Abrahams, "Codes with Monotonic Codeword Lengths," *Proc. Data Compression Conf. (DCC '93)*, CS Press, Los Alamitos, Calif., pp. 52–59, 1993.

[D439] B.K. Natarajan, "Filtering Random Noise via Data Compression," *Proc. Data Compression Conf. (DCC '93)*, CS Press, Los Alamitos, Calif., pp. 60–69, 1993.

[D440] A. Bookstein et al., "Can Random Fluctuation Be Exploited in Data Compression?" *Proc. Data Compression Conf. (DCC '93)*, CS Press, Los Alamitos, Calif., pp. 70–78, 1993.

[D441] G.H. Freeman, "Divergence and the Construction of Variable-to-Variable-Length Lossless Codes by Source-Word Extensions," *Proc. Data Compression Conf. (DCC '93)*, CS Press, Los Alamitos, Calif., pp. 79–88, 1993.

[D442] T. Linder, G. Lugosi, and K. Zeger, "Universality and Rates of Convergence in Lossy Source Coding," *Proc. Data Compression Conf. (DCC '93)*, CS Press, Los Alamitos, Calif., pp. 89–97, 1993.

[D443] P.G. Howard and J.S. Vitter, "Design and Analysis of Fast Text Compression Based on Quasi-Arithmetic Coding," *Proc. Data Compression Conf. (DCC '93)*, CS Press, Los Alamitos, Calif., pp. 98–107, 1993.

[D444] A. Moffat et al., "An Empirical Evaluation of Coding Methods for Multi-Symbol Alphabets," *Proc. Data Compression Conf. (DCC '93)*, CS Press, Los Alamitos, Calif., pp. 108–117, 1993.

[D445] G. Feygin, P.G. Gulak, and P. Chow, "Minimizing Error and VLSI Complexity in the Multiplication Free Approximation of Arithmetic Coding," *Proc. Data Compression Conf. (DCC '93)*, CS Press, Los Alamitos, Calif., pp. 118–127, 1993.

[D446] H. Printz and P. Stubley, "Multialphabet Arithmetic Coding at 16 MBytes/sec," *Proc. Data Compression Conf. (DCC '93)*, CS Press, Los Alamitos, Calif., pp. 128–137, 1993.

[D447] P.M. Fenwick, "Ziv–Lempel Encoding with Multi-Bit Flags," *Proc. Data Compression Conf. (DCC '93)*, CS Press, Los Alamitos, Calif., pp. 138–147, 1993.

[D448] I. Sadeh, "On Approximate String Matching," *Proc. Data Compression Conf. (DCC '93)*, CS Press, Los Alamitos, Calif., pp. 148–157, 1993.

[D449] J.T. Connor and L.E. Atlas, "Coding Theory and Regularization," *Proc. Data Compression Conf. (DCC '93)*, CS Press, Los Alamitos, Calif., pp. 158–167, 1993.

[D450] V. Bhaskaran, B.K. Natarajan, and K. Konstantinides, "Optimal Piecewise-Linear Compression of Images," *Proc. Data Compression Conf. (DCC '93)*, CS Press, Los Alamitos, Calif., pp. 168–177, 1993.

[D451] A.B. Watson, "Visually Optimal DCT Quantization Matrices for Individual Images," *Proc. Data Compression Conf. (DCC '93)*, CS Press, Los Alamitos, Calif., pp. 178–187, 1993.

[D452] D.M. Monro and B.G. Sherlock, "Optimum DCT Quantization," *Proc. Data Compression Conf. (DCC '93)*, CS Press, Los Alamitos, Calif., pp. 188–194, 1993.

[D453] J.D. Villasenor, "Full-Frame Compression of Tomographic Images Using the Discrete Fourier Transform," *Proc. Data Compression Conf. (DCC '93)*, CS Press, Los Alamitos, Calif., pp. 195–203, 1993.

[D454] A. Rios and M.R. Kabuka, "A High Performance Adaptive Image Compression System Using a Generative Neural Network: Dynamic Neural Network II (DANN II)," *Proc. Data Compression Conf. (DCC '93)*, CS Press, Los Alamitos, Calif., pp. 204–213, 1993.

[D455] J.M. Shapiro, "An Embedded Hierarchical Image Coder Using Zerotrees of Wavelet Coefficients," *Proc. Data Compression Conf. (DCC '93)*, CS Press, Los Alamitos, Calif., pp. 214–223, 1993.

[D456] J.M. Bradley and C.M. Brislawn, "Wavelet Transform-Vector Quantization Compression of Supercomputer Ocean Models," *Proc. Data Compression Conf. (DCC '93)*, CS Press, Los Alamitos, Calif., pp. 224–233, 1993.

[D457] K. Culik II, S. Dube, and P. Rajcani, "Efficient Compression of Wavelet Coefficients for Smooth and Fractal-Like Data," *Proc. Data Compression Conf. (DCC '93)*, CS Press, Los Alamitos, Calif., pp. 234–243, 1993.

[D458] H. Raittinen and K. Kaski, "Fractal Based Image Compression with Affine Transformations," *Proc. Data Compression Conf. (DCC '93)*, CS Press, Los Alamitos, Calif., pp. 244–253, 1993.

[D459] D.M. Monro, "Generalized Fractal Transforms: Complexity Issues," *Proc. Data Compression Conf. (DCC '93)*, CS Press, Los Alamitos, Calif., pp. 254–261, 1993.

[D460] X. Wu and Y. Fang, "Segmentation-Based Progressive Image Coding," *Proc. Data Compression Conf. (DCC '93)*, CS Press, Los Alamitos, Calif., pp. 262–271, 1993.

[D461] C.F. Barnes and E.J. Holder, "Classified Variable Rate Residual Vector Quantization Applied to Image Subband Coding," *Proc. Data Compression Conf. (DCC '93)*, CS Press, Los Alamitos, Calif., pp. 272–281, 1993.

[D462] A.C. Hung and T.H.-Y. Meng, "Adaptive Channel Optimization of Vector Quantized Data," *Proc. Data Compression Conf. (DCC '93)*, CS Press, Los Alamitos, Calif., pp. 282–291, 1993.

[D463] J. Lin and J.A. Storer, "Design and Performance of Tree-Structured Vector Quantizers," *Proc. Data Compression Conf. (DCC '93)*, CS Press, Los Alamitos, Calif., pp. 292–301, 1993.

[D464] B.D. Andrews et al., "A Mean-Removed Variation of Weighted Universal Vector Quantization for Image Coding," *Proc. Data Compression Conf. (DCC '93)*, CS Press, Los Alamitos, Calif., pp. 302–309, 1993.

[D465] H. Yokoo, "Application of AVL Trees to Adaptive Compression of Numerical Data," *Proc. Data Compression Conf. (DCC '93)*, CS Press, Los Alamitos, Calif., pp. 310–319, 1993.

[D466] G. Promhouse, "Tree Compacting Transformations," *Proc. Data Compression Conf. (DCC '93)*, CS Press, Los Alamitos, Calif., pp. 320–329, 1993.

[D467] A. Zandi, B. Iyer, and G. Langdon, "Sort Order Data Compression for Extended Alphabets," *Proc. Data Compression Conf. (DCC '93)*, CS Press, Los Alamitos, Calif., pp. 330–339, 1993.

[D468] S. Grumbach and F. Tahi, "Compression of DNA Sequences," *Proc. Data Compression Conf. (DCC '93)*, CS Press, Los Alamitos, Calif., pp. 340–350, 1993.

[D469] P.G. Howard and J.S. Vitter, "Fast and Efficient Lossless Image Compression," *Proc. Data Compression Conf. (DCC '93)*, CS Press, Los Alamitos, Calif., pp. 351–360, 1993.

[D470] J.E. Fowler and S.C. Ahalt, "Robust, Variable Bit-Rate Coding Using Entropy-Biased Codebooks," *Proc. Data Compression Conf. (DCC '93)*, CS Press, Los Alamitos, Calif., pp. 361–370, 1993.

[D471] F. Kossentini, W.C. Chung, and M.J.T. Smith, "Low Bit Rate Coding of Earth Science Images," *Proc. Data Compression Conf. (DCC '93)*, CS Press, Los Alamitos, Calif., pp. 371–380, 1993.

[D472] S. Arya and D.M. Mount, "Algorithms for Fast Vector Quantization," *Proc. Data Compression Conf. (DCC '93)*, CS Press, Los Alamitos, Calif., pp. 381–390, 1993.

[D473] T. Markas and J. Reif, "Multispectral Image Compression Algorithms," *Proc. Data Compression Conf. (DCC '93)*, CS Press, Los Alamitos, Calif., pp. 391–400, 1993.

[D474] R. Tawel, "Real-Time Focal-Plane Image Compression," *Proc. Data Compression Conf. (DCC '93)*, CS Press, Los Alamitos, Calif., pp. 401–409, 1993.

[D475] G.T. Tuttle, S. Fallahi, and A.A. Abidi, "A Low-Power Analog CMOS Vector Quantizer," *Proc. Data Compression Conf. (DCC '93)*, CS Press, Los Alamitos, Calif., pp. 410–419, 1993.

[D476] H.H. Taylor, D. Chin, and A.W. Jessup, "An MPEG Encoder Implementation on the Princeton Engine Video Supercomputer," *Proc. Data Compression Conf. (DCC '93)*, CS Press, Los Alamitos, Calif., pp. 420–430, 1993.

[D477] S. Forchhammer, "Adaptive Context for JBIG Compression of Bi-Level Halftone Images," *Proc. Data Compression Conf. (DCC '93)*, CS Press, Los Alamitos, Calif., p. 431, 1993.

[D478] Y.A. Ignatieff and E. Koch, "Binary Tree Dictionary Coding Using Logic Alphabet for Image Compression," *Proc. Data Compression Conf. (DCC '93)*, CS Press, Los Alamitos, Calif., p. 432, 1993.

[D479] G.G. Langdon, Jr., and M. Manohar, "Centering of Context-Dependent Components of Prediction Error Distributions of Images," *Proc. Data Compression Conf. (DCC '93)*, CS Press, Los Alamitos, Calif., p. 433, 1993.

[D480] A. Desoky, C. O'Connor, and P. Lankswert, "Coding of Gray Scale and Color Images by Polygon Segmentation," *Proc. Data Compression Conf. (DCC '93)*, CS Press, Los Alamitos, Calif., p. 434, 1993.

[D481] K.M. Liang, C.M. Huang, and R.W. Harris, "Comparison between Adaptive Search and Bit Allocation Algorithms for Image Compression Using Vector Quantization," *Proc. Data Compression Conf. (DCC '93)*, CS Press, Los Alamitos, Calif., p. 435, 1993.

[D482] M.A. Ghafourian and C.-M. Huang, "Comparison between Several Adaptive Search Vector Quantization Schemes and JPEG Standard for Image Compression," *Proc. Data Compression Conf. (DCC '93)*, CS Press, Los Alamitos, Calif., p. 436, 1993.

[D483] D. Glover and S.C. Kwatra, "Compressing Subbanded Image Data with Lempel–Ziv-Based Coders," *Proc. Data Compression Conf. (DCC '93)*, CS Press, Los Alamitos, Calif., p. 437, 1993.

[D484] K. Sathish and O. Johnson, "Compression and Restoration of SEG-Y Files," *Proc. Data Compression Conf. (DCC '93)*, CS Press, Los Alamitos, Calif., p. 438, 1993.

[D485] M.D. Dahlin et al., "CRAM: Hardware Support for End-to-End Compression," *Proc. Data Compression Conf. (DCC '93)*, CS Press, Los Alamitos, Calif., p. 439, 1993.

[D486] M.L. Incze and G.W. Lucas, "Data Compression for Environmental Data in the GEM System," *Proc. Data Compression Conf. (DCC '93)*, CS Press, Los Alamitos, Calif., p. 440, 1993.

[D487] K.W. Ohnesorge, P. Stucki, and M. Bichsel, "Data Models for Lossless Image Compression Using Arithmetic Coding," *Proc. Data Compression Conf. (DCC '93)*, CS Press, Los Alamitos, Calif., p. 441, 1993.

[D488] R.L. Kirlin, J. Fan, and S.D. Stearns, "Design of a Data Compression Scheme," *Proc. Data Compression Conf. (DCC '93)*, CS Press, Los Alamitos, Calif., p. 442, 1993.

[D489] G.D. Miller and J. Malla, "A Different Approach Using 'POLA' for Image Compression," *Proc. Data Compression Conf. (DCC '93)*, CS Press, Los Alamitos, Calif., p. 443, 1993.

[D490] M. Patel, N. MacLean, and G. Langdon, "An Economical Hardware-Oriented High-Speed Data Compression Scheme," *Proc. Data Compression Conf. (DCC '93)*, CS Press, Los Alamitos, Calif., p. 444, 1993.

[D491] O.S. Schoepke and G.C. Smith, "A Fast Decoding Algorithm for Arithmetic Coding," *Proc. Data Compression Conf. (DCC '93)*, CS Press, Los Alamitos, Calif., p. 445, 1993.

[D492] A.D. Samples, "Faster Dictionary Growth in Ziv–Lempel-Style Compression," *Proc. Data Compression Conf. (DCC '93)*, CS Press, Los Alamitos, Calif., p. 446, 1993.

[D493] S.-G. Miaou and J.T. Tou, "Fast Image Decompression for Telebrowsing of Images," *Proc. Data Compression Conf. (DCC '93)*, CS Press, Los Alamitos, Calif., p. 447, 1993.

[D494] N. Ranganathan, S.G. Romaniuk, and K.R. Namuduri, "A Feature-Based Heuristic Algorithm for Lossless Image Compression," *Proc. Data Compression Conf. (DCC '93)*, CS Press, Los Alamitos, Calif., p. 448, 1993.

[D495] M.J. Gormish and J.D. Allen, "Finite State Machine Binary Entropy Coding," *Proc. Data Compression Conf. (DCC '93)*, CS Press, Los Alamitos, Calif., p. 449, 1993.

[D496] M.G. Hinchey and T. Cahill, "Formal Methods and Compression/Decompression Techniques," *Proc. Data Compression Conf. (DCC '93)*, CS Press, Los Alamitos, Calif., p. 450, 1993.

[D497] R. Rinaldo and A. Zakhor, "Fractal Approximation of Images," *Proc. Data Compression Conf. (DCC '93)*, CS Press, Los Alamitos, Calif., p. 451, 1993.

[D498] G. Promhouse and M. Bauer, "Generalized Low Level Encoding," *Proc. Data Compression Conf. (DCC '93)*, CS Press, Los Alamitos, Calif., p. 452, 1993.

[D499] J.A. Foster, P.W. Oman, and K. Van Houten, "A Highly Compact Representation of Tree Structures," *Proc. Data Compression Conf. (DCC '93)*, CS Press, Los Alamitos, Calif., p. 453, 1993.

[D500] A. Razavi, "A High Performance JPEG Image Compression Chip Set for Multimedia Applications," *Proc. Data Compression Conf. (DCC '93)*, CS Press, Los Alamitos, Calif., p. 454, 1993.

[D501] M.-C. Lee, "High Speed Video Compression Using Generalized Multiscale Motion Compensation with Logarithmic Quantization," *Proc. Data Compression Conf. (DCC '93)*, CS Press, Los Alamitos, Calif., p. 455, 1993.

[D502] T.L. Yu, "Hybrid Dynamic Markov Modeling," *Proc. Data Compression Conf. (DCC '93)*, CS Press, Los Alamitos, Calif., p. 456, 1993.

[D503] C.-Y. (M.) Maa, "Identifying the Existence of Bar Codes in Compressed Images," *Proc. Data Compression Conf. (DCC '93)*, CS Press, Los Alamitos, Calif., p. 457, 1993.

[D504] M.-C. Lee, "Image Compression Using Generalized Multiscale Vector Quantization: A Product Code Vector Quantization Approach," *Proc. Data Compression Conf. (DCC '93)*, CS Press, Los Alamitos, Calif., p. 458, 1993.

[D505] A. Averbuch, D. Lazar, and M Israeli, "Image Compression Using Wavelet Transform and Multiresolution Decomposition," *Proc. Data Compression Conf. (DCC '93)*, CS Press, Los Alamitos, Calif., p. 459, 1993.

[D506] L. Huang, "Image Data Compression by Gray Scale Morphological Skeleton," *Proc. Data Compression Conf. (DCC '93)*, CS Press, Los Alamitos, Calif., p. 460, 1993.

[D507] K. Christiansen and W. Barrett, "An Improved Method for Color Quantization," *Proc. Data Compression Conf. (DCC '93)*, CS Press, Los Alamitos, Calif., p. 461, 1993.

[D508] G.M. Shebert and M. Kabuka, "An Improvement to the Neural Network Compression of Medical Image Data," *Proc. Data Compression Conf. (DCC '93)*, CS Press, Los Alamitos, Calif., p. 462, 1993.

[D509] Y.-L. Lin and S.S. Skiena, "Inducing Better Codes from Examples," *Proc. Data Compression Conf. (DCC '93)*, CS Press, Los Alamitos, Calif., p. 463, 1993.

[D510] A. Bookstein and S.T. Klein, "Is Huffman Coding Dead?" *Proc. Data Compression Conf. (DCC '93)*, CS Press, Los Alamitos, Calif., p. 464, 1993.

[D511] J.Y.H. Liao, J.D. Villasenor, and R. Jain, "JPEG-Compatible Hybrid Compression Using Supplemental Error Coding," *Proc. Data Compression Conf. (DCC '93)*, CS Press, Los Alamitos, Calif., p. 465, 1993.

[D512] T.-M. Koo, H. Lu, and D.D. Fisher, "A Method of Dictionary Compression for Spelling Checkers," *Proc. Data Compression Conf. (DCC '93)*, CS Press, Los Alamitos, Calif., p. 466, 1993.

[D513] N. Scaife and A. Gammerman, "Minimal Length Encoding and Its Application to a Large Set of Medical Data," *Proc. Data Compression Conf. (DCC '93)*, CS Press, Los Alamitos, Calif., p. 467, 1993.

[D514] R. Pruchnik, "Modeling by Multiplying Model: An Application to Arithmetic Coding," *Proc. Data Compression Conf. (DCC '93)*, CS Press, Los Alamitos, Calif., p. 468, 1993.

[D515] T. Ozcelik and A.K. Katsaggelos, "Motion Compensated Coding of Image Sequences without Transmitting Motion Vectors," *Proc. Data Compression Conf. (DCC '93)*, CS Press, Los Alamitos, Calif., p. 469, 1993.

[D516] C.-M. Huang, "Multi-Stage Adaptive Search Vector Quantization Image Compression," *Proc. Data Compression Conf. (DCC '93)*, CS Press, Los Alamitos, Calif., p. 470, 1993.

[D517] H.U. Khan and H.A. Fatmi, "A Novel Approach to Data Compression as a Pattern Recognition Problem," *Proc. Data Compression Conf. (DCC '93)*, CS Press, Los Alamitos, Calif., p. 471, 1993.

[D518] S. Fioravanti, "A Novel Lossless Predictor for VQ Schemes," *Proc. Data Compression Conf. (DCC '93)*, CS Press, Los Alamitos, Calif., p. 472, 1993.

[D519] B.W. Evans and R.L. Renner, "Optimal Bit Rate Allocation for Wavelet Transform Coding," *Proc. Data Compression Conf. (DCC '93)*, CS Press, Los Alamitos, Calif., p. 473, 1993.

[D520] F.G.B. De Natale, "Optimized Bi-Linear Interpolation and DCT: A Two-Source Coding for Image Compression," *Proc. Data Compression Conf. (DCC '93)*, CS Press, Los Alamitos, Calif., p. 474, 1993.

[D521] S. Venkataraman and P.M. Farrelle, "Optimum Quantization in Hybrid JPEG/Recursive Block Coding of Images," *Proc. Data Compression Conf. (DCC '93)*, CS Press, Los Alamitos, Calif., p. 475, 1993.

[D522] Y.Y. Zhang, "A Perfectly Parallel Thinning Algorithm with Two-Subiteration," *Proc. Data Compression Conf. (DCC '93)*, CS Press, Los Alamitos, Calif., p. 476, 1993.

[D523] C.H. Zheng and W. Refai, "Predictive Color Motion Image Coding Using Quadtree Decomposition and Concentric-Shell Partition Vector Quantization," *Proc. Data Compression Conf. (DCC '93)*, CS Press, Los Alamitos, Calif., p. 477, 1993.

[D524] D. Wongsawang and M. Okamoto, "A Predictive Data Compression with Self-Organizing Heuristics," *Proc. Data Compression Conf. (DCC '93)*, CS Press, Los Alamitos, Calif., p. 478, 1993.

[D525] O. Kiselyov and P. Fisher, "Pyramidal Image Decompositions: A New Look," *Proc. Data Compression Conf. (DCC '93)*, CS Press, Los Alamitos, Calif., p. 479, 1993.

[D526] H.-C. Huang and J.-L. Wu, "Real-Time Software-Based Moving Picture Coding (SBMPC) System," *Proc. Data Compression Conf. (DCC '93)*, CS Press, Los Alamitos, Calif., p. 480, 1993.

[D527] T.P. Bizon, M.J. Shalkhauser, and W.A. Whyte, Jr., "Real-Time Transmission of Digital Video Using Variable-Length Coding," *Proc. Data Compression Conf. (DCC '93)*, CS Press, Los Alamitos, Calif., p. 481, 1993.

[D528] X. Wu and Y. Fang, "Segmentation Coding by Minimum-Weight Graph Coloring," *Proc. Data Compression Conf. (DCC '93)*, CS Press, Los Alamitos, Calif., p. 482, 1993.

[D529] S.S. Ardalan, J. Foster, and H.L. Martin, "Speech Waveform Coding and Compression Using Adaptive Vector Quantization," *Proc. Data Compression Conf. (DCC '93)*, CS Press, Los Alamitos, Calif., p. 483, 1993.

[D530] G. Promhouse, "Stochastic Tree Compression," *Proc. Data Compression Conf. (DCC '93)*, CS Press, Los Alamitos, Calif., p. 484, 1993.

[D531] R.F. Haines and S.L. Chuang, "A Study of Video Frame Rate on the Perception of Compressed Dynamic Imagery," *Proc. Data Compression Conf. (DCC '93)*, CS Press, Los Alamitos, Calif., p. 485, 1993.

[D532] J. Kovacevic, "Subband Coding Systems Incorporating Quantizer Models," *Proc. Data Compression Conf. (DCC '93)*, CS Press, Los Alamitos, Calif., p. 486, 1993.

[D533] A.M. Eskiciouglu and P.S. Fisher, "A Survey of Quality Measures for Gray Scale Image Compression," *Proc. Data Compression Conf. (DCC '93)*, CS Press, Los Alamitos, Calif., p. 487, 1993.

[D534] P.M. Fenwick and P.C. Gutmann, "Table-Driven Arithmetic Coding," *Proc. Data Compression Conf. (DCC '93)*, CS Press, Los Alamitos, Calif., p. 488, 1993.

[D535] C. Fan and H. Ma, "A Ternary VSELP Speech Coder at 8000 BPS," *Proc. Data Compression Conf. (DCC '93)*, CS Press, Los Alamitos, Calif., p. 489, 1993.

[D536] Y.-F. Wong, "Ultrafast Principal Component Vector Quantization," *Proc. Data Compression Conf. (DCC '93)*, CS Press, Los Alamitos, Calif., p. 490, 1993.

[D537] J. Abrahams, "Universal Coding for Unequal Code Symbol Costs," *Proc. Data Compression Conf. (DCC '93)*, CS Press, Los Alamitos, Calif., p. 491, 1993.

[D538] B. Carpentieri and J.A. Storer, "A Video Coder Based on Split-Merge Displacement Estimation," *Proc. Data Compression Conf. (DCC '93)*, CS Press, Los Alamitos, Calif., p. 492, 1993.

[D539] R.P. Blanford, "Wavelet Encoding and Variable Resolution Progressive Transmission," *Proc. Data Compression Conf. (DCC '93)*, CS Press, Los Alamitos, Calif., p. 493, 1993.

[D540] A.E. Cetin, H. Koymen, and M.C. Aydin, "Multichannel ECG Data Compression by Multirate Signal Processing and Transform Domain Coding Techniques," *IEEE Trans. Biomedical Eng.*, Vol. 40, No. 5, pp. 495–499, May 1993.

[D541] A. Nicoulin et al., "Subband Image Coding Using Jointly Localized Filter Banks and Entropy Coding Based on Vector Quantization," *Optical Eng.*, Vol. 32, No. 7, pp. 1438–1450, July 1993.

[D542] R.W. Young and N.G. Kingsbury, "Video Compression Using Lapped Transforms for Motion Estimation/Compensation and Coding," *Optical Eng.*, Vol. 32, No. 7, pp. 1451–1463, July 1993.

[D543] L. Blanc-Feraud, M. Barlaud, and T. Gaidon, "Motion Estimation Involving Discontinuities in a Multiresolution Scheme," *Optical Eng.*, Vol. 32, No. 7, pp. 1475–1482, July 1993.

[D544] K.N. Ngan and W.L. Chooi, "Subband Motion Analysis," *Optical Eng.*, Vol. 32, No. 7, pp. 1483–1488, July 1993.

[D545] S.-W. Wu and A. Gersho, "Lapped Vector Quantization of Images," *Optical Eng.*, Vol. 32, No. 7, pp. 1489–1495, July 1993.

[D546] N. Mohsenian, S.A. Rizvi, and N.M. Nasrabadi, "Predictive Vector Quantization Using a Neural Network Approach," *Optical Eng.*, Vol. 32, No. 7, pp. 1503–1513, July 1993.

[D547] D.G. Daut, D. Zhao, and J.-C. Wu, "Double Predictor Differential Pulse Code Modulation Algorithm for Image Data Compression," *Optical Eng.*, Vol. 32, No. 7, pp. 1514–1523, July 1993.

[D548] C. Hwang, S. Venkatraman, and K.R. Rao, "Human Visual System Weighted Progressive Image Transmission Using Lapped Orthogonal Transform/Classified Vector Quantization," *Optical Eng.*, Vol. 32, No. 7, pp. 1524–1530, July 1993.

[D549] D.L. McLaren and A. Gersho, "Multiresolution High-Definition Television Compression Algorithm for Digital Video Tape Recording," *Optical Eng.*, Vol. 32, No. 7, pp. 1549–1558, July 1993.

[D550] F. Dufaux et al., "Motion-Compensated Generic Coding of Video Based on a Multiresolution Data Structure," *Optical Eng.*, Vol. 32, No. 7, pp. 1559–1570, July 1993.

[D551] H.-C. Huang, M. Ouhyoung, and J.-L. Wu, "Automatic Feature Point Extraction on a Human Face in Model Based Image Coding," *Optical Eng.*, Vol. 32, No. 7, pp. 1571–1580, July 1993.

[D552] O.-J. Kwon and R. Chellappa, "Segmentation-Based Image Compression," *Optical Eng.*, Vol. 32, No. 7, pp. 1581–1587, July 1993.

[D553] H. Li, M. Novak, and R. Forchheimer, "Fractal-Based Image Sequence Compression Scheme," *Optical Eng.*, Vol. 32, No. 7, pp. 1588–1595, July 1993.

[D554] H.-S. Hsu and W.-H. Tsai, "Moment-Preserving Edge Detection and Its Application to Image Data Compression," *Optical Eng.*, Vol. 32, No. 7, pp. 1596–1608, July 1993.

[D555] J.M. Shapiro, "Image Coding Using the Embedded Zerotree Wavelet Algorithm," *Proc. SPIE: Mathematical Imaging: Wavelet Applications in Signal and Image Processing*, Vol. 2034, SPIE Press, Bellingham, Wash., pp. 180–193, 1993.

[D556] Q. Liu et al., "Hybrid Technique Using Spline-Wavelet Packets and Vector Quantization for High-Rate Image Compression," *Proc. SPIE: Mathematical Imaging: Wavelet Applications in Signal and Image Processing*, Vol. 2034, SPIE Press, Bellingham, Wash., pp. 194–204, 1993.

[D557] G. Aharoni et al., "Local Cosine Transform: A Method for the Reduction of the Blocking Effect in JPEG," *Proc. SPIE: Mathematical Imaging: Wavelet Applications in Signal and Image Processing*, Vol. 2034, SPIE Press, Bellingham, Wash., pp. 205–217, 1993.

[D558] W.C. Powell and S.G. Wilson, "Lattice Quantization in the Wavelet Domain," *Proc. SPIE: Mathematical Imaging: Wavelet Applications in Signal and Image Processing*, Vol. 2034, SPIE Press, Bellingham, Wash., pp. 218–229, 1993.

[D559] F.O. Zeppenfeldt, J.B. Borger, and A. Koppes, "Optimal Thresholding in Wavelet Image Compression," *Proc. SPIE: Mathematical Imaging: Wavelet Applications in Signal and Image Processing*, Vol. 2034, SPIE Press, Bellingham, Wash., pp. 230–241, 1993.

[D560] F. Hartung and J.H. Husoy, "Wavelet and Subband Coding of Images: A Comparative Study," *Proc. SPIE: Mathematical Imaging: Wavelet Applications in Signal and Image Processing*, Vol. 2034, SPIE Press, Bellingham, Wash., pp. 242–253, 1993.

[D561] M. Chou and E. Lin, "Wavelet Compression through Wavelet Stieltjes Transform," *Proc. SPIE: Mathematical Imaging: Wavelet Applications in Signal and Image Processing*, Vol. 2034, SPIE Press, Bellingham, Wash., pp. 254–265, 1993.

[D562] B. Deng, B. Jawerth, and G. Peters, "Wavelet Probing for Compression-Based Segmentation," *Proc. SPIE: Mathematical Imaging: Wavelet Applications in Signal and Image Processing*, Vol. 2034, SPIE Press, Bellingham, Wash., pp. 266–276, 1993.

[D563] S. Bhama, H. Singh, and N.D. Phadte, "Parallelism for the Faster Implementation of the K-L Transform for Image Compression," *Pattern Recognition Letters*, Vol. 14, No. 8, pp. 651–660, Aug. 1993.

[D564] M.A. Bassiouni, N.S. Tzannes, and M.C. Tzannes, "High-Fidelity Integrated Lossless/Lossy Compression and Reconstruction of Images," *Optical Eng.*, Vol. 32, No. 8, pp. 1848–1853, Aug. 1993.

[D565] M. Kawashima et al., "Adaptation of the MPEG Video-Coding Algorithm to Network Applications," *IEEE Trans. Circuits and Systems for Video Technology*, Vol. 3, No. 4, pp. 261–269, Aug. 1993.

[D566] M.K. Marcellin, P. Sriram, and K.-L. Tong, "Transform Coding of Monochrome and Color Images Using Trellis Coded Quantization," *IEEE Trans. Circuits and Systems for Video Technology*, Vol. 3, No. 4, pp. 270–276, Aug. 1993.

[D567] P.L. Silsbee, A.C. Bovik, and D. Chen, "Visual Pattern Image Sequence Coding," *IEEE Trans. Circuits and Systems for Video Technology*, Vol. 3, No. 4, pp. 291–301, Aug. 1993.

[D568] J. Kraus, J. Reimers, and K. Gruger, "A VLSI Chip Set for DPCM Coding of HDTV Signals," *IEEE Trans. Circuits and Systems for Video Technology*, Vol. 3, No. 4, pp. 302–308, Aug. 1993.

[D569] K.N. Ngan, N.K. Sin, and H.C. Koh, "HDTV Coding Using Hybrid MRVQ/DCT," *IEEE Trans. Circuits and Systems for Video Technology*, Vol. 3, No. 4, pp. 320–323, Aug. 1993.

[D570] F.G.B. De Natale, G.S. Desoli, and D.D. Giusto, "Adaptive Least-Square Bilinear Interpolation (ALSBI): A New Approach to Image Data Compression," *Electronic Letters*, Vol. 29, No. 8, pp. 1638–1640, 2 Sept. 1993.

[D571] N. Beser, "Development of an AIAA Standard for Space Data Compression," *Proc. AIAA Conf. Computing in Aerospace '93*, p. 4483, 1993.

[D572] S. Jaggi, "An Investigative Study of Multispectral Data Compression for Remotely-Sensed Images," *Proc. AIAA Conf. Computing in Aerospace '93*, p. 4484, 1993.

[D573] R. Matci and J. Mosley, "Wavelet Transform-Adaptive Scalar Quantization of Multispectral Data," *Proc. AIAA Conf. Computing in Aerospace '93*, p. 4485, 1993.

[D574] K. Sayood, S. Magliveras, and N. Memon, "Techniques for Reversible Compression of Multispectral Data," *Proc. AIAA Conf. Computing in Aerospace '93*, p. 4486, 1993.

[D575] A. Watson, "Visual Optimization of DCT Quantization Matrices for Individual Images," *Proc. AIAA Conf. Computing in Aerospace '93*, p. 4512, 1993.

[D576] N. Beser, "Image Data Compression Metrics," *Proc. AIAA Conf. Computing in Aerospace '93*, p. 4513, 1993.

[D577] P. Fisher and A. Eskiciouglu, "Survey of Quality Measures for Gray Scale Image Compression," *Proc. AIAA Conf. Computing in Aerospace '93*, p. 4514, 1993.

[D578] A. Ahumada, "A Visual Detection Model for DCT Coefficient Quantization," *Proc. AIAA Conf. Computing in Aerospace '93*, p. 4515, 1993.

[D579] S.V. Belur, "SCRIPT: Source Coding by Repeated Iterative Partitioning Technique," *Proc. AIAA Conf. Computing in Aerospace '93*, p. 4538, 1993.

[D580] K. Ohnesorge, "Pixel Pyramid for Lossless Image Compression Using Arithmetic Coding," *Proc. AIAA Conf. Computing in Aerospace '93*, p. 4539, 1993.

[D581] P. Yeh, W. Miller, and R. Rice, "On the Optimality of a Universal Lossless Coder," *Proc. AIAA Conf. Computing in Aerospace '93*, p. 4540, 1993.

[D582] R. Rice, P. Yeh, and W. Miller, "Algorithms for High Speed Universal Noiseless Coding," *Proc. AIAA Conf. Computing in Aerospace '93*, p. 4541, 1993.

[D583] T. Markas, "Hardware Implementations of Data Compression Algorithms for Aerospace Applications," *Proc. AIAA Conf. Computing in Aerospace '93*, p. 4563, 1993.

[D584] J. Miko, W. Fong, and W. Miller, "A High Speed Lossless Data Compression System for Space Applications," *Proc. AIAA Conf. Computing in Aerospace '93*, p. 4564, 1993.

[D585] J. Venbrux et al., "A VLSI Chip Set Development for Lossless Data Compression," *Proc. AIAA Conf. Computing in Aerospace '93*, p. 4565, 1993.

[D586] S. Budge, "The Spirit III Radiometer Data Compression System," *Proc. AIAA Conf. Computing in Aerospace '93*, p. 4566, 1993.

[D587] P. Fisher and Z. Fan, "Chunked Finite Inductive Sequences and Compression of Text," *Proc. AIAA Conf. Computing in Aerospace '93*, p. 4594, 1993.

[D588] K. Prager, "A Real Time System for the Transmission of Remote Surveillance Data Over Low-Bandwidth Channels," *Proc. AIAA Conf. Computing in Aerospace '93*, p. 4595, 1993.

[D589] A. Sloan, "Fractal Image Compression and Copernicus Environmental Applications," *Proc. AIAA Conf. Computing in Aerospace '93*, p. 4596, 1993.

[D590] J. Williams and C. Yang, "Tactical Sensor Data Compression for Military Multimedia Systems," *Proc. AIAA Conf. Computing in Aerospace '93*, p. 4597, 1993.

[D591] P. Fisher and C. Angaye, "Text Compression Using FI Sequences," *Proc. AIAA Conf. Computing in Aerospace '93*, p. 4598, 1993.

[D592] M. Hilton and B. Jawerth, "Error Sensitivity of Wavelet Compressed IIR Sensor Images," *Proc. AIAA Conf. Computing in Aerospace '93*, p. 4667, 1993.

[D593] R. McFarland, "Compression of Telemetric Data," *Proc. AIAA Conf. Computing in Aerospace '93*, p. 4668, 1993.

[D594] F. Zeppenfeldt and J. Barger, "SAR Imagery Data Obtained after Application of Raw SAR Signal and SAR Image Compression," *Proc. AIAA Conf. Computing in Aerospace '93*, p. 4669, 1993.

[D595] D. Glover, "Transform Coding for Space Applications," *Proc. AIAA Conf. Computing in Aerospace '93*, p. 4670, 1993.

[D596] T. Bizon, M. Shalkhauser, and W. Whyte, Jr., "Real-Time Transmission of Digital Video Using Variable Length Coding," *Proc. AIAA Conf. Computing in Aerospace '93*, p. 4687, 1993.

[D597] M. Lee, "An Ultrafast Video Compression Scheme Using Generalized Multirate Motion Compensation," *Proc. AIAA Conf. Computing in Aerospace '93*, p. 4688, 1993.

[D598] C. Chakravarthy, K. Hong, and D. Vaman, "Adaptive Delta Modulation Based 2-D Subband Coding for Packet Video Under Lossy Conditions," *Proc. AIAA Conf. Computing in Aerospace '93*, p. 4689, 1993.

[D599] T. Ozcelik and A. Katsaggelos, "Image Sequence Coding without Motion Vector Transmission," *Proc. AIAA Conf. Computing in Aerospace '93*, p. 4690, 1993.

[D600] H. Taylor, D. Chin, and A. Jessup, "An MPEG Encoder Implementation on the Princeton Engine Video Supercomputer," *Proc. AIAA Conf. Computing in Aerospace '93*, p. 4691, 1993.

[D601] C.-H. Hsieh, D.-C. Chuang, and J.-S. Sue, "Image Compression Using Finite-State Vector Quantization with Derailment Compensation," *IEEE Trans. Circuits and Systems for Video Technology*, Vol. 3, No. 5, pp. 341–349, Oct. 1993.

[D602] J.E. Fowler, Jr., M.R. Carbonara, and S.C. Ahalt, "Image Coding Using Differential Vector Quantization," *IEEE Trans. Circuits and Systems for Video Technology*, Vol. 3, No. 5, pp. 350–367, Oct. 1993.

[D603] W. Philips, "ECG Data Compression with Time-Warped Polynomials," *IEEE Trans. Biomedical Eng.*, Vol. 40, No. 11, pp. 1095–1101, Nov. 1993.

[D604] Y. Yang, N.P. Galaatsanos, and A.K. Katsaggelos, "Regularized Reconstruction to Reduce Blocking Artifacts of Block Discrete Cosine Transform Compressed Images," *IEEE Trans. Circuits and Systems for Video Technology*, Vol. 3, No. 6, pp. 421–432, Dec. 1993.

[D605] A.E. Cetin, O.N. Gerek, and S. Ulukus, "Block Wavelet Transforms for Image Coding," *IEEE Trans. Circuits and Systems for Video Technology*, Vol. 3, No. 6, pp. 433–435, Dec. 1993.

[D606] K.H.-K. Chow and M.L. Liou, "Genetic Motion Search Algorithm for Video Compression," *IEEE Trans. Circuits and Systems for Video Technology*, Vol. 3, No. 6, pp. 440–445, Dec. 1993.

[D607] W.B. Pennebaker and J.L. Mitchell, *JPEG Still Image Data Compression Standard*, Van Nostrand Reinhold, New York, 1993.

[D608] E.D. Petajan and J. Mailhot, "Grand Alliance HDTV System," *Proc. SPIE: Image and Video Compression*, Vol. 2186, SPIE Press, Bellingham, Wash., pp. 254–265, 1994.

[D609] W.M. Refai, "Real-Time Transmission of Digital Video," *Proc. SPIE: Image and Video Compression*, Vol. 2186, SPIE Press, Bellingham, Wash., pp. 18–23, 1994.

[D610] K.W. Ohnesorge and M. Bichsel, "Fast Adaptive Arithmetic Coding," *Proc. SPIE: Image and Video Compression*, Vol. 2186, SPIE Press, Bellingham, Wash., pp. 24–28, 1994.

[D611] C. Fogg, "Survey of Software and Hardware VLC Architectures," *Proc. SPIE: Image and Video Compression*, Vol. 2186, SPIE Press, Bellingham, Wash., pp. 29–37, 1994.

[D612] E.L. Schwartz et al., "Superscalar Huffman Decoder Hardware Design," *Proc. SPIE: Image and Video Compression*, Vol. 2186, SPIE Press, Bellingham, Wash., pp. 38–48, 1994.

[D613] Z. Fan and R. Eschbach, "JPEG Decompression with Reduced Artifacts," *Proc. SPIE: Image and Video Compression*, Vol. 2186, SPIE Press, Bellingham, Wash., pp. 50–55, 1994.

[D614] D.A. Silverstein and S.A. Klein, "Restoration of Compressed Images," *Proc. SPIE: Image and Video Compression*, Vol. 2186, SPIE Press, Bellingham, Wash., pp. 56–64, 1994.

[D615] R. Yang, M. Gabbouj, and Y.A. Neuvo, "Nonlinear Preprocessing Scheme for JPEG-Based Image Coding," *Proc. SPIE: Image and Video Compression*, Vol. 2186, SPIE Press, Bellingham, Wash., pp. 65–74, 1994.

[D616] K.-J. Wong, P.-Y. Cheng, and C.-C.J. Kuo, "JPEG-Based Image Compression Scheme Using Fully Decomposed Wavelet Packet Transform," *Proc. SPIE: Image and Video Compression*, Vol. 2186, SPIE Press, Bellingham, Wash., pp. 75–86, 1994.

[D617] D. Houlding and J. Vaisey, "Low-Entropy Image Pyramids for Efficient Lossless Coding and Progressive Transmission," *Proc. SPIE: Image and Video Compression*, Vol. 2186, SPIE Press, Bellingham, Wash., pp. 88–97, 1994.

[D618] P.G. Howard, and J.S. Vitter, "Fast Progressive Lossless Image Compression," *Proc. SPIE: Image and Video Compression*, Vol. 2186, SPIE Press, Bellingham, Wash., pp. 98–109, 1994.

[D619] S. Bi and K. Sayood, "Simple High-Quality Lossy Image Coding Scheme," *Proc. SPIE: Image and Video Compression*, Vol. 2186, SPIE Press, Bellingham, Wash., pp. 110–120, 1994.

[D620] G. Lu and T.L. Yew, "Image Compression Using Partitioned Iterated Function Systems," *Proc. SPIE: Image and Video Compression*, Vol. 2186, SPIE Press, Bellingham, Wash., pp. 122–133, 1994.

[D621] I. Hussain and T.R. Reed, "Compression of Still Images Using Segmentation-Based Approximation," *Proc. SPIE: Image and Video Compression*, Vol. 2186, SPIE Press, Bellingham, Wash., pp. 134–145, 1994.

[D622] R. Sennhauser and K.W. Ohnesorge, "Document Image Compression Using Document Analysis and Block-Class-Specific Data Compression Methods," *Proc. SPIE: Image and Video Compression*, Vol. 2186, SPIE Press, Bellingham, Wash., pp. 146–155, 1994.

[D623] S.-H. Jung and S.K. Mitra, "Improved DCT-Based Image Coding and Decoding Method for Low-Bit-Rate Applications," *Proc. SPIE: Image and Video Compression*, Vol. 2186, SPIE Press, Bellingham, Wash., pp. 156–162, 1994.

[D624] Y.-F. Wong, "Combining Nonlinear Multiresolution System and Vector Quantization for Still Image Compression," *Proc. SPIE: Image and Video Compression*, Vol. 2186, SPIE Press, Bellingham, Wash., pp. 163–171, 1994.

[D625] J. Li and P.C. Yip, "Class of Smooth Block Transforms and Applications in Image Compression," *Proc. SPIE: Image and Video Compression*, Vol. 2186, SPIE Press, Bellingham, Wash., pp. 174–184, 1994.

[D626] A. Ortega, Z. Zhang, and M. Vetterli, "Modeling and Optimization of a Multiresolution Remote Image Retrieval System," *Proc. SPIE: Image and Video Compression*, Vol. 2186, SPIE Press, Bellingham, Wash., pp. 185–196, 1994.

[D627] K. Shen et al., "Overview of Parallel Processing Approaches to Image and Video Compression," *Proc. SPIE: Image and Video Compression*, Vol. 2186, SPIE Press, Bellingham, Wash., pp. 197–208, 1994.

[D628] C. Deutsch, A. Zaccarin, and M.T. Orchard, "Estimation Theoretic Approach for Robust Predictive Motion Field Segmentation," *Proc. SPIE: Image and Video Compression*, Vol. 2186, SPIE Press, Bellingham, Wash., pp. 210–221, 1994.

[D629] A. Deknuydt et al., "Space Domain Coding Method, Suitable for Coding Motion-Compensated Difference Images," *Proc. SPIE: Image and Video Compression*, Vol. 2186, SPIE Press, Bellingham, Wash., pp. 222–232, 1994.

[D630] N. Haddadi and C.-C.J. Kuo, "Multiple Bit-Rate Video Compression via Progressive Motion Field Coding," *Proc. SPIE: Image and Video Compression*, Vol. 2186, SPIE Press, Bellingham, Wash., pp. 233–244, 1994.

[D631] A.T. Erdem and M.I. Sezan, "Scalable Extension Of MPEG-2 for Coding 10-Bit Video," *Proc. SPIE: Image and Video Compression*, Vol. 2186, SPIE Press, Bellingham, Wash., pp. 245–256, 1994.

[D632] P. Devaney, D. Gnanaprakasam, and P.H. Westerink, "Segmentation-Based Image Compression for Video Cassette Recorders," *Proc. SPIE: Image and Video Compression*, Vol. 2186, SPIE Press, Bellingham, Wash., pp. 258–269, 1994.

[D633] G.S. Desoli, F.G. De Natale, and D.G. Giusto, "High-Compression Video Coding: A Novel Approach," *Proc. SPIE: Image and Video Compression*, Vol. 2186, SPIE Press, Bellingham, Wash., pp. 270–277, 1994.

[D634] J. Lee and B.W. Dickinson, "Motion-Compensated Subband Coding with Scene Adaptivity," *Proc. SPIE: Image and Video Compression*, Vol. 2186, SPIE Press, Bellingham, Wash., pp. 278–288, 1994.

[D635] M. Effros, P.A. Chou, and R.M. Gray, "Variable Dimension Weighted Universal Vector Quantization and Noiseless Coding," *Proc. Data Compression Conf. (DCC '94)*, CS Press, Los Alamitos, Calif., pp. 2–11, 1994.

[D636] K. Rose, D. Miller, and A. Gersho, "Entropy-Constrained Tree-Structured Vector Quantizer Design by the Minimum Cross Entropy Principle," *Proc. Data Compression Conf. (DCC '94)*, CS Press, Los Alamitos, Calif., pp. 12–21, 1994.

[D637] X. Wu and K. Zhang, "A Subjective Distortion Measure for Vector Quantization," *Proc. Data Compression Conf. (DCC '94)*, CS Press, Los Alamitos, Calif., pp. 22–31, 1994.

[D638] A.C. Hung and T.H.-Y. Meng, "Multidimensional Rotations for Quantization," *Proc. Data Compression Conf. (DCC '94)*, CS Press, Los Alamitos, Calif., pp. 32–41, 1994.

[D639] C.F. Barnes, "A New Multiple Path Search Technique for Residual Vector Quantizers," *Proc. Data Compression Conf. (DCC '94)*, CS Press, Los Alamitos, Calif., pp. 42–51, 1994.

[D640] N. Merhav and M. Feder, "The Minimax Redundancy Is a Lower Bound for Most Sources," *Proc. Data Compression Conf. (DCC '94)*, CS Press, Los Alamitos, Calif., pp. 52–61, 1994.

[D641] A. Bist, "Differential State Quantization of High Order Gauss–Markov Process," *Proc. Data Compression Conf. (DCC '94)*, CS Press, Los Alamitos, Calif., pp. 62–71, 1994.

[D642] S. Azhar et al., "Data Compression Techniques for Stock Market Prediction," *Proc. Data Compression Conf. (DCC '94)*, CS Press, Los Alamitos, Calif., pp. 72–82, 1994.

[D643] J. Abrahams, "Huffman-Type Codes for Infinite Source Distributions," *Proc. Data Compression Conf. (DCC '94)*, CS Press, Los Alamitos, Calif., pp. 83–89, 1994.

[D644] P.R. Stubley, "On the Redundancy of Optimum Fixed-to-Variable Length Codes," *Proc. Data Compression Conf. (DCC '94)*, CS Press, Los Alamitos, Calif., pp. 90–97, 1994.

[D645] P.R. Stubley, "Adaptive Variable-to-Variable Length Codes," *Proc. Data Compression Conf. (DCC '94)*, CS Press, Los Alamitos, Calif., pp. 98–105, 1994.

[D646] S. Inglis and I.H. Witten, "Compression-Based Template Matching," *Proc. Data Compression Conf. (DCC '94)*, CS Press, Los Alamitos, Calif., pp. 106–115, 1994.

[D647] A. Bookstein, S.T. Klein, and T. Raita, "Markov Models for Clusters in Concordance Compression," *Proc. Data Compression Conf. (DCC '94)*, CS Press, Los Alamitos, Calif., pp. 116–125, 1994.

[D648] A. Moffat, N. Sharman, and J. Zobel, "Static Compression for Dynamic Texts," *Proc. Data Compression Conf. (DCC '94)*, CS Press, Los Alamitos, Calif., pp. 126–135, 1994.

[D649] D.S. Hirschberg and L.M. Stauffer, "Parsing Algorithms for Dictionary Compression on the PRAM," *Proc. Data Compression Conf. (DCC '94)*, CS Press, Los Alamitos, Calif., pp. 136–145, 1994.

[D650] K. Ramachandran and M. Vetterli, "Syntax-Constrained Encoder Optimization Using Adaptive Quantization Thresholding for JPEG/MPEG Coders," *Proc. Data Compression Conf. (DCC '94)*, CS Press, Los Alamitos, Calif., pp. 146–155, 1994.

[D651] R.A. Vander Kam and P.W. Wong, "Customized JPEG Compression for Grayscale Printing," *Proc. Data Compression Conf. (DCC '94)*, CS Press, Los Alamitos, Calif., pp. 156–165, 1994.

[D652] S. Takamura and M. Takagi, "Lossless Image Compression with Lossy Image Using Adaptive Prediction," *Proc. Data Compression Conf. (DCC '94)*, CS Press, Los Alamitos, Calif., pp. 166–174, 1994.

[D653] D.T. Hoang, P.M. Long, and J.S. Vitter, "Explicit Bit Minimization for Motion-Compensated Video Coding," *Proc. Data Compression Conf. (DCC '94)*, CS Press, Los Alamitos, Calif., pp. 175–184, 1994.

[D654] X. Wang, S.M. Shende, and K. Sayood, "Online Compression of Video Sequences Using Adaptive VQ Codebooks," *Proc. Data Compression Conf. (DCC '94)*, CS Press, Los Alamitos, Calif., pp. 185–194, 1994.

[D655] R. Bhaskaran and S.C. Kwatra, "Compression of HDTV Signals for Low Bit-Rate Transmission Using Motion Compensated Subband Transform Coding and a Self-Organization Neural Network," *Proc. Data Compression Conf. (DCC '94)*, CS Press, Los Alamitos, Calif., pp. 195–204, 1994.

[D656] J.E. Fowler and S.C. Ahalt, "Differential Vector Quantization of Real-Time Video," *Proc. Data Compression Conf. (DCC '94)*, CS Press, Los Alamitos, Calif., pp. 205–214, 1994.

[D657] R.J. Gove, "The MVP: A Highly-Integrated Video Compression Chip," *Proc. Data Compression Conf. (DCC '94)*, CS Press, Los Alamitos, Calif., pp. 215–224, 1994.

[D658] P.C. Gutmann and T.C. Bell, "A Hybrid Approach to Text Compression," *Proc. Data Compression Conf. (DCC '94)*, pp. 225–233, 1994.

[D659] Y. Nakano et al., "Highly Efficient Universal Coding with Classifying to Subdictionaries for Text Compression," *Proc. Data Compression Conf. (DCC '94)*, CS Press, Los Alamitos, Calif., pp. 234–243, 1994.

[D660] C.G. Nevill-Manning, I.H. Witten, and D.L. Maulsby, "Compression by Induction of Hierarchical Grammars," *Proc. Data Compression Conf. (DCC '94)*, CS Press, Los Alamitos, Calif., pp. 244–253, 1994.

[D661] G. Feygin, P.G. Gulak, and P. Chow, "Architectural Advances in the VLSI Implementation of Arithmetic Coding for Binary Image Compression," *Proc. Data Compression Conf. (DCC '94)*, CS Press, Los Alamitos, Calif., pp. 254–263, 1994.

[D662] L. Huynh, "Multiplication and Division Free Adaptive Arithmetic Coding Techniques for Bi-Level Images," *Proc. Data Compression Conf. (DCC '94)*, CS Press, Los Alamitos, Calif., pp. 264–273, 1994.

[D663] K.O. Perlmutter et al., "Bayes Risk Weighted Tree-Structured Vector Quantization with Posterior Estimation," *Proc. Data Compression Conf. (DCC '94)*, CS Press, Los Alamitos, Calif., pp. 274–283, 1994.

[D664] X. Wu and Y. Fang, "Fast Bintree-Structured Image Coder for High Subjective Quality," *Proc. Data Compression Conf. (DCC '94)*, CS Press, Los Alamitos, Calif., pp. 284–293, 1994.

[D665] M.J. Ruf, "A High Performance Fixed Rate Compression Scheme for Still Image Transmission," *Proc. Data Compression Conf. (DCC '94)*, CS Press, Los Alamitos, Calif., pp. 294–303, 1994.

[D666] M.J. Slyz and D.L. Neuhoff, "A Nonlinear VQ-Based Predictive Lossless Image Coder," *Proc. Data Compression Conf. (DCC '94)*, CS Press, Los Alamitos, Calif., pp. 304–310, 1994.

[D667] S.R. Tate, "Band Ordering in Lossless Compression of Multispectral Images," *Proc. Data Compression Conf. (DCC '94)*, CS Press, Los Alamitos, Calif., pp. 311–320, 1994.

[D668] I. Linares, R.M. Mersereau, and M.J.T. Smith, "Enhancement of Block Transform Coded Images Using Residual Spectra Adaptive Postfiltering," *Proc. Data Compression Conf. (DCC '94)*, CS Press, Los Alamitos, Calif., pp. 321–330, 1994.

[D669] O. Kiselyov and P. Fisher, "Self-Similarity of the Multiresolutional Image/Video Decomposition: Smart Expansion as Compression of Still and Moving Images," *Proc. Data Compression Conf. (DCC '94)*, CS Press, Los Alamitos, Calif., pp. 331–340, 1994.

[D670] M.T. Orchard and K. Ramachandran, "An Investigation of Wavelet-Based Image Coding Using an Entropy-Constrained Quantization Framework," *Proc. Data Compression Conf. (DCC '94)*, CS Press, Los Alamitos, Calif., pp. 341–350, 1994.

[D671] J.D. Villasenor, B. Belzer, and J. Liao, "Filter Evaluation and Selection in Wavelet Image Compression," *Proc. Data Compression Conf. (DCC '94)*, CS Press, Los Alamitos, Calif., pp. 351–360, 1994.

[D672] J.A. Solomon, A.B. Watson, and A. Ahumada, "Visibility of DCT Basis Functions: Effects of Contrast Masking," *Proc. Data Compression Conf. (DCC '94)*, CS Press, Los Alamitos, Calif., pp. 361–370, 1994.

[D673] A.B. Watson, J.A. Solomon, and A.J. Ahumada, Jr., "Visibility of DCT Basis Functions: Effects of Display Resolution," *Proc. Data Compression Conf. (DCC '94)*, CS Press, Los Alamitos, Calif., pp. 371–379, 1994.

[D674] R. Zamir and M. Feder, "On Lattice Quantization Noise," *Proc. Data Compression Conf. (DCC '94)*, CS Press, Los Alamitos, Calif., pp. 380–389, 1994.

[D675] X. Ginesta and S.P. Kim, "Vector Quantization of Contextual Information for Lossless Image Compression," *Proc. Data Compression Conf. (DCC '94)*, CS Press, Los Alamitos, Calif., pp. 390–399, 1994.

[D676] R.D. Wesel and R.M. Gray, "Bayes Risk Weighted VQ and Learning VQ," *Proc. Data Compression Conf. (DCC '94)*, CS Press, Los Alamitos, Calif., pp. 400–409, 1994.

[D677] C. Constantinescu and J.A. Storer, "Improved Techniques for Single-Pass Adaptive VQ," *Proc. Data Compression Conf. (DCC '94)*, CS Press, Los Alamitos, Calif., pp. 410–419, 1994.

[D678] A. Das, A.V. Rao, and A. Gersho, "Variable Dimension Vector Quantization of Speech Spectra for Low Rate Vocoders," *Proc. Data Compression Conf. (DCC '94)*, CS Press, Los Alamitos, Calif., pp. 420–429, 1994.

[D679] T. Shamoon and C. Heegard, "A Rapidly Adaptive Lossless Compression Algorithm for High Fidelity Audio Coding," *Proc. Data Compression Conf. (DCC '94)*, CS Press, Los Alamitos, Calif., pp. 430–439, 1994.

[D680] B.K. Natarajan, "Sharper Bounds on Occam Filters and Application to Digital Video," *Proc. Data Compression Conf. (DCC '94)*, CS Press, Los Alamitos, Calif., pp. 440–450, 1994.

[D681] M.A. Turker and M. Severcan, "Adaptive Intraframe Coding for Very Low Bit-Rate Image Sequence Compression Using Classifier Constrained DCT-VQ," *Proc. Data Compression Conf. (DCC '94)*, CS Press, Los Alamitos, Calif., p. 452, 1994.

[D682] D.J. Craft, "Adaptive Lossless Data Compression," *Proc. Data Compression Conf. (DCC '94)*, CS Press, Los Alamitos, Calif., p. 453, 1994.

[D683] A. Ortega and M. Vetterli, "Adaptive Quantization without Side Information," *Proc. Data Compression Conf. (DCC '94)*, CS Press, Los Alamitos, Calif., p. 454, 1994.

[D684] K.-M. Cheung and P. Smyth, "Adaptive Source Coding Schemes for Geometrically Distributed Integer Alphabets," *Proc. Data Compression Conf. (DCC '94)*, CS Press, Los Alamitos, Calif., p. 455, 1994.

[D685] A.S. Mazer, "Advanced End-to-End Simulation for On-Board Processing (AESOP)," *Proc. Data Compression Conf. (DCC '94)*, CS Press, Los Alamitos, Calif., p. 456, 1994.

[D686] A. Milosavljevic, "Algorithmic Significance, Mutual Information and DNA Sequence Comparisons," *Proc. Data Compression Conf. (DCC '94)*, CS Press, Los Alamitos, Calif., p. 457, 1994.

[D687] L.A. Potter, "Applications of Run-Length Lists (RLL)," *Proc. Data Compression Conf. (DCC '94)*, CS Press, Los Alamitos, Calif., p. 458, 1994.

[D688] R.J. Stewart, Y.M. Fleming Lure, and C.S.J. Liou, "An Approach to Achieving Maximum Lossless Compression of Medical Images," *Proc. Data Compression Conf. (DCC '94)*, CS Press, Los Alamitos, Calif., p. 459, 1994.

[D689] H. Plantinga, "An Asymmetric, Semi-Adaptive Text Compression Algorithm," *Proc. Data Compression Conf. (DCC '94)*, CS Press, Los Alamitos, Calif., p. 460, 1994.

[D690] W.K. Ng and C.V. Ravishankar, "Attribute Enumerative Coding: A Compression Technique for Tuple Data Structures," *Proc. Data Compression Conf. (DCC '94)*, CS Press, Los Alamitos, Calif., p. 461, 1994.

[D691] E.E. Majani and M. Lightstone, "Bioorthogonal Wavelets for Data Compression," *Proc. Data Compression Conf. (DCC '94)*, CS Press, Los Alamitos, Calif., p. 462, 1994.

[D692] R.-Y. Wang, E.A. Riskin, and R. Ladner, "Codebook Organization to Enhance MAP Detection of Weighted Universal Vector Quantized Image Transmission over Noisy Channels," *Proc. Data Compression Conf. (DCC '94)*, CS Press, Los Alamitos, Calif., p. 463, 1994.

[D693] M.J. Gormish, "Combining Data Compression with Channel Modulation and/or Error Correction," *Proc. Data Compression Conf. (DCC '94)*, CS Press, Los Alamitos, Calif., p. 464, 1994.

[D694] R.M. Matic and J.I. Mosley, "A Comparison of Spectral Decorrelation and Rate Allocation Techniques for a Wavelet Transform-Based Multispectral Data Compression Algorithm," *Proc. Data Compression Conf. (DCC '94)*, CS Press, Los Alamitos, Calif., p. 465, 1994.

[D695] M.L. Hilton and P. Panda, "A Comparison of Wavelet Coding Sequences for Noisy Channels," *Proc. Data Compression Conf. (DCC '94)*, CS Press, Los Alamitos, Calif., p. 466, 1994.

[D696] C. Lambert-Nebout et al., "A Comparative Study of SAR Data Compression Schemes," *Proc. Data Compression Conf. (DCC '94)*, CS Press, Los Alamitos, Calif., p. 467, 1994.

[D697] A. Mukherjee and T. Acharya, "Compressed Pattern Matching," *Proc. Data Compression Conf. (DCC '94)*, CS Press, Los Alamitos, Calif., p. 468, 1994.

[D698] R.M. Davies and I.H. Witten, "Compressing Computer Programs," *Proc. Data Compression Conf. (DCC '94)*, CS Press, Los Alamitos, Calif., p. 469, 1994.

[D699] P. Franti and O. Nevalainen, "Compression of Binary Images by Composite Methods Based on the Block Coding," *Proc. Data Compression Conf. (DCC '94)*, CS Press, Los Alamitos, Calif., p. 470, 1994.

[D700] G. Langdon et al., "On Compression of Data from a Meteorological Station," *Proc. Data Compression Conf. (DCC '94)*, CS Press, Los Alamitos, Calif., p. 471, 1994.

[D701] J.M. Shapiro, S.A. Martucci, and M. Czigler, "Compression of Multispectral Landsat Imagery Using the Embedded Zerotree Wavelet (EZW) Algorithm," *Proc. Data Compression Conf. (DCC '94)*, CS Press, Los Alamitos, Calif., p. 472, 1994.

[D702] J. Danskin and P. Hanrahan, "Compression Performance of the Xremote Protocol," *Proc. Data Compression Conf. (DCC '94)*, CS Press, Los Alamitos, Calif., p. 473, 1994.

[D703] S.P. Kim, X. Ginesta, and M.T. Sun, "Context-Tree Based Lossless Image Compression," *Proc. Data Compression Conf. (DCC '94)*, CS Press, Los Alamitos, Calif., p. 474, 1994.

[D704] G.I. Davida and L. Rodrigues, "Data Compression Using Linear Feedback Shift Registers," *Proc. Data Compression Conf. (DCC '94)*, CS Press, Los Alamitos, Calif., p. 475, 1994.

[D705] J.N. Bradley and C.M. Brislawn, "Detector-Activated Predictive Wavelet Transform Image Coding," *Proc. Data Compression Conf. (DCC '94)*, CS Press, Los Alamitos, Calif., p. 476, 1994.

[D706] J. Jiang, "A Direct Implementation of Arithmetic Coding," *Proc. Data Compression Conf. (DCC '94)*, CS Press, Los Alamitos, Calif., p. 477, 1994.

[D707] C.-K. Chou and F. Ercal, "An Edge-Oriented Image Compression Technique Using Edge Prediction and Classified Vector Quantization," *Proc. Data Compression Conf. (DCC '94)*, p. 478, 1994.

[D708] A. Tatsaki, T. Stouraitis, and C. Goutis, "An Efficient Pyramid VQ-Based Image Compression Algorithm," *Proc. Data Compression Conf. (DCC '94)*, CS Press, Los Alamitos, Calif., p. 479, 1994.

[D709] M. Gooch and S.R. Jones, "An Experimental Investigation into Table Driven Data Compression Algorithms for Solid State Discs," *Proc. Data Compression Conf. (DCC '94)*, CS Press, Los Alamitos, Calif., p. 480, 1994.

[D710] P. Lee et al., "A Fast Algorithm for the 2-D Discrete Cosine Transform," *Proc. Data Compression Conf. (DCC '94)*, CS Press, Los Alamitos, Calif., p. 481, 1994.

[D711] M. Semenov, "Fast Image Compression Using Direct Quantisation of Colour Components," *Proc. Data Compression Conf. (DCC '94)*, CS Press, Los Alamitos, Calif., p. 482, 1994.

[D712] S.U.B. Sarma and P. Siy, "Fourier Based Tools for Compression and Vector Quantization," *Proc. Data Compression Conf. (DCC '94)*, CS Press, Los Alamitos, Calif., p. 483, 1994.

[D713] S. Abdallah and N. Tepedelenlioglu, "Fractal Interpolation Functions for Image Compression," *Proc. Data Compression Conf. (DCC '94)*, CS Press, Los Alamitos, Calif., p. 484, 1994.

[D714] T.M. Cover and R.D. Wesel, "A Gambling Estimate of the Rate Distortion Function for Images," *Proc. Data Compression Conf. (DCC '94)*, CS Press, Los Alamitos, Calif., p. 485, 1994.

[D715] G. Betzos, "Heuristic Algorithms for Quadtree Compression Using a Content Addressable Memory," *Proc. Data Compression Conf. (DCC '94)*, CS Press, Los Alamitos, Calif., p. 486, 1994.

[D716] W. Gao, D. Zhao, and W. Yang, "A High Bit Rates MPEG Video Coding Scheme," *Proc. Data Compression Conf. (DCC '94)*, CS Press, Los Alamitos, Calif., p. 487, 1994.

[D717] S. Chuang et al., "An Image Assessment Study of Image Acceptability of the Galileo Low Gain Antenna Mission," *Proc. Data Compression Conf. (DCC '94)*, CS Press, Los Alamitos, Calif., p. 488, 1994.

[D718] D.E. Tamir and K. Phillips, "Image Compression via Image Fragmentation and Heuristic Search Techniques," *Proc. Data Compression Conf. (DCC '94)*, CS Press, Los Alamitos, Calif., p. 489, 1994.

[D719] A.M. Eskicioglu, P.S. Fisher, and S. Chen, "Image Quality Measures and Their Performance," *Proc. Data Compression Conf. (DCC '94)*, CS Press, Los Alamitos, Calif., p. 490, 1994.

[D720] S. Yoshida et al., "Improvement of Sliding-Window Data Compression Using Splay-Tree Coding," *Proc. Data Compression Conf. (DCC '94)*, CS Press, Los Alamitos, Calif., p. 491, 1994.

[D721] J. Lin, "Improving the Performance of Tree-Structured Vector Quantizers," *Proc. Data Compression Conf. (DCC '94)*, CS Press, Los Alamitos, Calif., p. 492, 1994.

[D722] W. Chang, H.S. Soliman, and A.H. Sung, "A Learning Vector Quantization Neural Model for Image Data Compression," *Proc. Data Compression Conf. (DCC '94)*, CS Press, Los Alamitos, Calif., p. 493, 1994.

[D723] C.H. Chong, C.-M. Huang, and R.W. Harris, "Lossless Compression of Vector Quantization Indices," *Proc. Data Compression Conf. (DCC '94)*, CS Press, Los Alamitos, Calif., p. 494, 1994.

[D724] S. Kwong, C.H. Lee, and S.H. Tong, "A Lossless Data Compression Method for Chinese Characters," *Proc. Data Compression Conf. (DCC '94)*, CS Press, Los Alamitos, Calif., p. 495, 1994.

[D725] M.G. Albanesi, M. Ferretti, and S. Leoni, "Mapping Algorithms into ASIC: A Multi-Resolution Algorithm for Image Compression," *Proc. Data Compression Conf. (DCC '94)*, CS Press, Los Alamitos, Calif., p. 496, 1994.

[D726] M. Manohar et al., "Model-Based Vector Quantization," *Proc. Data Compression Conf. (DCC '94)*, CS Press, Los Alamitos, Calif., p. 497, 1994.

[D727] R.A. Baxter and D.L. Dowe, "Model Selection in Linear Regression Using the MML Criterion," *Proc. Data Compression Conf. (DCC '94)*, CS Press, Los Alamitos, Calif., p. 498, 1994.

[D728] L. Chen and W.K. Tsai, "Multiresolution Surface Approximation Using Vector Quantization in Image Compression," *Proc. Data Compression Conf. (DCC '94)*, CS Press, Los Alamitos, Calif., p. 499, 1994.

[D729] S. Schweid and T.K. Sarkar, "Neural Network Minimization Techniques for Multistage Orthogonal QMF Filters with Vanishing Moments," *Proc. Data Compression Conf. (DCC '94)*, CS Press, Los Alamitos, Calif., p. 500, 1994.

[D730] M.L. Hui and J.C.R. Tseng, "A New Access Control Scheme Based on Minimal Perfect Hashing Functions," *Proc. Data Compression Conf. (DCC '94)*, CS Press, Los Alamitos, Calif., p. 501, 1994.

[D731] D.D. Giusto, "Nonlinear-Predicted Vector Quantization," *Proc. Data Compression Conf. (DCC '94)*, CS Press, Los Alamitos, Calif., p. 502, 1994.

[D732] G.U. Sunada and T. Chen, "A Novel DCT Implementation Using Bit-Serial Arithmetic," *Proc. Data Compression Conf. (DCC '94)*, CS Press, Los Alamitos, Calif., p. 503, 1994.

[D733] K. Atteson, "Optimal Asymptotic Adaptive Text Compression Using Markov Chains," *Proc. Data Compression Conf. (DCC '94)*, CS Press, Los Alamitos, Calif., p. 504, 1994.

[D734] M. Lewis, "Optimal Predictors and Transform Coding Methods for the Data Compression of Digital Elevation Models," *Proc. Data Compression Conf. (DCC '94)*, CS Press, Los Alamitos, Calif., p. 505, 1994.

[D735] E. Hatton and G.H. Freeman, "The Optimal Symbol-Probability Estimate for Lossless Compression," *Proc. Data Compression Conf. (DCC '94)*, CS Press, Los Alamitos, Calif., p. 506, 1994.

[D736] R.G. Palmer, Jr., et al., "A Parallel Algorithm for a Tree Structured Vector Quantizer for Image Compression," *Proc. Data Compression Conf. (DCC '94)*, CS Press, Los Alamitos, Calif., p. 507, 1994.

[D737] G.D. Finlayson, S. Atkins, and M. Zastre, "Parallel Data Compression on a Transputer Network," *Proc. Data Compression Conf. (DCC '94)*, CS Press, Los Alamitos, Calif., p. 508, 1994.

[D738] B.W.Y. Wei and P.-J. Lan, "Parallel Decoding of Huffman Codes," *Proc. Data Compression Conf. (DCC '94)*, CS Press, Los Alamitos, Calif., p. 509, 1994.

[D739] M. Boliek, J.D. Allen, and E.L. Schwartz, "Parallel Entropy Coding Using Multiple Coders," *Proc. Data Compression Conf. (DCC '94)*, CS Press, Los Alamitos, Calif., p. 510, 1994.

[D740] J.D. Gorman and S.A. Werness, "Perceptual Compression of Magnitude-Detected Synthetic Aperture Radar Imagery," *Proc. Data Compression Conf. (DCC '94)*, CS Press, Los Alamitos, Calif., p. 511, 1994.

[D741] K.M. Liang, C.M. Huang, and R.W. Harris, "Pruned Tree and Bit Allocation Vector Quantization," *Proc. Data Compression Conf. (DCC '94)*, CS Press, Los Alamitos, Calif., p. 512, 1994.

[D742] C.-T. Chen et al., "Rapid Prototyping of a JPEG Image Compression System Using Synthesis Tools," *Proc. Data Compression Conf. (DCC '94)*, CS Press, Los Alamitos, Calif., p. 513, 1994.

[D743] K. Culik II and J. Kari, "A Recursive Algorithm for Image Compression with Finite Automata," *Proc. Data Compression Conf. (DCC '94)*, CS Press, Los Alamitos, Calif., p. 514, 1994.

[D744] S. Fioravanti, "A Region-Based Approach to Image Coding," *Proc. Data Compression Conf. (DCC '94)*, CS Press, Los Alamitos, Calif., p. 515, 1994.

[D745] S.S. Zahir, S.-W. Lee, and M. Kanefsky, "A Segmentation Based Prediction Algorithm," *Proc. Data Compression Conf. (DCC '94)*, CS Press, Los Alamitos, Calif., p. 516, 1994.

[D746] S. Bi and K. Sayood, "Set Quantizer," *Proc. Data Compression Conf. (DCC '94)*, CS Press, Los Alamitos, Calif., p. 517, 1994.

[D747] M.J. Turner, "Shell Coding of 3D Image Sets," *Proc. Data Compression Conf. (DCC '94)*, CS Press, Los Alamitos, Calif., p. 518, 1994.

[D748] A. Makur and K.V. Hari Narayanan, "Some Fast Search and Partial Search VQ Encoding Algorithms," *Proc. Data Compression Conf. (DCC '94)*, CS Press, Los Alamitos, Calif., p. 519, 1994.

[D749] W.K. Tsai and R. Lim, "Spatial Multi-Resolution Algorithm for Image Data Compression," *Proc. Data Compression Conf. (DCC '94)*, CS Press, Los Alamitos, Calif., p. 520, 1994.

[D750] T.L. Yu and K.W. Yu, "Study of Image Compression through Wavelet Decomposition and Approximate String Matching," *Proc. Data Compression Conf. (DCC '94)*, p. 521, 1994.

[D751] K. Hong, D.R. Vaman, and C.V. Chakravarthy, "Sub-Band Coding of Video Using 2-D Adaptive Deltamodulation for Packet Video Applications," *Proc. Data Compression Conf. (DCC '94)*, CS Press, Los Alamitos, Calif., p. 522, 1994.

[D752] R.-F. Chang and Y.-L. Huang, "Subband Coding Using Finite-State Vector Quantization by Exploiting Inter-band and Intra-band Correlations," *Proc. Data Compression Conf. (DCC '94)*, CS Press, Los Alamitos, Calif., p. 523, 1994.

[D753] S.D. Cabrera, S.-W. Wu, and G. Gonzalez, "Subband Coding Using Overcomplete Decompositions with Applications to Planetary Images," *Proc. Data Compression Conf. (DCC '94)*, CS Press, Los Alamitos, Calif., p. 524, 1994.

[D754] C.-C. Huang, C.-M. Huang, and R.W. Harris, "Subband Image Coding Using Pruned Multi-Stage Tree-Structured Vector Quantization," *Proc. Data Compression Conf. (DCC '94)*, CS Press, Los Alamitos, Calif., p. 525, 1994.

[D755] N.D. Memon and K. Sayood, "A Taxonomy for Lossless Image Compression," *Proc. Data Compression Conf. (DCC '94)*, CS Press, Los Alamitos, Calif., p. 526, 1994.

[D756] M.W. Maier and M.S. Moellenhoff, "Time Domain Evaluation of Compression Algorithms," *Proc. Data Compression Conf. (DCC '94)*, CS Press, Los Alamitos, Calif., p. 527, 1994.

[D757] M. Ali and T.G. Clarkson, "Using Linear Fractal Interpolation Functions to Compress Video Images," *Proc. Data Compression Conf. (DCC '94)*, CS Press, Los Alamitos, Calif., p. 528, 1994.

[D758] B. Gopinath and V. Phalke, "Using Spatial Locality for Trace Compression," *Proc. Data Compression Conf. (DCC '94)*, CS Press, Los Alamitos, Calif., p. 529, 1994.

[D759] H.A. Peterson, A.J. Ahumada, Jr., and A.B. Watson, "The Visibility of DCT Quantization Noise: Spatial Frequency Summation," *Proc. Data Compression Conf. (DCC '94)*, CS Press, Los Alamitos, Calif., p. 530, 1994.

[D760] K.W. Glander and K.P. Durre, "VLC Trios," *Proc. Data Compression Conf. (DCC '94)*, CS Press, Los Alamitos, Calif., p. 531, 1994.

[D761] B. Evans, B. Ringer, and M. Yeates, "Wavelet Compression Techniques for Hyperspectral Data," *Proc. Data Compression Conf. (DCC '94)*, CS Press, Los Alamitos, Calif., p. 532, 1994.

[D762] M. Khurrum and J.B. Jordan, "Edge-Data Compression Using Bezier Polynomials," *Proc. SPIE: Signal Processing, Sensor Fusion, and Target Recognition III*, Vol. 2232, SPIE Press, Bellingham, Wash., pp. 135–141, 1994.

[D763] Y. Liu, "Unification of Several Image Compression Methods," *Proc. SPIE: Hybrid Image and Signal Processing IV*, Vol. 2238, SPIE Press, Bellingham, Wash., pp. 92–106, 1994.

[D764] M.S. Schmalz, "Optical and Electro-Optical Architectures for the Compression and Encryption of Discrete Signals and Imagery: 1. Data Compression," *Proc. SPIE: Hybrid Image and Signal Processing IV*, Vol. 2238, SPIE Press, Bellingham, Wash., pp. 107–119, 1994.

[D765] M.S. Schmalz, "Optical and Electro-Optical Architectures for the Compression and Encryption of Discrete Signals and Imagery: 2. Data Encryption," *Proc. SPIE: Hybrid Image and Signal Processing IV*, Vol. 2238, SPIE Press, Bellingham, Wash., pp. 120–130, 1994.

[D766] M.S. Schmalz, "Optical and Electro-Optical Architectures for the Compression and Encryption of Discrete Signals and Imagery: 3. Optical Computation over Compression Data," *Proc. SPIE: Hybrid Image and Signal Processing IV,* Vol. 2238, SPIE Press, Bellingham, Wash., pp. 131–144, 1994.

[D767] N. Li, L. Van Eycken, and A.J. Oosterlinck, "Employing Frequency-Dependent Property of the Human Visual Systems (HVS) for DCT and Other Orthogonal Transform Coding," *Proc. SPIE: Hybrid Image and Signal Processing IV,* Vol. 2238, SPIE Press, Bellingham, Wash., pp. 145–152, 1994.

[D768] W. Philips, "Weakly Separable Bases for Fast Segmented Image Coding," *Proc. SPIE: Hybrid Image and Signal Processing IV,* Vol. 2238, SPIE Press, Bellingham, Wash., pp. 153–163, 1994.

[D769] S.C. Ahalt and J.E. Fowler, "Real-Time Video Compression Using Entropy Biased ANN Codebooks," *Proc. SPIE: Applications of Artificial Neural Networks V,* Vol. 2243, SPIE Press, Bellingham, Wash., pp. 254–265, 1994.

[D770] D. Anastassiou, "Digital Television," *Proc. IEEE,* Vol. 82, No. 4, pp. 510–519, Apr. 1994.

[D771] B. Jawerth, Y. Liu, and W. Sweldens, "Signal Compression with Smooth Local Trigonometric Bases," *Optical Eng.,* Vol. 33, No. 7, pp. 2125–2135, July 1994.

[D772] C-H.H. Chu, "Data Compression by Multiresolution Tree Search," *Optical Eng.,* Vol. 33, No. 7, pp. 2136–2142, July 1994.

[D773] J.W. Kim and S.U. Lee, "Hierarchical Variable Block Size Motion Estimation Technique for Motion Sequence Coding," *Optical Eng.,* Vol. 33, No. 8, pp. 2553–2561, Aug. 1994.

[D774] G.P. Abousleman, E. Gifford, and B.R. Hunt, "Enhancement and Compression Techniques for Hyperspectral Data," *Optical Eng.,* Vol. 33, No. 8, pp. 2562–2571, Aug. 1994.

[D775] J. Rosiene and I. Greenshields, "Standard Wavelet Basis Compression of Images," *Optical Eng.,* Vol. 33, No. 8, pp. 2572–2578, Aug. 1994.

[D776] K.L. Oehler and R.M. Gray, "Combining Image Compression and Classificiation Using Vector Quantization," *IEEE Trans. Pattern Analysis and Machine Intelligence,* Vol. PAMI-17, No. 5, pp. 461–473, May 1995.

Chapter 2
Chronological Critique

AN OVERVIEW

As a glance at the references furnished at the end of this chapter shows, nearly 100 studies contributing to the area of block truncation coding (BTC) and its derivatives have been identified through an exhaustive search of the literature published up to April 1995. (A couple of these came to light thanks to the anonymous reviewers.) The yearly level of activity and the cumulative growth in this area are portrayed in **Figure 2-1.** Following the introduction of BTC in 1978, there was a long period of rather lackluster activity, which was broken by a significant spurt in 1991. This spurt was probably triggered by the renewed interest in the overall field of data compression, fueled by an increase in commercial interests in the fields of picture and document transmission and HDTV, and further supported by telecommunication industry deregulation and other world events. The scope for hybrid techniques was, by and large, the single biggest factor in this increased attention to BTC. This growth in spurts is traced and discussed in the following sections, starting from its origins up to the latest developments reported in the open literature.

THE ORIGINS

Reverse chronological tracing of the origin of what has since come to be known as BTC shows that there seem to have been two independent and simultaneous efforts: one in Japan, by Kishimoto, Mitsuya, and Hoshida [B1, B2],[1] and the other in the United States at Purdue University, by Delp, Mitchell, and Carlton [B3], with both groups first reporting in the literature rather coincidentally in the second quarter of 1978. The latter used the term *block truncation coding* to denote what was then a new approach to image data compression. They introduced some of the initial concepts underlying this approach by setting them in the context of previously established data compression techniques, such as discrete cosine transforms (DCT) and predictive coding schemes (PCS).

---

[1]The numbers in parentheses starting with the letter B refer to the citations on block truncation coding studies listed at the end of this chapter.

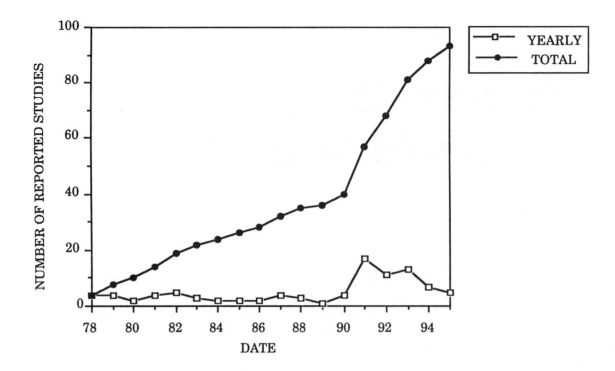

Figure 2-1. Yearly level of activity and cumulative growth in the BTC area.

Some preliminary results comparing the BTC approach with these established techniques were also included. (Some of the definitions employed in this study, such as that of sample variance—equation (1) of [B3]—were later modified [**B8**].[2] This changed some of the outputs as well.) In mid-1978, Kishimoto and associates [B4] published their results (in Japanese) in a regular journal forum of limited circulation.

The next study that appeared in 1979 was another conference paper by Delp and Mitchell [B5] on some analytical aspects of the moment-preserving quantizers, representing the generalization of the two-level BTC techniques to multilevels. While [B5] appeared chronologically before the more detailed study on BTC techniques by the same authors [**B8**], the latter represents a more general treatment; hence details of moment-preserving quantizers will be deferred until the specifics of the basic BTC techniques are presented and discussed.

Also in 1979, Murakami et al. [B6] presented an adaptive block coding technique based on variable block sizes and local characteristics of the image. Depending on the homogeneity of the region, the block size can be varied. In addition, the nature of information carried for the block can be varied, ranging from a single average intensity value to two standard gray levels as in traditional BTC, or in between, a reduced-bit description of the two gray levels whenever the block sizes are small. Specifically, the authors consider a four-mode adaptive procedure:

---

[2] Numbers in bold indicates that a reprint of this study has been included in Part B of this book.

- Mode A: a (4×4) block with average intensity only
- Mode B: a (4×4) block with two standard gray levels as under BTC
- Mode C: a (2×2) block with reduced-bit gray levels
- Mode D: a (2×2) block with standard gray levels as under BTC

A mode selection method simpler than the earlier one proposed in [B4] was also offered. Mode A becomes applicable whenever the difference in the two output gray levels under binary coding is smaller than a sufficiently small threshold value T_1. Mode B is to be selected whenever the output gray-level difference is between T_1 and a slightly larger threshold T_2 and the squared error (the difference between the input and output at each pixel) sum is less than a threshold T_3. Mode C and mode D are distinguished by a threshold T_4, once again on the difference in the two output intensity values. The paper [B6] provides further details on the bit-allocation procedure and other aspects required for the implementation of the adaptive procedure.

Following this study in chronology were the doctoral thesis and a like-titled university technical report by Delp [B7], which were both of very limited distribution. In September 1979, Delp and Mitchell published the first detailed account of their studies in the BTC area in a widely distributed forum [**B8**]. The specific terminology of BTC thus seems to be attributable to Delp and his associates. Also, to this date, they have continued reporting further work in this area.

BTC FUNDAMENTALS

Block truncation coding techniques, as discussed in the previous chapter, fall within the category of what has since been generalized as moment-preserving quantization methods of data compression. In its original form, the central idea was to preserve the first two sample moments of a small block (of size, let us say, $n \times n$) within the image under compression-oriented processing.

Let $\{x_i, i = 1,..., n^2\}$ be the n^2 intensity values of the pixel set in this sub-image block. Then the first two moments $\bar{x}$ and $\overline{x^2}$ the standard deviation σ, a function of these two moments, can be written as

$$\bar{x} = \frac{1}{n^2} \sum_{i=1}^{n^2} x_i \tag{2.1}$$

$$\overline{x^2} = \frac{1}{n^2} \sum_{i=1}^{n^2} x_i^2 \tag{2.2}$$

$$\sigma = \left(\overline{x^2} - \bar{x}^2 \right)^{1/2} \tag{2.3}$$

(In the referenced paper, it is not clear why the authors used σ with a bar on the top, generally indicative of an average of a variable. However, in their subsequent papers, this overbar has been dropped. But Halverson et al. continue this somewhat misleading notation in their follow-on studies.)

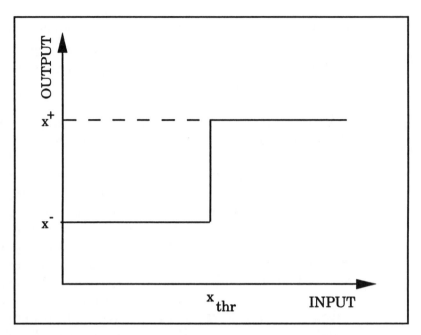

Figure 2-2. Input–output relationship of a binary quantizer.

The concept central to this analysis is to define a one-bit, that is, two-level quantizer, as shown in **Figure 2-2,** with a threshold x_{thr} and two output levels x^+ and x^- such that

$$\left.\begin{array}{l} x_i \geq x_{\mathrm{thr}} \Rightarrow y_i = x^+ \\ x_i < x_{\mathrm{thr}} \Rightarrow y_i = x^- \end{array}\right\} \forall i = 1,\ldots,n^2 \tag{2.4}$$

An intuitively obvious threshold in this context would be the mean value itself. The unknown output values x^+ and x^- can be determined by setting up the expressions that equate (preserve) the moments before and after quantization, as follows:

$$n^2\overline{x} = n^- x^- - n^+ x^+ \tag{2.5}$$

$$n^2\overline{x^2} = n^- \left[x^-\right]^2 - n^+ \left[x^+\right]^2 \tag{2.6}$$

where n^+ and n^- are, respectively, the number of pixels above and below the threshold (mean) value, which together add up to n^2 (the total number of pixels in the block).

Now, in equations (2.5) and (2.6), the only unknowns are x^- and x^+, since n^+ and n^- can be counted once the mean value is determined. Solving the simultaneous nonlinear equations (2.5) and (2.6) for x^- and x^+, we have

$$x^- = \overline{x} - \sigma\sqrt{\frac{n^+}{n^-}} \tag{2.7}$$

$$x^+ = \bar{x} + \sigma \sqrt{\frac{n^-}{n^+}} \qquad (2.8)$$

Thus, the output levels, x^- and x^+, are biased symmetrically about the mean value. Both the positive and negative biases are proportional to the standard deviation. However, these biases are weighted in opposite directions for the two cases. The weight for the lower output is determined as the square root of the ratio of the number of samples above the mean value to the number of samples below it. Likewise, the weight for the higher output is determined as the square root of the ratio of the number of samples below the mean value to the number of samples above it. It should be noted here that after these output values are computed, they will necessarily have to be rounded off to the number of bits allowed for their storage and transmission. This round-off process, however, affects to some extent the moments of the image data set and, to that extent, the claimed objective of preservation of moments is compromised.

As an illustrative example, consider an image block of (4×4):

$$X_{\mathrm{I}} = \begin{bmatrix} 136 & 27 & 144 & 216 \\ 172 & 83 & 43 & 219 \\ 200 & 254 & 1 & 128 \\ 64 & 32 & 96 & 25 \end{bmatrix}$$

For this input data set, X_{I} from equations (2.1)–(2.3), the mean and standard deviation can be determined to be $\bar{x} = 115$ and $\sigma = 77.93$, respectively.

Now, on compression, each block of output is defined by its mean value, its standard deviation, and an $(n \times n)$ binary matrix of 1s and 0s identifying each pixel as being above or below the thresholds. For the numerical example discussed above, setting the mean as the threshold value, the output compressed binary image block X_{o} can be written as

$$X_{\mathrm{O}} = \begin{bmatrix} 1 & 0 & 1 & 1 \\ 1 & 0 & 0 & 1 \\ 1 & 1 & 0 & 1 \\ 0 & 0 & 0 & 0 \end{bmatrix}$$

The counts of 1s and 0s give n^+ and n^-. In the above example, the number of output pixels above and below the threshold is $n^+ = 8$ and $n^- = 8$.

These counts, along with the mean and standard deviations, give the values x^+ and x^- when substituted into equations (2.7) and (2.8). In the case of the numerical example under consideration, the two output levels corresponding to the 0 and 1 bits become $x^- = 37$ and $x^+ = 193$, respectively.

Replacement of the 1s and 0s in the compressed image leads to an approximate equivalent of the original image. In the example illustrated above, the reconstructed image X_{R} is given by

$$X_{\mathrm{R}} = \begin{bmatrix} 193 & 37 & 193 & 193 \\ 193 & 37 & 37 & 193 \\ 193 & 193 & 37 & 193 \\ 37 & 37 & 37 & 37 \end{bmatrix}$$

It is clear from the above example that this is not a lossless compression scheme. The extent of loss or change depends on several factors, including the initial variance in the data. These factors are discussed in more detail in Chapter 3, wherein results corresponding to some real data sets are illustrated.

The extent of compression achieved by this process is a function of the number of bits used to describe the original intensities, the bits used to convey the mean and standard deviation values, and the block size. Obviously, the higher the block size, the higher the compression ratio and vice versa. The study deals with the extent of compression for a specific case of 8-bit intensity values and a (4×4) block size. To fully appreciate the true extent of compression achieved by the method, let us consider here a general case. If the pixel intensity in the image is described by, say, b bits/pixel, then we have a total of bn^2 bits describing the original image block of size $(n \times n)$. After compression, assuming that the mean and standard deviations are defined with the same number of bits b, we have a total of $n^2 + 2b$ bits for the compressed image. The compression ratio therefore becomes

$$R(n) = \frac{bn^2}{n^2 + 2b} \tag{2.9}$$

If, for example, 8 bits/pixel is used in the input image—the standard in most imagery applications—then we have a compression ratio given by

$$R(n) = \frac{8n^2}{n^2 + 16} \tag{2.10}$$

Here, for the case $n = 4$, equation (2.10) gives a compression ratio of 4. **Figure 2-3** shows a plot of the compression ratio as a function of n for various bit rates from 4 to 16. One could achieve a higher compression ratio than indicated by the above expressions by assigning fewer than b bits to the mean and standard deviation values. For example, in the case of 8-bit data, one could use only 6 bits for the mean value and just 4 bits for the standard deviation. For a block size of (4×4), this would increase the compression ratio to 4.923 with an output bit rate of 1.625 bits/pixel. One suggested enhancement in the literature [**B8**] is to use 10 bits jointly for the mean and standard deviation values, with the mean value being assigned more bits whenever the standard deviation is small, and vice versa. One could also visualize additional improvements by efficiently encoding the bit plane itself, as for example, through run-length encoding if the homogeneity of the image makes it worthwhile.

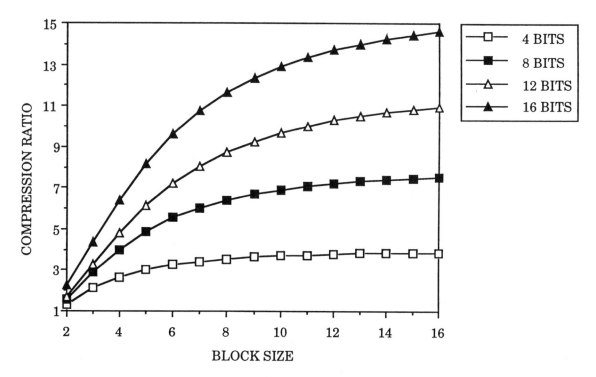

Figure 2-3. Compression ratio versus block size at different original image quantization levels.

The basic BTC approach outlined above is compared with two established quantization alternatives (based on use of fidelity criteria) to judge its relative performance. The two baseline fidelity criteria employed for this comparative evaluation were

- Minimum mean square error (MMSE) [D3]
- Minimum mean absolute error (MMAE) [D36]

Under the MMSE criterion, the first step is to sort the pixel intensities—that is, to develop a histogram of the image block. Let $\{x_i^s, i = 1, \ldots n^2\}$ be the sorted pixel intensities such that $x_i^s \leq x_{i+1}^s$. The higher and lower output values, x^+ and x^-, can be determined by minimizing the mean square error or equivalently, the square error function:

$$J_{\mathrm{S}} = \sum_{i=1}^{n^--1} \left(x_i^s - x^- \right)^2 + \sum_{i=n^-}^{n^+} \left(x_i^s - x^+ \right)^2 \tag{2.11}$$

Here,

$$x^- = \frac{1}{n^-} \sum_{i=1}^{n^--1} x_i^s \tag{2.12}$$

and

$$x^+ = \frac{1}{n^+} \sum_{i=n^-}^{n^+} x_i^s \qquad (2.13)$$

The threshold itself can be determined by exhaustively searching through the possible $(n^2 - 1)$ threshold points and choosing the one with the lowest mean square error function given by expression (2.11). The performance from the viewpoint of the data compression ratio achieved is the same as before.

The alternative of using the MMAE fidelity criterion can be defined along similar lines by substitution of the absolute values instead of squared values for the error at each pixel; that is,

$$J_A = \sum_{i=1}^{n^--1} \left| x_i^s - x^- \right| + \sum_{i=n^-}^{n^+} \left| x_i^s - x^+ \right| \qquad (2.14)$$

Here, x^- and x^+ are the median of the lower and higher intensity sets of pixels, $\{x_i^s, i = 1,\ldots,(n^- - 1)\}$ and $\{x_i^s, i = n^-,\ldots n^+\}$, respectively. The threshold is again determined by an exhaustive search through the $(n^2 - 1)$ points. The detailed results presented by Delp and Mitchell (Table I in [B8]) show that BTC is qualitatively comparable to the standard error-minimization techniques and computationally far more attractive.

A modification or, more appropriately, an extension of the basic BTC scheme proposed in this study is the relaxation of the constraint on the threshold to be equal to the mean value. If this threshold is a variable in addition to the two output levels, one can extend the scheme to preserve the third moment in addition to the first two moments. The problem can be reformulated as a determination of the output values x^- and x^+ (as before) and another variable n^+, which in essence determines the threshold point. In addition to the pair of equations (2.5) and (2.6), we now have a third equation:

$$n^2 \overline{x^3} = n^- \left[x^-\right]^3 - n^+ \left[x^+\right]^3 \qquad (2.15)$$

Solving the simultaneous equations (2.5), (2.6), and (2.15) for x^-, x^+, and n^+, we get

$$n^+ = \frac{n^2}{2} \left[1 + \alpha \left[\alpha^2 + 4\right]^{-1/2} \right] \qquad (2.16)$$

where

$$\alpha = \frac{3\overline{x}\left(\overline{x^2}\right) - \overline{x^3} - 2\overline{x}^3}{\sigma^3}; \qquad \sigma \neq 0 \qquad (2.17)$$

It should be noted in this context, that the equation on p. 332 in the referenced paper by Delp and Mitchell [B8] (which corresponds to equation (2.17) given above) is incorrect. This error is discussed at length in a later work by

Halverson [B19]. (This latter study is reviewed as to its contributions later on in this chapter.)

Thus, this first detailed study [**B8**] in BTC techniques laid the main foundation to the field and briefly hinted at its potential in the development of BTC-based hybrid approaches, which have been explored at length since.

The moment-preserving concept of BTC was generalized by Delp and Mitchell in a study [B5], which incidentally was presented prior to their earlier study [**B8**] owing to the publication time lag for transaction papers. Here in [B5], the authors explore generalizations first in terms of general probability functions in place of the nonparametric formulations assumed in the earlier study [**B8**]. The first three generalized moment-preserving equations, in place of equations (2.5), (2.6), and (2.15), can be expressed as

$$E(x) = x^- F(x_{\text{thr}}) + x^+ \left(1 - F(x_{\text{thr}})\right) \tag{2.18}$$

$$E(x^2) = [x^-]^2 F(x_{\text{thr}}) + [x^+]^2 \left(1 - F(x_{\text{thr}})\right) \tag{2.19}$$

$$E(x^3) = [x^-]^3 F(x_{\text{thr}}) + [x^+]^3 \left(1 - F(x_{\text{thr}})\right) \tag{2.20}$$

where $f(x)$ and $F(x)$ are, respectively, the density and distribution functions of the input x, $F(x_{\text{thr}}) = P(x < x_{\text{thr}})$, $[1 - F(x_{\text{thr}}) = P(x > x_{\text{thr}})]$, and E(.) is the expected value.

Equations (2.18), (2.19), and (2.20) are three simultaneous nonlinear algebraic equations in x^-, x^+, and $F(x_{\text{thr}})$. Solution to these equations requires that $F^{-1}(x_{\text{thr}})$ exists. It is possible to transform the input data such that it has zero mean and unit variance, and thus, without loss of generality, the first equation (2.18) can be set to zero and the second equation (2.19) to unity. Solving the resulting equations for x^- and x^+ in terms of $F(x_{\text{thr}})$, we have

$$x^- = -\left[\frac{[1 - F(x_{\text{thr}})]}{F(x_{\text{thr}})}\right]^{1/2} \tag{2.21}$$

$$x^+ = -\left[\frac{F(x_{\text{thr}})}{[1 - F(x_{\text{thr}})]}\right]^{1/2} \tag{2.22}$$

$$F(x_{\text{thr}}) = 0.5\left[1 + E(x^3)\left[4 + \{E(x^3)\}^2\right]^{-1/2}\right] \tag{2.23}$$

where

$$F(x_{\text{thr}}) = P(x < x_{\text{thr}}) \tag{2.24}$$

$$1 - F(x_{\text{thr}}) = P(x \geq x_{\text{thr}}) \tag{2.25}$$

Thus one can have closed-form solutions for the quantizer threshold and output levels for a general density function, which is not feasible under the more traditional MMSE criterion. The threshold x_{thr} is nominally the median of the data block and not the mean as was the case under the original BTC. The third moment is a measure of skewness of the data. The threshold is thus biased about (above or below) the median, depending on the sign and magnitude of this skewness. The moment-preserving quantizer as defined above can be generalized to a multilevel (say, N) quantizer, with N output levels and $(N-1)$ thresholds. Extrapolating the earlier analysis, it is easy to see that one needs to know and preserve $(2N-1)$ moments. As N increases, the computational load of determining these moments increases. Depending on the type of density function, one may be able to define recursive relationships between successive moments and use it to determine these moments. As before, assuming zero mean and unit variance, the equations preserving the moments become

$$E(x^q) = \sum_{i=1}^{N} x_{o_i}^q \left[F(x_{\text{thr1}}) - F(x_{\text{thr1-1}}) \right] \qquad (2.26)$$

Here, x_o's represent the output levels, x_{thr}'s represent the threshold, ($q = 1, 2, ..., 2N - 1$), $x_{\text{thr0}} = -\infty$, and $x_{\text{thr}N} = \infty$. Expression (2.26) represents $(2N - 1)$ nonlinear equations in terms of the output levels and thresholds. These equations are difficult to solve analytically, and one must resort to numerical approaches to their solutions. The study goes on to show that one could make some simplifying assumptions, such as $f(x)$ being even for classes of problems (that is, $f(x) = f(-x)$) and derive less complex equations for such cases. These simplified equations, again, can be solved analytically only for some specific low values of N (< 5). Beyond this, numerical methods must be used for solving these complex nonlinear equations. The generalized moment-preserving quantizer is compared with the traditional mean square error (MSE) quantizer. The latter preserves the first moment as in BTC, but unlike BTC its reconstructed image variance is always less than or equal to the original image variance; that is, it does not always preserve the second moment as BTC does. This comparison is based on assuming specific density functions for $f(x)$, since MSE-based derivations require knowledge of the distributions. The study [B5] backs up these conclusions with detailed numerical comparisons. Because preservation of the two moments (which relate directly to perceived picture qualities such as brightness and contrast) is desirable in practical image processing applications, BTC offers a more attractive alternative to the error minimization-based quantizers.

INITIAL APPLICATIONS

Shortly after the publication of [B5], in mid-1980, Mitchell and Delp [B9] presented a modified version of the BTC specifically designed to code and represent multilevel graphic information by taking advantage of the limited number of pixel intensities (far less than the normal 256 values in a standard gray-scale image). The sample mean and standard deviation for each block are coded jointly using a two-dimensional scheme under the premise that the mean is critical only in low-variance regions of the image and that its accuracy is less significant in high-variance regions. This permits definition of tables of permissible codes of values of mean and standard deviation, which can be constrained to be of specific length (for example, 128 code words for graphics of 32 gray levels and 64 code words for graphics with only 16 gray levels). This results in a higher compression ratio (because of the lower overhead in storing the mean and standard deviation values) than that achievable when the full range of possible values of mean and standard deviation is independently stored as under the original BTC construct. Although the mean square error is not explicitly minimized, the errors are concentrated in the high-variance regions, where, the authors claim, they are least noticeable. This claim is somewhat dubious as high-variance regions are not necessarily of less importance in every application. Application of a low-pass smoothing filter is observed to reduce the mean square error.

Mitchell et al. [B10] presented in 1980 a study comparing BTC with DCT, and a hybrid of DCT and DPCM in the context of some aerial reconnaissance photography. Professional photoanalysts were asked to subjectively compare the images compressed and reconstructed through the three approaches. Relative to its low computational demands, BTC performance was considered to be reasonably good.

Early in 1981, Goeddel and Bass [B11] presented a two-dimensional quantizer called quantum pattern coding (QPC). The QPC quantizer, although not a true member of the BTC class of techniques, parallels the BTC process to some extent. QPC defines a two-dimensional (2×2) quantizer with each pixel having one of three possible values: $+1$, -1, and 0. This gives a total of $3^4 = 81$ possible distinct arrays. The frequency pattern of these arrays is exploited in the coding process. Emphasizing this kinship of QPC with BTC, the authors compare their results with that obtained under BTC (as well as a couple of other methods). The mean square error under QPC is shown to be less than that under BTC for each of the three images considered in their study. However, the computational expense of QPC is roughly three times that of BTC (Table V of [B11]) although compromises that reduce the computations are offered by the authors to make QPC computationally competitive to BTC.

In a late-1981 conference, Arce and Gallagher [B12] discussed the role of median filter roots in the context of BTC. The truncated output block is encoded further by specifying it in the root signal space, which requires fewer bits than would be needed otherwise. This conference presentation was essentially a preliminary version of their 1983 journal paper [**B20**], which is discussed in more detail later on in this chapter.

At the same conference, Siegel and associates [B13] explored the potential for implementation of BTC techniques on a PASM, that is, a partitionable SIMD/MIMD (single-instruction multiple data stream)/(multiple-instruction multiple data stream) multimicroprocessor system, designed specifically for image-processing applications. The study starts with a detailed description of BTC, paying particular attention to computational aspects. This discussion on the computational aspects of BTC is of value to the uninitiated, especially from an implementation viewpoint (software as well as hardware). An overview of PASM follows this discussion. The parallel implementation of BTC on PASM for the coding phase is examined under two distinct scenarios: fixed–bit-rate BTC and variable–bit-rate BTC. For the basic fixed–bit-rate BTC scenario, the computations are structured purely as an SIMD process. For other variants of BTC (such as those involving only mean value transmission when the variance is small) that result in variable rates, both SIMD and MIMD implementations are investigated, with the latter being determined as the preferred method. For the decoding phase, the choice between SIMD and MIMD under the fixed–bit-rate approach is dependent upon the specific architecture used for the implementation. For the variable-rate approach, the choice is once again shown to be MIMD processing. This is a very detailed and interesting paper that offers good insight into the computational aspects of BTC; hence it is of particular value for anyone interested in actual implementation in a practical problem environment.

The BTC approach, which was originally designed for still pictures or snapshots at different instants of time, was applied late in 1981 to digital video bandwidth compression by Healy and Mitchell [**B14**]. This method, in addition to defining two-dimensional spatial blocks as required for still-image coding, adds a third dimension to the block in the temporal sense. This approach, as compared to the obvious alternative of applying two-dimensional BTC to a sequence of images independently, leads to a higher compression ratio since the overhead cost of carrying a single pair of mean and standard deviation values is spread over multiple frames. While this procedure is conceptually attractive, in practice, motion across image block spatial boundaries leads to poor temporal correlation in the decompressed image sequence. To address this problem, a registration scheme is proposed. Details of this global registration and motion detection process leading to an adaptive scheme of bit assignments are presented. Performance of the system in both noiseless and noisy channels is discussed to demonstrate the relative robustness of the system in the presence of channel noise. The paper offers a significantly detailed presentation of the problem of digital video bandwidth reduction and hence finds a place within the collection of reprints presented here.

In mid-1982, Mudge et al. [B16] presented the implementation aspects of BTC on a multimicroprocessor system PASM. This is essentially an extension of the work previously reported in [B13] and discussed earlier in this chapter. In [B16] the real-time implementation of parallel BTC algorithms is explored, using either fixed-length or variable-length output formats. The former is structured as an SIMD process and in the latter both SIMD and MIMD implementations are analyzed. The number of processors required to meet real-time needs driven by video rates of 60 frames/second is estimated using the then-current technology. Given the progress in the hardware arena since then, this problem deserves to be revisited.

BTC GENERALIZATIONS

Early in 1982, Ronson and Dewitte [B15] presented an adaptive BTC scheme involving the use of an edge-following algorithm. One of the inherent artifacts of BTC is the tendency for jagged edges in the reconstructed images. The purpose of the edge-following algorithm is to minimize this tendency by identifying the edge pixels and using an additional level (that is, three instead of the standard two levels) in these regions. This results in a relatively modest increase in the bit rate, but improves the appearance of the reconstructed images. Details of the edge-following algorithm are presented along with sample results of application of their methodology.

In the same year, Halverson, Griswold, and Wise [B17] presented, at the annual Princeton Conference on Information Science and Systems, their study on a generalized BTC quantizer, which was a forerunner to their more detailed like-titled journal publication [B23] later in 1984. Also appearing that year was a master's thesis by Lema [B18] on absolute-moment BTC, the gist of which appeared later as a paper [**B24**] in 1984. The details of these studies are accordingly deferred for later presentation in this chapter.

The 1982 study by Halverson [B19], as mentioned earlier, points out that there is an error in the expression derived for α (equation (2.17)) by Delp and Mitchell [**B8**]. The study discusses in great detail the problem of round-off errors caused by quantization of the output values x^+ and x^- as well as n^+ and the consequent effects on the preservation of the moments. It is indeed an interesting discussion on the practical implications of the alternatives available to the designer in terms of the order in which the different quantities can be rounded off and their relative merits.

In mid-1983, Arce and Gallagher [**B20**] discussed the role of median filter roots in a BTC approach to image coding. An appreciation of the method calls for a good understanding of median filter theory and related aspects. In a nutshell, the approach revolves around the idea of applying the median filter to convert the truncated binary output block into what is called the median root signal and store or transmit the code that specifies the root instead of the entire bit plane. This, in some sense, is a form of bit-plane encoding superimposed on the basic BTC technique. The study discusses alternatives such as a one-dimensional versus two-dimensional application of the filtering and root encoding concept. An elaborate mathematical model of the truncation process is discussed in great detail and offers possibly enticing food for thought for the mathematically inclined. This study has spawned a number of other studies wherein the basic concept of using the filter root signals for encoding the bit plane to gain additional compression has been extended to other generalized median filters such as stack filters.

In September 1983, Dewitte and Ronsin [B21] presented a three-stage compression scheme wherein the first stage is effectively the BTC scheme of determining the quantization scale and the binary matrix representation of the input block. The second stage consists of classifying this binary matrix into one of three categories:

- No edges (more or less homogeneous or near-uniform region)
- A single edge across the block
- A pair of edges across the block

The classification is accomplished by counting the number of transitions from 0 to 1 and 1 to 0 in the peripheral ring of the block. With 0 or more than 4 transitions, it is considered to be a no-edge case; with 2 transitions, a single-edge case; and with 4 transitions, a two-edge case. In the third stage, the classified block is matched to a specific model corresponding to its classification.

The paper provides details of the implementation of each of these stages and their interrelationships. Implementation experience with TV pictures showed that about 80 percent of the blocks belong to the first class of no edges, 12 percent are single-edge cases, and the remaining 8 percent are two-edge cases. This lopsided distribution in favor of blocks with no edges means that one can expect, in most instances, significantly lower bit rates without compromising image quality.

Around the same time, Uhl [B22] presented the next study in the BTC arena on adaptive BTC wherein the adaptation was driven mainly by edge orientations. Eight different classes or states, designed to preserve edge renditions along horizontal, vertical, and diagonal directions, are defined. The classification procedure required to identify the status of each block for implementing the adaptive procedure consists of five decision levels. The details of the procedure, which contains many ad hoc parameters, are beyond the scope of the high-level overview presented here.

Halverson, Griswold, and Wise [B23] presented a generalized version of the BTC algorithm in 1984. The two alternative methods of defining the quantizer thresholds (mean value chosen a priori and a variable value chosen to preserve, in addition, the third moment of the image block data) proposed by Delp and Mitchell [B8] are shown to be correspondingly generalizable to a larger class of pairs and triples of other higher-order sample moments. Examples to show that such generalization leads to improved qualitative performance are included. Equations (2.5) and (2.6), on generalization to the preservation of the higher-order moments of r and kr, can be rewritten as

$$n^2 \overline{x^r} = n_r^- \left[x_r^- \right]^r - n_r^+ \left[x_r^+ \right]^r \qquad (2.27)$$

$$n^2 \overline{x^{kr}} = n_r^- \left[x_r^- \right]^{kr} - n_r^+ \left[x_r^+ \right]^{kr} \qquad (2.28)$$

Noting that k is an integer, it is possible to show through transformation of variables that, when $k = 2$, a closed-form solution similar to one obtained previously is feasible through a quadratic formulation. The solutions can be written in the form

$$\left[x_r^- \right]^r = \overline{x^r} - \sigma_r \left[\frac{n^+}{n^-} \right]^{1/2} \qquad (2.29)$$

$$\left[x_r^+ \right]^r = \overline{x^r} + \sigma_r \left[\frac{n^-}{n^+} \right]^{1/2} \qquad (2.30)$$

where

$$\sigma_r = \left[\overline{x^{2r}} - \left(\overline{x^r} \right)^2 \right]^{1/2} \qquad (2.31)$$

Equation (2.31) expresses the rth-order standard deviation corresponding to the two moments, r and $2r$. These expressions effectively reduce to those derived earlier when $r = 1$. Equations (2.29) and (2.30) can be rewritten to define the output states as

$$x_r^- = \left[\overline{x^r} - \sigma_r \left[\frac{n^+}{n^-} \right]^{1/2} \right]^{1/r} \tag{2.32}$$

$$x_r^+ = \left[\overline{x^r} + \sigma_r \left[\frac{n^-}{n^+} \right]^{1/2} \right]^{1/r} \tag{2.33}$$

The quantization threshold for this general formulation can be expressed as

$$x_{\text{thr}} = \left[\overline{x^r} \right]^{1/r} \tag{2.34}$$

The authors state that closed-form solutions are not readily obtained for values of k other than 2 since the quadratic-equation solution will no longer be applicable. While it is true that the equations are no longer quadratic in form, closed-form solutions may be feasible for other equations: hence $k = 2$ represents a sufficient, but not always necessary, condition for obtaining closed-form solutions. The alternative approach of preserving three moments can also be generalized along the same lines by adding a third equation to equations (2.27) and (2.28):

$$n^2 \overline{x^{pr}} = n_r^- \left[x_r^- \right]^{pr} - n_r^+ \left[x_r^+ \right]^{pr} \tag{2.35}$$

Extending the logic of exploiting similarities, selection of $p = 3$ once again permits closed-form solutions to the three simultaneous equations (2.27), (2.28), and (2.35). Solution of these three simultaneous nonlinear equations leads, in addition to the two solutions (2.29) and (2.30), to

$$n^+ = \frac{n^2}{2} \left[1 + \alpha_r \left[\alpha_r^2 + 4 \right]^{-1/2} \right] \tag{2.36}$$

where

$$\alpha_r = \frac{3\overline{x^r}\,\overline{x^{2r}} - \overline{x^{3r}} - 2\left(\overline{x^r}\right)^3}{\sigma_r^3}; \qquad \sigma_r \neq 0 \tag{2.37}$$

The earlier study [B8] can therefore be viewed as a special case of this generalized study [B23] with $r = 1$, since all the equations corresponding to the general case reduce to the original set of equations when r is set to 1. However, the examples shown and discussed do *not* make a sufficiently convincing case for justifying the increased cost of this generalized approach [B23]. In fact, in the case of high-contrast facsimile, the quality actually decreases rapidly with increases in the value of r. The conclusion is that in some cases it may be justifiable to use $r = 2$, but $r > 2$ would rarely be advisable.

ABSOLUTE MOMENT BTC

Later in 1984, Lema and Mitchell [B24] reworked the BTC concept by modifying the objective to be the preservation of sample absolute moments rather than the standard moments used in all the prior published work. The resulting approach, called AMBTC (absolute-moment–based block truncation coding), is computationally more efficient and hence faster. The first absolute central moment is given by

$$\overline{x_a} = \frac{1}{n^2} \sum_{i=1}^{n^2} |x_i - \overline{x}| \tag{2.38}$$

The absolute central moment effectively contains the information of the dispersion about the mean, which is the conceptual equivalent of the standard deviation information derived under the original BTC. The computation of the first absolute central moment can be restructured through the simple algebraic manipulation of breaking up the summation in equation (2.38) into two ranges and rearranging the terms:

$$\overline{x_a} = \frac{2}{n^2} \left[\sum_{x_i \geq \overline{x}}^{n^2} x_i - \overline{x} n^+ \right] \tag{2.39}$$

Obviously, equation (2.39) is computationally less expensive to determine than the second moment employed in the earlier studies. Applying the principle of preservation of these two moments, we get the two simultaneous equations

$$n^2 \overline{x} = n^+ x^+ - n^- x^- \tag{2.40}$$

$$n^2 \overline{x_a} = n^+ (x^+ - \overline{x}) - n^- (x^- - \overline{x}) \tag{2.41}$$

Solving the two simultaneous equations (2.40) and (2.41), we get

$$x^+ = \overline{x} + \frac{n^2 \overline{x_a}}{2n^+} \tag{2.42}$$

$$x^- = \overline{x} - \frac{n^2 \overline{x_a}}{2n^-} \tag{2.43}$$

Equations (2.42) and (2.43) show that the output levels are once again biased symmetrically about the mean value as in the earlier case. Here, however, the biases are proportional to the absolute central moment (instead of the standard deviation) and inversely proportional to the number of samples on corresponding sides of the mean. Thus these biases under the AMBTC approach are simpler in form than the ones obtained under the classical BTC technique. Substitution of equation (2.39) in (2.42) and (2.43) gives

$$x^- = \frac{1}{n^-}\left[\sum_{x_i < \bar{x}} x_i\right] \qquad (2.44)$$

$$x^+ = \frac{1}{n^+}\left[\sum_{x_i \geq \bar{x}} x_i\right] \qquad (2.45)$$

Equations (2.44) and (2.45) are essentially the estimated conditional mean values, given that x is less or greater than the quantization threshold, which in this case is the mean value of the total set. This is similar to equations (2.12) and (2.13) derived for the MMSE case, with a general threshold x_{thr} determined to be optimal by an exhaustive search through all the possible threshold points. Here, however, we have a predetermined threshold—the mean value of the data block—and hence this approach represents a suboptimal solution as compared to the MMSE method. The authors show that if the histogram of the block is symmetric about the mean and n^2 is even, the mean square error is given by

$$e_{ms} = \sigma^2 - \left(\overline{x_a}\right)^2 \qquad (2.46)$$

Equation (2.46) shows that when the standard deviation equals the first absolute central moment, the mean square error becomes zero, that is, either when the gray level is constant or when half the pixels are above average by a constant quantity and half are below average to the same extent. Other thresholds—for example, the average between the minimum and maximum intensities, which have been reported to yield lower mean square errors under standard BTC—can also be used here to obtain better qualitative performance. The computational benefits of AMBTC are twofold. In the compression phase (that is, at the transmitter), computation of the absolute central moment is less expensive by far than the second moment since addition times are generally much less than multiplication times in most general-purpose digital processors. At the receiver (that is, during the decompression phase), the expressions for computation of the output levels are also much simpler. However, the computational savings at the receiver are not as impressive as those at the transmitter since the computations at the receiver are small to begin with and, hence, not a significant load. This fact is not brought out by Lema and Mitchell in their discussion highlighting the benefits of AMBTC over the basic version of BTC. The advantage of MMSE is also similarly somewhat exaggerated, as it is achieved only in special cases of symmetry as discussed above. However, they do report that AMBTC resulted in lower mean square errors as compared to classical BTC. The improvement in performance reported in their study is generally on the order of 10 percent, both in terms of mean square error and mean absolute error. The application of AMBTC to color images is also discussed in detail in this study. However, these details are more pertinent to the problem of color-image data processing and alternative color coordinate systems, such as RGB and YIQ. As such, these details are outside the scope of the main topic of this discussion. The reader is therefore referred to the original study [B24] for these application-specific details.

MORE BTC VARIANTS

In late 1985, Udpikar and Raina, in a brief communication [B25], presented an interesting alternative form of BTC wherein the mean and standard deviation statistics do not represent each block; instead, a pair of mean values, $\overline{x_L}$ and $\overline{x_H}$—one of the pixels above the overall mean and one of the pixels below the overall mean—is defined for the output levels:

$$x^- = \overline{x_L} = \frac{1}{n^-} \sum_{\substack{i=1 \\ x_i < \overline{x}}}^{n^2} x_i \tag{2.47}$$

$$x^+ = \overline{x_H} = \frac{1}{n^+} \sum_{\substack{i=1 \\ x_i \geq \overline{x}}}^{n^2} x_i \tag{2.48}$$

It can be easily shown that the two output levels under this structuring of the BTC are related by the expression

$$x^+ = x^- + \frac{1}{n^+}(\overline{x} - x^-) \tag{2.49}$$

The computation at the front end is less expensive because there is no need to compute the standard deviation; thus this method represents a computationally attractive alternative to the classical BTC. Additionally, the authors show that for the class of binary adaptive quantizers that use the mean as the threshold, the proposed upper and lower output levels, x^+ and x^-, represent the optimal in the mean square sense. This is shown by assuming a probability density $p(x)$ of the pixel intensities in a block and deriving the expression for mean square error as

$$\text{MSE} = \int_{-\infty}^{\overline{x}} (x - x^-)^2 p(x)dx + \int_{\overline{x}}^{\infty} (x - x^+)^2 p(x)dx \tag{2.50}$$

Differentiating equation (2.50) with respect to x^- and x^+ and setting the outcomes to zero gives

$$x^- = \frac{\int_{-\infty}^{\overline{x}} x\, p(x)d(x)}{\int_{-\infty}^{\overline{x}} p(x)d(x)} \tag{2.51}$$

$$x^+ = \frac{\int_{\overline{x}}^{\infty} x\, p(x)d(x)}{\int_{\overline{x}}^{\infty} p(x)d(x)} \tag{2.52}$$

These expressions are essentially the continuous-domain equivalents of the discrete versions defined earlier for the upper and lower mean values. Experimental results showing lower mean square errors for the new approach as compared to the classical BTC are also provided in support of the conclusions resulting from this error analysis. The authors conclude with a comment on the possibility of employing other statistical parameters in coder design, but offer no specifics.

At the end of 1985, Venkataraman and Rao [B26] presented a comparative study of BTC and another recently introduced data compression technology called vector quantization (VQ) in the context of image coding. A new scheme involving application of BTC to the image in the transform domain was also proposed in the study. It is shown how BTC applied in the orthonormal transform domain preserves the moments in the data domain also. By dropping a few of the coefficients with less variance in the transform domain (which will affect only the variance in the data domain), a higher compression ratio than would otherwise be possible can be achieved. However, most of the discussions in this study are in the area of VQ rather than BTC. The study also has a relatively long list of references covering the entire spectrum of data compression techniques.

The 1986 study by Frost and Minden [B27] presents a modification of BTC specifically designed to address the problem of data compression in the context of synthetic aperture radar (SAR) imagery. Block truncation coding is considered particularly well suited to SAR imagery applications wherein preservation of local statistics is considered particularly important. Results are provided to show that BTC produced images of suitable visual quality and preserved cultural features of interest. A further increase in the compression ratio is possible by taking advantage of the fact that in SAR images of homogeneous areas, the local mean and variance are proportional, and thus only the mean value need be saved and/or transmitted. The standard deviation is accordingly predicted to be σ_p, and with this assumption the BTC is modified as follows:

$$\sigma_p = \bar{x}N^{-1/2} \tag{2.53}$$

where N is number of looks for SAR. Using equation (2.53) in equations (2.7) and (2.8), we get the expressions for the output levels:

$$x^- = \bar{x}\left[1 - \sqrt{\frac{n^+}{Nn^-}}\right] \tag{2.54}$$

$$x^+ = \bar{x}\left[1 + \sqrt{\frac{n^-}{Nn^+}}\right] \tag{2.55}$$

Incidentally, there is a typographical error (a negative sign instead of a positive sign) in equation (14) of [B27], which corresponds to equation (2.55).

This modification to BTC, while producing images that are visually still acceptable, leads to a significant loss of contrast in the cultural features. This occurs mainly because nonhomogeneous regions containing cultural features and edges do not fit the traditional statistical radar model. An adaptive BTC algorithm is offered as an antidote to this problem. The adaptability lies in deciding when to use only the mean (that is, the modified BTC) and when to use both the mean and standard deviation (that is, the basic BTC) to describe a specific block of SAR imagery data. This decision is made by comparing the local area with a standard radar model and transmitting only the mean when the local area fits such a radar model. A simple test is offered to check whether the observed variance is greater than the predicted variance by a constant ratio k. This ratio is chosen so as to make the probability of rejecting the model small when it is in fact valid. This approach achieves a higher compression ratio than a standard BTC without the significant loss in the contrast of cultural features that occurs when only the mean values are transmitted across the entire set of image blocks. The disadvantage of such an adaptive procedure is that the number of bits required per block varies across the image. One therefore needs an extra bit as a flag to indicate whether the specific block is being compressed with the basic BTC or the modified BTC, that is, whether or not explicit standard deviation information is being carried for the block. This adds slightly to the overhead.

Another factor, not explicitly highlighted in the paper, is that standard deviation computations are needed for every block to determine the fit of the block to the standard radar model, even when this information is not actually transmitted. The paper reviews SAR image statistical models in terms of their point statistics and autocorrelation properties to show that the mean and variance of local areas are essentially redundant pieces of information in homogeneous regions. A further modification to remove the blocky appearance of the reconstructed image, produced by BTC as well as the adaptive BTC, is also proposed. This involves synthetic sampling in the decompression phase using pseudorandom numbers. The generation of pseudorandom numbers, however, adds to the computational expense. Experimental results covering the spectrum of these approaches are included in the study. An avenue worthy of further exploration, as pointed out by the authors themselves, is to assess the effect of N, the number of looks of SAR, on the quality of the reconstructed imagery.

Late in 1986, Ramamurthi and Gersho [B28] looked at a related problem, that of improving the reconstructed image resulting from the application of BTC and other similar techniques through specially designed nonlinear filter post-processing of the images.

Early in 1987, Udpikar and Raina [**B29**] presented a study on source encoding of the outputs of a block truncation coder. To this end, they proposed using vector quantization, which by then had gained attention as an efficient means of representing a sequence of discrete vectors with a smaller set of prototype vectors. The authors use their own version of the BTC reported earlier [B25], in which two mean values (instead of a mean and standard deviation as under classical BTC) describe the statistics of an image block, to illustrate their vector quantization strategy for achieving further gains in the compression ratio. The basic premise here is that vector quantizations can be applied separately both to the overhead statistical information (in this case the two means) and to the one-bit quantized output block. Quantization of the two mean values separately, as was suggested in the earlier study [B25], is inefficient since the joint distribution of the overall mean and the mean of the lower set is nonuniform. By treating the pair as a two-dimensional vector, vector quantization of this two-dimensional vector can improve the compression ratio. Similarly, treating the binary output block as an n^2-dimensional binary vector and applying vector quantization reduces the number of bits required for representation to less than n^2. The vector quantization method used in this study follows previously reported methodology, called the iterative training sequence-based approach, with the initial guess derived by a splitting algorithm. Details of these vector quantization algorithms, which are beyond the scope of this book, can be found in the abundant literature available on this topic (see, for example, the review by Nasrabadi and King [B33]).

Early in 1987, Ko and Lee [B30] explored and discussed the potential for real-time implementation of the absolute moment block truncation coding (AMBTC) previously proposed by Lema and Mitchell [**B24**]. They viewed BTC as a prime candidate for real-time hardware VLSI (very large-scale integration) implementation, when compared with other encoding schemes, based on its relatively modest computational demands. The real-time implementation envisaged five functional blocks:

- A four-line buffer memory
- A data processing unit
- A two-field memory
- A signal conditioner
- A control signal generator

Detailed descriptions of each of these blocks are presented along with their interrelationships. Experimental results demonstrating the feasibility of their implementation are also offered.

Chang, Kwok, and Curlander [B31] reported in mid-1987 on their evaluation of BTC along with four other coding techniques in the context of their application to SAR imagery (SEASAT) data. The other techniques studied here were

- Spatial domain techniques:
    Linear three-point predictor (LTPP)
    Microadaptive picture sequencing (MAPS)
- Transform domain techniques:
    Adaptive discrete cosine transform (ADCT)
    Adaptive Hadamard transform (AHT)

Various trade-off issues, such as rate distortion performance, computational complexity, algorithm flexibility, and compression ratio controllability, are addressed. The study first describes briefly the three spatial domain and two transform domain techniques. Based on the simulation results reported therein, the authors conclude that the transform domain techniques are better than the spatial domain techniques from the viewpoint of rate distortion performance. The trade-off is, of course, the higher computational and buffer requirements of these transform domain tools. Both LTTP and BTC offer good quality with 1 to 2 bits/pixel. Unlike LTTP, BTC requires no buffering of the input image. On the other hand, the compression ratio achievable under

MAPS, although more flexible than both LTPP and BTC, is not controllable. Furthermore, the problem of blocky appearance of the reconstructed output image is more pronounced under MAPS. However, MAPS does not require any buffering either. Thus the main advantages of BTC, as brought out by the study, are computational ease, controllability of the compaction level achievable, and flexibility with reasonably good image quality—that is, an overall well-balanced performance. The other techniques may have superior performance from one viewpoint but prove to be largely unsuitable from other viewpoints.

Another small increment to the progress of the BTC field is offered in the 1987 study by Griswold, Halverson, and Wise [B32]. The study presents an adaptive formulation of BTC, with the adaptability coming into play in terms of defining the order of the moments preserved by the generalized BTC proposed by these same authors in their earlier study [B23] on a selective block-by-block basis. Additionally, a choice between black-on-white (higher intensity numbers assigned to lighter gray levels) and white-on-black (higher intensity numbers assigned to darker gray levels) can be made for each block. Depending on the maximum order (r in equations (2.18)–(2.28)) of the moments, the number of options available for the adaptive strategy will be $2r$. No additional computational load or overhead bits are necessary to achieve this adaptability.

Nasrabadi and King [B33] presented in the latter half of 1988 a detailed review of image coding via vector quantization. Although vector quantization, the main subject matter of their review, is not our primary interest here, we cite this review because it covers, albeit in a passing fashion, the work of Udpikar and Raina [B29] on BTC image coding using vector quantization. In all, this survey [B33] covers more than a hundred studies.

Also in 1988, Wu and Coll [B34] presented a multilevel BTC for high-fidelity compression of composite imagery. Again in late 1988, Tsai [B35] presented a real-time architecture for VLSI implementation of the BTC algorithms. Chen and Tsai [B36] presented in 1989 a detailed survey of moment-preserving techniques, a first such attempt in this area that also included some new approaches.

THREE-LEVEL BTC

The next significant study is that of Alsaka and Lee [B37], who, in 1990, took a different approach as compared to the classical one by expanding the BTC concepts. Instead of the traditional two-level or binary quantization implied under the classical BTC, they proposed a three-level quantization, requiring 2 bits/pixel, instead of 1 bit/pixel. The range of the intensity spread in the image block, D, is given by

$$\Delta = \max[x_i] - \min[x_i]; \qquad i = 1,\ldots,n^2 \tag{2.56}$$

Two mean values, upper and lower, are defined as

$$\overline{x_H} = \max[x_i] - \Delta/3 \tag{2.57}$$

76

$$\overline{x_{\mathrm{L}}} = \min[x_i] + \Delta/3 \tag{2.58}$$

Under these definitions, the three (rather than the two under classical BTC) output levels are given by

$$x^+ = \tfrac{1}{2}\left[\overline{x_{\mathrm{H}}} + \max[x_i]\right] \tag{2.59}$$

$$x^- = \tfrac{1}{2}\left[\overline{x_{\mathrm{L}}} + \min[x_i]\right] \tag{2.60}$$

$$x^{\mathrm{M}} = \tfrac{1}{2}\left[\overline{x_{\mathrm{L}}} + \overline{x_{\mathrm{H}}}\right] \tag{2.61}$$

This obviously reduces the compression ratio achievable under their modification to

$$R(n) = \frac{bn^2}{2n^2 + 2b} \tag{2.62}$$

If $b = 8$, the standard bit rate for pixel data in most imagery applications, we have a compression ratio given by

$$R(n) = \frac{8n^2}{2n^2 + 16} \tag{2.63}$$

For $n = 4$, this gives a compression ratio of 2.67 instead of 4 under the classical BTC. Equating expressions for $R(n)$ for the two- and three-level BTC schemes (equations (2.9) and (2.62)), it can be shown that for equivalent compression ratios under both the schemes, the number of bits per pixel under the three-level BTC would have to be twice that under the classical BTC.

Equation (2.63) is shown in graphical form in **Figure 2.4.** Comparing **Figure 2.4** with **Figure 2.3,** we can see that the corresponding curves for given input quantization levels are lower for the three-level BTC and that the three-level BTC curves match the curves corresponding to twice the bit rate under the classical BTC scheme. Compensating for this loss in compression ratio are the benefits claimed in terms of reduced blocky appearance of the reconstructed images under the three-level quantization. The mean square error is also obviously reduced since there is a choice of three output levels instead of just two under the classical BTC. The experimental results included in the study support this observation in that the mean square error under the three-level BTC is less than that in the basic BTC, AMBTC, and entropy-preserving block truncation coding (EBTC). (The citation by Alsaka and Lee on EBTC refers to a University of Virginia report by Tzannes, Thacker, and Tzannes, which was unavailable; thus, a review of EBTC could not be included here.) Since no second-order moment is needed, the computational load is also less than that in the other methods cited above. It is, of course, to be kept in mind that all of these gains are paid for in terms of the lower compression ratio achieved under the three-level BTC.

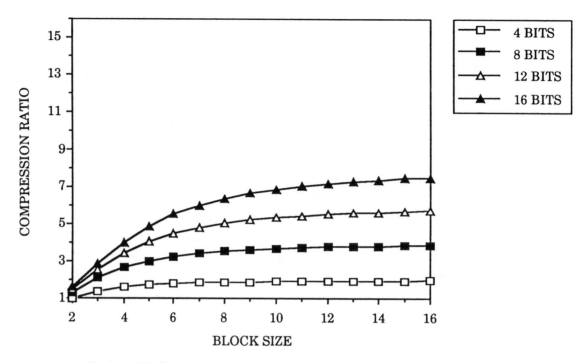

Figure 2.4 Compression ratio versus block size at different original image quantization levels under the three-level BTC scheme.

ADAPTIVE AND HIERARCHICAL BTC

Hui [B38] presented an adaptive BTC (ABTC) early in 1990 based on minimum mean square error (MMSE) principles. The contribution of the study is twofold: Development of an iterative MMSE-based implementation of BTC and an adaptive structure to take advantage of the local variations in the image. The new ABTC method offers, in essence, three choices—one-level, two-level, and four-level MMSE quantizers—for switching during the adaptive process. This switching is dictated by statistics of the locality of the image block, categorized into one of three classes:

- Low activity—most pixels having nearly the same intensity
- Medium activity—small transitions with no significant edges
- High activity—large transitions with contrasting edges

The iterative MMSE implementation requires even fewer complex computations compared to the classical BTC since it does not require any multiplication or square-root operations. The iterative process consists of computing the threshold as the average of the two output levels (initially set as the maximum and minimum intensities in the image block) and then recomputing the output levels to minimize the distortion of the reconstructed image using the threshold selected previously. This process of alternately updating the threshold and output levels is continued until no more changes in the output levels occur, that is, until stability is attained. Experimental evidence is included in support of the claim of improvement in performance (in terms of lower mean square errors) over traditional BTC, AMBTC, and two-level MMSE methods (Table I of [B38]).

Nasrabadi et al. [**B39**] presented in mid-1990 a hierarchical BTC (HBTC) for digital HDTV images. The technique is essentially a hybrid of BTC and a quadtree segmentation procedure. The quadtree procedure segments the image into homogeneous regions with little correlation between them and applies BTC to these regions separately. This permits one to use large blocks where there is high correlation and small blocks only in regions with low correlation. This results in a considerable gain in the overall level of compression achievable under this method as compared to a conventional BTC scheme in which block size is chosen to satisfy the requirements of the regions with low correlation. The quadtree segmentation procedure, a well-accepted tool in image analysis, recursively divides regions into four quadrants, or subregions, until the quadrants reach a desired level of homogeneity or a preset minimal size, thereby creating a tree-structured representation of the image with nodes at different levels. Application of BTC to each of these nodes in the hierarchy of the quadtree representation is thus viewed as a hierarchical block truncation coding (HBTC) technique; hence its name. A 10-bit joint quantization of the mean and standard deviation is used for each terminal node. Experimental results demonstrating the benefits of the HBTC approach relative to the traditional BTC in terms of higher compression ratios are included. The overhead of the quadtree segmentation procedure is not brought out, and thus the effective increase in computational expense is not properly accounted for in the overall assessment of the scheme. While this ommission does not invalidate the contribution of the study, it shows that a balanced view of the benefits of the approach has not been presented.

Chen and Bovik [B40] presented, at the end of 1990, a new approach to data compression called visual pattern image coding (VPIC). This is not, in a strict sense, a true BTC technique, but is included in this chronology since it has some similarities to BTC and VQ techniques, which have been used in conjunction with BTC. In essence, BTC attempts to preserve the low-frequency information (in the form of average intensity of the image block) and high-frequency information (in the form of standard deviation of the image block). Under VPIC, low-frequency information is coded essentially in the same manner as in BTC with image block average. Like VQ, VPIC also takes a codebook approach. However, unlike VQ, wherein the codebook is a function of the specific image under quantization, VPIC employs a universal codebook definition approach based on measured properties of human biological vision. This eliminates the traditional training phase of the VQ approach required for constructing the codebook. Thus Chen and Bovik attempt to combine certain features of BTC and certain features of VQ and modify the basis for codebook construction. However, VPIC does not qualify as a hybrid of BTC and VQ in the traditional sense of hybrid techniques, since hybrid techniques continue to carry recognizable portions of their components. The paper [B40] discusses at length the properties of biological vision and associated factors, including receptive fields, visual continuity and discontinuity constraints (image smoothness and detail), spatial frequency constraint, and viewing geometry. This discussion is followed by a detailed presentation of the design of visual patterns, which covers pattern design, image coding, and coding complexity analysis as well as decoding and post-processing. Fourteen basic edge patterns are defined for (4×4) block image data. A subset of these patterns is generally enough to code the images in most cases. Two versions of the VPIC algorithm are presented. The first uses four patterns for coding, and the second uses eight patterns while achieving slightly lower compression ratios than the first. Overall, the compression ratios achieved here under both versions are seen to be far higher than under BTC and compare favorably to those obtainable under VQ. However, the computations of VPIC are shown to be significantly (almost two orders of magnitude) less complex than those of VQ and comparable to simpler data compression techniques such as DPCM. This is expected to make VPIC a feasible candidate for real-time applications without necessarily requiring special-purpose hardware. Simulation results in support of the proposed scheme are offered. The study concludes with suggestions for further work, including possible improvements and new avenues for research.

Primarily, the visual pattern set defined here is by no means comprehensive or unique. Additional variations, such as edges of different orientations, line patterns, and curves, can be conceived and implemented. One could also resort to hybrid techniques—for example, in terms of using DPCM for coding the mean intensity values of the image blocks—to achieve higher compression ratios. It is to be noted in this context that VPIC is important in subband coding where the subbands contain edge information, as in line patterns, for example. In conclusion, this paper is not an easy one to summarize in a few simple words or equations since it involves many different qualitative concepts of visual perception and other related aspects that require lengthy explanations. The interested reader is therefore best served by the full paper.

NEURAL NET AND OTHER NOVELTIES

At the beginning of 1991, Tabatabai and Troudet [B41] presented a neural net–based architecture for segmentation of mixed gray-level and binary pictures. Block truncation coding can be looked upon as a method of classifying an image block into two classes of high- and low-intensity pixels for ensuing binary coding. In the classical approach, this classification is accomplished by statistical means. With the advent of neural nets, it has become fashionable among researchers to revisit all statistically addressed problems with a neural net approach. In keeping with this new trend, neural nets have been investigated as a means of solving this binary classification problem. The Hopfield neural network, one of the most prominent types of neural net, is an obvious candidate for this effort. At the top level, the image blocks (of size 16 × 16) are first classified either into character blocks or gray-level image blocks by employing an adaptive (16 × 16) neural net. The image blocks are further divided into smaller subblocks of size (4 × 4). Both the (16 × 16) character blocks and the (4 × 4) image subblocks are then quantized using a neural net–based segmentation approach, which is accomplished with a neural net–based binary quantization of the image blocks similar to BTC. However, instead of preserving the first and second moments, as under the BTC, the quantizer levels are obtained by maximizing the class separation measure of the pixels over the block. Although this process has an optimization flavor similar to the MMSE approach, it is quite unlike MMSE in both its conceptual and computational aspects. This significantly innovative study goes into great detail on the implementation and architectural aspects as well. However, such details are beyond the scope of this review, and accordingly the reader is referred to the original paper for these details.

Around the same period, Kamel, Sun, and Guan [B42] presented another variant of the BTC called the variable BTC (vBTC), in contrast to the traditional fixed-size BTC. The main thrust of this study, as the name implies, is to exploit the potential usefulness of subdividing the image block into subblocks successively until the standard deviation of the subblock reduces below a predefined threshold. Obviously the smallest useful block size would be (2×2). The largest size is defined by the largest homogeneous region in the given image. The main advantage of this hierarchical approach would be that in homogeneous areas one could use larger block sizes and reduce the size to the desired extent in areas with additional cultural details, such as edges. This adaptive approach would effectively permit a higher compression ratio without sacrificing the quality of the reconstructed image. This adaptive implementation would obviously entail additional overhead in terms of having to carry the variable block size information. This information is carried in the form of an index tree. The index tree is a quadtree with each node having either zero or four, corresponding to four subblocks created at each stage by halving both rows and columns. This mode of subdivision of the block is admittedly one of convenience and not necessarily unique. In addition, the authors suggest using an optimal threshold selection for each block or subblock, which is practically the same as the classical MMSE approach described and used as a benchmark under the original BTC study. The authors, however, fail to acknowledge this fact. They restructure the expression for the mean square error as

$$J_{\text{mse}} = 2\sigma^2 - 2\sigma\left[\frac{n^+}{n^-}\right]\left[\bar{x} - x^-\right] \tag{2.64}$$

Since the first term in equation (2.64) is a constant independent of the threshold, maximizing the negative second term is equivalent to the minimization of the mean square error function. This is achieved by an exhaustive search through the sorted image pixel data set.

Shortly thereafter, Weitzman and Mitchell [B43] offered a fast search procedure for the hybrid BTC–VQ algorithm proposed earlier by Udpikar and Raina [**B29**]. The major drawback therein is noted to be the significantly high computational expense of an otherwise very attractive algorithmic approach. The codebook generation process, which is central to the VQ phase of the approach, is structured not as a global search but as a localized search in a small subcodebook. These subcodebooks are not necessarily disjoint sets, in that some code-vectors can appear in multiple subcodebooks. Of course, this requires a presearch for the appropriate subcodebook. Thus for the approach to be effective, the savings in search time accomplished by having multiple subcodebooks should be greater than the additional expense incurred by the preselection process of identifying the right subcodebook. Furthermore, the code-vector identified by the new localized approach should be the same as that determined from the traditional global search. In practice, a suboptimal procedure cannot always be expected to achieve the optimal result, and thus it is possible in rare cases that a code-vector different from that obtainable with a global search may be selected. This probability is estimated to be less than 1 percent. The subcodebooks are roughly a third of the global one in size and thus the computational savings are considerable. The paper gives further implementation details of this approach. In summary, this study is basically one of computational efficiency enhancement in the second phase of the hybrid approach with little impact on the qualitative aspects. It does not in any way contribute to the BTC aspects of the methodology.

The benefits of employing BTC in predictive differential pulse code modulation (DPCM) coding of images were explored by Delp and Mitchell [**B44**] again in early 1991. Under DPCM, the difference between a pixel intensity and its predicted value is quantized and transmitted. The quality of the reconstructed image and the data compression achieved is determined by the predictor model and the quantizer. In this study, a BTC-based moment-preserving quantizer is used to quantize the difference signal. It is observed that preserving the moments of the difference signal cannot, in general, be expected to preserve the moments of the original image in the reconstructed one. However, even with this admitted drawback, the authors claim that the benefit of additional savings in the effective bit rate is worth the effort. While the results in themselves are not all that significant, the uniqueness of this study lies in exploring a new avenue in the field of hybrid techniques involving BTC.

Around the same time, Ma and Rajala [B45] applied AMBTC to subband coding of digital imagery data. The objective of this fusion of subband coding and AMBTC tools is to minimize the blocky appearance resulting from the application of AMBTC alone. The AMBTC method of Lema and Mitchell [**B24**], discussed earlier, forms the baseline for this study. The paper presents a summary of the AMBTC technique as well as the concept of subband coding, wherein the input signal is decomposed into narrow-frequency bands, or subbands, by a set of parallel filters, referred to as analysis filters. Each subband is separately coded, and at the reconstruction phase the coded subbands signals are decoded, interpolated, and filtered through synthesis filters before being combined to form a representation of the original signal.

Also early in 1991, Lu, Gough, and Davies [B46] discussed application of BTC to the compression of scientific data in Space. They presented a modified block truncation coding (MBTC) algorithm. The features of this modified algorithm are

- Lloyd optimal quantizer—instead of the normal BTC quantizer
- Differential coding—in place of absolute-value coding
- Entropy coding—whereby quantized outputs are further encoded
- Error control—whereby a preset error threshold is imposed

The method uses the algorithm proposed by Udpikar and Raina [B25] as the starting point for a recursive procedure. Modifying equations (2.47) and (2.48),

$$x^- = \overline{x_{\mathrm{L}}} = \frac{1}{n^-} \sum_{\substack{i=1 \\ x_i < x_{\mathrm{thr}}}}^{n^2} x_i \tag{2.65}$$

$$x^+ = \overline{x_{\mathrm{H}}} = \frac{1}{n^+} \sum_{\substack{i=1 \\ x_i \geq x_{\mathrm{thr}}}}^{n^2} x_i \tag{2.66}$$

where the initial value of x_{thr} is the mean value of x. A new value of x_{thr} is computed using x^+ and x^- as

$$x_{\mathrm{thr}} = \frac{\left[\overline{x_{\mathrm{H}}} + \overline{x_{\mathrm{L}}}\right]}{2} \tag{2.67}$$

The computations of x^+, x^-, and x_{thr} using equations (2.65), (2.66), and (2.67) are recursively continued until a stable set of values is obtained for these variables. The method uses this modified BTC as the building block and employs, in addition, a differential coding scheme (to take advantage of the nature of space science image data) along with entropy coding (consisting of short codewords for high-frequency data and longer ones for low-frequency data) and error control (by explicit determination of error through actual compression and decompression on-board prior to transmission) to achieve an overall performance significantly better than a simple BTC alone.

A little later, Roy and Nasrabadi [B47] presented a hierarchically structured BTC technique, which is essentially equivalent of the earlier work by Nasrabadi et al. [B39] except that the image data sets used to illustrate the method are different this time around. There is, however, no cross-reference between these two conceptually identical studies (the latter paper [B47] seems to have been submitted for publication a little earlier than the prior one [B39]), although they have a common author.

In mid-1991, at the annual IEEE International Symposium on Circuits and Systems, Nasipuri et al. [B48] presented an adaptive encoding technique for images that employed a pyramid architecture. This is similar in concept to the quadtree approach of Nasrabadi et al. [B39] and Roy and Nasrabadi [B47] in that block sizes are adaptively varied based on the level of homogeneity in the region. Instead of computing the variance and using it as the measure of homogeneity as was done in the quadtree approach [B39, B47], the range of intensities (the difference between the maximum and minimum values in the block) is used as the measure of homogeneity for dividing the blocks into subblocks. Instead of being viewed as branches of a tree, these subblocks are looked upon as parts of a pyramid structure. Thus, while there may be differences in the coding of these two procedures, there is little conceptual difference between the quadtree approach [B39, B47] and the pyramid approach [B48]. A detailed comparative analysis of the two sets of codes would perhaps be an interesting exercise.

At the same symposium, Ma and Rajala [B49] compared the AMBTC and MMSE quantizers. The Lagrange multiplier technique of optimization is employed to develop the interrelationship between AMBTC and the MMSE quantizers. Each of these schemes is separately embedded into a subband coding structure. From an implementation viewpoint, AMBTC is more practical than MMSE since AMBTC, unlike the MMSE quantizer, does not involve an iterated procedure for searching the optimum threshold. The Lagrangian method is used to show that when the threshold is set at the mean value, AMBTC indeed becomes identical to MMSE.

Once again, at this same conference, Zeng, Wang, and Neuvo [B50] delved further into the use of median filter roots in BTC image coding, which was first considered by Arce and Gallagher [B12, **B20**]. Instead of the one-dimensional window of width-three median filter employed by Arce and Gallagher, which preserves either row or column details only, a two-dimensional cross-window (five-point) median (CWM) filter and a separable (3 × 3) median (SM) filter are considered for BTC application in this study. Instead of the rate of 1.75 bits/pixel (for the scenario wherein the standard BTC requires 2 bits/pixel) obtained before, the new approach gives rates of 1.81 bits/pixel and 1.69 bits/pixel, respectively, for the two types of filters.

Zeng [B51], also in mid-1991, presented a short note on two interpolative BTC coding techniques based on the use of optimal stack filters in the minimum mean absolute error (MMAE) sense as the interpolator. It is claimed that the performance degradation is insignificant while resulting compression ratios are 25 to 37.5 percent higher under the two interpolative schemes as compared to the standard BTC approach.

HYBRID BTC AND OTHER INNOVATIONS

Once again in mid-1991, Efrati, Liciztin, and Mitchell [**B52**] investigated a hybrid approach of BTC and VQ that is sensitive to the presence of edges in the images. This is a modification of the approach put forth earlier by Udpikar and Raina [B25], which, although simple, had the problem of ragged edges, or the so-called staircase effect. The new method, called BTC–CVQ, employs a three-level reconstruction for the edge pixels separately from the nonedge pixels. Thus the vector quantization part of the technique calls for a pair of codebooks: one based on two-level quantization of the nonedge pixels and another based on three-level quantization for the edge pixels. For the former, the approach of Udpikar and Raina is directly adapted. For the latter, a training codebook containing different directional edges was created. Details of this procedure are beyond the scope of this review and the reader is referred to the original paper [**B52**]. Experimental results are offered in support of the claim of superior compression for acceptable quality of the reconstructed image.

Nasiopoulos, Ward, and Morse [**B53**] dealt with adaptive compression coding (ACC) in the latter half of 1991. The aim of this study was to develop a technique that can preserve edges, which is crucial in engineering as well as visual applications. Very high compression ratios—that is, low bit rates of 0.5 to 0.8 bits/pixel—are claimed for the approach. Once again, ACC also uses a quadtree coding reminiscent of other studies, such as those of Nasrabadi et al. [**B39,** B47], Kamel, Sun, and Guan [B42], and Nasipuri et al. [B48], which are not cited in [**B53**]. However, looking at the date of submission of the manuscript—August 1987 and revised in November 1989—it is clear that their efforts antedate most of these uncited studies. The basic BTC building block employed here is the absolute moment BTC (AMBTC) and hence all comparisons are made relative to AMBTC. The adaptability consists in making one of four choices for each image block of (4×4):

- Represent by average
- AMBTC
- AMBTC with lookup table
- Quadtree

A two-bit codeword overhead is obviously necessary to denote which choice has been made for the specific block. The study also includes extensive experimental results.

Shortly thereafter, Wu and Coll [**B54**] studied a hybrid coding approach involving VQ and DCT in conjunction with BTC. The positive contributions claimed for the different components of this hybrid are as follows:

- BTC—computational ease and edge-preservation properties
- VQ—high compression ratio and good subjective quality
- DCT—high fidelity and high compression ratio

The hybrid scheme is computationally more efficient than either VQ or DCT alone. The first piece of this trilogy is the BTC. The bit map generated by the BTC is then processed further using the VQ concept. Since the VQ is being applied to a binary map rather than the original 8-bit image, it is computationally much more efficient than when applied to the 8-bit image. Adaptive DCT coding with residual error feedback is the last leg of this process and is used to encode the high-mean and low-mean subimages. Compression ratios of about 10:1 are achievable with fidelity comparable to DCT or VQ alone, but with much lower computational loads. This compares favorably with the 8:1 ratio achievable from the earlier work of Udpikar and Raina [**B29**], which formed a hybrid using only the BTC and VQ concepts. The BTC building block for this hybrid is the absolute moment BTC of Lema and Mitchell [**B24**]. The VQ process, consisting of vector formation, codebook generation, and quantization, is made computationally efficient by using a lookup table (LUT) operation, a universal codebook (VQU) that avoids update for each input image, and a Hamming distance (instead of Euclidean distance) measure for assessing distortion.

The adaptive DCT phase of this hybrid process is explored using three alternative methods. In the first one, ADCT is directly implemented on both the high-mean and low-mean pseudo-subimages obtained by grouping all the high means and low means of the different BTC blocks of the original image. In the second, ADCT is applied either on the high or low mean and on the difference between the high- and low-mean subimages, thereby saving some additional bits in view of the lower entropy of the difference image. In the third method there is a further step along these same lines wherein, instead of the low-mean subimage, its reconstructed version is employed in the difference image using residual error feedback. The first method has the best performance and least computational complexity, but also the least compression benefits. At the other end, the second method has the poorest MSE performance, moderate computational complexity, and the most compression ratio gains. The third method, a compromise of sorts between these two, has high compression ratio and moderate MSE, but the most computational complexity. However, the high computational complexity is really not a serious factor since the size of these pseudo-subimages is very small so that effective computational loads are insignificant in the overall context. Accordingly, the authors recommend the third method as their choice for the third component of their hybrid approach.

Late in 1991, Qiu, Varley, and Terrell [B55] explored the use of Hopfield neural networks for BTC applications. However, the algorithm employed here is very similar, if not identical to that proposed in the much broader and more comprehensive study by Tabatabai and Troudet [B41], except for some minor details such as the constants in equations (11) and (12) of [B55], which differ by a factor of 2 from the corresponding ones in equations (3.8a) and (3.8b) of [B41]. However, this earlier work was not cited by Qiu, Varley, and Terrell.

Also in late 1991, Delp and Mitchell [B56] dealt with the underlying subject of moment-preserving quantization in a more general way than was attempted previously in their pioneering studies [B8, B9] and numerous other developments since that time. The earlier efforts were mostly based on a purely nonparametric approach that involved no a priori knowledge of the underlying probabilistic models for the image data sets. Here, the objective is to derive closed-form solutions to the moment-preserving quantization problem and compare them with those of minimum mean square error quantizers. The moment-preserving quantization problem is shown to be equivalent to the classical Gauss–Jacobi mechanical quadrature problem. The analysis starts with a representation of some of Delp and Mitchell's earlier results [B5] discussed earlier in this chapter for the binary level (equations (2.18) through (2.26)) and its generalization to N levels. This is followed by recognizing the equivalence of the problem to the Gauss–Jacobi mechanical quadrature. The output levels of the N-level quantizer are correspondingly the zeros of the Nth-degree orthogonal polynomial associated with the probability distribution function.

In their 1991 tutorial text on data compression techniques, Rabbani and Jones [B57] have briefly reviewed the area of block truncation coding schemes in the context of their overall review of the data compression area. Accordingly, the coverage of BTC is brief, about 15 pages, and touches upon both moment-preserving and error-minimizing quantizers. It also covers adaptive AMBTC and VQ encoding of the bit map and thus spans a fairly broad cross-section of the BTC area. In their list of references on lossy compression techniques, which contains 86 entries, 11 entries relate to BTC area. Although they list fewer than 15 percent of the available citations in the BTC area, the fact that these make up a significant portion, about 12 percent, of their total citations reflects the importance of BTC within the field of lossy compression techniques. However, this relatively recent book does not mention wavelet transforms in the coverage of transform coding techniques. Thus, 1991 was one of the most productive years in the development history of BTC techniques.

Early in 1992, Neagoe [**B58**] presented a hybrid block truncation coding (HBTC) technique as one possible option for the last stage of a cascade of four processing stages. The different stages of this cascade in order are as follows:

- Predictive ordering technique (POT)
- Feedback transform coding (FTC)
- Vertical subtraction of quantized coefficients (VSQC)
- Overshoot suppression (OS) or a hybrid BTC (HBTC)

Details of the first three stages are, however, outside the scope of our current study and as such are not presented here. HBTC is employed to derive a one-bit quantization of the error between the original image scanline and the one reconstructed by FTC while preserving its first two moments. Various combinations of these stages are evaluated in the paper, and the complex combinations attempted here offer image quality that is comparable to BTC with only slightly better compression. It is thus not clear whether the benefits are worth all the additional effort and the associated complexity.

Early in 1992, Overturf, Comer, and Delp [B59] offered a new way of employing BTC within a hybrid built on the concept of morphological pyramid decomposition. This conference presentation has since appeared in a revised and more detailed form in an archival journal (*IEEE Transactions on Image Processing* [B90]). An image pyramid consists of an ordered set of images derived from the original image with successively decreasing spatial resolution. If this set of images is viewed as a stack with the original image at the bottom, the set would resemble a pyramid; hence the name. Image coding using pyramid structures was first postulated by Burt and Adelson [D58], who introduced the concept of Laplacian image pyramids. Each level in this Laplacian pyramid consists of a difference image between the original image and its smoothed version generated by a Gaussian kernel–based linear smoothing operator. Other variants to this have also appeared in the literature: one by Ho and Gersho [D101], who employed vector quantization of the difference images with contour-based interpolation, and one by Sun and Margos [D102], who resorted to a nonlinear filter operator based on mathematical morphology concepts. In this BTC-oriented study by Overturf et al. [B59], quantization is performed using BTC with linear interpolation for image decoding. The method employs the morphological smoothing for the pyramidal decomposition of the original image. The study offers details of the pyramidal decomposition, interpolation, followed by the BTC-based quantization process. To some extent, the role of BTC in this study is peripheral, although the contribution of BTC to the overall process is recognized by comparing the results of using BTC quantization with those obtained with a scalar quantization. The comparison brings out the positive aspects of BTC, namely, better preservation of edge information within the image.

Also early in 1992, Zeng, Neuvo, and Venetsanopoulos [B60] presented a study on an interpolative approach in the context of BTC. This study is along the same lines as Zeng's earlier short note [B51], but here, instead of an optimal stack filter, a median filter is used in defining the two interpolative BTC (IBTC) algorithm alternatives. The authors even point out that the earlier approach of using the optimal stack filter improves the coding quality. However, in addition, the possibility of using VQ for the mean vectors in the interpolative coding is also investigated and is shown to be better than just BTC with VQ *à la* Udpikar and Raina [**B29**].

Again, early in 1992, Kruger [B61] presented a summary of BTC techniques in a magazine article. This introductory study mainly addresses the uninitiated in this field. Accordingly, the author maintains the depth of treatment of the subject matter at a level that would be appropriate to such an audience.

In mid-1992, Wu and Coll [**B62**] reported their investigations on the application of BTC techniques to color images. Color images in general can be looked upon as consisting of three monochromatic image planes—red, green, and blue (R/G/B). An obvious approach is to apply BTC to each of these planes separately. However, in practice, the R/G/B planes are likely to have high correlation since they are looking at the same objects within the same scene; thus they will have more or less the same underlying segmentations, although the actual intensity levels may differ significantly from color plane to color plane. One can, therefore, achieve an additional compression ratio of approximately 3:1 if one could use a single bitmap for all of the three primary color planes, except the quantization values would be different for each color plane. The question that arises then is, which of the three possible approximately similar bit-plane maps should one choose as the common representative for all the three. A little careful thought makes it clear that no single one would be optimal by itself. Accordingly, a fourth plane, which is in some sense optimally weighted to minimize noise and registration errors in all three planes, would be advisable. Development of a methodology to derive such a weighted plane represents the core of the contributions of this study. Details of this methodology, which minimizes the mean square error, are presented. An alternative scheme that joins the three planes through a bit-by-bit majority rule (among the R, G, and B bits at each pixel) into a single fused bitmap is also explored. Further compression, which reaches a total of up to 12:1 through the application of ADCT, differential coding, and error feedback techniques on the BTC output image, is also demonstrated.

In the latter half of 1992, Weitzman and Mitchell [B63] presented a variation of the BTC to take into account the interblock correlations that lead to a lower bit rate. The interblock correlations are taken into account by VQ coding the current-block high and low values relative to the high–low values of three other previously encoded nearest-neighbor blocks (blocks to the east, north, and northeast of the current block). This is less expensive than VQ coding the high–low values of each block directly. Additional savings are also obtained by dividing the truncation block into two interleaving matrices and transmitting alternate ones, with the other reconstructed through interpolation.

A little later in 1992, Wang and Neuvo [B64] offered a new approach to BTC based on mathematical morphology. The statistical descriptors of the blocks required by BTC—that is, the mean and variance of the block—can be encoded for transmission using what the authors call adaptive morphological predictors within a DPCM construct. The roots of the morphological filters are then used to compress the bit plane. The standard morphological operator set of dilation, erosion, opening, and closing is extended to the gray-scale domain and developed into an adaptive morphological algorithm (in a companion paper these authors presented at the same conference), which is employed here as the predictor in a DPCM system for achieving compression of the block statistics overhead. The BTC-derived bit plane is itself further compressed using the root signals of the morphological opening and closing. The performance of the new method is compared with standard BTC and BTC using median filter roots proposed by Arce and Gallagher [B12, **B20**].

Qui, Varley, and Terrell [B65], in late 1992, revisited the concept of deploying Hopfield neural networks in the BTC context and presented a variable block size BTC technique using a Hopfield neural network. However, the related work of Tabatabai and Troudet [**B41**] is not acknowledged.

In November 1992, Mitchell and Dorfan [B66] critically reviewed the first study by Qiu, Varley, and Terrell [B55] in which Hopfield neural networks are used for improving the performance of BTC. However, this study also fails to cite the first neural net–based BTC study by Tabatabai and Troudet [**B41**]. The authors contend that the solution obtained by Qiu et al. [B55], although better than the results obtained by Udpikar and Raina [B25], is suboptimal and point to three other BTC efforts that would give equally good performance. Of these references, one is partially their own earlier work [**B52**], and the second could not be traced since it does not appear in the quoted proceedings. The third refers only to a thresholding method that does not in itself deal with the compression problem, but could be extrapolated to it. The basic point made is that instead of a threshold based on the mean value, an iterative procedure computing the threshold based on the average of the upper and lower gray-level values (detailed earlier in these pages) is superior in performance. No comparison with the second study of Qiu, Varley, and Terrell [B65] is offered, possibly because it had appeared only just before theirs. Projecting ahead, one can expect to see this addressed in future studies by one of these authors.

Alcaim and Oliveira [B67] presented in late 1992 a vector quantization approach to reduce the bit rate required to encode the overhead information, namely the mean and standard deviation, associated with the application of the BTC technique to image data compression. This encoding of what the authors refer to as "side information" is accomplished by separate vector quantizers for each of the two arrays, instead of the single two-dimensional vector quantizer utilized in previous studies such as those of Udpikar and Raina [**B29**]. The two alternative vector quantization schemes are experimentally compared using nine monochrome images. Five of these images are employed for training and the remaining four, along with two from the training set, are used for testing. The peak signal-to-noise ratio is seen to be clearly higher under the new independent vector quantization scheme in all data sets and at all bit rates. As always the improvement is achieved with additional computational expense. The added expense, it is observed, can be minimized by using a VQ scheme of reduced complexity. Not pointed out in these discussions is the fact that such reduction can presumably be applied to the original two-dimensional VQ scheme also, and thus the relative increase in computational expense would continue to be a trade-off factor against the improvement in performance.

Deng and Cahill [B68] presented a hybrid of AMBTC, DPCM and quadtree in an overseas 1992 conference, the details of which were not available at the time of this writing.

In early 1993, Wang and Neuvo [B69] presented a study that concentrates on the properties of separable and cross-median filters. Although peripheral to the BTC area, this work has potential for application to BTC.

Chen et al. [B70] presented in the first half of 1993 a detailed discussion on a real-time video signal processing chip along with its potential for application in the BTC context. The VLSI chip combines within it both the BTC algorithm and a conventional motion compensation (MC) algorithm. The BTC algorithm used here is the basic binary quantizer. While this study does not advance the theory of BTC in any way, it helps to bring out the attractiveness of BTC relative to other compression techniques, such as DCT, in terms of the ease of implementation facilitated by the less complex computational demands of BTC. In effect, the paper promotes the case of BTC and is thus both a reflection of and an impetus to the renewed interest in BTC in recent years.

Qiu, Varley, and Terrell [B71] presented around the same time a brief paper on using the Hopfield neural network for variable bit rate BTC encoding image data. This further variant of their previous studies [B55, B65] once again fails to acknowledge other neural net–based BTC studies reported in the literature [**B41**, B66]. The approach here is to employ the network to define an optimal classification of an image block as either a high-detail or low-detail block to be coded accordingly. The variable bit rate arises from the fact that low-detail image can be represented by just the mean value without a bitmap, resulting in a low bit rate, while the high-detail image is represented in the traditional BTC manner with its relatively higher bit rate. Here, the cost function associated with this optimization problem includes the bitmap distributions explicitly. The resulting block effect caused by the variable bit rate scheme may be alleviated with a simple smoothing as a post-processing step. In view of this variable bit rate provision, the approach, as is to be expected, yields higher compression ratios than would otherwise be feasible. As always, this gain is at the expense of some increase in mean square error values. Mitchell [B72] reported in mid-1993 a correction to an earlier study [B66] in which he was co-author; this correction must be taken into account in the implementation of [B66].

Another contribution in this area is by Wen and Lu [**B73**] who, in mid-1993, reported their investigations on hybrid vector quantization. This study looks at VQ as the principal tool with BTC and DCT as optional add-on mechanisms for improving the performance of VQ. The authors present an algorithm that is claimed to combine the advantages of both the image quality benefits of the BTC–VQ hybrid and the high compression ratios of the

DCT–VQ hybrid. An obvious starting point of reference for this study should have been the work of Wu and Coll [**B54**] discussed earlier. However, the authors make no mention of this work, which was in fact reported very much earlier. While the three conceptual component blocks, BTC, VQ, and DCT, of the hybrid are the same under the two studies, the ways in which these building blocks are put together are very different. Here, DCT is the first rather than the last step of the hybrid process. The DCT employed here, on basic (8×8) image blocks, is called a partial DCT (PDCT) since the subsequent processing requires only four lowest frequency coefficients of DCT: $d(0,0)$, $d(0,1)$, $d(1,0)$, and $d(1,1)$. The ensuing process is much more interwoven and ad hoc and not all blocks go through the same logic. Based on a thresholding of two of the four DCT-derived coefficients, $d(0,1)$ and $d(1,0)$, the image block is classified as a smooth or edge region. These coefficients represent the brightness change in horizontal and vertical directions and the corresponding thresholds are experimentally chosen. This brings out a need for training phase of sorts, using some training image sets. The smooth-image blocks are then coded using classified vector quantization (CVQ) for three of the coefficients, $d(0,1)$, $d(1,0)$, and $d(1,1)$, while a full 8 bits are allotted for $d(0,0)$. The edge-image blocks, on the other hand, are subdivided into four (4×4) blocks and sequentially processed using BTC–VQ. The compression ratios are in the range of ~20. The main negative aspect is the need for training, which is not dealt with in much detail. It is not clear how robust the process is relative to such training and what other factors are essential to any process that involves a training phase. However, the authors do offer an alternative approach that is worth comparing with other proposed hybrid schemes. An independent, detailed comparative experimental study of these different hybrid schemes using a wide range of images as a common data base would therefore be a valuable contribution to the field.

The next study, also in July 1993, is by Oshri, Shelley, and Mitchell [B74] on the interpolative techniques applied to three-level (instead of two-level) BTC algorithms. This study extends the interpolation concepts employed by Zeng [B51] and his associates [B60] to the domain of three-level BTC as enunciated by Efrati, Liciztin, and Mitchell [**B52**].

Wu and Coll [**B75**] in the latter half of 1993 studied a multilevel BTC using a minmax error criterion. This is a fairly detailed paper and describes a scheme involving two passes through the data. The first pass employs a multilevel BTC instead of the traditional two-level BTC, in which the adaptive quantizer level allocation is through a process of minimizing the maximum quantization error in each block. These requantized or compressed data are processed through a combination of predictive coding, entropy coding, and vector quantization to gain additional compression in this second pass. Both interblock and intrablock predictions are employed in this step. The second pass can be either loss-free or lossy, depending on the level of compression desired. Of course, the first pass is necessarily lossy and thus the effective overall difference between the options available for the second pass would be only the extent of information loss.

A more recent study published immediately thereafter, toward the end of 1993, is that of Kurita and Otsu [B76], who offer an alternative approach to color image data compression. The method, which the authors called a color BTC (CBTC) algorithm, is based on a one-bit adaptive vector quantizer that employs the principal components derived by principal-components analysis of the R/G/B tricolor space. A modification to the scheme (MCBTC) is also proposed to reduce the truncation errors.

Skarbek and Pietrowcew [B77] present a study wherein they experimentally compare a number of BTC variants. Two different aspects, blocking and quantization, are chosen for this exercise. Three types of blocking are examined: standard 4×4 squared blocks, random shifting of partition origin in consecutive lines of blocks, and partition into 16-element blocks along the generalized Hilbert scan of the image. For quantization, the standard BTC binarization technique is augmented by error diffusion in the raster block scan as well as in the Hilbert scan. Several error criteria are employed in the evaluation process.

In late 1993, a study by Lo and Cham [B78] offered a new coding scheme called predictive classified address vector quantization (PCAVQ). It consists of a new two-stage classification method based on the three-level BTC technique that efficiently classifies blocks of an image into different classes having similar characteristics. The problem of blocky appearance in the resultant image is addressed with a predictive mean removal VQ technique. In addition, a simplified address VQ method is offered to increase the overall compression ratio. Simulations showing improved performance over the JPEG scheme are included.

In a short paper in late 1993, Zeng and Neuvo [B79] offered two alternative BTC schemes that employ vector quantization and median filters as the interpolator. The first interpolative scheme employs a quincunx subsampling with the missing pixels reconstructed by interpolation using the four surrounding pixels that form a cross. The second scheme uses alternate-row and alternate-column sampling and the missing samples are reconstructed in two steps: alternate pixels in the missing row are interpolated first using pixels along the diagonals, and the in-between pixels thereof are once again interpolated by the pixels that form a cross surrounding them. The interpolation is achieved as a median filter process. The method is compared with AMBTC. Vector quantization is used to code the overhead parameters (upper and lower intensity values). This combination of VQ with median filter–based interpolation is shown to perform better than a direct BTC–VQ scheme.

Two papers in Korean appeared in late 1993. The first, by Shin, Lee, and Lee [B80], presents an adaptive BTC using a human visual system (HVS). A category classification coefficient is introduced to reduce blocky appearance. The category classification coefficient is derived by combining the modified HVS and standard deviation values. The second paper, by Kim and Park [B81], offers an automatic variable BTC methodology. The block size is selected automatically on the basis of the discontinuity measure of blocks. This automated block size determination procedure is combined with classical BTC to derive the new methodology. The method is applied to color imagery by subsampling the I and Q chrominance components. Computer simulation results comparing the new method with prior methods are also included.

The renewed interest in BTC continued on into 1994. An example is the work of Chen and Liu [B82], who early in 1994 presented a video compression technique that is a combination of a motion compensation (MC) algorithm and an optimized block truncation technique (OBTC). It is shown that their hybrid OBTC-based system performs better than the conventional one, both from qualitative and implementational complexity viewpoints.

A further example of this interest is the publication by Mitchell, Zilverberg, and Avraham [B83], who offer a comparison of different BTC algorithms. This study, however, is limited to less than a sixth of the studies in this area reported thus far and is too brief to cover the full range of developments. In all, a total of seven algorithms—classical BTC [**B8**], AMBTC [**B24**], generalized BTC [B23], variable BTC [B42], modified BTC [B25], classified BTC–VQ [**B52**], and the so-called optimal approach (wherein the threshold is determined by exhaustive search to identify the one with minimum mean square error)—is applied to a set of seven standard test images and compared. The authors, not surprisingly, conclude that [**B52**] offers the best performance, followed closely by [B25] and [**B24**]. The computational aspects of the different methods are also taken into account in this relative assessment. An independent objective study of all the different BTC methods reported in the literature, including hybrids thereof (instead of just these seven), carried out at the same level of detail would be a worthwhile effort that can truly identify the most promising methodologies.

Chan and Chan [B84] combine VPIC and AMBTC through a look-up table to derive a more efficient form of processing. Visual patterns are used for subimages with significant edges and texture patterns are employed for high-variance data blocks within AMBTC. This mapping to the two pattern types is adaptively made based on mean square error.

A very recent article, a relatively detailed survey of the BTC area by Franti et al. [B85], appeared around the time of final production of this book. Accordingly, the coverage of these late-appearing studies is somewhat perfunctory, as insertion of additions at the time of going to press is arduous at best. In addition to presenting a survey, the authors present some of their own work in this area. The developments in BTC are viewed under three headings: Quantization, coding of quantized data, and coding of the resultant bit plane. With this breakdown, the authors put forth a new combination of the component approaches and compare the result with the standard JPEG approach. Although 78 references are cited, only about half of them deal with BTC and the rest cover other aspects of data compression. In effect, less than half of the collection reviewed here is covered by this survey. However, it does offer some additional insights and therefore provides material worthy of perusal by those actively involved in the BTC area.

Lo and Cham [B86] offer another hybrid coding scheme composed of a predictive classified vector quantization (PCVQ) and the three-level block truncation coding. The BTC technique is applied by dividing the image into different subsources and using a two-stage classification strategy. Each of the subsources is then further processed using the vector quantization approach. The results are compared favorably relative to the JPEG scheme. This is essentially an update of their earlier conference presentation [B78].

Mor, Swissa, and Mitchell [B87] presented towards the end of 1994 a variation of the three-level BTC that is claimed to be nearly optimal in the mean square error sense. Additionally, the method is intended to be computationally attractive in terms of its speed.

Wei and Chen [B88], in a short note, discuss the development of a systolic array for BTC implementation. The process is recursive in its computation of the sample mean of the block as well as in the generation of the bit plane and higher moments. The architecture is developed to suit VLSI implementation.

Yang and Tsai [B89], in the first of the papers of 1995, describe methods of enhancing BTC through the use of line and edge information. Toward this end, an adaptive bit-plane selection scheme is utilized based on a set of predefined bit planes. The advantages of the method over previous methods, in terms of lower bit rates and better image reconstruction quality, are discussed at length followed by the illustrative examples using the now inevitable Lena and mandrill images.

Overturf, Cover, and Delp [B90] offer an updated version of their previous study [B59] on color image coding using BTC quantization in conjunction with morphological pyramid decomposition, and is conceptually not very different from it ([B59] is discussed earlier in this chapter). This study, however, helps to emphasize the continuing interest in the area of hybrid techniques using BTC as one of its components.

Ma and Rajala [B91], in a brief note, discuss along with proofs some new properties of AMBTC. The study is intended to explore the fundamentals of AMBTC and incidentally strengthen the case for AMBTC as an attractive choice both from computational and conceptual viewpoints.

Quweider and Salari [B92], again in a short note, present a new gradient-based BTC algorithm. The algorithm is used in conjunction with a binary classification process to improve image quality in terms of reduced staircase effects common to block coding approaches and preservation of edges in the original image.

The most recent of the studies, identified just at the time of going to press, is that of Webb and Munson, Jr. [B93], who offer a potential remedy to the problem of image quality degradation associated with large block sizes in BTC implementation. The remedy offered takes the form of a modification to BTC centered around the use of error diffusion techniques that have been employed previously in half-toning applications.

The continued and, in fact, rejuvenated interest in the block truncation coding area shows that by no means are these going to be the last words to be written on the developments in the BTC area. As always, any survey attempt of this nature is nothing more than a snapshot taken at the time of the review process, and as such this anthology has been continually updated right up to the time of going to press.

REFERENCES
BTC TECHNIQUES

[B1]   T. Kishimoto, E. Mitsuya, and K. Hoshida, "A Method of Still Picture Coding by Using Statistical Properties" (in Japanese), *Proc. Nat'l Conf. Inst. Electronic Communication Eng., Japan*, No. 974, 1978.

[B2]   T. Kishimoto, E. Mitsuya, and K. Hoshida, "An Experiment of Still Picture Coding by Block Processing" (in Japanese), *Proc. Nat'l Conf. Inst. of Electronic Communication Eng., Japan*, No. 975, 1978.

[B3]   O.R. Mitchell, E.J. Delp, and S.J. Carlton, "Block Truncation Coding: A New Approach to Image Compression," *IEEE Int'l Conf. Comm.—Conf. Record I*, IEEE Press, Piscataway, N.J., pp. 12B.1.1–12B.1.4, 1978.

[B4]   T. Kishimoto, E. Mitsuya, and K. Hoshida, "Block Coding of Still Pictures" (in Japanese), *Technical Group of Communication Systems of the Inst. of Electronics and Communications Engineers of Japan*, pp. 63–69, July 1978.

[B5]   E.J. Delp and O.R. Mitchell, "Some Aspects of Moment Preserving Quantizers," *Conf. Record 1979 IEEE Int'l Conf. Comm. (ICC '79)*, Vol. I, IEEE Press, Piscataway, N.J., pp. 7.2.1–7.2.5, 1979.

[B6]   S. Murakami et al., "One Bit/Pel Coding of Still Pictures," *Conf. Record 1979 IEEE Int'l Conf. Comm. (ICC '79)*, Vol. I, IEEE Press, Piscataway, N.J., pp. 23.1.1–23.1.5, 1979.

[B7]   E.J. Delp, "Moment Preserving Quantization and Its Application in Block Truncation Coding," Ph.D. Dissertation, Purdue University, School of Electrical Engineering, West Lafayette, Indiana, Aug. 1979. (Also a like-titled Purdue University technical report by E.J. Delp and O.R. Mitchell, TR-EE-79-27, Aug. 1979.)

[B8]   E.J. Delp and O.R. Mitchell, "Image Compression Using Block Truncation Coding," *IEEE Trans. Comm.*, Vol. COM-27, No. 9, pp. 1335–1342, Sept. 1979.

[B9]   O.R. Mitchell and E.J. Delp, "Multilevel Graphics Representation Using Block Truncation Coding," *Proc. IEEE*, Vol. 68, No. 7, pp. 868–873, July 1980.

[B10]   O.R. Mitchell et al., "Image Coding for Photo Analysis," *Proc. Soc. Information Display*, Vol. 21/3, pp. 279–292, 1980.

[B11]   T.W. Goeddel and S.C. Bass, "A Two-Dimensional Quantizer for Coding Digital Imagery," *IEEE Trans. Comm.*, Vol. COM-29, No. 1, pp. 60–67, Jan. 1981.

[B12]   G.R. Arce and N.C. Gallagher, Jr., "Image Source Coding Using Median Filter Roots," *Proc. Ann. Allerton Conf. Communications, Control and Computing*, pp. 869–878, Oct. 1981.

[B13]   L.J. Siegel et al., "Block Truncation Coding on PASM," *Proc. Ann. Allerton Conf. Communications, Control and Computing*, pp. 891–900, Oct. 1981.

[B14]   D.J. Healy and O.R. Mitchell, "Digital Video Bandwidth Compression Using Block Truncation Coding," *IEEE Trans. Comm.*, Vol. COM-29, No. 12, pp. 1809–1817, Dec. 1981.

[B15]   J. Ronson and J. Dewitte, "Adaptive Block Truncation Coding Scheme Using an Edge Following Algorithm," *Proc. IEEE Int'l Conf. Acoustics, Speech, and Signal Processing*, IEEE Press, Piscataway, N.J., pp. 1235–1238, 1982.

[B16]   T.N. Mudge et al., "Image Coding Using the Multimicroprocessor System PASM," *Proc. IEEE Pattern Recognition and Image Processing*, CS Press, Los Alamitos, Calif., pp. 200-205, 1982.

[B17]   D.R. Halverson, N.C. Griswold, and G.L. Wise, "On Generalized Block Truncation Coding Quantizers for Image Compression," *Proc. Information Science and Systems Conf.*, Princeton, N.J., 1982.

[B18]   M.D. Lema, "Absolute Moment Block Truncation Coding and Its Application to Still Color Images," MSEE Thesis, Purdue University, School of Electrical Engineering, West Lafayette, Indiana, Aug. 1982.

[B19]   D.R. Halverson, "On the Implementation of a Block Truncation Coding Algorithm," *IEEE Trans. Comm.*, Vol. COM-30, No. 11, pp. 2482–2484, Nov. 1982.

[B20]   G.R. Arce and N.C. Gallagher, Jr., "BTC Image Coding Using Median Filter Roots," *IEEE Trans. Comm.*, Vol. COM-31, No. 6, pp. 784–793, June 1983.

[B21]   J. Dewitte and J. Ronsin, "Original Block Coding Scheme for Low Bit Rate Image Transmission," in *Signal Processing II: Theories and Applications—Proc. of EUSIPCO-83*, H.W. Schussler, ed., Elsevier Science Publishers B.V. (North-Holland), Amsterdam, pp. 143–146, 1983.

[B22] T.J. Uhl, "Adaptive Picture Data Compression Using Block Truncation Coding," in *Signal Processing II: Theories and Applications—Proc. of EUSIPCO-83*, H.W. Schussler ed., Elsevier Science Publishers B.V. (North-Holland), Amsterdam, pp. 147–150, 1983.

[B23] D.R. Halverson, N.C. Griswold, and G.L. Wise, "A Generalized Block Truncation Coding Algorithm for Image Compression," *IEEE Trans. Acoustics, Speech, and Signal Processing*, Vol. ASSP-32, No. 6, pp. 664–668, June 1984.

[B24] M.D. Lema and O.R. Mitchell, "Absolute Moment Block Truncation Coding and Applications to Color Images," *IEEE Trans. Comm.*, Vol. COM-32, No. 10, pp. 1148–1157, Oct. 1984.

[B25] V.R. Udpikar and J.P. Raina, "Modified Algorithm for Block Truncation Coding of Monochrome Images," *Electronics Letters*, Vol. 21, No. 20, pp. 900–902, 26 Sept. 1985.

[B26] S. Venkataraman and K.R. Rao, "Applications of Vector Quantizers and BTC in Image Coding," *Proc. Global Telecommunications Conf. (GLOBECOM '85)*, Vol. 2, IEEE Press, Piscataway, N.J., pp. 602–608, 1985.

[B27] V.S. Frost and G.J. Minden, "A Data Compression Technique for Synthetic Aperture Radar Images," *IEEE Trans. Aerospace and Electronic Systems*, Vol. AES-22, No. 1, pp. 47–54, Jan. 1986.

[B28] B. Ramamurthi and A. Gersho, "Nonlinear Space-Variant Postprocessing of Block Coded Images," *IEEE Trans. Acoustics, Speech and Signal Processing*, Vol. ASSP-34, No. 5, pp. 1258–1267, Oct. 1986.

[B29] V.R. Udpikar and J.P. Raina, "BTC Image Coding Using Vector Quantization," *IEEE Trans. Comm.*, Vol. COM-35, No. 3, pp. 352–356, Mar. 1987.

[B30] H.H. Ko and C.W. Lee, "Real Time Implementation of Block Truncation Coding for Picture Data Compression," *Proc. IEEE Int'l Conf. Acoustics, Speech, and Signal Processing*, IEEE Press, Piscataway, N.J., pp. 1067–1070, 1987.

[B31] C.Y. Chang, R. Kwok, and J.C. Curlander, "Image Coding of SAR Imagery," *Proc. Int'l Geoscience and Remote Sensing Symp. (IGARSS '87)*, pp. 699–704, 1987.

[B32] N.C. Griswold, D.R. Halverson, and G.L. Wise, "A Note on Adaptive Block Truncation Coding for Image Processing," *IEEE Trans. Acoustics, Speech, and Signal Processing*, Vol. ASSP-35, No. 8, pp. 1201–1203, Aug. 1987.

[B33] N.M. Nasrabadi and R.A. King, "Image Coding Using Vector Quantization: A Review," *IEEE Trans. Comm.*, Vol. COM-36, No. 8, pp. 957–971, Aug. 1988.

[B34] Y. Wu and D.C. Coll, "Multi-level Block Truncation Coding for High Fidelity Compression of Composite Imagery," *Proc. Canadian Conf. Electrical and Computer Eng.*, Vancouver, B.C., Canada, 1988.

[B35] Y.T. Tsai, "A Real-Time Architecture for an Error-Tolerant Picture Compression Algorithm in VLSI Implementation," in *VLSI Signal Processing III*, R.W. Brodersen and H.S. Moscovitz, eds., IEEE Press, New York, pp. 149–160, 1988.

[B36] L.H. Chen and W.H. Tsai, "Moment Preserving Techniques in Image Processing—A Survey and New Approaches," *Proc. Nat'l. Science Council, Part A: Physical Science and Eng.*, Vol. 13, pp. 280–301, 1989.

[B37] Y.A. Alsaka and D.A. Lee, "Three Level Block Truncation Coding," *Proc. 1990 IEEE Southeastcon*, Vol. 2, IEEE Press, Piscataway, N.J., pp. 420–423, 1990.

[B38] L. Hui, "An Adaptive Block Truncation Coding Algorithm for Image Compression," *Proc. 1990 Int'l Conf. Acoustics, Speech, and Signal Processing*, Vol. 4, IEEE Press, Piscataway, N.J., pp. 2233–2236, 1990.

[B39] N.M. Nasrabadi et al., "Hierarchical Block Truncation Coding of Digital HDTV Images," *IEEE Trans. Consumer Electronics*, Vol. 36, No. 3, pp. 254–261, Aug. 1990.

[B40] D. Chen and A.C. Bovik, "Visual Pattern Image Coding," *IEEE Trans. Comm.*, Vol. COM-38, No. 12, pp. 2137–2146, Dec. 1990.

[B41] A. Tabatabai and T.P. Troudet, "A Neural Net Based Architecture for the Segmentation of Mixed Gray-Level and Binary Pictures," *IEEE Trans. Circuits and Systems*, Vol. 38, No. 1, pp. 66–77, Jan. 1991.

[B42] M. Kamel, C.T. Sun, and L. Guan, "Image Compression by Variable Block Truncation Coding with Optimal Threshold," *IEEE Trans. Signal Processing*, Vol. 39, No. 1, pp. 208–212, Jan. 1991.

[B43] A. Weitzman and H.B. Mitchell, "Fast Multi-stage VQ Search for the BTC-VQ Algorithm," *Proc. 17th Convention of Electrical and Electronics Eng. in Israel*, Kfar Hamacccabiah, Ramat Gan, Israel, pp. 182–185, 1991.

[B44] E.J. Delp and O.R. Mitchell, "The Use of Block Truncation Coding in DPCM Image Coding," *IEEE Trans. Signal Processing*, Vol. 39, No. 4, pp. 967–971, Apr. 1991.

[B45] K.-K. Ma and S.A. Rajala, "Subband Coding of Digital Images Using Absolute Moment Block Truncation," *Proc. 1991 Int'l Conf. Acoustics, Speech, and Signal Processing*, Vol. 4, IEEE Press, Piscataway, N.J., pp. 2645–2648, 1991.

[B46] W-W. Lu, M.P. Gough, and P.N.H. Davies, "Scientific Data Compression for Space: A Modified Block Truncation Coding Algorithm," *Proc. SPIE: Data Structures and Target Classification*, Vol. 1470, SPIE Press, Bellingham, Wash., pp. 197–205, 1991.

[B47] J.U. Roy and N.M. Nasrabadi, "Hierarchical Block Truncation Coding," *Optical Eng.*, Vol. 30, No. 5, pp. 551–556, May 1991.

[B48] M. Nasipuri et al., "An Adaptive Image Encoding Technique Using Pyramid Architecture," *Proc. 1991 IEEE Int'l Symp. Circuits and Systems*, Vol. 1, IEEE Press, Piscataway, N.J., pp. 292–295, 1991.

[B49] K.-K. Ma and S.A. Rajala, "A Comparison of Absolute Moment Block Truncation Coding and the Minimum Mean Square Error Quantizer," *Proc. 1991 IEEE Int'l Symp. Circuits and Systems*, Vol. 1, IEEE Press, Piscataway, N.J., pp. 296–299, 1991.

[B50] B. Zeng, Q. Wang, and Y. Neuvo, "BTC Image Coding Using Two-Dimensional Median Filter Roots," *Proc. 1991 IEEE Int'l Symp. Circuits and Systems*, Vol. 1, IEEE Press, Piscataway, N.J., pp. 400–403, 1991.

[B51] B. Zeng, "Two Interpolative BTC Image Coding Schemes," *Electronics Letters*, Vol. 27, No. 13, pp. 1126–1128, 20 June 1991.

[B52] N. Efrati, H. Liciztin, and H.B. Mitchell, "Classified Block Truncation Coding–Vector Quantization: An Edge Sensitive Image Compression Algorithm," *Signal Processing: Image Communication*, Vol. 3, Nos. 2–3, pp. 275–283, June 1991.

[B53] P. Nasiopoulos, R.K. Ward, and D.J. Morse, "Adaptive Compression Coding," *IEEE Trans. Comm.*, Vol. COM-39, No. 8, pp. 1245–1254, Aug. 1991.

[B54] Y. Wu and D.C. Coll, "BTC-VQ-DCT Hybrid Coding of Digital Images," *IEEE Trans. Comm.*, Vol. COM-39, No. 9, pp. 1283–1287, Sept. 1991.

[B55] G. Qiu, M.R. Varley, and T.J. Terrell, "Improved Block Truncation Coding Using Hopfield Neural Network," *Electronics Letters*, Vol. 27, No. 21, pp. 1924–1926, 10 Oct. 1991.

[B56] E.J. Delp and O.R. Mitchell, "Moment Preserving Quantization," *IEEE Trans. Comm.*, Vol. COM-39, No. 11, pp. 1549–1558, Nov. 1991.

[B57] M. Rabbani and P.W. Jones, *Digital Image Compression Techniques,* SPIE Press Tutorial Text Series, Chapter 11, SPIE Press, Bellingham, Wash., pp. 129–143, 1991.

[B58] V.-E.I. Neagoe, "Predictive Ordering Technique and Feedback Transform Coding for Data Compression of Still Pictures," *IEEE Trans. Comm.*, Vol. COM-40, No. 2, pp. 385–396, Feb. 1992.

[B59] L.A. Overturf, M.L. Comer, and E.J. Delp, "Color Image Coding Using Morphological Pyramid Decomposition," *Proc. SPIE Conf. Human Vision, Visual Processing, and Digital Display III*, Vol. 1666, SPIE Press, Bellingham, Wash., pp. 265–275, 1992.

[B60] B. Zeng, Y. Neuvo, and A.N. Venetsanopoulos, "Interpolative BTC Image Coding," *Proc. 1992 Int'l Conf. Acoustics, Speech, and Signal Processing*, Vol. 3, IEEE Press, Piscataway, N.J., pp. 493–496, 1992.

[B61] A. Kruger, "Block Truncation Compression," *Dr. Dobb's J.*, pp. 48–55, Apr. 1992.

[B62] Y. Wu and D.C. Coll, "Single Bit-Map Block Truncation Coding of Color Images," *IEEE J. Selected Areas in Comm.*, Vol. 10, No. 5, pp. 952–959, June 1992.

[B63] A. Weitzman and H.B. Mitchell, "An Interblock BTC-VQ Image Coder," *Proc. 11th IAPR Int'l Conf. Pattern Recognition—Conf. C: Image, Speech, and Signal Analysis*, Vol. III, CS Press, Los Alamitos, Calif., pp. 426–429, 1992.

[B64] Q. Wang and Y. Neuvo, "BTC Image Coding Using Mathematical Morphology," *Proc. IEEE Int'l Conf. Systems Eng.*, IEEE Press, Piscataway, N.J., pp. 592–595, 1992.

[B65] G. Qiu, M.R. Varley, and T.J. Terrell, "Image Compression by a Variable Block Size BTC Technique Using Hopfield Neural Networks," *IEE Colloquium on Neural Networks for Image Processing Applications*, Digest No. 186, pp. 10/1–6, 1992.

[B66] H.B. Mitchell and M. Dorfan, "Block Truncation Coding Using Hopfield Neural Network," *Electronics Letters*, Vol. 28, No. 23, pp. 2144–2145, 5 Nov. 1992.

[B67] A. Alcaim and L.V. Oliveira, "Vector Quantization of the Side Information in BTC Image Coding," *Proc. Communications on the Move*, Vol. 1, pp. 345–349, 1992.

[B68] G. Deng and L.W. Cahill, "AMBTC-DPCM-Quad-Tree Hybrid Coding of Still Images," *1992 IEEE Region 10 Int'l Conf. (TENCON '92), Computers, Communications and Automation towards the 21st Century*, Vol. 1, IEEE Press, Piscataway, N.J., pp. 484–488, 1992.

[B69] Q.F. Wang and Y.J. Neuvo, "Deterministic Properties of Separable and Cross Median Filters with an Application to Block Truncation Coding," *Multidimensional Systems and Signal Processing*, Vol. 4, No. 1, pp. 23–38, Jan. 1993.

[B70] L.-G. Chen et al., "A Real-Time Video Signal Processing Chip," *IEEE Trans. Consumer Electronics*, Vol. 39, No. 2, pp. 82–92, May 1993.

[B71] G. Qiu, M.R. Varley, and T.J. Terrell, "Variable Bit Rate Block Truncation Coding for Image Compression Using Hopfield Neural Networks," *Proc. 3rd Int'l Conf. Artificial Neural Networks*, pp. 233–237, 1993.

[B72] H.B. Mitchell, "Block Truncation Coding Using Hopfield Neural Network—Correction," *Electronics Letters*, Vol. 29, No. 12, p. 1148, June 1993.

[B73] K.-A. Wen and C.-Y. Lu, "Hybrid Vector Quantization," *Applied Optics*, Vol. 32, No. 7, pp. 1496–1502, July 1993.

[B74] E. Oshri, N. Shelley, and H.B. Mitchell, "Interpolative Three-Level Block Truncation Coding Algorithm," *Electronics Letters*, Vol. 29, No. 14, pp. 1267–1268, 8 July 1993.

[B75] Y. Wu and D.C. Coll, "Multilevel Block Truncation Coding Using a Minimax Error Criterion for High-Fidelity Compression of Digital Images," *IEEE Trans. Comm.*, Vol. 41, No. 8, pp. 1179–1191, Aug. 1993.

[B76] T. Kurita and N. Otsu, "A Method of Block Truncation Coding for Color Image Compression." *IEEE Trans. Comm.*, Vol. 41, No. 9, pp. 1270–1274, Sept. 1993.

[B77] W. Skarbek and A. Pietrowcew, "Error Diffusion in Block Truncation Coding," *Proc. 5th Int'l Conf. Computer Analysis of Images and Patterns (CAIP '93)*, pp. 105–112, 1993.

[B78] K.-T. Lo and W.-K. Cham, "New Classified Vector Quantization of Images," *Proc. 1993 IEEE Region 10 Conf. (TENCON '93), Computer, Communication, Control and Power Eng.*, Vol. 3, IEEE Press, Piscataway, N.J., pp. 373–376, 1993.

[B79] B. Zeng and Y. Neuvo, "Interpolative BTC Image Coding with Vector Quantization," *IEEE Trans. Comm.*, Vol. 41, No. 10, pp. 1436–1438, Oct. 1993.

[B80] Y.D. Shin, B.L. Lee, and K.I. Lee, "An Adaptive Block Truncation Coding Using Human Visual Systems," *J. Korean Inst. Telematics and Electronics*, Vol. 30B, No. 12, pp. 67–72, Dec. 1993.

[B81] T.K. Kim and R.-H. Park, "Automatic Variable Block Truncation Coding Technique," *J. Korean Inst. Telematics and Electronics*, Vol. 30B, No. 12, pp. 73–86, Dec. 1993.

[B82] L.-G. Chen and Y.-C. Liu, "A High Quality MC-OBTC Codec for Video Signal Processing," *IEEE Trans. Circuits, Systems, and Video Technology*, Vol. 4, pp. 92–98, Feb. 1994.

[B83] H.B. Mitchell, N. Zilverberg, and M. Avraham, "A Comparison of Different Block Truncation Coding Algorithms for Image Compression," *Signal Processing: Image Communications*, Vol. 6, No. 1, pp. 77–82, Mar. 1994.

[B84] K.W. Chan and K.L. Chan, "An Adaptive Pattern Based Image Coding Technique Using Visual Pattern and Texture Pattern," *Proc. 1994 Int'l Symp. Speech, Image Processing, and Neural Networks*, Vol. 1, pp. 180–183, 1994.

[B85] P. Franti, O. Nevalainen, and T. Kaukoranta, "Compression of Digital Images by Block Truncation Coding: A Survey," *Computer J.,* Vol. 37, No. 4, pp. 308–332, 1994.

[B86] K.-T. Lo and W.-K. Cham, "New Predictive Classified Vector Quantization Scheme for Image Compression," *Electronics Letters*, Vol. 30, No. 16, pp. 1280–1282, 4 Aug. 1994.

[B87] I. Mor, Y. Swissa, and H.B. Mitchell, "A Fast Nearly Optimum Equi-Spaced 3-Level Block Truncation Coding Algoithm," *Signal Processing: Image Communication*, Vol. 6, No. 5, pp. 397–404, Oct. 1994.

[B88] C.-H. Wei and C.-F. Chen, "Systolic Array for Block Truncation Coding," *Electronics Letters*, Vol. 30, No. 23, pp. 1929–1930, 10 Nov. 1994.

[B89] C.-K. Yang and W.-H. Tsai, "Improving Block Truncation Coding by Line and Edge Information and Adaptive Bit Plane Selection for Gray-Scale Image Compression," *Pattern Recognition Letters*, Vol. 16, No. 1, pp. 67–75, Jan. 1995.

[B90] L.A. Overturf, M.L. Comer, and E.J. Delp, "Color Image Coding Using Morphological Pyramid Decomposition," *IEEE Trans. Image Processing*, Vol. 4, No. 2, pp. 177–185, Feb. 1995.

[B91] K.-K. Ma and S.A. Rajala, "New Properties of AMBTC (Absolute Moment Block Truncation Coding)," *IEEE Signal Processing Letters*, Vol. 2, No. 2, pp. 34–36, Feb. 1995.

[B92] M.K. Quweider and E. Salari, "Gradient-Based Block Truncation Coding," *Electronics Letters*, Vol. 31, No. 5, pp. 353–355, 2 Mar. 1995.

[B93] J.L.H. Webb and D.C. Munson, Jr., "Reduced-Rate Block Truncation Coding of Images Using Error Diffusion," *IEEE Signal Processing Letters*, Vol. 2, No. 4, pp. 68–69, Apr. 1995.

Chapter 3
Illustrative Insights

In this chapter, the results of this author's previously unpublished personal research in terms of some experiments conducted using multispectral imagery data sets are discussed. Potentially, these results offer additional conceptual and computational insights into BTC performance. Both two- and three-parameter BTC techniques were implemented and tested using several bands of the Landsat multispectral image data of size 256×256, covering the Huntsville area (a touch of parochial pride, if you will!).

BASIC TWO- AND THREE-LEVEL BTC APPROACHES

Under the basic version of BTC [**B8**], the two quantization levels (which correspond to the two states of the binary encoded output) are determined, as detailed in Chapter 2, by solving the two simultaneous linear equations (2.5) and (2.6) set up to ensure that the first two moments (average value and variance) remain unaltered under the encoding transformation. The threshold for the dichotomy of the data set is determined as the average value of the pixel intensities within the block being encoded. Instead of this simplistic approach, it is also possible to treat the threshold as a third unknown parameter to be determined by another equation designed to preserve the third-order moment of the data in addition to the first two moments that were preserved under the previous approach. The input to this program comprises the image to be compressed and a user-selected block size. The outputs are the compressed image file and two quantization level files. The compression ratio is determined as the size of the input image file divided by the combined size of the three output files (as-is or after being processed by a UNIX-based compress utility, which implements a modified Lempel–Ziv algorithm [D59]). The necessary decoding software was also implemented; this software uses the three output files of the compression program as input to generate a single decompressed image file as output.

Table 3-1 shows the results of these tests in terms of root mean square (RMS) and normalized mean square (NMS) error values for different block sizes and different bands of the Landsat multispectral data for the two-parameter case. The table also offers the nominal and observed compression ratios for these cases. The RMS errors, NMS errors, and compression ratio results are portrayed graphically in **Figures 3-1** through **3-6.** As shown in **Figure 3-1,** in accordance with expectations, the RMS error increases with block size in every case. But the variation in RMS error across the different data sets at any given block size is itself very large, and thus the extent of

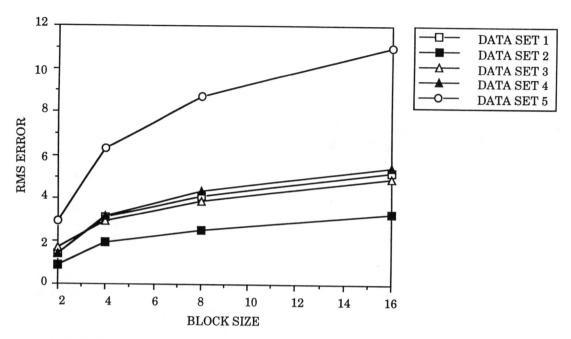

Figure 3-1. RMS Error versus block size for different data sets under the two-parameter BTC approach.

Table 3-1. Simulation results for the two-parameter BTC experiments

Data set	1	2	3	4	5	
Block size (nominal compression ratio)	RMS, NMS Errors and compression ratio					Average time (seconds)
2 × 2 (1.6)	1.44 0.0002 2.36	0.91 0.0004 2.57	1.69 0.0012 2.20	1.43 0.0010 2.10	3.10 0.0024 1.75	8
4 × 4 (4.0)	3.20 0.0009 4.57	1.97 0.0019 4.85	2.98 0.0047 4.44	3.18 0.0049 4.32	6.37 0.0095 3.94	5
8 × 8 (6.4)	4.68 0.0018 6.50	2.88 0.0039 7.00	4.29 0.0089 6.86	4.56 0.0100 6.70	8.99 0.0183 6.48	3
16 × 16 (7.5)	6.18 0.0031 7.89	3.81 0.0066 8.64	5.51 0.0136 8.71	5.67 0.0158 8.43	11.22 0.0280 8.34	2
Standard deviation of test data	12.01	7.54	11.15	14.23	25.34	

increase in RMS error with increase in block size varies significantly across the data sets. **Figure 3-2** portrays the approximately monotonic relationship that exists between the resulting RMS error and the standard deviation of the original data set. Thus, for a given tolerance on RMS error, block-size selection depends on the standard deviation of the data set, with higher standard deviations dictating lower block sizes and hence lower compression ratios. **Figure 3-3** shows the relationship between NMS errors and block size for the different data sets. Comparing this with **Figure 3-1,** we can see that

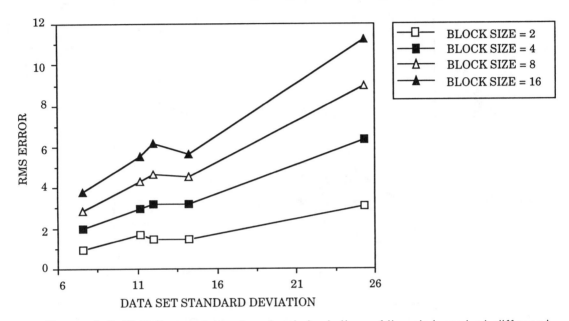

Figure 3-2. RMS Error versus standard deviation of the data set at different block sizes under the two-parameter BTC approach

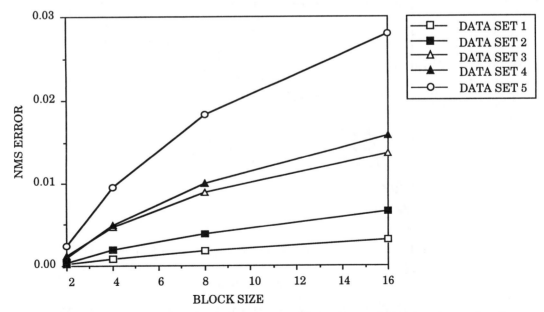

Figure 3-3. NMS Error versus block size for different data sets under the two-parameter BTC approach.

both errors show similar trends, but the spread between the minimum to maximum across different data sets is wider for the NMS errors. **Figure 3-4** depicts the relationship between NMS errors and standard deviations of the input image data sets. The monotonic trend, while similar to that seen for RMS errors in **Figure 3-2,** is broken in a more pronounced way by one data set (data set 1) that has unusually low NMS errors across all block sizes. This

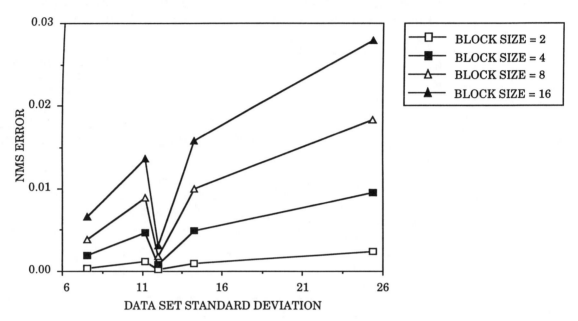

Figure 3-4. NMS Error versus standard deviation of the data set at different block sizes under the two-parameter BTC approach.

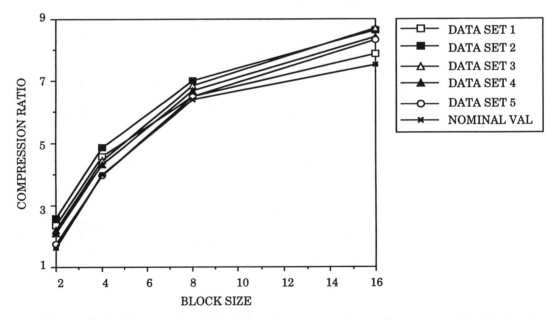

Figure 3-5. Observed and nominal compression ratios versus block size for different data sets under the two-parameter BTC approach.

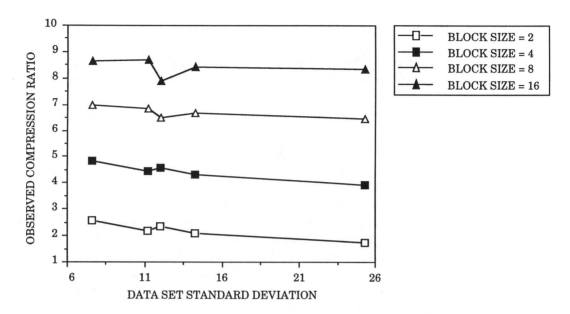

Figure 3-6. Observed compression ratio versus standard deviation of the data set at different block sizes under the two-parameter BTC approach.

points to the need for characterizing the data sets by measures other than the standard deviation for better understanding of the performance of the block truncation coding scheme. **Figure 3-5** shows the observed and nominal compression ratios at different block sizes for the different data sets. The variations of the observed compression ratio values across the different data sets are not as pronounced as those of RMS errors. This is easily observable in **Figure 3-6,** which shows the observed compression ratios versus standard deviation of the data sets at different block sizes. Thus, the effectiveness of the compression process as measured by compression ratios is less sensitive to variations in data set characteristics than when measured in terms of RMS error values.

Table 3-2 gives the equivalent results corresponding to the three-parameter case. These results are correspondingly portrayed in graphical form in **Figures 3-7** through **3-12.** The variations of RMS and NMS errors, as well as those of the observed compression ratios relative to block sizes and standard deviations of the data sets, are more or less similar to what was observed for the two-parameter case. The RMS and NMS errors (and the effective compression ratio) are dependent on the block statistics (standard deviation). The standard deviation of the entire data set is an indirect, but fairly representative, measure of this dependence. The computational loads in terms of average CPU time for the two- and three-parameter cases shown in Tables 3-1 and 3-2 are comparatively portrayed in **Figure 3-13.**

The test results show that the standard deviation of the data sets remains virtually unchanged by the compression and decompression cycle. It can be observed that as the standard deviation of the data set increases, the RMS error value increases and the effective compression ratio decreases. Accordingly, data set 2 has the best results and data set 5 shows the worst performance. The NMS, being a function not only of the absolute error but also the actual intensity range of the data, does not show this trend as clearly as the RMS error (which is a function of the absolute error only).

As can be seen by a comparison of these tables and figures, the fidelity of the retrieved image is marginally better under the three-parameter case than under the two-parameter case. The compression achieved is also slightly better under the three-parameter than that obtained under the two-parameter case. (It is to be noted that as the data sets used were small, the relative costs of the overhead due to header blocks are not negligible; hence the actual compression ratios obtained for larger data sets can be expected to be higher than those observed here.) These differences are marginal at small block sizes but become significant at larger block sizes. However, the cost of encoding increases under the three-parameter case (rather dramatically at larger block sizes reaching a ratio of 1:20 relative to the two-parameter case at a block size of 16), mainly because of the need for sorting of the data within the window. As is clear from the comparative plots shown in **Figure 3-13,** while the CPU time required drops monotonically with increase in block size under the two-parameter case, the time requirement under the three-parameter case drops initially but begins to increase as the savings due to the increase in block size is more than wiped out by the increase in the cost of sorting larger arrays (because the sort array length increases with the square of the block size). The decoding process being identical for the two- and three-parameter cases, there is no change in the CPU time requirements. The cost of decoding is indeed negligible (1–2 seconds for the data sets used in these tests) when compared to the encoding costs. In view of the significantly higher costs in terms of CPU time for the encoding phase under the three-parameter case, especially at higher block sizes, the improvement in performance does not seem to be cost-justified; hence as of this writing the two-parameter case is viewed as the candidate of choice for further study.

The two-parameter approach was evaluated further from the view point of actual compression achieved. Four different suboptions within this approach are possible. Under the first (BTC pack), the binary values corresponding to eight consecutive pixels can be packed into a single byte. This creates a compressed image one-eighth in size (except for the overhead contributed by the header blocks) and results in two additional quantization level files (whose sizes depends on the block size used for the BTC process). In many cases, these quantization parameter files can be further compressed using the CLIX compress facility. However, the packed-byte image shows no further compression using the CLIX utility. Alternatively, instead of packing the binary file, one could attempt run-length encoding of the binary file. Experimentation showed that this was not very effective. The third option (BTC 8 bit) is to apply the CLIX compress utility directly on the binary-valued 8-bit format file. The choice between this and the packed-byte option seems to be almost a tossup for block size values in the range of 2–4, with the results in favor of the packed-byte approach at a block size of 2 and switching slightly in favor of the other at a block size of 4. But at higher block sizes (>4), the CLIX utility leads to higher compression as compared to the set level of compression obtainable under the packed-byte option. Lastly, the binary data can conceivably be compressed using the CCITT group-4 format. Tests showed that, as was to be expected for nonhomogeneous files, this did not even match the compression ratios obtainable under the packed-byte format. Thus, pending evaluation of other binary file compaction alternatives reported in the literature, the CLIX utility shows the most compression (at all block sizes >4) and the packed-byte approach has the least computational overhead. Since the quantization level files can also be further compressed in many cases by using the CLIX utility, the actual compression obtained turns out to be generally greater than the theoretically predicted nominal values based on the block size shown as nominal compression ratios in Tables 3-1 and 3-2. The overhead contributed by the header blocks, however, tends to reduce the final effective compression to some extent. Other variations, such as packing both the quantization levels into a single file and storing running differences of quantization levels of successive block values, were also simulated, with no dramatic benefits in compression ratios. The most efficient of these variants, from the combined viewpoints of maximum scope for compression and minimum round-off errors, was to store the lower quantization level separately (after rounding off to the nearest integer) and the higher one as the incremental difference of the two (rounded off after differencing) each in its own file.

Table 3-2. Simulation results for the three-parameter BTC experiments

Data set	1	2	3	4	5	
Block size (nominal compression ratio)	RMS, NMS Errors and compression ratio					Average time (seconds)
2 × 2 (1.6)	1.41 0.0002 2.36	0.90 0.0004 2.57	1.68 0.0013 2.21	1.43 0.0011 2.10	2.93 0.0025 1.75	12
4 × 4 (4.0)	3.09 0.0009 4.57	1.93 0.0020 4.86	2.92 0.0047 4.46	3.16 0.0050 4.33	6.34 0.0095 3.95	8
8 × 8 (6.4)	4.08 0.0015 6.75	2.53 0.0036 7.27	3.88 0.0084 7.02	4.33 0.0095 6.86	8.73 0.0176 6.64	14
16 × 16 (7.5)	5.22 0.0025 8.96	3.27 0.0058 9.59	4.92 0.0129 9.38	5.47 0.0154 8.89	11.02 0.0281 8.63	42
Standard deviation of test data	12.01	7.54	11.15	14.23	25.34	

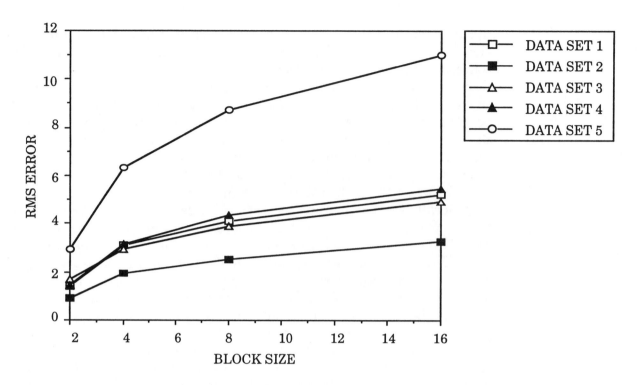

Figure 3-7. RMS Error versus block size for different data sets under the three-parameter BTC approach.

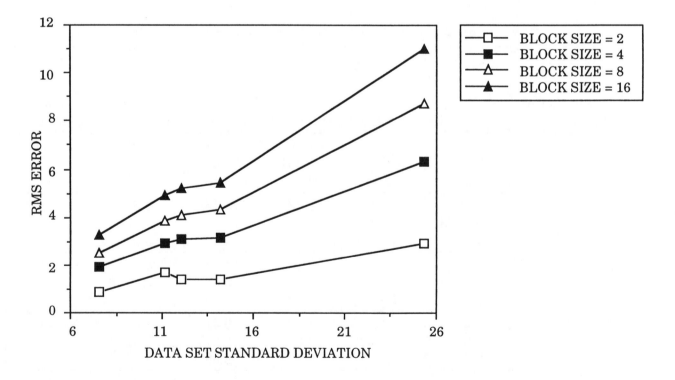

Figure 3-8. RMS Error versus standard deviation of the data set at different block sizes under the three-parameter BTC approach.

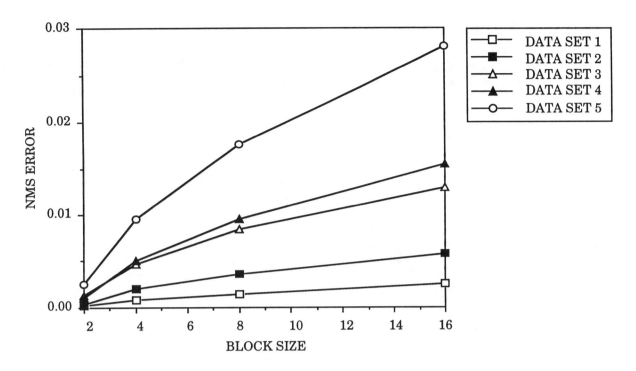

Figure 3-9. NMS Error versus block size for different data sets under the
three-parameter BTC approach.

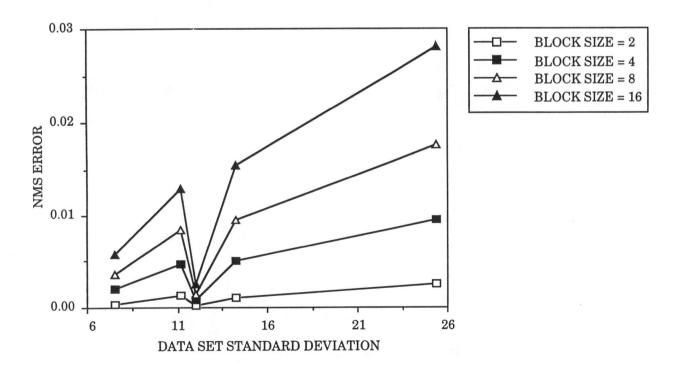

Figure 3-10. NMS Error versus standard deviation of the data set at
different block sizes under the three-parameter BTC approach.

The use of less than 8 bits for the quantization level values is known to improve the compression ratios but with some added costs in terms of loss of image fidelity. The actual extent of this trade-off was estimated in the context of one of the data sets as shown in Table 3-3.

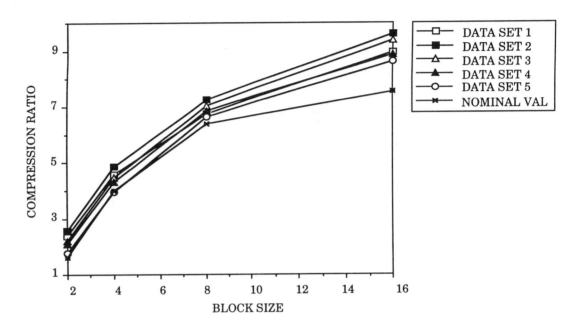

Figure 3-11. Observed and nominal compression ratios versus block size for different data sets under the three-parameter BTC approach.

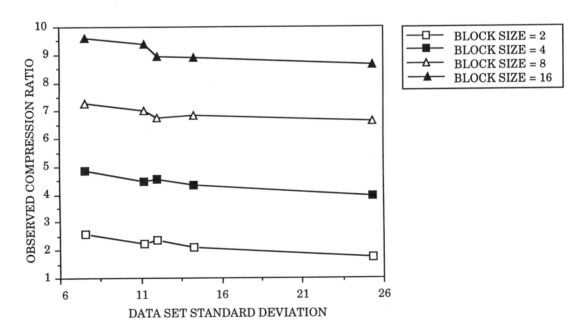

Figure 3-12. Observed compression ratio versus standard deviation of the data set at different block sizes under the three-parameter BTC approach.

110

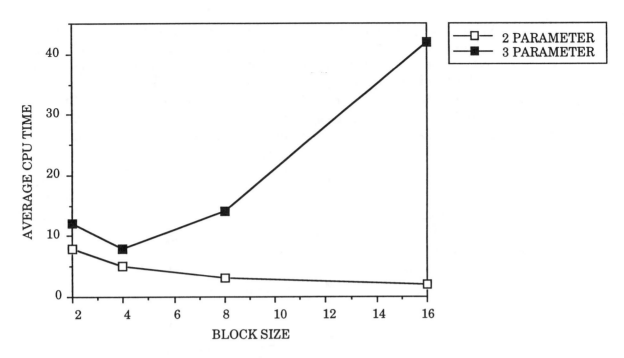

Figure 3-13. Average CPU time versus block size for the two- and three-parameter BTC approaches.

Table 3-3. Quantization effects under the two-parameter BTC approach

Number of bits	8	7	6	5	4
Block size	RMS, NMS Errors: Observed and nominal compression ratios				
2 × 2	1.44 0.0002 2.36 1.60	1.54 0.0002 2.84 1.78	1.82 0.0004 3.41 2.00	2.96 0.0010 4.00 2.29	4.43 0.0022 5.02 2.67
4 × 4	3.20 0.0009 4.57 4.00	3.23 0.0009 4.99 4.27	3.38 0.0010 5.39 4.57	3.85 0.0015 5.75 4.92	4.64 0.0024 6.25 5.33
8 × 8	4.68 0.0018 6.50 6.40	4.70 0.0018 6.69 6.56	4.82 0.0020 6.88 6.74	5.12 0.0024 7.04 6.92	5.73 0.0032 7.24 7.11
16 × 16	6.18 0.0031 7.89 7.53	6.20 0.0032 7.96 7.59	6.30 0.0033 8.02 7.64	6.56 0.0038 8.08 7.70	6.91 0.0044 8.15 7.76

As considerable coding effort would be needed to simulate the cases with less than 8 bits of storage for the parameters, the values were reduced to the equivalent number of significant bits and stored in the normal byte fashion, with the CLIX utility being used to estimate the effective compression. As can be seen by a perusal of Table 3-3, or more effectively in **Figures 3–14** through **3-21,** the effect of decreasing the number of quantization bits is more significant at smaller block sizes than at larger block sizes. The loss of fidelity

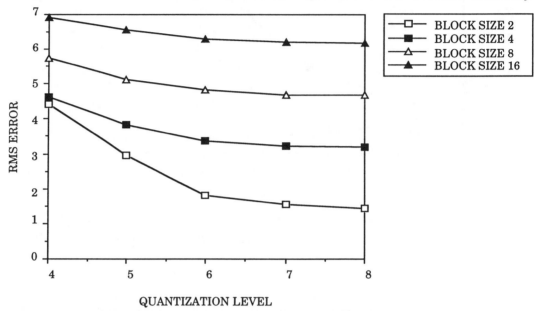

Figure 3-14. RMS Error versus quantization level for different block sizes under the two-parameter BTC approach.

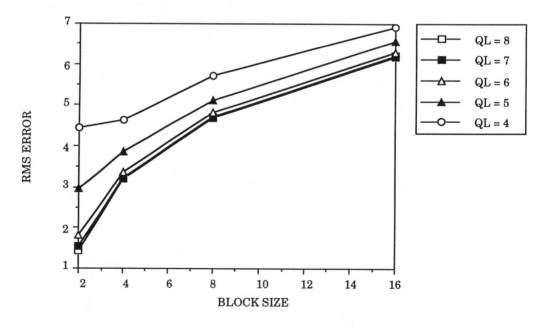

Figure 3-15. RMS Error versus block size at different quantization levels under the two-parameter BTC approach.

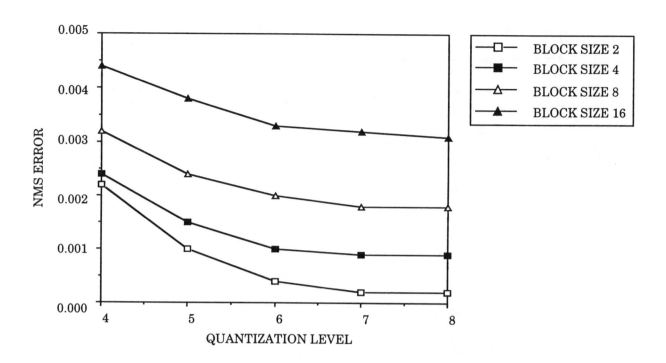

Figure 3-16. NMS Error versus quantization level for different block sizes under the two-parameter BTC approach.

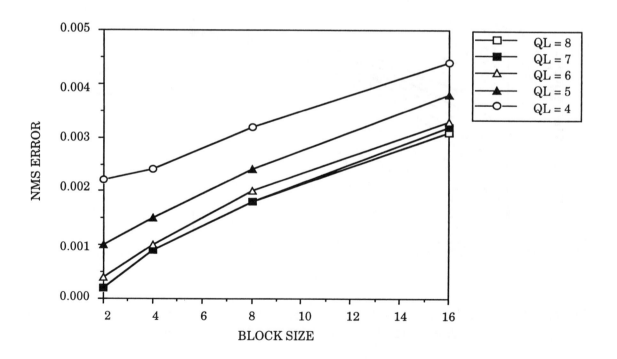

Figure 3-17. NMS Error versus block size at different quantization levels under the two-parameter BTC approach.

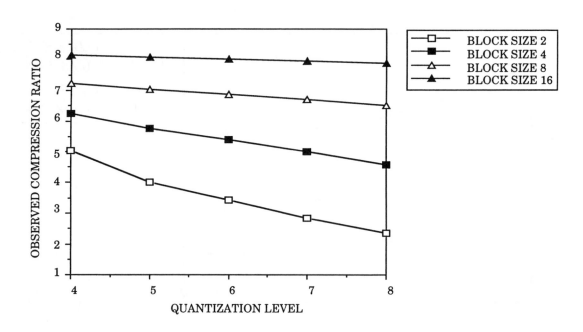

Figure 3-18. Observed compression ratio versus quantization level for different block sizes under the two-parameter BTC approach.

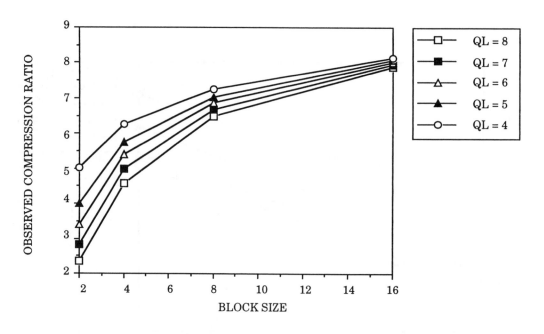

Figure 3-19. Observed compression ratio versus block size at different quantization levels under the two-parameter BTC approach.

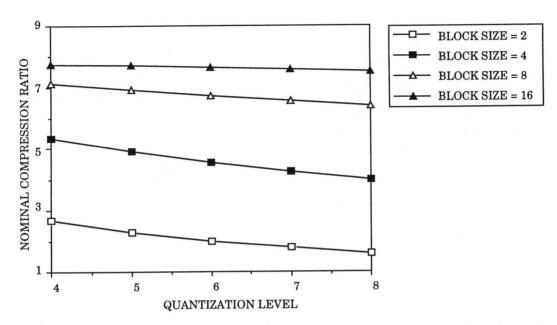

Figure 3-20. Nominal compression ratio versus quantization level for different block sizes under the two-parameter BTC approach.

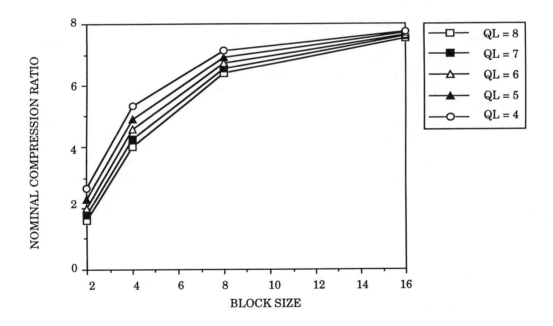

Figure 3-21. Nominal compression ratio versus block size at different quantization levels under the two-parameter BTC approach.

for a given improvement in compression ratio is more significant with a decrease in the bits used than with an increase in block sizes. The computational cost also increases by adapting the bit-reduction scheme both in the encoding and decoding phases. On the contrary, an increase in block size reduces the computational costs. In view of these facts, it is far better to increase the block sizes to meet the required compression levels rather than to reduce the number of bits of the output parameters. This would make the costs much lower both in loss of fidelity and computational loads.

Several algorithmic and conceptual modifications to the BTC have been considered by the author and others since then. An in-house modification was also conceived during this review effort. This consists of applying the block truncation scheme in a recursive manner as follows. For example, using a (4×4) block size leads to two parameters (quantization levels or mean and standard deviation) for each block. This results equivalently in two pseudo-images with one value for each of the (4×4) pixels, that is, an image of $(n/4) \times (n/4)$ in size. A compression to 2 bits/pixel (that is, a compression ratio of 4) is thus achieved with one level of application. This, again, can be coded further in block form, thereby increasing the compression. With two levels of application, a compression to 1.25 bits/pixel can be reached. Continued recursive application tends asymptotically toward a compression level of 1 bit/pixel (that is, a compression ratio of 8) using a basic block size of (4×4). Table 3-4 lists the compression ratios to be expected for different block sizes and multi-level applications. Simulation of this enhancement showed that the extra loss in image fidelity was greater than the added benefits of compression achieved by this recursive scheme and as such this was not pursued further.

Other recent variations of this approach have also been reported under the names *generalized block truncation coding* and *block separated component progressive coding,* wherein up to 2 bits/pixel (instead of 1 bit/pixel) can be used when necessary to handle blocks with relatively larger ranges. The progressive coding scheme (PCS) based on subsampling and predictive coding is applied to further increase the final compression ratios. These tools were part of the candidate set chosen for evaluation by the International Standards Organization (ISO) committee. A modification to the basic BTC scheme was developed by adapting some of the ideas underlying the 2-bit approach. This is discussed in more detail in the next section.

Table 3-4. Compression table (bits/pixel) under BTC

Image size Block size	2×2	4×4	8×8	16×16
2×2	5.0	3.75	2.75	2.375
4×4		2.0		1.25
8×8			1.25	
16×16				1.0625

MODIFIED BTC APPROACH

In this approach, the image is processed in blocks as under the basic approach. However, after determining the variance/standard deviation of the data within the block, a user-specified threshold is employed to decide on the encoding scheme to be used for the block. For blocks with a standard deviation greater than the user-specified threshold, the encoding procedure is the same as under the basic BTC approach. For blocks with standard deviation less than the user input threshold, the region is treated as homogeneous with intensity equal to the average intensity in the region. This effectively reduces the storage requirement for the block to that of storing an average value only—that is, 8 bits for the entire $n \times n$ pixels, or a compression ratio of n^2 for the block. This reduces the entropy of the output image and thereby increases the effective compression ratio for the entire image. The decoding process remains the same under the modified approach. Obviously, this scheme tends to reduce the fidelity of the retrieved image. In order to estimate the loss of fidelity the new scheme was simulated and tested using the same data set used earlier to facilitate comparisons. To avoid extensive software development effort, the encoding scheme was retained with 1 bit/pixel, even within the homogeneous blocks, but set to a uniform value of 1 within the block. Application of the UNIX-based CLIX utility takes advantage of this uniformity in gaining additional compression and thus provides a good estimate of the true underlying compression. The results of this simulation are shown in Table 3-5 and **Figures 3-22** through **3-27.**

Table 3-5. Standard deviation thresholding effects under the two-parameter BTC approach

Threshold Block size and nominal compression ratio	0	1	2	3	4
	RMS, NMS Errors and observed compression ratio				
2 × 2 1.6	1.44 0.0002 2.36	1.49 0.0002 2.44	1.70 0.0003 3.18	1.89 0.0004 3.82	2.05 0.0005 4.30
4 × 4 4.0	3.20 0.0009 4.57	3.20 0.0009 4.59	3.30 0.0010 5.78	3.41 0.0011 7.38	3.53 0.0012 8.58
8 × 8 6.4	4.68 0.0018 6.50	4.68 0.0018 6.50	4.72 0.0019 7.70	4.81 0.0020 10.16	4.89 0.0021 12.10
16 × 16 7.5	6.18 0.0031 7.89	6.18 0.0031 7.89	6.20 0.0032 8.56	6.26 0.0033 11.37	6.33 0.0034 13.65

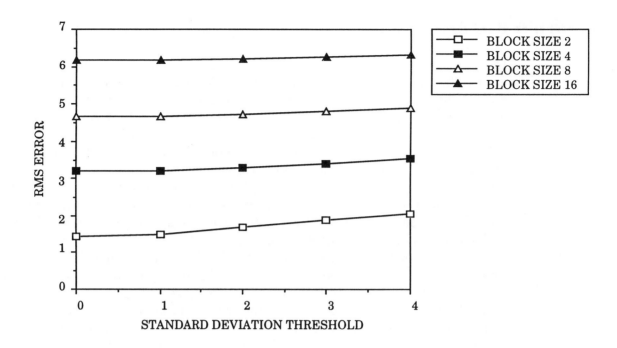

Figure 3-22. RMS Error versus standard deviation threshold for different block sizes under the two-parameter BTC approach.

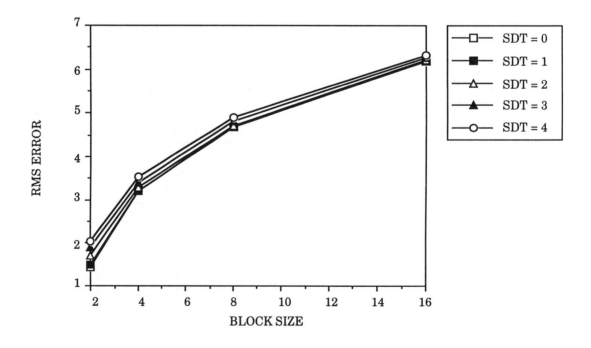

Figure 3-23. RMS Error versus block size at different standard deviation thresholds (SDT) under the two-parameter BTC approach.

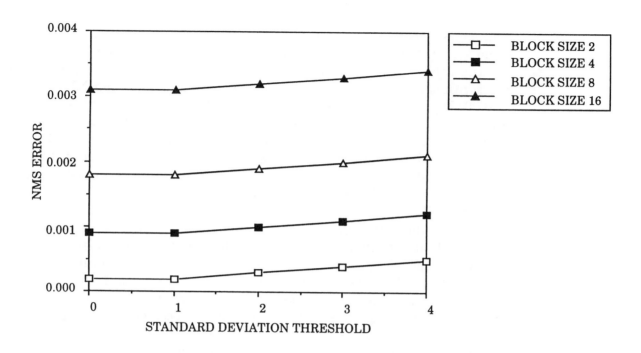

Figure 3-24. NMS Error versus standard deviation threshold for different block sizes under the two-parameter BTC approach.

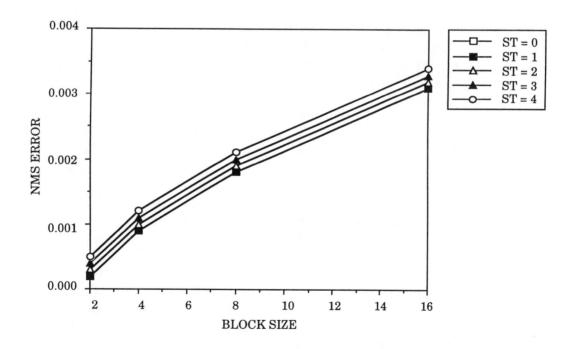

Figure 3-25. NMS Error versus block size at different standard deviation thresholds under the two-parameter BTC approach.

As shown therein, the benefit of this innovation is very significant. For example, setting a threshold of 4 on the standard deviation for the block increases the compression ratio for the case of 4×4 block size, from 4.57 to 8.58, with only a small increase in the RMS (3.20 to 3.53) and NMS (0.0009 to 0.0012) error values. This is even more dramatic for larger block sizes. Admittedly, RMS by itself does not provide any information about the blocky artifacts created within the thresholded block. The small increase in RMS may in fact hide an otherwise glaring visual fidelity loss. **Figures 3-22** and **3-23** clearly show this insensitivity of RMS error to the standard deviation threshold level. Similarly, Figures 3-24 and 3-25 show the same relationship under the NMS error measure. On the other hand, **Figures 3-26** and **3-27** bring out the large improvement in compression ratio with an increase in the standard deviation threshold. They also show how the compression ratio is positively affected by increase in block size. However, defining a uniform intensity over a large block tends to give a blocky appearance to the image, although the error measures remain relatively constant. An additional fringe benefit noticed during the simulation of this enhancement was that the CPU time required dropped as the threshold level increased because the cost of setting the bit for each pixel in the block is saved. This was particularly noticeable at lower block sizes where the CPU time was considerable in the first place. Therefore, it is best to provide this enhancement as a user-controllable option along with the block size.

The block size determines the size of the subregions showing a blocky visual appearance in the image, and the standard deviation threshold dictates the number or frequency of such subregions in the image. It should be noted that, even without this modification, the retrieved image tends to have a blocky appearance as only two intensity levels exist within any single block. Under the new scheme, some regions will end up with a single-intensity value instead of two. In view of these facts, for a given compression ratio, it is better to use relatively smaller block sizes and a threshold that would meet the compression requirements, rather than a small or no threshold and a relatively large block size that would satisfy the compression ratio requirements. The visual criterion dictates that it is far more important to have a smaller block size for these subregions than to have a smaller percentage of single-intensity subregions (as opposed to two-intensity subregions). This is supported by the quantitative simulation results as well. For example, looking at Table 3-5, a compression ratio of around 4 is achieved with less fidelity loss (almost 50 percent less as measured by NMS) by using a block size of 2 and a threshold of 4 rather than a block size of 4 and 0 threshold. Similarly, for a compression ratio of around 8, a block size of 4 and a threshold of 4 gives a fidelity loss measure of only about 40 percent of that encountered by adapting a block size of 16 and 0 threshold. In view of this remarkable increase in the compression ratio with very little added loss in the image fidelity (as measured by mean square error), this is considered a useful enhancement to the basic BTC methodology and should be included as a user controlled option in any design based on the BTC approach.

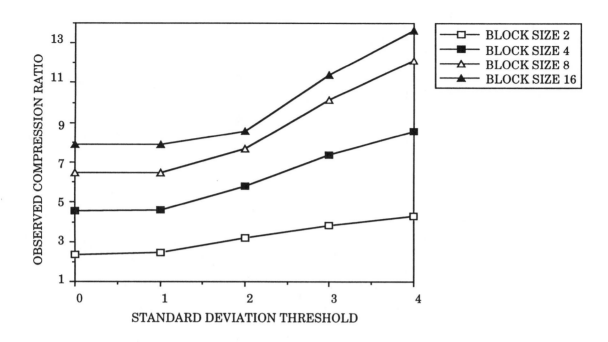

Figure 3-26. Observed compression ratio versus standard deviation threshold for different block sizes under the two-parameter BTC approach.

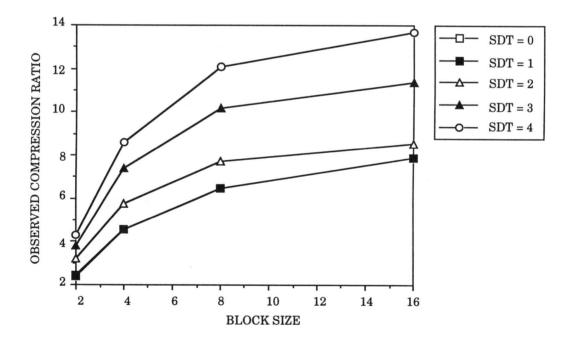

Figure 3-27. Observed compression ratio versus block size at different standard deviation thresholds under the two-parameter BTC approach.

121

GLOSSARY

ABAC	Adaptive Binary Arithmetic Coding
ACC	Adaptive Compression Coding
ADCT	Adaptive Discrete Cosine Transform
AHT	Adaptive Hadamard Transform
AMBTC	Absolute-Moment–Based BTC
BSCPC	Block-Separated Component Progressive Coding
BTC	Block Truncation Coding
CBTC	Color BTC
CCITT	International Committee on Telegraph and Telephone
CLIX	Unix-Based Compress Utility
CPU	Central Processing Unit
CVQ	Classified Vector Quantization
CWM	Cross Window Median
DC	Discrete Cosine
DCT	Discrete Cosine Transform
DPCM	Differential Pulse Code Modulation
EBTC	Entropy-Preserving BTC
FFT	Fast Fourier Transform
FT	Fourier Transform
FTC	Feedback Transform Coding
GBTC	Generalized BTC
HBTC	Hierarchical (or Hybrid) BTC
HDTV	High-Definition Television
IBTC	Interpolative BTC
IEEE	Institute of Electrical and Electronic Engineers
ISO	International Standards Organization
JPEG	Joint Photographic Experts Group
KL	Karhunen–Loeve
LTPP	Linear Three-Point Predictor
LUT	Lookup Table
MAE	Mean Absolute Error
MAPS	Microadaptive Picture Sequencing
MBTC	Modified BTC
MCBTC	Modified Color BTC

MIMD	Multiple Instruction Multiple Data
MMAE	Minimum Mean Absolute Error
MMSE	Minimum Mean Square Error
MPEG	Moving Picture Experts Group
MSE	Mean Square Error
NMS	Normalized Mean Square
NMSE	Normalized Mean Square Error
NRMS	Normalized Root Mean Square
OS	Overshoot Suppression
PASM	Partitionable SIMD/MIMD System
PCS	Progressive Coding Scheme
PDCT	Partial Discrete Cosine Transform
POT	Predictive Ordering Technique
QPC	Quantum Pattern Coding
RLE	Run-Length Encoding
RMS	Root Mean Square
SAR	Synthetic Aperture Radar
SIMD	Single Instruction Multiple Data
SM	Separable Median
SVD	Singular Value Decomposition
vBTC	Variable BTC
VLSI	Very Large Scale Integration
VPIC	Visual Pattern Image Coding
VQ	Vector Quantization
VSQC	Vertical Subtraction of Quantized Coefficients

PART B

In Part B, we present a collection of seventeen papers, which (in our opinion) represents a good cross-section of the significant developments reported in the area of block truncation coding. In addition to being restricted to English language literature, the selection is primarily limited to peer-reviewed papers; conference papers presenting preliminary results have specifically been excluded. While we pay appropriate homage to the originators of the basic BTC concepts by including a few early papers that lay the foundation for the papers that follow, our bias has been towards the inclusion of studies that tend to represent the more recent state of the art. One of the papers [B6], which was originally intended for inclusion, had to be dropped owing to publication-related difficulties.

Of course, all seventeen studies presented here as reprints have been discussed in detail in a chronological order in Chapter 2 together with another eighty or so studies that we were able to identify in this area. Here, these seventeen studies have been grouped into clusters under four chapter headings:

- Core Contributions (two papers)
- Appreciable Advances (four papers)
- Innovative Implementations (five papers)
- Harmonious Hybrids (six papers)

The progression in the number of studies under each heading is not purely coincidental. It reflects to some extent the direction of growth in the area. Each chapter, 4 through 7, starts with a brief overview of the papers presented therein, without repeating all of the details covered earlier in Chapter 2, followed by the actual reprints themselves. The last chapter provides food for thought on future research in the area.

Chapter 4
Core Contributions

In this chapter, two papers serve as representatives of the initial studies that provided the impetus for research and development in this area of data compression. An early paper, published in mid-1979 by Murakami et al. [B6], represents the pioneering efforts of a group of Japanese researchers whose team was one of two that seem to have independently come up with essentially similar results. However, because of publication-related difficulties, this could not be included here. Among the two included, the first, by Delp and Mitchell [**B8**], was also published about the same time. It is a comprehensive representation of the efforts of the other pioneering team, which was from the United States. The conceptual and implementation details of this study have been discussed at length in the previous chapter and hence are not repeated here. The second, by Healy and Mitchell [**B14**], which appeared a little later, is significant in that it was perhaps the first effort at looking at a sequence of images and thus created a wider range of interest in these techniques.

Chapter 4 Reprints

[B8] E.J. Delp and O.R. Mitchell, "Image Compression Using Block Truncation Coding," *IEEE Trans. Comm.*, Vol. COM-27, No. 9, pp. 1335–1342, Sept. 1979.

[B14] D.J. Healy and O.R. Mitchell, "Digital Video Bandwidth Compression Using Block Truncation Coding," *IEEE Trans. Comm.*, Vol. COM-29, No. 12, pp. 1809–1817, Dec. 1981.

Image Compression Using Block Truncation Coding

EDWARD J. DELP, STUDENT MEMBER, IEEE, AND
O. ROBERT MITCHELL, MEMBER, IEEE

Abstract—A new technique for image compression called Block Truncation Coding (BTC) is presented and compared with transform and other techniques. The BTC algorithm uses a two-level (one-bit) nonparametric quantizer that adapts to local properties of the image. The quantizer that shows great promise is one which preserves the local sample moments. This quantizer produces good quality images that appear to be enhanced at data rates of 1.5 bits/picture element. No large data storage is required, and the computation is small. The quantizer is compared with standard (minimum mean-square error and mean absolute error) one-bit quantizers. Modifications of the basic BTC algorithm are discussed along with the performance of BTC in the presence of channel errors.

I. INTRODUCTION

Since the beginning of the use of digital techniques for image processing, there has been a desire to find ways of coding images efficiently. The number of bits required to preserve high dynamic range and resolution in a typical PCM picture ranges from 10^6 to 10^8. Many, efficient image coding schemes have evolved [1], popular examples are the Cosine transform of Chen and Smith [2] and predictive coding (DPCM) [3].

In this paper we will present a new technique called Block Truncation Coding (BTC) that has been developed at Purdue University in the past two years [4]–[5]. This technique uses a one bit nonparametric quantizer adaptive over local regions of the image. The quantizer that shows great promise is one that preserves local statistics of the image.[1]

Paper approved by the Editor for Data Communication Systems of the IEEE Communications Society for publication after presentation at ICC'78, Toronto, Ont., Canada, June 1978. Manuscript received October 30, 1978; revised March 22, 1979. This work was supported by the Rome Air Development Center, Griffiss AFB-RADC, under Grant F75C0082 covering the period from April 1, 1977 to October 31, 1978.

The authors are with the School of Electrical Engineering, Purdue University, West Lafayette, IN 47907.

[1] At the time of presentation of our ICC paper [5], a method similar to BTC was presented in Japan by Kishimoto *et al.* [6]–[8].

In this paper the BTC algorithm is presented and compared with some common techniques of image compression. Modifications to BTC are presented including some hybrid techniques. The performance of BTC in the presence of channel errors is also discussed.

II. BASIC BTC ALGORITHM

For the study presented here the image will be divided into 4×4 pixel blocks, and the quantizer will have 2 levels. If one uses the classical quantization design of Max [9] which minimizes the mean square error, one must know, *a priori,* the probability density function of the pixels in each block. This same knowledge is also required for the absolute error fidelity criteria of Kassam [10]. Since in general it is not possible to find adequate density function models for typical imagery, we have used nonparametric quantizers for our coding schemes. Nonparametric quantizer design that minimizes either mean square error (denoted MSE) or mean absolute error (denoted MAE) will be presented in Section III. In this section we present the design of a nonparametric quantizer that preserves sample moments (denoted MP); the design of a parametric MP quantizer is presented in [11].

After dividing the picture into $n \times n$ blocks ($n = 4$ for our examples), the blocks are coded individually, each into a two level signal. The levels for each block are chosen such that the first two sample moments are preserved. Let $m = n^2$ and let $X_1, X_2, \cdots X_m$ be the values of the pixels in a block of the original picture.

Then the first and second sample moments and the sample variance are, respectively

$$\overline{X} = \frac{1}{m} \sum_{i=1}^{m} X_i$$

$$\overline{X^2} = \frac{1}{m} \sum_{i=1}^{m} X_i{}^2$$

$$\overline{\sigma^2} = \overline{X^2} - \overline{X}^2. \tag{1}$$

As with the design of any one bit quantizer, we find a threshold, X_{th}, and two output levels, a and b, such that

if $X_i \geqslant X_{th}$ output $= b$

if $X_i < X_{th}$ output $= a$

for $i = 1, 2, \cdots, m$. $\tag{2}$

For our first quantizer, we set $X_{th} = \overline{X}$, this reasonable assumption will be modified in Section IV to improve performance. The output levels a and b are found by solving the following equations:

Let $q =$ number of X_i's greater than $X_{th}(= \overline{X})$

then to preserve $\overline{X}$ and $\overline{X^2}$

$$m\overline{X} = (m - q)a + qb \tag{3}$$

and

$$m\overline{X^2} = (m - q)a^2 + qb^2$$

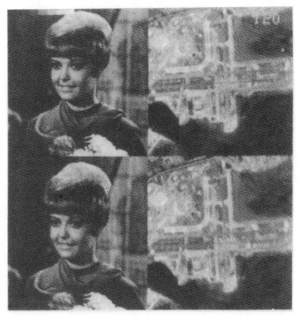

Figure 1. Results using the basic BTC algorithm. The original images (top) are 256×256 pixels with nominal 8 bits gray level resolution. The coded images (bottom) have a data rate of 2 bits/pixel.

Solving for a and b:

$$a = \overline{X} - \overline{\sigma} \sqrt{\left[\frac{q}{m-q} \right]}$$

$$b = \overline{X} + \overline{\sigma} \sqrt{\left[\frac{m-q}{q} \right]}. \tag{4}$$

Each block is then described by the values of $\overline{X}$, $\overline{\sigma}$ and an $n \times n$ bit plane consisting of 1's and 0's indicating whether pixels are above or below X_{th}. Assigning 8 bits each to $\overline{X}$ and $\overline{\sigma}$ results in a data rate of 2 bits/pixel. The receiver reconstructs the image block by calculating a and b from Equation 4 and assigning these values to pixels in accordance with the code in the bit plane. (An example of coding a 4×4 picture block is presented in the Appendix.)

Examples of this coding system are shown in Figure 1. The block boundaries are not visible in the reconstructed pictures nor is the quantization noise visible in regions of the picture where there is little change in luminance. Here the levels a and b are close together. They are widely spaced only in regions where large changes of luminance occur; but it is well known [13] that large changes of luminance mask noise. Thus BTC encoding makes use of the masking property in human vision. The most noticeable improvement of the reconstructed picture is a little raggedness of sharp edges. In the next section we will present methods for improving the image quality and reducing the bit rate.

Because the calculations are relatively simple and the storage of data small, BTC is fairly easy to implement. A recent study has shown that BTC can be realized on an integrated circuit chip [12].

III. OTHER NONPARAMETRIC QUANTIZER SCHEMES

As mentioned in Section II, other techniques can be used to design a one bit quantizer. Use of rate-distortion theory seems theoretically attractive but somewhat impractical for real images [14]–[15]. In this section we will discuss the use of the minimum mean square error (MSE) and minimum mean absolute error (MAE) fidelity criteria for one-bit nonparametric quantizers.

To use the MSE fidelity criterion, one proceeds by first constructing a histogram of the X_i's (i.e., sorting the X_i's). Let $Y_1, Y_2, \cdots Y_m$ be the sorted X_i's; i.e., $Y_1 \leq Y_2 \cdots \leq Y_m$. Again let q be the number of X_i's greater than X_{th}. Then a and b are found by minimizing

$$J_{\text{MSE}} = \sum_{i=1}^{m-q-1} (Y_i - a)^2 + \sum_{i=m-q}^{m} (Y_i - b)^2 \qquad (5)$$

where

$$a = \frac{1}{m-q} \sum_{i=1}^{m-q-1} Y_i$$

$$b = \frac{1}{q} \sum_{i=m-q}^{m} Y_i.$$

One obvious way to solve this problem is to try every possible threshold (there are at most $m - 1$ thresholds) and pick the one with smallest J_{MSE}. Assuming a and b have 8-bit resolution, this gives a data rate of 2 bits/pixel.

The problem of using the MAE fidelity criterion is very similar to the MSE. The values a and b are found by minimizing

$$J_{\text{MAE}} = \sum_{i=1}^{m-q-1} \left| Y_i - a \right| + \sum_{i=m-q}^{m} \left| Y_i - b \right| \qquad (6)$$

where

$$a = \text{median of } (Y_1, Y_2, \cdots, Y_{m-q-1})$$

$$b = \text{median of } (Y_{m-q}, \cdots, Y_m).$$

Here again the nonparametric quantizer is arrived at by an exhaustive search. Results using these quantizers and BTC are shown in Figures 2 and 3. As mentioned in Section II it is possible to use a parametric quantizer once the probability density function of the pixels is known (or guessed). In Figures 2 and 3 results are presented for a parametric MSE quantizer where the pixels are assumed to be uniformly distributed over each block. Table I has the computed mean square error and mean absolute error measures for each image. As anticipated the MSE quantizer has the smallest computed mean square error measure and the MAE quantizer has the smallest computed mean absolute error measure. The performance of BTC is quite good when compared to these standard fidelity criteria. The advantage of using a nonparametric MP quantizer is that the quantizer formulation is available in *closed form*; this greatly simplifies the computational load.

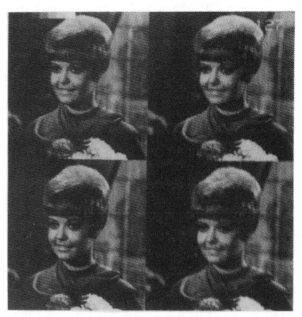

Figure 2. Results using various fidelity criterion. All data rates are 2.0 bits/pixel. Upper left: minimum mean square error; Upper right: minimum mean absolute error; Lower left: moment preserving; Lower right: minimum mean square error and also assuming image data uniformly distributed each block.

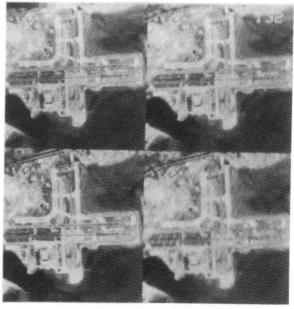

Figure 3. These four pictures were produced as described in Figure 2 using the other original.

IV. BTC MODIFICATIONS

In many image coding schemes it is desired to obtain data rates less than 2 bits/pixel. An obvious way of achieving this is to assign less than 8 bits to $\bar{X}$ and $\bar{\sigma}$. Experimental evidence has indicated that coding $\bar{X}$ with 6 bits and $\bar{\sigma}$ with 4 bits introduces only a few perceivable errors. Now the data rate is 1.63 bits/pixel. Better performance could be obtained by quan-

TABLE I
COMPUTED MEAN SQUARE ERROR AND MEAN ABSOLUTE
ERROR MEASURES FOR VARIOUS QUANTIZATION
SCHEMES

	Mean Square Error	Mean Absolute Error
Data from Figure 2:		
Using MSE quantizer	32.94	3.54
Using MAE quantizer	37.13	3.28
Using BTC	40.89	3.91
Using parametric MSE quantizer and assumed uniform density	44.64	4.23
Data from Figure 3:		
Using MSE quantizer	47.14	4.39
Using MAE quantizer	53.22	4.10
Using BTC	58.34	4.85
Using parametric MSE quantizer and assumed uniform density	64.02	5.42

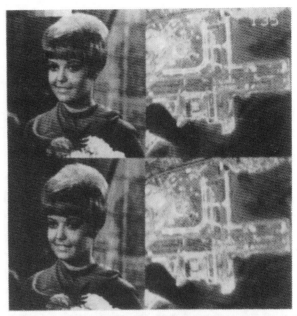

Figure 4. Results of BTC using third moment preserving threshold selection. Original images are at the top. Coded images are at the bottom. Data rate is 2.0 bits/pixel.

tizing $\bar{X}$ and $\bar{\sigma}$ jointly, using 10 bits. $\bar{X}$ is assigned most bits in blocks where $\bar{\sigma}$ is small and fewest bits where $\bar{\sigma}$ is large.

Additional savings could be realized by efficiently coding the bit plane. Entropy calculations indicate that 0.85 bits/pixel would be sufficient for the bit plane. Such small improvement does not justify the increased complexity of the system and the increased variability to error that efficient coding entails.

Setting the threshold of the quantizer at $\bar{X}$, removes a possible degree of freedom for optimizing the encoding. Allowing the threshold to be a variable permits the encoding to preserve not only the first two sample moments but also the third sample moment. To analyze this, we make use of the sorted pixel values Y_i. The third moment can be expressed as

$$\overline{X^3} = \frac{1}{m} \sum_{i=1}^{m} X_i{}^3 = \frac{1}{m} \sum_{i=1}^{m} Y_i{}^3. \tag{7}$$

The problem then is finding a, b, and q to preserve $\bar{X}$, $\overline{X^2}$, and $\overline{X^3}$ (q defines the threshold since it specifies the number of X_i's greater than X_{th}), Equation 3 now becomes

$$m\bar{X} = (m - q)a + qb$$
$$m\overline{X^2} = (m - q)a^2 + qb^2$$
$$m\overline{X^3} = (m - q)a^3 + qb^3. \tag{8}$$

Having the solutions

$$a = \bar{X} - \sigma \sqrt{\left[\frac{q}{m - q}\right]}$$

$$b = \bar{X} + \bar{\sigma} \sqrt{\left[\frac{m - q}{q}\right]}$$

$$q = \frac{m}{2}\left[1 + A\sqrt{\frac{1}{A^2 + 4}}\right] \tag{9}$$

where

$$A = \frac{3\bar{X}\overline{X^2} - \overline{X^3}2(\bar{X})^3}{\bar{\sigma}^3}$$

$$\bar{\sigma} \neq 0.$$

If $\bar{\sigma} = 0$, then $a = b = \bar{X}$.

In general the value of q obtained will not be an integer, so in practice it must be rounded to the nearest integer. An interesting interpretation of Equation 9 is that the threshold is nominally set to the sample median and biased higher or lower depending upon the value of the third sample moment which is a measure of skewness of the Y_i's. This threshold selection requires no extra computation at the receiver (decoder), but the transmitter (encoder) does have extra processing. This method of threshold selection is far easier to implement than are the nonparametric quantizers discussed in Section III since they require an exhaustive search.

Figure 4 shows results using this threshold selection. It improves subtle features (such as near edges) of the image that are usually important in analysis of aerial photography imagery. This improvement will be discussed in the following section.

V. PERFORMANCE EVALUATION OF BTC

Recent studies at Purdue University have evaluated various image coding techniques for transmitting aerial reconnaissance images over noisy channels [16]. BTC, transform, Hybrid [17] and one other technique were evaluated by professional photo analysts.

Although BTC did not perform as well as transform coding in the photo interpreters evaluation, it proved superior to the other techniques. In the presence of many channel errors, BTC was superior to all of the other techniques. Some images used in the study are shown in Figures 5-8. In these figures BTC is compared with the Chen and Smith [2] method of transform coding and Hybrid coding. The computed mean square errors and mean absolute errors are shown in Table II. Our study has shown that the mean square error and mean absolute error measure cannot be easily correlated with photo analysts' evaluations. In some cases, images with large mean square errors were evaluated higher than images with smaller mean square errors. It should be noted that BTC requires a significantly smaller computational load and much less memory than

Figure 5. Original image used in comparison study. Image is 512 ×
512 pixels with nominal 8 bits gray level resolution.

Figure 6. Results of coding original (Figure 5) using BTC with third
moment preserving threshold selection. Data rate is 1.63 bits/pixel.

Figure 7. Results of coding original (Figure 5) using Chen and Smith
[2] method of Cosine Transform coding. Data rate is 1.63 bits/pixel.

Figure 8. Results of coding original (Figure 5) using Hybrid coding
[17]. Data rate is 1.63 bits/pixel.

TABLE II
COMPUTED MEAN SQUARE ERROR AND MEAN ABSOLUTE
ERROR MEASURES FOR COMPARISON IMAGES SHOWN IN
FIGURES 6-11 AND FIGURE 13

	Mean Square Error	Mean Absolute Error
Figure 6	84.22	5.94
Figure 7	67.13	6.32
Figure 8	125.84	6.12
Figure 9	115.09	6.29
Figure 10	115.31	7.06
Figure 11	140.33	6.67
Figure 13	74.67	5.72

Figure 9. BTC coding with channel error probability of 10^{-3}. Data rate is 1.63 bits/pixel.

Figure 11. Hybrid coding with channel error probability of 10^{-3}. Data rate is 1.63 bits/pixel.

Figure 10. Chen and Smith coding with channel error probability of 10^{-3}. Data rate is 1.63 bits/pixel.

Figure 12. Enlarged section of image from Figure 6 (left) and Figure 7 (right).

transform or Hybrid coding. For instance, the Chen and Smith method requires the two-dimensional Cosine transform over every 16 × 16 image block and also requires multiple passes through the transform data to collect various statistics about the transform coefficients. It should also be mentioned that BTC requires no sophisticated error protection as do the other coding methods evaluated. Figures 9-11 show the results of each coding method in the presence of channel errors. The channel was assumed to be binary symmetric with the probability of a bit error of 10^{-3}.

One of the advantages of BTC is that luminance edges are emphasized. Figure 12 shows an enlarged section of an image coded using the Chen and Smith method and BTC. The edges using the transform coding method are not as sharp as the BTC image.

As with all noninformation preserving image coding, coding artifacts are produced in the image. It became apparent very early in this study that BTC produces artifacts that are very different than transform coding. They are usually seen in regions around edges and in low contrast areas containing a sloping gray level. As mentioned above, BTC does produce sharp edges; however, these edges do have a tendency to be ragged. Transform coding usually produces edges that are blurred and smooth. The second problem in low contrast regions is due to inherent quantization noise in the one bit quantizer. Here sloping gray levels can turn into false contours. Preliminary experiments have indicated that pre- and post-

133

Figure 13. Results of Hybrid Formulation of BTC. Data rate is 1.88 bits/pixel.

processing of the image can reduce the effects of both these artifacts while simultaneously reducing the mean square error and mean absolute error. It should be emphasized that these coding artifacts are problems in high resolution aerial reconnaissance images where minute objects are important. These coding artifacts usually are not visible in typical "head and shoulders" imagery.

VI. HYBRID FORMULATION OF BTC

BTC uses only first-order information and does not exploit the two-dimensional sturcture of the image within each block as do most other forms of image coding. For example in two-dimensional transform coding the transform coefficients contain information about variations in the picture in both directions. Also BTC generally has a poor response near the spatial frequency of 1/2 cycle per block.

One method to overcome this disadvantage is a hybrid formulation. First a highly compressed Cosine transform coded image is subtracted from the original image. For the results presented here the transform picture was obtained by taking the two-dimensional Cosine transform over 16 × 16 pixel blocks. Only the eight non-dc coefficients in the low frequency section of each block were retained. This corresponds to a zonal filtering method with a bit rate of 0.25 bits/pixel for the highly compressed image. BTC was then used on this difference picture and the recombination formed at the receiver. While this did increase the computational load, the improvement seemed to be significant enough to give this method further attention. Figure 13 presents results of this hybrid method. Table II has the mean square error and mean absolute error measures for Figure 13.

VII. CONCLUSIONS

A new, simple technique has been described with modifications to improve its performance. The resulting recon-structed image has artifacts quite different from those produced by other techniques, but the resulting images are comparable and in some ways superior to those produced by the most sophisticated techniques available. This method produces a coded image that is more robust in the presence of channel errors and requires very little error protection overhead.

ACKNOWLEDGMENT

The authors would like to thank Dr. John Gamble of the Rome Air Development Center for his helpful criticism of this work. We would also like to thank Richard P. Petroski and his colleagues of the Rome Research Corporation who provided the expert photo evaluations mentioned in Section V.

The authors would also like to thank Professor Steven Bass of Purdue for suggesting the hybrid formulation of BTC and Ali Tabatabai and Paul Stiling also of Purdue for providing the transform and Hybrid coded images.

APPENDIX

To illustrate coding a 4 × 4 picture block using Block Truncation Coding, let us quickly review the basic BTC algorithm:

a) the image is divided in small nonoverlapping blocks such as 4 × 4.

b) The first and second sample moments are computed.

c) A bit plane is constructed such that each pixel location is coded as a "one" or a "zero" depending on whether that pixel is greater than $\bar{X}$.

d) The bit plane, $\bar{X}$, and $\bar{\sigma}$ are sent to the receiver.

e) The picture block is reconstructed such that $\bar{X}$ and $\bar{\sigma}$ (alternatively $\overline{X^2}$) are preserved. That is, pixels in the bit plane that are "0" are set to "a" and the "1"'s are set to "b" in Equation 4. For example, suppose a 4 × 4 picture block is given by the following:

$$X_{ij} = \begin{bmatrix} 121 & 114 & 56 & 47 \\ 37 & 200 & 247 & 255 \\ 16 & 0 & 12 & 169 \\ 43 & 5 & 7 & 251 \end{bmatrix}$$

so

$$\bar{X} = 98.75$$

$$\bar{\sigma} = 92.95$$

$$q = 7$$

and

$$a = 16.7 \cong 17$$

$$b = 204.2 \cong 204$$

the bit plane is

$$\begin{bmatrix} 1 & 1 & 0 & 0 \\ 0 & 1 & 1 & 1 \\ 0 & 0 & 0 & 1 \\ 0 & 0 & 0 & 1 \end{bmatrix}$$

The reconstructed block becomes

$$\begin{bmatrix} 204 & 204 & 17 & 17 \\ 17 & 204 & 204 & 204 \\ 17 & 17 & 17 & 204 \\ 17 & 17 & 17 & 204 \end{bmatrix}$$

and the sample mean and variance are preserved.

REFERENCES

[1] A. Habibi, "Survey of Adaptive Image Coding Techniques," *IEEE Trans. on Communications,* Vol. COM-25, No. 11, pp. 1275-1284, Nov. 1977.

[2] W-H. Chen and C. H. Smith, "Adaptive Coding of Monochrome and Color Images," *IEEE Trans. on Communications,* Vol. COM-25, pp. 1285-1292, Nov. 1977.

[3] J. B. O'Neal, "Predictive Quantizing System (DPCM) for the Transmission of Television Signals," *BSTJ,* Vol. 45, pp. 689-721, May-June 1966.

[4] O. R. Mitchell and E. J. Delp, "Image Compression Using Block Truncation," Purdue University—Purdue Research Foundation, Record and Disclosure of Invention, dated April 8, 1977. This document is available from the authors.

[5] O. R. Mitchell, E. J. Delp, and S. G. Carlton, "Block Truncation Coding: A New Approach to Image Compression," *Conference Record, 1978 IEEE International Conference on Communications* (ICC'78), Vol. I, June 4-7, 1978, pp. 12B.1.1-12B.1.4.

[6] T. Kishimoto, E. Mitsuya, and K. Hoshida, "A Method of Still Picture Coding by Using Statistic Properties," (in Japanese) National Conference of the Institute of Electronics and Communications Engineers of Japan, March 1978, No. 974.

[7] T. Kishimoto, E. Mitsuya, and K. Hoshida, "An Experiment of Still Picture Coding by Block Processing" (in Japanese) National Conference of the Institute of Electronics and Communications Engineers of Japan, March 1978, No. 975.

[8] T. Kishimoto, E. Mitsuya, and K. Hoshida, "Block Coding of Still Pictures," (in Japanese), Technical Group of Communication System of the Institute of Electronics and Communication Engineers of Japan, pp. 63-69, July 1978.

[9] J. Max, "Quantizing for Minimum Distortion," *IRE Trans. on Info. Theory,* Vol. IT-6, pp. 7-12, March 1960.

[10] S. A. Kassam, "Quantization Based on the Mean-Absolute-Error Criterion," *IEEE Trans. on Communications,* Vol. COM-26, pp. 267-270, Feb. 1978.

[11] E. J. Delp and O. R. Mitchell, "Some Aspects of Moment Preserving Quantizers," in *Conf. Rec., 1979 IEEE International Conference on Communications,* (ICC'79), vol. I, June 10-14, pp. 7.2.1-7.2.5.

[12] W. L. Eversole, D. J. Mayer, F. B. Frazee, an T. F. Cheek, "Investigation of VLSI Technologies for Image Processing," *Proceedings: Image Understanding Workshop,* Pittsburgh, PA, Nov. 14-15, 1978. Sponsored by the Defense Advanced Research Projects Agency (DARPA), pp. 191-195. (Copies available from the Defense Documentation Center (DDC) under Accession No. ADA 052903).

[13] D. Jameson and L. M. Hurvich (editors), *Handbook of Sensory Physiology: Visual Psychophysics,* New York: Springer-Verlag, 1972.

[14] T. Berger, *Rate Distortion Theory,* Englewood Cliffs: Prentice-Hall, 1971.

[15] J. L. Munnos and D. J. Sakrison, "The Effects of a Visual Fidelity Criterion on the Encoding of Images," *IEEE Trans. on Information Theory,* Vol. IT-20, pp. 525-536, July 1974.

[16] O. R. Mitchell, S. C. Bass, E. J. Delp, and T. W. Goeddel, "Coding of Aerial Reconnaissance Images for Transmission over Noisy Channels," issued as Rome Air Development Center (RADC) Technical Report, Griffiss Air Force Base, NY. Report No. RADC-TR-78-210. (This report is available from the National Technical Information Service, Accession No. ADA 061539).

[17] A. Habibi, "Hybrid Coding of Pictorial Data," *IEEE Trans. Commun.,* Vol. COM-22, pp. 614-624, May 1974.

Digital Video Bandwidth Compression Using Block Truncation Coding

DONALD J. HEALY, STUDENT MEMBER, IEEE, AND O. ROBERT MITCHELL, MEMBER, IEEE

Abstract—A technique for bandwidth compression coding of sequential digitized video imagery is presented. The method uses adaptive one-bit quantization over small blocks of space and time. The system includes global registration and motion detection for optimal bit assignments. A comparison is made with a conditional replenishment technique using a motion compensated predictor described in the literature. The method presented produces reconstructed video sequences filmed from low altitude aircraft with slight degradation which is acceptable for many remote sensing applications at 0.9 bit/pixel data rate. Robust behavior in the presence of channel noise is demonstrated.

I. INTRODUCTION

THERE is interest in medium bandwidth transmission systems for digitized real-time moving imagery. Previous work in this area has been largely based on subsampling (spatial and temporal) and/or nearest neighbor prediction combined with some form of DPCM [1]–[5]. Computationally more complex motion compensated prediction methods have also been developed [6]–[9]. The data rate reduction reported here is an extension to three dimensions of the block truncation coding (BTC) technique using a moment preserving quantizer developed at Purdue University for coding still images [10]–[12]. Three constant data rate transmission systems employing BTC are introduced. A motion compensated prediction system described by Robbins and Netravali [8] has been implemented for comparison.

One intraframe and two interframe BTC systems are presented. The intraframe system achieves sufficient reconstruction at a data rate of 1.625 bits/pixel using a simple closed form adaptive quantizer which operates on two-dimensional 4 × 4 pixel blocks, thus requiring only four lines of storage. The interframe systems achieve additional bandwidth compression by simultaneously coding three frames using 4 × 4 × 3 pixel blocks. Large movements (e.g., due to camera motion) across block boundaries cause reduced temporal correlation and decreased reconstructed quality. This problem is overcome by using a fast registration method developed by Reeves and Rostampour [13] for background registration. The registered area and edge regions for three consecutive frames are identified. Nonregistered edge regions are coded using two-dimensional blocks. The registered area can be largely coded using three-dimensional blocks, except where there is movement across the background necessitating the selective use of two-dimensional blocks. Minimum mean square error and motion detection criteria optimize the distribution of two-dimensionally and three-dimensionally coded blocks within the registered area. Overall data rates as low as 0.9 bit/pixel are achieved using interframe BTC with little degradation in the reconstructed moving images. Robust behavior in the presence of channel noise is demonstrated.

II. BLOCK TRUNCATION CODING

A. Two-Dimensional Block Truncation Coding of Still Images

Block truncation coding (BTC) using a moment preserving quantizer is a technique originally applied to still pictures [10]–[12]. This method divides an image into $n \times n$ pixel blocks (typically $n = 4$), each of whose pixels are individually quantized to two levels, Y_0 and Y_1, such that the block sample mean η and variance σ^2 are preserved. If $X_1, X_2, \cdots, X_N$ are the original sampled values within a given block, then the sample mean is defined as

$$\eta = \frac{1}{N} \sum_{i=1}^{N} X_i = \bar{X} \tag{1}$$

and the sample variance is defined as

$$\sigma^2 = \frac{1}{N} \sum_{i=1}^{N} X_i^2 - \eta^2 = \overline{X^2} - \bar{X}^2. \tag{2}$$

It has been shown [10]–[12] that the first two sample moments $\bar{X}$ and $\overline{X^2}$ can be preserved using quantizer levels

$$Y_0 = \eta - \sigma\sqrt{q/p} \tag{3}$$

and

$$Y_1 = \eta + \sigma\sqrt{p/q} \tag{4}$$

where q and p are the number of pixels above and below the sample mean, respectively. Pixels below the sample mean are quantized to level Y_0 and the others to Y_1. Since the first two sample moments are preserved, (2) shows that the sample variance is also preserved. For each block, η, σ, and a bit plane (one bit per pixel to select quantizer level Y_0 or Y_1) are normally transmitted.

Using 4 × 4 pixel blocks and eight bits each for η and σ, the data rate is 2 bits/pixel (including 16 bits for the bit plane).

Manuscript received March 3, 1981; revised July 1, 1981. This paper was presented at the International Conference on Communications, Denver, CO, June 1981.

D. J. Healy is with the Department of Electrical Engineering, Georgia Institute of Technology, Atlanta, GA 30332.

O. R. Mitchell is with the School of Electrical Engineering, Purdue University, West Lafayette, IN 47907.

Fig. 1(b) exemplifies this coding technique. The original image in Fig. 1(a) has 8-bit intensity resolution. Advantages of BTC include computational simplicity and robust behavior in the presence of channel noise (the latter will be demonstrated later). Additionally, the adaptive one-bit quantizer preserves the dominant intensity variations at the expense of secondary changes which are less perceptible to the human visual system.

B. Simultaneous η-σ Quantization

Empirical evidence suggests that, on an 8-bit scale, quantizing σ values greater than 63 is unnecessary. Separately coding σ using six bits (0–63) and η using eight bits (0–255) would result in a data rate of $(16 + 14)/16 = 1.875$ bits/pixel. A two-dimensional quantizer is introduced which simultaneously codes η and σ using a total of 10 bits. The η-σ combinations are chosen such that the quantization error in η and σ increases with σ. This scheme is based on the observation that grey level quantization error is more visible in low variance regions. An example of two-dimensional BTC using this quantizer is shown in Fig. 1(c). The resulting data rate is $(16 + 10)/16 = 1.625$ bits/pixel. There is no significant degradation compared to Fig. 1(b). Table I shows the quantized output values of σ and the corresponding number of levels allowed for η. For any given σ, the η levels are distributed uniformly.

Instead of simultaneously quantizing η and σ using 10 bits, Fig. 1(d) shows the result of separately quantizing η and σ using five bits for each. The 32 resulting quantizer levels for each are uniformly distributed over the ranges 0–255 and 0–63 for η and σ, respectively. Note the false contours that appear in some low variance regions of the water. The two-dimensional quantizer clearly results in superior reconstruction.

C. Application to Moving Imagery

Intraframe coding of moving images using 2-D BTC was accomplished first. Each frame was coded independently. A typical frame coded in this manner is shown in Fig. 2(b). 30 frames/s were viewed by repeating each frame twice to achieve a 60 Hz field rate. No new artifacts were observed in the coded moving sequence which was recorded on video tape. Motion appeared continuous and clear, contrary to the suspicion of some researchers that the unique artifacts of BTC (e.g., sharp well-defined edges) would cause objectionable jerkiness when used in a moving image application.

An interframe BTC scheme was developed which uses three-dimensional (two spatial, one temporal) blocks to reduce the overall bit rate by spreading the η and σ overhead bits over more pixels. Specifically, three frames are simultaneously coded using blocks of size $4 \times 4 \times 3$ pixels. Using the 10-bit simultaneous η-σ quantizer described earlier, the resulting data rate for three-dimensional (3-D) blocks is $(48 + 10)/48 = 1.21$ bits/pixel.

However, satisfactory results cannot be obtained by coding all data using 3-D blocks. Although motion within a 3-D block is accurately represented using this technique, larger movements (across block boundaries) cause reduced temporal cor-

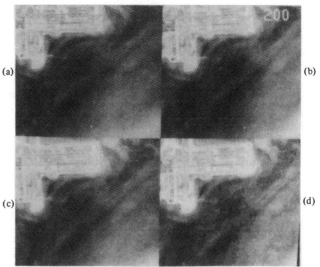

Fig. 1. (a) Original 240 × 256 section showing airport runways and ocean. (b) 2-D BTC with eight bits each for $\bar{\eta}$ and $\bar{\sigma}$. (c) 2-D BTC using 10-bit simultaneous $\bar{\eta}$-$\bar{\sigma}$ quantizer. (d) 2-D BTC using five bits each for $\bar{\eta}$ and $\bar{\sigma}$.

TABLE I
SIMULTANEOUS η-σ QUANTIZER USING 10 BITS

σ	Number of Uniformly Distributed η Levels
0	256
1, 2, 4	128
6, 8, 13, 19, 28	64
42, 56	32

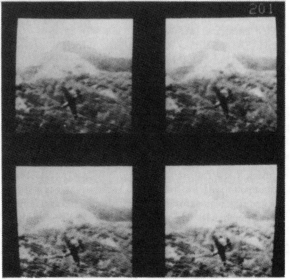

Fig. 2. (a) Original data—frame 1—100 rows × 200 columns. (b) BTC coding, 2-D blocks assigned everywhere (intraframe BTC system). (c) BTC coding, 450 2-D blocks assigned to edge regions first and then assigned starting at upper left until exhausted, remaining 800 blocks coded 3-D. (d) Same as (c) except 2-D blocks remaining after coding edges are optimally distributed to minimize mean square error (interframe BTC system with fixed 3-D/2-D block ratio).

137

relation. To overcome this problem, a registration algorithm is used to identify global translations. This translational information is used to segment each of the three frames into a registered rectangular background common to all three frames, and nonregisterable edge regions. The edge regions must be coded using 2-D blocks. However, the registered area can be largely coded using the lower data rate 3-D blocks, except where there is significant movement across block boundaries. Methods to select registered blocks for 2-D coding will be discussed in Section IV.

III. REGISTRATION

The registration algorithm [13] is designed to be implemented using parallel binary array processors which makes it quite suitable for the real time frame-to-frame processing that is required in this application. The algorithm consists of four stages.

1) Pseudomedian filtering to remove spurious noise spikes— a 3×3 block is formed by each pixel and its eight nearest neighbors. The center pixel of each row of the block is set equal to the median of that row. The median of the resulting center column is used as the value of the block's center pixel amplitude. This pseudomedian value will be within one rank order of the true median of the block.

2) Bit assignment for each pixel based on a threshold determined by the local maximum and minimum in the 15×15 block containing that pixel (i.e., threshold = (max + min)/2). Any pixel whose amplitude is below its calculated threshold is assigned 0; otherwise, it is assigned 1.

3) Balanced binary smoothing—this is intended to remove fine details by complementing any 1 or 0 when a majority of its 4-neighbors are equal to its complement. This smoothing algorithm is iterated four times.

4) Binary image registration—the present and previous frame binary images are translated vertically and horizontally to find the best match using a minimum mean square error criterion. The translational shift which yields the best match between two frames is transmitted as a vector to the receiver which can then identify the registered areas.

Steps 1) and 3) may not be necessary for good quality imagery. It has been found that registration to within one pixel accuracy can be easily achieved using this algorithm to quantify global translations (e.g., due to camera movement).

IV. BTC VIDEO TRANSMISSION SYSTEMS

The three BTC systems described below employ constant data rates and fixed length codes to retain robust performance in noise without excessive bit error protection encoding. All systems employ 10-bit simultaneous η-σ quantization.

A. Intraframe 2-D BTC

This is the system introduced previously which individually codes each frame using two-dimensional block truncation coding. Using 4×4 pixel blocks and the 10-bit η-σ quantizer results in a data rate of 1.625 bits/pixel. No registration information or bit error protection is employed with this system. This very simple system achieved adequate reconstruction, as shown in Fig. 2(b), while requiring only four lines of storage.

B. Interframe BTC with Fixed 3-D/2-D Block Ratio

The frame size used in the examples presented in this paper (100×200 pixels) results in 1250 2-D (4×4 pixel) blocks per frame. For each set of three frames a registered rectangular background is obtained as described earlier. The registered areas for the set of three frames are divided into 3-D blocks ($4 \times 4 \times 3$ pixels). To achieve a constant data rate, 800 of the registered blocks are coded using 3-D BTC. This leaves 450 2-D blocks available for each frame to code edge regions and the remaining registered areas.

This, of course, limits the allowable translations(background movement) to amounts which will achieve a registered image containing at least 800 3-D blocks. This requires a minimum of 64 percent of the pixels to be registered. It is easy to show that this restriction allows for a pure horizontal or a pure vertical displacement of 36 percent, or a combined displacement of 20 percent in each direction. This allows for very rapid background (or camera) motion. For the image sequences studied (filmed from moving aircraft), at least 989 blocks registered in each three-frame set. However, if translation did exceed limits, temporary frame repeating could easily be used to maintain the fixed data rate.

Once the edge regions have been coded, the remaining 2-D BTC blocks can be distributed in the registered area. In Fig. 2(c) assignment of 2-D BTC in the registered area was arbitrarily started at the top and continued until the available 2-D BTC blocks were exhausted. Improvement can be obtained by distributing the 2-D BTC blocks in the registered area to achieve minimum mean square error (MMSE). This is accomplished by calculating the resulting MSE using 2-D and 3-D BTC for each registered 3-D block, and assigning 2-D BTC where the resulting MSE improvement is greatest. As previously discussed, it is desirable to assign 2-D blocks to those registered areas where there is significant movement across block boundaries. The MMSE technique effectively accomplishes this task. Fig. 2(d), which used the MMSE criteria, achieves superior reconstruction of the airplane which is moving across the registered area.

Each set of three frames contains $100 \times 200 \times 3 = 60\,000$ pixels. There are $450 \times 3 = 1350$ 2-D coded blocks and 800 3-D coded blocks. Using the 10-bit η-σ quantizer requires

$$(1350 + 800) \times 10 = 21\,500$$

bits. The receiver must know which registered blocks are 2-D coded and which are 3-D coded. This requires a maximum of 1250 bits. To register a three-frame group two translational vectors are needed, corresponding to the horizontal and vertical movements of frame 2 relative to frame 1 and frame 3 relative to frame 2. Each of the two translation vectors (horizontal: ±200; vertical: ±100) requires no more than 17 bits. Bit plane transmission uses an additional 60 000 bits, resulting in an overall data rate of

$$(21\,500 + 1250 + (17 \times 2) + 60\,000)/60\,000 = 1.38$$

bits/pixel. In the presence of channel noise, bit error protection is appropriate for the translation vectors and the bits that identify 2-D BTC blocks within the registered area. The resulting error protected data rate (calculated in Section V) is 1.39 bits/pixel.

C. Interframe BTC with Adaptive Mode Selection

Rather than fixing the number of 2-D BTC blocks as described above, this system achieves a constant data rate by adaptively selecting one of four transmission modes for each group of three frames. Again, a registered area for each frame is identified and edge regions are coded using 2-D BTC. Data rate reduction is primarily accomplished by transmitting only one or two of the three available bit planes for selected 3-D blocks within the registered area. To aid in this selection process, a moving-area detection algorithm is used to segment the registered region into moving and stationary blocks. Another algorithm is used to identify each stationary BTC block whose three bit-planes differ only at isolated pixel locations. Before describing the four available modes, it is appropriate to digress and detail these algorithms.

1) Moving-Area Detection: A given spatial pixel location within a registered area is identified as moving or stationary (with respect to the registered background) based on the operations described below which are performed on the original data. Some interim results of these procedures performed on the registered areas of frames 1–3 are illustrated in Fig. 3.

First, the absolute differences between frame 2's registered area and the registered areas of frames 1 and 3 are calculated. The maximum of the two differences at each location is obtained as shown in Fig. 3(a). A histogram of these maximum absolute differences is used to select the highest threshold such that a chosen percentage (3 percent is used here) of the differences is greater than or equal to the threshold. Maximum absolute differences below the threshold are set equal to 0 and the others are set equal to 1 [shown in Fig. 3(b)]. The resulting bit plane is submitted to two iterations of the pseudomedian filter also used in the registration procedure. The filtered result is shown in Fig. 3(c). This effectively removes isolated pixels and lines (horizontal, vertical, or diagonal) which are one pixel wide, while leaving intact lines of uniform width greater than one pixel. The resulting spatial locations containing 1's and 0's are identified as moving or stationary, respectively. A registered block is defined as moving if it contains any moving pixels. Fig. 3(d) shows the moving blocks for this example.

With this thresholding approach to motion detection, the use of a maximum absolute difference criterion is superior to using a sum of absolute differences and to using mean square differences. Consider a hypothetical case with a background of uniform intensity of 100 and a moving object with a uniform intensity of 125 which covers 4 percent of the background at any given instant. The positions of the object for frames 1–3 are shown in Fig. 4. A sum of absolute differences gives a value of 50 at position 2 and a value of 25 at positions 1 and 3. Since position 2 covers 4 percent (>3 percent) of the background, the threshold will be set equal to 50 and the movement across positions 1 and 3 is not detected. Contrarily, the

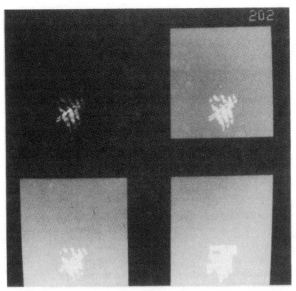

Fig. 3. Motion detection steps for registered area in frames 1–3. (a) Maximum differences. (b) Threshold of (a). (c) Pseudomedian filter of (b). (d) Moving blocks.

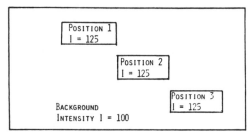

Fig. 4. Hypothetical block movement.

maximum absolute difference criterion results in a value of 25 at all three positions, resulting in a threshold of 25 and accurate motion detection. A similar argument can be made to show the inferiority of a mean square difference approach.

Using the thresholding and pseudomedian filtering technique described above, the smallest detectable moving area is a 2 × 2 pixel region. For the data in frames 1–3, 61 moving blocks were detected containing 534 moving pixels in a registered area of 1104 blocks. In a typical 123 frame sequence, the number of moving blocks per frame ranged from 33 to 74.

2) Identification and Removal of Isolated Bit Plane Differences: The purpose of this procedure is to identify each 3-D BTC block whose three bit planes match or can be made to match by removing only isolated differences. Blocks identified as matchable are made available for single bit plane transmission as required to achieve the selected data rate. A 4 × 4 difference bit plane is generated for each of the three frames as follows: for each frame bit plane a pixel location in its difference bit plane is set equal to 1 if and only if the corresponding BTC bit is the complement of both of the corresponding BTC bits in other two frames. This procedure not only identifies the spatial locations at which BTC bit differences exist, but also identifies which frame caused the difference. An example of such a set of difference planes is shown in Fig. 5(a). A dif-

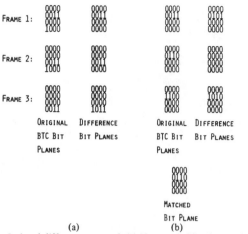

FRAME 1:

FRAME 2:

FRAME 3:

ORIGINAL   DIFFERENCE   ORIGINAL   DIFFERENCE
BTC BIT   BIT PLANES   BTC BIT   BIT PLANES
PLANES   PLANES

MATCHED
BIT PLANE

(a)   (b)

Fig. 5.   Isolated difference removal. (a) Nonmatchable. (b) Matchable.

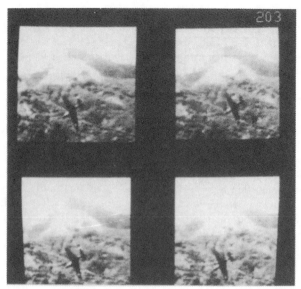

Fig. 6.   (a) Original frame 2. (b)–(d) Mode 1 with no isolated difference removal: (b) Frame 1 (MSE = 50.7). (c) Frame 2 (MSE = 55.2). (d) Frame 3 (MSE = 64.2). Data rate is 1.28 bits/pixel.

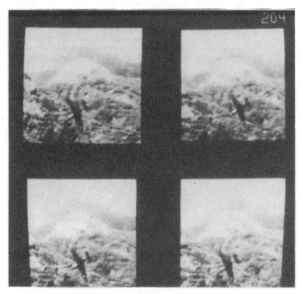

Fig. 7.   (a) Original frame 3. (b)–(d) Mode 1 with 280 matched blocks using isolated difference removal. (b) Frame 1 (MSE = 53.1). (c) Frame 2 (MSE = 58.1). (d) Frame 3 (MSE = 66.9). Data rate is 1.16 bits/pixel.

ference is defined as removable if and only if none of its existing neighbors (horizontal or vertical) in its own plane is a 1. In this example the difference shown at (row, column) location (4, 1) in frame 3's difference plane is removable since both of its existing neighbors are 0. None of the other differences is removable. Since not all of the differences are removable, a 3-D BTC block containing this bit configuration would not be identified as matchable, and the BTC bit planes would not be altered. The opposite situation is presented in Fig. 5(b). In this case all differences are removable, and such a 3-D BTC block would be identified as matchable.

Figs. 6 and 7 exemplify coded registered areas obtained both without the removal of isolated differences and with the removal of isolated differences, respectively. For this group of three frames, 46 blocks match without removing any differences, resulting in a data rate of 1.28 bits/pixel. By removing up to eight isolated differences per block, 280 blocks were identified as matchable, resulting in a data rate of 1.16 bits/ pixel. These data rates are based on Mode 1 operation described later. No substantial differences are observed among the reconstructed images. As ascertainable from Fig. 5, this technique will match (remove intrablock movement) if the movement exists only along a path (or streak) one pixel wide, but it will not match or remove movement if the movement occupies a wider path.

3) Adaptive Mode Selection: A fixed data rate is achieved by adaptively selecting one of the four modes described below for each group of three frames. The transmitter uses the lowest possible mode number for three consecutive frames which can achieve the operator selected data rate. Higher numbered modes achieve more compression by selectively eliminating data. A flow chart for this system's transmitter is given in Fig. 8.

Mode 1: Moving blocks and edge regions are coded using 2-D BTC. Data rate reduction is achieved in the registered area by sending only one 2-D bit plane for 3-D BTC blocks which either match in each of the three frames or can be made to match by removing isolated bit differences using the algorithm described earlier. Isolated bit differences are removed from matchable blocks as required to achieve the operator

selected data rate, starting with those blocks which have the fewest differences. At the receiver the reconstructed frame 2 data plane for matched blocks is repeated three times. All three bit planes are transmitted for remaining matchable blocks, if any, and for nonmatchable blocks.

Mode 2: Further data rate reduction is achieved in this mode by transmitting only one 4 × 4 bit plane (from frame 2) or two 4 × 4 bit planes (from frames 1 and 3) for nonmatchable blocks. Other blocks are coded as in Mode 1. When required to achieve the desired data rate, some nonmatchable blocks are selected for 2-D BTC transmission of frame 2 only.

140

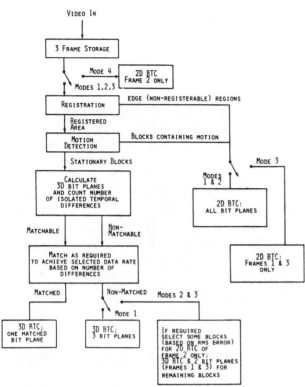

Fig. 8. Transmitter for BTC adaptive mode selection system.

The blocks selected are chosen so as to minimize the maximum rms error in any reconstructed frame 1 or frame 3 block. Two different coding techniques have been studied for the other nonmatchable blocks for which two bit planes are transmitted.

In the first method the transmitter calculates η and σ based only on the data in frames 1 and 3. As the receiver the decoded η and σ values and the two bit planes are used to reconstruct frames 1 and 3 per BTC equations (3) and (4). Frame 2 is obtained by averaging the corresponding reconstructed intensities in frames 1 and 3.

The second method retains intuitively desirable temporal averaging while still preserving the overall mean and variance. The transmitter calculates η and σ using all three data planes, although only two bit planes are transmitted. At the receiver a three-level (0, 1, and $\frac{1}{2}$) averaged bit plane for frame 2 is constructed by averaging the corresponding bit values received for frames 1 and 3. The reconstructed quantizer levels corresponding to 0, 1, and $\frac{1}{2}$ are Y_0, Y_1, and $(Y_0 + Y_1)/2$. It can be shown that η and σ are preserved by calculating Y_0 and Y_1 as follows.

$$Y_0 = \eta - \frac{\sigma(N - p + q)}{\sqrt{(p+q)N - (p-q)^2}} \tag{5}$$

and

$$Y_1 = \eta + \frac{\sigma(N + p - q)}{\sqrt{(p+q)N - (p-q)^2}} \tag{6}$$

where N is the number of pixels per 3-D block (i.e., 48), and p and q are the number of 0's and 1's, respectively, in the reconstructed bit planes. Thus there are $N - (p + q)$ averaged bit values equal to $\frac{1}{2}$.

The averaged bit BTC equations (5) and (6) are easily shown to reduce to (3) and (4) when only 0's and 1's are allowed. In this case $N = p + q$. Substituting this value for N and simplifying gives the desired result.

For a set of 123 frames the averaged reconstruction intensity method consistently resulted in lower MSE for frames 1 and 3, while the average bit BTC method resulted in lower MSE for frame 2. This is generally expected since the former method ignores frame 2's data and concentrates on coding frames 1 and 3. The Mode 2 examples given in Fig. 10 used the averaged bit BTC method. This method is preferred since it treats frame 2 more equitably by using its data in the η-σ calculations.

Mode 3: Only the first and third frames are coded (using 2-D BTC) for moving blocks and edge regions. Matchable stationary blocks are transmitted as in Modes 1 and 2. As in Mode 2, only frame 2's data may be transmitted for selected nonmatchable blocks. For the other nonmatchable blocks 3-D BTC is used for frames 1 and 3 only.

At the receiver frame 2 is obtained by repeating the first reconstructed frame for all block types. For stationary blocks for which two bit planes are received, reconstruction of frames 1 and 3 is accomplished using the standard BTC equations (3) and (4). When only one bit plane is received, frames 1 and 3 are reconstructed by repeating the received frame 2 data.

Mode 4: In this emergency mode only frame 2 is coded for transmission using 2-D BTC. Frame repeating is used at the receiver. No registration information is used. Allowing 20 000 bits for the bit planes, $(10 \times 1250) = 12 500$ bits for η-σ values, and two bits for the mode number, the Mode 4 data rate is

$$(20\,000 + 12\,500 + 2)/60\,000 = 0.54$$

bit/pixel. This represents a lower bound for the data rate achievable using this system.

Data rate selection is accomplished by fixing the number of bits allowed for transmitting each group of three frames. The number of bits required for Mode 1 is calculated based on the matchability criterion described previously. If the number of bits required for Mode 1 exceeds the number available, similar calculations are accomplished for Mode 2 and, if necessary, Modes 3 and 4. In this manner the lowest mode number compatible with the data and selected data rate is chosen.

V. PERFORMANCE

A. In a Noiseless Channel

The various coding schemes described above have been implemented and video tapes have been produced to observe reconstruction quality. Data rates as low as 0.9 bit/pixel have been achieved using the adaptive mode selection system operating in Mode 2 with little visible degradation compared to the original. Modes 1 and 2 are preferred since no significant data are eliminated. Lower data rates are achievable if Mode 3 or

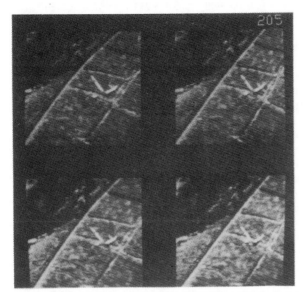

Fig. 9. Original data sequence. Each frame is 100 × 200 pixels. (a) Frame 100. (b) Frame 101. (c) Frame 102. (d) Frame 103.

Mode 4 operation is allowed but image degradation is more noticeable. In all cases motion appears continuous and clear.

Coding reconstruction comparisons are shown in Figs. 9-12. Four sequential original frames are shown in Fig. 9. The results of using the adaptive mode system (Mode 2) at 0.9 bit/pixel (including error protection as described later) on these four frames are shown in Fig. 10. As a comparison, the method of [8] motion-compensated conditional replenishment (MCR) has been implemented, and results on the same originals are shown in Fig. 11. The average data rate is 0.7 bit/pixel, and the peak data rate is 1.29 bits/pixel (for the worst case frame) using optimum entropy coding, but no error protection.

When comparing video sequences from each of these two coding methods, we have found the primary advantage of BTC over MCR coding is the lack of temporal correlation of the coding error over many frames. The conditional replenishment methods such as MCR do not update those pixels which are within some allowed error distance of their predicted values. When the error threshold is high (to allow low data rates) this effect is visible as a stationary low contrast pattern superimposed on the moving image (comparable to viewing the sequence through a "dirty window"). Shown in Fig. 12 is an indication of the difference in techniques. A sequence of two images has been compared pixel by pixel and those pixels which do not match are set to zero. Frames 102 and 103 were used. As seen in Fig. 12, very few points match in the original (due to camera motion), but the motion-compensated scheme produces many matching points that are within error tolerance. BTC, on the other hand, works with blocks consisting of three frames so that the same errors do not continue for more than three consecutive frames. Thus, the error patterns are not correlated over long periods of time and do not exhibit a "dirty window" effect.

B. With Channel Noise

For the BTC systems introduced here, bit errors in the bit plane or coded η-σ values only result in isolated reconstruc-

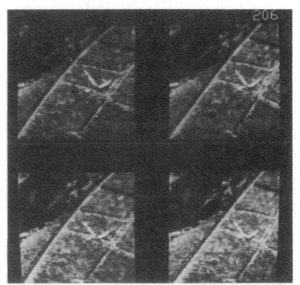

Fig. 10. Reconstruction of BTC adaptive mode system, Mode 2, 0.9 bit/pixel including error protection. Frames 100-102 are in the same coding group. (a) Frame 100 (MSE = 44.1). (b) Frame 101 (MSE = 49.3). (c) Frame 102 (MSE = 47.2). (d) Frame 103 (MSE = 47.4).

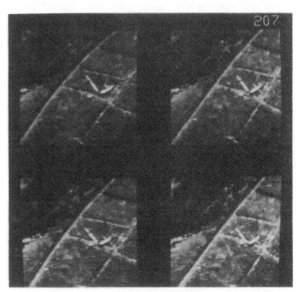

Fig. 11. Reconstruction of motion compensated, conditional replenishment system (MCR) [8], average data rate 0.7 bit/pixel (no error protection), maximum absolute error = 16. (a) Frame 100 (MSE = 50.7). (b) Frame 101 (MSE = 48.1). (c) Frame 102 (MSE = 48.6). (d) Frame 103 (MSE = 48.8).

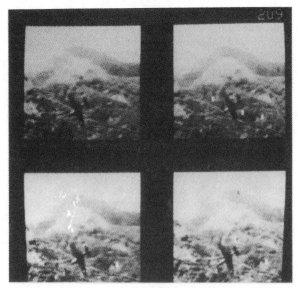

Fig. 12. Matching points between two consecutive frames. Nonmatching points are set to zero. (a) Fig. 9(c) and (d) original data, few matches due to camera motion. (b) Fig. 11(c) and (d), MCR system, many matches due to motion-compensation conditional replenishment method. (c) Fig. 10(b) and (c), BTC adaptive mode system, many matches because frames are within the same coding group. (d) Fig. 10(c) and (d), BTC adaptive mode system, few matches because frames are not in the same coding group.

Fig. 13. Effect of channel errors on BTC fixed 3-D/2-D ratio system. Channel error rate = 10^{-3}. (a) Original data, frame 2. (b) Reconstructed frame 1. (c) Reconstructed frame 2. (d) Reconstructed frame 3.

tion errors. The maximum temporal duration of an error is 0.1 s (three frames at the television rate). Hence, error protection encoding for these bits is unwarranted. For the intraframe 2-D BTC system no error protection is needed since only η-σ and bit planes are transmitted. However, certain critical overhead bits should be error protected in the interframe BTC systems. These include 1284 bits per set of three frames used in the fixed 3-D/2-D block ratio system for 3-D and 2-D block identification and for translation vector encoding. In the adaptive mode system, error protection is appropriate for the 1286 overhead bits required for the mode number, translation vectors, and identification of matchable blocks.

In order to maintain a constant data rate and receiver bit synchronzation, fixed length codes are preferred. For example, using a (127,92) BCH code [14] will reduce an unprotected bit error rate of 10^{-3} to the point where only one in 1.67×10^7 groups of three frames will have incorrectly decoded overhead bits. At the television frame rate this corresponds to 0.1 s of bad frames every 17 days. 14 (127,92) blocks or 1778 bits are required to code 1286 overhead bits for each group of frames. The resulting overall data rate increase is less than 0.01 bit/pixel.

Proper operation of any conditional replenishment system (e.g., MCR) requires that the transmitter and receiver prediction algorithms operate on the same data. If channel noise is permitted to cause errors in the received update information the transmitter will no longer be able to accurately calculate and correct receiver predictions. When DPCM is employed, as is usually the case, errors become cumulative. The problem is further compounded by the use of variable length coding (e.g.,

Huffman coding) required to achieve low data rates. Under these conditions all transmitted bits should be error protected in the presence of channel noise, requiring a substantial increase in the data rates.

The BTC system performs well in the presence of channel noise. Shown in Fig. 13 are three consecutive reconstructed frames when a random channel error rate of $P_E = 10^{-3}$ is present. The most visible errors are errors in the mean of 2-D and 3-D blocks.

VI. CONCLUSIONS

Block truncation coding has been shown to be a simple and effective technique for compression of digitized video image data. The inherent one-bit quantizer tends to enhance edges by preserving dominant intensity variations at the expense of secondary changes which are less perceptible to the human visual system. Moving reconstructed 100 × 200 pixel images coded at data rates as low as 0.9 bit/pixel have shown little distortion and very little loss of resolution compared to the 8 bit/pixel original images. Reconstructed motion is continuous and clear, exhibiting no blurring or other objectionable artifacts present in many high compression video systems. Large translations due to camera movement are reproduced accurately.

Implementation of a simple intraframe BTC system operating at 1.6 bits/pixel requires only four lines of video storage and produces a fixed data length code over each block. The transmitter need only calculate a sample mean and sample standard deviation, use a table lookup for the two-dimensional quantizer, and threshold the image block at the sample mean to produce the bit plane. This can be done at TV data rates with appropriate hardware. Operator selected data rates of 0.6–

1.6 bits/pixel can be achieved using interframe BTC systems requiring three frames of random access memory, buffering memory, and various one-bit frame memories for registration, differencing, and moving area detection. Such a system is most suitable presently for low frame rate video transmission. The registration algorithm and the block segmented nature of BTC allow implementation using parallel architectures.

The interframe BTC systems produce a fixed length code over each set of three frames. This can be useful in receiver synchronization and video editing. Very few bits are control bits which require channel error protection. Error protection of these bits results in less than a 0.01 bit/pixel increase in the overall data rate. Channel errors in the unprotected bits only result in spatially isolated reconstruction errors with maximum duration of three frames. Even the effects of errors in the protected control bits last only three frames.

Bandwidth compression for digitized video data using the BTC techniques described here seems quite practical. The large degree of parallel processing possible enhances the attractiveness of these systems for real-time sequential image coding. Robust performance of 0.9 bit/pixel over noisy channels has been demonstrated.

REFERENCES

[1] F. W. Mounts, "Low resolution TV: An experimental digital system for evaluating bandwidth-reduction techniques," *Bell Syst. Tech. J.*, vol. 46, pp. 167–198, Jan. 1967.

[2] B. G. Haskell, F. W. Mounts, and J. C. Candy, "Interframe coding of videotelephone pictures," *Proc. IEEE*, vol.60, pp. 792–800, July 1972.

[3] H. G. Musmann and J. Klie, "TV-transmission using a 64 kbits/s transmission rate," in *Proc. Int. Conf. Commun.*, Boston, MA, June 10–13, 1979, vol. 2, pp. 23.3.1–23.3.5.

[4] R. Lippmann, "Techniques of DPCM picture coding for RPV TV," in *Proc. Int. Conf. Commun.*, Boston, MA, June 10–13, 1979, vol. 3, pp. 52.4.1–52.4.5.

[5] B. G. Haskell, "Differential addressing of clusters of changed picture elements for interframe coding of videotelephone signals," *IEEE Trans. Commun.*, vol. COM-24, pp. 140–144, Jan. 1976.

[6] A. N. Netravali and J. A. Stuller, "Motion-compensated transform coding," *Bell Syst. Tech. J.*, vol. 58, pp. 1703–1718, Sept. 1979.

[7] A. N. Netravali and J. D. Robbins, "Motion-compensated television coding: Part I," *Bell Syst. Tech. J.*, vol. 58, pp. 631–670, Mar. 1979.

[8] J. D. Robbins and A. N. Netravali, "Interframe television coding using movement compensation," in *Proc. Int. Conf. Commun.*, Boston, MA, June 10–13, 1979, vol. 2, pp. 23.4.1–23.4.5.

[9] J. A. Stuller and A. N. Netravali, "Transform domain motion estimation," *Bell Syst. Tech. J.*, vol. 58, pp. 1673–1702, Sept. 1979.

[10] O. R. Mitchell, E. J. Delp, and S. G. Carlton, "Block truncation coding: A new approach to image compression," in *Proc. Int. Conf. Commun.*, Toronto, Ont., Canada, June 1978, pp. 12B.1.1–12B.1.4.

[11] E. J. Delp, "Moment preserving quantization and its application in block truncation coding," Ph.D. dissertation, School Elec. Eng., Purdue Univ., West Lafayette, IN, Aug. 1979.

[12] E. J. Delp and O. R. Mitchell, "Image compression using block truncation coding," *IEEE Trans. Commun.*, vol. COM-27, Sept. 1979.

[13] A. P. Reeves and A. Rostampour, "Computation cost of image registration with a parallel binary array processor," *IEEE Trans. Pattern Anal. Machine Intell.*, to be published.

[14] S. Lin, *An Introduction to Error-Correcting Codes*. Englewood Cliffs, NJ: Prentice-Hall, 1970, ch. 6.

Chapter 5
Appreciable Advances

In this chapter we present four papers selected to represent advancements of the field over the years. However, the selection is weighted more toward recent contributions as it encompasses the earlier ones in a conceptual sense. Furthermore, it is indicative of the spurt in activity that occurred in this area around 1991. The first one, published in 1983 by Arce and Gallagher [**B20**], looked at the BTC area from an interestingly different and unique perspective. The second selection on hierarchical block truncation coding, published in 1990 by Nasrabadi et al. [**B39**], is representative of a series of efforts [B46, B47] centered around the concept of adaptive coding using quadtrees. The third, by Nasiopoulos et al. [**B53**], which appeared in 1991 (but was submitted for publication much earlier than other related efforts) is also aimed towards development of adaptive coding schemes. However, its adaptability involves more than just quadtrees, which is just one component thereof. The last one in this set is by the founders of this field, Delp and Mitchell, who, also in 1991, presented [**B56**] a broad generalization of the BTC approach.

Chapter 5 Reprints

[**B20**] G.R. Arce and N.C. Gallagher, Jr., "BTC Image Coding Using Median Filter Roots," *IEEE Trans. Comm.*, Vol. COM-31, No. 6, pp. 784–793, June 1983.

[**B39**] N.M. Nasrabadi et al., "Hierarchical Block Truncation Coding of Digital HDTV Images," *IEEE Trans. Consumer Electronics*, Vol. 36, No. 3, pp. 254–261, Aug. 1990.

[**B53**] P. Nasiopoulos, R.K. Ward, and D.J. Morse, "Adaptive Compression Coding," *IEEE Trans. Comm.*, Vol. COM-39, No. 8, pp. 1245–1254, Aug. 1991.

[**B56**] E.J. Delp and O.R. Mitchell, "Moment Preserving Quantization," *IEEE Trans. Comm.*, Vol. COM-39, No. 11, pp. 1549–1558, Nov. 1991.

BTC Image Coding Using Median Filter Roots

GONZALO R. ARCE, MEMBER, IEEE, AND NEAL C. GALLAGHER, JR., MEMBER, IEEE

Abstract—In this paper we source encode the truncated block used in block truncation coding. It is shown that the truncated block is well approximated by wide-sense Markoff statistics; a signal having these characteristics has a high probability of belonging to the root signal set of median filters. Because the root signal space is much smaller than the binary space, it takes fewer bits to specify the truncated block in the root signal space, obtaining in this manner rate compression. Using two-dimensional filtering we can reduce the standard BTC rate of 1.63 bits/pel to 1.31 bits/pel. Using one-dimensional filtering along with a trellis encoder, rates close to 1.1 bits/pel are obtained with this fixed-length coding method.

I. INTRODUCTION

BLOCK truncation coding is a coding method that has been proposed by Delp and Mitchell for coding images in the spatial domain [1]. Its performance and simplicity make this coding method very attractive for real-time image transmission. The bit rate attainable with standard BTC is about 1.63 bits/pel for intraframe coding. In many applications such as real-time moving imagery, transmission rates of about 1 bit/ pixel are desired. Unfortunately, the simple BTC algorithm does not attain such rates with reasonably small distortion. Researchers have used interframe systems to reduce the rate, but at the same time have added complexity to the original simple technique method [2]. In this analysis, we develop a simple fixed-length coding method that uses the statistical properties of the BTC imagery to reduce the bit rate.

The BTC algorithm is simple; the image is divided into non-overlapping blocks of 4 by 4 pels. Each block is quantized into two levels (1 bit/pel); the levels are chosen to preserve the first two moments of the block. The block is transmitted as a binary plane along with information on the mean and the standard deviation of the block. A two-dimensional quantizer is used to simultaneously code the mean and the standard deviation using 10 bits per block. The criterion used for the design of the two-dimensional quantizer is that the grey level quantization error is more pronounced in low variance regions [1]. At the receiver, the samples which have a value above the threshold are set to

$$b = \eta + \sigma \sqrt{\frac{k-q}{q}} \tag{1}$$

and the samples lying below the threshold are set to

$$a = \eta - \sigma \sqrt{\frac{q}{k-q}} \tag{2}$$

where η and σ denote the mean and the standard deviation of the block, respectively, k is 16 (total number of samples), and q is the number of samples lying above the threshold level. The process is illustrated in Fig. 1(a)-(c), where the original block, the bit plane, and the reconstructed block are shown, respectively. There are many variations on this basic algorithm that in some cases yield better performance. Some modifications preserve three moments instead of just two. In some cases by preserving the nth and the $2n$th sample moments, an improved performance can be obtained in a mean square absolute sense, for some positive integer n [3]. The truncation process is just a hard limiter shown in Fig. 2. In general, image signals are modeled as having exponential correlations of the form

$$R(\Delta x, \Delta y) = e^{-\alpha|\Delta x| - \beta|\Delta y|}$$

where Δx and Δy are the distances between the pels, in the x and y direction. Since here we only discuss one-dimensional filtering, the input signal to the hard limiter has an autocorrelation of the form

$$R(\Delta x) = e^{-\alpha|\Delta x|} \tag{3}$$

where α ranges between 0.05 and 0.3, depending on the image characteristics.

If we let the input image be a continuous Gaussian random process with correlation as shown in (3), the correlation of the truncated signal can be shown to be [4]

$$R_{yy}(\Delta x) = \frac{2}{\pi} \sin^{-1}(e^{-\alpha|\Delta x|}). \tag{4}$$

We see that the bit plane retains some correlation. Let us gain

Paper approved by the Editor for Signal Processing and Communication Electronics of the IEEE Communications Society for publication after presentation in part at the 19th Annual Allerton Conference on Communication, Control, and Computing, Monticello, IL, October 1981. Manuscript received July 30, 1982. This work was supported by the National Science Foundation under Grant ECS 8024302.

G. R. Arce was with the Department of Electrical Engineering, Purdue University, West Lafayette, IN 47907. He is now with the Department of Electrical Engineering, University of Delaware, Newark, DE 19711.

N. C. Gallagher is with the Lawrence Livermore National Laboratory, Livermore, CA 94550, on leave from the Department of Electrical Engineering, Purdue University, West Lafayette, IN 47907.

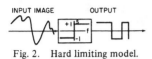

```
10 10 11 12        1 1 1 1        12 12 12 12
10  9 12 15        1 0 1 1        12  3 12 12
 3  4 12 15        0 0 1 1         3  3 12 12
 2  4 10 15        0 0 1 1         3  3 12 12
     (a)             (b)              (c)
```

Fig. 1.   Truncating process: $\eta = 9.6$, $\sigma = 4.2$, $q = 11$, $a = 3$, and $b = 12$. (a) Original block. (b) Truncated block. (c) Reconstructed.

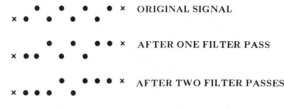

Fig. 2.   Hard limiting model.

some intuition in the truncating process. From (4) we obtain

$$e^{-\alpha|\Delta x|} = \frac{\pi}{2} R_{yy}(\Delta x) - \frac{\left[\dfrac{\pi}{2} R_{yy}(\Delta x)\right]^3}{3!} + \frac{\left[\dfrac{\pi}{2} R_{yy}(\Delta x)\right]^5}{5!} - \cdots.$$

Since R_{yy} is bounded by one, we can approximate the series by

$$e^{-\alpha|\Delta x|} \cong \frac{\pi}{2} R_{yy}(\Delta x) - \frac{\left[\dfrac{\pi}{2} R_{yy}(\Delta x)\right]^3}{3!}.$$

For Δx large, we see that the output autocorrelation is just the input autocorrelation scaled by $2/\pi$. From (3) and (4) we find

$$\frac{R_{yy}'(\Delta x)}{R_{xx}'(\Delta x)} = \frac{2}{\pi\sqrt{1 - e^{-2\alpha|\Delta x|}}} \quad \text{for } |\Delta x| > 0;$$

hence, for small Δx the output autocorrelation decays much faster than the input autocorrelation. This tells us that most of the redundancy in the bit plane is among very close neighbors. In fact, it is this correlation that we remove in this coding scheme. Since each binary block has to be sent separately, we cannot use run length coding [5] or any other standard scheme to encode the bit plane; instead we use median filters.

Median filtering is a very simple nonlinear digital operation. Briefly, we slide across the entire signal a window that spans three sample points. At each point, we compute the median of the three adjacent samples spanned by the window, and replace the center sample by the calculated median. To account for startup and end effects at the two endpoints of the signal, a sample is appended to the beginning and end of the signal. The values of the appended samples are equal to the first and last sample values of the signal, respectively. This filter has the property that if a signal is repeatedly median filtered, the output after each filter pass converges to a signal invariant to further median filtering. The signal set invariant to the filter is called "*the root signal set.*" A description of this signal can be found in [6]; for our purposes it is enough

to mention that this set is much smaller than the binary space; moreover, the root signals are constrained to be locally monotone. The next example will illustrate the one-dimensional median filtering process, where the x's denote the appended samples.

Example 1:

```
      •   •   •   •  ×   ORIGINAL SIGNAL
 ×  •   •   •   •

          •   •   •  ×   AFTER ONE FILTER PASS
 ×  • •   •   •

          •   •  •  ×    AFTER TWO FILTER PASSES
 ×  •  •   •

              •  •  •  ×  AFTER THREE FILTER PASSES
 ×  •  •  •              (ROOT SIGNAL)
```

The number of binary root signals R_n for a filter of window size 3 and signal length n is related to the Fibonacci sequence (f_n) by

$$R_n = 2f_{n+1} \qquad n \geq 1,$$

where

$$f_n = \frac{1}{\sqrt{5}}\left[\left(\frac{1 + \sqrt{5}}{2}\right)^n - \left(\frac{1 - \sqrt{5}}{2}\right)^n\right].$$

Hence, for a row of the block, $n = 4$ and $R_4 = 10$.

II. ROOT CODING

The plan is to median filter the truncated block into a root signal and, instead of transmitting the block in the binary domain, send a code specifying the root. Signals in the bit plane are modeled as hard-limited Gaussian signals; as such, they are approximated as wide-sense Markovian. Thus, it is shown that the block signals have a very high probability of belonging to the root signal set. Since the root signal set is smaller than the general binary space, we need fewer bits to represent a block in the root domain; hence, we obtain compression. In the process of median filtering the bit plane, we have the option of filtering the block in two dimensions (obtain a single root for the entire block), or of filtering in one dimension (obtain one root for each row of the block). The next example shows the one-dimensional filtering process for the block shown in Fig. 1.

Example 2:

```
1 1 1 1        1 1 1 1        12 12 12 12
1 0 1 1        1 1 1 1        12 12 12 12
0 0 1 1        0 0 1 1         3  3 12 12
0 0 1 1        0 0 1 1         3  3 12 12

 BTC Block    Filtered Block    Reconstructed
```

The tree structure of the two-dimensional root signal set is very complicated; here we will present two-dimensional results for illustration purposes only. First, let us describe the one-dimensional process. Each row of the block consists of four bits; with conventional BTC, we need 16 bits to

147

Fig. 3. PCM and 2D root coded (top: L, R): BTC and 1-D root coded (bottom: L, R) at 8, 1.3, 1.6, and 1.3 bits/pel, respectively.

specify the bit plane. Using our root space along with the statistical nature of the bit plane, we only require 12 bits (3 bits to specify the eight possible roots of each row), reducing the bit rate in this way from 1.63 to 1.31 bits/pel. It can be shown that only one filter pass is required to reduce the input row to a root signal. Using two-dimensional filtering, we require about 13 bits to represent the block; this number is obtained by building a tree structure for the two-dimensional root signal space and finding the number of roots for a 4 × 4 signal. Fig. 3 shows the PCM figure, the two-dimensional root coded picture, the conventional BTC, and the one-dimensional root coded picture (top: left, right; bottom: left, right, respectively).[1]

III. MATHEMATICAL MODEL FOR THE TRUNCATION PROCESS

In order to evaluate this coding method, we must look analytically and experimentally at the distortion introduced by this process. The first part of the analysis is the modeling of the one-dimensional filtering of the image. Referring back to Fig. 2 we observe that the occurrence probability distribution for each of the signals in the bit plane is closely related to the distribution of the duration of excursions of Gaussian

[1] The original in this coding analysis is the conventional BTC image.

fluctuations. Rice [7] derives an approximate probability density of having an upper excursion of length τ, given that the excursion started at the origin. For such a distribution, the expected number of zero crossings in a finite interval is proportional to

$$\frac{1}{\pi} \left(-\frac{\psi''(0)}{\psi(0)} \right)^{1/2}$$

where $\psi(\tau) = R(\tau)$ is the autocorrelation function. Since

$$\psi_0'' = \frac{\partial^2 e^{-\alpha|\tau|}}{\partial \tau^2} \to \infty \qquad \text{as } \tau \to 0,$$

the expected number of crossings becomes unbounded. This shows that we cannot treat the input image as a continuous signal, but as a discrete random process. Denote the input image samples by $\{f_n, f_{n+1}, f_{n+2}, f_{n+3}\}$ and their truncated binary versions by $\{s_n, s_{n+1}, s_{n+2}, s_{n+3}\}$ (row of the truncated block). Let the four input image samples be jointly normal. Obtaining the occurrence probability for the root signal set amounts to integrating the 4-variate normal distribution within the limits specified by the root sequence. A simpler model is obtained by only considering the correlation among neighbors in the input signal. With this approximation, the binary plane can be described approximately by a first-order Markoff process [8]. Consider the occurrence probability of a sample row "0011." For the Markoff model, we can write

$$\Pr\left(s_{n+3} = 0, s_{n+2} = 0, s_{n+1} = 1, s_n = 1\right)$$

$$= \Pr\left(s_{n+3} = 0 \,|\, s_{n+2} = 0\right) \Pr\left(s_{n+2} = 0 \,|\, s_{n+1} = 1\right)$$

$$\times \Pr\left(s_{n+1} = 1 \,|\, s_n = 1\right) \Pr\left(s_n = 1\right) \qquad (5)$$

where again $\{s_n, s_{n+1}, s_{n+2}, s_{n+3}\}$ are the samples in a row of the truncated block. In order to obtain the probability of occurrence of any signal in the plane, we only need the transition probabilities. Denote the probability of a change of bit value between two consecutive pels as

$$P_1 = \Pr\left(s_{n+1} = 0 \,|\, s_n = 1\right) = \Pr\left(s_{n+1} = 1 \,|\, s_n = 0\right)$$

and

$$P_0 = 1 - P_1$$

the probability of a sequence of two equal valued bits. Following the Markoff model, and letting the random variables f_n and f_{n+1} be jointly normal with correlation coefficient ρ, then P_1 is the area spanned by the bivariate normal density in the second and fourth quadrant. In this case

$$\rho = e^{-\alpha}; \quad \beta = \cos^{-1}\rho.$$

Then it is simple to show that

$$P_1 = \frac{\beta}{\pi}, \quad \text{and} \quad P_0 = 1 - \frac{\beta}{\pi}. \qquad (6)$$

Table I shows each root sequence along with its probability of occurrence. As an illustration for $\alpha = 0.15$, $\Pr\left(\text{row} \in \text{root}\right) = 0.81$ and $\Pr\left(\text{row} \notin \text{root}\right) = 2P_1^2 P_0 = 0.19$. The analytical results are in agreement with the experimental probabilities that we have computed. Table I also shows the theoretical values and the experimental values for each probability occurrence.

IV. DISTORTION ANALYSIS

By selecting different subsets within the root signal set, we can obtain higher data compression at a cost of higher probability of distortion. In order to evaluate the different subsets, we will locate them in a rate distortion plane along with optimum upper and lower bound functions. To calculate the rate distortion function, we require the knowledge of the bit plane autocorrelation; a derivation of it is in order.

As before, we model the bit plane as a Markoff process. For mathematical simplicity define a random variable x such that

$$x_n = \begin{cases} 1 & \text{if } s_n = 1 \\ 0 & \text{if } s_n = 0. \end{cases}$$

TABLE I
PROBABILITY DISTRIBUTION FOR THE ROOT SPACE

Root #	Sequence	Pr(root/α)	Pr(root/α = 0.2)	Pr(root/Fig. 5.7)
1	0000	$1/2\,P_0^3$	0.256	0.20
2	0001	$1/2\,P_0^2\,P_1$	0.064	0.08
3	0011	$1/2\,P_0^2\,P_1$	0.064	0.11
4	0110	$1/2\,P_0\,P_1^2$	0.015	0.02
5	0111	$1/2\,P_0^2\,P_1$	0.064	0.07
6	1000	$1/2\,P_0^2\,P_1$	0.064	0.09
7	1001	$1/2\,P_0\,P_1^2$	0.015	0.02
8	1100	$1/2\,P_0^2\,P_1$	0.064	0.12
9	1110	$1/2\,P_0^2\,P_1$	0.064	0.09
10	1111	$1/2\,P_0^3$	0.256	0.20

Next, define a two-state Markoff space, where the state is the value of x

state 0: $x_n = 0$

state 1: $x_n = 1$.

The symmetric Markoff transition matrix is

$$P = \begin{bmatrix} P_0 & P_1 \\ P_1 & P_0 \end{bmatrix}$$

where P_0 and P_1 are given in (6). The k-step transition probability matrix is given by

$$P^k = \frac{1}{2} \begin{bmatrix} \lambda_1^{\,k} + \lambda_2^{\,k} & \lambda_1^{\,k} - \lambda_2^{\,k} \\ \lambda_1^{\,k} - \lambda_2^{\,k} & \lambda_1^{\,k} + \lambda_2^{\,k} \end{bmatrix}$$

where

$$\lambda_1 = P_0 + P_1 \quad \text{and} \quad \lambda_2 = P_0 - P_1$$

are the eigenvalues of P. Denote the probability of a bit having a value of zero in the truncated block by Q_0, and the probability of it being one by Q_1. The autocorrelation of the truncated block is

$$E(x_i x_j) = \Pr\left(x_i = 1, x_j = 1\right).$$

In terms of the eigenvalues, the above expression becomes

$$E(x_i x_j) = Q_1\left(\lambda_1^{\,|j-i|} + \lambda_2^{\,|j-i|}\right) = R(i, j). \qquad (7)$$

Since the threshold of the truncation is the mean of the block and the input distribution about the mean is symmetric, $Q_0 =$

$\frac{1}{2}$. The autocorrelation is then simplified to

$$R(i,j) = \tfrac{1}{2}(P_0 + P_1)^{|j-i|} + \tfrac{1}{2}(P_0 - P_1)^{|j-i|}. \qquad (8)$$

For sources with memory, the rate distortion function $R(D)$ is known exactly for only a few special cases. On the other hand, bounds to $R(D)$ are simple to calculate for stationary and ergodic sources.

Define the square error distortion measure as

$$d(x_i - x_f) = \sum (x_i - x_f)^2 \qquad (9)$$

where x_i and x_f are the input and filtered samples of the block, respectively. Notice that for this process the square and difference distortion measures are the same. Then, for any discrete zero mean source with spectral density $\Phi(\omega)$ and squared error distortion measure, the rate distortion upper bound becomes [9]

$$R_{UB}(D) \leqslant \frac{1}{4\pi} \int_{-\pi}^{\pi} \max\left[0, \log \frac{\Phi(\omega)}{\Theta}\right] d\omega \qquad (10)$$

where Θ satisfies

$$D = \frac{1}{2\pi} \int_{-\pi}^{\pi} \min\left[\Theta, \Phi(\omega)\right] d\omega$$

where

$$\Phi(\omega) = \sum_{k=-\infty}^{\infty} \phi_k e^{-ik\omega}$$

and

$$\phi_k = E(x_i, x_{i+k}).$$

In this case,

$$\phi_k = \tfrac{1}{2}(\lambda_1{}^k + \lambda_2{}^k)$$

and

$$\Phi(\omega) = \sum_{k=-\infty}^{\infty} \tfrac{1}{2}(\lambda_1{}^k + \lambda_2{}^k) e^{-ik\omega}.$$

Simplifying $\Phi(\omega)$ we get

$$\Phi(\omega) = \frac{1}{2}\left[\frac{1 - \lambda_2{}^2}{1 - 2\lambda_2 \cos\omega + \lambda_2{}^2}\right]$$

$$+ \frac{1}{2}\left[\frac{1 - \lambda_1{}^2}{1 - 2\lambda_1 \cos\omega + \lambda_1{}^2}\right] \qquad (11)$$

for

$$\Theta < \frac{1}{2}\left[\frac{1 - \lambda_2}{1 + \lambda_2} + \frac{1 - \lambda_1}{1 + \lambda_1}\right], \qquad \Theta = D.$$

Placing (11) into (10), the rate distortion upper bound is obtained:

$$R_{UB}(D) = \frac{1}{4\pi} \int_{-\pi}^{\pi} \log\left[\frac{1}{2D}\left(\frac{1 - \lambda_2{}^2}{1 - 2\lambda_2 \cos\omega + \lambda_2{}^2}\right.\right.$$

$$\left.\left. + \frac{1 - \lambda_1{}^2}{1 - 2\lambda_1 \cos\omega + \lambda_1{}^2}\right)\right] d\omega$$

$$\text{for } 0 < D < \frac{1}{2}\left[\frac{1 - \lambda_2}{1 + \lambda_2}\right].$$

Evaluating the above integral we obtain

$$R_{UB}(D) = \frac{1}{2}\log_2\left(\frac{1 - \lambda_2{}^2}{2D}\right)$$

$$\text{for } 0 < D < \frac{1}{2}\left[\frac{1 - \lambda_2}{1 + \lambda_2}\right].$$

Now we obtain the lower bound. Recall that our process is generated by a Markov source with the transition matrix shown below:

$$P = \begin{bmatrix} P_0 & P_1 \\ P_1 & P_0 \end{bmatrix}.$$

For a symmetric first-order two-state Markov source with a transition matrix shown above, the lower rate distortion bound for a difference distortion measure is [10]

$$R_{LB}(D) = h(P_1) - h(D)$$

where $h(x) = -x \log_2 x - (1-x) \log_2 (1-x)$. Furthermore, $R_{LB}(D) = R(D)$ for $0 < D < D_c$, where

$$D_c = \frac{1}{2} - \frac{1}{2}\sqrt{1 - \left[\frac{P_1}{P_0}\right]^2}.$$

Although a square and a difference distortion measure were used to respectively evaluate R_{UB} and R_{LB}, they can be plotted in the same distortion scale since for this process the two measures are the same.

Denote an input sequence to the filter by seq_j, $j = 1, \cdots, 16$. The distortion introduced by the filtering process is

$$D_f = \sum_{\text{seq}_j}\left[\sum_{x_i \in \text{seq}_j} (x_i - x_f)^2\right] P_r(\text{seq}_j) \qquad (12)$$

where the inner term is the distortion measure for the jth sequence and the last term denotes the probability of occurrence for such a jth sequence. Recall that x takes on the values $+1$ and 0. Then, for each bit that is changed by the filtering process, the distortion is 1. Since the sequences that belong to the root signal space introduce no distortion, and by noticing that all the nonroot signals differ from their filtered ver-

TABLE II
CONDITIONAL TRANSITION PROBABILITIES

j	$Pr\left\{\dfrac{\Upsilon_{k+1}^{j}}{\Upsilon_{k}^{2}}\right\}$	Experimental* values
1	0.38	0.22
2	0.32	0.29
3	0.12	0.21
5	0.034	0.08
6	0.034	0.04
8	0.015	0.03
9	0.06	0.09
10	0.06	0.09

*For Fig. 7

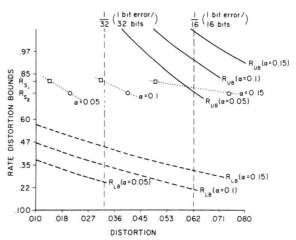

Fig. 4.   Rate distortion plane.

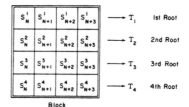

Fig. 5.   Root random variables.

sion by only one bit, (12) can be written as $D_f = P(\text{row} \notin \text{root})$. Referring to Table I, roots 4 and 7 are much less likely to occur than the rest of the root set. If we delete these two roots from the space, we only need 12 bits to encode the bit plane. If the entire root signal space is used, we need about 13.4 bits to encode the plane. Let $S1$ be the entire root signal set, and $S2$ be a subset of $S1$, where we exclude roots 7 and 4. In terms of the Markov transition probabilities, the distortion introduced by the filtering process using sets $S1$ and $S2$ are

$$D_{f1} = (2P_0 P_1{}^2 + P_1{}^3)$$

and

$$D_{f2} = (3P_0 P_1{}^2 + P_1{}^3).$$

Fig. 4 illustrates the optimum bounds R_{LB} and R_{UB} along with the root coding points for the two sets. Regardless of the input source autocorrelation parameter α, the coding rate is fixed at 0.83 bits per bit plane sample for the set $S1$, and 0.75 for $S2$. These two rates are shown on the rate axis as R_{s1} and R_{s2}, respectively. Hence, for a given source autocorrelation parameter α, the root coding rate distortion points, for the sets S_1 and S_2, are shown by a square and a circle. Notice that the coding scheme has good performance when coding highly correlated images since, for the distortion introduced by the scheme, the rate is close to the lower bound. As can be expected for highly uncorrelated sources, the coding rate distortion points will approach the upper bound. Fig. 4 shows that if the image has high correlation, the filtering process will modify the average 1 bit in four entire blocks. If the input image has low correlation the expected distortion is about 1 bit per block (recall there are 16 bits per block).

V. SEQUENTIAL ANALYSIS

In the one-dimensional root coding we have taken advantage of the x axis correlation only. By removing some mutual information in the y axis, we can reduce the bit rate even further. One approach would be to model the source as a two-dimensional Markov process and by an analysis similar to the one-dimensional case, one can remove the x and y image correlation. Here, we avoid that complicated approach and remove y axis redundancy by a sequential root analysis.

Each block is coded by four consecutive roots, where each root has four samples. Each root is treated as a random variable that can take ten possible states (see Fig. 5). The distribution for this random variable was obtained in the previous section. Denote the root class j and the kth root signal of the block by

$$\Upsilon_k{}^j, \qquad \text{where } 1 \leqslant j \leqslant 10, \quad 1 \leqslant k \leqslant 4.$$

As mentioned before, each root signal has four components

$$\Upsilon_k{}^j \equiv (s_n{}^k, s_{n+1}{}^k, s_{n+2}{}^k, s_{n+3}{}^k)$$

where k denotes the root's vertical location within the block, and the lower subscript is the column of the block; Fig. 5 shows the above block description. For instance, the binary root block shown in Example 2 is represented by the sequence $\Upsilon_1{}^1, \Upsilon_2{}^1, \Upsilon_3{}^3, \Upsilon_4{}^3$. The conditional probability of two con-

151

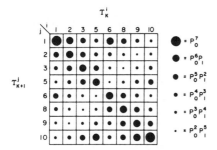

Fig. 6.   Root transition probabilities.

secutive roots in the y direction, given the first one, is

$$\Pr\left(\Upsilon_{k+1}{}^j | \Upsilon_k{}^i\right) = \frac{\Pr\left(\Upsilon_k{}^i | \Upsilon_{k+1}{}^j\right) \Pr\left(\Upsilon_{k+1}{}^j\right)}{\Pr\left(\Upsilon_k{}^i\right)} \qquad (13)$$

where

$$\Pr\left(\Upsilon_k{}^i\right) = \sum_{j=1}^{10} \Pr\left(\Upsilon_k{}^i | \Upsilon_{k+1}{}^j\right) \Pr\left(\Upsilon_{k+1}{}^j\right). \qquad (14)$$

Define the difference measure

$$d_n = |[s_n{}^k - s_n{}^{k+1}]| \quad \text{and} \quad d_T = \sum_{i=n}^{n+3} d_i.$$

Applying the Markoff model in the vertical direction,

$$\Pr\left(\Upsilon_k{}^i | \Upsilon_{k+1}{}^j\right) = P_0{}^{4-d_T} P_1{}^{d_T} \qquad (15)$$

and

$$\Pr\left(\Upsilon_k{}^i, \Upsilon_{k+1}{}^j\right) = [P_0{}^{4-d_T} P_1{}^{d_T}] \Pr\left(\Upsilon_{k+1}{}^j\right). \qquad (16)$$

It is important to note that P_0 and P_1 in (16) are the transition probabilities in the vertical direction. In general, the correlation in the horizontal axis is higher than the correlation in the vertical direction. This is so because of the horizontal sampling process. If we ignore this fact in computing (16), values differing by up to 20 percent of the true transition probabilities can be obtained. The joint probabilities (16) among all values of the root random variable are easily obtained. The experimental and the theoretical values for the transition probabilities from root 2 are shown in Table II. It should be mentioned that diagonal correlation among samples was ignored; therefore, we can expect some variance around the theoretical transition probabilities. Fig. 6 shows joint probability matrix, where all the possible transition probabilities are shown. The probability is proportional to the area of the black dot (i.e., the greater the probability, the greater the area of the dot). Note that there are some very unlikely root transition paths. By restricting certain transition paths, we can reduce the bit rate with a low probability of distortion. This method of encoding is based on a trellis. The trellis will allow all transitions which have high probability of

occurrence. As an example, we will encode an image where only four transitions are allowed. We allow 3 bits to the first row in order to start the state trellis with an exact location, and 2 bits for each transition. The trellis used in the example is specified by the allowed transitions with greater probability of occurrence. In cases where there are two transitions with equal probability that are being considered for the last allowed transition in the trellis, arbitrary selection is done. Fig. 7 shows a BTC coded image and the trellis compressed image, at 16 bits/block and 9 bits/block, respectively.

VI. COMPARISON WITH OTHER TECHNIQUES

The BTC coding method has also been used for coding graphics, which differ from pictures in that they generally have fewer quantization levels and are not real world scenes. In [11] a method to reduce the bit plane data is presented. In the original BTC algorithm, 16 bits are required to represent the block. The method introduced in [11] is based on a look-up table where the bit plane is represented with 8 bits only. For a 32-level picture, the bit rate is reduced from 1.437 to 0.937 bit/pixel, where a two-dimensional quantizer was used to code simultaneously the mean and standard deviation of the block. In this section, we implement a trellis coder that codes the bit plane with 8 bits and then we compare the performance of both methods.

The table look-up is based on the occurrence probability of certain bit plane patterns. Referring to Fig. 8, a set of 8 pels in the 4 by 4 block will specify the value of the other bits in the plane. The value of the circle pels are the ones transmitted, and the value of the other are defined according to the following logical table [11].

$B = 1$ iff $[(A \text{ and } D) = 1]$ or $[(F \text{ and } J) = 1]$

$C = 1$ iff $[(A \text{ and } D) = 1]$ or $[(G \text{ and } K) = 1]$

$E = 1$ iff $[(A \text{ and } M) = 1]$ or $[(F \text{ and } G) = 1]$

$H = 1$ iff $[(D \text{ and } P) = 1]$ or $[(F \text{ and } G) = 1]$

$I = 1$ iff $[(A \text{ and } M) = 1]$ or $[(J \text{ and } K) = 1]$

$L = 1$ iff $[(D \text{ and } P) = 1]$ or $[(J \text{ and } K) = 1]$

$N = 1$ iff $[(M \text{ and } P) = 1]$ or $[(F \text{ and } J) = 1]$

$O = 1$ iff $[(M \text{ and } P) = 1]$ or $[(G \text{ and } K) = 1]$.

The logic behind the table will preserve the edges of the block.

A trellis coder using 8 bits/block was then implemented. Fig. 9 shows the original 32-level pictures which will be coded at the same bit rate. Fig. 10 shows the trellis coded pictures (top left and bottom left) and the table look-up coded pictures (top right and bottom right), all of them at the same bit rate of 0.94 bit/pel. We see by these examples that the trellis code adapts better to the different bit plane patterns of the pictures.

VII. CONCLUSION

A new method of coding block truncated images is presented. The fixed-length intraframe coding method uses the

(a)

(b)

Fig. 7.   (a) Trellis coded image at 1.1 bits/pel. (b) BTC coded image
at 1.6 bits/pel.

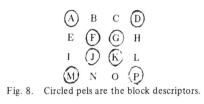

Fig. 8. Circled pels are the block descriptors.

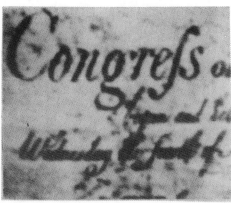

Fig. 9. Original PCM pictures (5 bits/pel).

Fig. 10. Trellis coded (top and bottom: left) and table look-up coded
pictures (top and bottom: right).

statistical properties of BTC imagery along with a simple nonlinear digital filter, namely a median filter. This filter maps the input binary block into a root signal space which is smaller than the binary space. With high probability, the BTC binary block is not distorted. The performance of this coding scheme is evaluated in a rate-distortion plane, showing a good performance for correlated data. In order to use the vertical dependence among image samples, a trellis encoder is used in which we obtain higher data compression at a cost of higher probability of distortion.

REFERENCES

[1] E. J. Delp and O. R. Mitchell, "Image compression using BTC," *IEEE Trans. Commun.*, vol. COM-27, Sept. 1979.
[2] D. Healy and O. R. Mitchell, "Digital video bandwidth compression using BTC," *IEEE Trans. Commun.*, vol. COM-29, Dec. 1981.
[3] D. R. Halverson, N. C. Griswold, and G. L. Wise, "On generalized block truncation coding quantizers for image compression," in *Proc. Inform. Sci. Syst. Conf.*, Princeton, NJ, 1982.
[4] A. Papoulis, *Probability, Random Variables and Stochastic Processes*. New York: McGraw-Hill, 1965.
[5] T. S. Huang, "Coding of two tone images," *IEEE Trans. Commun.*, vol. COM-25, Nov. 1977.
[6] G. R. Arce and N. C. Gallagher, Jr., "State description for the root signal set of median filters," *IEEE Trans. Acoust., Speech, Signal Processing*, vol. ASSP-30, Dec. 1982.
[7] S. O. Rice, "Mathematical analysis of random noise," *Bell Syst. Tech J.*, vols. 23, 24, 1944, 1945.
[8] J. Capon, "A probabilistic model for the runlength coding of pictures," *IRE Trans. Inform. Theory*, vol. IT-5, Dec. 1959.
[9] J. Viterbi and K. Omura, *Principles of Digital Communications and Coding*. New York: McGraw-Hill, 1979.
[10] R. M. Gray, "Rate distortion functions for finite-state finite-alphabet Markov sources," *IEEE Trans. Inform. Theory*, vol. IT-17, Mar. 1971.
[11] O. R. Mitchell and E. J. Delp, "Multilevel graphics representation using block truncation coding," *Proc. IEEE*, vol. 68, July 1980.

HIERARCHICAL BLOCK TRUNCATION CODING OF DIGITAL HDTV IMAGES

Nasser M. Nasrabadi, Chang Y. Choo,
Thomas Harries and Jim Smallcomb
Electrical Engineering Department
Worcester Polytechnic Institute

ABSTRACT

In this paper a source coding technique is presented for compressing HDTV digital images for B-ISDN visual services. The proposed source coding technique is called Hierarchical Block Truncation Coding (HBTC). It is a combination of the Block Truncation Coding technique and a Quadtree segmentation method. The quadtree segmentation is used to decompose an image into homogeneous regions so that the BTC method can exploit the non-stationarity of the image data. Bit rates around 1.46 bits/pixel is achieved with this method. Experimental results for several HDTV images are presented.

I. INTRODUCTION

Introduction of broadband integrated service digital network (B-ISDN) with its wide bandwidth capability will make visual communications services feasible in future communication networks. Digital transmission of High Definition TV pictures and graphics is an important aspect of the B-ISDN video services which will broaden the application of the current visual services. However, the main problem in digital transmission of high quality images is the huge bandwidth requirement. In this paper a simple source coding technique is introduced to compress digital HDTV images for transmission systems (CCITT H4-Level [1]) having bandwidth around 140 Mbits/sec.

The aim of this paper is to investigate the application of BTC technique for encoding HDTV images and introduce a Hierarchical Block Truncation Coding (HBTC) method which is very suitable for encoding high resolution HDTV images. Block Truncation Coding (BTC) technique was introduced by Delp and Mitchell [2-3] as a simple source coding method to achieve good quality image reproduction by preserving the first two statistical moments of an image, the mean and the variance. The method significantly reduces the amount of computation required by more traditional coding methods, such as transform or hybrid coding, yet it still produces an acceptable quality of reproduction. BTC retains the sharp edges in an image without blurring, although some edges may appear ragged in the reconstruction.

The bit rate achieved by BTC, however, is not as low as the rates for conventional transform coders [4]. The bit rate can be reduced further by exploiting the non-stationary characteristics typical of digital images. Because the original BTC algorithm uniformly partitions the image into small blocks of equal size, it fails to exploit the local characteristics of the image data. A non-uniform partitioning would be a more efficient method to exploit these characteristics by forming large regions in areas of high pixel correlation, and smaller regions where there is little correlation.

This paper introduces a new BTC method where a uniform quadtree decomposition technique is used to segment the image data into different regions such that there is very little correlation between the regions. Since the blocks are not of uniform size, the number of bits required to encode all of the blocks is less than that required by the conventional BTC method.

Section II describes the Block Truncation Coding method and some of its variations which have been explored in the past. Section III reviews the quadtree segmentation technique. Section IV explains the proposed Hierarchical Block Truncation Coding (HBTC) method using quadtree segmentation and its application to high resolution HDTV images. Section V discusses the experimental results of HBTC in comparison with the conventional BTC encoder. Finally, section VI summarizes our conclusions.

II. BLOCK TRUNCATION CODING

The conventional BTC algorithm subdivides an image into uniform blocks, typically 4×4 pixels in size. For each block, the mean (μ) and the standard deviation (σ) are computed, and a bit plane pattern is created. The bit plane results from a two-level quantization of the block, where pixels with values greater than or equal to the block mean are represented by 1 and pixels with values less than the block mean are represented by 0. The image is reconstructed by computing two values for each block, based on the encoded moments of that block. One value (a) is assigned to the 0-valued pixels in the bit plane, the other (b) is assigned to the 1-valued pixels. The reconstruction values are given by:

$$a = \mu - \sigma \sqrt{q/(n-q)}, \qquad (1a)$$

$$b = \mu + \sigma \sqrt{(n-q)/q}, \qquad (1b)$$

where n is the number of pixels in the block, and q is the number of pixels greater than or equal to the block mean threshold. Figure 1 demonstrates the BTC process for a sample 4×4 block.

Joint quantization of the mean and the standard deviation produces a better reconstruction than separate quantization into the same number of bits. Table 1 shows a typical 10 bit quantization scheme by Healy and Mitchell [5] for a 256 grey level image. The standard deviation of each block is quantized to the nearest value given in the table and the mean grey level of that block is quantized according to the

number of levels designated for that σ. This method is superior to separately quantizing the mean with a 6 bit quantizer and the standard deviation with a 4 bit quantizer. The quantizer's divisions are based on the observation that errors in grey level quantization are most noticeable in areas with the lowest variance [2-3]. With this 10 bit quantizer and uniform blocks of 4×4 pixels, the BTC algorithm provides a constant bit rate of 1.625 bits per pixel.

$$
\begin{array}{cccc}
2 & 9 & 12 & 15 \\
2 & 11 & 11 & 9 \\
2 & 3 & 12 & 15 \\
3 & 3 & 4 & 14 \\
\end{array}
\qquad
\begin{array}{l}
m = 7.94 \\
s = 4.91
\end{array}
$$

(a) original block

$$
\begin{array}{cccc}
0 & 1 & 1 & 1 \\
0 & 1 & 1 & 1 \\
0 & 0 & 1 & 1 \\
0 & 0 & 0 & 1 \\
\end{array}
\qquad q = 9
$$

(b) bit plane

$$
\begin{array}{cccc}
2 & 12 & 12 & 12 \\
2 & 12 & 12 & 12 \\
2 & 2 & 12 & 12 \\
2 & 2 & 2 & 12 \\
\end{array}
\qquad
\begin{array}{l}
a = 2.3 \\
b = 12.3
\end{array}
$$

(c) reconstructed block

Figure 1. Illustration of Block Truncation Coding

Table 1. Simultaneous Mean-Standard Deviation Quantizer using 10 Bits

standard deviation	number of uniformly distributed mean values
0	256
1, 2, 4	128
6, 8, 13, 19, 28	64
42, 56	32

Halverson, Griswold, and Wise [6] developed a generalized BTC algorithm which preserves the nth and $2n^{th}$ moments of each local block. That is, while the original method preserves the first and second moments of each block, the generalized version can preserve the second and fourth moments, or the third and sixth moments, etc. While these alternative moment pairs can maintain, or even improve, image

157

quality, the use of very high moments is not recommended because of quantization overflow problems which reduce image quality.

Lema and Mitchell [7] proposed a minimal computational variation of the BTC technique which preserves the first absolute central moment in place of the standard deviation. This change eliminates the need to find square roots and simplifies the reconstruction value equations. The resulting images are comparable, if not superior, to those encoded with the standard deviation. Absolute moment BTC (AMBTC) is recommended for applications in which minimizing computational time is crucial. Lema and Mitchell also applied AMBTC to color images, separately encoding each of the Y, I, and Q planes, and obtaining bit rates as low as 2.13 bpp.

Healy and Mitchell applied BTC to moving images in [5]. They extended the BTC technique to 3 dimensions by encoding blocks of 4×4 pixels by 3 frames deep. Edges of motion are more accurately reproduced by encoding them as 2 dimensional blocks, so this method requires the identification and registration of the areas of greatest movement within the sequence. The remainder of the image is incorporated into 3-d blocks. The process is very detailed, requires somewhat more memory than conventional BTC, and produces an average bit rate of 0.9 bpp.

Further work on the BTC algorithm has improved the bit rate by encoding the bit plane. Arce and Gallagher [8] used a median filter to smooth the bit plane, thereby reducing the possible combinations of ones and zeros. Those patterns with the highest probability of occurrence are encoded, using fewer bits than the original bit plane requires, and reducing the bit rate to 1.3 bpp. Similarly, Udpikar and Raina [9] vector quantized both the statistical information (equivalent to joint quantization, discussed earlier) and the bit planes to reduce the bit rate to about 1.0 bpp.

III. QUADTREE SEGMENTATION

For HDTV images the bit rate can be reduced further by exploiting the inherent non-stationary characteristics of high resolution digital images. Because the original BTC algorithm uniformly partitions the image into small blocks of equal size, it fails to exploit the local characteristics of the image data. A non-uniform partitioning would be a more efficient method to exploit these characteristics by forming large regions in areas of high pixel correlation, and smaller regions where there is little correlation. This non-uniform segmentation is especially suitable for high resolution HDTV images.

A simple segmentation technique is the quadtree method [10-11] which subdivides a region of an image into four equal blocks if a given criterion is not met by that region. It continues to divide each subdivision until the criterion is met or a minimum block size is reached. Typically, an image is initially divided into a set of large blocks (32 pixels square, for instance). The variance is computed and compared to a threshold for each of these blocks. Any sub-blocks created by failure of the variance test undergo the same procedure, with subdivision continuing until a block either reaches a minimum size or has a variance below the threshold. Each block tested constitutes a node of the quadtree. A node for which no further subdivision is needed is called a leaf, or terminal, node. The tree structure and accompanying encoding for each leaf node are stored or transmitted for later reconstruction. Figure 2 illustrates the procedure.

The structure of the quadtree depends on the inter-pixel correlations of the image that it represents. Areas with the highest correlation, that is, little (uniform) variation, compose the leaf nodes at the lowest levels in the quadtree, which represent the large uniform blocks. These areas are often slowly varying backgrounds behind the image subject. Areas with the most variation (least correlation) fall into the highest levels of the quadtree. Since almost the same information is encoded by the BTC for each block regardless of its size, the largest and the most highly correlated areas require fewer bits per pixel and the smallest areas are encoded at the highest bit rate, in accordance with their more detailed structure.

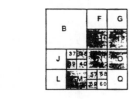

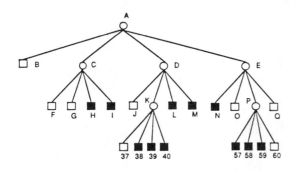

Figure 2. A typical quadtree representation of an image or region.

IV. HIERARCHICAL BLOCK TRUNCATION CODING

We call the application of block truncation coding to the leaf nodes of a quadtree segmented image the Hierarchical Block Truncation Coding (HBTC) method. The image is initially divided into uniform blocks of 32×32 pixels. Quadtree segmentation is performed on each of these blocks; each is checked against a predefined variance threshold, then subdivided until the threshold is not exceeded. The minimum block size is 4×4 pixels. For each terminal node, the mean and the standard deviation are found and are jointly quantized into 10 bits, according to table 1. Next, a bit plane is created, using the block mean as the threshold. The quadtree structure and the encoded information for each leaf node is transmitted or stored for later reconstruction.

HBTC reduces the bit rate from that required by BTC because it exploits the non-stationarity of the image data. Although the overhead of the tree structure is required, the 10-bit statistical quantizer is shared by blocks of different sizes, instead of only 4×4 blocks. The hierarchical approach requires only a little more memory than BTC; 32 lines of an image must be stored at a time.

V. EXPERIMENTAL RESULTS

Performance of the HBTC technique was compared to that of the conventional BTC method on several HDTV images of resolution 1152×1440 by 8 bits/pixel. For example, the original image (Castle) shown in Figure 3 (a) was encoded by an HBTC encoder at a bit rate around 1.444 bpp with a SNR=31.17 dB as shown in Figure 3 (b), a significant reduction when compared with the BTC encoder. Figure 3 (c) shows the same encoded image by BTC at a bit rate of 1.625 bpp with almost the same SNR=31.82 dB. Another HDTV image (Calendar) shown in Figure 4 (a) was encoded by HBTC at 1.434 bpp with a SNR=27.80 dB. The corresponding bit rate with the BTC encoder was 1.625 bpp with a SNR=27.96 dB. Similarly, Figure 5 (a), (b) and (c) represent the original, HBTC and BTC encoded images. Finally Figure 6 (a), (b) and (c) represent the quadtree segmented test images.

Table 2 compares the bit rates and reconstruction quality of of the images encoded in this study. As a measure of quality, the mean squared error (MSE) between the original image and its reconstruction was found. This was also translated into a signal- to-noise ratio (SNR) according to:

$$SNR = -10 \log_{10} \left(\frac{MSE}{255^2} \right) \qquad (2)$$

(where 255 is the maximum possible pixel value). Variance thresholds of 150, 120, and 90 were used for the blocks of size 32×32, 16×16 and 8×8 during the segmentation of these images.

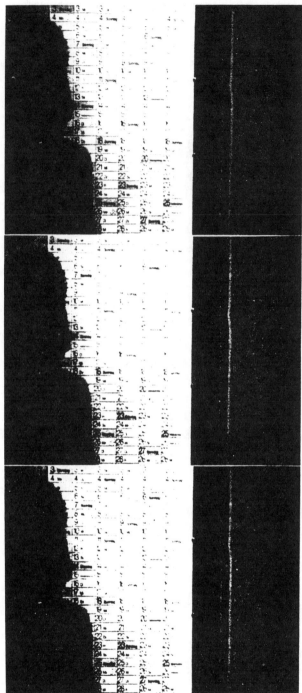

Figure 3. (a) Original HDTV image, and reconstructed images from

(b) HBTC, bit rate = 1.444 bits/pixel, MSE=49.61, SNR=31.17 dB.

(c) BTC, bit rate = 1.625 bits/pixel, MSE=42.74, SNR=31.82 dB.

Figure 4. (a) Original HDTV image, and reconstructed images from

(b) HBTC, bit rate = 1.434 bits/pixel, MSE=107.73, SNR=27.81 dB.

(c) BTC, bit rate = 1.625 bits/pixel, MSE=103.90, SNR=27.96 dB.

Figure 5. (a) Original HDTV image, and reconstructed images from

(b) HBTC, bit rate = 1.447 bits/pixel, MSE=64.74, SNR=30.02 dB.

(c) BTC, bit rate = 1.625 bits/pixel, MSE=56.28, SNR=30.63 dB.

Figure 6. Quadtree segmented HDTV images.

161

Table 2. RESULTS FROM ENCODING STILL IMAGES

Image	Castle	Calendar	Girl
BTC			
BPP	1.625	1.625	1.625
MSE	42.742	103.900	56.277
SNR (dB)	31.822	27.965	30.627
HBTC			
BPP	1.444	1.434	1.447
MSE	49.606	107.730	64.739
SNR (dB)	31.175	27.807	30.019
% area by block size			
32 X 32	17.63	17.75	13.63
16 X 16	9.06	12.41	12.72
8 X 8	15.45	12.93	15.60
4 X 4	57.86	56.91	58.05

A consequence of applying BTC to areas larger than the standard 4×4 disturbing contouring artifacts can be seen in the encoded images. As block size increases, monotonically changing areas are reconstructed with false contours where the division between pixels above and below the block mean occurs. This problem is strongly dependent on the threshold used during segmentation. These artifacts are reduced as the threshold is decreased, but an increase in the bit rate will also occur. A compromise between compression and quality must be made for each image, based on individual image characteristics. One way to correct the false contours would be a post-processing smoother, but it must distinguish between the true and false contours in order to maintain sharpness at the true edges.

VI. CONCLUSIONS

In this paper we have shown that a greater image compression can be achieved by using Hierarchical BTC method, in conjunction with quad-tree segmentation, than by applying BTC to an image with uniform block divisions since the correlation of uniform areas is exploited. This is especially true for appropriate images such as HDTV with large uniform areas. When encoding original images, there is a degradation in image quality which depends on the segmentation threshold. Other coding methods may further reduce the bit rate, but HBTC maintains the simplicity that makes Block Truncation Coding an attractive coding alternative.

REFERENCES

[1] H Gaggioni and D. Le Gall, "Digital Transmission and Coding for the Broadband ISDN," IEEE Trans. on Consumer Electronics, vol. CE-34, no.1, pp. 16-35, Feb. 1988.

[2] E. J. Delp and O. R. Mitchell, "Image Compression using Block Truncation Coding," IEEE Trans. on Communications, vol. COM-27, no.9, pp. 1335-1342, 1979.

[3] O. R. Mitchell and E. J. Delp, "Multilevel Graphics Representation Using Block Truncation Coding," Proc. of the IEEE, vol. 68, no. 7, pp. 868-873, 1980.

[4] W. H. Chen and C. H. Smith, "Adaptive Coding of Monochrome and Color Images," IEEE Trans. Commun., vol. COM-25, pp. 1285-1292, Nov. 1977.

[5] D. J. Healy and O. R. Mitchell, "Digital Video Bandwidth Compression Using Block Truncation Coding," IEEE Trans. on Commun., vol. COM-29, no. 12, PP. 1809-1817, Dec. 1981.

[6] D. R. Halverson, N. C. Griswold, and G. L. Wise, "A Generalized Block Truncation Coding Algorithm for Image Compression," IEEE Trans. on Acoustics, Speech, and Signal Proc., vol. ASSP-32, no. 3, pp. 664-668, 1984.

[7] M. D. Lema and O. R. Mitchell, "Absolute Moment Block Truncation Coding and its Application to Color Images," IEEE Trans. on Commun., vol. COM-32, no. 10, pp. 1148-1157, 1984.

[8] G. R. Arce and N. C. Gallagher, Jr., "BTC Image Coding Using Median Filter Roots," IEEE Trans. on Commun., vol. COM-31, no. 6, pp. 784-793, 1983.

[9] V. R. Udpikar and J. P. Raina, "BTC Image Coding Using Vector Quantization," IEEE Trans. on Commun., vol. COM-35, no. 3, pp. 352-356, 1987.

[10] A. Klinger and C. R. Dyer, "Experiment on Picture Representation Using Regular Decomposition," Computer Graphics and Image Processing, vol. 5, no. 1, pp. 68-105, 1976.

[11] H. Samet, "The Quadtree and Related Hierarchical Data Structure," ACM Computing Surveys, vol. 16, no. 2, pp. 188-260, June 1984.

Adaptive Compression Coding

Panos Nasiopoulos, Rabab K. Ward, and Daryl J. Morse

Abstract—A compression technique which preserves edges in compressed pictures is developed. It is desirable to build edge preservation characteristics in compression methods since many applications in engineering and vision depend on edge information.

In this paper we present a compression algorithm which adapts itself to the local nature of the image. Smooth regions are represented by their averages and edges are preserved using quad trees. Textured regions are encoded using BTC (block truncation coding) and a modification of BTC using look-up tables. We developed the latter (BTC with look-up tables) so as 1) to improve on the compression ratio of BTC and 2) to leave the visual quality of compression exactly the same as that of BTC.

A threshold using a range which is the difference between the maximum and the minimum grey levels in a 4×4 pixel quadrant is used. At the recommended value of the threshold (equal to 18), the quality of the compressed textured regions is very high, the same as that of AMBTC (absolute moment block truncation coding) but the edge preservation quality is far superior to that of AMBTC. This significant improvement is achieved at compression levels (1.1–1.2 b/pixel) which are better than that of AMBTC (1.63).

Compression levels below (0.5–0.8) b/pixel may be achieved. The high quality of edge preservation of this method does not change at these low compression levels or as the threshold value changes. However, a postfilter is needed to improve the blocky appearance in the smooth and textured regions.

I. Introduction

THE AIM of this study is to obtain high-quality compressed images with high-compression ratios and with edge preservation characteristics. Edge preservation is important in many engineering applications such as in vision, robotics, and recognition. Examples of applications which rely on edge information include identification of the types of specific objects such as apples, oranges, houses, military and civilian aircraft, etc. In robotics, edge detection is used for the recognition of tools and their positions. In biomedical engineering, applications such as recognition of the different kinds of blood cells and sizes of tumors also rely on edge information. Block truncation coding (BTC) is known to give high-quality compressed images, however, by its nature BTC results in ragged edges and introduces noise at edges. In this work we rely on BTC for compression but we improve the quality of the compressed edges and also improve the compression ratios.

Paper approved by the Editor for Image Processing of the IEEE Communications Society. Manuscript received August 20, 1987; revised November 6, 1989.

P. Nasiopoulos is with Vancouver Community College, Langara Campus, Vancouver, B.C., Canada.

R. K. Ward is with the Department of Electrical Engineering, University of British Columbia, Vancouver, B.C. V6T 1W5, Canada.

D. J. Morse is with Microtel Pacific Research, Burnaby, B.C. V7A 4E8.

IEEE Log Number 9100831.

BTC is a well documented spatial image compression algorithm with a simplicity which leads to easy implementation and a variety of applications. Since its introduction by Delp and Mitchell [1], BTC has been applied to graphics [3], digital video [2], and color digital imagery [5]. The operation of BTC is simple. The image is divided into nonoverlapping, four by four pixel blocks, which are coded individually by passing them through a 1 b quantizer. The quantization levels can be chosen to fit several different criteria. In the original algorithm [1], the levels are chosen to preserve the first and second sample moments. Quantization which preserves combinations of the first, second, and third sample moments is possible, as is preservation of the nth and $2n$th sample moments [10]. Another algorithm, absolute moment BTC, preserves the first sample moment and the first absolute central sample moment [5]. These variations of BTC achieve a compressed data rate of 1.625 b/pixel if two-dimensional quantization is used to store the moments.

It has been shown for BTC that correlation remains in the pixels of the binary block generated by the quantizer [11]. The compressed data rate is reduced to 1.375 b/pixel if the roots of the median filter are used to represent the binary block. A compressed data rate of 1.1875 b/pixel is achieved if the binary block is coded with trellis coding. These modifications increase the compression ratio but unfortunately this is done at the expense of increased image degradation and algorithm complexity, especially at 1.1875 b/pixel.

These variations of BTC are fundamentally similar, relying on a uniform operator which does not adapt to the local statistics of the image. A positive aspect of BTC is that it exploits the masking property of the human vision system, whereby errors in a textured region of an image are less visible than are errors in a uniform region. As a result, it codes heavily detailed or textured regions compactly without introducing obvious artifacts. However, BTC does not perform equally well in other types of regions. It introduces artifacts which cause a noisy, ragged appearance in regions which contain an edge. Also, the data representation used by BTC is inefficient in regions where the pixel intensities are relatively constant.

An algorithm which adapts to the local statistics of the image should be able to preserve edges while coding smooth regions more compactly than BTC. Adaptive compression coding (ACC) is formed by combining BTC with quad-tree coding for regions which are smooth and regions which contain an edge. Compression ratio is improved by first representing regions which contain relatively constant intensity by their average intensity and second by representing the 16 binary bits of BTC by seven bits via a look-up table. The latter is only done for the BTC blocks where the intensities of the two output levels of BTC differ by less than 20. Image quality is improved by representing regions which contain an edge by a quad tree containing original pixels. ACC achieves high-quality compressed pictures with data rates from 1.1 to 1.2 b/pixel. Good quality pictures may be obtained at 0.5–0.8 b/pixel if a post smoothing filter is applied. This is to smooth the blocky appearance of the picture at those compression levels. More important is the edge preservation nature of ACC. Edges are preserved at all compression ratios. This makes ACC very useful in applications where edge preservation is important such as robot vision and other recognition applications. The adaptive algorithm is more complex than BTC, resulting in an increased compression time. However, the data representations used by ACC result in a decreased decompression time.

II. THE ADAPTIVE COMPRESSION CODING ALGORITHM

Consider a four by four pixel block of an image. It is desired that the 4×4 block be placed in one of three categories. The first category is that where either the intensities of the pixels in the block are relatively uniform. The second category is that where the block contains an edge. The third category is that where the block contains a random or pseudorandom pattern or texture.

Coding the image compactly, without introducing unreasonable distortion, requires that a different method be used in each case. In the first case, the block is represented by its average. In the second case, the block is represented by a quad-tree. BTC has proven to be effective under the conditions of the third case. For the latter, if the intensities of the two output levels of BTC differ by 20 or less a different version of BTC is used. This version uses look-up tables. When look-up tables are used the 16 binary bits of BTC are encoded into 7 b only. Experiments have shown that using the look-up tables in the above manner does not alter the visual appearance of the compressed image at all.

The test to determine whether or not a block is relatively uniform (smooth) and thus could be represented by its average, uses the range which is the difference between the maximum and the minimum intensities in the block. This is compared to a preset threshold usually in the range 13–50. This threshold shall be called the smoothness threshold. Another good candidate to detect smoothness, besides the smoothness range, would have been the variance of the intensities in the block. However, the range is better in detecting the small portions of lines or edges which might be present in the block. The range always detects such features, while the variance might miss them. A good value for the smoothness threshold is found to be equal to 18. This value produces the best results in terms of image quality, RMSE and image compression values (1.1–1.2 b/pixel). At high values of the smoothness threshold (e.g., 40) more blocks are represented by their averages and better compression rates (0.7–0.8) are obtained. However, more blockiness appears in the picture and a postsmoothing filter is here needed. The edge preservation of the filter is not affected by the variations in the smoothness threshold.

III. QUAD-TREE CODING

If the 4×4 block is not represented by its average then

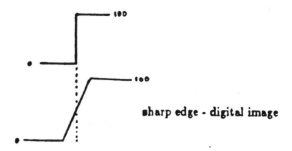

sharp edge - digital image

Fig. 1. Representation of a sharp edge in a digital image.

it is assumed to either contain an edge or to have texture. A test to determine that, uses a different threshold that is fixed in value and equal to 120. This threshold shall be called the edge detection threshold. If the range (difference between the maximum and minimum intensities) is less than this threshold, the block is assumed to be of a texture nature. In this case, BTC or BTC with look-up tables is used for coding. Otherwise, the 4×4 block is assumed to have an edge. If an edge is detected then quad tree encoding is used. The procedure to determine which of the 2×2 pixels subquadrants contain the edge is described below.

Our experiments have shown that a value of 120 for the edge detection threshold in a 4×4 block is very good in reproducing the edges without artifacts (as in BTC). If an edge is detected then that block is divided into its four 2×2 blocks. Afterwards, the range for each 2×2 block is compared to a threshold which is equal to half of the one used for detecting edges in the 4×4 original block, namely a value of 60 is now used. The reason for using half of the original value of the threshold is that a sharp edge is in fact represented by a gradual step. This is due to the low-pass filtering effect of the lens of the camera which results in a slight blurring of the image. The result here is that a sharp edge will look more like a ramp than a step function. In the unlikely event that the lens used is perfect, and the edges are in fact perfect step function, then the above procedure does not alter the results. Fig. 1 illustrates the rationale behind this idea.

For the 4×4 blocks which have a sharp edge, the original intensities of those 2×2 blocks which contain the edge will be saved, the other 2×2 blocks will be represented by their averages.

IV. AMBTC AND LOOK-UP TABLES

BTC encodes every 4×4 block of the image by its average, variance, and 16 binary bits. Each bit indicates whether or not the original intensity at a pixel is above the average intensity value. The absolute moment BTC encodes the first absolute moment instead of the variance. After decoding every pixel takes one of the following two values depending on whether the binary bit is 0 or 1. The two levels are

$$A = \overline{x} - \frac{16\overline{\alpha}}{2(16 - q)}$$
$$B = \overline{x} + \frac{16\overline{\alpha}}{2q}$$

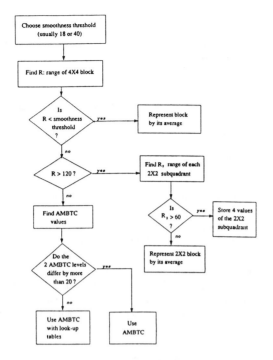

Fig. 2. Flowchart of ACC.

where $\bar{x}$ and $\bar{\alpha}$ are the average and the first absolute moment of the original intensities and q is the number of pixels with intensities equal or greater than the average.

AMBTC attains a compression ratio of 8 : 1.625 if a two-dimensional quantizer is used for the mean and the first absolute moment. Further compression may be achieved if the 16 binary bits are represented by fewer bits. Methods which make this possible include using look-up tables [2] and the roots of the median filter [6]. Another simple method which uses a look-up table only for areas with very low contrast is proposed and used here. This method uses BTC only if the difference between the two output levels is less than or equal to 20 otherwise a look-up table is used. The look up table has 2^7 entries, i.e., the 16 binary bits are represented by 7 b. The look-up table is constructed so that to preserve horizontal, vertical and diagonal straight edges, thin lines, stripes (2 pixels wide), corners and U shapes which run horizontally and vertically. These are shown in the Appendix.

Extensive experimentation has shown that if the difference of the two output levels of BTC is equal to or less than 20 then there is no change whatsoever in the visual quality of the AMBTC compressed picture. The compression ratios using AMBTC with this look-up table are not as high as those in [2] and [6] but the quality here is much superior. The flowchart of ACC is shown in Fig. 2.

V. Data Identification

A two-bit codeword is needed for each 4×4 block since for such a block four possibilities exist. These are the possibilities of representing the block by its average, AMBTC, AMBTC with look-up table and quad-tree. This codeword is followed by the relevant values i.e. the averages of the intensities (8 b

each), the values for AMBTC (26 b), AMBTC with look-up tables (17 b). If an edge exists within a 4×4 quadrant we need to specify which of the 2×2 blocks that edge passes through. For such 2×2 blocks the most significant bit of the word used to store the information for that block is used to identify whether the block has an edge or the mean of the intensities is stored. If the mean is stored, 7 b are used to represent the mean instead of the usual 8. In this case the original value of the mean is divided by 2 before the compression. During decompression this value is multiplied by 2. If the 2×2 block contains an edge then the 4 original intensities have to be stored. In this case one of these intensities is represented by 7 b.

VI. Filter

As the value of the smoothness threshold used to detect smoothness increases, more areas of the image are represented by their averages. At these high compression levels the edges are still reproduced as accurately as before, but degradation becomes significant as many textured regions are smoothed over and the picture will have a blocky appearance in those regions. The reason for having that blocky appearance is that the blocks which were represented by their averages have intensity values which are not close together and their boundaries can be seen. (Fig. 3.)

Since it might be desirable to reach very low data rates and still obtain good quality compressed pictures, an adaptive filter should be applied to those areas where the "blocky" artifacts appear. This gives back the image its lost continuity and improve the compression ratio of ACC. The adaptive filter designed for this case is based on a 3×3 averaging filter.

After the reconstruction of the image is complete, the picture is scanned (for those edges which give the picture its blocky appearance) using an 8×8 window. The range of the window is compared to the smoothness threshold value used. If it is smaller, then the area is smoothed by a 3×3 averaging filter. This method takes care of the blocky appearance of the reconstructed image, but the smoothed regions now look flat and artificial. In order to give back to the image the lost "texture," Gaussian random noise is added to the averaged areas.

VII. Comparison with AMBTC

The version of BTC which is used as the basis for the implementation of adaptive compression coding (ACC) is absolute moment block truncation coding (AMBTC) because the latter is a more efficient version of BTC. The AMBTC algorithm used was implemented using two-dimensional encoding for the sample moments, giving a compressed data rate of 1.625 b/pixel [Figs. 4(a), 5(a), 6(a)].

Assessing the capabilities of the adaptive algorithm requires a comparison of the processing speed, image quality, and compression ratio using images with varying statistics. Three test images are described in Table I.

The comparison is done using three different values for the smoothness-thresholds. The first threshold value yields a very high-quality picture [Figs. 4(c), 5(c), 6(c)]. The second value gives a high-quality, low-data rate image and the third is a

Fig. 4. (a) Results of compression using BTC, rate = 1.63 b/pixel and RMSE = 7.63.

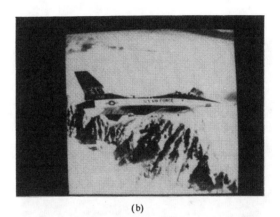

(b)

Fig. 4. (b) Results of compression using ACC (threshold = 13) rate = 1.21 and RMSE = 5.75.

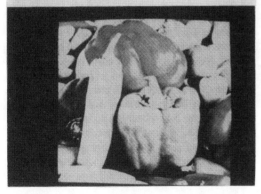

Fig. 3. Original pictures of Jet, Girl, and Peppers.

high-threshold value to demonstrate the upper limit of ACC using the adaptive filter discussed in the previous section [Figs. 4(d), 5(d), 6(c)].

A visual evaluation of the images is very important. The pictures from the adaptive compression coding technique appear much better than those of AMBTC. It is known that root mean square error, RMSE, is not an especially accurate measure of visual fidelity, so besides the RMSE the difference pictures were chosen as a mean for the visual analysis of the images [Figs. 4(f)–(h), 5(f)–(h), 6(f)–(h)]. The edges of the images from AMBTC are noisy and have ragged appearance. The images from the ACC algorithm do not appear as degraded as the RMSE would suggest because most of the edges are perfectly preserved. This indicates that the degree of edge preservation is an important characteristic of any image coding algorithm. At low-compression rate, degradation

(c)

Fig. 4. (c) Results of compression using ACC (threshold = 18) rate = 1.14 and RMSE = 5.90.

becomes significant due to the fact that many textured regions are smoothed as the number of blocks represented by their average increases.

167

(d)

Fig. 4.   (d) Results of compression using ACC (threshold = 40) rate = 0.81 and RMSE = 7.04.

Fig. 4.   (g) Difference picture of Fig. 4(c).

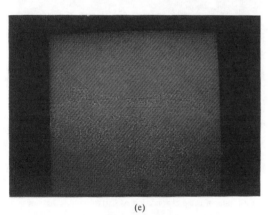

(e)

Fig. 4.   (e) Difference picture of Fig. 4(a).

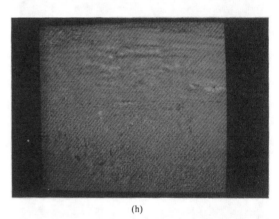

(h)

Fig. 4.   (h) Difference picture of Fig. 4(d).

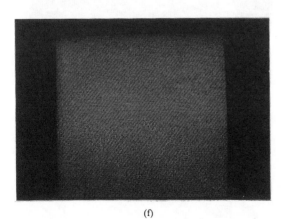

(f)

Fig. 4.   (f) Difference picture of Fig. 4(b).

(a)

Fig. 5.   (a) Results of compression using BTC rate = 1.63 b/pixel and RMSE = 6.61.

168

(e)

Fig. 5. (b) Results of compression using ACC (threshold = 13) rate = 1.36 and RMSE = 5.47.

Fig. 5. (e) Difference picture of Fig. 5(a).

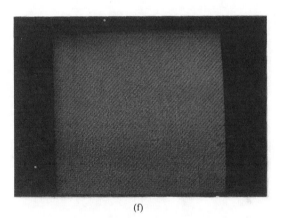

(c)

(f)

Fig. 5. (c) Results of compression using ACC (threshold = 18) rate = 1.25 and RMSE = 5.70.

Fig. 5. (f) Difference picture of Fig. 5(b).

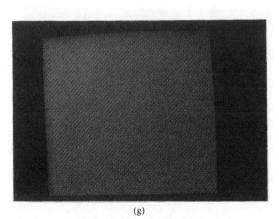

(d)

(g)

Fig. 5. (d) Results of compression using ACC (threshold = 40) rate = 0.76 and RMSE = 9.10.

Fig. 5. (g) Difference picture of Fig. 5(c).

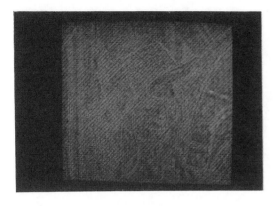

(h)

Fig. 5. (h) Difference picture of Fig. 5(d).

(c)

Fig. 6. (c) Results of compression using ACC (threshold = 18) rate = 1.17 and RMSE = 4.75.

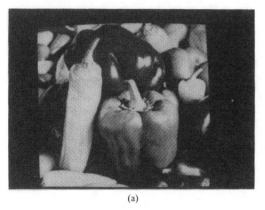

(a)

Fig. 6. (a) Results of compression using BTC, rate = 1.63 b/pixel and RMSE = 5.69.

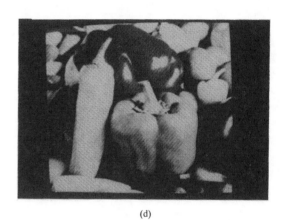

(d)

Fig. 6. (d) Results of compression using ACC (threshold = 40) rate = 0.70 and RMSE = 8.40.

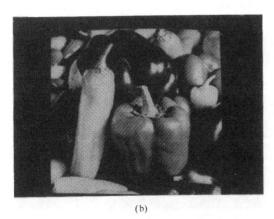

(b)

Fig. 6. (b) Results of compression using ACC (threshold = 13) rate = 1.30 and RMSE = 4.60.

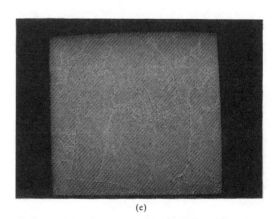

(e)

Fig. 6. (e) Difference picture of Fig. 6(a).

(f)

Fig. 6. (f) Difference picture of Fig. 6(b).

(g)

Fig. 6. (g) Difference picture of Fig. 6(c).

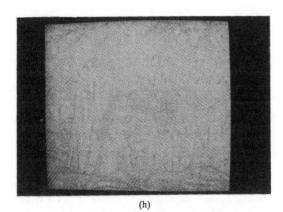

(h)

Fig. 6. (h) Difference picture of Fig. 6(d).

TABLE I
TEST IMAGES

image	size	b/pixel
F16	512×512	8
Girl	512×512	8
Peppers	512×512	8

TABLE II
COMPRESSION RATES WITH AND WITHOUT LOOK-UP TABLES

Image	Range	Rate without Look up tables	Rate With Look up tables	RMSE
F16AMBTC		1.63	1.63	7.63
F16	13	1.29	1.21	5.75
F16	18	1.20	1.14	5.90
F16	40	0.96	0.81	7.04
GirlAMBTC		1.63	1.63	6.61
Girl	13	1.52	1.36	5.47
Girl	18	1.37	1.25	5.70
Girl	40	0.89	0.76	9.10
PeppersAMBTC		1.63	1.63	5.69
Peppers	13	1.46	1.3	4.6
Peppers	18	1.30	1.17	4.75
Peppers	40	0.80	0.70	8.40

The compressed data rates and the RMSE for AMBTC and ACC using three different thresholds are shown in Table II. For high quality images ACC yields lower RMSE than that of AMBTC. At the upper limits of the method, smoothing becomes significant and the RMSE obtained is larger than that of AMBTC.

Because BTC algorithms are non-adaptive, their compression and decompression times are relatively constant for all images. Compression using the adaptive algorithm is approximately two times slower than AMBTC (up to four times if look-up tables are used) and varies slightly from image to image. Decompression though is approximately the same as that of AMBTC for high-quality images. As the threshold value increases and the compressed data rates become lower the decompression time becomes significantly faster than that of BTC.

VIII. CONCLUSION

We have developed a compression technique which is very successful in preserving the edges of pictures. Edge preservation is important since many enhancement and recognition algorithms depend on edge information. Our algorithm not only preserves edges but also achieves high quality compressed images which compare in quality to those produced by BTC. Most significantly we managed to obtain the high quality and the edge preservation characteristics at compression ratios (1.1–1.2 b/pixel) which were much lower than that of AMBTC (1.63).

Compression ratios as low as 0.5–0.8 b/pixel are possible. The high-quality edge preservation characteristics at these compression ratios is still maintained, however, a postfilter is needed to improve the quality of the smooth and textured regions.

TABLE III
Look-Up Tables Representing Different Cases of Edges

1 1 0 0	1 1 1 0			0 1 1 0	0 0 0 0
1 0 0 0	1 1 0 0			0 1 1 0	0 0 0 0
0 0 0 0	1 0 0 0			0 1 1 0	1 0 0 0
0 0 0 0	0 0 0 0			0 1 1 0	0 1 0 0
1 1 1 1	1 1 1 1	1 1 0 0	0 0 0 0	1 1 1 1	0 0 0 0
1 1 1 0	1 1 1 1	1 1 0 0	1 1 1 1	1 0 0 0	0 1 1 1
1 1 0 0	1 1 1 0	1 1 0 0	1 1 1 1	1 0 0 0	0 1 0 0
1 0 0 0	1 1 0 0	1 1 0 0	0 0 0 0	1 0 0 0	0 1 0 0
1 1 1 1		0 0 0 0		0 0 0 0	0 0 0 1
1 1 1 1		0 0 0 0		0 0 0 0	0 0 0 1
1 1 1 1		1 1 1 1		0 0 1 1	0 0 0 1
1 1 1 0		1 1 1 1		0 0 1 0	1 1 1 1
0 0 1 1	0 1 1 1	1 1 1 1	0 0 0 0	0 0 1 0	0 1 0 0
0 0 0 1	0 0 1 1	1 1 1 1	0 1 1 1	0 0 1 0	1 1 0 0
0 0 0 0	0 0 0 1	1 1 0 0	0 1 1 1	1 1 1 0	0 0 0 0
0 0 0 0	0 0 0 0	1 1 0 0	0 1 1 0	0 0 0 0	0 0 0 0
1 1 1 1	1 1 1 1	1 1 1 1	0 0 0 0	1 0 0 0	0 1 0 0
0 1 1 1	1 1 1 1	1 1 1 1	1 1 1 0	1 0 0 0	0 1 0 0
0 0 1 1	0 1 1 1	0 0 1 1	1 1 1 0	1 0 0 0	0 1 1 1
0 0 0 1	0 0 1 1	0 0 1 1	0 1 1 0	1 1 1 1	0 0 0 0
1 1 1 1	0 1 1 0	1 1 0 0	0 1 1 0	0 0 1 0	1 1 1 1
1 1 1 1	1 1 0 0	1 1 0 0	0 1 1 1	0 0 1 1	0 0 0 1
1 1 1 1	1 0 0 0	1 1 1 1	0 1 1 1	0 0 0 0	0 0 0 1
0 1 1 1	0 0 0 0	1 1 1 1	0 0 0 0	0 0 0 0	0 0 0 1
0 0 1 1	0 0 0 1	0 0 1 1	0 1 1 0	0 0 0 0	0 0 0 0
0 1 1 0	0 0 1 1	0 0 1 1	1 1 1 0	1 1 1 0	0 0 0 0
1 1 0 0	0 1 1 0	1 1 1 1	1 1 1 0	0 0 1 0	1 1 0 0
1 0 0 0	1 1 0 0	1 1 1 1	0 0 0 0	0 0 1 0	0 1 0 0
	0 1 1 0	0 1 0 0	0 0 1 0	1 1 1 1	1 1 1 1
	0 0 1 1	1 0 0 0	0 1 0 0	0 0 1 1	1 1 0 0
	0 0 0 1	0 0 0 0	1 0 0 0	0 0 1 1	1 1 0 0
	0 0 0 0	0 0 0 0	0 0 0 0	1 1 1 1	1 1 1 1
1 1 0 0	1 0 0 0	0 0 0 1	0 0 0 0	1 1 1 1	1 0 0 1
0 1 1 0	1 1 0 0	0 0 1 0	0 0 0 1	1 1 1 1	1 0 0 1
0 0 1 1	0 1 1 0	0 1 0 0	0 0 1 0	1 0 0 1	1 1 1 1
0 0 0 1	0 0 1 1	1 0 0 0	0 1 0 0	1 0 0 1	1 1 1 1
1 1 1 1	1 1 1 1	0 0 0 0		0 1 0 0	0 0 1 0
0 0 0 0	1 1 1 1	0 0 0 0		0 1 0 0	0 0 1 0
0 0 0 0	0 0 0 0	0 0 0 1		0 1 0 0	0 0 1 0
0 0 0 0	0 0 0 0	0 0 1 0		0 1 0 0	0 0 1 0
1 1 1 1	0 0 0 1	0 0 1 0	0 1 0 0	1 1 0 0	0 1 1 1
1 1 1 1	0 0 0 1	0 0 0 1	0 0 1 0	1 1 0 0	0 1 1 1
1 1 1 1	0 0 0 1	0 0 0 0	0 0 0 1	1 1 1 0	0 0 1 1
0 0 0 0	0 0 0 1	0 0 0 0	0 0 0 0	1 1 1 0	0 0 1 1
0 0 1 1	0 1 1 1	1 0 0 0	0 0 0 0		
0 0 1 1	0 1 1 1	0 1 0 0	1 0 0 0		
0 0 1 1	0 1 1 1	0 0 1 0	0 1 0 0		
0 0 1 1	0 1 1 1	0 0 0 1	0 0 1 0		

APPENDIX I

The 128 look-up tables are chosen to represent different cases of edges. Most of the edges are chosen to have width of at least two pixels. This is justified because edges are almost never represented as step functions but more like gradual steps.

In Table III only 64 of the 128 tables are shown. The other 64 tables are chosen to be the inverse representation of the first 64.

REFERENCES

[1] E.J. Delp and R. Mitchell, "Image compression using block truncation coding," *IEEE Trans. Commun.*, vol. COM-27, pp. 1335–1342, Sept. 1979.

[2] D.J. Healy and O.R. Mitchell, "Digital video bandwidth compressing block truncation coding," *IEEE Trans. Commun.*, vol. COM-29, pp. 1809–1817, Dec. 1981.

[3] E.J. Delp and O.R. Mitchell, "Multilevel graphics representation using block truncation coding," *Proc. IEEE*, vol. 68, pp. 868–873, July 1980.

[4] A.N. Netravali and J.O. Limb, "Picture coding: A review," *Proc. IEEE*,

vol. 68, pp. 366–403, Mar. 1981.

[5] M. D. Lema and O. R. Mitchell, "Absolute moment block truncation coding and its application to colour images," *IEEE Trans. Commun.*, vol. COM-32, pp. 1148–1157, Oct. 1984.

[6] J. L. Mannos and D. J. Sakrison, "The effects of a visual fidelity criterion on the encoding of images," *IEEE Trans. Inform. Theory*, vol. IT-20, pp. 525–536, July 1974.

[7] A. K. Jain, "Image data compression: A review," *Proc. IEEE*, vol. 69, pp. 349–389, 1981.

[8] Z. L. Budrikis, "Visual fidelity criterion and modeling," *Proc. IEEE*, vol. 60, pp. 771–778, July 1972.

[9] M. Kunt, A. Ikonomopoulos, and M. Kocher, "Second-generation image-coding techniques," *Proc. IEEE*, vol. 73, pp. 549–574, 1985.

[10] D. R. Halverson, N. C. Griswold, and G. L. Wise, "A generalized block truncation coding algorithm for image compression," *IEEE Trans. Acoust., Speech, Signal Processing*, vol. ASSP-32, pp. 664–668, June 1984.

[11] G. R. Arce and N. C. Gallagher, Jr., "BTC image coding using median filter roots," *IEEE Trans. Commun.*, vol. COM-31, pp. 784–793, June 1983.

[12] A. Rosenfeld and C. Kak, *Digital Picture Processing, Second Edition*. New York: Academic, 1982, vol. 1, pp. 176–181.

Transactions Papers

Moment Preserving Quantization

Edward J. Delp, *Senior Member, IEEE*, and Owen Robert Mitchell, *Senior Member, IEEE*

Abstract—In this paper, we present a new criteria for quantizer design whereby moments of the input and output of the quantizer are preserved. The moment preserving (MP) quantizer is shown to be related to the Gauss–Jacobi mechanical quadrature. The output levels of the N-level MP quantizer are shown to be the N zeros of an Nth degree orthogonal polynomial associated with the input probability distribution function. The $N-1$ thresholds of the MP quantizer are shown to be related to the Christoffel numbers through the Separation Theorem of Chebyshev–Markov–Stieltjes. The statistical convergence of the MP quantizer is also investigated. MP quantizer tables are presented for the uniform, Gaussian and Laplacian density functions. The moment preserving quantizer is shown to be related to block truncation coding.

I. INTRODUCTION

SINCE the advent of the use of pulse code modulation (PCM) systems there has been great interest in the design of quantizers. It was observed that nonuniform quantizers possessed properties that could be used to achieve results such as smaller mean square error or enhanced subjective performance in areas such as speech and image processing [1]–[3]. These types of quantizers are designed for a particular input probability distribution function relative to a particular performance index or fidelity criterion. The most popular fidelity criterion used is that of the mean square error (MSE) between the input and output with the quantizer designed to minimize this mean square error [4]. Other pointwise measure have also been proposed, e.g., mean absolute error [5]. Studies have shown that pointwise fidelity criteria cannot be used reliably in image coding [6]–[9].

In previous papers [10]–[11] we have demonstrated that a new criterion for quantizer design, that of preserving the moments of the input and output of the quantizer, can be used very successfully for image coding schemes. The coding algorithm, known as block truncation coding (BTC), used a small number of levels and a nonparametric form of the moment preserving quantizer. By nonparametric we mean that the quantizer was designed to fit the actual data; no *a priori* probability distribution was assumed. The BTC algorithm has been extended to include color images [12], time-varying

imagery [13], vector quantizers [14], [15], different sets of moments [16], and variations of the basic algorithm [17], [18]. All of these studies of BTC have shown that preserving moments in an image is important at very low data rates, which is not indicated by minimum mean square error [19].

In this paper we present the general solution to the moment preserving (MP) quantizer problem. We will compare the MP quantizer to standard quantization design, e.g., minimum mean square error quantizers. We will show that quantizers which preserve moments are easy to derive in closed form when the input probability density function is symmetric and the number of levels is relatively small. We will further show that the moment preserving quantization problem can be formulated as the classical Gauss–Jacobi mechanical quadrature problem where the output levels of the quantizer are the zeros of orthogonal polynomials associated with the input probability distribution. The thresholds of the quantizer are then related to the so-called Christoffel numbers.

II. MOMENT PRESERVING QUANTIZATION

We will approach the problem of using the MP criterion by first examining the problem of a two-level MP quantizer and then generalizing the result to N levels. The notation used here is that of Max [4].

Let the random variable X denote the input to the quantizer whose probability distribution function is $F(x)$, $x \in [a, b]$. The interval $[a, b]$ can be finite, infinite, or semi-infinite. Let Y denote the random variable at the output of the quantizer. For a two level quantizer, the random variable Y is discrete and takes on the values $\{y_1, y_2\}$ with probabilities $P_1 = \mathrm{Prob}(Y = y_1)$ and $P_2 = \mathrm{Prob}(Y = y_2)$. The output Y takes on the value y_1 whenever the input X is below some threshold x_1 otherwise; the output is y_2. Therefore, in general, to design any two-level quantizer one must choose the two output levels y_1 and y_2 and the input threshold x_1. When using a design criterion of having the two-level quantizer preserve moments of the input it is necessary that the quantizer preserve the first three moments of the input, otherwise one of the three parameters would have to be known (or guessed) initially. To specify the quantizer one must solve the following equations for y_1, y_2, and x_1:

$$E[Y] = E[X] = y_1 P_1 + y_2 P_2$$
$$E[Y^2] = E[X^2] = y_1^2 P_1 + y_2^2 P_2$$
$$E[Y^3] = E[X^3] = y_1^3 P_1 + y_2^3 P_2$$
$$P_1 + P_2 = 1. \tag{1}$$

Paper approved by the Editor for Quantization, Speech/Image Coding of the IEEE Communications Society. Manuscript received January 24, 1989; revised July 24, 1990.

E. J. Delp is with the Computer Vision and Image Processing Laboratory, School of Electrical Engineering, Purdue University, West Lafayette, IN 47907.

O. R. Mitchell is with the Department of Electrical Engineering, University of Texas at Arlington, Arlington, TX 76019.

IEEE Log Number 9101570.

Where the expectation operator is defined by the Lebesgue–Stieltjes integral

$$E[X^i] = \int_a^b x^i \, dF(x), \quad \text{and} \quad y_1 \le x_1 \le y_2.$$

We shall assume throughout this presentation that the moments exist and are finite. Equation (1) can be rewritten as

$$m_1 = y_1 F(x_1) + y_2(1 - F(x_1))$$
$$m_2 = y_1^2 F(x_1) + y_2^2(1 - F(x_1))$$
$$m_3 = y_1^3 F(x_1) + y_2^3(1 - F(x_1)) \qquad (2)$$

where $m_i = E[X^i]$

$$P_1 = \mathrm{Prob}(X \le x_1) = F(x_1)$$
$$P_2 = \mathrm{Prob}(X > x_1) = 1 - F(x_1).$$

By solving (2) for y_1, y_2, and x_1 the quantizer obtained is such that the first three moments of X are identical to those of Y. To find x_1 we shall assume $F^{-1}(\cdot)$ exists.

Without loss of generality we shall further assume that $m_1 = 0$ and $m_2 = 1$, i.e., X is zero mean and unit variance. Equation (2) becomes

$$0 = y_1 F(x_1) + y_2(1 - F(x_1))$$
$$1 = y_1^2 F(x_1) + y_2^2(1 - F(x_1))$$
$$m_3 = y_1^3 F(x_1) + y_2^3(1 - F(x_1)). \qquad (3)$$

By solving the first two equations for y_1 and y_2 in terms of $F(x_1)$ and using these solutions in the last equation we arrive at the desired results

$$y_1 = -\sqrt{\frac{1 - F(x_1)}{F(x_1)}} = -\sqrt{\frac{P_2}{P_1}}$$

$$y_2 = \sqrt{\frac{F(x_1)}{1 - F(x_1)}} = \sqrt{\frac{P_1}{P_2}}$$

$$F(x_1) = \frac{1}{2} + \frac{m_3}{2}\sqrt{\frac{1}{4 + m_3^2}}. \qquad (4)$$

This result is interesting in that the quantizer can be written in closed form. When using other fidelity criteria, such as mean square error, it is usually impossible to obtain a closed form expression for the quantizer. The above result in (4) also indicates that the threshold x_1 is nominally the *median* of X and not the mean as one would expect. The third moment m_3 is in general a signed number and can be thought of as a measure of skewness in the distribution function. This result indicates that the threshold is biased above or below the median according to the sign and magnitude of this skewness. These results are similar to those of block truncation coding, the difference being that BTC uses sample moments [10]. It should be noted that at this point we have no guarantee that $y_1 \le x_1 \le y_2$. This problem will be addressed below.

The MP quantizer can be generalized to N-levels. One needs to recognize that for the N-level quantizer there are N output levels and $N - 1$ thresholds. So if we desire an N-level MP quantizer we need to know the first $2N - 1$

TABLE I
Summary of the Closed Formed Relationships of a Moment Preserving Quantizer When the Input Density is Symmetric, Where $m_i = E[X^i]$

$N = 2$	$y_1 = -y_2 = -1$
	$x_1 = 0$
$N = 3$	$y_1 = y_3 = -\sqrt{m_4}$
	$y_2 = 0$
	$x_1 = -x_2$
	where $F(x_1) = \frac{1}{2m_4}$
$N = 4$	$y_1 = -y_4 = -\left(1 + \left[\frac{1 - 2F(x_1)}{2F(x_1)}(m_4 - 1)\right]^{1/2}\right)^{1/2}$
	$y_2 = -y_3 = -\left(1 - \left[\frac{2F(x_1)}{1 - 2F(x_1)}(m_4 - 1)\right]^{1/2}\right)^{1/2}$
	$x_1 = -x_3$
	$x_2 = 0$
	where $F(x_1) = \frac{1}{4} - \frac{R}{4}\sqrt{\frac{1}{4 + R^2}}$
	$R = \frac{(m_6 - 1) - 3(m_4 - 1)}{(m_4 - 1)^{3/2}}$

moments, i.e., the N-level MP quantizer preserves $2N - 1$ moments. This will be shown below and in the Appendix to guarantee the uniqueness of the quantizer. For large N this does lead to the problem of knowing a large set of moments for a given distribution. However, for most probability distribution functions we are interested in, one can exploit recursion relationships among the moments.

To arrive at the desired quantizer we need to find N output levels $\{y_1, y_2, \cdots, y_N\}$ and $N - 1$ thresholds $\{x_1, \cdots, x_{N-1}\}$; with $y_1 \le x_1 \le y_2 \cdots x_{N-1} \le y_N$. We again assume $m_1 = 0$ and $m_2 = 1$. We must solve

$$m_n = \int_a^b x^n \, dF(x) = \sum_{i=1}^N y_i^n P_i$$

for

$$n = 0, 1, 2, \cdots, 2N - 1 \qquad (5)$$

where

$$x_0 = a,$$
$$x_N = b,$$
$$m_n = E[X^n],$$
$$P_i = F(x_i) - F(x_{i-1}) = \mathrm{Prob}(Y = y_i).$$

For a large class of practical problems where $F(x)$ admits a probability density function $f(x)$ and if $f(x)$ is even, i.e., $f(x) = f(-x)$, then the complexity of (5) is simplified since $m_n \equiv 0$ for n odd and the quantizer itself is symmetric. For a symmetrical density function a closed-form solution has been obtained for $N = 2, 3, 4$. These results are summarized in Table I.

Equation (5) can be recognized as a form of the Gauss–Jacobi mechanical quadrature [20]. The output levels y_i of a N-level MP quantizer are the zeros of the Nth degree orthogonal polynomial associated with $F(x)$. The P_i are the Christoffel numbers and the x_i and y_i alternate by the Separation Theorem of Chebyshev–Markov–Stieltjes [20]. A brief review of orthogonal polynomials, the Gauss–Jacobi

175

mechanical quadrature, and the Separation Theorem is presented in the Appendix.

Tables II–IV show the MP quantizer thresholds and output levels for uniform, Gaussian and Laplacian probability distribution functions. The polynomials were generated using the standard recursion relation of (A1). The zeros (output levels) were obtained by numerical methods using the IMSL package. The thresholds were obtained by using the fact that

$$F(x_i) = \sum_{j=1}^{i} P_j$$

and

$$x_i = F^{-1}(\cdot).$$

This assumes $F(x)$ has no points of discontinuity. For the uniform density the polynomials are the Legendre polynomials and for the Gaussian density the polynomials are the Hermite polynomials [20].

For comparison purposes we also computed the mean square error of the quantizer and the entropy of the output. Since

$$E[Y^2] = E[X^2] = 1$$

the mean square error becomes

$$E\left[(Y - X)^2\right] = 2\left(1 - \sum_{i=1}^{N} y_i \int_{x_{i-1}}^{x_i} x \, dF(x)\right). \quad (6)$$

Figs. 1–3 show plots of the mean square error versus N. Table V shows the minimum mean square error (MSE) quantizer for $N = 8$, for the uniform, Gaussian, and Laplacian densities [4], [21].

The results for the MP quantizer for a uniform density are interesting in that as N increases the output levels tend to group closely to end points of the density function. In fact it can be shown that on a finite interval the zeros of any orthogonal polynomial for a fixed N are denser near the end points [20].

The results for the other two density functions on an infinite interval exhibit one of the disadvantages of the MP quantizer; the outputs at y_0 and y_N have a tendency to spread out much further than the MSE quantizer. What this says is that the quantizer assigns output levels that have a small probability of occurrence. For example, the Laplacian MP quantizer for $N = 16$ assigns levels out beyond 20 standard deviation units as compared to the MSE quantizer which only assigns levels out to four standard deviation units. These assignments of small probability output levels are reflected by the low values of the entropy for all three of the MP quantizers. This indicates that it would be very hard to evaluate the MP quantizer for large values of N (say larger than 30) because the output levels would be assigned such small probability of occurrence that one could have problems with computational accuracy. Also, it is no easy task to compute the zeros of a polynomial of high degree. These types of problems do not manifest themselves in the MSE quantizer due to the types of algorithms used to determine the output levels and input thresholds [4].

TABLE II
POSITIVE THRESHOLDS AND POSITIVE OUTPUT LEVELS FOR A MP QUANTIZER ($N = 2-16$) FOR A ZERO MEAN, UNIT VARIANCE UNIFORM PROBABILITY DENSITY FUNCTION. (mse = MEAN SQUARE ERROR)

	output levels	thresholds
$N = 2$ entropy 1.00 mse 0.2679	1.00	0.00
$N = 3$ entropy 1.547 mse 0.1352	0.00 1.3416	0.7698
$N = 4$ entropy 1.9321 mse 0.015	0.5889 1.4915	0.0 1.1295
$N = 5$ entropy 2.2325 mse 0.0545	0.00 0.9327 1.5695	0.4927 1.3217
$N = 6$ entropy 2.4794 mse 0.039	0.4133 1.1452 1.6151	0.0 0.8105 1.4353
$N = 7$ entropy 2.6893 mse 0.02927	0.00 0.7029 1.2894 1.6439	0.3620 1.0233 1.5078
$N = 8$ entropy 2.8722 mse 0.0228	0.3177 0.9102 1.3799	0.00 0.6282 1.1715
$N = 9$ entropy 3.0342 mse 0.0182	0.00 0.5616 1.0624 1.4480 1.6769	0.2860 0.8270 1.2784 1.5913
$N = 10$ entropy 3.1796 mse 0.0149	0.2579 0.7507 1.1768 1.4983 1.6869	0.00 0.5119 0.9782 1.3577 1.6166
$N = 11$ entropy 3.3116 mse 0.0124	0.00 0.4669 0.8991 1.2647 1.5364 1.6943	0.2364 0.6915 1.0955 1.4181 1.6356
$N = 12$	0.2169 0.6371 1.0172 1.3335 1.5660 1.7001	0.00 0.4315 0.8359 1.1878 1.4651 1.6503

Continued on next page

176

TABLE II   (continued)

	output levels	thresholds
entropy 3.4325 mse 0.0105		
N = 13	0.00	0.2014
	0.3991	0.5933
	0.7768	0.9533
	1.1126	1.2618
	1.3883	1.5023
	1.5893	1.6619
	1.7046	
entropy 3.5439 mse 0.0090		
N = 14	0.1872	0.00
	0.5527	0.3728
	0.8924	0.7283
	1.1904	1.0496
	1.4327	1.3219
	1.6081	1.5324
	1.7083	1.64122
entropy 3.6474 mse 0.0078		
N = 15	0.00	0.1754
	0.3485	0.5191
	0.6827	0.8416
	0.9889	1.1296
	0.2547	1.3713
	1.4691	1.5569
	1.6234	1.6788
	1.7113	
entropy 3.7439 mse 0.0068		
N = 16	0.1646	0.0
	0.4878	0.3281
	0.7933	0.6444
	1.0702	0.9374
	1.3084	1.1965
	1.4993	1.4124
	1.6361	1.5772
	1.7137	1.6850
entropy 3.8343 mse 0.0061		

TABLE III

POSITIVE THRESHOLDS AND POSITIVE OUTPUT LEVELS FOR A MP QUANTIZER ($N = 2-16$) FOR A ZERO MEAN, UNIT VARIANCE GAUSSIAN PROBABILITY DENSITY FUNCTION. (mse = MEAN SQUARE ERROR)

	output levels	thresholds
N = 2	1.00	0.00
entropy 1.00 mse 0.4042		
N = 3	0.00	0.9673
	1.7321	
entropy 1.2516 mse 0.2689		
N = 4	0.7419	0.00
	2.3344	1.6866
entropy 1.4423 mse 0.2032		
N = 5	0.00	0.7277
	1.3557	2.2820
	2.8570	

TABLE III   (continued)

	output levels	thresholds
entropy 1.5936 mse 0.1626		
N = 6	0.6167	0.00
	1.8892	1.3338
	3.3242	2.8003
entropy 1.7188 mse 0.1362		
N = 7	0.00	0.6081
	1.1544	1.8624
	2.3667	3.2648
	3.7504	
entropy 1.8255 mse 0.1166		
N = 8	0.5391	0.00
	1.6365	1.1408
	2.8025	2.3364
	4.1445	3.6890
entropy 1.9185 mse 0.1024		
N = 9	0.00	0.5332
	1.0233	1.6193
	2.0768	2.7694
	3.2054	4.0818
entropy 2.0008 mse 0.0909		
N = 10	0.4849	0.00
	1.465	1.0137
	2.4843	2.0568
	3.5818	3.1702
	4.8595	4.4491
entropy 2.0748 mse 0.0820		
N = 11	0.00	0.4805
	0.9288	1.4537
	1.8760	2.4620
	2.8651	3.5449
	3.9361	4.7951
	5.1880	
entropy 2.1419 mse 0.0745		
N = 12	0.4444	0.00
	1.3404	0.9216
	2.2595	1.8615
	3.2237	2.8409
	4.2718	3.8979
	5.5009	5.1232
entropy 2.2032 mse 0.06841		
N = 13	0.00	0.4409
	0.8567	1.3309
	1.7254	2.2429
	2.6207	3.1978
	3.5634	4.2324
	4.5914	5.4358
	5.8002	
entropy 2.2598 mse 0.0631		
N = 14	0.4126	0.00
	1.2427	0.8509
	2.0883	1.7142
	2.9630	2.6026
	3.8869	3.5363
	4.8969	4.5512
	6.0874	5.7349

Continued on next page

TABLE III *(continued)*

	output levels	thresholds
entropy 2.2598 mse 0.0631		
$N = 14$	0.4126	0.00
	1.2427	0.8509
	2.0883	1.7142
	2.9630	2.6026
	3.8869	3.5363
	4.8969	4.5512
	6.0874	5.7349
entropy 2.3123 mse 0.0587		
$N = 15$	0.00	0.4096
	0.7991	1.2352
	1.6067	2.0755
	2.4324	2.4435
	3.2891	3.8586
	4.1962	4.8560
	5.1901	6.0221
	6.3639	
entropy 2.3611 mse 0.0547		
$N = 16$	0.3868	0.00
	1.1638	0.7943
	1.9519	1.5977
	2.7602	2.4182
	3.6009	3.2683
	4.4929	4.1670
	5.4722	5.1485
	6.6308	6.2986
entropy 2.4069 mse 0.0519		

TABLE IV
POSITIVE THRESHOLDS AND POSITIVE OUTPUT LEVELS FOR A MP QUANTIZER ($N = 2-16$) FOR A ZERO MEAN, UNIT VARIANCE LAPLACIAN PROBABILITY DENSITY FUNCTION. (mse = MEAN SQUARE ERROR)

	output levels	thresholds
$N = 2$	1.00	0.00
entropy 1.00 mse 0.5858		
$N = 3$	0.00	1.2669
	2.4495	
entropy 0.8166 mse 0.3882		
$N = 4$	0.8183	0.00
	4.0163	2.7193
entropy 1.1491 mse 0.3744		
$N = 5$	0.00	1.0213
	1.9942	4.3414
	5.7175	
entropy 1.0417 mse 0.2928		
$N = 6$	0.7371	0.00
	3.2972	2.2191
	7.4655	6.0272
entropy 1.2593 mse 0.2969		

TABLE IV *(continued)*

	output levels	thresholds
$N = 7$	0.00	0.9078
	1.7802	3.5842
	4.7376	7.7924
	9.2806	
entropy 1.1716 mse 0.2466		
$N = 8$	0.6882	0.00
	2.9425	1.9745
	6.2421	5.0278
	11.1214	9.5909
entropy 1.3387 mse 0.2549		
$N = 9$	0.00	0.83906
	1.6493	3.1963
	4.2342	6.5607
	7.8246	11.4370
	13.0037	
entropy 1.2614 mse 0.2185		
$N = 10$	0.6545	0.00
	2.7208	1.8226
	5.5928	4.4910
	9.4470	8.1405
	14.9024	13.3038
entropy 1.3997 mse 0.2279		
$N = 11$	0.00	0.7916
	1.5585	2.9499
	3.9134	5.8867
	7.0302	9.7778
	11.1210	15.2028
	16.8298	
entropy 1.3292 mse 0.1993		
$N = 12$	0.6293	0.00
	2.5652	1.7164
	5.1716	4.1535
	8.5122	7.3272
	12.8225	11.4467
	18.7686	17.1161
entropy 1.4488 mse 0.2089		
$N = 13$	0.00	0.7562
	1.4905	2.7756
	3.6856	5.4432
	6.5668	8.8279
	10.0490	13.1566
	14.5613	19.0530
	20.7287	
entropy 1.3832 mse 0.1851		
$N = 14$	0.6094	0.00
	2.4481	1.6368
	4.8695	3.9076
	7.8878	6.7842
	11.6177	10.3646
	16.3204	14.8893
	22.6971	21.0000
entropy 1.4897 mse 0.1945		

Continued on next page

	output levels	thresholds
TABLE IV (continued)		
$N = 15$	0.00	0.7284
	1.4370	2.6438
	3.5130	5.1223
	6.1276	8.1854
	9.3240	11.9454
	13.2273	16.6528
	18.1078	22.9651
	24.6821	
entropy 1.4279		
mse 0.1741		
$N = 16$	0.5932	0.00
	2.3557	1.5740
	4.6388	3.7202
	7.4314	6.3876
	10.7942	9.6242
	14.8614	13.5532
	19.9108	18.4339
	26.6735	24.9387
entropy 1.5246		
mse 0.1832		

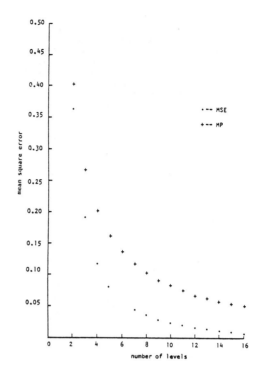

Fig. 2. Mean square error versus the number of quantizer levels (N) for both the minimum mean square error and moment preserving quantizers for a zero mean, unit variance Gaussian probability distribution.

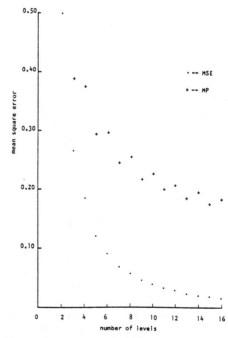

Fig. 3. Mean square error versus the number of quantizer levels (N) for both the minimum mean square error and moment preserving quantizers for a zero mean, unit variance Laplacian probability distribution.

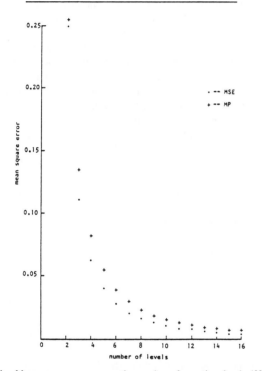

Fig. 1. Mean square error versus the number of quantizer levels (N) for both the minimum mean square error and moment preserving quantizers for zero mean, unit variance uniform probability distribution.

For probability distributions on an infinite or semi-infinite interval the moment sequence diverges. This will also tend to limit the maximum value one can use for N because of computational accuracy. In the next section we discuss the convergence properties of the MP quantizer and the quantization noise.

III. CONVERGENCE OF THE MP QUANTIZER

In this section we examine the convergence properties of the MP quantizer for large N. Let Y_N denote the random variable at the output of the quantizer with N levels. We desire to investigate under what circumstances does

$$Y_N \underset{N \to \infty}{\to} X,$$

i.e., does Y_N approach X in some sense when N is large.

TABLE V
POSITIVE THRESHOLDS AND POSITIVE OUTPUT LEVELS
FOR A MINIMUM MEAN SQUARE ERROR QUANTIZER
($N = 8$) FOR A ZERO MEAN, UNIT VARIANCE UNIFORM,
GAUSSIAN, AND LAPLACIAN PROBABLY DENSITY
FUNCTIONS. AFTER MAX [4] AND ADAMS AND GRIESLER
[31] (mse = MEAN SQUARE ERROR)

	output levels	thresholds
$N = 8$	0.2165	0.00
(uniform)	0.6495	0.43
	1.0825	0.8660
	1.5155	1.2990
entropy 3.000		
mse 0.0156		
$N = 8$	0.2451	0.00
(Gaussian)	0.7560	0.5006
	1.344	1.050
	2.152	1.748
entropy 2.825		
mse 0.0345		
$N = 8$	0.2334	0.00
(Laplacian)	0.8330	0.5332
	1.6725	1.2527
	3.0867	2.3796
entropy 2.5654		
mse 0.0545		

In particular does Y_N converge to X in mean square or in distribution? These can be stated as follows:

1) Y_N converges to X in mean square, denoted as $Y_N \overset{ms}{\to} X$, if $E\left[(Y_N - X)^2\right] \to 0$ as $N \to \infty$;

2) Y_N converges to X in distribution, denoted as $Y_N \overset{d}{\to} X$, if $F_N(x) \to F(x)$ as $N \to \infty$ where $F_N(x)$ is the probability distribution of Y_N.

Convergence in mean square guarantees convergence in distribution.

Convergence in distribution seems somewhat attractive for the MP quantizer since, as $N \to \infty$, Y_N, and X have the same moments. We know that for each moment sequence

$$m_k(N) = E\left[Y_N^k\right]$$
$$k = 0, 1, 2, 3, \cdots$$

there exists some integer R_k depending on k, such that if $N > R_k$ then $E\left[X^k\right] = m_k(N)$. In other words all the moment sequences are converging. Hence, if the moments of $F_N(x)$ are converging will that imply convergence in distribution? This well-known problem is discussed in [25] and can be restated by asking under what circumstances will the moments completely characterize the input distribution, i.e., given the moments, can the distribution be found? This leads to the classical moment problems of Stieltjes, Hausdorff, and Hamburger [22]. The work of Aheizer [23], Krein [22], and Shohat and Tamarkin [24] address the moment problem very elegantly. The Stieltjes moment problem is defined on the semi-infinite interval. The Hamburger moment problem is defined on the infinite interval. We will only mention the results for the Hamburger problem; the results are analogous for the Stieltjes problem. On a finite interval (Hausdorff) every probability distribution is characterized by its moments [25],

[20]. This says that on a finite interval we have convergence in distribution of the MP quantizer. A theorem due to Riesz [24] states that the orthogonal polynomials associated with $F(x)$ are closed if and only if $F(x)$ is characterized by its moments. Since the orthogonal polynomials are closed on any finite interval this implies that any distribution on a finite interval is characterized by its moments.

A sufficient condition that the Hamburger moment problem be determined, i.e., that the distribution is characterized by its moments, is that

$$\sum_{i=1}^{\infty} (m_{2i})^{-\frac{1}{2i}} = \infty \qquad (7)$$

or more generally (see [24])

$$\sum_{n=1}^{\infty} \left(\inf_{i \geq n}(m_{2i})^{\frac{1}{2i}}\right)^{-1} = \infty.$$

What the above does is put conditions on the rate of increase of the even moments of $F(x)$. A much more restrictive sufficient condition, but perhaps more intuitive, is that a probability distribution is characterized by its moments if its characteristic function is analytic in a neighborhood of the real line [25]. The above conditions can be extended to the Stieltjes problem.

Thus, if the input distribution $F(x)$ is characterized by its moments, the MP quantizer converges in distribution. The three distributions discussed in Section II are characterized by their moments, hence they converge in distribution. An example of a distribution not characterized by its moments is log-normal [25].

Mean square convergence is much more difficult. We will only show mean square convergence on a finite interval. We will then state some necessary conditions for mean square convergence on an finite or semi-infinite interval. For mean square convergence we must show

$$E\left[(Y_N - X)^2\right] \to 0 \quad \text{as } N \to \infty.$$

From (8) we have

$$E\left[(Y_N - X)^2\right] = 2\left(1 - \sum_{i=1}^{N} y_{iN} \int_{x_{i-1,N}}^{x_{i,N}} x \, dF(x)\right)$$

where the output levels and thresholds are also indexed by N. Essentially, what we need to show is

$$\lim_{N \to \infty} \sum_{i=1}^{N} y_{iN} \int_{x_{i-1,N}}^{x_{i,N}} x \, dF(x) = \int_{a}^{b} x^2 \, dF(x) = 1$$
$$\text{note } y_{iN} \in [x_{i-1,N}, x_{i,N}]. \qquad (8)$$

We shall assume $F(x)$ is absolutely continuous to avoid any problems mentioned by the Separation Theorem (see the Appendix). Before proceeding we will state a theorem concerning the distance between consecutive zeros.

Theorem 1: (Szego, [20]): Assume $F(x)$ admits a density $f(x)$ on the finite interval $[a, b]$ with $f(x) \geq \nu > 0$. Let

$y_{1N} < y_{2N}, < \cdots < y_{NN}$ be the zeros of the associated Nth-order polynomial $\Psi_N(x)$. Let

$$y_{kN} = \frac{1}{2}(a+b) + \frac{1}{2}(b-a)\cos\theta_{kN}$$

with

$$0 < \theta_{kN} < \pi, \qquad k = 1, 2, \cdots, N$$

then

$$\theta_{k+1} - \theta_k < K\frac{\log N}{N}. \qquad (9)$$

The proof is omitted. Note that K is determined only by ν, a, b and does not depend on $f(x)$. Therefore

$$\lim_{N\to\infty} (\theta_{k+1,N} - \theta_{kN}) = 0$$

We now can state the following.

Theorem 2: The MP quantizer convergences in mean square on a finite interval.

Proof: We will require the assumptions of Theorem 1 (i.e., $f(x) \geq \nu > 0$). Since the quantizer represents a formal partition of $[a, b]$ we use Theorems A2 and A3 and the Separation Theorem (Theorem A6). These theorems provide (along with Theorem 1):

$$\lim_{N\to\infty} |y_{k+1,N} - y_{kN}| = 0$$
$$\lim_{N\to\infty} |x_{k+1,N} - x_{kN}| = 0$$
$$\text{for all } k.$$

Therefore, (8) is immediately specified. For mean square convergence on an infinite interval we need a theorem similar to Theorem 1 plus the additional end point conditions:

$$\lim_{N\to\infty} y_{1N} \int_{-\infty}^{x_{1N}} x\,dF(x) = 0$$

and

$$\lim_{N\to\infty} y_{NN} \int_{x_{N-1,N}}^{\infty} x\,dF(x) = 0.$$

Hence, we need to show that $y_{1N} \to -\infty$ slower than $\int_{-\infty}^{x_{1N}} x\,dF(x) \to 0$ and similarly for the other end point.

We have not been successful at showing a general result in this case. It is very difficult to make statements concerning the zeros of general orthogonal polynomials. This difficulty should be compared to the minimum mean square error quantizer (MSE) where convergence in mean square is guaranteed if the input distribution has finite variance.

As to how well the MSE quantizer preserves moments it can be shown that MSE quantizer always preserves m_1 but in general $E[Y^2] < E[X^2]$ [26]. It can further be shown that

$$E\left[(Y-X)^2\right] = E[X^2] - E[Y^2]$$

hence convergence in mean square guarantees that the second moment series converges.

Finally, before leaving this section let us briefly discuss the quantization error of the MP quantizer. Let

$$\epsilon_q = Y - X$$

be the error in quantizing X with an N-level MP quantizer. So we have

$$Y = X + \epsilon_q$$

hence

$$E[\epsilon_q] = 0 \qquad (17)$$

and

$$E[Y^2] = E[X^2] + 2E[X\epsilon_q] + E[\epsilon_q^2] \qquad (18)$$

or

$$E[\epsilon_q^2] = -2E[X\epsilon_q].$$

Thus,

$$E[X\epsilon_q] \leq 0 \qquad (20)$$

since

$$E[\epsilon_q^2] \geq 0.$$

This says that the quantization noise is negatively correlated with the input. This negative correlation has been empirically observed in block truncation coding [10]. Negative correlation of the quantization noise can be also shown for the MSE quantizer [26].

IV. CONCLUSION

We have presented a method of designing quantizers based on a new criterion of preserving moments. We have shown how these quantizers compare with classical quantization design. Block truncation coding can be seen as a special case of a MP quantizer where the orthogonal polynomials are discrete and defined on the pixel gray level interval. One could use the results presented above to easily extend BTC to many more levels and higher dimensional vector quantizers than previously reported [14], [16].

APPENDIX

A very brief review of orthogonal polynomials is presented in this section. We will present only material needed to understand the MP quantizer problem. For a complete discussion of orthogonal polynomials the reader is referred to the literature, particularly the classical work of Szego [20], the somewhat dated but still relevant bibliography by Shohat [27], and the work of Askey [28], Jackson [29], Davis [30], and Krylov [31]. The notation used in this section is a slight modification of Szego's notation.

Let the probability distribution function $F(x)$ be a fixed nondecreasing real-valued function with infinitely many points of increase in the finite or infinite interval $[a, b]$. The class of functions $g(x)$ which are measurable with respect to $F(x)$ and for which the Lebesgue–Stieltjes integral:

$$\int_a^b |g(x)|^2 \, dF(x)$$

is finite is known as $L_F^2(a, b)$.

Let π_n denote the set of all polynomials $\{\rho(x)\} \in L_F^2(a, b)$ with degree less than or equal to n. Hence π_n is a subspace of $L_F^2(a, b)$.

Definition A1: Let the probability distribution function $F(x)$ having moments

$$m_n = \int_a^b x^n \, dF(x) \qquad n = 0, 1, 2, \cdots$$

that exist and are finite. If we orthogonalize the set of functions $\{x^n\}$, $n = 0, 1, 2, \cdots$ using a Gram–Schmidt procedure we can obtain a set of orthogonal polynomials

$$p_0(x), p_1(x), \cdots, p_n(x), \cdots,$$

i.e.,

$$\int_a^b p_n(x) p_m(x) \, dF(x) = k_n \delta_{nm}$$

where δ_{nm} is the Kronecker delta. A similar definition holds if $F(x)$ admits a density function $f(x)$. The set $\{p_n(x)\}$ of orthogonal polynomials is said to be associated with $F(x)$ [or $f(x)$]. We shall use the notation $\{\Psi_n(x)\}$ to denote the normalized set of $\{p_n(x)\}$. If $F(x)$ has only a finite number of points of increase then we obtain a finite system of polynomials.

The following recurrence relationship holds for any three consecutive orthonormal polynomials:

$$x\Psi_n(x) = \frac{a_n}{a_{n+1}} \Psi_{n+1}(x) + \left(\frac{b_n}{a_n} - \frac{b_{n+1}}{a_{n+1}} \right) \Psi_n(x) + \frac{a_{n-1}}{a_n} \Psi_{n-1}(x). \tag{A1}$$

where a_n is the coefficient of x^n in $\Psi_n(x)$ and b_n is the coefficient of x^{n-1} in $\Psi_n(x)$. See Jackson [29].

We now turn our attention to some elementary properties of the zeros of orthogonal polynomials. The following theorems are stated without proof (see Szego [20] or Davis [30]).

Theorem A1: The zeros of real orthogonal polynomials are real, simple and if $[a, b]$ is a finite interval the zeros are located in the interior of $[a, b]$.

Theorem A2: Let $z_1 < z_2 < \cdots < z_n$ be the zeros of $\Psi_n(x)$; $z_0 = a$ and $z_{n+1} = b$. Then each interval $[z_i, z_{i+1}]$, $i = 0, 1, 2, \cdots, n$, contains exactly one zero of $\Psi_{n+1}(x)$.

Theorem A3: Between two zeros of $\Psi_n(x)$ there is at least one zero of $\Psi_m(x)$, $m > n$. These three theorems are used when we discuss the convergence of the MP quantizer.

We now state the three theorems that totally specify the MP quantizer problem.

Theorem A4: (Gauss–Jacobi Mechanical Quadrature) Let $z_1 < z_2 < \cdots < z_n$ denote the zeros of $\Psi_n(x)$, there exist real numbers $\lambda_1, \lambda_2, \cdots, \lambda_n$ such that

$$\int_a^b \rho(x) \, dF(x) = \sum_{i=1}^n \lambda_i \rho(z_i) \tag{A2}$$

whenever $\rho(x) \in \pi_{2n-1}$. The distribution $F(x)$ and the integer n uniquely determine the numbers λ_i. The λ_i are known as the Christoffel numbers.

The proof is omitted (see Szego [20]). Note that the λ_k's are independent of $\rho(x)$.

The result above is often used in numerical integration where $\rho(x)$ is replaced by a general function $g(x) \in L_F^2(a, b)$. The error can be predicted and n can be chosen to find the degree of accuracy needed [30]. In the next two theorems we state some important properties of the Christoffel numbers.

Theorem A5: The Christoffel numbers, λ_k are positive, and

$$\sum_{k=1}^n \lambda_k = \int_a^b dF(x) = F(b) - F(a) = 1. \tag{A3}$$

The proof is omitted.

One way of finding the Christoffel numbers is

$$\lambda_k^{-1} = \sum_{m=0}^n \Psi_m^2(z_k)$$
$$k = 1, 2, \cdots, n. \tag{A4}$$

From the above result of the positiveness of the λ_k's, and noting the properties of $F(x)$ previously stated, there exists numbers $q_1 < q_2 < \cdots q_{n-1}$, $a < q_1$, $q_{n-1} < b$ such that

$$\lambda_k = F(q_k) - F(q_{k-1})$$
$$k = 1, 2, \cdots, n$$
$$q_0 = a$$
$$q_n = b. \tag{A5}$$

We should of course worry about points of discontinuity of $F(x)$ but this does not effect the results of Theorem A4. Also the q_k's are not in general uniquely determined. However, for most cases of practical interest $F^{-1}(\cdot)$ will exist. We shall now present the Separation Theorem of Chebyshev–Markov–Stieltjes which along with Theorems A4 and A5 will specify the MP quantizing.

Theorem A6: (Separation Theorem) The zeros $z_1 < z_2 < \cdots < z_n$ alternate with the numbers $q_1 < q_2 \cdots q_n$ that is

$$q_k < z_k < q_{k+1}.$$

Hence, Theorem A5 could be written as

$$\int_a^b \rho(x) \, dF(x) = \sum_{k=1}^n \rho(z_k)(F(x_k) - F(x_{k-1})). \tag{A6}$$

The proof is omitted. Szego [20] presents three proofs of this theorem.

REFERENCES

[1] P. F. Panter and W. Dite, "Quantization distortion in pulse-counte modulation with nonuniform spacing of levels," *Proc. IRE,* vol. 39, pp. 44–48, Jan. 1951.

[2] N. S. Jayant, "Digital coding of speech waveforms: PCM, DPCM, and DM quantizers," *Proc. IEEE,* vol. 62, pp. 611–632, May 1974.

[3] D. J. Sharma and A. N. Netravali, "Design of quantizers for DPCM coding of picture signals," *IEEE Trans. Commun.,* vol. COM-25, pp. 1267–1274, Nov. 1977.

[4] J. Max, "Quantizing for minimum distortion," *IRE Trans. Inform. Theory,* vol. IT-6, pp. 7–12, Mar. 1960.

[5] S. A. Kassam, "Quantization based on the mean-absolute-error criterion," *IEEE Trans. Commun.,* vol. COM-26, pp. 267–270, Feb. 1978.

[6] Z. L. Budrikis, "Visual fidelity criterion and modelling," *Proc. IEEE,* vol. 60, pp. 771–779, July 1972.

[7] J. L. Munnos and D. J. Sakrison, "The effects of a visual fidelity criterion on the encoding of images," *IEEE Trans. Inform. Theory,* vol. IT-20, pp. 525–536, July 1974.

[8] D. J. Sakrison, "On the role of the observer and a distortion measure in image transmission," *IEEE Trans. Commun.,* vol. COM-25, pp. 1251–1267, Nov. 1977.

[9] G. C. Higgins, "Image quality criteria," *J. Appl. Photograph. Eng.,* vol. 3, pp. 53–60, Spring 1977.

[10] E. J. Delp and O. R. Mitchell, "Image compression using block truncation coding," *IEEE Trans. Commun.,* vol. COM-27, pp. 1335–1341, Sept. 1979.

[11] O. R. Mitchell and E. J. Delp, "Multilevel graphics representation using block truncation coding," *Proc. IEEE,* vol. 68, pp. 868–873, July 1980.

[12] M. D. Lema and O. R. Mitchell, "Absolute moment block truncation coding and its application to color images," *IEEE Trans. Commun.,* vol. COM-32, pp. 1148–1157, Oct. 1984.

[13] D. J. Healy and O. R Mitchell, "Digital video bandwidth compression using block truncation coding," *IEEE Trans. Commun.,* vol. COM-29, pp. 1809–1817, Dec. 1981.

[14] V. R. Udpikar and J. P. Raina, "BTC image coding using vector quantization," *IEEE Trans. Commun.,* vol. COM-35, pp. 352–356, Mar. 1987.

[15] N. M. Nasrabadi and R. A. King, "Image coding using vector quantization: A review," *IEEE Trans. Commun.,* vol. 36, pp. 957–971, Aug. 1988.

[16] D. R. Halverson, N. C. Griswold, and G. L. Wise, "A generalized block truncation coding algorithm for image compression," *IEEE Trans. Acoust., Speech Signal Processing,* vol. ASSP-32, pp. 664–668, June 1984.

[17] N. C. Griswold, D. R. Halverson, and G. L. Wise, "A note on adaptive block truncation coding for image processing," *IEEE Trans. Acoust. Speech, Signal Processing,* vol. ASSP-35, pp. 1201–1203, Aug. 1987.

[18] G. R. Arce and N. C. Gallagher, "BTC image coding using median filter roots," *IEEE Trans. Commun.,* vol. COM-31, pp. 784–793, June 1983.

[19] O. R. Mitchell, S. C. Bass, E. J. Delp, T. W. Goeddel, and T. S. Huang, "Image coding for photo analysis," in *Proc. Soc. Inform. Display,* vol. 21, no. 3, 1980, pp. 279–292.

[20] G. Szego, *Orthogonal Polynomials.* American Mathematical Society, vol. 23, 1975.

[21] W. C. Adams and C. E. Giesler, "Quantizing characteristics for signals having laplacian amplitude probability density function," *IEEE Trans. Commun.,* vol. COM-26, pp. 1295–1297, Aug. 1978.

[22] N. I. Akheizer and M. Krein, *Some Questions in the Theory of Moments,* American Mathematical Society, Translations of Mathematical Monographs, vol. 2, 1962.

[23] N. I. Akhiezer, *The Classical Moment Problem.* New York: Hafner, 1961 (translated by N. Kemmer).

[24] J. A. Shohat and J. D. Tamarkin, *The Problems of Moments.* American Mathematical Society, Mathematical Survey, no. 1, 1943.

[25] W. Feller, *An Introduction to Probability Theory and Its Applications.* New York: Wiley, 1971, vol. 2.

[26] J. A. Bucklew and N. C. Gallagher, "A note on optimum quantization," *IEEE Trans. Inform. Theory,* vol. IT-25, pp. 365–366, May 1979.

[27] J. A. Shohat, (Ed.) *A Bibliography on Orthogonal Polynomials.* Nat. Res. Council Bulletin no. 103, 1940.

[28] R. Askey, *Orthogonal Polynomials and Special Functions.* Philadelphia, PA, SIAM, Regional Conference Series, Nov. 21, 1975.

[29] D. Jackson, *Fourier Series and Orthogonal Polynomials.* American Mathematical Society, Mathematical Monograph No. 6, 1941.

[30] P. J. Davis, *Interpolation and Approximation.* New York: Ginn, 1963.

[31] V. I. Krylov, *Approximate Calculation of Integrals.* New York: MacMillian, 1962. (translated by A. H. Stroud).

Chapter 6
Innovative Implementations

This chapter includes five studies that illustrate innovations made in implementation of BTC for specific applications. The first, published by Lema and Mitchell [B24] in 1984, is an outgrowth of the first author's Master's thesis published a little earlier; it is a much referenced article on absolute moment BTC applied to color imagery, which has special considerations. The second, published by Frost and Minden [B27] in 1986, shows the scope for application of BTC in synthetic aperture radar (SAR) imagery, which is of special interest to a large audience in a variety of application areas. The third, published by Tabatabai and Troudet [B41] in 1991, celebrates the marriage of BTC with the immensely popular area of neural nets. The fourth is an innovative application to color images published by Wu and Coll [B62] in 1992. The last, a very recent article by the same authors [B75], describes a multilevel BTC, which could fit in under the next category as well with its hybrid exploration aspects.

Chapter 6 Reprints

[B24] M.D. Lema and O.R. Mitchell, "Absolute Moment Block Truncation Coding and Applications to Color Images," *IEEE Trans. Comm.*, Vol. COM-32, No. 10, pp. 1148–1157, Oct. 1984.

[B27] V.S. Frost and G.J. Minden, "A Data Compression Technique for Synthetic Aperture Radar Images," *IEEE Trans. Aerospace and Electronic Systems*, Vol. AES-22, No. 1, pp. 47–54, Jan. 1986.

[B41] A. Tabatabai and T.P. Troudet, "A Neural Net Based Architecture for the Segmentation of Mixed Gray-Level and Binary Pictures," *IEEE Trans. Circuits and Systems*, Vol. 38, No. 1, pp. 66–77, Jan. 1991.

[B62] Y. Wu and D.C. Coll, "Single Bit-Map Block Truncation Coding of Color Images," *IEEE J. Selected Areas in Comm.*, Vol. 10, No. 5, pp. 952–959, June 1992.

[B75] Y. Wu and D.C. Coll, "Multilevel Block Truncation Coding Using a Minimax Error Criterion for High-Fidelity Compression of Digital Images," *IEEE Trans. Comm.*, Vol. 41, pp. 1179–1191, Aug. 1993.

Absolute Moment Block Truncation Coding and Its Application to Color Images

MAXIMO D. LEMA AND O. ROBERT MITCHELL

Abstract—A new quantization method that uses the criterion of preserving sample absolute moments is presented. This is based on the same basic idea for block truncation coding of Delp and Mitchell but it is simpler in any practical implementation. Moreover, output equations are those for a two-level nonparametric minimum mean square error quantizer when the threshold is fixed to the sample mean. The application of this method to single frame color images is developed. A color image coding system that uses absolute moment block truncation coding of luminance and chroma information is presented. Resulting color images show reasonable performance with bit rates as low as 2.13 bits/pixel.

I. INTRODUCTION

This paper presents a new quantization method that uses the idea of preserving moments as a design criterion of the quantizer. An extensive study of moment-preserving quantization was done by Delp in [2] and was applied to still images

Paper approved by the Editor for Signal Processing and Communication Electronics of the IEEE Communications Society for publication without oral presentation. Manuscript received November 22, 1982; revised August 4, 1983. This work was supported in part by the U.S. Army Research Office.

M. D. Lema is with the Department of Electrical Engineering, Purdue University, West Lafayette, IN 47907, and the Empresa Nacional de Telecommunicaciones (ENTEL), Argentina.

O. R. Mitchell is with the Department of Electrical Engineering, Purdue University, West Lafayette, IN 47907.

by Delp and Mitchell [1], [3] and to moving imagery by Healy and Mitchell [4]. A major application of moment-preserving quantization leads to what is known as block truncation coding or BTC. This coding method takes a finite number of samples and tries to preserve their first two sample moments, assigning a two-level quantizer designed for that goal. The equations of the quantizer are relatively simple, and block truncation coding has shown robust behavior in the presence of channel noise [1]. It also gives good reconstructed images, since the method preserves local characteristics of spatial blocks of the image important to the human observer. The method computes for each of these blocks the sample mean and the sample standard deviation, that is,

$$\bar{\eta} = \frac{1}{m} \sum_{i=1}^{m} x_i \tag{1}$$

$$\bar{\sigma} = \left\{ \frac{1}{m} \sum_{i=1}^{m} x_i{}^2 - \bar{\eta}^2 \right\}^{1/2} \tag{2}$$

where m is the total number of pixels in the block, and x_i represents the grey value of each pixel.

Both values are transmitted along with a bit plane which contains ones in those places where $x_i \geqslant \bar{\eta}$ and zeros otherwise. At the receiver, the block is reconstructed with a two-level quantizer that preserves the sample mean and the sample variance. The output values that achieve this goal are (see [1])

$$a = \bar{\eta} - \bar{\sigma} \sqrt{\frac{q}{m-q}} \qquad \text{for } x_i < \eta \tag{3}$$

$$b = \bar{\eta} + \bar{\sigma} \sqrt{\frac{m-q}{q}} \qquad \text{for } x_i \geqslant \eta \tag{4}$$

where q is the number of pixels greater than or equal to $\bar{\eta}$.

The method presented in this paper preserves absolute moments rather than standard moments (see [5]). It will be shown that this method gives similar pictorial results to block truncation coding but it gives simpler equations which lead to faster computation and smaller mean square error than BTC. The relation between AMBTC and the nonparametric minimum mean square error (MMSE) two-level quantizer is given in Section III.

An application of this method to color images is discussed. The problem of coding color images starts with the trichromatic nature of human color vision and the correlation that generally exists between color planes of actual pictures. It is therefore important to consider some decorrelating operation. A system that uses absolute moment preservation is presented. Finally, results from coding actual color images with the proposed system are given.

II. ABSOLUTE MOMENT BLOCK TRUNCATION CODING (AMBTC)

Since the principal idea used in block truncation coding is to achieve compression while preserving some sample moments, there exist other variants that lead to simpler results. Here, a new method of coding still images that preserves absolute sample moments is presented. Let us call it absolute moment block truncation coding or AMBTC.

Let a digitized image be divided into blocks of $n \times n$ pixels. Each block is quantized in such a way that each resulting block has the same sample mean and the same sample first absolute central moment of each original block. Let x_i be the grey level of a pixel in the block where $1 \leq i \leq m$ and $m = n^2$. Consequently, it is necessary to calculate the sample mean

$$\bar{\eta} = \frac{1}{m} \sum_{i=1}^{m} x_i \tag{5}$$

and the sample first absolute central moment

$$\bar{\alpha} = \frac{1}{m} \sum_{i=1}^{m} |x_i - \bar{\eta}|. \tag{6}$$

The mean value contains information about central tendency; this is the same central tendency information used by Delp and Mitchell in the original BTC [1]. On the other hand, the sample first absolute central moment contains information about dispersion about the mean. The corresponding value used by Delp and Mitchell is the sample standard deviation. Therefore, two of the most important local characteristics of the spatial block grey levels are preserved: central tendency and deviation from the center.

The sample first absolute central moment can be calculated in a simple way as follows: from (6)

$$m\bar{\alpha} = \sum_{\text{for} x_i \geq \bar{\eta}} x_i - \bar{\eta} \sum_{\text{for} x_i \geq \bar{\eta}} 1 - \sum_{\text{for} x_i < \bar{\eta}} x_i$$

$$+ \bar{\eta} \sum_{\text{for} x_i < \bar{\eta}} 1 \tag{7}$$

where $\bar{\eta}$ is the decision threshold of the quantizer (see Fig. 1). Since q is the number of pixels above the threshold, then

$$q = \sum_{\text{for} x_i \geq \bar{\eta}} 1 \quad \text{and} \quad m - q = \sum_{\text{for} x_i < \bar{\eta}} 1$$

then, from (5)

$$m\bar{\eta} = \sum_{\text{for} x_i \geq \bar{\eta}} x_i + \sum_{\text{for} x_i < \bar{\eta}} x_i.$$

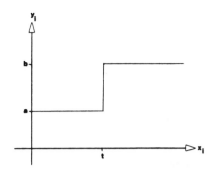

Fig. 1. Input–output relation for a typical two-level quantizer.

Inserting into (7)

$$m\bar{\alpha} = \sum_{\text{for} x_i \geq \bar{\eta}} x_i - \bar{\eta}q - m\bar{\eta} + \sum_{\text{for} x_i \geq \bar{\eta}} x_i + \bar{\eta}(m - q)$$

$$\bar{\alpha} = \frac{2}{m} \left[\sum_{\text{for} x_i \geq \bar{\eta}} x_i - \bar{\eta}q \right]. \tag{8}$$

Equation (8) is a more efficient way of computing $\bar{\alpha}$. Let us define a quantity that will be useful:

$$\bar{\gamma} = \frac{m\bar{\alpha}}{2} = \sum_{\text{for} x_i \geq \bar{\eta}} x_i - \bar{\eta}q. \tag{9}$$

In order to preserve the moments given in (5) and (6), it is necessary to assign two values, a and b, at the output of the two-level quantizer (see Fig. 1) such that

$$m\bar{\eta} = \sum_{i=1}^{m} y_i = qb + (m - q)a \tag{10}$$

$$m\bar{\alpha} = \sum_{i=1}^{m} |y_i - \bar{\eta}| = q(b - \bar{\eta}) - (m - q)(a - \bar{\eta}). \tag{11}$$

From (10) the value of a is

$$a = \frac{m\bar{\eta} - qb}{m - q}. \tag{12}$$

Inserting into (11) the value of b is

$$b = \bar{\eta} + \frac{\bar{\gamma}}{q}. \tag{13}$$

Replacing it into (12) we obtain the value of a:

$$a = \bar{\eta} - \frac{\bar{\gamma}}{m - q}. \tag{14}$$

The behavior of this quantizer can be analyzed by examining (13) and (14). For the case in which all the pixels have equal grey value, the deviation information is equal to zero and both a and b are set to the mean value, which is also the correct value for each pixel. On the other hand, if the pixels are dispersed about the mean, the value assigned to b is the mean plus a *bias* that depends directly on the dispersion and inversely on the number of pixels above the mean. Similar reasoning can be made for the value a. A numerical quantization example of a typical block is presented in the Appendix.

Fig. 2. Original 512 × 480 image with 8 bits/pixel.

Fig. 4. AMBTC reconstructed image using 4 × 4 pixel blocks, 6 bits for each sample mean, and 4 bits for each sample first absolute central moment. The bit rate is 1.625 bits/pixel. The mean square error is 30.00.

Fig. 3. Standard BTC reconstructed image using 4 × 4 pixel blocks, 6 bits for each sample mean, and 4 bits for each sample standard deviation. The bit rate is 1.625 bits/pixel. The mean square error is 32.35.

Fig. 5. Original 256 × 240 image with 8 bits/pixel.

Results from applying BTC and AMBTC to actual images are shown in the figures. Fig. 2 is an original image of 512 × 480 pixels with 8 bits per pixel (256 grey levels). Fig. 3 is the same image after being passed through a standard BTC quantizer using 4 × 4 pixel blocks, 6 bits for the sample mean and 4 bits for the sample standard deviation. Fig. 4 is the same original after being passed through an AMBTC quantizer using 4 × 4 pixel blocks, 6 bits for the mean and 4 bits for the first absolute central moment. In Figs. 5-7 we present another original image with less resolution than the previous so that coding errors are more visible. Fig. 5 is an original of 256 × 240 pixels with 8 bits/pixel. Fig. 6 is the quantized BTC image. Fig. 7 is the quantized AMBTC image. All the images were reconstructed using the same rate, 1.625 bits/pixel, but the mean square error for those using AMBTC is smaller. It has been found that the major artifacts are the same as those

noted by Delp in [2], which are edge raggedness, and misrepresentation of some midrange values due to their assignment to either high or low value.

III. ERRORS IN AMBTC

In order to compare this quantizer to the two-level MMSE quantizer, let us substitute (9) into (13) and (14). The result is

$$a = (1/(m - q)) \sum_{x_i < \bar{\eta}} x_i \tag{15}$$

$$b = (1/q) \sum_{x_i \geqslant \bar{\eta}} x_i. \tag{16}$$

Fig. 6. Standard BTC reconstructed image using 4 × 4 pixel blocks, 6 bits for each sample mean, and 4 bits for each sample standard deviation. The bit rate is 1.625 bits/pixel. The mean square error is 32.72.

Fig. 7. AMBTC reconstructed image using 4 × 4 pixel blocks, 6 bits for each sample mean, and 4 bits for each sample first absolute central moment. The bit rate is 1.625 bits/pixel. The mean square error is 30.73.

Note that a and b are estimated conditional means given that x is less or greater than $\bar{\eta}$, respectively.

On the other hand, as is shown in [1], the nonparametric MMSE two-level quantizer would give the same form of equations but with a general threshold t instead of $\bar{\eta}$. Unfortunately, there is no closed form relation to find t and an iterative procedure is suggested in [1]. Therefore, the output equations of AMBTC are those of a suboptimum implementation of a nonparametric MMSE quantizer in which the threshold is fixed to the mean $\bar{\eta}$. This result could explain the better mean square error performance of AMBTC when compared to standard BTC.

In order to analyze the error introduced by this non-parametric quantizer, let us define a deterministic mean square error as

$$\text{MSE} = \frac{1}{m} \sum_{i=1}^{m} (y_i - x_i)^2. \tag{17}$$

Let us define

$$g(\bar{\eta}) = \sum_{x_i < \bar{\eta}} x_i. \tag{18}$$

Then

$$a = g(\bar{\eta})/(m - q) \tag{19}$$

$$b = (m\bar{\eta} - g(\bar{\eta}))/q \tag{20}$$

so

$$\text{MSE} = \frac{1}{m} \sum_{i=1}^{m} [x_i^2 + y_i^2 - 2x_i y_i]. \tag{21}$$

After replacing values for y_i we get

$$\text{MSE} = \overline{x^2} - \frac{g(\bar{\eta})^2}{m(m - q)} - \frac{(m\bar{\eta} - g(\bar{\eta}))^2}{mq} \tag{22}$$

where

$$\overline{x^2} = \frac{1}{m} \sum_{i=1}^{m} x_i^2.$$

If the histogram of the block is symmetric about the sample mean and m is even, we have $q = m - q = m/2$. From (9)

$$g(\bar{\eta}) = \frac{m}{2} (\bar{\eta} - \bar{\alpha})$$

$$m\bar{\eta} - g(\bar{\eta}) = \frac{m}{2} (\bar{\eta} + \bar{\alpha}).$$

Replacing these values into the expression for the mean square error, we get

$$\text{MSE} = \bar{\sigma}^2 - \bar{\alpha}^2. \tag{23}$$

It is important to note here, that in those cases where the standard deviation equals the first absolute central moment, the error becomes zero. This situation occurs, for example, when all the pixels have the same grey level or when half of them take a value $\eta + A$ and the other half take a value of $\eta - A$ for any fixed A.

Other values for the threshold could be used. Goeddel and Bass [6] report that using $t = (x_{\min} + x_{\max})/2$ as a threshold yields lower mean square errors in standard BTC, where $x_{\min}$ and $x_{\max}$ are the minimum and maximum values of the pixels in a block. This fact was verified by the authors for some images and current research is being done aimed to find other measures of central tendency which could yield even lower mean square errors.

IV. Advantages of AMBTC

In the case that the quantizer is used to transmit an image from a transmitter to a receiver, it is necessary to compute at the transmitter two quantities using either BTC or AMBTC. These two quantities are the sample mean and the information about deviation from the center, which is the sample standard deviation for BTC and the sample first absolute central moment for AMBTC. Since computation of central information is the

189

Fig. 8. A composite of the first nine original images listed in Table I and used for testing of the reconstruction error for the coding techniques.

TABLE I
RESULTS SHOWING THE MEAN SQUARE ERROR AND THE MEAN ABSO-
LUTE ERROR FOR SEVERAL IMAGES TESTED AT THE LABORATORY FOR
IMAGE PROCESSING AT PURDUE. ALL IMAGES ARE 1.625 BITS/PIXEL.

Image	mse		mae	
	AMBTC	BTC	AMBTC	BTC
Airport2	54.97	59.42	4.98	5.21
Girl	45.35	48.70	4.55	4.75
Couple	39.40	41.80	4.08	4.18
Crowd	70.46	75.40	5.20	5.38
Aerial	140.50	151.50	8.44	8.80
Moon	42.80	46.77	4.89	5.23
X-ray	144.50	157.80	8.23	8.74
Gems	130.40	142.60	7.80	8.35
Cork	400.00	433.70	14.50	15.37
Shuttle	30.00	32.35	3.60	3.74

same for both methods, let us compare the necessary computations for deviation information. For standard BTC is it necessary to compute a sum of m values, see (2), each of them squared, while in the case of AMBTC it is only necessary to compute the sum of values given in (6). Since the multiplication time in most digital processors is several times greater than the addition time, by using AMBTC the total calculation time at the transmitter is significantly reduced.

A similar situation occurs at the receiver. For standard BTC is it necessary to evaluate two quotients and two square roots, see (3) and (4), while using AMBTC those calculations simplify to only two quotients, see (13) and (14). Consequently, the processing time at the receiver is also substantially reduced. The savings in time achieved by AMBTC might suggest the name of *fast BTC* for this method.

The rest of the characteristics of AMBTC remain the same as those of BTC since the philosophy of both methods is substantially the same.

An additional advantage of AMBTC is the minimum mean square error achieved under symmetry conditions stated before. As expected, for all the images tested in the Laboratory for Image Processing at Purdue University, AMBTC achieved smaller mean square error than standard BTC. Results for some of these images (see Fig. 8) are shown in Table I.

V. APPLICATION OF AMBTC TO COLOR IMAGES

A. The Color Signal

Because of the trichromatic nature of the human vision, we can assume that the color signal that we want to code lies in a three-dimensional space. Election of the coordinate system to represent this signal is often limited by practical situations. Because of the monitoring system available, we have used the NTSC receiver phosphor primary system [8] in the implementation of color AMBTC. This system defines three primaries R, G, and B such that

$$0 \leqslant R \leqslant 1; \quad 0 \leqslant G \leqslant 1; \quad 0 \leqslant B \leqslant 1. \tag{24}$$

The relationship between this group of primaries and other coordinate systems is given in the literature [8]. From this point we assume that our gamut of color is limited to the reproducible colors in the NTSC primary system. Taking into account the boundaries for R, G, and B, the solid of all reproducible colors is a cube such as in Fig. 9.

B. Correlation Between Color Planes

In typical color image data, there exists a high degree of correlation between the planes R, G, and B. It is well known that more efficient coding is achieved when the different output signals are decorrelated. It is therefore convenient to perform some decorrelating operation on the planes R, G, and B before trying to apply AMBTC to the three signals. It is also desired to have an invertible transformation. The ideal decorrelation operation is a Karhunen–Loeve transform that would theoretically achieve total decorrelation between planes. However, such an approach leads to lengthy computations of eigenvalues and eigenvectors and depends on the image statistics. Thus, it is impractical.

There exist other transformations that, although they do not achieve optimum results, are close to the optimum case and are much simpler in practical implementation. We will make use of one particular transformation, the NTSC R-G-B to Y-I-Q transformation. This is the method used in the NTSC color TV system. Also, as is shown in [9], [10], it has RGB component space energy compaction properties comparable to Karhunen–Loeve for most images.

The direct R-G-B to Y-I-Q transformation is given by

$$\begin{bmatrix} Y \\ I \\ Q \end{bmatrix} = L \begin{bmatrix} R \\ G \\ B \end{bmatrix}; \quad \text{where } L = \begin{bmatrix} 0.299 & 0.587 & 0.114 \\ 0.596 & -0.274 & -0.322 \\ 0.211 & -0.523 & 0.312 \end{bmatrix} \tag{25}$$

and the inverse Y-I-Q to R-G-B transformation is given by

$$\begin{bmatrix} R \\ G \\ B \end{bmatrix} = L^{-1} \begin{bmatrix} Y \\ I \\ Q \end{bmatrix}; \quad \text{where } L^{-1} = \begin{bmatrix} 1.000 & 0.956 & 0.621 \\ 1.000 & -0.272 & -0.647 \\ 1.000 & -1.106 & 1.703 \end{bmatrix}. \tag{26}$$

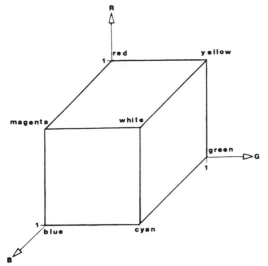

Fig. 9.   Cube of NTSC colors in the *R-G-B* NTSC space of primaries.

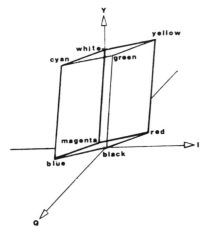

Fig. 10.   Resulting solid of colors in the *Y-I-Q* space obtained by mapping the cube in Fig. 9 with the *RGB* to *YIQ* transformation.

The range of the Y, I, and Q signals using (24) and (25) is

$$0 \leqslant Y \leqslant 1 \qquad (27)$$

$$-0.596 \leqslant I \leqslant 0.596 \qquad (28)$$

$$-0.523 \leqslant Q \leqslant 0.523. \qquad (29)$$

Mapping the cube of Fig. 9 in the *R-G-B* space to the *Y-I-Q* space results in the solid shown in Fig. 10.

C. AMBTC Color System

Suppose that we have three color planes R, G, and B of NTSC primaries for a given image. The goal is to transmit that image achieving compression and having a reconstructed image with an acceptable quality for the human observer. The proposed system diagram is shown in Fig. 11. In that diagram, the R, G, and B signals pass through a linear transformation given in (25) to get the NTSC Y, I, and Q signals. In order to get a high compression and remembering that the human eye is more sensitive to spatial variations of Y, fairly sensitive to spatial variations of I, and less to Q, the I signal is subsampled by taking averaging windows of 2 × 2 pixels and the Q signal is subsampled by taking averaging windows of 4 ×

4 pixels. Noninteger values could have been used for this decimation; however, they are integers to mantain simplicity in the system. The outputs of this filtering stage are Y', I', Q', which are coded with three separate AMBTC coders. At the receiver the signals are reconstructed in AMBTC quantizers. In order to keep the sizes correct, signals Y''', I''', Q''' are obtained by taking bilinear interpolations of two points for I and four points for Q in each direction (x and y). Finally, using a linear transformation L^{-1}, the reconstructed planes $\hat{R}$, $\hat{G}$, $\hat{B}$ are obtained.

D. Problems in the Practical Implementation

The system proposed above presents certain problems that one has to solve in any practical case. Looking at Fig. 9, we can see that only those points that lie inside the cube of *R-G-B* space are reproducible NTSC colors. On the other hand, only those points that lie inside the solid of Fig. 10 in the *Y-I-Q* space are reproducible NTSC colors in the mapped *R-G-B* cube. Our problem then is to not allow the reconstructed Y, I, and Q signals to fall outside the solid of Fig. 10 in order to have reproducible colors when they are converted again into *R-G-B* signals. This problem arises in the proposed system since each of the signals suffers different distortions in their paths. Those distortions sometimes give place to groups of Y'', I'', Q'' values that are outside the reproducible color solid.

Consequently, it is necessary to modify this situation using some specified criterion. We will propose two methods of correcting the errors. One, which we call "correction by truncation," is relatively simple to implement. The other, which we call "correction by preserving luminance," tries to preserve an important quantity for the human observer, the luminance of the image.

Correction by Truncation: This method consists in keeping the received *R-G-B* value within the bounds for these signals. If the received group is inside the cube of Fig. 9 we take this group as our reconstructed point $\hat{R}$, $\hat{G}$, $\hat{B}$. In the case that one or more signals (R, G, or B) are outside the permitted range, we take the corresponding quantity to its nearest reproducible bound. For example:

$$R'' = 0.5 \qquad \hat{R} = 0.5$$
$$G'' = 1.2 \qquad \hat{G} = 1.0$$
$$B'' = -0.3 \qquad \hat{B} = 0.0.$$

Correction by Preserving Luminance: This approach is based on the fact that the luminance signal Y is the signal that suffers the least distortion in our system (see Fig. 11). Therefore, we would like to preserve the received value of Y.

It turns out that it is more convenient to analyze this problem in the *Y-I-Q* space. In this space, the planes with constant luminance intersect the solid of Fig. 10, forming regions *I-Q* that show all reproducible values for a given Y. These regions are shown for several luminance values in Fig. 12. As we can see, there are six possible lines which define the borders of those regions and they move on the *I-Q* plane according to the value of Y. The equations of those lines come from intersecting each one of the six faces of the solid of Fig. 10 with a plane of constant luminance. From (26) they are

$$\text{for } G = 1: \qquad I = (Y - 1)/0.272 - 2.378Q \qquad (30)$$
$$\text{for } R = 1: \qquad I = (1 - Y)/0.956 - 0.649Q$$
$$\text{for } B = 1: \qquad I = (Y - 1)/1.106 + 1.539Q$$
$$\text{for } G = 0: \qquad I = Y/0.272 - 2.378Q$$
$$\text{for } R = 0: \qquad I = -Y/0.956 - 0.649Q$$
$$\text{for } B = 0: \qquad I = Y/1.106 + 1.539Q.$$

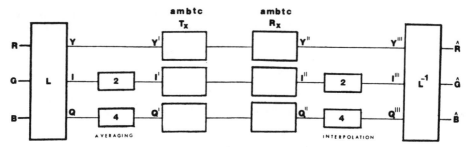

Fig. 11. Proposed AMBTC color system.

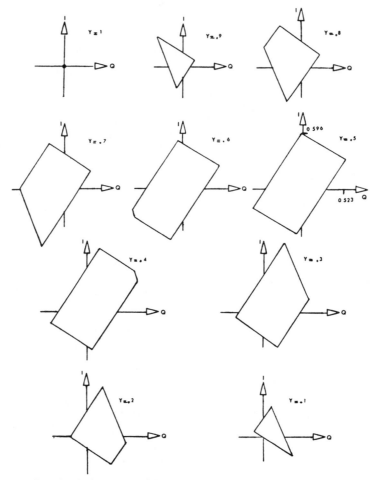

Fig. 12. Regions in plane *I-Q* obtained by intersecting the solid of Fig. 10 with constant luminance planes.

In general, the regions are defined by less than six border lines; however, all of them were used in the correction algorithm. We will study the correcting method, making use of Fig. 13. The received value is given by Y_R, I_R, Q_R and the corrected value is $\hat{Y}$, $\hat{I}$, $\hat{Q}$. Therefore, $Y = Y_R$ is the value that determines the particular shape of the *I-Q* region. It must be noted that, given a particular line defined by the previous equations, the reproducible point is always on the semiplane divided by this line that contains the origin. The correction algorithm simply takes a received point, and for each of the lines defined by (30) asks the following question: is the received pair (I_R, Q_R) in the semiplane divided by the current line that contains the origin?. If the answer is yes, the question is made for the next line. If the answer if no, it corrects *I*

and *Q*. The corrected values of $\hat{I}$ and $\hat{Q}$ are obtained taking the intersection of the current border line and a line that passes through the received point and the origin. Suppose that the current line equation is

$$I = fQ + g \tag{31}$$

where *f* and *g* depend on the received luminance value and on the line under analysis [see (30)]. The corrected value of $\hat{Q}$ is then

$$\hat{Q} = \frac{g}{\left(\dfrac{I_R}{Q_R} - f\right)} \qquad \text{for } Q_R \neq 0 \tag{32}$$

192

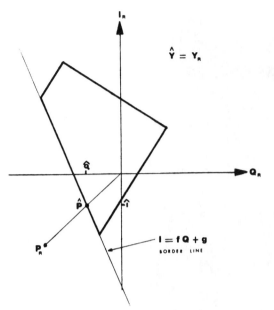

Fig. 13. Analyzing the method of correction of unreproducible colors by preserving luminance.

$$\hat{Q} = 0 \qquad \text{for } Q_R = 0$$

and $\hat{I}$ is

$$\hat{I} = f\hat{Q} + g. \tag{33}$$

Now, the algorithm takes as received values the new ones and continues with the question for the next border line. When all six lines where examined, the corrected value is $(Y_R, \hat{I}, \hat{Q})$.

The luminance preserving method also preserves the color hue, and only the saturation is varied to conform the coordinate values to a reproducible color.

E. Results of the System for Actual Images

The system proposed in Fig. 11 has been tested, having as input a 256 × 256 pixel color image with 8 bits per pixel for each color plane, that is, 24 bits per pixel. The original image is in the upper left corner of Fig. 14. The image on the upper right corner of Fig. 14 was obtained with the proposed system using correction by preserving luminance. The image on the lower left corner of Fig. 14 was obtained using correction by truncation. The differences between these two corrected images are minor. The bit rate of both is 2.13 bits/pixel at the input of the receiver. This bit rate is achieved in the following manner: bit rate for Y, 26/16 bits/pixel; bit rate for I, 26/64 bits/pixel; bit rate for Q, 26/256 bits/pixel.

Since the original has 24 bits/pixel, a good deal of compression has been achieved, more than 11 : 1. Note also that the color information does not need many additional bits. Indeed, the bit rate of I plus the bit rate of Q is about 0.5 bits/pixel or a third part of the luminance's bit rate.

In order to evaluate errors introduced by the system, let us define the relative mean square error for one color plane (as in [10]) as the average of square differences divided by the estimated variance of the plane. We then can define an average total error as

$$\epsilon_T{}^2 = (\epsilon_R{}^2 + \epsilon_G{}^2 + \epsilon_B{}^2)/3. \tag{34}$$

All these errors were evaluated for the images in Fig. 14. The values of the original variances are

$$\bar{\sigma}_R{}^2 = 587 \qquad \bar{\sigma}_G{}^2 = 189 \qquad \bar{\sigma}_B{}^2 = 252.$$

For the image obtained using correction by truncation, the errors are

$$\epsilon_R{}^2 = 12 \text{ percent} \quad \epsilon_G{}^2 = 24.2 \text{ percent} \quad \epsilon_B{}^2 = 34.3 \text{ percent}$$

$$\epsilon_T{}^2 = 23.5 \text{ percent}.$$

For the image obtained using correction by preserving luminance, the corresponding values are

$$\epsilon_R{}^2 = 13.3 \text{ percent} \quad \epsilon_G{}^2 = 24.4 \text{ percent} \quad \epsilon_B{}^2 = 34.2 \text{ percent}$$

$$\epsilon_T{}^2 = 24 \text{ percent}.$$

Although the errors of the second set of values are slightly bigger than the first one, the advantage of the method that corrects by preserving luminance is that it keeps a low error on the reconstructed luminance which can be useful in some cases. Furthermore, results of a subjective test using five untrained persons showed that four of them chose the image obtained using correction by preserving luminance.

The principal artifact of the reconstructed upper right and lower left images in Fig. 14 is that they present some false contours in regions of slow changes in luminance and in chrominance. This is more noticeable in the background of the upper right and lower left images of Fig. 14. In order to improve these images, an AMBTC quantizer that uses two-dimensional quantization for $\bar{\eta}$ and $\bar{\alpha}$ has been implemented. The major idea in using this type of quantizer is given by Healy and Mitchell in [4]. They explain that in low variance zones, the value of the mean is very important for the observer, and therefore, it is convenient to assign more bits to the mean. On the other hand, in high variance zones, the mean is not critical for the human and fewer bits can be assigned to the mean.

Reference [4, Table I] shows the characteristics of the joint quantizer used. The resulting image, using three AMBTC 10 bit two-dimensional quantizers in the color system of Fig. 11, is shown in the lower right corner of Fig. 14. As expected, the false contours have disappeared. Some chroma errors are still present in this image, especially under the lips and other parts of the face. These chroma errors could be due to the high subsampling in one of the signals that carries color, the Q signal. However, the image on the lower left of Fig. 14 has a great similarity with the original. The errors for this image are

$$\epsilon_R{}^2 = 12 \text{ percent} \quad \epsilon_G{}^2 = 22 \text{ percent} \quad \epsilon_B{}^2 = 33 \text{ percent}$$

$$\epsilon_T{}^2 = 22.3 \text{ percent}.$$

The errors obtained for this two-dimensional quantized image are smaller than those of both previous methods.

VI. Conclusion

An improvement in BTC can be obtained by preserving absolute moments. This method is called absolute moment block truncation coding or AMBTC. Both computing speed and reconstructed image quality are improved by preserving absolute moments instead of standard moments. The new method has the same general characteristics as BTC which include low storage requirements and an extremely simple coding and decoding technique. Color images can also be coded using this method. The block size for the chroma data can be increased by less frequent spatial sampling, resulting in good quality reconstructed color imagery.

Appendix

To illustrate absolute moment block truncation coding, let us present the following example. The image to be coded has been divided into nonoverlapping blocks of 4 × 4 pixels.

Fig. 14. Upper left: original 256 × 256 color image (8 bits/color = 24 bits/pixel). Upper right: reconstruction using AMBTC and correction by preserving luminance (2.13 bits/pixel). Lower left: reconstruction using AMBTC and correction by truncation (2.13 bits/pixel). Lower right: reconstruction using AMBTC, correction by truncation, and a 10 bit two-dimensional quantizer for each mean and deviation (also 2.13 bits/pixel).

Suppose that one of the blocks is

$$X = \begin{bmatrix} 121 & 114 & 56 & 47 \\ 37 & 200 & 247 & 255 \\ 16 & 0 & 12 & 169 \\ 43 & 5 & 7 & 251 \end{bmatrix}$$

Using (5) and (6), the corresponding sample moment values are

$$\bar{\eta} = 98.75 \quad \text{and} \quad \bar{\alpha} = 83.22 \quad \text{or} \quad \bar{\gamma} = \frac{m\bar{\alpha}}{2} = 665.76.$$

Taking the mean value as threshold, the bit plane is

$$B = \begin{bmatrix} 1 & 1 & 0 & 0 \\ 0 & 1 & 1 & 1 \\ 0 & 0 & 0 & 1 \\ 0 & 0 & 0 & 1 \end{bmatrix}$$

$\bar{\eta}$, $\bar{\gamma}$, and B are sent to the receiver. At that point, a and b are computed using (13) and (14):

$$a = 24.8 \quad b = 193.8$$

so, the reconstructed block becomes

$$X_R = \begin{bmatrix} 193.8 & 193.8 & 24.8 & 24.8 \\ 24.8 & 193.8 & 193.8 & 193.8 \\ 24.8 & 24.8 & 24.8 & 193.8 \\ 24.8 & 24.8 & 24.8 & 193.8 \end{bmatrix}$$

One can check that X_R has the same sample mean and the same sample first absolute central moment as the original block X. The mean square error for this example is MSE = 1605.

This example was taken to be the same as that presented in [1] by Delp and Mitchell, which gives the following reconstructed plane using standard BTC:

$$X_{R\,btc} = \begin{bmatrix} 204.1 & 204.1 & 16.8 & 16.8 \\ 16.8 & 204.1 & 204.1 & 204.1 \\ 16.8 & 16.8 & 16.8 & 204.1 \\ 16.8 & 16.8 & 16.8 & 204.1 \end{bmatrix}$$

and the mean square error for this example, using standard BTC, is MSE = 1687. Note that the necessary quantity of information to be transmitted is given by

$$\frac{N_\eta + N_\alpha + m}{m} \quad [\text{bits/pixel}]$$

where N_η is the number of bits of the $\bar{\eta}$ value; N_α is the number of bits of the $\bar{\alpha}$ value; and m the number of pixels in the block. Typical values for N_η are 6–8 bits and for N_α are 4–6 bits, which gives about 1.675–1.875 bits/pixel.

REFERENCES

[1] E. J. Delp and O. R. Mitchell, "Image compression using block truncation coding," *IEEE Trans. Commun.*, vol. COM-27, pp. 1335–1342, Sept. 1979.
[2] E. J. Delp, "Moment preserving quantization and its application in block truncation coding," Ph.D. dissertation, Purdue Univ., West Lafayette, IN, Aug. 1979.
[3] E. J. Delp and O. R. Mitchell, "Multilevel graphics representation using block truncation coding," *Proc. IEEE*, vol. 68, pp. 868–873, July 1980.
[4] D. J. Healy and O. R. Mitchell, "Digital video bandwidth compression using block truncation coding," *IEEE Trans. Commun.*, vol. COM-29, pp. 1809–1817, Dec. 1981.

[5] M. D. Lema, "Absolute moment block truncation coding and its application to still color images," M.S.E.E. thesis, Purdue Univ., West Lafayette, IN, Aug. 1982.

[6] T. W. Goeddel and S. C. Bass, "A two-dimensional quantizer for coding digital imagery," *IEEE Trans. Commun.,* vol. COM-29, pp. 60–67, Jan. 1981.

[7] D. G. Fink, *Television Engineering Handbook,* New York: McGraw-Hill, 1957.

[8] W. K. Pratt, *Digital Image Processing,* New York: Wiley, 1978, p. 737.

[9] C. B. Rubinstein and J. O. Limb, "Statistical dependence between components of a differentially quantized color signal," *IEEE Trans. Commun. Technol.,* vol. COM-20, pp. 890–899, Oct. 1972.

[10] W. K. Pratt, "Spatial transform coding of color images," *IEEE Trans. Commun. Technol.,* vol. COM-19, pp. 980–992, Dec. 1971.

A Data Compression Technique for Synthetic Aperture Radar Images

V.S. FROST, Member, IEEE
G.J. MINDEN, Member, IEEE
University of Kansas
Telecommunications & Information
Sciences Laboratory

A data compression technique is developed for synthetic aperture radar (SAR) imagery. The technique is based on an SAR image model and is designed to preserve the local statistics in the image by an adaptive variable rate modification of block truncation coding (BTC). A data rate of approximately 1.6 bit/pixel is achieved with the technique while maintaining the image quality and cultural (pointlike) targets. The algorithm requires no large data storage and is computationally simple.

Manuscript received January 30, 1985; revised August 7, 1985.

This work was supported by NASA under Grant NAGN-381.

Authors' address: Department of Electrical and Computer Engineering, Telecommunications and Information Sciences Laboratory, University of Kansas Center for Research, Lawrence, KS 66045.

I. INTRODUCTION

This paper describes an efficient image data compression technique which has been specifically designed for synthetic aperture radar (SAR) images. SAR has become an important class of imaging sensor for both civilian and military applications. As with other imaging systems there is a need to transmit and store SAR images, and thus there has been considerable interest in efficient coding algorithms for SAR [1–3].

The aim of data compression is to minimize the data rate while maintaining the information contained in the signal using as simple an algorithm as possible. Thus a desirable property of an image encoding algorithm is fidelity; i.e., the reconstructed (received) image should preserve all of the "important" features of the sensed image. For example, in some radar applications cultural features which appear in SAR images as small bright features are important and should be faithfully reproduced. In the geologic analysis of SAR images, texture [4] is important and thus should be preserved. Image fidelity (quality) is a difficult quantity to measure [5] because it is application dependent. Image data compression algorithms are also compared on the basis of their compressing capability, i.e., the number of bits per image sample in the coded image. Implementation complexity is also an important consideration in evaluating data compression algorithms [6]. The technique described below preserves important image features (e.g., cultural features) at about 1.6 bit/sample and is simple to implement.

Standard compression techniques primarily fall into two broad categories, predictive and transform coding. Predictive coding is performed in the spatial domain and attempts to remove the local redundancies in the image. Transform coding is performed by an energy preserving transformation of the image into another image so that the maximum information is placed into a minimum number of transform components [6]. Many different transforms, e.g., Fourier, Cosine, Karhunen–Loeve, have been used. Transform coding tends to be more complex than predictive coding. It is shown in Section II that predictive coding is not effective for SAR images, and further, it is argued that transform coding is not a viable alternative because of the low correlation observed in SAR images even though it has been tried [1].

The technique developed here is a modification of the block truncation coding (BTC) algorithm developed in [7]. BTC is suitable for SAR images because it preserves the local statistics of the image. In SAR these statistics are important. In BTC the image is divided into small blocks (e.g., 4×4) of picture elements (pixels) and for each block a 1 bit quartizer is applied such that the block can be reconstructed with the moments (e.g., mean and variance) preserved. Clearly, in addition to the bit mask (quantized block), supplementary information is needed. In the BTC the supplementary information is the sample mean $\bar{x}$ and standard deviation S_x. For example, a BTC system using 4×4 blocks of picture elements (pixels) (with 8 bit/pixel) and 8 bits to code $\bar{x}$ and S_x results in a 4 to 1 compression or 2 bit/pixel. Reducing the number of mean and standard deviation code bits as well as further coding of the bit mask can result in further compression [7, 8].

Direct application of the BTC algorithm [7] (2 bit/pixel) to SAR images produced reconstructed images that were of suitable quality visually and preserved cultural features. These results are presented in Section VI. A further reduction in bit rate was achieved by observing that the local mean and variance are proportional in SAR images of homogeneous areas, and thus, it is required to transmit only the mean. This modification results in a 5.3 to 1 compression or 1.5 bit/pixel (using the above example).

This modification did produce reconstructed images of acceptable quality; however, significant contrast was lost for cultural features. This weakness was overcome by developing an adaptive BTC algorithm. The adaptive BTC algorithm sends only the mean if the local area (block) fits the standard radar model. For those blocks where the model does not fit, both the mean and standard deviation are transmitted.

Using this adaptive approach, a 5 to 1 compression or about 1.6 bit/pixel was achieved with the quality of the original 2 bit/pixel BTC algorithm. Now a variable number of bits per block is required for the adaptive BTC technique. However, this modification to the BTC algorithm does not significantly increase its complexity.

A statistical model for SAR images is reviewed in Section II. The original BTC technique is discussed in Section III. The modifications to the BTC algorithm for SAR images are described in the following section. The BTC, modified BTC (mean only), and adaptive BTC were implemented and tested using SEASAT-A SAR imagery. These results are presented in Section VI. The SAR image data compression described here is simple, produces reconstructed images of adequate quality for many applications, and tends to preserve cultural futures.

II. STATISTICAL MODEL FOR RADAR IMAGES

A. Point Statistics

An imaging radar illuminates areas of the terrain within its field of view and records the value of the power returned from nonoverlapping resolution cells on the ground. A resolution cell is typically made up of a large number of scatterers, and under some mild assumptions we can model the signal received by the radar (before detection) as a narrowband Gaussian random process. Then with a square-law detector, the value of the received power P from a resolution cell has the probability density function (pdf) [9–11]

$$f_p(p) = \mu^{-1} \exp(-p/\mu), \qquad p \geq 0$$
$$= 0, \qquad p < 0 \tag{1}$$

where $E\{P\} = \mu$.

In most imaging radars several independent measurements of the reflected power for each resolution cell are obtained and are averaged to form the image intensity value $Y(t_1, t_2)$ for the resolution cell with a spatial location (t_1, t_2). The pdf of Y is the gamma distribution [9, 10] of the form

$$f_y(y) = \frac{y^{N-1} (\mu/N)^{-N} \exp(-yN/\mu)}{\Gamma(N)}, \qquad y \geq 0$$
$$= 0, \qquad y < 0 \tag{2}$$

where N is the number of independent measurements (or "looks"),

$$Y = \frac{1}{N} \sum_{i=1}^{N} P_i; \qquad \Gamma(N) = (N-1)!.$$

The mean value μ of the power reflected from a resolution cell is proportional to the radar reflectivity X of the resolution cell, and we can assume that $\mu = X$ without any loss of generality. Since the radar reflectivity changes from resolution cell to resolution cell, we can model the reflectivity as a random variable X (or a random process $X(t_1, t_2)$) and write (2) as a conditional pdf of the form

$$f_{Y|X}(y|x) = \frac{y^{N-1} x^{-N} \exp(-yN/x)}{\Gamma(N) N^{-N}}. \tag{3}$$

The conditional pdf given in (3) is based on the observation that X is not in general a constant, i.e., it changes from area to area. Even the characteristics of a homogeneous target area can change about some average as different parts of the target are illuminated. These within-field variations have been measured using radar data [16].

We assume a Swerling type II [10] target model to describe the statistical characteristics of the echo on a per-pixel basis and then let the mean reflectivity X vary to model the SAR image of a large heterogeneous scene. With an appropriate change of variable we obtain the relationship between X and Y:

$$Y(t_1, t_2) = \frac{X(t_1, t_2) Z(t_1, t_2)}{2N} \tag{4}$$

where Z has a standard chi-square distribution with $2N$ degrees of freedom [10], and X and Z are statistically independent.

Specific factors in the image formation process can be modeled by passing $Y(t_1, t_2)$ through a linear system. The transfer function of this system would model the image response due to antenna, correlator, and receiver and induce a spatial correlation. This is the model previously proposed in [17]. However, the low spatial correlation observed for this and other studies [12] suggest that these effects are not significant. The observed low spatial correlation is most likely due to the sampling of a lowpass random process at approximately the Nyquist rate which occurs in the digital formation of SAR images. Thus if the reciprocal of the system bandwidth is a measure of the size of a resolution cell, then adjacent pixels sampled at approximately the Nyquist rate will exhibit a low correlation.

Note that $Z(t_1, t_2)$ represents the speckle noise in SAR images. Here we have explicitly shown that X and Z are functions of position; however, for notational convenience the spatial dependence will be dropped. It can be easily shown that for a given X

$$E[Y/X] = \mu \tag{5}$$

$$\sigma^2_{Y/X} = \mu^2/N. \tag{6}$$

For our purposes, we can see that if we are considering a "homogeneous" target (i.e., $E\{X\} = \mu$), then we can predict the variance given the mean. This observation is the basis for the modified BTC algorithm.

B. Autocorrelation Properties of SAR Images

The feasibility of using either predictive or transform coding for SAR image can be discussed in terms of the image correlations properties. On a local level, i.e., inside a homogeneous area, the model (4) indicates that adjacent pixels are uncorrelated. This is quite different compared with images collected with noncoherent sensors. For noncoherent sensors, e.g., LANDSAT or aerial photographs, pixels in homogenous areas are highly correlated. The low correlation of adjacent pixels has been observed previously [12]. The presence of a low correlation of adjacent pixels suggests that predictive coding will not be as effective on SAR data as it is on optical images.

However, transform coding can operate over larger regions and thus the regional correlation properties of SAR images needs to be considered. Fig. 1 presents a typical one-dimensional autocorrelation[1] in the row and column directions of an SAR image of terrain (see Fig. 4 for the image). Note that this autocorrelation function decays very rapidly. The presence of some correlation indicates that transform coding is possible; however, the rapid decay implies that the size of the transform window must be large, thus greatly increasing the memory and computational requirements of the compression algorithm. A sophisticated transform coding algorithm for SAR images has been reported [1]. The technique described in [1] uses row/column deletion (resampling) and transform coding; however, the algorithm is computationally intensive and requires substantial amounts of memory.

Reexamining the SAR image model (4) we notice that the mean and variance of each local area (within a larger homogeneous region) are redundant, and thus a coding algorithm which preserves these image attributes would be suitable for SAR. In the next section, the BTC

[1]The record contained 512 pixels and the autocorrelation function was obtained using fast Fourier transform (FFT) techniques as described in [18].

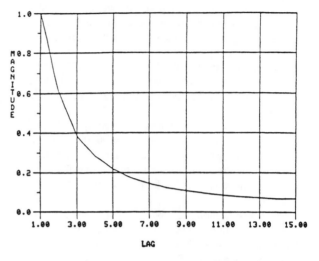

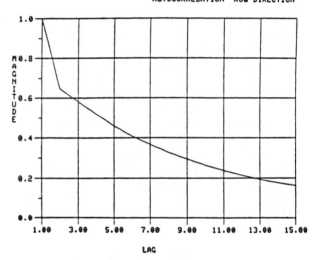

Fig. 1. SAR image autocorrelation function of terrain.

algorithm which does preserve these features is discussed, and it is modified to fit the above SAR image models.

III. REVIEW OF BTC

Let $\bar{y}$ and S_y denote the sample mean and standard deviation of a block (e.g., 4×4) of pixels in an SAR image. That is,

$$\bar{y} = \frac{1}{m} \sum_{i=1}^{m} y_i \tag{7}$$

and

$$S_y^2 = \overline{(y^2)} - (\bar{y}^2) \tag{8}$$

with

$$\overline{(y^2)} = \frac{1}{m} \sum_{i=1}^{m} y_i^2 \tag{9}$$

198

where m is the number of pixels in the block and y_i is the pixel intensity. In BTC a 1 bit quantizer is used for each pixel in the block with the quantizing threshold set at $\bar{y}$. That is, if $y_i \geq \bar{y}$ then that pixel location is coded with a 1, otherwise with a 0. A bit mask is thus formed. This bit mask along with $\bar{y}$ and S_y is transmitted/stored.

At the receiver, a level A is assigned to a point if that pixel location within the block contained a 0 and a level B if a 1 was contained. Levels A and B are selected to preserve the moments of the block. These levels can be simply found as [7, 13]

$$A = \bar{y} - S_y \frac{\sqrt{q}}{m - q} \quad \tag{10}$$

and

$$B = \bar{y} + S_y \frac{\sqrt{m - q}}{q} \tag{11}$$

where q is the number of ones in the received block. For a 4×4 block and using 8 bits to code $\bar{y}$ and S_y results in 4 to 1 compression ratio or 2 bit/pixel.

IV. MODIFIED BTC

Based on the SAR image model, we can predict the standard deviation for a block based on the sample mean. Let the predicted standard deviation be

$$\sigma_p = \bar{y}/\sqrt{N} \tag{12}$$

where N is the number of looks for the SAR. The BTC technique described in Section III is then applied at the source. Now only the sample mean and the bit mask are transmitted. At the receiver, levels A and B are reconstructed using

$$A = \bar{y}\left[1 - \sqrt{\frac{q}{N(m-q)}}\right] \tag{13}$$

and

$$B = \bar{y}\left[1 - \sqrt{\frac{m-q}{Nq}}\right]. \tag{14}$$

For a 4×4 block and using 8 bits to code the sample mean a compression ratio of 5.3 to 1 or a data rate of 1.5 bit/pixel is obtained.

It was found that this technique produced reconstructed images of homogeneous areas almost identical to the 2 bit/pixel technique. However, contrast was lost on cultural features relative to the initial BTC method. The reason for this is obvious. Regions containing cultural features (and edges) do not fit the SAR model of (4). To overcome this weakness an adaptive variable bit rate BTC was developed.

V. ADAPTIVE VARIABLE BIT RATE BTC

The goal of the adaptive BTC technique is to use the modified BTC for those image blocks where it is appropriate, i.e., where the model fits, and to use the original BTC algorithm otherwise.

The model does not adequately describe the SAR image for heterogeneous local areas which contain a mixture of pixels from two or more targets or cultural features. It is these regions where the original BTC technique will be more effective. A simple test based on the predicted and sample variances was developed to indicate if the data from an image block fits the SAR model. Specifically, if $k S_y^2 > \sigma_p^2$ (where k is a constant) then the model does not fit the data. That is, if the observed (sample) variance is "too much" greater than the predicted variance then it would be expected that the model does not provide an adequate description for the data. The proportionality constant k must be selected such that the probability of rejecting the model when the model is valid, P_F, is small, i.e.,

$$P_F = P(k S_y^2 > \sigma_p^2 \,|\, \text{model is valid}). \tag{15}$$

From the theory of confidence intervals [14] we know that we can find a β such that

$$P(m S_y^2/\sigma_p^2 > \beta) = P(\sigma_p^2 < m S_y^2/\beta) = P_F. \tag{16}$$

The above equation indicates that the probability that $m S_y^2/\beta$ (here $k = m/\beta$) is greater than the unknown parameter σ_p^2 is P_F when the SAR model fits the data. The predicted variance σ_p^2 is calculated using (12). Therefore the SAR model is not appropriate if

$$\bar{y}^2/N < (m/\beta) S_y^2 \tag{17}$$

or

$$\bar{y}^2/S_y^2 < mN/\beta \tag{18}$$

where β is selected to force P_F to be small, e.g., 10^{-3}. Note that $\bar{y}^2/S_y^2$ is an estimate for the number of looks used in the SAR processing based on the m pixels in the block. This ratio will be referred to as the local number of looks.

Assuming that the pixel intensities are Gaussian distributed (which is true for large N) the random variable $m S_y^2/\sigma_p^2$ has a χ^2 distribution with $m - 1$ degrees of freedom. Thus P_F can be estimated. For example, let $m = 16$ (i.e., 4×4 blocks) and $N = 4$ then for a $P_F = 0.005$, $\beta = 32.8$, $k \approx 0.5$, and $mN/\beta \approx 2$. In this case we would expect that the sample standard deviations would be needlessly transmitted only for 1 in every 200 blocks.

The adaptive BTC algorithm for each block is implemented as shown in Fig. 2. At the transmitter, the sample mean and standard deviation are calculated and the bit mask is formed as specified in the original BTC algorithm. An estimate for the number of looks $\bar{y}^2/S_y^2$ is calculated next and compared to a threshold mN/β. If the local number of looks is less than the threshold, then a flag is set on and a data block is sent which contains the bit mask, sample mean, sample standard deviation, and the flag bit indicating the presence of the standard deviation. If the local number of looks exceeds the

```
SendAdaptiveBTC( InputImage, Threshold )
    DO for each row of blocks
        DO for each column of blocks
            Compute BlockMean and BlockStandardDeviation
            Send( BlockMean )
            IF ( (BlockMean / BlockStandardDeviation) < Threshold )
                THEN Send( 1 )
                     Send( BlockStandardDeviation )
                ELSE Send( 0 )
            DO for each row of block
                DO for each column of block
                    IF ( Pixel > BlockMean )
                        THEN Send( 1 )
                        ELSE Send( 0 )
                OD
        OD
    OD
```

```
ReceiveAdaptiveBTC
    DO for each row of blocks
        DO for each column of blocks
            Receive( BlockMean )
            Receive( BlockSDFlag )
            IF ( BlockSDFlag = 1 )
                THEN Receive( BlockStandardDeviation )
                ELSE BlockStandardDeviation := BlockMean / sqrt( N )
            A := BlockMean - BlockStandardDeviation * sqrt( q / m - q )
            B := BlockMean - BlockStandardDeviation * sqrt( q / m - q )
            DO for each row of pixels
                DO for each column of pixels
                    Receive( PixelFlag )
                    IF ( PixelFlag = 0 )
                        THEN Pixel := A
                        ELSE Pixel := B
                OD
        OD
    OD
```

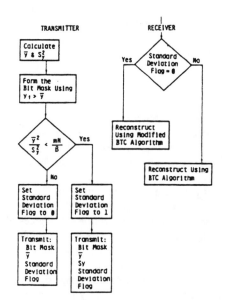

Fig. 2. Adaptive BTC algorithm and flow diagram.

threshold, then it is highly probable that the SAR model is valid and thus the standard deviation present flag is set off and a block is sent which contains only the bit mask, sample mean, and the flag. At the receiver the flag is tested. If it is on, the original BTC reconstruction algorithm is applied, i.e., (10), (11); otherwise the modified BTC algorithm (13), (14) is used to reconstruct the image.

The adaptive BTC algorithm described above automatically adds 1/16 bit/pixel overhead, the standard deviation present flag. It was found that for SEASAT-A SAR images the quality of the original BTC technique was maintained using the adaptive approach at approximately 1.6 bit/pixel.

The BTC algorithm produces reconstructed images which have a blocky appearance [13] when displayed with magnification. This characteristic is also evident when the BTC algorithm is applied to SAR images. However, the image reconstruction algorithm in the adaptive BTC technique can be modified to remove this blocky appearance.

When the SAR image model, e.g., (2), is valid and only the mean is transmitted we know that a pixel marked with a 1(0) can be modeled by a conditional pdf, i.e., the pdf given in (2) is conditioned on the event that the sample is above (below) the mean. Synthetic sampling (using pseudorandom numbers) can be used in the reconstruction to map pixels marked with a 1(0) into a gray level based on the appropriate conditional pdf. As is shown in the following section, using pseudorandom numbers in the reconstruction algorithm does effectively remove the blockness. Unfortunately, generation of pseudorandom numbers is computationally intensive; thus this modification increases the computational complexity of the algorithm. In some applications this refinement is not required.

In the following sections the four compression algorithms, original, modified BTC, adaptive BTC, and adaptive BTC with pseudorandom reconstruction are compared.

VI. RESULTS

The compression algorithms, BTC, modified BTC, adaptive BTC, and adaptive BTC with pseudorandom reconstruction have been applied to SEASAT-A SAR imagery, and their performance is discussed here. As mentioned previously, image quality is difficult to quantify. Here the performance evaluation is based on two criteria: 1) the faithful reproduction of cultural features, and 2) the general appearance of the reconstructed image relative to the original.

The SEASAT-A SAR imagery used here had a resolution of 25×25 m with N in the range of 3 to 4 depending on the specific implementation of the SAR processor. Each pixel intensity was represented by 8 bits (0–255 grey levels). (For more details about the sensor see [15].) For all the compression algorithms described here, the sample mean was coded using 8 bit/block. Also, a 4×4 pixel block was used in all cases. In the original BTC algorithm the standard deviation was also coded using 8 bit/block resulting in a 2 bit/pixel data rate.

The modified BTC algorithm resulted in a 1.5 bit/pixel data rate. In the adaptive BTC algorithm, the standard deviation was coded using 7 bit/block, then allowing for the 1 overhead bit results in a maximum of 32 bit/block. Thus in the adaptive BTC technique each block is coded into 25 or 32 bits depending on the statistics of the pixel intensities of the block. A threshold of 2.0 on the local number of looks was used in all cases. The data rate of the adaptive BTC algorithm is variable. However, in most cases it was about 1.6 bit/pixel.

The response of the first three algorithms to a "pointlike" target is shown one-dimensionally in Fig. 3. Fig. 3(a) represents an intensity profile of 100 pixels from a SEASAT-SAR image. There is one bright feature in the center of this profile. The target-to-background contrast in Fig. 3 is about 9 dB. The target-to-background contrast is the ratio (in dB) of the intensity of the target to the average of the background. Fig. 3(b) is the reconstructed profile using the original BTC technique. The target is still quite evident, the average background level has remained the same as expected and the target level has been reduced. The target-to-background contrast is about 7.5 dB, a loss of 1.5 dB. The result of the modified BTC algorithm is shown in Fig. 3(c). In this

case, the target-to-background loss is about 3.4 dB. This loss is not considered acceptable. The adaptive BTC algorithm, Fig. 3(d), restored the profile to that given by the original BTC at a small cost in data rate from 1.5 bit/pixel to 1.58 bit/pixel. There is little difference between the original and adaptive BTC results (Figs. 3(b) and 3(d); this observation is true for all the results presented here.

A scene containing a variety of terrain features is shown in Fig. 4. This scene is composed of 512×512 pixels. The three compressed images favorably compare to the original in terms of reproducing the terrain features. However, there is some difference in scale of the texture in the homogeneous regions caused by the block nature of the block coding technique. These differences are more easily seen in the agricultural scene shown in Fig. 5. The texture patterns in the reconstructed images appear as speckle patterns. This might be attributed to the

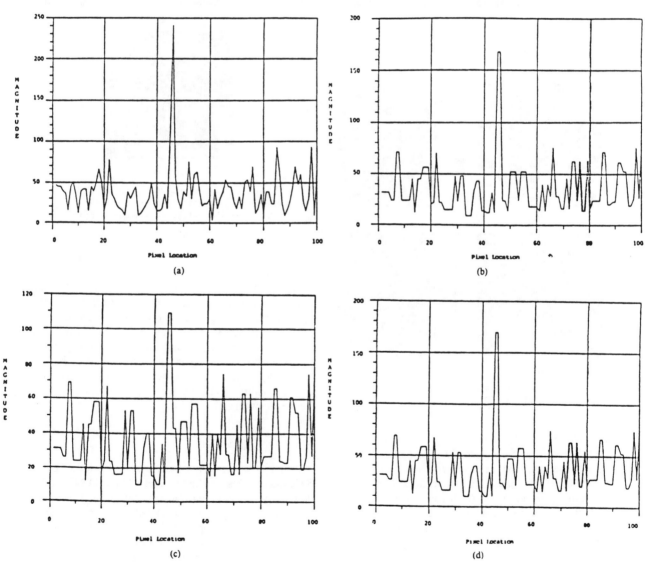

Fig. 3. Cultural feature response of the compression algorithms. (a) Original. (b) BTC. (c) Modified BTC. (d) Adaptive BTC.

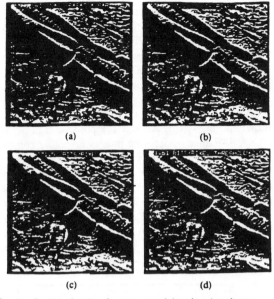

Fig. 4.   Results of coding for scene containing elevation changes.
(a) Original. (b) BTC. (c) Modified BTC. (d) Adaptive BTC.

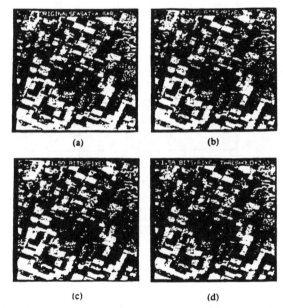

Fig. 5.   Results of coding for agricultural scene. (a) Original. (b) BTC.
(c) Modified BTC. (d) Adaptive BTC.

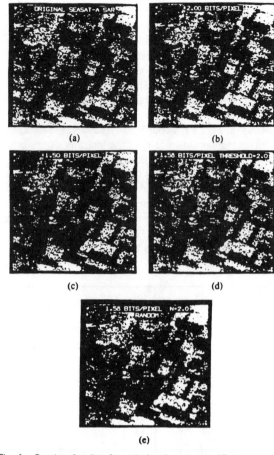

Fig. 6.   Results of coding for agricultural scene: magnified.
(a) Original. (b) BTC. (c) Modified BTC. (d) Adaptive BTC.
(e) Adaptive BTC with pseudorandom reconstruction.

compression algorithm's two level quantization of the pixels in each block: the algorithm is mapping all the up fades to one value and the down fades to another value.

The upper left corner of the agricultural scene is shown magnified in Fig. 6. At this scale the "blockyness" property [13] of the algorithm is clearly illustrated. However, the shape of most cultural features is preserved. Specifically, the features identified as 1, 2, and 3 on the original SEASAT-A image, Fig. 6(a), are preserved in shape in all three (6(b), (c), and (d)) reconstructed images. Note the loss of contrast for the

pointlike target (feature 2) between the original BTC and the modified BTC. The result of the adaptive BTC algorithm using pseudorandom reconstruction is shown in Fig. 6(e). As expected this refinement reduced the blocky appearance of the reconstructed image. The properties of the BTC algorithm are also evident in Fig. 7. This scene contains a water body, a dam, and a power transmission line (the row of bright points near the bottom of the scene). Again, the shape of these features is preserved and the modified BTC algorithm shows a loss of contrast for the point targets.

VII. CONCLUSIONS

A data compression technique has been developed for SAR images. The method was tested on SEASAT-A SAR data and found to produce images with a suitable quality for a variety of applications. The algorithm developed here is an extension of the BTC technique developed in [7]. The specific statistical properties of SAR data were used to improve the data compression ratio. A compression ratio of 5 to 1 (data rate of 1.6 bit/pixel) was obtained. Further minor reductions in data rate might

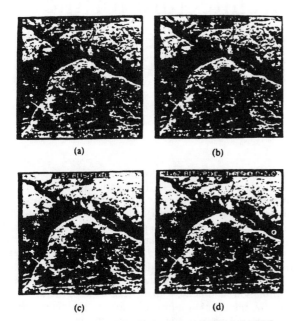

Fig. 7. Results of coding for general scene. (a) Original. (b) BTC.
(c) Modified BTC. (d) Adaptive BTC.

be possible by reducing the number of bits used to represent the sample mean and standard deviation as suggested in [8]. The benefit of such a reduction would have to be considered based on the application of the sensor. Also, further study is needed to evaluate the effect of changing the number of looks of the SAR on the quality of the reconstructed images.

The technique presented here requires no large data storage, as opposed to transform coding methods [1], and is computationally simple so that a single chip implementation is possible [7]. As the SAR image formation moves closer to a real-time operation and is thus performed on the sensor, data compression techniques such as the one presented here will provide the system designer with additional tradeoffs for transmitting and storing the data.

ACKNOWLEDGMENT

The author would like to thank Dr. K.S. Shanmugan for his helpful criticism of this work. Also, the help of E. Watson and D. Boberg for processing the images is recognized.

REFERENCES

[1]   Kashef, B.G., and Tam, K.K. (1983)
        Synthetic aperture radar image bandwidth compression.
        In *Proceedings of the SPIE, 432* (Aug. 1983), 45–53.
[2]   Lipes, R.G., and Butman, S.A. (1977)
        Bandwidth compression of synthetic aperture radar imagery
        by quantization of raw radar data.
        In *Proceedings of the SPIE, 119* (1977), 107–114.
[3]   Wu, C. (1976)
        Considerations on data compression of synthetic aperture
        radar images.
        In *Proceedings of the SPIE, 87* (1976), 134–140.
[4]   Shanmugan, K.S., et al. (1981)
        Textural features for radar image analysis.
        *IEEE Transactions on Geoscience and Remote Sensing,
        GE-19,* 3 (July 1981), 153–156.
[5]   Moore, R.K. (1979)
        Tradeoff between picture element dimensions and
        noncoherent averaging in side-looking airborne radar.
        *IEEE Transactions on Aerospace and Electronic Systems,
        AES-15,* 5 (Sept. 1979), 697–708.
[6]   Jain, A.K. (1981)
        Image data compression: a review. *IEEE Proceedings, 69,* 3
        (Mar. 1981), 349–384.
[7]   Delp, E.J., and Mitchell, O.R. (1979)
        Image compression using block truncation coding.
        IEEE Transactions on Communication, COM-27, 9 (Sept.
        1979), 1335–1342.
[8]   Arce, G.R., and Gallaghen, N.C. (1984)
        BTC image coding using median filter roots.
        IEEE Transactions on Communications, COM-31, 6 (June
        1984), 784–793.
[9]   Porcello, L.J., Massey, N.G., Innes, R.B., and Marks, J.M.
        (1976)
        Speckle reduction in synthetic aperture radars.
        Journal Optical Society of America, 66, 11 (Nov. 1976),
        1305–1311.
[10] Meyer, D.P., and Mayer, H.A. (1973)
        Radar Target Detection.
        New York: Academic Press, 1973, pp. 36–65.
[11] Mitchell, R.L. (1974)
        Models of extended targets and their coherent radar images.
        Proceedings of the IEEE, 62, 6 (June 1974), 754–758.
[12] Lee, J.S. (1981)
        Speckle analysis and smoothing of synthetic aperture radar
        images.
        Computer Graphics and Image Processing, 1 (Dec. 1981),
        17–32.
[13] Rosenfeld, A., and Kak, A. (1982)
        Digital Picture Processing.
        New York: Academic Press, 1982.
[14] Hogg, R.V., and Craig, A.T. (1970)
        Introduction to Mathematical Statistics.
        London: MacMillan, 1970.
[15] Jordan, R.L. (1980)
        The SEASAT—A synthetic aperture radar system.
        IEEE Journal of Oceanic Engineering, OE-2, 2 (Apr. 1980),
        154–165.
[16] Ulaby, F.T., Li, R.Y., and Shanmugan, K.S. (1982)
        Crop classification using airborne radar and LANDSAT data.
        *IEEE Transactions on Geoscience and Remote Sensing, GE-
        20* (Jan. 1982), 42–51.
[17] Frost, V.S., Stiles, J.A., Shanmugan, K.S., and Holtzman, J.C.
        (1982)
        A model for radar images and its application to adaptive
        digital filtering of multiplicative noise.
        *IEEE Transactions on Pattern Analysis and Machine
        Intelligence, PAMI-4,* 2 (1982).
[18] Bendat, J.S., and Piersol, A.G. (1971)
        Random Data, Analysis and Measurement Procedures.
        New York: Wiley-Interscience, 1971.

A Neural Net Based Architecture for the Segmentation of Mixed Gray-Level and Binary Pictures

Ali Tabatabai, *Member, IEEE*, and Terry P. Troudet

Abstract —A neural net based architecture is proposed to perform segmentation in real time for mixed gray-level and binary pictures. In this approach, the composite picture is divided into 16×16 pixel blocks, which are identified as character blocks or image blocks on the basis of a dichotomy measure computed by an adaptive 16×16 neural net. For compression purpose, each image block is further divided into 4×4 subblocks and, similar to the classical block truncation coding (BTC) scheme, a one-bit nonparametric quantizer is used to encode 16×16 character and 4×4 image blocks. In this case, however, the binary map and quantizer levels are obtained through a neural net segmentor over each block. The efficiency of the neural segmentation in terms of computational speed, data compression, and quality of the compressed picture is demonstrated. The effect of weight quantization is also discussed. VLSI implementations of such adaptive neural nets in CMOS technology are described and simulated in real time for a maximum block size of 256 pixels.

I. Introduction

THE growing significance of neural signal processing and the increasing attraction of analog VLSI implementation are the motivation for this paper. The span of expertise required to satisfy these interests ranges from algorithm, through architecture and circuit design, to simulation. The purpose of this paper is twofold: 1) to show an example of how to bridge these fields by describing the design of an image compression system that integrates both coding and implementation aspects, and 2) to outline the benefits and advantages of such an approach. In the coding part, we describe a segmentation-based coding scheme for composite pictures. We then proceed to present an architectural methodology for the neural implementation of our proposed coding scheme. Here, the composite picture refers to the class of pictures that contain both printed/handwritten text and multilevel images. Such pictures are often used in business facsimile and audiographics conferencing systems where both types of information are usually present.

In the last several years, much of the research in image compression techniques has been focused on either gray-level or binary images with surprisingly little attention given to the coding of composite pictures. It is, however, well understood that an efficient data compression technique for such pictures should consist of a segmentation part that divides a picture into character and image planes, and a coding part

that encodes each plane according to binary and gray-level coding techniques [1], [2]. This clearly agrees with the fact that the ultimate success of any image compression technique depends on how well it determines features within a given image and then chooses a coding method that best fits those features [3]. As an example, Yasuda *et al.* [1] proposed a method for compression of check images. In their method the image was first divided into character planes composed of character pels on a uniform background (i.e., essential information) and nonessential background or picture. Subsequently, the position information of the character pels on a character plane was conditionally entropy coded, whereas their gray-level intensity values were coded by using an adaptive predictive coding scheme. Later, Gharavi and Netravali [2] treated the composite compression problem in a more general context. In their approach, a segmentation scheme was applied to classify each picture element as a character (bilevel) or image (multilevel) pel. The extracted character pels were coded by using CCITT compatible binary coding techniques. A differential pulse coded modulation (DPCM) was used to code image pels. In the latter case, the bit stream corresponding to the DPCM code assignments was processed so as to change the statistics of run lengths and thus make CCITT run-length code more efficient.

In terms of implementation, in particular in the field of real-time signal processing, data speed, together with the complexity of many algorithms, imposes severe computational demands that often cannot be satisfied by general purpose digital microprocessors. These demands, in principle, can be met by new system architectures that increase the degree of parallelism of the digital microprocessing, and that tailor the hardware architecture to the application itself (e.g., use of application specific IC, ASIC). Custom VLSI, however, is not the only possible approach to the implementation of real-time signal processors. A second alternative is to take advantage, whenever possible, of the massively parallel structure of neural networks, which together with the analog nature of the signal processing, provides an attractive real-time processing capability. In this latter case, the task is to tailor the representation of the application to an algorithm that can be directly run on a general purpose neural network architecture, either programmable or trainable, and thus avoid the design of an ASIC. Although applications of analog VLSI to data processing have received considerably less attention than digital VLSI, the former technology is extremely attractive and futuristic to overcomes the Von Neuman bottlenecks that are characteristic of general purpose digital microprocessors.

In this paper, we focus on such design methodology by

Manuscript received May 22, 1989; revised February 21, 1990. This paper was recommended by Associate Editor Y. F. Huang.

A. Tabatabai is with Bell Communications Research, Red Bank, NJ 07701-7020.

T. P. Troudet was with Bell Communications Research. He is now with Sverdrup Technology, NASA Lewis Research Group, Cleveland, OH 44135.

IEEE Log Number 9040418.

recognizing the potential that a neural net has to offer, and we wish to exploit it. We thus propose a parallel processing scheme of segmentation/coding to be run on an adaptive programmable neural net. and we discuss the symbiotic aspects of our software/hardware integration as a possible methodological guideline for future work. The basic idea of segmentation is covered in Section II, where the difference between sequential/parallel pixel classification is emphasized. The concept of neural segmentation is introduced in Section III, and an adaptive Hopfield [4]–[6] net architecture is proposed for the segmentation/coding of character/image blocks. The choice of synaptic weights and the effect of weight quantization on the quality of the reconstructed picture are discussed through a stochastic simulation of the net. This leads in Section IV to an electronic implementation of neural net segmentor, whose efficiency and real-time performance are estimated through a computer simulation of the analog processing. The conclusions and summary appear in Section V.

II. Segmentation

The key idea behind our segmentation scheme is that, due to its binary nature, a strong dichotomy should exist in a character block. In view of the above, it therefore becomes necessary to choose an appropriate dichotomy measure. First we start by defining a class separability criterion according to the discriminant analysis discussed in [7] and [8]. More specifically, we use a measure that has been suggested in [8] as a means to select a threshold automatically from a gray-level histogram. A brief discussion of the steps leading to the derivation of such a measure is given below.

Assume the pixels within a block are dichotomized into two classes, Ω_1 and Ω_2, by a threshold at intensity level $L \in \alpha$, where α is the set of all integers less than 256. One can thus write

$$P_1 = Pr\,(\text{Class } \Omega_1) = \sum_{x=0}^{L} p_x = P(L) \qquad (2.1a)$$

where

$$p_x = \frac{n_x}{n} \qquad (2.1b)$$

n_x Number of occurrences of intensity level x (2.1c)

n Total number of pixels within a block (2.1d)

and

$$P_2 = Pr\,(\text{Class } \Omega_2) = 1 - P(L). \qquad (2.1e)$$

Similarly, the class means m_1, m_2 and class variances σ_1^2, σ_2^2 are given by

$$m_1 = E[X|\Omega_1] = \frac{m(L)}{P(L)} \qquad (2.2a)$$

$$m(L) = \sum_{x=0}^{x=L} xp_x \qquad (2.2b)$$

$$m_2 = E[X|\Omega_2] = \frac{m_0 - m(L)}{1 - P(L)} \qquad (2.2c)$$

$$\sigma_i^2 = E\left[(X - m_i)^2|\Omega_i\right], \qquad i = 1,2. \qquad (2.2d)$$

Here, the term m_0 denotes the mixture mean and is expressed by

$$m_0 = E[X] = m_1 P_1 + m_2 P_2. \qquad (2.3)$$

In the discriminant analysis of statistics, within-class and between-class scatter matrices are used to formulate criteria of class separability [7]. A within-class scatter matrix S_W shows the scatter of the samples around the class mean, and is expressed by

$$S_W = \sum_{i=1}^{2} P_i \sigma_i^2. \qquad (2.4a)$$

On the other hand, the between-class scatter matrix S_B is denoted by

$$S_B = \sum_{i=1}^{2} P_i (m_i - m_0)^2 = \frac{[P(L)m_0 - m(L)]^2}{P(L)[1 - P(L)]}. \qquad (2.4b)$$

Using definitions (2.4a) and (2.4b), we can write the class-separation measure as [7]

$$J(L) = \frac{S_B}{S_B + S_W} = \frac{S_B}{\sigma_0^2}. \qquad (2.5)$$

Here σ_0^2 denotes the mixture variance, and the last term on the right-hand side of (2.5) was obtained by using the relation $\sigma_0^2 = S_W + S_B$. We now define the dichotomy measure J as [7], [8]

$$J = \max_L \left(\frac{S_B}{\sigma_0^2}\right) = \max_L \left(1 - \frac{S_W}{\sigma_0^2}\right) = 1 - \min_L \left(\frac{S_W}{\sigma_0^2}\right), \qquad L \in \alpha. \qquad (2.6a)$$

Since σ_0^2 is independent of the threshold intensity level L, it follows from (2.6a) that

$$J = 1 - \frac{\min_L (S_W)}{\sigma_0^2} \qquad (2.6b)$$

or, equivalently

$$J = 1 - \frac{\min_L \left(n_1 \sigma_1^2 + n_2 \sigma_2^2\right)}{(n_1 + n_2)\sigma_0^2} \qquad (2.7)$$

where n_1 and n_2 denote the number of pixels in each class, respectively. It can be easily shown that the class-separation measure J, as defined by (2.6) or (2.7), has several important characteristics. Namely,

1) for an ideal character block (i.e., noise-free), the measure is maximum and equal to one;
2) for blocks with uniform brightness values (e.g.; background only), the measure takes the minimum value of zero;
3) the measure is invariant under scaling and translation of pixel values.

In our segmentation approach, by taking into account the above, we divide a composite picture into nonoverlapping blocks of size 16×16 (e.g., $n = 256$). A dichotomy measure is then calculated for each block, and, if its value exceeds a certain specified threshold J_0, it is classified as a character block. Otherwise, it is classified as an image block [9].

One iteration of the segmentation algorithm defined in (2.1)–(2.7) consists of first defining a possible partition of the image blocks in two classes, Ω_1 and Ω_2, followed by the calculation of the corresponding between-class scatter matrix S_B. The pixel segmentation results from the maximization of S_B over all the possible sets of partitions $\{\Omega_1, \Omega_2\}$. In order to estimate the speed limitation of performing the segmentation on a general-purpose microprocessor, the algorithm of (2.1)–(2.7) was written in the assembly language, and was run on an AT&T 6386E Work Group System (WGS) processor. The processor is based on a 32-bit 20-MHz Intel 80386 microprocessor, and to speed up operations on floating point numbers, an Intel 80387 math coprocessor was also used. Accordingly, it took on the average about 20 ms to maximize S_B over a 16×16 block.

As was pointed out in the introduction, the most common way to reduce such speed limitations is to increase the degree of parallelism of the hardware within the limits of digital VLSI technology through the realization of an ASIC. For this application, however, it is proposed to take full advantage of the inherently parallel nature of the segmentation by *simultaneously* classifying the pixel intensities and minimizing the class-separation measure on a fully parallel and easy-to-implement neural architecture.

III. Hopfield Neural Net: The Concept of Computational Energy

Hopfield [4]–[6] has demonstrated that analog neural-like cells can be highly and selectively interconnected so as to give rise to *collective* computational properties and provide such networks with extreme computational efficiency. Collective computational properties emerge from the existence of a computational energy that is a function of the neural cells' outputs and whose minima coincide with the stable states of the net. For a given set of inputs, the neural net output converges towards one of the minima of the computational energy, and thus can be used for the resolution of optimization problems, provided appropriate connections and input currents of the net can be found. Hopfield [5] has shown that an educated guess of appropriate "synaptic" connections and input currents can be obtained in a simple manner from the simulation of a neural network of discrete output neurons, where only one neuron at a time is updated. This update is often referred to as the stochastic model, owing to its asynchronous nature. The interest of the stochastic model lies in its numerical simplicity together with the fact that it provides a good estimation of the collective nature of the neural computation independently of its practical implementation (i.e., without appealing to complicated neural dynamics). It is, however, emphasized that due to the sequential nature of the update and the discrete output approximation of the neurons, the stochastic model does not address in any way whatsoever the real-time performance of a parallel update of the net, i.e., a synchronous update with continuous-valued output neurons.

Since it is the collective nature of the neural computation that governs its ability to lead to the expected solution, the dimensionless parameter values derived from the stochastic model can be scaled to determine the electronic characteristics that maximize the real-time performance of a practical implementation. This will be done in Section IV by integrating the set of nonlinearly coupled differential equations that represent the time evolution of the interconnected neurons.

3.1. General Principles of the Stochastic Model

In the stochastic model, a "neuron" represents a two-state cell, i.e., one whose output ν is either 0 or 1, which is connected to the other neurons and changes its state according to the state of the other neurons. If T_{ij} is the strength (or weight) of the connection from neuron j to neuron i, the contribution of neuron j's output to neuron i's input is $T_{ij}\nu_j$. If the external current fed into neuron i is represented by I_i^{ext}, the total input signal to neuron i is

$$u_i = \sum_j T_{ij}\nu_j + I_i^{\text{ext}}. \qquad (3.1)$$

When neuron i is updated, its output ν_i changes according to the threshold rule

$$u_i = \sum_j T_{ij}\nu_j + I_i^{\text{ext}} \geq u_i^0 \to \nu_i = 1 \qquad (3.2a)$$

$$u_i = \sum_j T_{ij}\nu_j + I_i^{\text{ext}} < u_i^0 \to \nu_i = 0 \qquad (3.2b)$$

where u_i^0 is the intrinsic threshold of neuron i.

Hopfield has shown that if $T_{ii} = 0$ (i.e., no self-connection) and $T_{ij} = T_{ji}$ (i.e., symmetric connections), the functional of the neuron output states

$$E[\nu_1, \nu_2, \cdots, \nu_k, \cdots] = -\frac{1}{2}\sum_{ij}\nu_i T_{ij}\nu_j - \sum_i I_i^{\text{ext}}\nu_i \quad (3.3)$$

decreases during asynchronous updating of the net. As a result, when the neurons are updated one at a time according to the algorithm defined by (3.2), the neural net ultimately converges towards a minimum of the computational energy $E[\nu_1, \nu_2, \cdots, \nu_k, \cdots]$. The neural computation of a given optimization problem amounts, therefore, to finding a neural network architecture for which the problem can be reduced or approximated by the minimization of a functional of the form (3.3). This in return defines the appropriate values of the weights T_{ij} and currents I_i^{ext}:

$$T_{ij} = -\frac{\partial^2 E[\nu_1, \nu_2, \cdots, \nu_k, \cdots]}{\partial \nu_i \partial \nu_j} \qquad (3.4a)$$

$$I_i^{\text{ext}} = -\frac{\partial E[\nu_1, \nu_2, \cdots, \nu_k, \cdots]}{\partial \nu_i}\bigg|_{\nu=0} \qquad (3.4b)$$

where $\nu^T = [\nu_1, \nu_2, \cdots, \nu_n]$. In addition, practical realizations of neural cells, whether electronic or photonic, inherently have a finite gain that is responsible for a gradual change of their output around the threshold, as shown in Fig. 6 (in contrast to the ideal two-state neuron whose output is a Heaviside distribution of its input). As a result, the collective computational properties of a practical realization of a neural network differ from the collective computational properties of the stochastic model where only one neuron at a time is updated and for an input–output relation of the neurons with infinite gain. In spite of these limitations, and as will be confirmed in the next sections, the essential characteristics of the stochastic model remain in the limit of synchronous updating and for a finite gain in the input–output relation of the neurons. The simplicity of the stochastic model actually makes it a very convenient tool to pre-estimate the expected performance of practical realizations of neural networks, whether electronic or photonic.

3.2. Stochastic Model of Neural Net Segmentor

Equation (2.6a) requires the determination of the threshold intensity L, which separates the block pixels into two subclasses, Ω_1 and Ω_2, for which $J(L)$, (2.5), reaches its maximum value. Similarly, the optimal value of L that minimizes the within-class scatter value $S_w(L)$, (2.6b), also minimizes the functional

$$E_w(L) = (n_1 + n_2)^2 S_w(L) = n_1^2\sigma_1^2 + n_2^2\sigma_2^2 + n_1 n_2(\sigma_1^2 + \sigma_2^2)$$
$$(3.5)$$

since $n = n_1 + n_2$ is the total fixed number of pixels per block.

Given a block of n pixels, a binary variable ν is associated to each pixel in order to partition the block into two subclasses, Ω_1 and Ω_2, such that pixel $i \in \Omega_1$ if $\nu_i = 1$, and pixel $i \in \Omega_2$ if $\nu_i = 0$. From the definition (3.3), the presence of the crossed-term $n_1 n_2(\sigma_1^2 + \sigma_2^2)$ in the RHS of (3.5) prohibits identifying $E_w(L)$ as the computational energy of a linear neural network whose weights T_{ij} are independent of the states of the neurons. Although, in principle, it is possible to envision a nonlinear neural segmentation, its practical realization would be drastically more complex and may be premature for the present state of the art of analog VLSI. A satisfactory approximation to the segmentation problem that is compatible with a linear neural net architecture is to minimize the functional $E^{(0)}(L)$:

$$E^{(0)}(L) = n_1^2\sigma_1^2 + n_2^2\sigma_2^2 \qquad (3.6a)$$

whose variations are bounded by the variations of $E_w(L)$:

$$E_w(L) \geq E^{(0)}(L) \geq 0. \qquad (3.6b)$$

If X_i and X_j represent the intensities of pixels i and j, the functional $E^{(0)}(L)$ can be expressed in quadratic form in terms of the neuron output states. Thus

$$E^{(0)}(\nu^T) = \sum_{i,j=1}^{n} \nu_i\nu_j\left(X_i^2 - X_iX_j\right)$$
$$+ \sum_{i,j=1}^{n} (1-\nu_i)(1-\nu_j)\left(X_i^2 - X_iX_j\right) \quad (3.7)$$

can be interpreted as the computational energy of an array of n fully interconnected neurons representing a 1/1 mapping of the block pixels.

As will be demonstrated in Section 4.3.1, the class-separation resulting from the minimization of $E^{(0)}(L)$ approximates well the class-separation resulting from the minimization of $E_w(L)$ (or $S_w(L)$). It is precisely the possibility of extracting a functional, which exhibits class-separation properties, and at the same time can be implemented on a linear neural net architecture, that motivates our choice of the segmentation scheme defined in Section II. Like creativity that emerges from the synergistic interaction between vertical and lateral thinkings [10], this result indicates that, for an analog implementation, much is to be gained by modifying the perspective of the problem that one would have in the framework of a digital implementation; it further demonstrates how crucial it is to take into account the hardware characteristics of analog parallel processing when designing algorithms to be executed by neural network architectures.

For an ideal character block, i.e., noise-free, the minimizations of $E_w(L)$ and $E^{(0)}(L)$ with respect to L lead to the

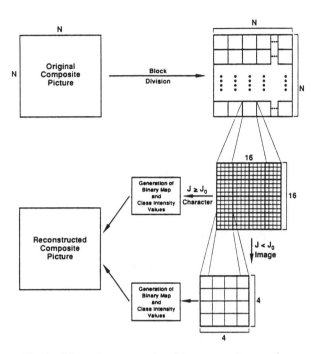

Fig. 1. Schematic representation of the segmentation procedure.

same set of subclasses, $\{\Omega_1, \Omega_2\}$, for which $J(L)$ has its maximum value, i.e., $J(L) = 1$. The functional $E^{(0)}(L)$ is thus a good candidate to class-separate strongly dichotomized blocks and approximate their class-separation measure by neural computation. Since the distinction between character and image blocks is made on the basis of the threshold rule J_0 (see Section II), we choose J_0 close to unity. In practical applications, strongly dichotomized blocks can be identified as character blocks by minimizing $E^{(0)}(L)$.

On the other hand, although $E^{(0)}(L)$ may not be as good to class-separate weakly dichotomized blocks, the resulting approximation of $J(L)$ will always be smaller than the exact value resulting from the minimization of $E_w(L)$. A block that is identified as an image block, on the basis of the threshold rule J_0, is still an image block on the basis of the same threshold rule when $E_w(L)$ is replaced by $E^{(0)}(L)$.

An adaptive neural net architecture [9] is now proposed in order to minimize the functional $E^{(0)}(L)$ in real time, and its ability to perform the segmentation of mixed-gray level and binary picture is analyzed by taking the example of a composite picture.

3.2.1. Adaptive Neural Net Architecture:

With the computational energy $E^{(0)}(L)$ defined in (3.6a) and (3.7), the input of neuron i that maps pixel i is connected to the output of neuron j by the weight

$$T_{ij} = -\frac{\partial^2 E^{(0)}[\nu_1, \nu_2, \cdots, \nu_n]}{\partial\nu_i\partial\nu_j} = -2(X_i - X_j)^2 \quad (3.8a)$$

and receives the external current

$$I_i^{ext} = -\frac{\partial E^{(0)}[\nu_1, \nu_2, \cdots, \nu_n]}{\partial\nu_i}\bigg|_{\nu=0} = \sum_j (X_i - X_j)^2. \quad (3.8b)$$

For a given block, the pixel intensities $\{X_i\}$ adaptively define the weights T_{ij} and the currents I_i^{ext} of the neural net segmentor. Assuming that all neuron outputs are identical at the beginning of the computation. (3.8) shows that the neurons associated to pixels that have the same intensity value present the same time evolution. and ultimately converge in the same subclass. Neurons associated to pixels of different intensity values tend to "repel" each other. since $T_{ij} < 0$, and the repulsion is stronger as the pixel intensity values are further apart. This interneuron repulsion is modulated by the "attractive" current I_i^{ext}, which is stronger as the intensity value of pixel i is further away from the rest of the pixel population. The neural class-separation of pixels that is the result of these two antagonistic effects is analyzed in the context of the architecture described in Fig. 1.

As shown in Fig. 1, the original composite picture is divided into 16×16 blocks of 256 pixels each. and the weights and currents are loaded in the 16×16 neural net from the values of the pixel intensities of each 16×16 block. As the neurons are asynchronously updated in the limit of the stochastic model, the pixels are progressively separated in two classes $\{\nu_i = 1|\Omega_1\}$ and $\{\nu_i = 0|\Omega_2\}$. When the 16×16 binary map $\{\nu\}$ remains stable under further updating, the block is identified as a character-block if $J \geq J_0$. Thus by substituting the identities

$$2(n_1 + n_2)^2 \sigma_0^2 = \sum_{i,j=1}^{n} (X_i - X_j)^2 \quad (3.9a)$$

$$2n_1^2 \sigma_1^2 = \sum_{i,j=1}^{n} \nu_i \nu_j (X_i - X_j)^2 \quad (3.9b)$$

$$2n_2^2 \sigma_2^2 = \sum_{i,j=1}^{n} (1 - \nu_i)(1 - \nu_j)(X_i - X_j)^2 \quad (3.9c)$$

in (2.7), we can write

$$\frac{1 - J_0}{n_1 + n_2} \sum_{i,j=1}^{n} (X_i - X_j)^2 \geq \frac{1}{n_1} \sum_{i,j=1}^{n} \nu_i \nu_j (X_i - X_j)^2$$

$$+ \frac{1}{n_2} \sum_{i,j=1}^{n} (1 - \nu_i)(1 - \nu_j)(X_i - X_j)^2 \quad (3.10)$$

where $n_1 = \sum_{i=1}^{n} \nu_i$, $n_2 = \sum_{i=1}^{n}(1 - \nu_i)$, and J_0 is the threshold of class-separation measure, $1 \geq J_0 \geq 0$. When a block is identified as a character block, data compression is achieved by assigning to the pixels of the same class the average intensity value of their class, i.e., $m_1 = \sum_{i=1}^{n} \nu_i X_i / n_1$ for Ω_1 and $m_2 = \sum_{i=1}^{n}(1 - \nu_i)X_i / n_2$ for Ω_2.

If condition (3.10) is not satisfied. the block is identified as an image block, and it is further divided into 4×4 sub-blocks as represented in Fig. 1. Each 4×4 sub-block is subsequently segmented by an adaptive 4×4 neural net. Like character blocks, data compression for the 4×4 sub-blocks can be achieved by assigning to the pixels of the same class the average intensity value of their class. Binary maps and class intensity values generated by the 16×16 and 4×4 neural net segmentors are used to reconstruct the composite picture.

In fact. such an approach is similar to the classical block truncation coding (BTC) first proposed by Delp and Mitchell [11]. Here, however. rather than preserving the moments. the quantizer levels are obtained by maximizing the class separation measure of the pixels over small blocks of image (i.e.. 16×16, or 4×4). In order to measure the efficiency of neural segmentation in relation to data compression, one can evaluate the average number of bits per pixel that is required

to reconstruct the composite picture in the architecture of Fig. 1. If 8 bits per pixel are used to define the pixel intensity values of the original composite picture. the average number of bits per pixel of the reconstructed picture is

$$\eta = \frac{17B + 32I}{16(B + I)} \quad (3.11)$$

where B is the number of blocks identified as character blocks, and I the number of blocks identified as image blocks. The maximum number of bits per pixel $\eta_{max} = 2$ is obtained for $B = 0$, i.e., when all the pixel blocks are identified as image blocks. While this case corresponds to the lowest compression rate, it provides the best quality picture that can be expected from the architecture proposed in Fig. 1. The minimum number of bits per pixel $\eta_{min} = 1.06$ is obtained for $I = 0$, i.e., when all pixel blocks are identified as character blocks. The case where $I = 0$ provides the least quality expected for the reconstructed image but at the same time leads to the maximum rate of data compression.

Through B and I, the rate of data compression depends upon the value of the class-separation threshold J_0. If $J_0 = 1$, all the blocks are treated as image blocks, i.e., $B = 0$. If $J_0 = 0$. all the blocks are treated as character blocks. i.e., $I = 0$. The flexibility of choosing appropriate intermediate values of J_0 between 0 and 1, in order to compromise between picture quality and data compression, is functionally reminiscent of the process by which the eye operates in order to obtain proper resolution. For a page of text consisting either of strongly dichotomized characters or white background. the quality of the reconstructed document is to a large extent insensitive to the choice of J_0. In that case, one can choose $J_0 = 0$ in order to maximize the compression rate to $\eta_{min} = 1.06$. For a composite picture with mixed gray-level, the threshold J_0 can be adaptively chosen so as to provide an adequate quality of the reconstructed picture.

As emphasized in Section I. the primary goal of this work is to demonstrate the general principles and the efficiency of a neural net approach to the segmentation of composite pictures. In particular, it does not address the problem of defining an architecture that would be optimal from all points of view of data compression, picture quality, and computational efficiency. Clearly, the architecture proposed in Fig. 1 is not optimal from the sole point of view of data compression. For example, the correlations that are typical of character blocks can be utilized to restrain the number of bits to be transmitted by compressing the binary maps of such blocks through binary coding techniques [12], [13], such as arithmetic coding technique (ACT) [14]. Further compression of the binary maps generated by the 4×4 neural net can also be achieved through the use of additional coding techniques [15].

By reconstructing the composite picture from the binary maps and class intensity values generated by the net segmentors, the architecture of Fig. 1 makes it possible to analyze not only quantitatively but also qualitatively the neural segmentation.

3.2.2. Performance of the Stochastic Neural Segmentation: For the composite picture of Fig. 2(a), the reconstructed picture is depicted in Fig. 2(d) after convergence of the neural segmentation and for the threshold value $J_0 = 0.90$. For comparison, Fig. 2(b) and (c) depict the reconstructed pictures after segmenting the blocks by minimizing the

208

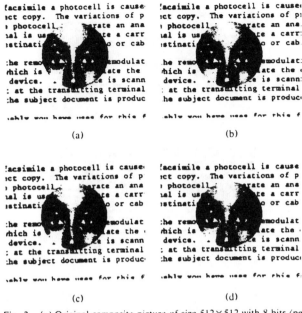

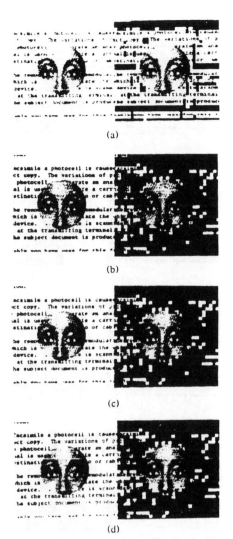

Fig. 2. (a) Original composite picture of size 512×512 with 8 bits/pel intensity values. (b) The image of Fig. 2(a) has been segmented into character/image blocks by minimizing the within-class scatter value $S_w(L)$ (i.e., (2.4a)), with a threshold $J_0 = 0.90$. The compressed picture is obtained by using a BTC-like coding scheme (i.e., using binary map and class intensity values of 16×16 character blocks and 4×4 image blocks). (c) The image of Fig. 2(a) has been segmented into character/image blocks by minimizing the within-class scatter value $E^{(1)}(L)$ (i.e., (3.6a)), with a threshold intensity $J_0 = 0.90$. Similar to Fig. 2(b), picture reconstruction is obtained by using binary map and class intensity values of 16×16 character blocks and 4×4 image blocks. (d) Reconstruction of the image of Fig. 2(a) after neural net segmentation, with four full asynchronous updatings of the 16×16 neural net and for a threshold $J_0 = 0.90$. The character/image identification of the blocks is made from (3.9) after class-separation by the 16×16 nets. The image blocks are divided in 4×4 sub-blocks, which are then compressed by 4×4 neural nets.

Fig. 3. The result of the segmentation of Fig. 2(a) by the stochastic model of neural net segmentor (Section 3.2) at various stages of neural computation. The threshold intensity value is $J_0 = 0.90$. The right-hand side illustrates the degree of character/image block segmentation by showing the character blocks in dark square and coded 4×4 image blocks. The left-hand side represents both coded 16×16 character blocks and 4×4 image blocks. (a) Zero asynchronous updatings of the 16×16 neural net. (b) Two full asynchronous updatings. (c) Four full asynchronous updatings. (d) Six full asynchronous updatings.

within-class scatter value $S_w(L)$ and the functional $E^{(1)}(L)$, respectively.

In the example of Fig. 2(a), the original composite picture has been divided into 1024 blocks of 16×16. For this picture where the pixel intensities are represented by 8 bits, i.e., $255 \geq X \geq 0$, the neural segmentation of the 16×16 pixel blocks is found to have nominally converged after six full updatings of the 16×16 arrays of neurons. After four full updatings, the neural segmentation has already converged for 1022 blocks out of the 1024 blocks of the composite picture. For the choices of $J_0 = 0.90$ or $J_0 = 0.92$, the two remaining blocks are yet correctly identified as image blocks, i.e., $J \leq J_0$, by the 16×16 neural nets. As a result, for the choices of J_0 given above, the character/image segmentation of the composite picture actually converges after only four full updatings of the 16×16 nets. In addition, the dynamic evolution of the 16×16 net, which is illustrated in the sets of Figs. 3 and 4 for $J_0 = 0.90$ and $J_0 = 0.92$, respectively, shows that the reconstructed picture has reached its expected quality after only two full updatings of the net. For the class-separation threshold $J_0 = 0.90$, the set of Fig. 3 shows the reconstructed picture (LHS) and indicates the character/image nature of the blocks (RHS) after zero, two,

four, and six full updatings of the 16×16 and 4×4 neural nets. The same process is illustrated in the set of Fig. 4 for $J_0 = 0.92$.

When comparing the segmentation of the 16×16 net with the exact minimization of the functional $E^{(1)}(L)$, (3.6a), one finds the same class-separation for 1018 blocks of the composite picture. However, the class-separation measures of the six remaining blocks, for which the 16×16 net gets trapped into local minima of the computational energy $E^{(1)}(L)$, are less than 0.80 in both neural and exact segmentations. If the dynamic range of J_0 is narrowed between 0.90 and 1 (which seems to be sufficient for most common composite pictures), these six local minima are in both cases identified as image blocks, so that the minimization of $E^{(1)}(L)$ and the neural segmentation leads to the same character/

209

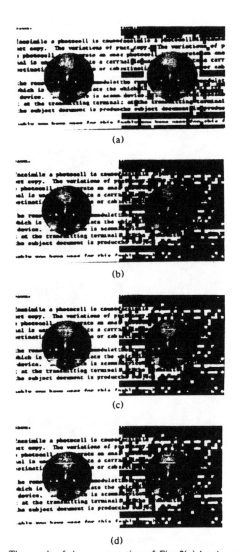

(a)

(b)

(c)

(d)

Fig. 4. The result of the segmentation of Fig. 2(a) by the stochastic model of neural net segmentor at various stages of neural computation, for a threshold $J_0 = 0.92$, as described in Fig. 3.

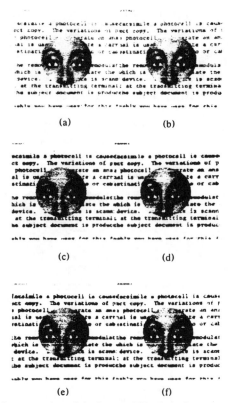

(a)   (b)

(c)   (d)

(e)   (f)

Fig. 5. Reconstruction of the image of Fig. 2(a) after convergence of the asynchronous neural net segmentation with a quantization of the synaptic weights and for a threshold $J_0 = 0.90$. (a) The reconstructed picture without weight-quantization. The differences of pixel intensities that define the synaptic weights have been quantized modulo (b) 8, (c) 16, (d) 32, (e) 64, and (f) 128.

image identification of the 16×16 blocks of Fig. 2(a). All the image blocks are further divided into 4×4 sub-blocks, which are subsequently segmented by 4×4 neural nets. For the picture of Fig. 2(a), only 0.5% of the 4×4 sub-blocks are misclassified by the 4×4 neural nets, and the resulting quantized intensities of the pixels are all within a maximum deviation of 4% from the values obtained by direct minimization of $E^{(0)}(L)$. A comparison between Fig. 2(c) and (d) suggests the same degree of quality between the picture segmented by the neural net and the picture segmented by direct minimization of $E^{(0)}(L)$.

For $J_0 = 0.90$, 297 blocks of the 1024 blocks of Fig. 2(a) are identified as image blocks by the neural net, and 727 as character blocks. For these values, (3.11) leads to $\eta_{net} = 1.33$ bit/pel for the segmented pictures reconstructed in Figs. 3(c) and (d). For the same value of the class separation threshold J_0, the maximization of $J(L)$, (2.6a), provides 224 image blocks and 800 character blocks leading to $\eta_{exact} = 1.27$ bit/pel. With $J_0 = 0.90$, the neural net architecture achieves

95% of the data compression that would be obtained by maximizing the exact class-separation measure for each block of Fig. 2(a).

For $J_0 = 0.92$, 426 blocks of the 1024 blocks of Fig. 2(a) are identified as image blocks by the neural net, and 598 as character blocks. For these values, (3.11) leads to $\eta_{net} = 1.45$ bit/pel for the segmented pictures of Figs. 4(c) and (d). For the same value of the class separation threshold J_0, the maximization of $J(L)$ provides 318 image blocks and 706 character blocks, leading to $\eta_{exact} = 1.35$ bit/pel. In this case, the neural net segmentation only achieves 92.5% of the compression rate of the "exact" segmentation.

3.2.3. Influence of Synaptic Weights Quantization: An important issue in the practical realization of neural networks is the influence of the quantization of the weights on the algorithmic performance of the nets. Whether photonic or electronic, the physical devices that are used to modulate the interneuron connections are intrinsically limited in their dynamic range. In the category of spatial light modulators, this limited dynamic range can go from 1 bit for liquid crystals up to 7 bits for acousto-optic devices. In the electronic domain, although analog VLSI appears very promising, it is not yet clear how accurate an analog update of the weights can be, and it is therefore desirable to adaptively activate the weights within a minimum dynamic range. Due to its simplicity, the stochastic model is well suited to analyze the influence of

TABLE I
Compression Rate of the Neural Segmentation for Fig. 2(a)
as a Function of the Number of Bits
Used to Address the Weights

$n_{\text{bit}}^{\text{weight}}$	5	4	3	2	1
η	1.33	1.33	1.32	1.30	1.34

weight quantization on the rate of data compression and quality of the segmented picture.

An efficient quantization of the weights T_{ij} and currents I_i^{ext} defined in (3.8) can be achieved by truncating the differences of pixel intensity values $|X_i - X_j|$ modulo 8, 16, 32, 64, or 128. For the above set of quantizers, the weights can be addressed by 5, 4, 3, 2, or 1 bit, respectively, instead of the original 8 bits corresponding to the full variation of the $|X_i - X_j|$'s over the interval $[0, 255]$.

As seen on the set of Fig. 5, the quality of the character component of the reconstructed picture depends very little upon the degree of weight quantization. If the character block represents a constant background, the population of pixel intensity values is well peaked around its average. Such a block, which consists of a single class of pixels (the other class having no pixel), is already class-separated and therefore segmented. If a character block represents an ideal character (or a portion of ideal character), it is naturally dichotomized in two classes of pixels whose intensities are well peaked around a low intensity value X_{low}, corresponding to the dark zone of the character, and around a high intensity value X_{high}, corresponding to the bright zone of the background. The synaptic weights between pixels of the same class (or intensity zone) are $T_{ij} \approx 0$, while the synaptic weights between pixels of different classes (or intensity zones) are $|T_{ij}| \approx 2(X_{\text{high}} - X_{\text{low}})^2 \gg 1$, so that a strongly dichotomized block can be well class-separated even if the weights are substantially quantized. Table I reports the rate of data compression after neural segmentation of the picture represented in Fig. 2(a) for different values of the number of bits used to address the quantized values of the synaptic weights. The quality of the image component of the reconstructed picture is, however, noticeably altered if the weights are addressed by less than 3 bits, like in Fig. 5(e) and (f). For a strong quantization of the weights, the resolution or segmentation power of the net is too low to class-separate the pixels of weakly dichotomized blocks. In this case, the assigned intensity is essentially the average of the block–pixel intensities, and the reconstructed picture looks blurry, as shown in Fig. 5(e) and (f).

IV. Electronic Implementation

The knowledge gained about the parameters of the neural net from the simulation of the stochastic model is now applied and extended to an electronic implementation of neural net segmentor. In this electronic implementation, the neurons are finite gain transistors interconnected by resistances that are inversely proportional to the weights derived from the computational energy defined in (3.7). In contrast to the asynchronous updating and the binary output approximation of the stochastic model, the neurons of the electronic implementation change their output voltage continuously and in parallel. Each neuron thereby affects and is affected in real-time by the rest of the network that evolves collec-

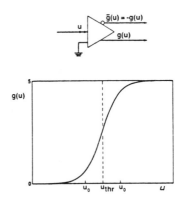

Fig. 6. Input–output relation of an amplifier. In the high gain limit where $u_0 \ll 1$, the direct output of a neuron is 5 V if its input is beyond the threshold voltage u_{thr}, and 0 V otherwise.

tively to segment the picture block. The time needed for the net to stabilize will be estimated by solving the set of the associated Kirchhoff equations. The efficiency of the neural segmentation by block will be then evaluated in terms of picture quality and compression rate. As in Fig. 1, the electronic architecture proposed for the segmentation consists of a parallel arrangement of 16×16 adaptive neural nets sequentially followed by a parallel arrangement of 4×4 adaptive neural nets. Since all the weights T_{ij} are negative, these electronic neural networks are essentially arrays of *inverting* amplifiers, the neural cells or "neurons," that represent a 1/1 mapping of the block pixels, and that are interconnected through resistances whose values can be adaptively varied according to the intensity values of the corresponding pixels.

4.1. Neural Cell and Neural Connection

Each neural cell has its input connected to the output of multiple other neural cells by means of wires of finite resistance and capacitance, and changes its output on the basis of threshold logic. If u is the input voltage of a neural cell, its output voltage is $\bar{g}(u) = -g(u)$, where $g(u)$ is a sigmoid of the form given in Fig. 6 and modeled for the simulation by

$$g(u) = 2.5\left[1 + \tanh\left(\frac{u - u_{\text{thr}}}{u_0}\right)\right]. \tag{4.1}$$

The threshold potential u_{thr} and the gain defined as $G = 2.5/u_0$ can be chosen to provide the desired characteristics of the neural cells. In the high-gain amplifier limit where $u_0 \ll 1$ (hard limiting node), the sigmoid of Fig. 6 reduces to the Heaviside distribution where the output voltage $g(u)$ is either $+5$ V or 0 V depending upon the input voltage being above or below the threshold potential u_{thr}, respectively. In the low-gain amplifier limit where $u_0 \gg 1$, the output potential varies smoothly from 0 to 5 V as a function of the input potential.

The dynamics of a neuron are defined from the distribution of the currents between its input and the outputs of the other connected neurons. As shown in Fig. 7, the total current at the input of neuron "i" is the sum of the current I_i^{ext} externally fed into neuron "i" and the current flowing

211

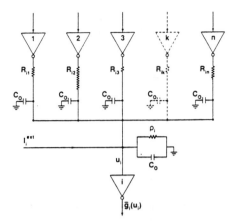

Fig. 7. Interneuron connections of the neural array.

from the other connected neurons

$$I_i^{\text{total}}(t) = \sum_{j=1}^{j=n} \left(\frac{\bar{g}_j(u_j(t-\gamma_j))}{R_{ij}} - \frac{u_j(t)}{R_{ij}} \right) + I_i^{\text{ext}} \quad (4.2)$$

where $u_j(t)$ is the input voltage of neuron "j," and γ_j is the propagation delay it takes for a voltage u_j at the input of neuron "j" to yield at time t the output voltage $\bar{g}_j(u_j(t-\gamma_j))$. The total current $I_i^{\text{total}}(t)$ charges the equivalent capacitance $C = (n+1)C_0$ of the circuit connected to neuron "i" according to the equation

$$I_i^{\text{total}}(t) = \frac{u_i(t)}{\rho_i} + C\frac{du_i(t)}{dt} \quad (4.3)$$

where ρ_i is the input resistance of neuron i. The time evolution of the input voltage of neuron "i" as a function of the input voltages of the other neurons is consequently given by the time-differential equation

$$\frac{du_i(t)}{dt} = -\frac{u_i(t)}{\tau_i} + \sum_{j=1}^{n} \frac{\bar{g}_j(u_j(t-\gamma_j))}{R_{ij}C} + \frac{I_i^{\text{ext}}}{C} \quad (4.4)$$

where $\tau_i = C/(1/\rho_i + \sum_{j=1}^{j=n}1/R_{ij})$ is the time constant of neuron "i." The output state of each neuron changes according to the states of the other connected neurons, and the dichotomization of a block of n pixels is estimated from the resolution of the n coupled differential equations (4.4) for $n \geq i \geq 1$.

4.2. Real-Time Simulation

As indicated in Section 3.2.2, the original picture of Fig. 2(a) is subdivided into 1024 blocks of 16×16 pixels whose intensities define adaptively the synaptic weights and input currents of the 16×16 neural net. The coupled differential equations (4.4) that describe the neural dynamics of the segmentation of these 16×16 blocks have been numerically integrated according to the discrete algorithm described in [16]. Each neuron output is initially set to zero by feeding a strong negative current at its input, at $t = 0$. The state of a neuron is defined as a logical 0, i.e., $\nu = 0$, if its voltage output $\bar{g}(u)$ is above -2.5 V, and as a logical 1, i.e., $\nu = 1$, if its voltage output $\bar{g}(u)$ is below -2.5 V. The presence of (electronic) noise has been simulated at the input of each

TABLE II
ELECTRONIC CHARACTERISTICS OF A NEURON OF THE ADAPTIVE
NEURAL NET SEGMENTORS IN CMOS TECHNOLOGY

Neuron	G	u_{thr}	ρ	γ
Mean Value	$729 = 3^6$	$+20$ mV	20 kΩ	6 ns
Distribution	10%	10%	10%	30%

neuron by a Gaussian of 10 μV, leading to output voltage fluctuations of approximately 10 mV during a low-to-high or high-to-low transition. During the analog computation, the pixels of each 16×16 block are progressively separated into two classes $\{\nu_i = 1\}$ or $\{\nu_i = 0\}$ as the neural net converges towards a stationary state. Although it may be possible to compare $J(L)$ with J_0 by analog means, a digital resolution of (3.10) is clearly desirable for an optimal character/image identification of the blocks. This means that the threshold J_0 can be loaded in a floating point unit whose input is connected to the output of a 16×16 adaptive net and whose output controls the analog computation of the corresponding 4×4 adaptive nets. Like the human eye accommodates to provide adequate focus, the threshold J_0 can be adaptively varied to provide adequate picture quality.

4.3. Electronic Characteristics and Performance

The electronic characteristics chosen for a neuron segmentor are reported in Table II for CMOS technology where G, u_{thr}, ρ, and γ denote the average gain, offset input resistance, and propagation delay of the amplifiers, respectively. In both 16×16 and 4×4 neural nets, neurons with the above characteristics are connected by variable resistances with a capacitance $C_0 = 2$ pF per connection [17].

4.3.1. 16×16 Adaptive Neural Net: For the 16×16 adaptive net, the differences $\Delta X_{ij} = |X_i - X_j|$ between the intensities X_i and X_j of pixels i and j have been quantized modulo 32. The discrete values of the resistances R_{ij} connecting neuron "j" to neuron "i" resulting from this quantization are reported in Table III as a function of the differences of intensity values ΔX_{ij}.

Although the time of nominal convergence of the 16×16 neural segmentation with the characteristics of Tables II and III is estimated to be 2 μs, a satisfactory class-separation of the blocks of Fig. 2(a) is obtained after only 200 ns of analog computation. In Table IV, the number of character blocks, B, and the number of image-blocks, I, obtained after 200 ns of 16×16 neural segmentation are compared with the values (B_0, I_0) corresponding to the exact minimization of $S_w(L)$, (2.6b), for several values of the class-separation threshold J_0.

The result of the segmentation of the picture of Fig. 2(a) can be visualized in Fig. 8(d), (e), and (f), for $J_0 = 0.90$, $J_0 = 0.91$, and $J_0 = 0.92$, respectively. Since the computational energy introduced in Section III is defined up to a positive multiplicative factor, the result of the neural computation is unchanged if the weights T_{ij} and currents I_i^{ext} defined in (3.8) are multiplied by a common positive factor. As discussed in [16], the time constants of the neurons increase linearly with the equivalent resistance of the interconnections, while the power dissipated in heat is inversely proportional to it. The choice of the common multiplicative factor is a compromise between speed performance and acceptable heat dissipation. For the set of resistances of Table III that leads to an effective convergence time of 200

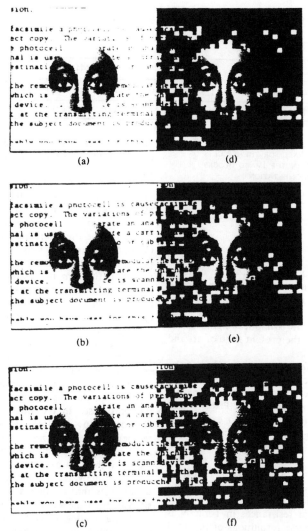

Fig. 8. Reconstruction of the image of Fig. 2(a) and representation of the character/image status of the blocks after convergence of the continuous neural segmentation described in Section 4.2. The time of analog computation is 200 ns for the 16×16 net and 2 μs for the 4×4 net. The reconstructed picture after segmentation by the 16×16 net followed by the segmentation by the 4×4 net for (a) $J_0 = 0.90$, (b) $J_0 = 0.91$, and (c) $J_0 = 0.92$. The result of the segmentation by the 16×16 net for (d) $J_0 = 0.90$, (e) $J_0 = 0.91$, and (f) $J_0 = 0.92$.

TABLE III
DISCRETE VALUES OF RESISTANCES OF THE 16×16 ADAPTIVE NET AS A FUNCTION OF THE DIFFERENCES OF INTENSITY BETWEEN PIXELS

ΔX_{ij}	0 → 31	32 → 63	64 → 95	96 → 127	128 → 159	160 → 191	192 → 223	224 → 255
R_{ij}	∞	6.4 MΩ	1.6 MΩ	711 kΩ	400 kΩ	256 kΩ	177 kΩ	130 kΩ

TABLE IV
NUMBER OF CHARACTER BLOCKS AND IMAGE BLOCKS, (B, I), AFTER 200 ns OF 16×16 NEURAL SEGMENTATION FOR DIFFERENT CLASS-SEPARATION THRESHOLDS J_0; (B_0, I_0) CORRESPONDS TO THE EXACT MINIMIZATION OF $S_w(L)$

J_0	0.90	0.91	0.92
(B, I)	(764, 260)	(715, 309)	(637, 387)
(B_0, I_0)	(800, 224)	(769, 255)	(706, 318)

ns for the segmentation, the average power dissipated in the 16×16 is estimated to be approximately 700 mW in CMOS technology, where the activation power of the amplifiers is of the order of the μW and can be neglected.

It should be noted that in order to segment a 16×16 block, the synaptic weights of the net have to be updated according to the values of the pixel intensities as shown in (3.8) or Table III. Recent papers [18]–[21] indicate that analog circuit techniques based on floating gate devices can reduce the size of synapses and increase their functionality.

213

TABLE V

DISCRETE VALUES OF RESISTANCES OF THE 4×4 ADAPTIVE NET AS A FUNCTION OF THE
DIFFERENCES OF INTENSITIES BETWEEN PIXELS

ΔX_{ij}	$0 \rightarrow 7$		$8 \rightarrow 15$		$16 \rightarrow 23$		$24 \rightarrow 32$
R_{ij}	∞		25.5 MΩ		6.4 MΩ		2.8 MΩ

ΔX_{ij}	$32 \rightarrow 63$	$64 \rightarrow 95$	$96 \rightarrow 127$	$128 \rightarrow 159$	$160 \rightarrow 191$	$192 \rightarrow 223$	$224 \rightarrow 255$
R_{ij}	1.6 MΩ	711 kΩ	400 kΩ	256 kΩ	177 kΩ	130 kΩ	100 kΩ

TABLE VI

AVERAGE NUMBER OF BITS PER PIXEL FOR THE RESULTS OF
TABLE V AFTER COMPRESSION OF THE IMAGE BLOCKS
VIA 4×4 NEURAL SEGMENTATION

J_0	0.90	0.91	0.92
η	1.30	1.35	1.42

The necessary time to set up a synaptic weight is essentially of the order of the access time of the ROM, which changes the conductance according to the amount of charge trapped on the floating gate [18], [21]. A reasonable upper bound for the setup time of a 16×16 block would be of the order of μs for a parallel analog update of the synaptic weights corresponding to a single neuron, with the present state of art and technology.

4.3.2. 4 × 4 Adaptive Neural Net: For a given value of the threshold J_0, binary maps and class intensity values assignment of the image-blocks can be obtained through a neural segmentation of each of their 4×4 sub-blocks. Pixels whose intensity difference is large, and are likely to exhibit the characteristics of a character sub-block, can still be separated by a weight quantization similar to the one of the 16×16 net. When pixels have a small difference of intensity, and are likely to exhibit the characteristics of an image sub-block, a finer weight quantization is needed to separate the pixels and preserve as much as possible of the mixed gray-level aspect of the picture. The set of resistances in Table V is proposed to achieve fine and coarse resolutions of the 4×4 neural net. The electronic characteristics of the neurons are the same as in Table II.

Fig. 8(a)–(c) represents the reconstructed picture of Fig. 2(a) after 2μs of 4×4 neural segmentation for $J_0 = 0.90$, $J_0 = 0.91$, and $J_0 = 0.92$, respectively. The average power dissipated in a 4×4 array of 4×4 neural nets during this computation is estimated to be 20 mW.

For the results of the 16×16 neural segmentation given in Table IV, the average number of bit/pel of the reconstructed pictures of Fig. 8(a)–(c) is reported in Table VI.

V. CONCLUSION

This preliminary study has demonstrated the ability of neural computation to compress in real-time mixed gray-level and binary pictures, opening the way to a broader range of applications in the image processing area. A composite picture is segmented and subsequently reconstructed from the binary maps and class intensity values calculated by an adaptive 16×16 neural net(s) for the character blocks, and by an adaptive 4×4 neural net(s) for the image blocks. With this neural net based architecture, picture quality can be adjusted with an average number of bit/pel between 1.06

and 2 by varying the threshold J_0, which controls the ratio of character blocks versus image blocks of the composite picture.

As emphasized, the rate of data compression can be lowered (below 1 bit/pel) by using the neural net segmentors as preprocessors, and subsequently coding the resulting binary maps and class intensity values by techniques such as ACT [14] for the character blocks, and vector quantization (VQ), or pattern matching, for the image blocks [15]. Such a possible architecture is represented in Fig. 9. In order to fully benefit from the extreme performance of the analog computation and, at the same time, lower the rate of data compression with an adjustable picture quality, this approach is presently being extended to an all neural net architecture through a vector quantization scheme.

Such an integrative approach is in natural agreement with the structural concept of sixth generation computers [22] consisting essentially of a CPU interacting continuously with peripheral arrangements, serial or parallel, of adaptive neural nets. In the present application, the CPU consists of a microprocessor that evaluates the class-separation measure $J(L)$ of the 16×16 blocks from the binary maps of the neural segmentation. If $J(L) \geq J_0$, the block is identified as a character block whose binary map and class intensity values are given by the neural segmentation. If $J(L) < J_0$, the microprocessor activates a parallel arrangement of adaptive 4×4 neural nets that computes the binary maps and class intensity values of the 4×4 sub-blocks of the image blocks.

Also, as analog VLSI matures, in particular in the domain of integrated analog memory, it may be possible to reduce the overall processing time through an all-parallel setup of the synaptic memories. If such is the case, submicron VLSI technology or higher speed electronics would be extremely beneficial for speeding up the convergence of the neural computation by decreasing the switching time of each individual neuron, thus possibly reducing the total time of the segmentation to tens of nanoseconds. In addition, since the neural net is a direct spatial mapping of the picture, it may be possible to include in the segmentation the spatial correlation that exists between pixels within a block by affixing different time constants to neurons of different neighborhood. Finally, we feel the most important aspects of our proposed image compression system can be summarized as follows:

1) Both segmentation and coding can be directly run on a general purpose analog neural network that is programmable and of extremely simple functionality, and has massively parallel processing capability, thus eliminating the need for designing a digital ASIC.
2) The approach can serve as a methodological guideline for future applications that can benefit from such a software/hardware integration.

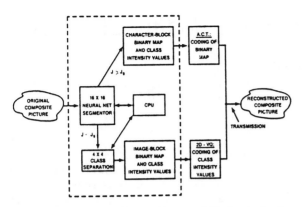

Fig. 9. Possible extension of the architecture of Fig. 1 to further lower the data compression rate below 1 bit/pel.

3) The distributed nature of the architecture enhances the immunity to system crash following malfunction/deterioration of some elements of the network.

VI. Acknowledgment

The authors would like to thank Dr. F. Troudet for inspiring discussions, and the referees for their comments and suggestions that have helped them clarify the paper. The second author wishes to acknowledge the support of Sverdrup Technology, Inc. and NASA during the revision stage of this work.

References

[1] Y. Yasuda, M. Dubois, and T. S. Huang, "Data compression for check processing machines," *Proc. IEEE*, vol. 68, pp. 874–885, July 1980.

[2] H. Gharavi and A. N. Netravali, "CCITT compatible coding of multilevel pictures," *BSTJ*, vol. 62, pp. 2765–2778, Nov. 1983.

[3] R. Gonzalez and P. Wintz, *Digital Image Processing*, 2nd ed. Reading, MA: Addison Wesley, p. 328.

[4] J. J. Hopfield, "Neural networks and physical systems with emergent collective computational abilities," in *Proc. Natl. Acad. Sci. USA*, vol. 79, pp. 2554–2558, 1982.

[5] ____, "Neurons with graded response have collective computational properties like those of two-state neurons," in *Proc. Natl. Acad. Sci. USA*, vol. 81, pp. 3088–3092, 1984.

[6] J. J. Hopfield and D. W. Tank, "Neural computation of decisions in optimization problems," *Biol. Cybern.*, vol. 52, pp. 141–152, 1985.

[7] K. Fukunaga, *Introduction to the Statistical Pattern Recognition*. New York: Academic Press, 1972.

[8] N. Otsu, "A threshold selection method from gray-level histograms," *IEEE Trans. Syst., Man, Cybern.*, vol. SMC-9, pp. 62–66, Jan. 1979.

[9] T. P. Troudet and A. Tabatabai, "An adaptive neural net approach to the segmentation of mixed gray-level and binary pictures," in *Proc. IEEE Int. Conf. Neural Networks*, vol. I, pp. 585–592, July 1988.

[10] F. Troudet, "Can creativity be taught," Cleveland State University, unpublished report, Dec. 1988.

[11] E. Delp and O. R. Mitchell, "Image compression using block truncation coding," *IEEE Trans. Commun.*, vol. COM-27, pp. 1335–1342, Sept. 1979.

[12] T. S. Huang, "Coding of two-tone images," *IEEE Trans. Commun.*, vol. COM-15, pp. 1406–1424, Nov. 1977.

[13] R. Hunter and A. H. Robinson, "International digital facsimile coding standards," *Proc. IEEE*, vol. 68, pp. 854–867, July 1980.

[14] G. G. Langdon and J. Rissanen, "Compression of black-white images with arithmetic coding," *IEEE Trans. Commun.*, vol. COM-29, pp. 858–867, June 1981.

[15] V. R. Udpikar and J. P. Raina, "BTC image coding using vector quantization," *IEEE Trans. Commun.*, vol. COM-35, pp. 352–356, Mar. 1987.

[16] T. P. Troudet and S. M. Walters, "Neural network architecture for crossbar switch control," this issue, pp. 42–56.

[17] J. Alspector and R. Allen, "Advanced research in VLSI," in *Proc. 1987 Stanford Conference*, Paul Losleben, Ed. Cambridge, MA: M.I.T. Press, 1987.

[18] J. Alspector, R. B. Allen, V. Hu, and S. Satyanarayana, "Stochastic learning networks and their electronic implementation," presented at Conf. Neural Information Processing Systems—Natural and Synthetic, Denver, CO, Nov. 1987.

[19] Z. Czamul, "Design of voltage-controlled linear transconductance elements with a matched pair of FET transistors," *IEEE Trans. Circuits Syst.*, vol. CAS-33, 1986.

[20] M. Banu and Y. Tsividis, "Floating voltage-controlled resistors in CMOS technology," *Electron. Lett.*, Vol. 18, pp. 678–679, 1982.

[21] D. Frohman-Bentchkowsky, "FAMOS—a new semiconductor charge storage device," *Solid State Electronics*, Vol. 17, 1974.

[22] M. A. Arbib, "Neural computing and sixth generation computers," Video-Conference Course, Center for Neural Engineering, University of Southern California, Feb. 1988.

Single Bit-Map Block Truncation Coding of Color Images

Yiyan Wu, *Member, IEEE,* and David C. Coll, *Senior Member, IEEE*

Abstract—This paper describes a color-image data compression technique based on block truncation coding (BTC). BTC is first implemented to encode a weighted trichromatic image. The bit map generated is then used to compress each of the R, G, and B signals separately, removing the intercolor correlations. The weighted trichromatic signal is generated by properly weighting R, G, and B signals so that the reconstructed R, G, and B signals have minimum mean square error (MSE). Another approach using a bit-wise majority rule on the R, G, and B BTC bit maps is also discussed. The algorithm preserves the spatial details in the image content and has low computational complexity. An 8:1 compression can be achieved. The truncated data is further compressed using adaptive DCT. Differential coding and error feedback techniques are also implemented to reduce the bit rate and improve the MSE performance. The total compression ratio is about 12:1. By exploiting human visual system characteristics, a 14:1 compression of NTSC color TV components can be achieved.

I. Introduction

BLOCK truncation coding (BTC) [1]–[5] uses a two-level moment-preserving quantizer that adapts to local properties to compress achromatic images. It has the advantages of preserving single pixel resolution and edges and having low computational complexity. The original algorithm preserves the block mean and the block standard deviation [1], [2]. Other choices of the moment result either in less MSE or less computational complexity [4], [5]. The BTC output data set includes a binary plane (bit map) which defines the quantization level for each pixel and two 8-bit parameters for each block, e.g., the block mean and standard deviation [1], or two reconstruction level codes [5]. The compression ratio for 4 × 4 blocks is 4:1, resulting in a transmission rate of 2 bits/pixel. If a 10-bit two-dimensional vector quantizer is used to coarsely quantize the mean and standard deviation [1] or the two reconstruction levels [5], [6], a rate of 1.625 bits/pixel can be achieved.

The bit map (1 bit/pixel) occupies more than 61% of the output code. Although some efforts have been made to compress the bit map [6], the subjective results are not quite satisfactory.

Color images, based upon the trichromatic nature of the human vision [7], consist of three planes—red, green, and blue (R, G, and B). There are very high correlations between the images in these planes. Actually, in a color image camera the R, G, and B signals are generated by three identical image sensors with R, G, or B optical filters placed in front of them. Thus, the three planes contain the same objects and, more importantly, by-and-large the same contours, although their intensity levels might be totally different. However, geometric distortions from the three sensors as well as the optical filters and some random noises from the different parts of the system might result in slight contour distortions or misregistrations in the three-color planes.

If BTC is implemented to encode the R, G, and B planes separately, the three resulting bit maps will be quite similar or almost identical, since the BTC is a two-level quantizer that adapts to local properties of the image. This motivates the use of one bit map to quantize all three of the color planes. Thus, only one out of three bit maps needs to be preserved, which means a savings of up to 40% in the bit rate.

The problem with this approach is deciding which single bit map should be used to quantize the three planes. As mentioned before, there are misregistrations and random noises involved in the color planes. Meanwhile, part of the color components in one plane might not correlate with other planes. Thus, no one of the R, G, or B bit maps alone provides optimal performance. A fourth plane must be generated by properly weighting the corresponding R, G, and B components such that it has less misregistrations and random noises with respect to all three color planes, and the uncorrelated components are best compromised. The BTC bit map of the "weighted plane" (W-plane) is, then, used to quantize the R, G, and B planes and a better mean square error (MSE) performance can be achieved.

In this paper, Section II briefly reviews block truncation coding. Section III discusses the generation of W-plane theoretically based upon the least MSE guideline. The post-BTC data compression used to achieve a higher compression ratio is also presented. Section IV describes the compression of NTSC color TV components. Section V presents the conclusions.

II. Block Truncation Coding

In BTC, the image is first partitioned into nonoverlapping $m \times m$ pixel blocks, in which there will likely be fairly high pixel-to-pixel correlation [1]–[5].

Manuscript received December 28, 1989; revised July 3, 1990.
Y. Wu is with the Communications Research Centre, Ottawa, Ont., Canada K2H 8S2.
D. C. Coll is with the Department of Systems and Computer Engineering, Carleton University, Ottawa, Ont., Canada K1S 5B6.
IEEE Log Number 9107591.

In Delp and Mitchell's algorithm [1], each pixel block is coded individually into a two-level signal. The levels for each block are chosen such that the first two moments, $\overline{X}$, and σ^2, are preserved. This algorithm has more computation than Lema and Mitchell's Absolute Moment BTC algorithm described in [5], since σ^2 must be calculated. In that algorithm, the pixels in each block are sorted into high-mean and low-mean groups, preserving the mean absolute moment or minimizing the mean absolute error in each block. The mean intensity

$$\overline{X} = \frac{1}{l} \sum_{i=1}^{l} x(i) \tag{1}$$

is used as the threshold for the 1-bit quantizer, where $x(i)$ is the value of ith pixel in the block and l is the number of pixels in a block, i.e., $m \times m$. If

$$x(i) \leq \overline{X} \quad \text{or} \quad x(i) > \overline{X} \tag{2}$$

$\overline{X}_L$ or $\overline{X}_H$, respectively, is assigned to the quantizer output levels, where

$$\overline{X}_L = \frac{1}{l - q} \sum_{x(i) < \overline{X}} x(i) \tag{3}$$

$$\overline{X}_H = \frac{1}{q} \sum_{x(i) \geq \overline{X}} x(i) \tag{4}$$

and q is the number of pixels having a value higher than $\overline{X}$. Hence, the outputs of the BTC for each block include two numbers which specify the high-mean, $\overline{X}_H$, and low-mean, $\overline{X}_L$; and a bit map which specifies the states, $\overline{X}_H$ or $\overline{X}_L$, of each output pixel. It can be understood that

$$\overline{X}_L < \overline{X}_H. \tag{5}$$

This algorithm has the potential of low computational complexity with no multiplications involved, and real-time implementation has been reported [8].

A two-dimensional vector quantizer was used to further compress the $\overline{X}_L$ and $\overline{X}_H$. A 10-bit vector quantizer having satisfactory visual results has been demonstrated [2], [6]. For a 4×4 block size, the resulting bit rate is:

$$1 + \frac{10}{16} = 1.625 \text{ bits/pixel.} \tag{6}$$

Halverson *et al.* [4] generalized BTC to include a family of moment-preserving quantizers with the potential of improving performance. It has been proved that the selection of the quantizer threshold and levels can be generalized for much larger classes of pairs and triples of sample moments, respectively. Performance improvements were demonstrated from the standpoint of peak signal-to-noise ratio. However, the application of the BTC algorithm for the higher moments case is often hampered by overflow problems and increased computational complexity.

In this paper, Lema's algorithm is used because of its computational simplicity (note: no matter which algorithm is used, the resulting bit maps are identical since they all use the same quantization threshold $\overline{X}$).

III. BTC of Color Images

Table I shows the MSE values resulting from implementing BTC individually on the R, G, and B planes of Fig. 1.

A. BTC of Color Images Using Single Bit Map

As mentioned in Section I, because of the similarities among the bit maps, the BTC bit map of one of the R, G, or B planes can be used to quantize the other two color planes. Let $QBM(i)$ represent the quantization bit map and q the number of 1's on the bit map in one $m \times m$ block. Then, (3) and (4) are modified as:

$$\overline{X}_1 = \frac{1}{l - q} \sum_{QBM(i) = 0} x(i) \tag{7}$$

$$\overline{X}_2 = \frac{1}{q} \sum_{QBM(i) = 1} x(i). \tag{8}$$

Here we use $\overline{X}_1$ and $\overline{X}_2$ instead of $\overline{X}_L$ and $\overline{X}_H$, since there is a possibility that $\overline{X}_1 > \overline{X}_2$ and the blocks are inverted. For instance, although the three bit maps might have the same contours, the 0's and 1's in some blocks of certain maps could be inverted so that 0's might represent the low values in a block and 1's represent the high values on one bit map and vice-versa on another. However, if there is no misregistration and noise involved, implementing a bit-inverted map in (7) and (8) will not result in any mistakes in the decoded plane since, in this case, $\overline{X}_1 > \overline{X}_2$.

The MSE results of using the bit map, derived from the R, G, or B planes as the quantization bit map, are displayed in Table I. It can be seen that the average MSE of reconstructed R, G, and B planes is up to 50% higher than that resulting from direct BTC of the color planes. Using different bit maps (R, G, or B) as the quantization bit map also results in different average MSE.

Table I also shows the correlations between the quantization bit map and the direct BTC bit maps [21], where

Correlation ρ

$$= \frac{\text{number of identical bits} - \text{number of different bits}}{\text{total bits}}$$

and the percentage of inverted blocks, where $\overline{X}_1 > \overline{X}_2$. These two parameters partially indicated the similarity between bit maps. The correlation can never be 1 because of the existence of misregistrations, random noises, and uncorrelated color components, the effects of which can be reduced as shown in the next section.

B. Minimum MSE Approach

Assuming each color plane consists of two parts

$$R = R' + n_R$$

$$G = G' + n_G$$

$$B = B' + n_B \tag{9}$$

TABLE I
MSE PERFORMANCE OF BTC OF R, G, AND B PLANES

		R-Plane	G-Plane	B-Plane	Y-Plane	W-Plane	Average of RGB
BTC	MSE	26.27	42.71	29.78	32.42	27.54	32.92
R map	MSE	26.27	63.46	59.93	*	*	48.89
	Bit-Map Corr. ρ	1	0.39	0.20	*	*	
	Inverted Blocks	0	12.03%	29.96%	*	*	
G map	MSE	35.81	42.71	46.68	*	*	41.73
	Bit-Map Corr. ρ	0.39	1	0.49	*	*	
	Inverted Blocks	10.67%	0	2.554%	*	*	
B map	MSE	49.24	62.84	29.78	*	*	47.29
	Bit-Map Corr. ρ	0.20	0.49	1	*	*	
	Inverted Blocks	26.41%	2.351%	0	*	*	
W map	MSE	33.05	46.41	39.75	*	27.54	39.74
	Bit-Map Corr. ρ	0.47	0.74	0.66	*	1	
	Inverted Blocks	5.280%	0.052%	0.195%	*	0	
M map	MSE	34.19	45.73	43.34	*	*	41.09
	Bit-Map Corr. ρ	0.55	0.84	0.65	*	*	
	Inverted Blocks	4.207%	0.053%	0.624%	*	*	
Y map	MSE	32.34	44.25	45.89	32.42	*	40.82
	Bit-Map Corr. ρ	0.50	0.85	0.52	1	*	
	Inverted Blocks	3.523%	0.000%	1.307%	0	*	

Fig. 1. Original diagram.

where n_R, n_G, and n_B represent the equivalent "noises" caused by misregistrations, random noises, and uncorrelated color components, which are assumed to be independent identically distributed (i.i.d.) random variables [9]. R', G', and B' are color components that have very high intercolor-plane correlations such that, if BTC is used to code each of them, the resulting bit maps would be identical or, in other words, the correlations can be removed by using a single quantization bit map.

Our purpose is to generate a fourth plane, W, by properly weighting the R, G, and B planes, i.e.,

$$W = \alpha R + \beta G + \gamma B \qquad (10)$$

where α, β, and γ are constants and

$$\alpha + \beta + \gamma = 1 \qquad (11)$$

to reduce the effects of n_R, n_G, and n_B and minimize the MSE in the reconstructed planes.

The differences between the W-plane and the color planes are:

$$\begin{bmatrix} W - R \\ W - G \\ W - B \end{bmatrix} = \begin{bmatrix} \alpha - 1 & \beta & \gamma \\ \alpha & \beta - 1 & \gamma \\ \alpha & \beta & \gamma - 1 \end{bmatrix} \begin{bmatrix} R \\ G \\ B \end{bmatrix}. \qquad (12)$$

Assuming the uncorrelated components in the difference planes are n_{W-R}, n_{W-G}, and n_{W-B}, the standard deviations are:

$$\begin{bmatrix} \sigma^2(n_{W-R}) \\ \sigma^2(n_{W-G}) \\ \sigma^2(n_{W-B}) \end{bmatrix}$$

$$= \begin{bmatrix} (\alpha - 1)^2 & \beta^2 & \gamma^2 \\ \alpha^2 & (\beta - 1)^2 & \gamma^2 \\ \alpha^2 & \beta^2 & (\gamma - 1)^2 \end{bmatrix} \begin{bmatrix} \sigma^2(n_R) \\ \sigma^2(n_G) \\ \sigma^2(n_B) \end{bmatrix}. \qquad (13)$$

The total "noise" energy is:

$$\sigma^2_{\text{total}} = \sigma^2(n_{W-R}) + \sigma^2(n_{W-G}) + \sigma^2(n_{W-B})$$

$$= (1 - 2\alpha + 3\alpha^2)\sigma^2(n_R) + (1 - 2\beta + 3\beta^2)$$

$$\cdot \sigma^2(n_R) + (1 - 2\gamma + 3\gamma^2)\sigma^2(n_R). \qquad (14)$$

It can be shown that σ^2_{total} is minimized by taking partial derivatives in respect to α, β, and γ and setting the results to zero. In this case,

$$\alpha = \beta = \gamma = \tfrac{1}{3} \qquad (15)$$

which also satisfies (11). Thus, the MSE optimized W-plane is:

$$W = \frac{R + G + B}{3}. \qquad (16)$$

Actually, (16) is an averaging process which calculates the average of the corresponding pixels of identical address from the R, G, and B planes and uses them as W-plane pixels. This process can reduce the uncorrelated components in W-plane [9]. For example, if

$$\sigma^2(n_R) = \sigma^2(n_G) = \sigma^2(n_B) = \sigma^2 \qquad (17)$$

then

$$\sigma^2(n_W) = \tfrac{1}{9}\sigma^2 + \tfrac{1}{9}\sigma^2 + \tfrac{1}{9}\sigma^2 = \tfrac{1}{3}\sigma^2. \qquad (18)$$

Substituting (15) and (17) into (13),

$$\min \{\sigma^2(n_{W-R,G,B})\} = \tfrac{2}{3}\sigma^2 \qquad (19)$$

while the uncorrelated components between the two color planes, e.g., between R and B, is

$$\sigma^2(n_{R-B}) = \sigma^2(n_R - n_G) = 2\sigma^2 \qquad (20)$$

which is three times higher than (18).

We have minimized the error caused by misregistrations, random noises, and uncorrelated color components between the W-plane and the color planes. Since BTC is an one-bit quantization process, there should be less difference between the BTC bit maps of the W-plane and of the color planes as opposed to the other cases. This can be shown by the reduction in the number of inverted bits, inverted blocks, and, more important, the MSE values in Table I, when the W-plane bit map is used as the quantization map.

The system diagram of MSE-optimized single bit map BTC of color images is shown in Fig. 2, where a single quantization bit map is implemented to quantize all three color planes to remove the interplane correlations.

The input color planes are first weighted together, using (10), to obtain a W-plane. Then, BTC is implemented on the W-plane to generate a quantization bit map. Based on the bit map, using (7) and (8), the R, G, and B planes undergo BTC. The resulting quantization data from each block, $\overline{X}_{R1}$, $\overline{X}_{R2}$, $\overline{X}_{G1}$, $\overline{X}_{G2}$, $\overline{X}_{B1}$, and $\overline{X}_{B2}$ go through post-quantization data compression.

For 24 bits/pixel (R, G, B) input data and a 4 × 4 block size (if no post-quantization data compression scheme is implemented), the overall bit rate is:

$$1 + \frac{3 \times 2 \times 8}{16} = 4 \text{ bits/color } - \text{ tuples} \qquad (21)$$

or a 6 : 1 compression. If a 10-bit two-dimensional vector quantizer [2], [6] is used to code the BTC output data $\overline{X}_{R,G,B1}$ and $\overline{X}_{R,G,B2}$, the overall bit rate is:

$$1 + \frac{3 \times 10}{16} = 2.875 \text{ bits/color } - \text{ tuples.} \qquad (22)$$

The compression ratio is 8.35 : 1.

C. Bit-Map Majority Rule Approach

Another approach to generation of the quantization bit map is using majority rule on R, G, and B bit maps. BTC is first implemented on the R, G, and B planes. The re-

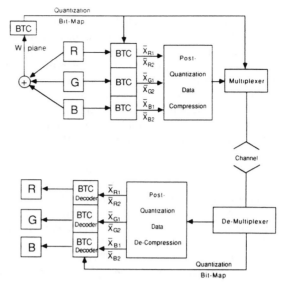

Fig. 2. System diagram of MSE-optimized single bit-map BTC of color images.

sulting bit maps are $BM_R(i, j)$, $BM_G(i, j)$, and $BM_B(i, j)$, where (i, j) specifies the bit-map element address and the bit-map sample space is $\{0, 1\}$. Let $QBM(i, j)$ represent the quantization bit map, then:

$$QBM(i, j) = \text{Majority } \{BM_R(i, j), BM_G(i, j), BM_B(i, j)\}$$

$$= BM_R(i, j) \cdot BM_G(i, j) + BM_R(i, j)$$

$$\cdot BM_B(i, j) + BM_G(i, j) \cdot BM_B(i, j). \qquad (23)$$

The MSE performance of using the majority-rule bit map, M-map, to encode the R, G, and B planes is shown in Table I. It can be seen that bit-map correlations between the M-map and the R, G, and B maps are higher than other cases. On the other hand, the average MSE value is higher than the minimum MSE approach.

To generate the quantization bit map, three BTC processes must be implemented to code the R, G, and B planes in the majority rule approach, while only one BTC process must be conducted in the minimum MSE approach. The total computational complexity of the majority rule approach is about 50% higher than that of the minimum MSE approach.

From the above discussion, minimum MSE approach is a better choice.

D. Post-Quantization Data Compression Using Adaptive DCT

After BTC of the R, G, and B planes using the W-plane bit map as the quantization bit map, there are seven sets of data to be transmitted (Fig. 2), i.e., one quantization bit map, and, for each block, six quantization levels— $\overline{X}_{R1}$, $\overline{X}_{R2}$, $\overline{X}_{G1}$, $\overline{X}_{G2}$, $\overline{X}_{B1}$, and $\overline{X}_{B2}$. Each of these quantization levels is a "mean" of certain pixels inside a quantization block, as defined by (7) and (8).

If quantization levels from each BTC block are grouped together as raster files, we can form six subsampled images—R_1, R_2, G_1, G_2, B_1, and B_2. For a 512×512 input image with 4×4 blocks, each subsampled image is 128×128. The subsampled images have details and features which must be preserved, since any distortion involved here will be distributed over all of the pixels in each reconstructed BTC block of respected color planes.

The coding algorithm used to compress these subsampled images must have high fidelity, even at the cost of a "high" bit rate, since the real bit rate is the subsampled-image bit rate divided by the BTC block size, i.e., 4×4. On the other hand, moderate computational complexity is acceptable because the subimage size is relatively small.

Adaptive discrete cosine transform (DCT) coding [10]–[12], which adaptively allocates bits in the transform domain based on fidelity requirements, has very high fidelity and seems a good candidate for the compression of the subsampled images. Although DCT coding tends to smear edges because some high-frequency components are discarded as part of the encoding procedure, the edges have already been preserved by the BTC preprocessing.

There are three ways to DCT-encode the subimages:
1) direct coding;
2) direct-differential coding;
3) direct-differential coding with residual error feedback.

1) Error Analysis for Three DCT Coding Algorithms

Method I: Adaptive DCT [10] is directly implemented on the six subimages separately [Fig. 3(a)]. Let $\hat{R}_1$ and $\hat{R}_2$ be reconstructed mean-subsampled images from the R plane, then

$$\hat{R}_1 = Q(R_1) = R_1 + e_{R1} \quad (24)$$

and

$$\hat{R}_2 = Q(R_2) = R_2 + e_{R2} \quad (25)$$

where the operator $Q(\cdot)$ represents the coding/decoding process, which can be thought of as a requantization of the input subimages, and e_{R1} and e_{R2} are quantization errors. Assuming e_{R1} and e_{R2} are independent identically distributed (i.i.d.) random variables (RV's), the total average coding error energy is:

$$\overline{e^2}(R_1, R_2) = \overline{e_{R1}^2} + \overline{e_{R2}^2} = 2\overline{e^2}. \quad (26)$$

Similar results can be obtained for the other color's subsampled images.

Method II: Six subimages are sorted into three pairs according to their colors, i.e., $\{R_1, R_2\}$, $\{G_1, G_2\}$, and $\{B_1, B_2\}$. Adaptive DCT is implemented on R_1 (G_1, and B_1) and the difference image $R_2 - R_1$ ($G_2 - G_1$, and $B_2 - B_1$):

$$R_{2-1} = R_2 - R_1 \quad (27)$$

in Fig. 3(b). Since a difference image usually has less entropy, i.e.,

$$H(R_{2-1}) \le H(R_1) \quad \text{and} \quad H(R_{2-1}) \le H(R_2)$$

less bits can be used to code R_{2-1} (G_{2-1} and B_{2-1}) than R_1 or R_2 (G_1 or G_2, and B_1 or B_2) for the same fidelity.

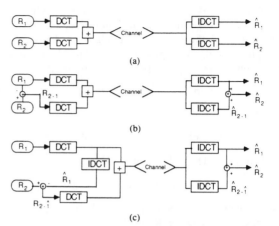

Fig. 3. Adaptive DCT coding of a subsampled color plane (red plane).

Thus,

$$\hat{R}_{2-1} = Q(R_{2-1}) = R_{2-1} + e(R_{2-1}). \quad (28)$$

From (24) and (28),

$$\hat{R}_2' = Q(R_1) + Q(R_{2-1})$$
$$= R_{2-1} + R_1 + e_{2-1} + e_1. \quad (29)$$

From (24) and (29), the total energy for an R-plane subsampled image is:

$$\overline{e^2}(R_1, R_{2-1}) = \overline{e^2(R_{2-1}) + e_{R1}^2 + e_{R1}^2} = 3\overline{e^2}. \quad (30)$$

Method III: Six subimages are sorted into three pairs according to their colors, i.e., $\{R_1, R_2\}$, $\{G_1, G_2\}$, and $\{B_1, B_2\}$. Adaptive DCT is implemented on R_1 (G_1, and B_1) and the difference image $R_2 - \hat{R}_1$ ($G_2 - \hat{G}_1$, and $B_2 - \hat{B}_1$) using residual error feedback [13]–[15], as shown in Fig. 3(c) where $\hat{R}_1$ ($\hat{G}_1$ and $\hat{B}_1$) is the reconstructed R_1 (G_1 and B_1). Hence, for the R channel,

$$\hat{R}_{2-1} = Q(R_1 - \hat{R}_1). \quad (31)$$

Inserting (24),

$$\hat{R}_{2-1} = Q(R_2 - R_1 + e_{R1}) = Q(R_{2-1} + e_{R1}). \quad (32)$$

For simplicity, assuming the quantization process $Q(\cdot)$ is linear,

$$\hat{R}_{2-1} \approx \hat{R}_{2-1} + Q(e_{R1}) = R_{2-1} + e(R_{2-1}) + Q(e_{R1}). \quad (33)$$

From (24) and (33),

$$\overline{e^2}(R_1, R_2 - \hat{R}_1) = \overline{e^2}(R_{2-1}) + e_{R1}^2 + Q^2(e_{R1})$$
$$= 2\overline{e^2} + \overline{Q^2(e)}. \quad (34)$$

$Q(e)$ is the quantizer output due to the quantization error e. Usually, e can be modeled as *white Gaussian noise* [16], which has a "flat" spectrum, or relatively "wide" bandwidth. Since most of quantizers have a lowpass-type frequency response, $Q(e)$ must have less energy than e, i.e.,

$$\overline{Q^2(e)} < \overline{e^2}. \quad (35)$$

220

On the other hand, e has a *Gaussian distribution* [9] in the time domain with zero mean. Most of the time, its amplitude is relatively small. When e is less than the quantizer step size, or threshold, there will be no output from the coding/decoding process $Q(\cdot)$

$$\overline{Q^2(e)} \approx 0, \qquad \text{when } e \approx 0. \qquad (36)$$

From (35) and (36),

$$0 < \overline{Q^2(e)} < \overline{e^2}. \qquad (37)$$

Thus,

$$2\overline{e^2} \leq \overline{e^2}(R_1, R_2, -\hat{R}_1) \leq 3\overline{e^2}. \qquad (38)$$

Comparing (26), (36), and (38), the error performance of the three methods can be related as:

$$\overline{e^2}(R_1, R_2) \leq \overline{e^2}(R_1, R_2 - \hat{R}_1) \leq \overline{e^2}(R_1, R_2 - R_1). \qquad (39)$$

Method I has the best MSE performance and least computational complexity, but the highest bit rate since the correlations between the two subimages are not removed. Method II has the worst MSE, moderate computational complexity, and low bit rate. Method III has moderate MSE, high computational complexity (about 50% more computation than the other methods), and low bit rate. Since the size of the subimages is relatively small, sixteen times less than the original image, the computational complexity is trivial. Considering low bit rate and MSE performance, Method III is the best candidate. The MSE performance of the three schemes are listed in Table II and the reconstructed image (Method III) is shown in Fig. 4.

2) Computational Complexity of Single Bit-Map BTC and Adaptive DCT versus Direct Adaptive DCT: For single bit-map BTC and adaptive DCT coding (SBMBTC-DCT), the BTC part requires few computations per pixel with respect to DCT, which is, with residual error feedback [17]–[19],

$$\frac{36 \cdot \log_2 N}{N_b \times N_b} \text{ multiplication/addition per pixel} \qquad (40)$$

where N_b is the BTC block size, N is the DCT block size. If $N_b = 4$ and $N = 16$, then:

$$\frac{36 \cdot \log_2 N}{N_b \times N_b} = 9 \text{ multiplication/addition per pixel.} \qquad (41)$$

For direct adaptive DCT coding, the computation is:

$$12 \cdot \log_2 N \text{ multiplication/addition per pixel}$$

and for $N = 16$,

$$12 \cdot \log_2 N = 48 \text{ multiplication/addition per pixel.}$$

SBMBTC-DCT, with residual error feedback, is about five times faster than direct DCT. Without residual error feedback, it is about eight times faster than direct DCT.

3) Channel Error Effects on Single Bit-Map BTC Data: SBMBTC-DCT data contain a quantization bit map

TABLE II
MSE PERFORMANCE OF SBMBTC-DCT CODING

Plane	Method	Bit Rate (bits/pixel)	MSE
R	I	0.400	44.3
	II	0.369	46.9
	III	0.369	44.5
G	I	0.438	55.2
	II	0.400	59.4
	III	0.400	56.8
B	I	0.388	49.8
	II	0.356	52.7
	III	0.356	50.3
Total (including) bit map	I	2.225	49.8
	II	2.125	52.9
	III	2.125	50.5

Fig. 4. Reconstructed RGB image (12 : 1 compression).

and six subsampled images which are further compressed using DCT coding (Fig. 2).

If transmission errors hit the bit map, the only effects in the reconstructed images are the conversion of $\overline{X}_{R,G,B1}$ into $\overline{X}_{R,G,B2}$, or vice versa, for error-contaminated bits. The errors will not propagate and the error effects are limited just like error effects to PCM-coded data.

Since DCT coding is error robust, any error in the six DCT-coded subsampled image data will distributed over all transform block [16]. The visual effects will be limited.

From the above discussions, SBMBTC-DCT coding has very strong error robustness.

IV. COMPRESSION OF NTSC COLOR TV COMPONENTS

In the NTSC color television system, the R, G, and B signals are combined to form a luminance signal Y and two chrominance signals I and Q, which are related by [7]:

$$\begin{bmatrix} Y \\ I \\ Q \end{bmatrix} = L \begin{bmatrix} R \\ G \\ B \end{bmatrix} = \begin{bmatrix} 0.299 & 0.587 & 0.114 \\ 0.596 & -0.274 & -0.322 \\ 0.211 & -0.523 & 0.312 \end{bmatrix} \begin{bmatrix} R \\ G \\ B \end{bmatrix}. \qquad (42)$$

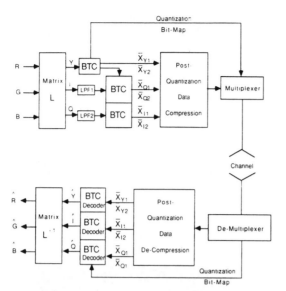

Fig. 5. System diagram of SBMBTC-DCT coding of NTSC components.

The inverse transform is

$$\begin{bmatrix} R \\ G \\ B \end{bmatrix} = L^{-1} \begin{bmatrix} Y \\ I \\ Q \end{bmatrix}$$

$$= \begin{bmatrix} 1.000 & 0.956 & 0.621 \\ 1.000 & -0.272 & -0.647 \\ 1.000 & -1.106 & 1.703 \end{bmatrix} \begin{bmatrix} Y \\ I \\ Q \end{bmatrix}. \quad (43)$$

Since the human visual system is very sensitive to the spatial variations of Y, less sensitive to I, and much less sensitive to Q [7], we can lowpass-filter the I signal with a 3×3 averaging filter and the Q signal with a 5×5 averaging filter, and code the resulting signals using SMBTC-DCT coding. Since Y is a combination of R, G, and B, i.e.,

$$Y = 0.299R + 0.587G + 0.114B \quad (44)$$

comparing with (10)

$$\alpha = 0.299, \quad \beta = 0.587 \quad \gamma = 0.114 \quad (45)$$

to maintain a relatively high fidelity coding of Y to satisfy the human visual system. Y is directly coded by BTC, and its bit map is used as the quantization bit map to code the lowpass-filtered I and Q signals.

The system diagram is shown in Fig. 5. Actually, the lowpass filtering process can be combined in the DCT coding process by discarding high-frequency components in the DCT domain. The MSE performance is listed in Table III. Comparing with Table II, a coding gain of approximately 0.5 bits/color-tuples can be obtained, because of the coarse coding of I and Q signals. The compression ratio is about 14:1. Fig. 6 displays the reconstructed image (Method III).

The bit rates of other test images are listed in Table IV. It can be seen that the test image "Baboon," which has

TABLE III
MSE PERFORMANCE OF SBMBTC-DCT CODING OF NTSC COLOR COMPONENTS

Plane	Method	Bit Rate (bits/pixel)	MSE
Y	I	0.419	39.4
	II	0.388	42.7
	III	0.388	40.8
I	I	0.200	18.7
	II	0.169	19.8
	III	0.169	19.2
Q	I	0.131	14.6
	II	0.119	15.3
	III	0.119	14.9
Total (including bit map)	I	1.750	
	II	1.675	
	III	1.675	

Fig. 6. Reconstructed NTSC image (14:1 compression).

TABLE IV
BIT RATE OF SBMBTC-DCT CODING OF NTSC COLOR COMPONENTS

Plane	Bit Rate (bits/pixel)		
	Baboon	Kodak Girl	Ken
Y	0.531	0.392	0.326
I	0.394	0.213	0.138
Q	0.171	0.154	0.122
Total (including bit map)	2.033	1.759	1.586
Compression Ratio	11.8:1	13.6:1	15.1:1

a large region containing high-frequency details, has a compression ratio about 12:1. The test image "Ken," which is a head-and-shoulder teleconferencing image, has a compression ratio about 15:1. The test image "Kodak Girl," which contains a head-and-shoulder pose plus some other objects, has a compression ratio of about 13.6:1. The average compression ratio of SBMBTC-DCT coding is between 12:1 to 15:1.

V. Conclusion

This paper describes a color-image data compression technique using block truncation coding (BTC). A quantization bit map is used to BTC all three color planes, which removes the intercolor correlations. The quantized data are further compressed using adaptive DCT coding. Differential coding and residual error feedback techniques are implemented to reduce the bit rate and improve the MSE performance. The algorithm preserves the spatial details in the image content because of the implementation of BTC and has lower computational complexity than DCT coding. The total compression ratio is about 12 : 1. For NTSC color TV components, the compression can be 14 : 1.

References

[1] E. J. Delp and O. R. Mitchell, "Image compression using block truncation coding," *IEEE Trans. Commun.*, vol. COM-27, pp. 1335–1342, Sept. 1979.

[2] D. J. Healy and O. R. Mitchell, "Digital video bandwidth compression using block truncation coding," *IEEE Trans. Commun.*, vol. COM-29, pp. 1809–1817, Dec. 1981.

[3] G. R. Arce and N. C. Gallagher, Jr., "BTC image using median filter roots," *IEEE Trans. Commun.*, vol. COM-31, June 1983.

[4] D. R. Halverson. "A generalized BTC algorithm for image compression," *IEEE Trans. Acoust., Speech and Signal Process.*, vol. ASSP-32, pp. 664–668, 1984.

[5] M. D. Lema and O. R. Mitchell, "Absolute moment block truncation coding and application to color image," *IEEE Trans. Commun.*, vol. COM-32, pp. 1148–1157, Oct. 1984.

[6] V. R. Udpikar and J. P. Raina, "BTC image coding using vector quantization," *IEEE Trans. Commun.*, vol. 35, pp. 352–356, Mar. 1987.

[7] W. K. Pratt, *Digital Image Processing.* New York: Wiley, 1978.

[8] H. H. Ko and C. W. Lee, "Real time implementation of block truncation coding for picture data compression," presented at Proc. ICASSP'87, 1987.

[9] A. Papoulis, *Probability, Random Variables, and Stochastic Processes.* New York: McGraw-Hill, 1984.

[10] W. H. Chen and W. Pratt, "Scene adaptive coder," *IEEE Trans. Commun.*, vol. COM-32, pp. 225–232, Mar. 1984.

[11] CCITT Document 420, "Adaptive discrete cosine transform coding scheme for still image telecommunication services," Jan. 1988.

[12] Y. Wu, "Data compression of meteorological satellite photo imagery for transmission," M. Eng. Thesis, Carleton Univ., Ottawa, Canada, 1986.

[13] J. R. Jain and A. K. Jain, "Displacement measurement and its application in interframe image coding," *IEEE Trans. Commun.*, vol. COM-29, pp. 1799–1808, Dec. 1981.

[14] J. A. Roese et al., "Interframe cosine transform image coding," *IEEE Trans. Commun.*, vol. COM-25, pp. 1329–1338, Nov. 1977.

[15] L. Wang and M. Goldberg, "Lossless progressive image transmission by residual vector quantization," in *Proc. 13th Biennial Symp. Commun.*, Kingston, Ont., Canada, June 1986, pp. c.1.9–c.1.12.

[16] N. S. Jayant and P. Noll, *Digital Coding of Waveforms.* Englewood Cliffs, NJ: Prentice-Hall, 1984.

[17] W. Chen, C. H. Smith, and S. C. Fralick, "A fast computational algorithm for the discrete cosine transform," *IEEE Trans. Commun.*, vol. COM-25, no. 9, pp. 1008–1017, Sept. 1977.

[18] M. J. Navasimha and A. M. Peterson, "On the computation of the discrete cosine transform," *IEEE Trans. Commun.*, vol. COM-16, no. 6, pp. 934–936, June 1978.

[19] Z. Wang, "Reconsideration of a fast computational algorithm for the discrete cosine transform," *IEEE Trans. Commun.*, vol. 21, pp. 121–123, Jan. 1983.

[20] D. C. Coll and Y. Wu, "High fidelity compression of composite meteorological imagery," presented at *Proc. 14th Biennial Symp. Commun.*, Kingston, Ont., Canada, May 1988.

[21] S. W. Golomb et al., *Digital Communications with Space Applications.* Englewood Cliffs, NJ: Prentice-Hall, 1964.

Multilevel Block Truncation Coding Using a Minimax Error Criterion for High-Fidelity Compression of Digital Images

Yiyan Wu, *Member, IEEE,* and David C. Coll, *Senior Member, IEEE*

Abstract—This paper describes an encoding technique—multilevel block truncation coding—that preserves the spatial details in digital images while achieving a reasonable compression ratio. An adaptive quantizer-level allocation scheme is introduced, which minimizes the maximum quantization error in each block and substantially reduces the computational complexity in the allocation of optimal quantization levels. A 3.2:1 compression can be achieved by the multilevel block truncation coding itself. The truncated, or requantized, data are further compressed in a second pass using combined techniques of predictive coding, entropy coding, and vector quantization. The second pass compression can be lossless or lossy. The total compression ratios are about 4.1:1 for lossless second-pass compression, and 6.2:1 for lossy second-pass compression. The subjective results of the coding algorithm are quite satisfactory, with no perceived visual degradation.

I. INTRODUCTION

MOST image coding algorithms, such as transform coding, predictive coding [1], [2], and vector quantization [23]–[27], are based on a mean-square error (MSE) fidelity criterion [3], [4]. The major disadvantage of MSE-based coding schemes is that they act, more or less, like low-pass filters. The high-frequency details are blurred or even filtered out in the reconstructed image since they normally have low probability, and thus may be discarded without a large contribution to the MSE. This low-pass filter effect is acceptable for some images, such as television and teleconferencing pictures. On the other hand, some scientific images such as satellite remote sensing, synthetic aperture radar (SAR), and medical imagery contain very-high-resolution artifacts coinciding with sharp edges and sudden single-pixel-width changes in gray level which can be crucial in the image application and must be preserved. As well, these images have large data sets which require massive storage space and result in substantial transmission times when the images are communicated over data networks. Finding a way to compress such images while maintaining high fidelity is very important; and, because the images are widely distributed, the decompression algorithms are expected to run efficiently on general-purpose computers, with no special-purpose hardware required.

Block truncation coding (BTC) [5]–[9] uses a two-level moment-preserving quantizer that adapts to local properties of the image. It has the advantages of preserving single-pixel resolution and edges and having low computational complexity. The original algorithm preserves the block mean and the block standard deviation [5], [6]. Other choices of the moments result either in less MSE or less computational complexity [8], [9]. However, a two-level quantization is simply not able to code a highly busy image with satisfactory fidelity [10]. To achieve high fidelity, we use a multilevel quantizer with a minimax error criterion, rather than the conventional two-level moment-preserving quantizer. In Section II, an algorithm using a minimax quantization error criterion is developed to allocate the quantizer levels to obtain a close replica of the original image and to be robust to the pixel statistical distribution within each pixel block. A fast searching algorithm is introduced to find the optimal quantizer levels, based on minimax quantization error. Sections III–VI discuss the postquantization compression of the coded data using combined techniques of predictive coding, entropy coding, and vector quantization.

The images used to test the coding algorithm are composite satellite imagery (CSI) [11], Picture I, and a standard test image, Picture II. CSI is a pictorial satellite remote sensing image overlaid with computer-generated graphics. The graphical portions are very distinctive in gray level relative to the surrounding pixels, and should be coded losslessly so that, in the reconstructed image, they can be identified. The pictorial portion contains high-frequency details which must be well preserved.

The contents of CSI are very random with first-order entropy around 7 b/pixel and first-order conditional entropies of about 5 b/pixel. For the standard image, Picture II, the first-order entropy is also around 7 b/pixel, but the conditional entropy is only about 4 b/pixel.

The test results of our coding algorithm are quite satisfactory. No visual degradation is perceived.

Paper approved by the Editor for Image Communications Systems of the IEEE Communications Society. Manuscript received October 26, 1989; revised May 18, 1990. This paper was presented in part at the Picture Coding Symposium'90, Cambridge, MA, March 1990.

Y. Wu was with the Department of Systems and Computer Engineering, Carleton University, Ottawa, Ont., Canada K1S 5B6. He is now with the Communications Research Center, P.O. Box 11490, Station H, Ottawa, Ont., Canada K2H 8S2.

D. C. Coll is with the Department of Systems and Computer Engineering, Carleton University, Ottawa, Ont., Canada K1S 5B6.

IEEE Log Number 9211216.

II. MINIMAX ERROR MULTILEVEL BTC AND ITS QUANTIZER LEVEL FAST ALLOCATION SCHEME

Picture I. CSI original image.

Picture II. Original image (Girl).

Picture III. CSI reconstructed image (4, 8).

Picture IV. Reconstructed image (4, 8).

A. Minimax Error Multi-Level BTC

In multilevel block truncation coding, the image is partitioned into $M \times M$ pixel blocks. Assume that the *random variable* (r.v.) X represents the pixel values in a block and,

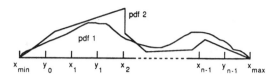

Fig. 1. Block pixel probability distribution functions.

in the first case, is continuously distributed over an interval $[x_{\min}, x_{\max}]$, such as pdf 1 and pdf 2 shown in Fig. 1. An *N-level quantizer* is used to quantize X. The N output values of the quantizer are

$$\{y_n\} = y_0, y_1, \cdots, y_{N-1}$$

where

$$y_0 \leq y_1 \leq \cdots \leq y_{N-1}. \tag{1}$$

The $N - 1$ threshold values are

$$\{x_n\} = x_1, x_2, \cdots, x_{N-1}$$

and

$$x_1 \leq x_2 \leq \cdots \leq x_{N-1}. \tag{2}$$

An output value $y_r, y_r \in \{y_n\}$ is assigned to represent the pixel values in the interval $[x_r, x_{r+1}]$, where $x_r, x_{r+1} \in \{x_n\}$. Thus,

$$x_r \leq y_r \leq x_{r+1}. \tag{3}$$

The maximum absolute quantization error on the interval is

$$|e_{r\,\max}| = \max\{x_{r+1} - y_r, y_r - x_r\}.$$

To minimize $e_{r\,\max}$, the y_r must be set to the midpoint of $[x_r, x_{r+1}]$, i.e.,

$$y_r = \frac{x_r + x_{r+1}}{2} \tag{4}$$

and

$$\min\{|e_{r\,\max}|\} = x_{r+1} - y_r = y_r - x_r = \frac{x_{r+1} - x_r}{2}. \tag{5}$$

If the entire sample interval $[x_{\min}, x_{\max}]$ is partitioned into N *equal-length intervals* by $\{x_n\}$ and the N output values $y_0, y_1, \cdots, y_{N-1}$ are set to the midpoint of each interval $(x_{\min}, x_1), (x_1, x_2), \cdots, (x_{N-1}, x_{\max})$, respectively, then on each interval (x_r, x_{r+1}),

$$|e_{r\,\max}| = \frac{x_{r+1} - x_r}{2} = \frac{x_{\max} - x_{\min}}{2N} \tag{6}$$

which also means

$$|e_{0\,\max}| = |e_{1\,\max}| = \cdots = |e_{N-1}| = \frac{x_{\max} - x_{\min}}{2N} \tag{7}$$

and

$$\min\{|e_{\max}|\} = \frac{x_{\max} - x_{\min}}{2N}. \tag{8}$$

One important point of the above results is that only the continuity of the pdf of the input r.v. X over the interval $[x_{\min}, x_{\max}]$ is mentioned, but not the type of the pdf. This means that (8) is valid as long as the pdf is continuous.

225

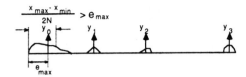

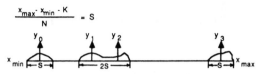

Fig. 2. Block histogram with "zero" intervals.

Fig. 3. The case where nonzero components can be partitioned into N equal-length intervals.

In the more general case, portions of the pdf which are zero within the interval $[x_{\min}, x_{\max}]$, i.e., if $\{x_m\}$ is a subset of $\{x\}$, and $f(x_m) = 0$, might result in, see Fig. 2,

$$|e_{\max}| < \frac{x_{\max} - x_{\min}}{2N}. \tag{9}$$

In an extreme case, i.e., when there are fewer than N nonzero points on the interval $[x_{\min}, x_{\max}]$,

$$|e_{\max}| = 0. \tag{10}$$

Hence, (8) is the upper bound of $\min\{|e_{\max}|\}$, and (10) is the lower bound. Thus,

$$0 \le \min\{|e_{\max}|\} \le \frac{x_{\max} - x_{\min}}{2N}. \tag{11}$$

For the general case, when there are K block histogram components, where $K \le x_{\max} - x_{\min} - 1$, on the interval $[x_{\min}, x_{\max}]$ that are equal to zero ($f(x_{\max}) \neq 0$ and $f(x_{\min}) \neq 0$)], it can be proven that

$$\frac{x_{\max} - x_{\min} - K}{2N} \le \min\{|e_{\max}|\} \le \frac{x_{\max} - x_{\min}}{2N}. \tag{12}$$

The equality on the left side of (12) holds only if the *nonzero components* can be partitioned into N *equal-length intervals*; see Fig. 3.

Actually, (12) is a more general expression of (11).

B. Fast Quantizer Level Allocation Scheme

So far, the lower and upper bounds of $\min\{|e_{\max}|\}$ have been found, (12). The next step is to find the best threshold allocation to obtain $\min\{|e_{\max}|\}$.

Fig. 4(a) is a typical input data histogram $f(x)$ over the interval $[x_{\min}, x_{\max}]$. Assuming that a four-level quantizer is used, $N = 4$. There will be $N - 1 = 3$ thresholds, x_1, x_2, and x_3, and the thresholds are equally placed with spacing

$$\frac{x_{\max} - x_{\min}}{N};$$

see Fig. 4(b). This partition will give the upper bound of $\min\{|e_{\max}|\}$, the right side of (12). However, there are "zeros" on the sample interval, which means, from (12), that $\min\{|e_{\max}|\}$ can be less.

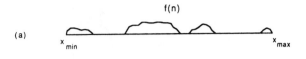

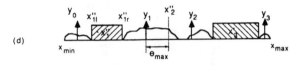

Fig. 4. An example of the threshold-dilation algorithm to fast search output levels which minimize $|e_{\max}|$ over a pixel block.

Since threshold x_3 is located on a "zero" interval, if we "dilate" x_3 to mask out "zeros," see Fig. 4(c), then y_3 will have a better error performance, where

$$y_3 = \frac{x'_{3r} + x_{\max}}{2}.$$

Now, the new threshold x'_3 occupies an interval (x'_{3l}, x'_{3r}). The next step is to reallocate x'_1 and x'_2 to partition $[x_{\min}, x'_{3l}]$ into equal-length intervals; see Fig. 4(c). Again, x'_1 can be dilated and mask out some "zeros." y_0 can be set as

$$y_0 = \frac{x_{\min} + x''_{1l}}{2}.$$

The new x''_2 is allocated using

$$x''_2 = \frac{x''_{1r} + x'_{3l}}{2}$$

and

$$y_1 = \frac{x''_{1r} + x''_2}{2}$$
$$y_2 = \frac{x''_2 + x'_{3l}}{2}.$$

Thus,

$$\min|e_{\max}| = x''_2 - y_1 = y_2 - x''_2 < \frac{x_{\max} - x_{\min}}{2N}.$$

From Fig. 4(d), not all "zeros" have been masked out. Hence, (12) should be modified as

$$\frac{x_{\min} - x_{\min} - K'}{2N} \le \min\{|e_{\max}|\} \le \frac{x_{\max} - x_{\min}}{2N} \tag{13}$$

where K' is the number of "zeros" that have actually been masked out in the threshold dilation procedure.

The above example also gives a computationally efficient method to reduce $|e_{\max}|$. For a sample interval $[x_{\min}, x_{\max}]$,

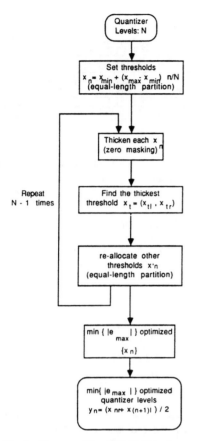

Fig. 5. Diagram of threshold-dilation scheme.

TABLE I
MSE Performance Comparison of Different Quantizers

Quantizer	Distribution	MSE	
		4 by 4 block	8 by 8 block
Max	Laplacian	203	208
	Gaussian	73.6	134
	Uniform	66.3	116
Conventional 2-Level BTC		72.1	172
4-Level BTC (moment preserving)		15.2	34.0
4-Level BTC (minimax)		11.6	31.0

Table I shows the MSE performance of various four-level quantizers. Max quantizers [3], optimized to Laplacian, Gaussian, and uniform distributions [2], and multilevel BTC using absolute moment-preserving quantizers [9], are compared with the minimax multilevel BTC. Different block sizes are used. Max quantizers assume a distribution, and the results in Table I show clearly that the test images tend towards a uniform distribution. A Lloyd–Max iterative quantization algorithm [2], [3] could result in lower MSE, but would require extensive computation. The multilevel BTC quantization algorithm minimizes the maximum error within each quantization block regardless of distribution. It can be seen, Table I, that the two multilevel BTC schemes have much better MSE performance than the Max quantizers because they are adaptive to the local statistics. The minimax multilevel BTC has the lowest MSE.

The most attractive feature of BTC is its computational simplicity. No computation at all is necessary for decoding of BTC data. LUT's may be used to assign the pixel values. The whole process can be implemented on a standard byte-oriented general-purpose computer, as appropriate for widely disseminated products [12].

III. Compression of Quantization Level Data

In minimax error multilevel block truncation coding, a four-level (2 b) quantizer is used to quantize the image data based on the minimax quantization error scheme within each pixel block. The quantized data set includes a quaternary plane which defines the quantization level for each pixel and four 8 b quantization level codes for each block. The bit rate for $M \times M$ blocks is

$$\text{bit rate} = 2 + \frac{4 \times 8}{M \times M} \text{ b/pixel}$$

which, for $M = 8$, is 2.5 b/pixel.

There are correlations between the quantization levels and within the quantization map. This section will discuss the further, lossless compression of the quantization levels.

Second-order predictors are used to remove the inter- and intrablock correlations between quantization levels. A variable length code is designed to code the four quantization level prediction errors losslessly. The algorithm is not sensitive to statistical variations in the data, has less encoding and decoding delay than the Huffman code, and is relatively robust to transmission or storage errors.

A. Intrablock Prediction

For each quantization level y_n, where $n = 0, 1, 2, 3$, the sample space is $[0, 255]$, and within each block,

$$y_0 \leq y_1 \leq y_2 \leq y_3. \tag{15}$$

the direct search for $\min\{|e_{\max}|\}$ will take $C^N_{x_{\max}-x_{\min}+1}$ iterations, where

$$C^N_{x_{\max}-x_{\min}+1} = \frac{(x_{\max} - x_{\min} + 1)!}{N! \, (x_{\max} - x_{\min} + 1 - N)!}. \tag{14}$$

When $N = 4$ and $x_{\max} - x_{\min} + 1 = 40$, $C^4_{40} = 91\,390$. Using the "threshold-dilation" scheme, only $N - 1 = 3$ iterations are needed.

Fig. 5 is a diagram of the "threshold-dilation" scheme. First, the $N - 1$ thresholds x_n are preset, equally spaced. Second, each threshold is dilated, and the thickest one, x_t, which masked out the most zeros is selected. Based on the x_t, the other $N - 2$ thresholds are reallocated, and then step 2 is repeated until all of the thresholds have been allocated.

C. Performance of Minimax Error Multilevel BTC

In this section, the performance of minimax error multilevel BTC is tested on CSI. Different block sizes are used, and the results are compared with other quantizers.

One of the advantages of the "threshold dilation" quantizer-level allocation scheme is that it will assign the exact value to overlay pixels in CSI. The overlay pixel level is normally quite distinct from surrounding satellite imagery pixels; see Picture I. Thus, the "threshold dilation" scheme will automatically mask out the distinguishing "zeros," and assign the exact value to overlay pixels.

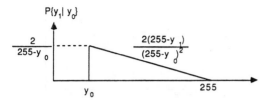

Fig. 6. Triangular distribution.

TABLE II
VALUES OF PIXEL CORRELATION COEFFICIENTS OF DIFFERENT IMAGES

CSI (with overlays)														
m	1	2	3	4	5	6	7	8	9	10	11	12	13	14	15
$\rho(m)$	.80	.74	.70	.67	.64	.61	.59	.57	.55	.54	.52	.51	.50	.48	.47
CSI (without overlays)														
m	1	2	3	4	5	6	7	8	9	10	11	12	13	14	15
$\rho(m)$	.90	.84	.79	.76	.72	.70	.67	.65	.63	.61	.59	.58	.56	.54	.53
Girl with Hat														
m	1	2	3	4	5	6	7	8	9	10	11	12	13	14	15
$\rho(m)$	.97	.93	.89	.86	.83	.80	.78	.75	.73	.71	.69	.67	.65	.63	.62

Individually, each quantization level is specified by 8 b. For a four-level quantizer, 32 b are required to represent all four of them. However, the quantization levels are related. For example, once y_0 is allocated on the sample space [0, 255], the sample space for y_1 reduces to $[y_0, 255]$. Thus,

$$\{y_0\} \in [0, 255] \tag{16}$$

$$\{y_1\} \in [y_0, 255] \tag{17}$$

$$\{y_2\} \in [y_1, 255] \tag{18}$$

$$\{y_3\} \in [y_2, 255]. \tag{19}$$

Assuming y_1 has a triangular distribution over $[y_0, 255]$, Fig. 6, since y_1 is more likely to be located close to y_0,

$$P\{y_1|y_0\} = \frac{2 \cdot (255 - y_1)}{(255 - y_0)^2}. \tag{20}$$

If y_0 is uniformly distributed over [0, 255], the first-order conditional entropy is

$$H\{y_1|y_0\} = -\sum_{y_0=0}^{255} \sum_{y_1=y_0}^{255} \frac{2(255 - y_1)}{256(255 - y_0)^2}$$
$$\cdot \log_2 \frac{2(255 - y_1)}{(255 - y_0)^2} = 6.33 \text{ b}, \tag{21}$$

which is less than 8 b. Similarly, other pairwise conditional entropies are

$$H\{y_2|y_1\} = H\{y_3|y_2\} = H\{y_1|y_0\} = 6.33 \text{ b}. \tag{22}$$

From (22), if entropy coding is used to code the quantization levels, the estimated bit rate will be about

$$H\{y_0\} + \sum_{n=1}^{3} H\{y_n|y_{n-1}\} =$$
$$8 + 3 \times 6.33 = 26.99 \text{ b/block}, \tag{23}$$

which is less than the original 32 b.

One way to remove the correlation between quantization levels is to use differential PCM coding on the differences between quantization levels. If y_0 is known, $y_1 - y_0$ gives all the information required to obtain y_1. Assuming that y_n and y_{n-1} are two random variables with the same variance $\sigma_n^2 = \sigma_{n-1}^2$, the variance of their difference is

$$\sigma^2(y_n - y_{n-1}) = \sigma_n^2 - 2\rho_{n,n-1}\sigma_n\sigma_{n-1} + \sigma_{n-1}^2$$
$$= 2\sigma_n^2[1 - \rho_{n,n-1}] \tag{24}$$

where $\rho_{n,n-1}$ is the cross-correlation coefficient of $\{y_n\}$ and $\{y_{n-1}\}$. For 8×8 block size,

$$\rho(7) \le \rho_{n,n-1} \le \rho(1)$$

where $\rho(m)$ are pixel correlation coefficients and m indicates pixel distance. Table II shows some pixel correlation coefficients of different test images. It can be seen that, for $m \le 7, \rho(m) > 0.5$. From (24), $\sigma^2(y_n - y_{n-1}) < \sigma_n^2$, which means $y_n - y_{n-1}$ has less dynamic range than y_n. In information theory [13], [19],

$$\text{entropy} \propto \log_2 \sigma.$$

Thus, $y_n - y_{n-1}$ has less entropy than y_n.

For the composite satellite imagery, the calculated results are

$$H\{y_1\} = 6.41 \text{ b}$$
$$H\{y_1 - y_0\} = 5.33 \text{ b}$$
$$H\{y_2 - y_1\} = 5.11 \text{ b}$$
$$H\{y_3 - y_2\} = 5.62 \text{ b}. \tag{25}$$

Comparing (25) and (22), it can be seen that the measured differential entropies $H\{y_n - y_{n-1}\}$ are lower than the theoretically deduced conditional entropies $H\{y_n|y_{n-1}\}$. This is because, to obtain (22), we assumed that the sample intervals for y_{n-1} and y_n, where $n = 1, 2, 3$ are [0, 255] and $[y_{n-1}, 255]$, respectively, while the sample intervals for $y_n - y_{n-1}$ in the real case are much less than that. In (25), $H\{y_1 - y_0\}$ and $H\{y_3 - y_2\}$ have slightly higher entropies than $H\{y_2 - y_1\}$. This is the effect of overlay pixels, since whenever there are overlays on a block, either or both y_0 and y_3 will automatically be allocated to represent the overlays. This will result in wider sampler intervals of $y_3 - y_2$ and $y_1 - y_0$, and thus increase the entropies.

From (25), the lower bound on the number of bits required to represent the quantization levels is

$$6.41 + 5.33 + 5.11 + 5.62 = 22.47 \text{ b/block}. \tag{26}$$

B. Interblock Prediction

So far, differential encoding has been used to remove the intrablock correlations between quantization levels. In (23), there is, however, a first-order entropy $H\{y_0\}$ which has a much higher value than the differential entropies. Interblock correlation may be used to further reduce the entropy.

Assume that blocks k and $k - 1$ are two adjacent blocks $y_{m,k}$ and $y_{m,k-1}$, where $m = 0, 1, 2, 3$ are the quantization levels on blocks k and $k - 1$. Substituting into (24),

$$\sigma^2(y_{m,k} - y_{m,k-1}) = 2\sigma_{y_k}^2(m)[1 - \rho_{k,k-1}(m)]. \tag{27}$$

Here, for an 8×8 block size,

$$\rho(15) \le \rho_{k,k-1} \le \rho(1). \tag{28}$$

Since $\rho(15) > 0.5$, see Table I, $\sigma^2(y_{m,k} - y_{m,k-1}) < \sigma^2_{m,k}$, which means that there will be coding gain by using interblock differential coding.

In our minimax error multilevel block truncation coding, the two outermost quantization levels (y_0 and y_3) are most influenced by overlays. As mentioned before, whenever there are overlays on a block, either or both outermost quantization levels will be used to represent the overlays by our threshold dilation scheme, while the other quantization levels are less affected by the overlays. Thus, interblock prediction on y_1 or y_2 can achieve higher coding gain than on y_0 or y_3. For composite images, the test results are

$$H\{y_{0,k} - y_{0,k-1}\} = 6.00 \text{ b}$$
$$H\{y_{1,k} - y_{1,k-1}\} = 5.68 \text{ b}$$
$$H\{y_{2,k} - y_{2,k-1}\} = 5.88 \text{ b}$$
$$H\{y_{3,k} - y_{3,k-1}\} = 6.64 \text{ b}. \tag{29}$$

From (25) and (29), the lower bound of the number of bits required to interblock code y_1 and intrablock code the other levels is

$$5.33 + 5.68 + 5.11 + 5.62 = 21.74 \text{ b}. \tag{30}$$

A gain of 0.73 b over (26) is achieved. Tests on other images also show coding gains. For the Girl image, the gain is 0.48 b.

In (29), quantization levels in previous blocks are used to differentially code the present ones, which actually is first-order prediction. Usually, it is advantageous to implement a second-order predictor. It not only will achieve a coding gain, but will also introduce an error "leakage" [2]. If two previous blocks, the block on the left, $y_m(k_v, k_h - 1)$, and the block on top of the present block, $y_m(k_v - 1, k_h)$, are used to predict the present block, $y_m(k_v, k_h)$, it may be expressed as

$$y_m(k_v, k_h) = e_m(k_v, k_h) + [y_m(k_v - 1, k_h) + y_m(k_v, k_h - 1)]/2$$

where e_m is the prediction error. Assuming that transmission or storage error noise is involved in either $y_m(k_v - 1, k_h)$ or $y_m(k_v, k_h - 1)$,

$$y'_m(k_v, k_h) = e_m(k_v, k_h) + \frac{y_m(k_v - 1, k_h) + y_m(k_v, k_h - 1) + \text{noise}}{2}$$
$$= e_m(k_v, k_h) + \frac{y_m(k_v - 1, k_h) + y_m(k_v, k_h - 1)}{2} + \frac{\text{noise}}{2}$$
$$= y_m(k_v, k_h) + \frac{\text{noise}}{2}.$$

It can be seen that noise will be attenuated by half [2]. Thus, for an 8 b image, any reconstructed image can recover from the error within eight prediction steps.

The coding gain is not very high because of the relatively low interblock correlation. Therefore, it is not worth implementing predictors of higher order than second for the interblock prediction since the computational complexity and memory space will increase and very small coding gain will be achieved. Test results support this argument. For a compos-

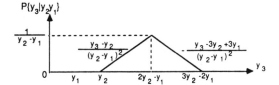

Fig. 7. Symmetric triangular distribution.

ite satellite image, the coding gain is only 0.04 b for a third-order predictor.

C. Higher Order Prediction

From information theory [13], if y_1 and y_2 are known, it should be possible to better predict y_3.

In our minimax error BTC, not considering the effects of the threshold dilation scheme, the quantization levels should be equally spaced. At this time, if two quantization levels, e.g., y_1 and y_2, are known, we can calculate the exact values of y_0 and y_3, which are

$$y_0 = y_1 - (y_2 - y_1)$$
$$y_3 = y_2 + (y_2 - y_1) \tag{31}$$

or

$$y_1 - y_0 - (y_2 - y_1) = 0$$
$$y_3 - y_2 - (y_2 - y_1) = 0. \tag{32}$$

With the effects of threshold dilation, we have

$$y_1 - y_0 - (y_2 - y_1) = e_0$$
$$y_3 - y_2 - (y_2 - y_1) = e_3 \tag{33}$$

where e_0 and e_3 are prediction errors.

For simplicity, assuming e_3 has a symmetric triangular distribution, see Fig. 7.

$$\{e_3\} \in [y_2, 3y_2 - 2y_1] \tag{34}$$

$$P\{y_3|y_2, y_1\} = \begin{cases} \dfrac{y_3 - y_2}{(y_2 - y_1)^2} & y_3 \leq 2y_2 - y_1 \\[2mm] \dfrac{-y_3 + 3y_2 - 2y_1}{(y_2 - y_1)^2} & y_3 > 2y_2 - y_1. \end{cases} \tag{35}$$

Then

$$H\{y_3|y_2, y_1\} = -\sum_{y_1}\sum_{y_2}\sum_{y_3} P\{y_3, y_2, y_1\} \cdot \log_2 P\{y_3|y_2, y_1\} = 3.51 \text{ b}. \tag{36}$$

which is an 2.82 b gain over (21). Similarly,

$$H\{y_0|y_1, y_2\} = H\{y_2|y_1, y_0\} = H\{y_3|y_2, y_1\} = 3.51 \text{ b}.$$

It can also show that e_0 and e_3, the second-order prediction errors, have smaller variances than those in (24), the first-order prediction errors, and therefore, have smaller entropies.

The entropy measurement also confirms that

$$H(e_0) = 3.97 \text{ b}$$
$$H(e_3) = 4.41 \text{ b} \quad \text{for composite satellite imagery}$$
$$H(e_0) = 3.25 \text{ b}$$
$$H(e_3) = 3.24 \text{ b} \quad \text{for the Girl image}. \tag{37}$$

Comparing (36) and (37) shows that the experimental measurements are close to the theoretically deduced result. (Note: (37) also shows that the threshold dilation scheme works well; otherwise, the prediction error $e_n = 0$, (32), and $H(e_n) = 0$.)

The total measured prediction error entropy now is

$$3.97 + 5.48 + 5.11 + 4.41 = 18.97 \text{ b}$$
$$\text{for composite satellite imagery}$$
$$3.25 + 5.79 + 4.58 + 3.24 = 16.86 \text{ b}$$
$$\text{for the Girl image}. \tag{38}$$

D. Coding of Prediction Errors

We have, so far, successfully reduced the entropies by implementing intra- and interblock prediction coding. The next step is to losslessly code the prediction errors. Equation (38) gives the lower bound of the bit rate. The most straightforward way is to entropy code, e.g., Huffman code, the prediction errors e_n, $n = 0, 1, 2, 3$ individually, which will result in a bit rate quite close to (38). However, the penalties of using an entropy code are as follows.

1) The code cannot recover from transmission and storage errors; any error involvement will destroy the rest of the image;

2) Entropy coding has long coding delays. For encoding, the whole image has to be gone through once to obtain the statistics which are needed to generate the codebook; for decoding, the coded data have to be read in bit-by-bit to follow the code tree, which makes the decoding process very slow running on a general-purpose computer.

3) A codebook has to be stored or transmitted for decoding. For a 512×512 image, 8×8 block size, and four-level quantizer, each prediction error has a dynamic range $[-255, +255]$, or 511 possible codebook entries, requiring 9 b. If Huffman coding is used, the longest codeword might be more than 9 b. On the other hand, in any practical situation, the maximum code length will be limited by the hardware configuration [114 – 118], e.g., to 16 b. Assuming that the maximum code length is 16 b, then each codebook entry will have 16 b, and

average overhead bits/block =
$$\frac{511 \times 16 \times 4 \times 8 \times 8}{512 \times 512} \simeq 8.0 \text{ b/block}. \tag{39}$$

Our solution is to develop a suboptimal code which has fixed length overhead for each block and variable size codewords. According to Shannon's rate-distortion theory, a better performance is always achievable in theory by coding vectors instead of scalars, even though the data source is memoryless [78]. A four-dimensional quantizer is used to quantize the prediction errors $\{e_0, e_1, e_2, e_3\}$ simultaneously, which results in a saving of overhead bits.

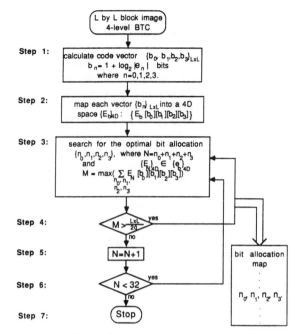

Fig. 8. Flowchart of the optimal bit allocation algorithm.

A bit allocation algorithm is used to efficiently allocate code bits. The allocation algorithm has the following steps.

Step 1: For an $L \times L$ block image, calculate the code-bit vector $\{b_0, b_1, b_2, b_3\}_{L \times L}$, where b_n, $n = 0, 1, 2, 3$ is the number of bits required to represent each prediction error $\{e_n\}$, and

$$b_n = 1 + \log_2 |e_n| \text{ bits}.$$

The added 1 bit is a sign bit.

Step 2: Map each vector $\{b_0, b_1, b_2, b_3\}_{L \times L}$ into a four-dimensional space $\{E_b\}_{4D}$,

$$\{E_b[b_0][b_1][b_2][b_3]\}.$$

Step 3: For an N-bit code, four-dimensionally search for the optimal bit allocation $\{n_0, n_1, n_2, n_3\}$, where the number of bits in the code $N = n_0 + n_1 + n_2 + n_3$ and $\{E_N\}_{4D} \in \{E_b\}_{4D}$, and calculate

$$M = \max\left(\sum_{n_0, n_1, n_2, n_3} E_N[n_0][n_1][n_2][n_3]\right)$$

where M is the number of error vectors $\{b_0, b_1, b_2, b_3\}_{L \times L}$ covered by $\{n_0, n_1, n_2, n_3\}$.

Step 4: If $M > (L \times L)/20$ and $\{n_0, n_1, n_2, n_3\}$ is not an entry in the bit allocation map, enter it into the bit allocation may and go back to Step 3. Otherwise, continue.

Step 5: $N = N + 1$; prepare for the next search.

Step 6: If $N < 32$, go to Step 3; search for next bit allocation vector. Otherwise, continue.

Step 7: Stop.

The flowchart of the algorithm is given in Fig. 8.

The bit allocation program was run on a series of satellite images and standard images, such as the Girl image. The

TABLE III
MULTIDIMENSION VARIABLE BLOCK CODE BIT ALLOCATION MAP

No.	overhead code (binary)	bit allocation map e_0	e_1	e_2	e_3	code bits (per block)	code bits & overhead bits
1	$(0000)_b$	2	3	3	2	10	14
2	$(0001)_b$	2	4	3	3	12	16
3	$(0010)_b$	1	2	8	1	12	16
4	$(0011)_b$	3	3	4	2	12	16
5	$(0100)_b$	3	4	4	3	14	18
6	$(0101)_b$	2	5	4	3	14	18
7	$(0110)_b$	3	5	4	4	16	20
8	$(0111)_b$	4	4	5	3	16	20
9	$(1000)_b$	3	6	5	4	18	22
10	$(1001)_b$	4	4	5	5	18	22
11	$(1010)_b$	4	6	5	5	20	24
12	$(1011)_b$	5	6	6	5	22	26
13	$(1100)_b$	3	5	5	9	22	26
14	$(1101)_b$	5	7	6	6	24	28
15	$(1110)_b$	9	7	5	3	24	28
16	$(1111)_b$	8	8	8	8	32	36
error entropy (CSI)		4.0	5.5	5.1	4.4	19.0 bits	
error entropy (girl)		3.2	5.8	4.6	3.2	16.8 bits	

TABLE IV
QUANTIZATION LEVEL PREDICTION ERROR ENTROPIES AND BIT RATES

images	error entropies e_0	e_1	e_2	e_3	total entropy (per block)	original bits (per block)	code bits (per block)	code bits & overhead bits
CSI (visual)	4.0	5.5	5.1	4.4	19.0	32	16.4	20.4
CSI (no OL)	3.5	5.3	4.9	3.9	17.6	32	15.1	19.1
CSI (Nir)	4.0	5.5	5.1	4.3	18.9	32	16.4	20.4
CSI (4mic)	3.6	5.3	5.3	4.4	18.6	32	16.2	20.2
CSI (11mic)	3.7	5.3	4.9	4.0	17.9	32	15.6	19.6
CSI (12mic)	3.9	5.3	5.0	4.3	18.5	32	16.1	20.1
Girl	3.2	5.8	4.6	3.2	16.8	32	15.2	19.2

TABLE V
BIT RATE CHANGE DUE TO STATISTIC MISMATCH

code bits per block	CSI Vis	CSI Nir	CSI 4mic	CSI 11mic	CSI 12mic	girl
optimized bit allocation map	16.4	16.3	16.0	15.5	16.0	14.9
bit allocation map of CSI Vis	16.4	16.4	16.2	15.6	16.1	15.2

resulting bit allocation maps are very similar. Table III is a typical bit allocation map.

In Table III, overhead code 1111_b is actually an escape sequence for those blocks with illdistributed quantization levels where prediction fails and the error dynamic range is more than 8 b. The four bytes, 32 b, after 1111_b are used to represent the four quantization levels. Code 13, $\{3, 5, 5, 9\}$, and code 15 $\{9, 7, 5, 3\}$, are for blocks with white and black overlays, respectively.

Table IV shows quantization level prediction error entropies and code bit rates for different images, where the bit allocation map in Table III is used. Although the bit allocation map in Table III is originally optimized to code visual-band CSI, it works well for other images. Table V shows the test results of code bits per block of different images using a statistically optimized bit allocation map and a bit allocation map optimized to visual-band CSI. It can be seen that the bit rate increase due to statistical mismatch is within 0.3 b/block or 0.0047 b/pixel.

Another interesting result is that, comparing total entropy and code bits in Table IV, the number of code bits is actually less than the entropy. This is because the multidimensional quantizer provides a simultaneous quantization of four quantization levels, while the entropy measures the four prediction errors separately.

The overhead of our algorithm is 4 b/block, which equals only 1 b for each prediction error. From (39), the overhead is about 8 b/block for a 512×512 image is a Huffman code is used to code the prediction errors.

In this section, a lossless coding algorithm has been developed to compress the quantization levels of the minimax error four-level BTC coding. Second-order predictors are used to remove the inter- and intrablock correlations between quantization levels. A variable length code is designed to four-dimensionally code for four quantization level prediction errors losslessly. The algorithm is not sensitive to the statistical variations in the data, has shorter encoding and decoding delay, and is relatively robust to transmission and storage errors. The compression ratio is about 2:1.

IV. LOSSLESS QUATERNARY PLANE DATA COMPRESSION

This section will introduce an algorithm which further compresses the quaternary plane. The correlation of quaternary plane elements is evaluated mathematically, which shows that there is redundancy between quaternary plane elements and that most of the redundancy in the plane is among very close neighbors. Based on this result, a four-element packing scheme is used to map the quaternary plane into a byte-oriented data set which then is coded using a variable length block code.

A. Correlation of Quaternary Plane Elements

The input image data can be modeled as a sample of a first-order Markov process for which the correlation between pixels is proportional to their geometric separation [20].

Fig. 9 shows the correlation functions of 8 b original data, two-level and four-level BTC truncated planes. It can be seen that correlation of four-level truncated data decays much faster than that of the input data. It also indicates that most of the redundancy in the quaternary plane is among very close neighbors. If we partition the quaternary plane into very small blocks, e.g., 2×2, and pack each block into a byte, we form another data set, in which each byte actually is a four-dimensional vector and, intuitively, there should be some correlations between those vector bytes.

B. Lossless Coding of Four-Dimensional Vector Pattern

The motivation for mapping the quaternary plane into a four-dimensional vector-byte file can also be traced back to rate distortion theory, which indicates that better performance can be achieved by coding vectors instead of scalars.

Fig. 10 shows the histogram of a byte-vector file. It can be seen that some of the vector components have mush higher frequency than others, which means that some of the 2×2 patterns occur much more often in the quaternary plane because of the existence of local correlations. The uneven and spiky distribution of the histogram indicates that entropy coding can be used to compress the four-element packed data. The entropy of the histogram in Fig. 10 is 6.07 b/vector or 1.52 b/element, which is less than the previous 1.96 b/element. Tables VI and VII list some high probability patterns of CSI and the Girl image, where the patterns are sorted by the order of their appearance frequency.

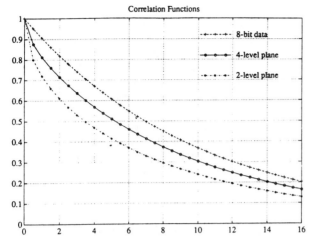

Fig. 9. Correlation functions of raw and truncated data.

Legend: 8-bit data; 4-level plane; 2-level plane

Title of plot: Correlation Functions

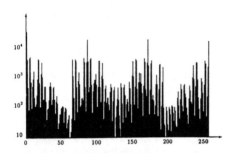

Fig. 10. 4-D Vector-byte file histogram.

TABLE VI
HIGH-PROBABILITY PATTERNS (CIS)

No.	pattern	prob.	total prob.	No.	pattern	prob.	total prob.
The first 4 high prob. patterns: G 1				25		1.157 %	7.209 %
0	00/00	12.77 %	12.77 %	26		1.139 %	8.348 %
1	11/11	6.932 %	19.70 %	27		1.128 %	9.476 %
2	22/22	6.745 %	26.45 %	28		1.109 %	10.58 %
3	33/33	5.889 %	32.34 %	29		1.107 %	11.69 %
The next 16 patterns: G 2				30		1.103 %	12.79 %
4		1.803 %	1.803 %	31		1.062 %	13.86 %
5		1.674 %	3.477 %	32		1.013 %	14.87 %
6		1.643 %	5.121 %	33		0.991 %	15.86 %
7		1.612 %	6.762 %	34		0.954 %	16.81 %
8		1.549 %	8.311 %	35		0.908 %	17.72 %
9		1.530 %	9.841 %	36		0.868 %	18.59 %
10		1.483 %	11.32 %	37		0.846 %	19.43 %
11		1.475 %	12.80 %	38		0.781 %	20.22 %
12		1.466 %	14.27 %	39		0.779 %	20.99 %
13		1.429 %	15.69 %	40		0.586 %	21.58 %
14		1.429 %	17.12 %	41		0.512 %	22.09 %
15		1.420 %	18.54 %	42		0.475 %	22.57 %
16		1.323 %	19.87 %	43		0.456 %	23.02 %
17		1.310 %	21.18 %	44		0.447 %	23.47 %
18		1.303 %	22.48 %	45		0.447 %	23.92 %
19		1.288 %	23.77 %	46		0.407 %	24.32 %
The next 32 patterns: G 3				47		0.385 %	24.71 %
20		1.264 %	1.264 %	48		0.383 %	25.09 %
21		1.234 %	2.498 %	49		0.379 %	25.47 %
22		1.201 %	3.699 %	50		0.375 %	25.84 %
23		1.190 %	4.889 %	51		0.367 %	26.21 %
24		1.163 %	6.052 %	The rest of patterns: G 4			17.68 %

TABLE VII
HIGH-PROBABILITY PATTERNS (GIRL)

No.	pattern	prob.	total prob.	No.	pattern	prob.	total prob.
The first 4 high prob. patterns: G 1				25		1.174 %	7.378 %
0	33/33	9.384 %	9.384 %	26		1.165 %	8.542 %
1	00/00	6.331 %	15.72 %	27		1.152 %	9.694 %
2	22/22	4.231 %	19.95 %	28		1.152 %	10.84 %
3	11/11	3.696 %	23.64 %	29		1.117 %	11.96 %
The next 16 patterns: G 2				30		1.113 %	13.07 %
4		2.095 %	2.095 %	31		1.074 %	14.15 %
5		2.047 %	4.142 %	32		1.047 %	15.19 %
6		1.867 %	6.009 %	33		1.043 %	16.24 %
7		1.865 %	7.873 %	34		1.034 %	17.27 %
8		1.776 %	9.650 %	35		1.036 %	18.27 %
9		1.680 %	11.34 %	36		0.951 %	19.22 %
10		1.645 %	12.98 %	37		0.916 %	20.14 %
11		1.498 %	14.48 %	38		0.807 %	20.94 %
12		1.463 %	15.95 %	39		0.772 %	21.72 %
13		1.459 %	17.40 %	40		0.715 %	22.73 %
14		1.439 %	18.84 %	41		0.711 %	23.14 %
15		1.430 %	20.27 %	42		0.663 %	23.81 %
16		1.410 %	21.68 %	43		0.632 %	24.44 %
17		1.371 %	23.05 %	44		0.599 %	25.04 %
18		1.341 %	24.40 %	45		0.580 %	25.62 %
19		1.330 %	25.73 %	46		0.579 %	26.20 %
The next 32 patterns: G 3				47		0.531 %	26.73 %
20		1.284 %	1.284 %	48		0.474 %	27.20 %
21		1.273 %	2.558 %	49		0.470 %	27.67 %
22		1.246 %	3.803 %	50		0.468 %	28.14 %
23		1.216 %	5.019 %	51		0.435 %	28.57 %
24		1.185 %	6.204 %	The rest of patterns: G 4			22.05 %

In Tables VI and VII, the patterns are classified into four groups:

- Group 1: the first four high probability patterns.
- Group 2: the next 16 patterns after Group 1.
- Group 3: the next 32 patterns after Group 2.
- Group 4: the rest of the patterns.

There is a total of 256 possible patterns. Among them, patterns in Group 1, Group 2, and Group 3 each cover approximately 25% of the total probability, Table VI and VII. This feature repeats on dozens of test images. Based on the fact, a variable block entropy code is designed to encode the four-element patterns.

A 2 b header, or prefix, is used to indicate the group number from 1 to 4. After the *header code,* a variable length *pattern code* is used to represent the patterns. For Group 1 patterns, a 2 b pattern code is used to indicate the four different patterns. For Groups 2, 3, and 4, the pattern codes are 4, 5, and 8 b, respectively. It can be understood that the Group 4 header code is an escape sequence; the pattern codes following it are actually carrying the original 8 b pattern. Thus, there is no need to send look-up table (LUT) contents for Group 4 patterns for decoding. On the other hand, Group 1, 2, and 3 patterns must be transmitted as overhead to the decoding end to form a decoding LUT. There is a total of 52 8-b, byte, patterns in the LUT. However, from out experiments, the Group 1 patterns are always unilevel patterns, i.e., $\frac{0\ 0}{0\ 0}$, $\frac{1\ 1}{1\ 1}$, $\frac{2\ 2}{2\ 2}$, and $\frac{3\ 3}{3\ 3}$ since their probabilities are several times higher than the others. Although their order in Group 1 might change, compare Tables VI and VII, it is irrelevant to select the order as long as these unilevel patterns are assigned in Group 1. Under this condition, a preset order in the LUT can be used without affecting coding/decoding and coded data size. Thus, an extra 4 out of 52 bytes, 4%, can be saved in the overhead. Now, the overhead has 48 bytes, or 384 b. For a 512×512 image, overhead takes only 0.0015 b/pixel. Since those unilevel patterns will never appear in the overhead data, they can be assigned as control sequences, to be used later.

C. Compression Overhead Using the Pattern Symmetry Property

The symmetry of the image correlation function can also be used to reduce the overhead. For an image with *isotropic* pixel correlation, its rotationally symmetric patterns, e.g., $\begin{smallmatrix}0&0\\1&1\end{smallmatrix}$, $\begin{smallmatrix}1&1\\0&0\end{smallmatrix}$, $\begin{smallmatrix}0&1\\0&1\end{smallmatrix}$, and $\begin{smallmatrix}1&0\\1&0\end{smallmatrix}$, are expected to have similar probabilities, which means that they very likely belong to the same Group. For example, in Table VI Group 2 patterns, 12 out of the 16 patterns can be formed from three rotationally symmetric patterns, i.e., $\begin{smallmatrix}0&0\\1&1\end{smallmatrix}$, $\begin{smallmatrix}1&1\\2&2\end{smallmatrix}$, and $\begin{smallmatrix}0&0\\0&1\end{smallmatrix}$, simply by rotating each of them 90°, 180°, and 270° clockwise. As mentioned before, once a set of patterns belongs to the same Group, their order is not important since they will be assigned to the same length of code, and changing their order within the Group would not affect the size of encoded data. For the rotationally symmetric patterns, we can simply send one out of four of them preceded by an escape code to indicate that the following patterns are rotated.

As for *separable* correlation, patterns symmetric about vertical, horizontal, and diagonal axes are expected to have similar probabilities. (Note: patterns $\begin{smallmatrix}1&2\\1&2\end{smallmatrix}$ and $\begin{smallmatrix}2&1\\2&1\end{smallmatrix}$ are by symmetric about the vertical axis, patterns $\begin{smallmatrix}1&2\\2&2\end{smallmatrix}$ and $\begin{smallmatrix}2&2\\1&2\end{smallmatrix}$ are horizontally symmetric, and patterns $\begin{smallmatrix}2&1\\1&1\end{smallmatrix}$ and $\begin{smallmatrix}1&1\\1&2\end{smallmatrix}$ are diagonal symmetric). These properties can also be used to compress overhead.

Table VIII shows the LUT's of CSI and the Girl image before and after compression. It can be seen that about 2:1 compression is achieved. (In Table VIII, R, V, H, D, and N stand for rotational, vertical, horizontal, diagonal symmetry, and noncoded patterns. Patterns $\begin{smallmatrix}0&0\\0&0\end{smallmatrix}$, $\begin{smallmatrix}1&1\\1&1\end{smallmatrix}$, $\begin{smallmatrix}2&2\\2&2\end{smallmatrix}$, and $\begin{smallmatrix}3&3\\3&3\end{smallmatrix}$ are used as the control sequences Ctrl_R, Ctrl_V, Ctrl_H, and Ctrl_D, respectively.)

D. Quaternary Plane Encoding Diagram

Fig. 11 is a diagram of the quaternary plane encoder. It has the following steps.

Step 1: Decompose the quaternary plane, 2 b/element, into 2×2 patterns, and pack each pattern, a four-dimensional vector, into a byte to form a four-dimensional vector file.

Step 2: Calculate the histogram of a four-dimensional vector file.

Step 3: Sort histogram components in decreasing order.

Step 4: Search the sorted histogram within each "Group" for pattern symmetry properties.

Step 5: Based on sorted histogram and pattern symmetry properties, generate an encoding LUT which also, as the overhead, is to be transmitted to form the decoding LUT.

Step 6: Encode the vector file using the encoding LUT.

In Step 3, sorting 256 histogram components in decreasing order requires

$$\sum_{n=1}^{255} (256 - n) = 255 \cdot \frac{1 + 255}{2} = 32\,640 \qquad (40)$$

searching loops. However, sorting the first 52 components is all that is really needed in our encoding algorithm, which requires

$$\sum_{n=1}^{52} (256 - n) = 52 \cdot \frac{255 + 204}{2} = 11\,934 \qquad (41)$$

TABLE VIII
OVERHEAD CODE BEFORE AND AFTER COMPRESSION

CSI No.	patterns	code	code type	Girl No.	patterns	code	code type
1			Ctrl_LR	1	V		Ctrl_LR
2	R		R	2	V		R
3	R		R	3	V		Ctrl_LV
4	R		R	4	V		V
5	R		Ctrl_LD	5	V		V
6	R		D	6	V		V
7	R		N	7	D		Ctrl_LH
8	R		N	8	D		H
9	R		Ctrl_LR	9	R		Ctrl_LD
10	D		R	10	H		D
11	R		R	11	R		D
12	R		R	12	D		Ctrl_LH
13	D		R	13	D		R
14	N		Ctrl_LV	14	R		R
15	R		V	15	R		R
16	R		V	16	D		Ctrl_LH
17	R		Ctrl_LH	17	H		H
18	N		H	18	R		H
19	D		Ctrl_LD	19	D		H
20	D		D	20	R		H
21	R		D	21	H		H
22	V		D	22	H		H
23	R		D	23	H		H
24	R		N	24	D		Ctrl_LD
25	V		N	25	R		D
26	N			26	H		D
27	R			27	R		N
28	H			28	R		N
29	R			29	H		
30	R			30	R		
31	V			31	R		
32	R			32	R		
33	R			33	R		
34	R			34	H		
35	R			35	H		
36	R			36	H		
37	H			37	H		
38	R			38	D		
39	D			39	H		
40	R			40	R		
41	H			41	D		
42	D			42	R		
43	D			43	H		
44	D			44	R		
45	R			45	R		
46	D			46	N		
47	R			47	R		
48	D			48	N		

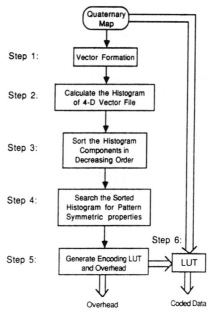

Fig. 11. Quaternary plane encoding diagram.

Quaternary Map

Step 1: Vector Formation

Step 2: Calculate the Histogram of 4-D Vector File

Step 3: Sort the Histogram Components in Decreasing Order

Step 4: Search the Sorted Histogram for Pattern Symmetric properties

Step 5: Generate Encoding LUT and Overhead

Step 6: LUT

Overhead   Coded Data

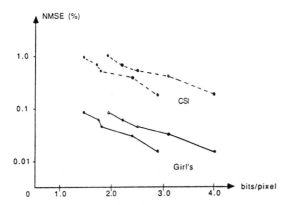

Fig. 12. MSE performances of BTC with various quantization levels and block sizes.

TABLE IX
MSE PERFORMANCES OF BTC WITH VARIOUS QUANTIZATION LEVELS
AND BLOCK SIZES

	no post-comp	with post-comp	Girl	CSI
(L,N)	bits/pixel	bits/pixel	NMSE	NMSE
(4,4)	4.0	2.9	0.014 %	0.170 %
(3,4)	3.08	2.4	0.029 %	0.358 %
(4,8)	2.5	1.8	0.042 %	0.465 %
(3,6)	2.25	1.75	0.054 %	0.615 %
(3,8)	1.955	1.5	0.077 %	0.868 %
(4,16)	2.125	1.5	0.162 %	0.909 %

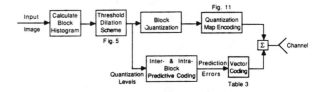

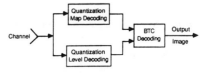

Fig. 13. Multilevel BTC coding system diagram.

searching loops. This pruning scheme can achieve about a 3:1 saving of searching computation.

E. The Possibility of Using a Larger Pattern Size

So far, we have used a 2×2 size pattern on the quaternary plane. If a larger size, e.g., 3×3, is used, there are 18 b in the nine-dimensional vector and 262 144 possible patterns. If we sort histogram components in decreasing order, Step 3 in Fig. 11, there are 3.44×10^{10} searching loops! Even with the pruning, e.g., sorting the first 20% of the components, (41), there are 1.24×10^{10} searching loops, which proves to be several hours of computation on a 10 MIPS machine. Meanwhile, the overhead will contain $262\,144 \times 20\% = 52\,429$ 18-b patterns, or 117 965 bytes, which is unrealistic.

On the other hand, as proved before, most of the redundancy in the quaternary plane is among very close neighbors. Increasing the pattern size might not obtain much coding gain. This can be proved by entropies. For 2×2 patterns, the average entropy is 1.52 b/element, while for 3×3 patterns, it is 1.46 b/element. There is only 0.06 b/element entropy gain.

Thus, for our quaternary plane coding algorithm, increasing the pattern size is pointless. It will increase the computational complexity, overhead data, and would not obtain much coding gain because of the data correlation property.

V. MSE PERFORMANCE OF MINIMAX ERROR MULTILEVEL BLOCK TRUNCATION CODING WITH LOSSLESS POSTQUANTIZATION COMPRESSION

In previous sections, minimax error quaternary block truncation coding was introduced. One of the disadvantages of the original bilevel block truncation coding [45]–[46] is that is has a limited range of rate distortion–bit rate tradeoff by employing different block sizes [22]. Since we have extended the bilevel BTC into multilevel BTC, various quantization levels and block sizes can be implemented which will result in different bit rates and distortions. The MSE performances are shown in Fig. 12 and the MSE values are listed in Table IX. The results of implementing lossless postquantization data compression, Sections III and IV are also displayed.

In Table IX, (L, N) stands for L-level, $N \times N$ block multilevel BTC. The original and reconstructed pictures are shown in Pictures I and IV. The entire multilevel BTC encoding system diagram is shown in Fig. 13.

VI. QUATERNARY PLANE DATA COMPRESSION USING VECTOR QUANTIZATION

In previous sections, we have shown that there are correlations, or redundancies, on the quaternary plane, and an algorithm of lossless compression of the quaternary plane has been developed. This section will discuss the lossy compression of the quaternary planes.

Vector quantization (VQ) is a recently developed technique for data compression [76], [77]. VQ provides a high compression ratio, fast, look-up-table (LUT)-based decoding, and competitive subjective performance, but the encoding procedure is quite time consuming, and sharp edges tend to be filtered out in the reconstructed images. Since the quaternary plane elements have very small dynamic range (2 b/element), it is possible to implement a simple LUT-based VQ encoding procedure which speeds up the encoding process substantially. The sharp edges and gray level sudden changes in the original image have already been preserved by the preceding quaternary BTC, so that they are not filtered out by the subsequent VQ coding.

The typical VQ block size is 4×4. For 8 b/pixel digital imagery, there are 2^{128} representation vectors in the image sample space. It is impossible to build an encoding LUT to map each of these input vectors into a corresponding codeword. This implies that the encoder must perform an exhaustive search through the entire codebook to find the minimum distortion codeword for each input vector. The computation involved in this vector-matching procedure is enormous. Tree-structured VQ methods [23] are substantially simpler than full search VQ, but require much larger code-

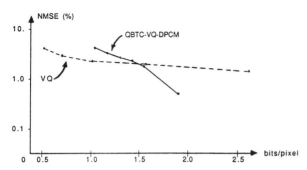

Fig. 14.   MSE performances of BTC–VQ–DPCM coding and VQ.

TABLE X
MSE PERFORMANCES OF BTC–VQ–DPCM CODING AND VQ

QBTC-VQ-DPCM Coding			Vector Quantization	
codebook size	NMSE (%)	bit rate	NMSE (%)	bit rate
QBTC(4,8)	0.4650	1.9	*	*
1024	1.6510	1.55	1.4184	2.625
512	1.8817	1.425	1.7899	1.5625
256	2.3259	1.30	2.2017	1.00
128	2.8364	1.175	2.5842	0.6875
64	3.4997	1.05	3.7612	0.50

book storage, and the codewords selected do not, in general, minimize the distortion.

In our special case, VQ is implemented on the quaternary plane, which can be realized by a simple LUT operation, drastically reducing the VQ coding complexity.

The quaternary plane is decomposed into 4×2 blocks. Each block can be packed into a 16 b word forming an eight-dimensional vector. The total number of representation vectors is only $2^{16} = 64K$. It is reasonable to design a 64 Kword encoding LUT to quickly encode the input vector. Once the LUT is built, it takes almost no time to quantize a word-packed vector.

The MSE performances, for 256×256 CSI, are shown in Fig. 14 and Table X where, for comparison, the conventional VQ (VQA) performances are also listed. The codebook used in quaternary plane VQ is generated from a group of training images that includes standard images, satellite images, and radar images. The LBG algorithm [26] was used to generate the codebook. A 64 Kword encoding LUT for VQ of the quaternary plane can be built from the codebook through an exhaustive search.

Comparing QBTC–VQ–DPCM coding with conventional VQ, Table X, our algorithm has comparable MSE performance at a moderate bit rate. On the other hand, QBTC–VQ–DPCM coding has much less computational complexity since VQ is implemented on the quaternary plane and a LUT-based encoding can be used.

VII. CONCLUSIONS

This paper describes an encoding technique—multilevel block truncation coding—that preserves the spatial details in digital images and which is specifically designed for the transmission of high-resolution images. It is a general extension of block truncation coding (BTC), wherein a multilevel quantizer is implemented instead of the usual two-level quantizer to obtain higher fidelity. A fast-searching algorithm using a minimax quantization error criterion has been developed to allocate the quantizer levels to obtain a close replica of the original image, and to be insensitive to variations in the pixel statistical distribution within each pixel block. The output of the multilevel BTC coding consists of a multilevel plane, which specifies the quantization levels assigned to each pixel, and the quantization level codes for each block. Second-stage compression of these coded data using combined techniques of predictive coding, entropy coding, and vector quantization is also described. Both inter- and intrablock prediction are used to predict the quantization levels, and the prediction errors are coded by a specially designed lossless vector-entropy coding. Vector quantization is implemented to further remove the redundancy within the multilevel plane. This compression can be lossless or lossy. In addition, the technique has very simple computational complexity.

REFERENCES

[1] A. K. Jain, "Image data compression: A review," *Proc. IEEE*, vol. 69, pp. 349–389, Mar. 1981.
[2] N. S. Jayant and P. Noll, *Digital Coding of Waveforms*. Englewood Cliffs, NJ: Prentice-Hall, 1984.
[3] J. Max, "Quantizing for minimum distortion," *IRE Trans. Inform. Theory*, vol. IT-6, pp. 7–12, Mar. 1960.
[4] F. Lu and G. L. Wise, "A further investigation of Max's algorithm for optimum quantization," *IEEE Trans. Commun.*, vol. COM-33, pp. 746–751, July 1985.
[5] E. J. Delp and O. R. Mitchell, "Image compression using block truncation coding," *IEEE Trans. Commun.*, vol. COM-27, pp. 1335–1342, Sept. 1979.
[6] D. J. Healy and O. R. Mitchell, "Digital video bandwidth compression using block truncation coding," *IEEE Trans. Commun.*, vol. COM-29, pp. 1809–1817, Dec. 1981.
[7] G. R. Arce and N. C. Gallagher, Jr., "BTC image using median filter roots," *IEEE Trans. Commun.*, vol. COM-31, June 1983.
[8] D. R. Halverson, "A generalized BTC algorithm for image compression," *IEEE Trans. Acoust., Speech, Signal Processing*, vol. ASSP-32, pp. 664–668, 1984.
[9] M. D. Lema and O. R. Mitchell, "Absolute moment block truncation coding and application to colour image," *IEEE Trans. Commun.*, vol. COM-32, pp. 1148–1157, Oct. 1984.
[10] J. Raby, A. Brunswick, and C. Sliper, "Advances in block truncation coding with applications to digital terrain elevation data," in *Proc. IEEE Conf. NACOM*, 1986.
[11] D. C. Coll and Y. Wu, "High fidelity compression of composite meteorological imagery," in *Proc. 14th Biennial Symp. Commun.*, Kingston, Ont., Canada, May 1988.
[12] D. C. Coll, H. J. Schneider, and D. M. Taylor, "A multi-purpose display station for meteorological products," presented at the 3rd Int. Conf. Interactive Inform. and Processing Syst. for Meteorology, Oceanography and Hydrology, New Orleans, LA, Jan. 1987.
[13] A. Papoulis, *Probability, Random Variables, and Stochastic Processes*. New York: McGraw-Hill, 1984.
[14] H. Murakami, S. Matsumoto, and H. Yamamoto, "Algorithm for construction of variable length code with limited maximum word length," *IEEE Trans. Commun.*, vol. COM-32, pp. 1157–1159, Oct. 1984.
[15] H. Garten, "On variable length codes under hardware constraints," *IEEE Trans. Commun.*, vol. COM-33, pp. 491–494, May 1985.
[16] J. P. Lameillieure and I. Bruyland, "Comments on 'Algorithm for construction of variable length code with limited maximum word length,'" *IEEE Trans. Commun.*, vol. COM-34, pp. 1252–1253, Dec. 1986.
[17] H. Gharavi, "Conditional run-length and variable-length coding of digital pictures," *IEEE Trans. Commun.*, vol. COM-35, pp. 671–677, June 1987.
[18] C. H. Lu, "Comments of 'Algorithm for construction of variable length code with limited maximum word length,'" *IEEE Trans. Commun.*, vol. 36, pp. 373–375, Mar. 1988.
[19] C. E. Shannon, "A mathematical theory of communications," *Bell Syst. Tech. J.*, vol. 27, pp. 379–423, 623–656, 1948.

[20] W. K. Pratt, *Digital Image Processing.* New York: Wiley, 1978.

[21] T. S. Huang, "Coding of two-tone images," *IEEE Trans. Commun.,* pp. 1410–1424, Nov. 1977.

[22] C. Y. Chen, R. Kwok, and J. C. Curlander, "Image coding of SAR imagery," in *Proc. IGARSS'87 Symp.,* Ann Arbor, MI, May 1987, pp. 699–704.

[23] N. M. Nasrabadi and R. A. King, "Image coding using vector quantization: A review," *IEEE Trans. Commun.,* vol. 36, pp. 957–971, Aug. 1988.

[24] M. Goldberg, P. R. Boucher, and S. Shlien, "Image compression using adaptive vector quantization," *IEEE Trans. Commun.,* vol. COM-34, pp. 180–187, Feb. 1986.

[25] J. Makhoul, S. Roucos, and H. Gish, "Vector quantization in speech coding," *Proc. IEEE,* vol. COM-33, pp. 1551–1588, Nov. 1985.

[26] Y. Linde, A. Buzo, and R. M. Gray, "An algorithm for vector quantizer design," *IEEE Trans. Commun.,* vol. COM-28, pp. 84–95, Jan. 1980.

[27] R. Aravind and A. Gersho, "Image compression based upon vector quantization with finite memory," *Opt. Eng.,* July 1987.

[28] Y. Wu and D. C. Coll, "Multi-level block truncation coding for high fidelity compression of composite imagery," in *Proc. Canadian Conf. Elec. Comput. Eng.,* Vancouver, B.C., Canada, 1988.

Chapter 7
Harmonious Hybrids

A window to the future of BTC techniques as it were, this chapter with its six studies deals mainly with efforts aimed at developing promising hybrid approaches involving BTC. The first one is the 1987 study by Udpikar and Raina [**B29**], who were the first to explore the hybridization of BTC using vector quantization. The second is the 1991 paper by Delp and Mitchell [**B44**] on using BTC as a post-processor to DPCM. The third, by Efrati, Liciztin, and Mitchell [**B52**], which also appeared in 1991, is a further development of the earlier study of Udpikar and Raina. It is included not only to show the emphasis placed on VQ techniques in the search for potentially powerful hybrids, but also to give sample representation to this group of active researchers. The next is a triple-component hybrid reported by Wu and Coll [**B54**] once again in 1991. This includes, in addition to BTC and VQ, DCT as the third leg. The fifth in this series is the 1992 work of Neagoe [**B58**], which is a mix of several techniques, one of which is BTC. The last one, by Wen and Lu [**B73**], which appeared in 1993, is once again a hybrid of BTC, VQ, and DCT. However, the actual method of development of the hybrid is much different from the earlier one by Wu and Coll.

Chapter 7 Reprints

[**B29**] V.R. Udpikar and J.P. Raina, "BTC Image Coding Using Vector Quantization," *IEEE Trans. Comm.*, Vol. COM-35, No. 3, pp. 352–356, Mar. 1987.

[**B44**] E.J. Delp and O.R. Mitchell, "The Use of Block Truncation Coding in DPCM Image Coding," *IEEE Trans. Signal Processing*, Vol. 39, No. 4, pp. 967–971, Apr. 1991.

[**B52**] N. Efrati, H. Liciztin, and H.B. Mitchell, "Classified Block Truncation Coding-Vector Quantization: An Edge Sensitive Image Compression Algorithm," *Signal Processing: Image Comm.*, Vol. 3, Nos. 2–3, pp. 275–283, June 1991.

[**B54**] Y. Wu and D.C. Coll, "BTC-VQ-DCT Hybrid Coding of Digital Images," *IEEE Trans. Comm.*, Vol. COM-39, No. 9, pp. 1283–1287, Sept. 1991.

[**B58**] V.E.I. Neagoe, "Predictive Ordering Technique and Feedback Transform Coding for Data Compression of Still Pictures," *IEEE Trans. Comm.*, Vol. COM-40, No. 2, pp. 385–396, Feb. 1992.

[**B73**] K.-A. Wen and C.-Y. Lu, "Hybrid Vector Quantization," *Applied Optics*, Vol. 32, No. 7, pp. 1496–1502, July 1993.

BTC Image Coding Using Vector Quantization

VISHWAS R. UDPIKAR AND JEWAN P. RAINA

Abstract—This paper describes source encoding of the outputs of a block truncation coder (BTC), namely, the overhead statistical information and the truncated block. The statistical overhead and the truncated

Paper approved by the Editor for Image Processing of the IEEE Communications Society. Manuscript received February 12, 1986; revised October 24, 1986.

The authors are with the Television Engineering/Fiber Optic Laboratory, Department of Electrical Engineering, Indian Institute of Technology, Madras-600 036, India.

IEEE Log Number 8612586.

block exhibit properties which can be effectively used for their quantization as vectors. Vector quantization of these BTC outputs results into reduction of the bit rate of the coder. The bit rate reduces up to 1.5 bits/pel if vector quantization is used on one of the outputs; i.e., either the overhead information or the truncated block. By vector quantizing both the BTC outputs the bit rate can be reduced up to 1.0 bits/pel without introducing many perceivable errors in the reconstructed output.

I. INTRODUCTION

BTC is a recent technique used for compression of monochrome image data. Essentially, it is a one-bit adaptive moment-preserving quantizer that preserves certain statistical moments of small blocks of the input image in the quantized output [1]. The original algorithm preserves the block mean and the block standard deviation. There have been other choices of the moments resulting either in less mean square error (mse) [2] and/or less computational complexity [3].

The coding algorithm described in [3] preserves the higher mean and the lower mean of the small blocks. So the statistical overhead to be coded per block is a pair of mean values. The truncated block of the BTC output is the bit plane representing the block consisting of a one-bit output of the quantizer for every pel in the block. These are the two sets of data we intend to compress using separate vector quantizers (VQ).

A VQ is a system for mapping a sequence of discrete vectors into a finite number of representative vectors [4]. The aim of vector quantization is to reduce the number of bits necessary to represent the input vectors. In this paper, we present the results of compressing the above-mentioned overhead information (a two-dimensional vector of mean values) and the truncated block (a multidimensional binary vector) using suitable VQ's. Other important efforts to improve the coding efficiency of BTC are reported in [5] and [6].

Section II of the paper describes the BTC algorithm of [3] with the features that make it suitable for further data compression using vector quantization. Section III describes the vector quantization schemes developed for the two sets of data. In Section IV, we present the simulation results of coding and reconstructing a typical monochrome image using BTC and VQ.

II. BLOCK TRUNCATION CODING

In this coding algorithm the one bit quantizer preserves the first-order statistical information, namely, the lower mean $\bar{X}_L$ and the higher mean $\bar{X}_H$ of $m \times m$ pels blocks of the input image data [3]. The mean $\bar{X}$ of the pels in the block is taken as the one bit quantizer threshold.

From [3],

$$\text{quantizer threshold} = \bar{X},$$

$$\text{quantizer output levels: } \bar{X}_L \cdots x(i) < \bar{X}$$

$$\bar{X}_H \cdots x(i) \geq \bar{X}, \qquad (1)$$

and

$$\bar{X} = \frac{1}{l} \sum_{i=1}^{l} x(i)$$

$$\bar{X}_L = \frac{1}{l-q} \sum_{\substack{i=1 \\ x(i) < \bar{X}}}^{l} x(i)$$

$$\bar{X}_H = \frac{1}{q} \sum_{\substack{i=1 \\ x(i) \geq \bar{X}}}^{l} x(i). \qquad (2)$$

In these expressions

l Number of pels in a block; i.e., $m \times m$.
$x(i)$ Value of the ith pel in the block.
q Number of pels having value higher than $\bar{X}$.

It is also shown that

$$\bar{X}_H = \bar{X}_L + \frac{1}{q} (\bar{X} - \bar{X}_L) \qquad (3)$$

Thus a BTC coder computes $\bar{X}$, $\bar{X}_L$ and transmits their quantized values to the decoder along with the 1-bit output of the quantizer.

Hence the bit rate of the coding scheme is given by

$$\gamma = \frac{l+a+b}{l} \qquad (4)$$

where a and b are the number of bits used in quantization of $\bar{X}$ and $\bar{X}_L$, respectively.

It is natural to expect the lower mean $\bar{X}_L$ to be high in the blocks where the mean $\bar{X}$ is high. Further the lower mean $\bar{X}_L$ is always lower than the mean $\bar{X}$. So a plot of points with $\bar{X}$ as the abscissa and $\bar{X}_L$ as the ordinate will occupy a narrow region near and below the line $y = x$. The spread of the distribution of these points will depend upon the contrast characteristics of the input image, the extreme case being that of zero contrast for an image of a constant gray level. In this case, there will be only one point at $y = 0$ and $x =$ the constant gray level. Fig. 1(a) shows a typical image of size 512 × 512 pels with reasonably good contrast. Fig. 1(b) shows the plot of $(\bar{X}, \bar{X}_L)$ for this image. Fig. 1(c) shows a similar plot for a low contrast real image.

Thus we have seen that the distribution of points $(\bar{X}, \bar{X}_L)$ for a real image is nonuniform in the two-dimensional domain. Quantizing $\bar{X}$ and $\bar{X}_L$ independently as in [3] is inefficient because it will distribute the representative points uniformly over the region bounded by $x = 0$, $x = \bar{X}$ max, $y = 0$, $y = \bar{X}_L$ max. If the pair $\bar{X}$ and $\bar{X}_L$ are treated as a two-dimensional vector and if a suitable VQ is used for coding the vector, the number of bits necessary for their representation can be reduced.

Let us now focus our attention on the other BTC output, namely, the truncated block. A simple representation for the truncated block is in the form of a sequence of 1's and 0's; (b_0, b_1, $\cdots$, b_{l-1}). Using a hard-limiting model for the truncation process of (1), it can be shown that the correlation between the input image pels is retained between the adjacent elements of the truncated block. In fact, the truncated block can be shown to approximate with Markov statistics, if the input image is modeled as a Markov process [6].

To study the distribution properties of the truncated block similar to the overhead information, we consider a hypothetical 2 × 2 truncated block as shown in Fig. 2(a). Fig. 2(b) shows a convenient two-dimensional plot representation of the block where the dots stand for different combinations of the elements of the truncated block. Due to the above-mentioned property of the truncated block, there will be more numbers of blocks represented by dots located in the neighborhood of the line $y = x$.

Generalizing this, the $m \times m$ truncated blocks of the BTC output will be distributed nonuniformly in the l-dimensional binary space. Assigning 1 bit to represent each element in the truncated block as in [3], amounts to uniformly representing all the points in the l-dimensional binary space, and thus is inefficient. If the truncated block is treated as an l-dimensional binary vector, and if a suitable VQ is used for coding it, then the number of bits used to represent the truncated block can be reduced below l.

(a)

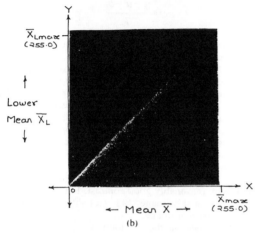

(b)

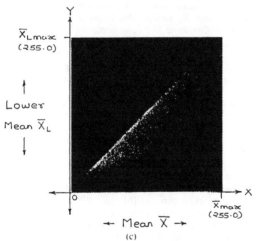

(c)

Fig. 1. (a) Original monochrome image (512 × 512 pels, 8 bits/pel). (b) Plot of mean vectors ($\bar{X}$, $\bar{X}_L$) (block size 4 × 4). (c) Plot of mean vectors ($\bar{X}$, $\bar{X}_L$) (for a low-contrast image).

III. Vector Quantization of the BTC Output

An N level k-dimensional VQ maps an input vector $V = (v_0, v_1, \cdots v_{k-1})$ into a reproduction vector $\hat{V}$. The reproduction vector belongs to a finite reproduction alphabet of N vectors [7]. There are a number of techniques available for the design of VQ's for a given class of input vectors [4]. A technique described in [7] uses an iterative procedure to arrive at an optimum VQ based on a long training sequence of input vectors. The other commonly used technique employs the knowledge of the probability distribution of the input vectors. We consider the training sequence based approach since prior

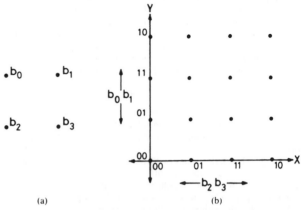

(a)　　　　　　　　　(b)

Fig. 2. (a) A 2 × 2 truncated block. (b) Truncated blocks representation as vectors.

knowledge of the distribution of vectors constructed from the BTC output is not available.

In the training sequence based approach, an initial N-level reproduction alphabet is assumed and an iterative procedure is carried out that alternates between optimum partitioning of training sequence vectors and computation of centroids of the partitions thus formed. The procedure runs until a prespecified distortion criterion is met for the training sequence vectors [7]. Normally used distortion measure is the average mse between the training sequence vectors and the reproduction vectors. The initial guess for the reproduction alphabet can either be drawn from the training sequence itself or can be arrived at iteratively using a splitting algorithm [4].

A. VQ for the Mean Vector ($\bar{X}$, $\bar{X}_L$)

Since $\bar{X}$ and $\bar{X}_L$ are available as numerical quantities, the VQ used for them is exactly identical to the training sequence based VQ in [7]. The initial guess of $N1$ quantizer vectors is obtained by splitting algorithm. The Euclidean center of a partition is used as its centroid.

B. VQ for the Truncated Block Vector (b_0, b_1, $\cdots b_{l-1}$)

Since the individual elements of these vectors are binary, the distortion measure and the centroid need to be redefined. We define the distortion measure as the distance between two binary vectors, which in turn is the number of positions in which the elements of the two binary vectors differ. The centroid of a partition is found by considering the elements of all vectors in the partition. A binary element of the centroid vector is "1" only if there are more than 50 percent of 1's in the same element of the vectors in the partition. Otherwise it is "0." The Appendix gives a sample computation of the distance measure and the centroid for a four-dimensional binary vector. The initial guess for the reproduction alphabet is formed by taking $N2$ unique vectors from the training sequence where $N2$ is the number of quantizer vectors. This is done because splitting of binary vectors cannot be done effectively.

IV. Simulation Results

The image of Fig. 1(a) is used for the simulation of coding with a block size of 4 × 4 pels; i.e., $l = 16$. The procedure used is as follows.

1) 1024 training sequence vectors for the means ($\bar{X}$, $\bar{X}_L$) and the truncated block (b_0, b_1, $\cdots b_{15}$) are constructed from the image whose pels range from 0 to 255.

2) An optimum 256 level; i.e., $N1 = 256$, VQ is designed for the mean vector using a threshold in the distortion criterion of 1.0 percent and a perturbation of 3.0 [4], [7]. Fig. 3 shows the vector plot of the 256 quantizer vectors.

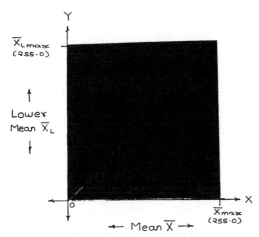

Fig. 3. Plot of $(\bar{X}, \bar{X}_L)$ quantizer vectors ($N1 = 256$).

3) an optimum 256 level; i.e., $N2 = 256$, VQ is designed for the truncated block vectors using a threshold in the distortion criterion of 1.0 percent.

4) Simulation of BTC with vector quantization is carried out on the typical image for following conditions.

a) VQ for $(\bar{X}, \bar{X}_L)$ alone with 16 bits for the truncated block. This corresponds with 1.5 bits/pel.

b) VQ for the truncated block alone with 8 bits each for $\bar{X}$ and $\bar{X}_L$. This corresponds with 1.5 bits/pel.

c) VQ's for both the mean vector and the truncated block vector. This corresponds with 1.0 bits/pel.

Fig. 4(a), (b), and (c) show the respective images after coding and reconstruction. As is seen from the reconstructed images, not many perceivable errors are introduced by this data compression even at a bit-rate around 1.0 bits/pel.

V. DISCUSSION

1) A comment about the vector quantization of the overhead information is perhaps warranted. In [5], similar joint quantization of the overhead information is done using a visual property to mask errors introduced by joint quantization. This suggests the possibility of weighting the distribution of mean vectors in our case, to further reduce the bit rate without introducing many visible errors.

2) Vector quantization described here is more convenient for hardware implementation as compared to similar efforts in [8] and [9]. This is because the vector with large dimensionality is binary in our case and thus enjoys all the advantages of logic processing as compared to numerical processing needed in the design of conventional VQ's.

VI. CONCLUSION

Statistical properties of the output of BTC coder are found to be useful in their vector quantization. VQ's designed using these properties improve the coding efficiency of the BTC coder. Suitable training sequence-based VQ's for a typical monochrome image reduce the bit rate up to 1.0 bits/s. The VQ design approach used, leaves open the option of real-time hardware implementation.

APPENDIX

1) Sample distance measure computation:

4-dimensional input vectors		Distance measure
1010	0101	4.0
1010	1101	3.0
1000	0000	1.0
1111	0000	4.0

(a)

(b)

(c)

Fig. 4. (a) mse = 22.0 at 1.5 bits/pel. (b) mse = 23.5 at 1.5 bits/pel. (c) mse = 28.1 at 1.0 bits/pel.

2) Sample centroid computation:

4-dimensional input vectors

	0001
	0100
	0000
	0010
	1101
	1001
Centroid	0001

REFERENCES

[1] E. J. Delp and O. R. Mitchell, "Image compression using BTC," *IEEE Trans. Commun.*, vol. COM-27, pp. 1335-1342, Sept. 1979.

[2] D. R. Halverson, "A generalized BTC algorithm for image compression," *IEEE Trans. Acoust., Speech, Signal Processing*, vol. ASSP-32, pp. 664-668, June 1984.

[3] V. Udpikar and J. P. Raina, "A modified algorithm for block truncation coding of monochrome images," *Electron. Lett.*, vol. 21, pp. 900-902, Sept. 26, 1985.

[4] R. M. Gray, "Vector quantization," *IEEE ASSP Magazine*, vol. 1, pp. 4–29, Apr. 1984.

[5] D. J. Healy and O. R. Mitchell, "Digital video bandwidth compression using BTC," *IEEE Trans. Commun.*, vol. COM-29, pp. 1809–1817, Dec. 1981.

[6] A. R. Gonzalo and N. C. Gallagher, "BTC image coding using median filter roots," *IEEE Trans. Commun.*, vol. COM-31, pp. 784–792, June 1983.

[7] Y. Linde, A. Buzo, and R. M. Gray, "An algorithm for vector quantizer design," *IEEE Trans. Commun.*, vol. COM-28, pp. 84–95, Jan. 1980.

[8] T. Murakami, K. Asai, and E. Yamazaki, "Vector quantizer of video signals," *Electron. Lett.*, vol. 7, pp. 1005–1006, Nov. 1982.

[9] R. L. Baker and R. M. Gray, "Differential vector quantization of achromatic imagery," in *Proc. Int. Picture Coding Symp.*, Mar. 1983.

The Use of Block Truncation Coding in DPCM Image Coding

Edward J. Delp and O. Robert Mitchell

Abstract—In this correspondence we present the results of using block truncation coding (BTC) in predictive differential pulse code modulation (DPCM) coding of images. BTC is based on the use of a moment preserving (MP) quantizer that is designed such that the quantizer preserves statistical moments of the input and output. We show that while it is theoretically impossible to preserve moments in the reconstructed image, as is normally done in BTC, the DPCM/BTC system works quite well at data rates of 1.18 b/pixel. The performance of the DPCM/BTC system is compared to classical mimimum mean-square error quantizers. These methods are also compared in the presence of channel errors.

I. Introduction

Differential pulse code modulation (DPCM) has been widely used in image bandwidth compression [1]-[3]. In DPCM the difference

Manuscript received January 18, 1989; revised June 4, 1990.

E. J. Delp is with the Computer Vision and Image Processing Laboratory, School of Electrical Engineering, Purdue University, West Lafayette, IN 47907.

O. R. Mitchell is with the Department of Electrical Engineering, University of Texas-Arlington, Arlington, TX 76019.

IEEE Log Number 9042278.

between a pixel gray level value and a predicted gray level value is quantized and transmitted (encoded). At the receiver (decoder) the quantized difference signal and predictor model are used to reconstruct the image. The performance of DPCM is based on the predictor model and the difference quantizer. The design of DPCM quantizers has been widely discussed in the literature [4]–[6].

In this correspondence we will examine the use of a moment preserving (MP) quantizer for the difference signal [7], [8]. This MP quantizer has previously been shown to work quite well in an adaptive PCM coding scheme known as block truncation coding (BTC) [8]–[10]. The combination of BTC and DPCM has not been examined, in particular, the effect of preserving moments in the difference signal in the quantizer-feedback scheme. In this correspondence we will show that preserving moments in the difference signal will not, in general, preserve moments in the decoded image. Despite this problem, we will show that the BTC/DPCM coding scheme works quite well at a data rate of 1.18 b/pixel when the quantizer has two levels (1 b).

II. Moment Preserving Quantizers in DPCM

In this section the use of a moment preserving (MP) quantizer in DPCM will be discussed. In [8], [9] we presented the basic moment preserving block adaptive quantization scheme that has become known as block truncation coding (BTC). This quantizer preserved up to the first three sample moments in the original and decoded image. This concept was extended in [10] to a larger set of moments. In [7] we completely generalized moment preserving quantization by showing that an N level MP quantizer can be related to the Gauss–Jacobi mechanical *quadrature* problem of numerical integration. The output levels of the MP quantizer are the zeroes of the Nth order orthogonal polynomial associated with the input probability distribution function. The question that arises is can a MP quantizer be used in the feedback system of a predictive coder and still preserve moments in the reconstructed image?

The classical DPCM block diagram is shown in Fig. 1. The MP quantizer used preserves the moments of the difference signal. In particular, for a 1-b MP quantizer, where the threshold of the quantizer is the mean of the difference signal, only the first two moments of the difference signal are preserved [8]. The question then is if the first two moments of the difference signal are preserved are the first two moments of the input signal preserved in the reconstructed signal, i.e., does

$$E[e_n] = E[\bar{e}_n] \qquad E[Y_n] = E[\bar{Y}_n]$$
$$\text{and} \qquad \Rightarrow \qquad \text{and}$$
$$E[e_n^2] = E[\bar{e}_n^2] \qquad E[Y_n^2] = E[\bar{Y}_n^2] \qquad (1)$$

where

$e_n = n$th difference signal,
$\bar{e}_n = n$th quantized difference signal,
$Y_n = n$th input signal,
$\bar{Y}_n = n$th reconstructed signal,
$\hat{Y}_n = n$th predicted (and quantized) signal.

In this analysis we will limit the MP quantizer to a two level quantizer with the mean as the threshold. The predictor, shown in Fig. 1, can be either one or two dimensional. For the analysis presented in this section, we will index the predictor by only a single variable without loss of generality. It is easy to show:

$$\bar{e}_n - e_n = \bar{Y}_n - Y_n = E_n \qquad (2)$$

where E_n is the quantization error in the nth sample. It is also possible to show that the first moment of the reconstructed signal is preserved if the first moment of the difference signal is preserved. From (1) and (2) we have

$$E[\bar{e}_n] - E[e_n] = E[\bar{Y}_n] - E[Y_n]$$
$$\text{but} \quad E[\bar{e}_n] = E[e_n] \quad \text{hence } E[\bar{Y}_n] = E[Y_n].$$

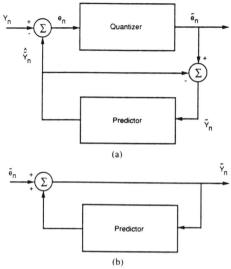

Fig. 1. The differential pulse code modulation block diagram. (a) Transmitter (encoder). (b) Receiver (decoder).

Given that the second moment of the difference is preserved $E[\bar{e}_n^2] = E[e_n^2]$ and the results above, the second moment of the reconstructed picture is preserved ($E[Y_n^2] = E[\bar{Y}_n^2]$) if and only if $E[\hat{Y}_n E_n] = 0$. What this says is that the quantization error E_n and the predicted quantized signal $\hat{Y}_n$ must be orthogonal. We can show this by rewriting (2) as

$$\bar{e}_n = (\bar{Y}_n - Y_n) + e_n$$
$$E[\bar{e}_n^2] = E[(\bar{Y}_n - Y_n)^2] + 2E[e_n(\bar{Y}_n - Y_n)] + E[e_n^2]$$
$$0 = E[\bar{Y}_n^2] - 2E[\bar{Y}_n Y_n] + E[Y_n^2] + 2E[e_n(\bar{Y}_n - Y_n)]$$

since $E[\bar{e}_n^2] = E[e_n^2]$

$$E[\bar{Y}_n^2] = -E[Y_n^2] + 2E[\bar{Y}_n Y_n - e_n(\bar{Y}_n - Y_n)]$$

but $e_n = Y_n - \hat{Y}$ hence $E[\bar{Y}_n^2] = E[Y_n^2] + 2E[\hat{Y}_n E_n]$.

$$(3)$$

Therefore $\quad E[\bar{Y}_n^2] = E[Y_n^2] \quad$ if $E[\hat{Y}_n E_n] = 0. \quad (4)$

Equation (4) can be alternatively written as (using (2)) $E[\hat{Y}_n(\bar{e}_n - e_n)] = 0$. One could argue heuristically that if the quantization error was uncorrelated with the input then (4) could be met. Alternatively, another heuristic argument could be put forth assuming $\bar{Y}_n$ is the optimal predictor (in the mean-square sense) and $\bar{e}_n \simeq e_n$. Hence, using the orthogonality principle we have the desired condition. Unfortunately, neither of the arguments can be successfully applied. Since the quantization error is negatively correlated with the input signal [7], and since our application involves a 1-b quantizer, the quantization error is relatively large. This result could obviously be extended to any number of moments; however, the above is sufficient to indicate that preserving the moments of the difference signal usually will not preserve the moments in the reconstruction.

III. Some Preliminaries Relative to DPCM Coding

The results of Section II are quite disappointing in that preserving moments in the difference signal will not preserve moments in the reconstructed image. Despite this result we decided to perform an empirical study using a MP quantizer to assess the performance of the predictive BTC scheme. To perform this study we choose to use a fixed nonadaptive predictor. We make no claim of optimality by assuming a fixed predictor, however, we are only interested in

Fig. 2. Original image used in comparison study. Image is 512 × 512 pixels with 8-b gray level resolution.

Fig. 3. Results using DPCM and the MP quantizer with data rate of 1.18 b/pixel.

investigating the performance of the quantizer. Throughout this correspondence we shall assume a two-dimensional half-plane predictor identical to the Gauss–Markov model we previously developed in [11] for other image coding applications:

$$\hat{Y}(i, j) = \theta_1 Y(i - 1, j) + \theta_2 Y(i - 1, j - 1) + \theta_3 Y(i, j - 1).$$

We shall fix the predictor coefficients at $\theta_1 = 0.8$, $\theta_2 = -0.6$, and $\theta_3 = 0.8$. This will eliminate the overhead information that would be necessary if the predictor model adapted at every block. This predictor has no "leak" associated with it, i.e., the predictor model is marginally stable and has shown to work well in other applications [11], [12].

Previous studies have indicated that the difference signal contains the relatively high frequency content of the input signal. For the application of image coding this would indicate that edge information is contained in the difference signal. We have previously shown that BTC works quite well on edge data [8], [9] and hence should preserve the edge structure in the difference signal.

IV. Comparison Study Using Predictive BTC

O'Neal [2] has shown that the difference signal in predictive coding can be modeled as having a Laplacian probability density function. In this section we will compare the use of the minimum mean-square error 1-b quantizer for a Laplacian density [13] with that of 1-b predictive BTC. We will base our comparison on computed mean-square and mean absolute error and subjective evaluation.

The coding scheme used is one where the quantizer adapts at every block of pixels. For this study the block size will be 8 × 8. The two quantizer schemes require that sample moments be calculated in order that quantizer parameters be obtained. We shall assume that the sample moments of the error signal represent a "reasonable" estimator of the moments. These sample moments are obtained by first doing an open-loop prediction of the error signal; the quantizer parameters are obtained and then the loop is closed for closed-loop prediction and quantization.

For each 8 × 8 block, a bit plane (the quantizer output) and open-loop sample mean and variance are obtained ($k = 64$):

$$\overline{m}_e = \frac{1}{k} \sum_{i=1}^{k} e_k$$

$$\overline{\sigma}_e^2 = \frac{1}{k} \sum_{i=1}^{k} (e_k - \overline{m}_e)^2.$$

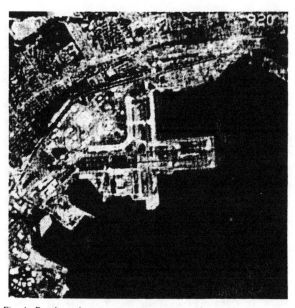

Fig. 4. Results using mean-square error quantizer with data rate of 1.18 b/pixel.

The output of the encoder for each 8 × 8 block is $\overline{m}_e$, $\overline{\sigma}_e$, and a 8 × 8 b plane indicating where in the block the difference signal is above or below $\overline{m}_e$. Empirical evidence indicates it is necessary to assign $\overline{m}_e$ only 4 b and $\overline{\sigma}_e$ only 3 b [9]; this leads to a data rate of 1.18 b/pixel. This should be contrasted to the data rate obtained by BTC of 1.625 b/pixel [8]. For each 8 × 8 block at the decoder, $\overline{m}_e$, $\overline{\sigma}_e$, and the 8 × 8 b plane are used to reconstruct the difference signal and the image either by using the BTC equations in [8] or the Laplacian quantization table in [13].

The predictor model tends to add a little smoothing to the reconstructed image which makes the image cosmetically more pleasing. Fig. 2 shows the original image used for this study. Coded images using these two quantizers are shown in Figs. 3 and 4 along with frame difference pictures between the original and coded images in Figs. 5 and 6. The computed mean square errors and mean absolute

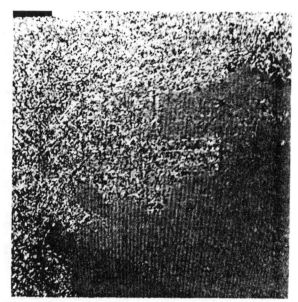

Fig. 5. The difference picture of Figs. 3 and 2. Medium gray corresponds to no coding artifacts. Gray scale expanded by factor of 5.

Fig. 7. Results using DPCM coding using a MP quantizer with channel (bit) error probability of 10^{-3}. Data rate is 1.18 b/pixel.

Fig. 6. The difference picture of Figs. 4 and 2. Medium gray corresponds to no coding artifacts. Gray scale expanded by factor of 5.

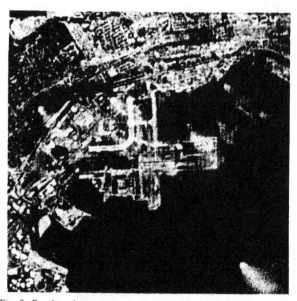

Fig. 8. Results using mean-square error quantizer with channel (bit) error probability of 10^{-3}. Data rate is 1.18 b/pixel.

TABLE I
COMPUTED MEAN-SQUARE ERROR AND MEAN ABSOLUTE ERROR MEASURES
FOR THE TWO DPCM CODING SCHEMES

	Mean Square Error	Mean Absolute Error
Figure 3	113.01	6.59
Figure 4	122.86	6.17

errors are shown in Table I. While the error measures are not significantly different, the predicitive BTC coded image of Fig. 3 looks sharper than Fig. 4's. We feel that the predictive BTC has smaller mean-square error because it preserves the edge structure in the difference signal better and also the Laplacian probability density model will be invalid in these edge regions. The blurring in Fig. 4 can be seen by observing the edge information that is "lost" as

evident in Fig. 6. The mean-square errors are large because in general the open-loop prediction causes the apparent average gray level in each block to change. Only a small shift in average gray level will cause a relatively large change in the computed mean-square error. Figs. 7 and 8 show results in the presence of channel errors. These reconstructed channel error images are interesting in that the 45° bias in the predictor is quite apparent. Errors propagate along the 45° axis because the predictor has no "leak" in that direction [2], [12]. In the horizontal or vertical direction the predictor has "leak," therefore error propagation is not as evident.

V. CONCLUSIONS

Despite the theoretical results in Section II, the empirical study indicates that the MP quantizer can be used quite satisfactorily in

DPCM and in fact its use complements that of regular BTC; i.e, when data rates of less than 1.5 b/pixel are desired it is better to use the differential scheme than to use regular BTC. In the predictive scheme discussed here we can take advantage of two differences from regular BTC. The fact that it is necessary only to assign 7 b to $\overline{m}_e$ and $\overline{\sigma}_e$ and the ability to go to a larger block size (8×8). This larger block size minimizes the effect of quantizer overhead and allows a lower data rate. The differential scheme still retains the relative simplicity of BTC although the prediction process adds some complications in the encoding and decoding.

REFERENCES

[1] D. J. Connor. R. F. W. Pense, and W. G. Scholes, "Television coding using two-dimensional spatial prediction," *Bell Syst. Tech. J.*, vol. 50, pp. 1049-1061, Mar. 1971.

[2] J. B. O'Neal, "Predictive quantizing systems (differential pulse code modulation) for the transmission of television signals," *Bell Syst. Tech. J.*, vol. 45, pp. 689-721, May/June 1966.

[3] M. Kunt, A. Ikonomopolous, and M. Kocher, "Second generation image coding techniques," *Proc. IEEE*, vol. 73, no. 4, pp. 549-574, Apr. 1985.

[4] J. O. Limb and F. W. Mounts, "Digital differential quantizers for television," *Bell Syst. Tech. J.*, vol. 48, pp. 2583-2599, Sept. 1969.

[5] D. J. Sharma and A. N. Netravali, "Design of quantizers for dpcm coding of picture signals," *IEEE Trans. Commun.*, vol. COM-25, no. 11, pp. 1267-1274, Nov. 1977.

[6] P. Pirsch, "Design of dpcm quantizers for video signals using subjective tests," *IEEE Trans. Commun.*, vol. COM-29, no. 7, pp. 990-1000, July 1981.

[7] E. J. Delp and O. R. Mitchell, "Moment preserving quantization," *IEEE Trans. Commun.*, to be published.

[8] E. J. Delp and O. R. Mitchell, "Image compression using block truncation coding," *IEEE Trans. Commun.*, vol COM-25, no. 9, pp. 1335-1342, Sept. 1979.

[9] O. R. Mitchell and E. J. Delp, "Multilevel graphics representation using block truncation coding," *Proc. IEEE*, vol. 68, no. 7, pp. 868-873, July 1980.

[10] D. R. Halverson, N. C. Griswold, and G. L. Wise, "A generalized block truncation coding algorithm for image compression," *IEEE Trans. Acoust., Speech, Signal Processing*, vol. ASSP-32, no. 3, pp. 664-668, June 1984.

[11] E. J. Delp, R. L. Kashyap, and O. R. Mitchell, "Image data compression using autoregressive time series models," *Patt. Recog.*, vol. 11, no. 5/6, pp. 313-323, 1979.

[12] P. Pirsch, "Stability conditions for dpcm coders," *IEEE Trans. Commun.*, vol. COM-30, no. 5, pp. 1174-1184, May 1982.

[13] W. C. Adams and C. E. Giesler, "Quantizing characteristics for signals having Laplacian amplitude probability density function," *IEEE Trans. Commun.*, vol. COM-26, no. 8, pp. 1295-1297, Aug. 1978.

Classified block truncation coding–vector quantization: An edge sensitive image compression algorithm

Noam Efrati, Hillel Liciztin
Ben Gurion University of the Negev, Beer Sheva, Israel

H.B. Mitchell
Signal Processing & Computing Division, Elta Electronics Industries Ltd, Ashdod, Israel

Received 17 July 1990
Revised 8 January 1991

Abstract. Block truncation coding–vector quantization (BTC–VQ) is an extremely simple non-adaptive block-based image compression technique. It has a relatively low compression ratio; however, the simplicity of the algorithm makes it an attractive option. Its main drawback is the fact that the reconstructed pictures suffer from ragged edges. In this paper we show that by allowing the algorithm to adapt to the local picture statistics and by paying particular attention to the nature and reproduction of edges in the picture we are able to substantially improve the visual picture quality and at the same time allow for a moderate increase in the compression ratio.

Keywords. Vector quantization, block truncation coding, image coding.

1. Introduction

Block truncation coding–vector quantization (BTC–VQ) is a simple hybrid image compression algorithm recently developed by Udpikar and Raina [6], which obtains a bit-rate of 1.5 bit/pixel.[1] At these bit-rates the extreme simplicity and ease of implementation makes the BTC–VQ algorithm a very attractive option. The main drawback in the algorithm is that the reconstructed image often exhibits the 'staircase' effect [4] especially in areas where the contrast in the picture is high.

In this paper we describe a modified version of the BTC–VQ algorithm in which we take into account both the nature and the importance of edge reproduction in a picture. As a result of these modifications we have been able to reduce the bit-rate in regions without edges and so reduce the overall bit-rate while at the same time improving the image quality. The changes introduced do not significantly affect the simplicity or the speed of the new algorithm.

We start by describing the block truncation code (BTC) algorithm [1, 6] on which all the methods are based. In BTC the image is divided into non-overlapping blocks of fixed size 4×4 pixels. In each block the pixels are divided into two groups: 'high' pixels whose gray levels are higher than, or equal to, the average gray level $\bar{x}$ in the block and 'low' pixels whose gray levels are less than $\bar{x}$. The relative positions of the high and low pixels are specified

---

[1] Udpikar and Raina describe two image compression schemes: One with a bit-rate of 1.5 bit/pixel and the other with a bit-rate of 1.0 bit/pixel. In this paper our primary interest is to show how the picture quality may be significantly improved whilst maintaining the same bit-rate. Consequently, we have used the simpler compression scheme with a bit-rate of 1.5 bit/pixel.

by the truncation block $T_2(i,j)$:

$$T_2 = \begin{cases} 1 & \text{if } x(i,j) \geqslant \bar{x}, & \text{(1a)} \\ 0 & \text{if } x(i,j) < \bar{x}, & \text{(1b)} \end{cases}$$

where $x(i,j)$ is the gray level intensity at pixel (i,j). Compression of the picture takes place by transmitting, for each data block, the truncation block $T_2(i,j)$ (1 bit/pixel) and two representative gray levels a_2 and b_2 (8 bits per level). Then at the receiver the reconstructed image is formed according to

$$x_r = \begin{cases} b_2 & \text{if } T_2(i,j) = 1, & \text{(2a)} \\ a_2 & \text{if } T_2(i,j) = 0. & \text{(2b)} \end{cases}$$

The representative gray levels a_2 and b_2 are defined as follows:

$$a_2 = \frac{\sum x(i,j)[1 - T_2(i,j)]}{[16 - \sum T_2(i,j)]}, \tag{3a}$$

$$b_2 = \frac{\sum x(i,j) T_2(i,j)}{\sum T_2(i,j)}. \tag{3b}$$

We obtained a substantial improvement in picture quality by repeating the classification procedure given by (1) and (3) using $(a_2 + b_2)/2$ as a new threshold. We found that one iteration was generally sufficient. This is clearly seen in Table 1 which shows how the mean square error falls as a function of the number of iterations. In all further references to the BTC algorithm we imply the use of a single iteration.

Notwithstanding this modification two main disadvantages in the BTC algorithm remain: (1) The algorithm is only capable of providing us with fairly low bit-rates of 32 bits/block or 2 bits/pixel. (2) The reconstructed image suffers in a moderate way from the staircase effect [4], i.e., straight edges in the original picture appear ragged in the reconstructed image. It should be noted that even though the data blocks with an edge running across them constitute a small fraction of a typical picture the perceived quality of an image suffers dramatically when the edge blocks are reconstructed poorly.

Table 1
MSE versus iteration

Picture	Iter no.	MSE BTC 2-level	BTC 3-level
Lenna	0	40.7	20.1
	1	37.6	17.4
	2	36.9	16.8
	5	36.8	16.6
	10	36.8	16.6
Gremlin	0	17.6	8.7
	1	16.6	7.8
	2	16.5	7.7
	5	16.5	7.6
	10	16.5	7.6

Both of these problem areas have been tackled separately in the past. In this paper we present a modification of the BTC algorithm (called BTC–CVQ) which combines a low bit-rate with a significant reduction in the severity of the staircase effect.

Sections 2 and 3 describe past modifications to the BTC algorithm. In Section 2 we describe the staircase effect and the work of Ronson and DeWitte [2, 5] and Walach et al. [8]. In Section 3 we describe how Updikar and Raina [7] were able to substantially increase the compression ratio by using vector quantization. The new BTC–CVQ scheme is described in Section 4. Experimental results are presented in Section 5. Finally, a concluding summary is given in Section 6.

2. The staircase effect

In order to identify the origin of the staircase effect in the BTC algorithm, Ronson and DeWitte [5] carried out a statistical survey on a sequence of typical television pictures. They identified a class of pixels whose gray levels were best reconstructed by $(a_2 + b_2)/2$ (rather than the levels a_2 or b_2). The positions of these pixels were found to be closely correlated with an edge crossing the block. They found a substantial reduction in the severity of the staircase effect by simply using the three gray levels

a_2, b_2 and $(a_2+b_2)/2$ in all edge blocks (i.e., blocks with one or two edges running across them).

Walach et al. [8] likewise found a marked decrease in the staircase effect when all high contrast data blocks (i.e., blocks with high $r_2 = b_2 - a_2$) are encoded with the three reconstruction levels a_2, b_2 and $(a_2+b_2)/2$.

A 3-level BTC algorithm which we have found works very well is summarized in (4)–(7).

First each block is encoded using the 2-level BTC algorithm. Then the pixels are tested against two thresholds t_1 and t_2, where

$$t_1 = (3b_2 + a_2)/4, \tag{4a}$$

$$t_2 = (3a_2 + b_2)/4. \tag{4b}$$

The 'high' pixels have gray levels $x(i,j)$ which are greater than, or equal to, t_1. The 'low' pixels have gray levels which are less than, or equal to, t_2. The remaining pixels have 'intermediate' gray levels between t_1 and t_2.

The 3-level truncation block-matrix $T_3(i,j)$ indicates whether the pixel (i,j) is a 'high', a 'low' or an 'intermediate' pixel:

$$T_3(i,j) = \begin{cases} 1 & \text{if } x(i,j) \geq t_1, \\ 0 & \text{if } t_2 < x(i,j) < t_1, \\ -1 & \text{if } x(i,j) \leq t_2. \end{cases} \tag{5}$$

The values chosen for the representative gray levels are a_3, b_3 and $(a_3+b_3)/2$, where

$$a_3 = \frac{\sum x(i,j)[T_3(i,j) - |T_3(i,j)|]}{\sum [T_3(i,j) - |T_3(i,j)|]}, \tag{6a}$$

$$b_3 = \frac{\sum x(i,j)[T_3(i,j) + |T_3(i,j)|]}{\sum [T_3(i,j) + |T_3(i,j)|]}. \tag{6b}$$

At the receiver the reconstructed image is formed according to

$$x_r(i,j) = \begin{cases} b_3 & \text{if } T_3(i,j) = +1, & \text{(7a)} \\ (a_3+b_3)/2 & \text{if } T_3(i,j) = 0, & \text{(7b)} \\ a_3 & \text{if } T_3(i,j) = -1. & \text{(7c)} \end{cases}$$

As in the case of the 2-level algorithm we obtained a substantial improvement in picture quality by repeating the encoding procedure using

$(a_3 + 3b_3)/4$ for t_1 and $(b_3 + 3a_3)/4$ for t_2. In all further references to the 3-level encoding algorithm we imply this modification has been used.

3. Vector quantization

Udpikar and Raina [7] showed how to reduce the bit-rate in the BTC algorithm by compressing the truncation block-matrix T_2 using vector quantization (VQ) techniques. Off-line a set of representative truncation block-matrices K_2 (a codebook) are formed. Then, for each data block, instead of transmitting the true truncation block-matrix T_2, they find the code-matrix K_2 closest to T_2 and transmit its index k_2. By using only 256 code matrices the bit-rate goes down from 32 bit/block to 24 bit/block (2 bit/pixel to 1.5 bit/pixel).

Udpikar and Raina used the LBG algorithm [3] to create the codebook of K_2 matrices. The main steps in the algorithm are

(1) Form a trainbook by taking a large number of different pictures. Divide each picture into blocks of size 4×4 pixels and BTC encode each block.

(2) Form an initial codebook by randomly selecting 256 matrices from the training book.

(3) Find the closest (i.e., minimum MSE) codebook matrix for each matrix T_2 in the training book.

(4) For each codebook matrix K_2 label all the T_2 matrices which are closest to it with the same index k_2.

(5) For each index k_2 find the centroid of all the T_2 matrices with the label k_2. The centroids are the new codebook matrices.

(6) Repeat steps (3) to (5) until no further changes occur in the codebook matrices.

Each code-matrix K_2 was formed into a single stream of 16 bits and for this reason we often refer to it as a code-vector rather than a code-matrix.

The problem of the staircase effect (ragged edges), however, was made worse by VQ for two reasons:

(1) The T_2-vector training sequence was populated with only a small fraction of edge blocks. The edge blocks, which are essential for good quality reproduction, are therefore poorly represented in the codebook.

(2) Even if the codebook contained sufficient edge code-vectors the MSE measure did not ensure that an edge block was coded with an edge vector.

A straightforward solution to the problem of ragged edges in VQ was put forward by Ramamurthi and Gersho [4]. They use a preprocessing stage in which the individual data blocks are classified into various classes before VQ. Each class has its own codebook and the appropriate code-vector is selected using the MSE distortion measure. The general technique is known as classified VQ.

4. Classified block truncation coding–vector quantization (BTC–CVQ)

In this section we present the new BTC–CVQ algorithm. In designing the new algorithm we were guided by the following four principles:

(1) The correct encoding of edges is most important if the reconstructed images are to be of a high quality,

(2) A minimum of 3 reconstruction levels is required to correctly encode edges,

(3) The staircase effect is most severe when high contrast edges are present, and

(4) A classified VQ technique has the intrinsic flexibility to handle the problem of encoding edges at a high quality.

Based on these principles we constructed two codebooks for the new algorithm. The first codebook contains a set of 2-level code-vectors K_2 and is used for encoding the non-edge T_2 vectors. The second codebook contains a set of 3-level code-vectors K_3 and is used for encoding the edge T_3 vectors.

For the K_2 codebook we used the prescription given by Udpikar and Raina [7] (see Section 3).

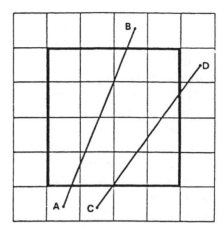

Fig. 1. Matrix used for creation of edge code-book.

For the K_3 codebook we required a trainbook of blocks which had a single significant edge running across them. The number of such edges in any one picture is limited. Thus to create a trainbook which is sufficiently rich (i.e., spans all edge directions and widths) would require an inordinate number of pictures. For this reason we decided to artificially construct the T_3 trainbook. The codebook was then constructed by applying the LBG algorithm to the trainbook using the MSE as the distortion measure.

To artificially create an edge block our aim is to divide the truncation block into three regions: one high gray level region, one low level region and one transition or edge region. In order to do this we used the matrix of unit squares shown in Fig. 1. This consists of an inner matrix of 4×4 squares and represents the pixels in the truncation block and surrounding this is an envelope one square wide of 'border' squares.

The elements in the trainbook were then generated by the following algorithm:

(1) Draw two straight lines AB and CD between the centers of any four border squares such that AB and CD do not cross one another.

(2) Label all squares in the 4×4 block and whose centers lie to the left of AB with a '+1', and all squares whose centers lie to the right of CD are labelled with a '−1'. For the remaining squares give the value '0'.

(3) Eliminate all patterns with zero squares of sign '+1' and/or zero squares of sign '−1'.

(4) Generate a second pattern by simply interchanging '+1' and '−1'.

(5) Eliminate all duplicate patterns.

The total number of edge patterns thus generated was 1064. These formed the T_3 training book from which the K_3 code-book was derived.

To classify the data blocks in the picture we used the following simple algorithm:

(1) Apply the standard Sobel operator to all pixels in the block and declare all pixels whose Sobel function is greater than a given threshold THR_1 to be 'edge' pixels.

(2) Declare a data block to be an edge block if the number of edge pixels equals or exceeds a threshold THR_2.

Empirically we found that $THR_2 = 7$ was optimum. The threshold THR_1 was set adaptively according to the picture type. Generally, we obtained the best results when the number of edge pixels was limited to between 10% and 20% of the total number of pixels in the picture.

The steps in the encoding algorithm are

(1) Divide the picture into non-overlapping squares of size 4×4 pixels.

(2) Encode the individual blocks according to the 2-level BTC algorithm as described in Section 1 (eqs. (1) and (3)).

(3) Classify the block according to whether it has an edge running across it or not.

(4) Encode individual edge blocks according to the 3-level BTC algorithm as described in Section 2 (eqs. (4)–(6)).

(5) Search the appropriate codebook (for edge blocks we search in the K_3 codebook and for no-edge blocks we search in the K_2 codebook) and find the closest code-vector K_3 or K_2 (and the corresponding index k_3 or k_2) using the MSE criterion for closeness.

(6) Transmit a 1-bit flag which indicates whether the block is an edge block (flag = 1) or a no-edge block (flag = 0).

(7) Transmit the representative levels a_3 and b_3 (for edge blocks) or a_2 and b_2 (for no-edge

blocks) with 8 bits for each level.

(8) Transmit the index k_3 or k_2.

The decoding algorithm is effectively the reverse of the above procedure:

(1) Identify data block as an edge block or as a no-edge block according to the received flag bit.

(2) For edge blocks set the truncation block matrix $T_3(i, j)$ equal to the code-matrix $K_3(i, j)$ which corresponds to the received code index k_3.

(3) Reconstruct no-edge blocks according to (7).

(4) For no-edge blocks set the truncation block matrix $T_2(i, j)$ equal to the code-matrix $K_2(i, j)$ which corresponds to the received code index k_2.

(5) Reconstruct edge blocks according to (2).

5. Experimental results

In this section we present the visual and statistical results obtained as a result of applying the new algorithm on two test pictures. For comparison purposes we also present the results obtained with the BTC–VQ algorithm. Note that the BTC–VQ algorithm used here includes an iteration step as described in Section 3.

Figures 2(a) and 3(a) show the two test pictures which were not included in the set of pictures used to form the training book. Each picture measures 512×512 pixels, is monochromatic and is 8 bits deep.

The image obtained with the BTC–VQ algorithm (Figs. 2(b) and 3(b)) are of moderate quality: the presence of ragged edges is clearly visible and widespread.

Encoding the test pictures with the new algorithm at approximately the same bit-rate (1.5 bit/pixel) shows a marked improvement. The staircase effect has virtually disappeared and areas far away from the edges are well reproduced (Figs. 2(c) and 3(c)). This improvement is also evident in the reduction in the MSE by nearly half (Table 2).

Fig. 2. (a) Original 8-bit deep monochromatic picture. Size 512 × 512 pixels. (b) Reconstructed picture obtained with the standard BTC–VQ algorithm. Notice the ragged edges along the rim and the outline of the hat. (c) Reconstructed picture obtained using the new classified BTC–VQ algorithm. The codebook size for the edge blocks was 512 and for the no-edge blocks was 128. Notice how the ragged edges have virtually disappeared. (d) Reconstructed picture obtained using the new classified BTC–VQ algorithm. The codebook size for the edge blocks was 512 and for the no-edge blocks was 64. (e) Reconstructed picture obtained using the new classified BTC–VQ algorithm. The codebook size for the edge blocks was 256 and for the no-edge blocks was 64. (f) Spatial distribution of edge no-edge blocks.

Fig. 3. (a) Original 8-bit deep monochromatic picture. Size 512 × 512 pixels. (b) Reconstructed picture obtained with the standard BTC–VQ algorithm. Notice the ragged edges along the outline of the mouth and the hands. (c) Reconstructed picture obtained using the new classified BTC–VQ algorithm. The codebook size for the edge blocks was 512 and for the no-edge blocks was 128. Notice how the ragged edges have virtually disappeared. (d) Reconstructed picture obtained using the new classified BTC–VQ algorithm. The codebook size for the edge blocks was 512 and for the no-edge blocks was 64. (e) Reconstructed picture obtained using the new classified BTC–VQ algorithm. The codebook size for the edge blocks was 256 and for the no-edge blocks was 64. (f) Spatial distribution of edge/no-edge blocks.

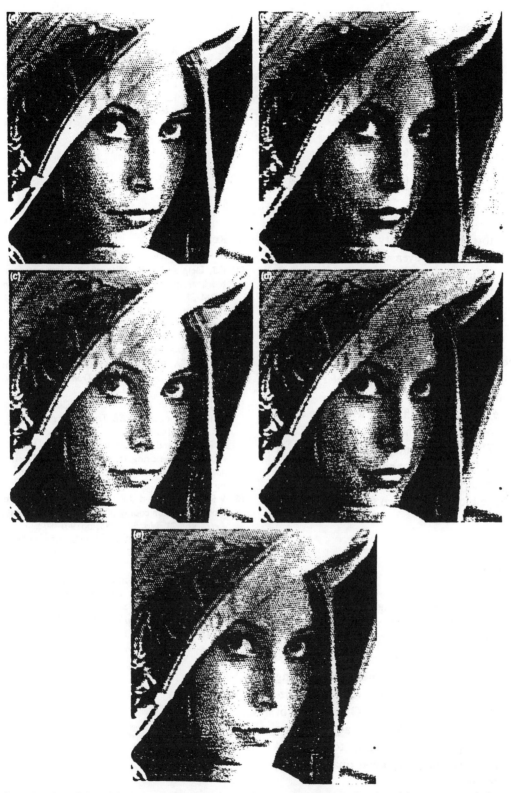

Fig. 4. (a) Central region of the original picture (Fig. 2(a)) at an enlarged scale. (b) Central region of the reconstructed picture (Fig. 2(b)) obtained with the standard BTC-VQ algorithm at an enlarged scale. (c) Central region of the reconstructed picture (Fig. 2(c)) obtained using the new classified BTC-VQ algorithm at an enlarged scale. The codebook size for the edge blocks was 512 and for the no-edge blocks was 128. (d) Central region of the reconstructed picture (Fig. 2(d)) obtained using the new classified BTC-VQ algorithm at an enlarged scale. The codebook size for the edge blocks was 512 and for the no-edge blocks was 64. (e) Central region of the reconstructed picture (Fig. 2(e)) obtained using the new classified BTC-VQ algorithm at an enlarged scale. The codebook sizes for the edge blocks was 256 and for the no-edge blocks was 64.

Table 2
Summary of encoding results

| Picture | Fig. | Codebook sizes | | MSE | Bit-rate | % edge |
		Edge	No-edge		bit/pixel	blocks
Lenna	2(b)	—	256	121.9	1.50	—
	(c)	512	128	59.6	1.52	17
	(d)	512	64	61.8	1.46	17
	(e)	256	128	63.8	1.51	17
Gremlin	3(b)	—	256	62.9	1.50	—
	(c)	512	128	25.1	1.51	15
	(d)	512	64	37.0	1.46	15
	(e)	256	128	27.7	1.50	15

Furthermore, the high fidelity obtained with the new algorithm remains even when the bit-rate is reduced by using smaller code-books. Thus Figs. 2(c, d, e) and 3(c, d, e) show barely perceptible degradations in visual quality as the codebook sizes are progressively reduced from 512(edge)/128(no-edge) to 512/64 and to 256/64.

This conclusion is clearly demonstrated in Fig. 4(a–e) which show the central region of Fig. 2(a–e) at an enlarged scale.

The edge/no-edge classification was made using the Sobel operator thresholds $THR_1 = 15\%$ and $THR_2 = 7$. The final percentage of edge blocks in Figs. 2(a) and 3(a) is 17% and 15%, respectively. Figs. 2(f) and 3(f) show the spatial distribution of edge/no-edge blocks in the two test pictures.

6. Conclusion

We have shown that the image quality obtained with the standard BTC–VQ algorithm may be substantially improved by taking into account both the nature and the importance of edge reproduction. The new algorithm was formed by combining the basic philosophy of classified vector quantization with the relatively simple BTC algorithm of Ronson and DeWitte [5]. With this algorithm we are able to compress pictures down to 1.45 bit/pixel whilst maintaining very good quality in the reconstructed image.

7. References

[1] E.J. Delp and O.R. Mitchell, "Image compression using block truncation coding", *IEEE Trans. Commun.*, Vol. COM-27, 1979, pp. 1335–1342.

[2] J. DeWitte and J. Ronson, "Original block coding scheme for low bit rate image transmission", in: H.W. Schüssler, ed., *Signal Processing II: Theories and Applications, Proc. EUSIPCO-83*, Elsevier, Amsterdam, 1983.

[3] Y. Linde, A. Buzo and R.M. Gray, "An algorithm for vector quantizer design", *IEEE Trans. Commun.*, Vol. COM-28, No. 1, 1980, pp. 84–95.

[4] B. Ramamurthi and A. Gersho, "Classified vector quantization of images", *IEEE Trans. Commun.*, Vol. COM-34, No. 1, pp. 1105–1115.

[5] J. Ronson and J. DeWitte, "Adaptive block truncation coding scheme using an edge following algorithm", *Internat. Conf. Acoust. Speech Signal Process. 82*, 1982, pp. 1235–1238.

[6] V.R. Udpikar and J.P. Raina, "Modified algorithm for block truncation coding of monochrome images", *Electron. Lett.*, Vol. 21, No. 20, 1985, pp. 901–902.

[7] V. Udpikar and J.P. Raina, "BTC image coding using vector quantization", *IEEE Trans. Commun.*, Vol. COM-35, No. 3, 1987, pp. 352–356.

[8] E. Walach, D. Chevion and E. Karnin, "On modification of block truncation coding approach to image compression", in: H.W. Schüssler, ed., *Signal Processing II: Theories and Applications, Proc. EUSIPCO-83*, Elsevier, Amsterdam, 1983.

BTC-VQ-DCT Hybrid Coding of Digital Images

Yiyan Wu and David C. Coll

Abstract— This paper presents a hybrid BVD-VQ-DCT image coding algorithm which combines the simple computation and edge preservation properties of BTC and the high fidelity and high-compression ratio of adaptive DCT with the high-compression ratio and good subjective performance of VQ, and which may be implemented with significantly lower coding delays than either VQ or DCT alone. The bit-map generated by BTC is decomposed into a set of vectors which are vector quantized. Since the space of the BTC bit-map is much smaller than that of the original 8 b image, a LUT-based VQ encoder has been designed to "fast encode" the bit-map. Adaptive DCT coding using residual error feedback is implemented to encode the high-mean and low-mean subimages. The overall computational complexity of BTC-VQ-DCT coding is much less than either DCT and VQ, while the fidelity performance is competitive. The algorithm has strong edge-preserving ability because of the implementation of BTC as a precompress decimation. The total compression ratio is about 10:1.

I. Introduction

THE performance of an image compression algorithm may be evaluated in terms of computational complexity, compression ratio, and fidelity. A "good" algorithm has low-computational complexity, high-compression ratio and high fidelity. Unfortunately, all three cannot be achieved simultaneously. The algorithm described in this paper combines the attributes of block truncation coding (BTC), vector quantization (VQ), and adaptive discrete cosine transform (ADCT) coding to achieve reasonable compression ratios quickly while maintaining high spatial fidelity.

BTC has very few computations, edge-preserving ability and single pixel resolution; but only a medium compression ratio. VQ provides high-compression ratio; fast, look-up-table (LUT)-based decoding and competitive subjective performance; but the encoding procedure is quite time consuming. ADCT coding has high-compression ratio, especially at low bit rates, and good mean square error (MSE) performance but both encoding and decoding processes are computationally complex.

The hybrid BTC-VQ-DCT image coding algorithm presented combines the simple computation and edge preservation properties of BTC and the high fidelity and high compression ratio of adaptive DCT with the high-compression ratio and good subjective performance of VQ, and may be implemented

Paper approved by the Editor for Image Communications Systems of the IEEE Communications Society. Manuscript received June 20, 1989; revised December 19, 1989. This paper was presented in part at the 14th Biennial Conference on Communications, Kingston, Ont., Canada, May 1988.

The authors are with the Department of Systems and Computer Engineering, Carleton University, Ottawa, Ont. KIS 5B6, Canada.

IEEE Log Number 9101506.

with significantly lower coding delays than either VQ or DCT alone.

BTC as developed by Delp and Mitchell [1] is, essentially, a 1 b adaptive moment-preserving quantization process, which preserves certain statistical moments of small blocks of the input image. Udpikar and Raina introduced BTC-VQ coding [2], which achieved an 8:1 compression ratio, but it did not remove the interblock redundancy. In BTC-VQ-DCT coding the DCT coding is implemented to remove both the inter- and intrablock redundancy.

The overall computational complexity of BTC-VQ-DCT coding is much less than either DCT or VQ, while the fidelity performance is competitive. The compression ratio is about 10:1.

II. BTC-VQ-DCT Coding

BTC-VQ-DCT coding has three phases.

- *Phase I:* BTC coding of the input image, which compresses blocks of the original $N \times N$ image into a "bit-map" and two reduced-sized gray-level images which are composed of the "high-mean" and "low-mean" pixel values of each BTC block, Fig. 4(c). The primary compression ratio of Phase I is 4:1 for 4×4 blocks.
- *Phase II:* VQ is implemented on the bit-map to further remove the intrablock redundancy. A universal 64 K codebook is built to quickly vector quantize the bit-map through the use of a LUT. The compression ratio in this phase is between 1.6:1 and 2.67:1.
- *Phase III:* Adaptive DCT is implemented to compress the $N/4$ by $N/4$ high- and low-mean subimages, which removes both inter- and intrablock correlations among high- and low-mean pixel values. Residual error feedback is used to reduce the MSE and bit rate. The compression ratio is about 3:1.

A. Phase I: BTC Encoding of the Input Image

BTC as described in [1], [2] is, essentially, a 1 b adaptive moment-preserving quantization process, which preserves certain statistical moments of small blocks of the input image in the quantized output. The original algorithm preserves the mean and standard deviation in each block [1]. Other quantization schemes result in less *mean square error* (MSE) [3], *mean absolute error* (MAE) [4], and *minimize absolute error* [5].

The algorithm used is absolute moment BTC, described in [4]. The pixels in each block are quantized into high-mean and low-mean, minimizing the mean absolute error in each block. This algorithm has the potential of low computational complexity with no multiplications involved.

In each pixel block, the block mean is used as the threshold for the 1 b quantizer. The outputs of the BTC for each block include two numbers which specify the high-mean, mean of pixel values greater than the block average, and low-mean, mean of pixels less than or equal to the block average; and a bit-map which specifies the high or low state of each output pixel. A 4×4 block is used and each pixel is represented by an 8 b number. The resulting bit rate is 2 b/pixel; and the compression ratio of Phase I is 4:1.

B. Phase II: VQ Encoding of the Bit-Map

Generally, VQ requires the following major steps [6]: *vector formation, codebook generation, and quantization.*

In our special case, VQ is implemented on the bit-map, thereby drastically reducing the VQ coding complexity in three ways: 1) VQ can be realized by a simple LUT operation, 2) *universal codebook VQ* (VQU) [8], which does not require codebook generation or an update process for each input image, can be used instead of *adaptive VQ* (VQA) [7], and 3) Hamming distance may be used to measure the distortion rather than Euclidean distance, which can speed up the process of codebook and encoding-LUT generation.

The bit-map, from Phase I, is decomposed into 4×4 blocks. The total number of representation vectors is only $2^{16} = 64$ K. With such a small vector sample space, the controversy of whether the universal codebook VQ or the adaptive codebook VQ approach is superior [18], [19] is actually phased out.

The MSE performances are shown in Table I where a codebook with $N_c = 256$ codewords is implemented. It can be seen that the *normalized mean square error* (NMSE) of BTC-VQU and BTC-VQA differ by only 0.4 dB, when applied to Fig. 4(a). Comparing the computational complexity of VQA where the codebook must be generated for each image by implementing the time consuming LBG algorithm [9], over VQU where there is no codebook generation during the coding procedure, VQU seems a better choice.

Since we are encoding a bit-map, simple Hamming distance may be used as the distortion measurement instead of Euclidean distance. In other words, we choose to represent each block by a vector which differs from it in the fewest number of places. However, in the codebook and encoding-LUT generation procedures, there is the possibility that there could be more than one codeword with the same Hamming distance from the input vector. Among them, we choose the one with the same number of "0's (or "1's) in the bit-map block. This selection scheme might not improve the MSE value by much, since the situation does not arise very often. However, the moments are still preserved in each BTC block.

The codebook used in VQU is generated from a group of training images that includes standard images, satellite images, and radar images.

C. Phase III: Adaptive DCT Encoding of the High- and Low-Mean Subimages

If we group the high-means, and the low-means, from each BTC block together as raster files, we can form two subsampled images—high-mean and low-mean subimages. For a 512×512 input image with 4×4 blocks, the subsampled images are 128×128 in size. The subsampled-images have details and features which must be preserved, since any distortion involved here will be distributed over all of the pixels in each reconstructed BTC block. Adaptive DCT coding [10]–[12], which adaptively allocates bits in the transform domain based on fidelity requirements, may have very high fidelity, and is a good candidate for the compression of the subsampled-images. Although DCT coding tends to smear edges because some high frequency components are discarded as part of the encoding procedure, the edges in the original image have already been preserved by the BTC preprocessing.

The high- and low-mean subimages from Phase I may be DCT encoded with direct coding, direct-differential coding or direct-differential coding with residual error feedback. These are diagrammed in Fig. 1.

In Method I, adaptive DCT [10] is directly implemented on both the high-mean subimage, S_H. and the low-mean subimage, S_L, Fig. 1(a).

In Method II, adaptive DCT is implemented on S_L or S_H, and the difference image,

$$S_{H-L} = S_H - S_L,$$

in Fig. 1(b). Since a difference image usually has less entropy, fewer bits can be used to code S_{H-L} than S_H or S_L for the same fidelity.

In Method III, adaptive DCT is implemented on S_L and the difference image $S_H - S_{\hat{L}}$. using residual error feedback [15]–[17] as shown in Fig. 1(c) where $S_{\hat{L}}$ is the reconstructed S_L.

Method I has the best MSE performance and least computational complexity, but the highest bit rate since the correlations between the two subimages are not removed. Method II has the worst MSE, moderate computational complexity and low bit rate. Method III has moderate MSE, high computational complexity (about 25% more computation than the other methods) and low bit rate. However, since the size of the subimages is relatively small (16 times less than the original image) the computational complexity is trivial. Considering low bit rate and MSE performance Method III is the best candidate.

The MSE simulation results are displayed in Table I. Method III is selected for use in the hybrid algorithm. The entire system diagram of BTC-VQ-DCT coding is shown in Fig. 2.

Simulation results show that the DCT coding bit rate should be around 2–3 b/subsampled-pixel, or higher, to achieve satisfactory subjective results for the reconstructed image. If the DCT coding bit rate is lower than that, false contours will appear in the reconstructed image, which then looks like a coarsely quantized image.

III. SYSTEM PERFORMANCES

A. Computational Complexity of BTC-VQ-DCT Versus Direct VQ and DCT

In direct VQ, the computational complexity, multiplica-

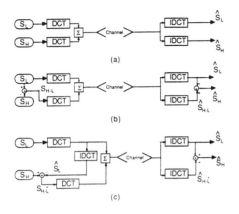

(a)

(b)

(c)

Fig. 1.   Adaptive DCT coding of high-mean and low-mean subimages.

TABLE I
MSE Performance of Computer Simulation Results [Fig. 4(a)],
Codebook Size = 256

	MSE	NMSE		bits/pixel
BTC	25.1	0.0700 %	31.55 dB	2.0
BTC-VQU	37.9	0.1058 %	29.76 dB	1.5
BTC-VQA	33.2	0.0928 %	30.32 dB	1.5156
BTC-DCT$_{L.H}$	31.9	0.0891 %	30.50 dB	1.375
BTC-DCT$_{L.H-L}$	35.3	0.0985 %	30.07 dB	1.3125
BTC-DCT$_{L.H-L}$	32.1	0.0896 %	30.48 dB	1.3125
BTC-VQU-DCT$_{L.H}$	45.8	0.1278 %	28.93 dB	0.875
BTC-VQU-DCT$_{L.H-L}$	48.8	0.1362 %	28.66 dB	0.8125
BTC-VQU-DCT$_{L.H-L}$	46.2	0.1289 %	28.90 dB	0.8125
BTC-VQA-DCT$_{L.H}$	40.8	0.1139 %	29.43 dB	0.875
BTC-VQA-DCT$_{L.H-L}$	43.9	0.1225 %	29.12 dB	0.8125
BTC-VQA-DCT$_{L.H-L}$	41.2	0.1151 %	29.39 dB	0.8125

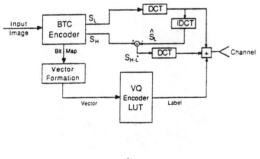

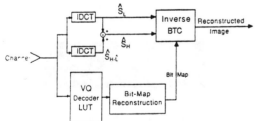

Fig. 2.   BTC-VQ-DCT coding system diagram.

tion/addition per pixel, is proportional to N_c, which is the number of codewords in the codebook. For direct DCT with an $N \times N$ block size, the computational complexity is about $4 \cdot \log_2 N$ multiplications/additions per pixel. For BTC-

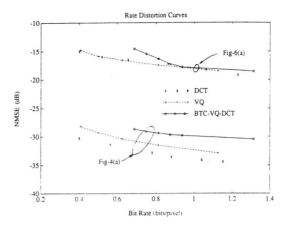

Fig. 3.   Rate distortion curves of VQ, DCT, and BTC-VQ-DCT.

DCT, the BTC part requires only two additions per pixel; the LUT-based VQ needs no computation but only vector formation and addressing; the DCT part, with residual error feedback, requires

$$\frac{10 \cdot \log_2 N}{N_b \times N_b} \text{ multiplications/additions per pixel}$$

where N_b is the BTC block size. Table II compares the computational requirements of the three coding algorithms, for $N_b = 4$, $N = 16$, and $N_c = 256$ where k_n, $n = 1, 2, 3$ is a scale constant, which represents other computer operations, e.g., memory access, data type conversions, etc. Usually, $1 < k_n < 2$. From Table II, the computation associated with BTC-VQ-DCT with residual error feedback is 6.4 times less than that of DCT and 102.4 times less than that of VQ. The advantage of BTC-VQ-DCT is quite clear.

Fig. 5(a) and Fig. 6(b) show the reconstructed images at bit rates of 0.8125 b/pixel and 0.875 b/pixel, respectively.

B. Encoding and Decoding Delay of VQ, DCT, and BTC-VQ-DCT

Coding delay, usually, is directly related to the computational complexity. Among the three coding algorithms, VQ has the most computational complexity. However, most of its computations are at the encoding end, the decoding process is simply a LUT. For DCT, the computations are almost equally divided between encoder and decoder. For BTC-VQ-DCT with residual error feedback, encoding costs about 2/3 of the computation and decoding 1/3. Hence, from Table II, considering encoding delay, the favorable order is BTC-VQ-DCT, DCT and VQ; for decoding delay, it is VQ, BTC-VQ-DCT, and DCT; while for the overall coding delay, it is BTC-VQ-DCT, DCT, and VQ.

C. Error Performance of VQ, DCT, and BTC-VQ-DCT

Table III lists the test results of BTC-VQ-DCT coding for different VQ block sizes where R_b, R_m, and R_{total} are bit rates of coding the bit-map, mean subimages, and total bit rate, respectively. Two test images are used, Fig. 4(a), a standard test image, and Fig. 6(a), a satellite image overlain

TABLE II
COMPUTATION INTENSITIES OF VQ, DCT, AND BTC-VQ-DCT

	Computational Complexity	Multi/Add per Pixel	$k_n = 1$
VQ	$k_1 \cdot N_c$	256	$N_c = 256$
DCT	$k_2 \cdot 4 \cdot \log_2 N$	16	$N_b = 4$
BCT-VQ-DCT	$k_3 \cdot (10 \cdot \log_2 N)/N_b^2$	2.5	$N = 16$

TABLE III
SIMULATION RESULTS OF BTC-VQ-DCT

R_b bpp	R_m bpp	R_{total}	NMSE (%) Fig.4(a)	NMSE (%) Fig.6(a)
1.0	0.3125	1.3125	0.0896	1.397
0.625	0.3125	0.9375	0.1100	1.651
0.5625	0.3125	0.875	0.1197	1.882
0.5	0.3125	0.8125	0.1289	2.325
0.4375	0.3125	0.75	0.1373	2.836
0.375	0.3125	0.6875	0.1596	3.500

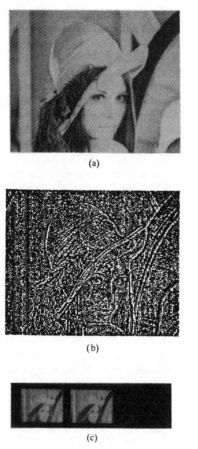

(a)

(b)

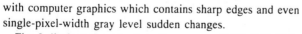

(c)

Fig. 4. (a) Original image. (b) BTC bit-map. (c) High- and low-mean images and their difference image.

(a)

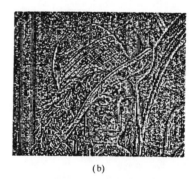

(b)

(c)

Fig. 5. (a) Reconstructed image (0.8125 b/pixel). (b) Coded bit-map. (c) Coded high- and low-mean images and their difference image.

with computer graphics which contains sharp edges and even single-pixel-width gray level sudden changes.

Fig. 3 displays the rate distortion curves of VQ [13], [14], DCT [10] and BTC-VQ-DCT. It can be seen that, for the simple image shown in Fig. 4(a), VQ and DCT have better MSE performance than BTC-VQ-DCT. However, for the complex image shown in Fig. 6(a), BTC-VQ-DCT has competitive NMSE at a bit rate higher than 0.8 b/pixel, because its BTC precoding has high edge preserving ability. For bit rates

260

(a)

(b)

Fig. 6. (a) Satellite image. (b) Reconstructed image (0.875 b/pixel).

lower than 0.8 b/pixel, VQ of the bit-map simply cannot provide satisfactory fidelity; however, because BTC-VQ-DCT has much less computational complexity than either VQ or DCT, it may be used satisfactorily at bit rates greater than 0.8 b/pixel [19].

IV. CONCLUSION

This paper presents a multistage, hybrid image coding algorithm which combines the simple computation and edge preservation advantages of BTC, the high fidelity and compression ratio of adaptive DCT, and the high-compression ratio and good subjective performance of VQ, with an overall computational complexity that is much less than either DCT and VQ, while the fidelity performance is competitive. Good performances at a compression ratio of about 10:1 are demonstrated.

REFERENCES

[1] E. J. Delp and O. R. Mitchell, "Image compression using BTC," *IEEE Trans. Commun.*, vol. COM-29, pp. 1335–1342, Dec. 1979.
[2] V. R. Udpikar and J. P. Raina, "BTC image coding using vector quantization," *IEEE Trans. Commun.*, vol. COM-35, pp. 352–356, Mar. 1987.
[3] D. R. Halverson, N. C. Griswold, and G. L. Wise, "A generalized BTC algorithm for image compression," *IEEE Trans. Acoust., Speech, Signal Processing*, vol. ASSP-32, pp. 664–668, June 1984.
[4] M. D. Lema and O. R. Mitchell, "Absolute moment block truncation coding and applications to colour image," *IEEE Trans. Commun.*, vol. COM-32, pp. 1148–1157, Oct. 1984.
[5] Y. Wu and D. C. Coll, "Multi-level block truncation coding for high fidelity compression of composite imagery," in *Proc. Canadian Conf. Elect. Comput. Eng.*, Vancouver, B. C., Canada, 1988.
[6] N. M. Nasrabadi and R. A. King, "Image coding using vector quantization: A review," *IEEE Trans. Commun.*, vol. 36, pp. 957–971, Aug. 1988.
[7] M. Goldberg, P. R. Boucher, and S. Shlien, "Image compression using adaptive vector quantization," *IEEE Trans. Commun.*, vol. COM-34, pp. 180–187, Feb. 1986.
[8] J. Makhoul, S. Roucos, and H. Gish, "Vector quantization in speech coding," *Proc. IEEE*, vol. 73, pp. 1551–1588, Nov. 1985.
[9] Y. Linde, A. Buzo, and R. M. Gray, "An algorithm for vector quantizer design," *IEEE Trans. Commun.*, vol. COM-28, pp. 84–95, Jan. 1980.
[10] W. H. Chen and W. Pratt, "Scene adaptive coder," *IEEE Trans. Commun.*, vol. COM-32, pp. 225–232, Mar. 1984.
[11] CCITT Document No. 420, "Adaptive discrete cosine transform coding scheme for still image telecommunication services," Jan. 1988.
[12] Y. Wu, "Data compression of meteorological satellite photo imagery for transmission," M. Eng. thesis, Carleton Univ., Ottawa, Ont., Canada, 1986.
[13] A. Papoulis, *Probability, Random Variables, and Stochastic Processes.* New York: McGraw-Hill, 1984.
[14] A. Gersho and B. Ramamurthi, "Image coding using vector quantization," in *Proc. IEEE ICASSP 1982*, pp. 428–431.
[15] J. R. Jain and A. K. Jain, "Displacement measurement and its application in interframe image coding," *IEEE Trans. Commun.*, vol. 29, pp. 1799–1808, Dec. 1981.
[16] J. A. Roese *et al.*, "Interframe cosine transform image coding," *IEEE Trans. Commun.*, vol. COM-25, pp. 1329–1338, Nov. 1977.
[17] L. Wang and M. Goldberg, "Lossless progressive image transmission by residual vector quantization," in *Proc. 13th Biennial Symp. Commun.*, Kingston, Ont., Canada, June 1986, pp. c.1.9–c.1.12.
[18] R. Aravind and A. Gersho, "Image compression based upon vector quantization with finite memory," *Opt. Eng.*, July 1987.
[19] Y. Wu, "Multi-stage hybrid coding of digital images." Ph.D. dissertation, Dep. Syst. and Comput. Eng., Carleton Univ., Ottawa, Ont., Canada, Apr. 1990.
[20] N. S. Jayant and P. Noll, *Digital Coding of Waveforms —Principles and Applications to Speech and Video.* Engelwood Cliffs, NJ: Prentice-Hall, 1984.

Predictive Ordering Technique and Feedback Transform Coding for Data Compression of Still Pictures

Victor-Emil I. Neagoe, *Senior Member, IEEE*

Abstract—This paper presents a new method for efficient image coding, consisting of a cascade of the following processing stages: i) predictive ordering technique (POT); ii) feedback transform coding (FTC); iii) vertical subtraction of quantized coefficients (VSQC); iv) predictive coding refinements in the signal space consisting of either overshoot suppression (OS) as a first variant or hybrid block truncation coding (HBTC) as a second one. The POT algorithm uses the vertical correlation between adjacent pels to change the relative order of elements along a scan line, by putting them in decreasing order of amplitudes (taking as reference the previously received scan line); this ordering concentrates the signal energy into "low generalized frequency" regions. The FTC method is an iterative procedure for increasing with a given step the number of nonzero elements that belong to the orthogonally transformed picture vector, until the mean square error criterion is satisfied (the error representing the difference between the original image vector and the last reconstructed iteration). The VSQC computes the discrete differences between the quantized transform coefficients of the same order belonging to adjacent scan lines. The OS algorithm detects and eliminates the spatial reconstruction errors, whose absolute values exceed a given threshold. The HBTC uses a one-bit nonparametric quantization of the error vector representing the difference between the original picture vector and the last reconstructed vector (satisfying the FTC criterion), so that the first two sample moments are preserved. The reconstructed pictures are presented with their coding fidelity performances (mean square quantization error, mean absolute error and signal-to-noise ratio), using as test pictures a portrait and a LANDSAT image. Good quality images at low bit rate (0.55–1.1) bits/pixel have been obtained.

I. Introduction

AS a consequence of the rapidly increasing demand for image transmission or storage and of the advances in computer technology, it is becoming advantageous to use sophisticated data processing techniques to improve the efficiency of picture transmission or storage [1]–[3]. For still images (such as weather maps, earth-resource pictures, medical images, and other multitone facsimile material), much of the processing can be done off line, so that the complexity of the implementation may be increased in comparison with the real time applications, with a view to obtaining a higher data compression ratio.

Paper approved by the Editor for Image Processing of the IEEE Communications Society. Manuscript received August 31, 1987; revised September 19, 1989.

The author is with the Faculty of Electronics and Telecommunications, Polytechnic Institute of Bucharest, Bucharest, Romania 77206.

IEEE Log Number 9106312.

There are two classical methods for image data compression: i) predictive coding (including the differential pulse code modulation (DPCM), which uses the redundancy in the original picture space [1], [2], [3]; ii) transform coding, which uses a unitary (energy preserving) transformation from the image space into another one, so that the maximum information can be concentrated into only a few "generalized frequency" samples [1]–[3], [12]. Some hybrid techniques use combinations of these two methods [1]–[5]. Recent progress in picture coding has led to high efficiency methods using local operators or contour—texture description [3].

Our idea for the first stage of the proposed coding method springs out from a series of papers by Netravali *et al.* [6], [7], who studied some ordering techniques for efficient coding of two-tone facsimile pictures; the method of Netravali changes the order of elements in a scan line, with reference to the previous one or with reference to a two-dimensional predictor pattern for increasing the average lengths of the black and white runs in the ordered line, thus implying the increasing of the run-length coding (RLC) efficiency. Why not extend the above ordering technique for multitone pictures, as a preprocessing stage to increase the efficiency of a subsequent orthogonal transformation? Therefore, we propose a Predictive Ordering Technique (POT) to change the relative order of elements along a scan line, so that they can be put in the decreasing order of their amplitudes; we consider as reference the previous received scan line.

For the second stage of our proposed method, we introduce the idea of feedback transform coding (FTC); according to this technique, the number of picture vector coefficients considered to be nonzero within an orthogonal transformation space is adaptively increased until the mean square error between the original picture vector and the reconstructed one becomes less than or equal to a given value (for our application, we associated a vector to each picture scan line). The priority order of retaining the image vector coefficients may be given by their energy levels, that are *a priori* estimated for every picture strip of p television lines. Alternatively, we may retain the transform coefficients according to the natural order of their indices (a variant without any order estimation).

The third stage is the vertical subtraction of quantized coefficients (VSQC) (representing a variant of Habibi's hybrid coding [1], [2], [4], [5]), which computes the differences between the rounded-off transform coefficients of the same order, belonging to adjacent lines. The adaptive character of

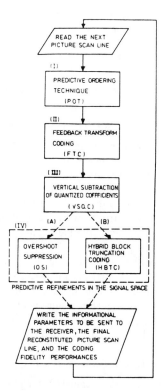

Fig. 1. General structure of the proposed hybrid coding cascade [POT-FTC-VSQC-(OS or HBTC)].

the algorithm is given by the fact that the bit allocation pattern is estimated for every picture.

This VSQC stage does not introduce any errors excepting the ones given by the rounding-off of the transform coefficients.

The fourth stage of the proposed processing cascade contains some predictive refinements within the original picture space, applying either an overshoot suppression (OS) (usually used in some Adaptive Delta Modulation methods, like those of M. Oliver [8] and L. Weis et al. [9]), to eliminate the peak reconstruction errors, or a Hybrid Block Truncation Coding (HBTC) (the method suggested by Mitchell and Delp [10] and developed by the author of this paper, which consists of an adaptive one-bit quantization of the error image representing the difference between the original picture vector (scan line) and the FTC reconstructed one, so that the first two sample moments are preserved.

The general structure of the proposed method presented in Fig. 1 has the above mentioned processing stages:

   i) predictive ordering technique (POT);
   ii) feedback transform coding (FTC);
   iii) vertical subtraction of quantized coefficients (VSQC);
   iv) predictive coding refinements in the signal space, consisting of overshoot suppression (OS) or hybrid block truncation coding (HBTC).

II. Predictive Ordering Technique (POT)

The first stage of the proposed coding method for multitone images (Fig. 1) is a preprocessing algorithm, called predictive

ordering technique (POT). According to this technique, the relative order of the picture elements along a scan line is changed, so that the pixels are placed in the decreasing order of their amplitudes; instead of ordering the pixel values themselves, the predictors of picture elements are ordered. The algorithm has two steps (like the one of Netravali et al. [6], [7] for two-tone pictures):

   1) prediction;
   2) ordering.

A. Prediction

We associate a predictor to every pixel. For the variant presented below, the predictor has the value of the adjacent pel of the previously received scan line (reconstructed after feedback transform coding, vertical subtraction and predictive coding refinements, see Fig. 1). One can also use a two-dimensional predictor containing several pels.

Denote by $X_{i,k}$ the picture value associated to the element of coordinates (i, k) where $i = 1, \cdots, m$ represents the scan line index and $k = 1, 2, \cdots, n$ is the pixel discrete abscissa (from left to right).

Let $P_{i+1,k}$ be the prediction of the picture sample $X_{i+1,k}$, i.e.,

$$P_{i+1,k} = \hat{X}_{i,k} \qquad (1)$$

where $\hat{X}_{i,k}$ represents the value of the pixel of coordinates (i, k) reconstructed after feedback transform coding, vertical subtraction of quantized coefficients, and predictive coding refinements.

Assume that the first scan line is sent without any coding to the receiver, as a reference, i.e.,

$$\hat{X}_{1,k} = X_{1,k} \qquad (k = 1, \cdots, n). \qquad (2)$$

B. Ordering

Suppose we have the ith received scan line

$$\hat{X}^{(i)} = \left(\hat{X}_{i,1} \cdots \hat{X}_{i,n} \right)^t \qquad (3)$$

where t denotes transposition.

We change the relative order of the $\hat{X}^{(i)}$'s elements, putting them in the decreasing order. Thus, we obtain the vector

$$Z^{(i)} = \left(\hat{X}_{i,i_1} \cdots \hat{X}_{i,i_n} \right)^t = (Z_{i,1} \cdots Z_{i,n})^t. \qquad (4)$$

with

$$\hat{X}_{i,i_1} \geqslant \hat{X}_{i,i_2} \geqslant \cdots \geqslant \hat{X}_{i,i_n} \qquad (5)$$

where i_h $(h = 1, \cdots, n)$ represents the position (discrete abscissa having the origin at the left edge of picture) in the unordered picture scan line of the element which has the position h in the ordered line $(i_1, i_2, \cdots, i_n \in \{1, 2, \cdots, n\})$.

Since we should define a unique ordering mapping, assume that if we have two neighboring elements

$$\hat{X}_{i,i_k} = \hat{X}_{i,i_{k+1}}. \qquad (6)$$

then

$$i_k < i_{k+1}. \tag{7}$$

It means that for two equal elements, when we order the line, we have to place on the left side the element which is nearer the left side in the unordered line.

Denote by K_i the ordering index vector

$$K_i = (i_1 i_2 \cdots i_n)^t. \tag{8}$$

Now, we order the elements of the $(i+1)$th original line

$$X^{(i+1)} = (X_{i+1.1} \cdots X_{i+1.n})^t, \tag{9}$$

considering as a reference the previous scan line reconstructed after it had been processed by FTC, VSQC, and by OS or, respectively, HBTC. According to (3), (4), and (9), we obtain the transformation of $X^{(i+1)}$ into

$$Z^{(i+1)} = (X_{i+1.i_1} \cdots X_{i+1.i_n})^t. \tag{10}$$

The purpose of the above ordering is to artificially increase the redundancy of the elements within the picture scan line using the vertical pixel correlation, so that the energy of the image scan line vector is concentrated only in a few low "generalized frequency" samples. The more the adjacent lines "i" and "$i+1$" are correlated, the fewer pairs of adjacent elements $(X_{i+1.i_k} : X_{i+1.i_{k+1}})$ are, for which $X_{i+1.i_k} < X_{i+1.i_{k+1}}$.

After FTC processing, we obtain a reconstruction of the vector $Z^{(i+1)}$, namely,

$$\hat{Z}^{(i+1)} = \left(\hat{Z}_{i+1.1} \cdots \hat{Z}_{i+1.n} \right)^t. \tag{11}$$

It can be expressed as

$$\hat{Z}^{(i+1)} = \left(\hat{X}_{i+1.i_1} \cdots \hat{X}_{i+1.i_n} \right)^t. \tag{12}$$

We can find again the reconstructed scan line after FTC processing

$$\hat{X}^{(i+1)} = \left(\hat{X}_{i+1.1} \cdots \hat{X}_n \right)^t. \tag{13}$$

The element $\hat{Z}_{i+1.h}$ taking the position h in the vector $\hat{Z}^{(i+1)}$ will have the position i_h in the vector $\hat{X}^{(i+1)}$ ($h = 1. \cdots. n$).

The predictive ordering transform (POT) expressed by the relations (3)–(10) can be equivalently expressed in the matrix form

$$Z^{(i+1)} = \phi_i^t X^{(i+1)} \tag{14}$$

where ϕ_i is an "$n \times n$" orthogonal and normalized matrix (the ordering matrix)

$$\phi_i = \left(\phi_1^{(i)} \cdots \phi_n^{(i)} \right). \tag{15}$$

having its general column vector $\phi_h^{(i)}$ given by

$$\phi_h^{(i)} = \begin{matrix} (0 & & 0 & 1 & 0 & & 0)^t \\ \uparrow & \cdots & \uparrow & \uparrow & \uparrow & \cdots & \uparrow \\ 1 & & i_h-1 & i_h & i_h+1 & & h \end{matrix}. \tag{16}$$

The inverse predictive ordering transform (IPOT) is expressed by the relation

$$\hat{X}^{(i+1)} = \phi_i \hat{Z}^{(i+1)}. \tag{17}$$

The flow-chart of the algorithm is given in Fig. 4.

III. FEEDBACK TRANSFORM CODING

As a second stage of the proposed method, we introduce an algorithm called feedback transform coding (FTC). It consists of an adaptive strategy of increasing with a given step the number of picture vector coefficients considered to be nonzero within an orthogonal transformation space, until the root mean square error between the original picture vector and the reconstructed one, after the last iteration, becomes less than or equal to a given value. The priority of retaining the image vector coefficients corresponds to one of the following two variants: a) the coefficients are selected in the decreasing order of their energies and the order of sample energies is estimated for every picture segment of p vectors; b) the transform coefficients are retained according to the natural order of their indices (a variant without estimation).

A. Estimation of the Transform Coefficient Energy Order

Assume a given picture segment having "p" sublocks (particularly, scan lines), each of them being represented as an n-dimensional vector $U^{(i)}$ ($i = 1.2. \cdots. p$).

On each vector $U^{(i)}$, we apply an orthogonal transform expressed by the matrix Ψ

$$W^{(i)} = \Psi U^{(i)} = (W_{i,1} \cdots W_{i,n})^t. \tag{18}$$

We have to evaluate the corresponding energy vector E, in the domain of the transformation

$$E = (c_1 \cdots c_n)^t. \tag{19}$$

having as a general element

$$e_h = \frac{1}{p} \sum_{i=1}^{p} (W_{i,h})^2, \quad (h = 1.2. \cdots. n). \tag{20}$$

Then, we order the energies c_h, obtaining the ordered energy vector

$$F = (e_{j_1} \cdots e_{j_n})^t \tag{21}$$

with

$$c_{j_1} \geqslant \cdots \geqslant c_{j_n} \quad (j_1. \cdots. j_n \in \{1.2. \cdots. n\}). \tag{22}$$

The ordering index vector is

$$J = (j_1. \cdots. j_n). \tag{23}$$

Remark 1: For the presented coding method, the FTC is a stage which follows the POT. Therefore, the estimation of the

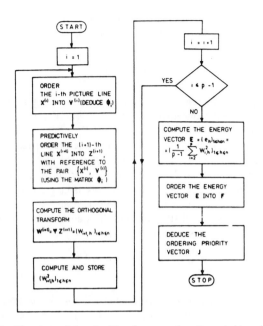

Fig. 2. Flowchart of the algorithm for computing the ordering priority vector J.

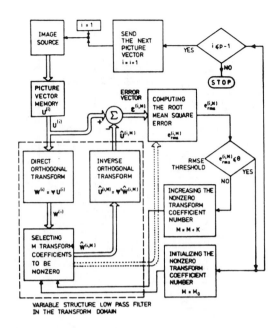

Fig. 3. Block diagram of the feedback transform coding (FTC).

transform coefficient energies has to reflect the previous POT. The image to be coded is segmented in areas of "p" scanning lines, each of them having n elements. The ordering index vector J is deduced for every such segment according to the flow-chart given in Fig. 2.

Remark 2: To achieve a reduction of the computational complexity, we may eliminate the estimation of the transform coefficient energy order, by retaining the transform coefficients, according to the natural order of their indexes. It means, we assume in (23) that

$$J = (1, 2, \cdots, n). \tag{23'}$$

B. Feedback Transform Coding

First, we will present the general FTC algorithm and second, we will consider it as a stage of the proposed cascaded coding method.

Assume a segmentation of a given picture region into p subregions and associate to such a subregion an n-dimensional vector $U^{(i)}$ ($i = 1, 2, \cdots, p$). An orthogonal transform applied to the vector $U^{(i)}$ will transform it into $W^{(i)}$ [see relation (18)]. We retain only $M = M_o$ transform coefficients, namely, those having as indexes the first M elements of the previously estimated vector J [relation (23)]; consider the other $(n - M)$ elements to be zero. Denote $\hat{W}^{(i,M)}$ the truncated version of the vector $W^{(i)}$. Then, dealing again with the picture domain, according to the relation

$$\hat{U}^{(i,M)} = \Psi^t \hat{W}^{(i,M)}. \tag{24}$$

evaluate the error vector

$$\varepsilon^{(i,M)} = U^{(i)} - \hat{U}^{(i,M)} = \left(\varepsilon_{i,1}^{(M)} \cdots \varepsilon_{i,n}^{(M)} \right)^t \tag{25}$$

and compute the root mean square error

$$e_{\mathrm{rms}}^{(i,M)} = \sqrt{ \frac{1}{n} \sum_{h=1}^{n} \left(\varepsilon_{i,h}^{(M)} \right)^2 }. \tag{26}$$

The mean square error for the spatial and transform domain are identical insofar as the unitary transforms are concerned [12]. Then, the root mean square truncation error $e_{\mathrm{rms}}^{(i,M)}$ given by relation (26) may also be expressed as

$$e_{\mathrm{rms}}^{(i,M)} = \sqrt{ \frac{1}{n} \sum_{h} (W_{i,h})^2 }, \quad \hat{h} = \{ h = j_{M+1}, \cdots, j_n \} \tag{27}$$

where $W_{i,h}$ are the elements of the vector $W^{(i)}$ [relation (18)] and the integers $j_{M+1}, \cdots, j_n$ have the significance given by relations (19), (20)–(23).

If $e_{\mathrm{rms}}^{(i,M)}$ is less than or equal to a given threshold Θ, then we pass to the next vector $U^{(i+1)}$. If it is not, increase M

$$M = M + K \tag{28}$$

where K is a fixed integer step (e.g., $K = 1$). We consider those M elements of the vector $W^{(i)}$ to be nonzero, corresponding to the priority order given by the vector J, and the process will continue in this manner until $e_{\mathrm{rms}}^{(i,M)}$ becomes less than or equal to Θ, according to the description given in Fig. 3.

Regarding the FTC algorithm as a stage of the presented coding cascade (the previous stage being POT), its operation is obvious from the flow-chart given in Fig. 4 (it corresponds to an image segment of sizes m, n).

The expression (27) of the root mean square error leads to an important reduction of the FTC computational complexity as shown in Figs. 3 and 4. Indeed, it is not necessary to return to the original picture domain for every FTC iteration, but

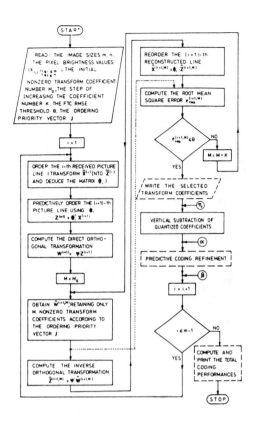

Fig. 4. Flowchart of the POT–FTC processing cascade.

one can remain within the transformation domain, to evaluate the truncation error. Increasing M to $M + K$ (relation (28)) is equivalent to reducing the mean square truncation error according to the recurrence relation

$$c_{\text{rms}}^{(i,M+K)} = \sqrt{\left(c_{\text{rms}}^{(i,M)}\right)^2 - R(i; M, K)}. \quad (29)$$

where

$$R(i; M, K) = \frac{1}{n} \sum_{\hat{h}} (W_{i,h})^2,$$

$$\hat{h} = \{h = j_{M+1}, \cdots, j_{M+K}\}. \quad (30)$$

This implies some short-cuts within the flow-charts given in Figs. 3 and 4 (see the dotted lines). One can remark that such a short-cut is useful during the FTC iteration process only; before the predictive coding refinements it is compulsory to compute the vector $\hat{X}^{(i+1,M)} = \hat{X}^{(i+1)}$.

IV. Vertical Subtraction of Quantized Coefficients (VSQC)

In order to improve the coding efficiency by removing the redundancy in the vertical direction, we used a very simple variant of the hybrid coding method proposed by Habibi [1], [2], [4], [5]. After the FTC stage, we first rounded-off the transform coefficients to the nearest integers (it is equivalent to quantize the coefficients by an analog-to-digital converter).

Second, we computed the difference between every pair of discrete (rounded-off) coefficients of the same order belonging to adjacent television lines

$$e(i, h) = W_{i,h}^* - W_{i-1,h}^* \quad (31)$$

where i is the line index ($i = 3, 4, \cdots, m$) and h signifies the transform coefficient order ($h = 1, 2, \cdots, n$); $W_{i,h}^*$ represents the digitization of the coefficient $W_{i,h}$.

We called the presented processing stage the vertical subtraction of quantized coefficients (VSQC). The algorithm has an adaptive character, the bit allocation pattern is estimated for every picture to be coded; this adaptivity is connected to the asynchronous character of our coding cascade. To evaluate the bit pattern, we firstly compute the transform coefficient discrete difference statistics expressed by

$$e(h) = \max_{i \in \{3, 4, \cdots, m\}} |e(i, h)|: \quad h = 1, 2, \cdots, n. \quad (32)$$

Hence, the number of bits allocated for the quantized coefficient difference of order h (including the bit of sign) is given by

$$b(h) = \begin{cases} 0, & \text{for } e(h) = 0 \\ \text{Integer}\{\log_2 e(h)\} + 2, & \text{for } e(h) \geqslant 1 \end{cases}$$
$$(h = 1, 2, \cdots, n) \quad (33)$$

Remark 3: We have to point out that the only degradation introduced by the VSQC is caused by the quantization of the transform coefficients; the coefficient subtraction itself is an exact mood of efficient signal representation (without any approximation errors).

V. Predictive Coding Refinements in the Picture Signal Space

The FTC, as a second stage of the presented coding method, ensures that the root mean square error between each scan line and the last iteration reconstructed line is less than or equal to a given threshold Θ. Since the mean square error corresponds to an overall criterion for the whole scan line, we intend to impose an additional control, taking into account the individual pel reconstruction errors. We further consider one of the two following predictive refinement variants: overshoot suppression (OS) and hybrid block truncation coding (HBTC). We will further neglect the rounding-off errors introduced by the VSQC, assuming $W_{i,h}^* \cong W_{i,h}$.

A. Overshoot Suppression (OS)

To check the peak spatial errors, we used the refinement of overshoot suppression (OS), inspired from some adaptive delta modulation techniques [8], [9]. The OS detects and eliminates the individual quantization errors which exceed a given threshold δ.

Denote by $\hat{X}^{(i+1)}$ the final FTC reconstructed picture scan line $\left(\hat{X}^{(i+1)} = \hat{X}^{(i+1,M)}\right)$ where M is the minimum integer belonging to the set $\{1, \cdots, n\}$, so that $c_{\text{rms}}^{(i+1,M)} \leqslant 0$, according to the root mean square error criterion, and also denote by $\varepsilon^{(i+1)}$ the corresponding error vector

$$\varepsilon^{(i+1)} = X^{(i+1)} - \hat{X}^{(i+1)} = (\varepsilon_{i+1.1} \cdots \varepsilon_{i+1.n})^t. \quad (34)$$

If one of the absolute values of the above mentioned vector elements exceeds a certain threshold

$$|\varepsilon_{i+1,h}| > \delta. \quad (\delta > 0, h = 1, \cdots, n) \quad (35)$$

a correction information is transmitted for such a pixel, containing the following:

a) the position of the corresponding pixel, expressed by the integer h;

b) the sign and the absolute value of the pixel reconstruction error $\varepsilon_{i+1,h}$.

To encode the pixel position, $\log_2 n$ bits are required. To encode the absolute error, three possibilities are available: (b_1) to quantize the error modulus with the same resolution as the original image pixels; (b_2) to quantize the error modulus with a reduced number of quantization levels; (b_3) to estimate the mean overshoot absolute error for each scan line and to approximate all the overshoot moduli of that line to be equal to their mean $\sigma^{(i+1)}$

$$\sigma^{(i+1)} = \frac{1}{s_{i+1}} \sum_{\substack{h \\ (\varepsilon_{i+1,h}| > \delta)}} |\varepsilon_{i+1,h}| \quad (36)$$

where s_{i+1} is the number of overshoots.

The flow chart of the OS algorithm is given in Fig. 5(a).

B. Hybrid Block Truncation Coding (HBTC)

Compared to the preceding coding improvement by overshoot suppression, the technique called hybrid block truncation coding (HBTC) has the advantage that it introduces a correction over all the pixels in the scan line (not only on the peak error pixels). It represents the development of an idea suggested by Delp and Mitchell [10]. Within our processing cascade, the above mentioned technique (used as a fourth stage) provides a one-bit quantization of the error picture vector between the original scan line and the FTC reconstructed one, so that the first two sample moments are preserved.

Given the picture reconstruction error vector $\varepsilon^{(i+1)}$ [corresponding to the $(i + 1)$th scan line, see relation (34)], we quantize this vector with one bit per element, obtaining

$$\gamma^{(i+1)} = (\gamma_{i+1,1} \cdots \gamma_{i+1,n})^t \quad (37)$$

with

$$\gamma_{i+1,h} = \begin{cases} 1. & \text{for } \varepsilon_{i+1,h} \geqslant 0 \\ 0. & \text{for } \varepsilon_{i+1,h} < 0 \end{cases}$$
$$(i = 1, \cdots, m - 1: h = 1, \cdots, n) \quad (38)$$

Then, we compute the variables α_{i+1} and β_{i+1} characterizing the adaptive quantization and deduce the final reconstruction vector

$$\hat{X}^{(i+1)} = \left(\tilde{X}_{i+1,1} \cdots \tilde{X}_{i+1,n} \right)^t. \quad (i = 1, \cdots, m - 1) \quad (39)$$

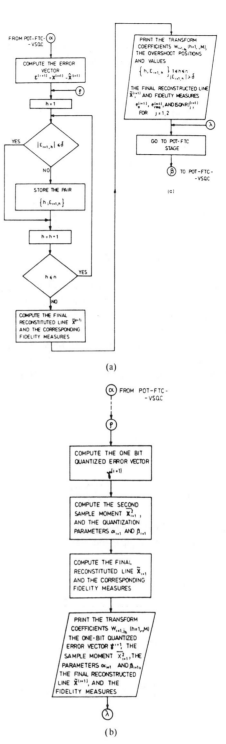

(a)

(b)

Fig. 5. Flowchart of predictive coding refinements. (a) Overshoot suppression (OS). (b) Hybrid block truncation coding (HBTC).

where

$$\tilde{X}_{i+1,h} = \begin{cases} X_{i+1,h} + \alpha_{i+1}. & \text{for } \gamma_{i+1,h} = 1 \\ X_{i+1,h} - \beta_{i+1}. & \text{for } \gamma_{i+1,h} = 0 \end{cases}.$$
$$(\alpha_{i+1} > 0. \beta_{i+1} > 0) \quad (40)$$

267

Let q_{i+1} be the number of $\gamma_{i+1,h}$'s having the value "1". The variables α_{i+1} and β_{i+1} are obtained from the conditions of preserving the first two sample moments

$$\sum_{h=1}^{n} \hat{X}_{i+1,h} + \alpha_{i+1} q_{i+1} - \beta_{i+1}(n - q_{i+1}) = \sum_{h=1}^{n} X_{i+1,h} \quad (41)$$

$$\sum_{h=1}^{n} \hat{X}_{i+1,h}^2 + 2\left(\alpha_{i+1} \sum_{\tilde{h}} \hat{X}_{i+1,h}^2 - \beta_{i+1} \sum_{\tilde{\tilde{h}}} \hat{X}_{i+1,h}^2 \right)$$
$$+ q_{i+1} \alpha_{i+1}^2 + (n - q_{i+1})\beta_{i+1}^2 = \sum_{h=1}^{n} X_{i+1,h}^2 \quad (42)$$

where

$$\tilde{h} = \{h / \gamma_{i+1,h} = 1\}; \quad \tilde{\tilde{h}} = \{h / \gamma_{i+1,h} = 0\}. \quad (43)$$

We further consider the following reasonable assumptions:

i) One always retains the first element $W_{i+1,1}$ of the vector $W^{(i+1)}$ [respectively, $j_1 = 1$, in relation (23)];

ii) All the elements belonging to the first row of the orthogonal matrix are equal. This is the most frequent case; e.g., it corresponds to the discrete cosine transform.

Based on the assumptions i) and ii), it is easy to prove that

$$\sum_{h=1}^{n} X_{i+1,h} = \sum_{h=1}^{n} \hat{X}_{i+1,h} = \frac{1}{\sqrt{n}} W_{i+1,1} = \frac{1}{\sqrt{n}} \hat{W}_{i+1,1}$$
$$(44)$$

and

$$F_{i+1} = \sum_{h=1}^{n} X_{i+1,h}^2 - \sum_{h=1}^{n} \hat{X}_{i+1,h}^2 > 0, \quad (45)$$

for any truncation with $1 \leqslant M < n$ (see Section III).

According to (44) and (45), the relations (41), (42), and (43) become

$$q_{i+1}\alpha_{i+1} + (n - q_{i+1})\beta_{i+1} = 0, \quad (46)$$

$$q_{i+1}\alpha_{i+1}^2 + (n - q_{i+1})\beta_{i+1}^2 + 2\left(\sum_{\tilde{h}} \hat{X}_{i+1,h} \right)\alpha_{i+1}$$
$$- 2\left(\sum_{\tilde{\tilde{h}}} \hat{X}_{i+1,h} \right)\beta_{i+1} - F_{i+1} = 0 \quad (47)$$

where $\tilde{h}$ and $\tilde{\tilde{h}}$ are given by relations (43).

It can be deduced that there are unique positive solutions of the system (46) and (47), given by the expressions

$$\alpha_{i+1} = \frac{1}{n q_{i+1}}$$
$$\cdot \left(\eta_{i+1} + \sqrt{\eta_{i+1}^2 + n q_{i+1}(n - q_{i+1})F_{i+1}} \right). \quad (48)$$

$$\beta_{i+1} = \frac{q_{i+1}}{n - q_{i+1}} \alpha_{i+1} \quad (49)$$

where

$$\eta_{i+1} = q_{i+1} \sum_{\tilde{\tilde{h}}} \hat{X}_{i+1,h} - (n - q_{i+1}) \sum_{\tilde{h}} \hat{X}_{i+1,h}. \quad (50)$$

$[i = 1, \cdots, m - 1; \tilde{h}$ and $\tilde{\tilde{h}}$ are given by (43)].

Remark 4: In the case of HBTC, the following information must be sent to the receiver, for the $(i + 1)$th scan line $(i = 1, \cdots, m - 1)$:

a) the transform coefficients $W_{i+1,j_1}, \cdots, W_{i+1,j_M}$; taking into account the QCVS stage, the transmission of the above coefficients is equivalent to transmitting the rounded-off coefficients of the second line and the discrete coefficient differences starting from the third line;

b) the one-bit quantized error vector

$$\gamma^{(i+1)};$$

c) the second sample moment

$$\overline{X}_{i+1}^2 = \frac{1}{n} \sum_{h=1}^{n} X_{i+1,h}^2; \quad (51)$$

$$\left(\text{based on this moment, one can compute} \right.$$

$$\left. F_{i+1} = n\overline{X}_{i+1}^2 - \sum_{h=1}^{n} \hat{X}_{i+1,h}^2 \right). \quad (52)$$

Remark 5: Moreover, we observe that instead of $\overline{X}_{i+1}^2$ we may transmit the parameter α_{i+1} to the receiver. From $\gamma^{(i+1)}$, we can deduce q_{i+1} and then β_{i+1} [using relation (49)].

VI. COMPUTER SIMULATION RESULTS

To test the proposed hybrid coding cascade, we used two pictures: a) a portrait (Răsvan) and b) a LANDSAT picture segment.

Every test picture has a resolution of $m = 512$ lines, each line having $n = 504$ pixels. Each pixel is digitized to 6 bits PCM ($V_{pp} = 63$).

Among the well-known orthogonal transforms, we chose the discrete cosine transform (DCT), [1], [2], [12], [13], which has very good compression properties. The orthogonal and normalized matrix of the above transform is given by the following formula:

$$\Psi = (\Psi_{kj})_{\substack{1 \leqslant k \leqslant n \\ 1 \leqslant j \leqslant n}}$$
$$= \left(\sqrt{\frac{2}{n}} \, c(k) \cos\left(\frac{(2j - 1)(k - 1)\pi}{2n} \right) \right)_{\substack{1 \leqslant k \leqslant n \\ 1 \leqslant j \leqslant n}} \quad (53)$$

where

$$c(k) = \begin{cases} 1/\sqrt{2}, & \text{for } k = 1 \\ 1, & \text{for } k = 2, 3, \cdots, n. \end{cases}$$

We also used the modified variant

$$\tilde{\Psi} = \frac{1}{\sqrt{n}} \Psi, \quad (54)$$

TABLE I
PERFORMANCES OF THE PROPOSED CODING METHODS

CODING VARIANT	TEST IMAGE	MEAN ABSOLUTE ERROR		ROOT MEAN SQUARE ERROR		SIGNAL-TO-QUANTIZATION NOISE RATIO SQNR (dB)	AVERAGE NUMBER OF RETAINED DCT COEFFICIENTS PER LINE $\overline{M}$	AVERAGE NUMBER OF OVER SHOOTS PER LINE $\overline{n}_\varepsilon$	AVERAGE BIT RATE PER PIXEL R_B (bits/pel)
		unnormalized e_a	normalized $(e_a)_N$ (%)	unnormalized e_{rms}	normalized $(e_{rms})_N$ (%)				
POT-FTC-E-OS ($\Theta = 4.5$: $M_o = 4$: $K = 4$: $\delta = 6$)	PORTRAIT	2.04	3.24	2.58	4.10	27.75	4.09	31.48	0.95
POT-FTC-E-HBTC ($\Theta = 4.5$: $M_o = 4$: $K = 4$)	PORTRAIT	0.86	1.36	1.52	2.41	32.35	4.09	—	1.10
POT-FTC-VSQC ($\Theta = 4.3$: $M_o = 1$: $K = 1$)	PORTRAIT	3.76	5.97	4.82	7.65	22.33	73.05	—	0.22
POT-FTC-VSQC-OS $\Theta = 4.3$ $M_o = 1$ $K = 1$ $\delta = 8$	PORTRAIT	2.70	4.28	3.44	5.46	25.26	3.48	21.48	0.55
	LANDSAT	2.85	4.52	3.54	5.62	25.00	19.84	34.15	0.93
$\delta = 12$	PORTRAIT	3.15	5.00	4.14	6.57	23.65	13.27	4.98	0.21
	LANDSAT	3.51	5.57	4.42	7.01	23.07	49.73	6.00	0.38
POT-FTC-VSQC-HBTC ($\Theta = 4.5$: $M_o = 1$: $K = 1$)	LANDSAT	2.85	4.52	3.54	5.62	25.00	9.80	—	1.08
BTC (FOR COMPARISON)	PORTRAIT	0.51	0.81	3.07	4.87	26.25	—	—	1.19
	LANDSAT	1.78	2.82	6.24	9.90	20.08	—	—	1.19

performing a multiplication of the transform coefficients of the first DCT variant by $\frac{1}{\sqrt{n}}$, which implies that after rounding-off the coefficients, we can encode them using a reduced number of bits. We need a multiplication by $\sqrt{n}$ at the receiver, in order to preserve the direct-inverse transformation cascade of the DCT.

To perform a fast DCT, we used the algorithm of Makhoul [13], deriving the DCT of an n-point real signal, by using an n-point discrete Fourier transform (DFT) of a reordered version of the original signal (instead of a $2n$-point DFT of the even extension of the signal like the traditional methods). To compute a fast DFT, we used the methods of Winograd [14] and Burrus et al. [15] based on an efficient way to obtain convolution. For the dimension of $n = 504$, we used the following factorization in relatively prime numbers: $504 = 7 \cdot 8 \cdot 9$.

As a fast ordering algorithm, needed in POT stage, we considered a variant given in [16].

To evaluate the coding performances, we used the following fidelity measures:

i) the average sample-mean absolute error

$$e_a = \frac{1}{mn} \sum_{i=1}^{m} \sum_{k=1}^{n} \left| X_{i,k} - \tilde{X}_{i,k} \right|; \qquad (55)$$

ii) the root of average sample-mean square error

$$e_{rms} = \sqrt{\frac{1}{mn} \sum_{i=1}^{m} \sum_{k=1}^{n} \left(X_{i,k} - \tilde{X}_{i,k} \right)^2}; \qquad (56)$$

iii) the signal-to-quantization noise ratio

$$\mathrm{SQNR} = 20 \log_{10} \frac{63}{e_{rms}} \quad (\mathrm{dB}). \qquad (57)$$

We tested the following variants of the proposed method.

1) POT-FTC-E-OS: The symbol E marks the variant of adaptive estimation of the transform coefficient energy order [relation (23)] for every strip of $p = 16$ lines, the whole image being segmented into 32 strips. For the DCT, we

269

considered the variant corresponding to relation (53). We chose the parameters of FTC-OS to be: $\Theta = 4.5$; $M_o = 4$; $K = 4$; $\delta = 6$.

2) POT-FTC-E-HBTC: The symbol E has the same significance as that of variant 1). The parameters Θ, M_o, and K are the same.

3) POT-FTC-VSQC: This variant has the following characteristics:

a) It does not need the stage of coefficient energy order estimation, by retaining the coefficients according to the natural order of their indexes.

b) The DCT uses the variant $\tilde{\Psi}$ [relation (54)], in order to increase the data compression performances.

c) It encodes the vertical differences of the quantized DCT coefficients (VSQC).

d) The pattern of bit allocation for the vertical differences of the quantized coefficients is adaptively estimated for every picture to be coded.

e) We used the parameters $\Theta = 4.3$; $M_o = 1$; $K = 1$.

f) This variant does not involve any predictive refinement in the signal space (neither OS, nor HBTC).

Remark 6: As a consequence of the DCT coefficient quantization, the rmse may increase beyond the threshold Θ (see, for example, Table V). This is caused by the fact we considered the exact values of retained coefficients (without rounding-off) within the feedback loop.

4) POT-FTC-VSQC-OS: This stage has the characteristics a)–e) of the previous variant, but it contains the stage of overshoot suppression (OS) as well.

5) POT-FTC-VSQC-HBTC: Compared to the variant 4), it is characterized by the substitution of the OS-stage by the HBTC stage.

6) BTC: For comparison, we considered the block truncation coding (BTC) method of Mitchell and Delp [10] corresponding to a picture segmentation of 8×8 pixels and the encoding of the levels a and b (see [10]) having 6 bits each.

The general coding performances of the experimented variants are given in Table I.

The original and reconstructed images processed by the proposed methods as well as by the BTC (for comparison) are given in Figs. 6 and 7.

VII. CONCLUDING REMARKS

1) The proposed picture data compression method essentially consists of a hybrid cascade having four processing stages. The predictive ordering technique (POT) and the feedback transform coding (FTC), can be individually considered as being two new methods.

2) The proposed coding cascade provides an asynchronous compressed bit stream.

3) According to the POT, one changes the pixel order, by placing the pixels in a decreasing order of their brightness, taking as a reference the previous received scan line. This ordering provides a concentration of the signal energy into "low generalized frequency" regions, so that if we further use an orthogonal transformation of the ordered scan line, we can retain only a few orthogonal transform coefficients for obtain-

(a)

(b)

(c)

Fig. 6. Original and reconstructed coded pictures for PORTRAIT (Răsvan) as a test image. (a) Original ($V_{pp} = 63$). (b) POT-FTC–E-OS ($\Theta = 4.5$; $M_o = 4$; $K = 4$; $\delta = 6$; $R_B = 0.95$ bits/pixel). (c) POT-FTC-E-HBTC ($\Theta = 4.5$; $M_o = 4$; $K = 4$; $R_B = 1.10$ bits/pixel). (d) POT-FTC-VSQC ($\Theta = 4.3$; $M_o = 1$; $K = 1$; $R_B = 0.22$ bits/pixel). (e) POT-FTC-VSQC-OS ($\Theta = 4.3$; $M_o = 1$; $K = 1$; $\delta = 8$; $R_B = 0.55$ bits/pixel). (f) POT-FTC-VSQC-OS ($\Theta = 4.3$; $M_o = 1$; $K = 1$; $\delta = 12$; $R_B = 0.21$ bits/pixel). (g) POT-FTC-VSQC-HBTC ($\Theta = 4.5$; $M_o = 1$; $K = 1$; $R_B = 1.05$ bits/pixel). (h) BTC (8×8 pixel segmentation; $R_B = 1.19$ bits/pixel).

ing very good coding fidelity performances. We can deduce that the efficiency of the POT followed by transform coding increases with the correlation coefficient between vertically adjacent pixels.

4) As we have already mentioned, within our scheme, the POT must be followed by an orthogonal transformation. We have proposed an improved version of the transform coding, called feedback transform coding (FTC). The FTC ensures a rigorous control of the root mean square error (rmse), by adjusting the number of nonzero transform coefficients of each picture vector so that the rmse is less than or equal to a

(d)

(g)

(e)

(h)

Fig. 6. (Continued)

(f)

Fig. 6. (Continued)

given threshold. The coding performances are functions of the threshold value, Θ.

5) The variants of the proposed method which use an adaptive estimation of the coefficient energy order for every strip of 16 lines (POT-FTC-E-OS and POT-FTC-E-HBTC) lead to high quality encoded pictures, but increase the processing time by the coefficient order estimation step. The coding variants without estimation of the coefficient energy order retain the DCT coefficients in the natural order of their indexes; these variants have the advantage of reducing substantially the computation time for a certain decreasing of picture quality.

6) The third coding stage called vertical subtraction of quantized coefficients (VSQC) is a simple variant of the hybrid coding; it encodes the exact differences between the quantized DCT coefficients of the same order belonging to adjacent lines. The VSQC has an adaptive character, the pattern of bit allocation being adaptively estimated for every picture to be coded.

7) The fourth stage of the proposed processing cascade represents a predictive refinement in the signal space, consisting of one of the two subsequent variants: a) overshoot suppression (OS), which detects and eliminates the individual reconstruction errors by transmitting the overshoot positions and values; b) hybrid block truncation coding (HBTC), which consists of transmitting a one bit quantization error pattern and a significant constant per line to preserve the first two sample moments for any picture line.

8) The OS variant performances are very sensitive to the value chosen for the OS threshold, δ. By decreasing δ, we obtain higher quality pictures, but the average number of overshoots per line increases, so that the coding efficiency becomes smaller. The greatest number of bits required by this stage corresponds to the encoding of the overshoot pattern (especially the overshoot positions). The variant leads to good quality images with an average bit rate of $(0.55-0.95)$ bits/pel.

9) The HBTC ensures the control not only of the peak error pixels, but also of all the pixels of the picture line, reconstructed after the previous processing stages; it provides a spatial homogeneousness of the error decrease, leading to very good quality images. It has the limitation that the average bit rate can not be decreased under about 1 bit/pel.

10) The quality of the best reconstructed pictures obtained by the algorithm presented in this paper is similar to that of the BTC and the compression is slightly better. We consider the proposed method to be an interesting and useful image coding algorithm, that may be improved and extended to obtain more efficient results.

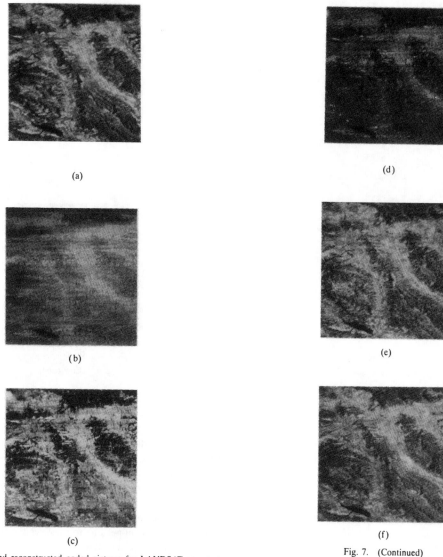

(a)

(b)

(c)

(d)

(e)

(f)

Fig. 7. Original and reconstructed coded-pictures for LANDSAT as a test image. (a) Original ($V_{pp} = 63$). (b) POT-FTC-VSQC ($\Theta = 4.3$; $M_o = 1$; $K = 1$; $R_B = 0.38$ bits/pixel). (c) POT-FTC-VSQC-OS ($\Theta = 4.3$; $M_o = 1$; $K = 1$; $\delta = 8$; $R_B = 0.93$ bits/pixel). (d) POT-FTC-VSQC-OS ($\Theta = 4.3$; $M_o = 1$; $K = 1$; $\delta = 12$; $R_B = 0.38$ bits/pixel). (e) **POT-FTC-VSQC-HBTC** ($\Theta = 4.5$; $M_o = 1$; $K = 1$; $R_B = 1.08$ bits/pixel). (f) BTC (8×8 pixel segmentation; $R_B = 1.19$ bits/pixel).

Fig. 7. (Continued)

11) We suggest the following ways of improving the data compression performances of our proposed method:

i) to compress the two-tone picture which corresponds either to the error matrix, $\{\gamma_{i,j}\}_{\substack{2 \leqslant i \leqslant 512 \\ 1 \leqslant j \leqslant 504}}$, for the HBTC variant, or to the two-tone image having as black pixels the overshoot ones, for the OS variant; to compress such error images, we can use typical techniques, suitable to black and white pictures [6], [7];

ii) to apply a sophisticated quantization scheme of the transform coefficient differences, corresponding to the stages FTC–VSQC.

iii) to use a refined scheme to quantize the overshoot values, for the OS variant.

ACKNOWLEDGMENT

The author would like to thank Mr. W. Prak and Mr. F. Preda for their contribution to the FORTRAN simulation program as well as Mr. N. Teodorescu and Mr. F. Talpes for the access to their image processing computer. The author also wishes to thank some of the referees for their comments.

REFERENCES

[1] A. N. Netravali and J. D. Limb, "Picture coding: A review," *Proc. IEEE*, vol. 68, pp. 366–406, Mar. 1980.
[2] A. K. Jain, "Image data compression: A review," *Proc. IEEE*, vol. 69, pp. 349–389, Mar. 1981.
[3] M. Kunt, A. Ikonomopoulos, and M. Kocher, "Second Generation Image-Coding Techniques," *Proc. IEEE*, vol. 73, pp. 549–574, Apr. 1985.
[4] A. Habibi, "Hybrid coding of pictorial data," *IEEE Trans. Commun.*, vol. COM-22, pp. 614–624, May 1974.
[5] A. Habibi, "An adaptive strategy for hybrid image coding," *IEEE Trans. Commun.*, vol. COM-29, pp. 1736–1740, Dec. 1981.

[6] A. N. Netravali, F. W. Mounts, and E. G. Bowen, "Ordering techniques for coding of two-tone facsimile pictures," *Bell Syst. Tech. J.*, vol. 55, pp. 1359–1552, Dec. 1976.

[7] A. N. Netravali and F. W. Mounts, "Ordering techniques for facsimile coding," *Proc. IEEE*, vol. 68, pp. 796–807, July 1980.

[8] M. Oliver, "An adaptive delta modulation with overshoot suppression for video signals," *IEEE Trans. Commun.*, vol. COM-21, pp. 243–247, Mar. 1973.

[9] L. Weis, I. M. Pazz, and D. L. Schilling, "Video encoding using an adaptive digital delta modulator with overshoot suppression," *IEEE Trans. Commun.*, vol. COM-23, pp. 905–920, Sept. 1975.

[10] E. J. Delp and O. R. Mitchell, "Image compression using block truncation coding," *IEEE Trans. Commun.*, vol. COM-27, pp. 1335–1342, Sept. 1979.

[11] V. E. Neagoe, "Predictive ordering and linear approximation for image data compression," *IEEE Trans. Commun.*, vol. 36, Oct. 1988.

[12] N. Ahmed and K. R. Rao, *Orthogonal Transforms for Digital Signal Processing*. New York: Springer-Verlag, 1975.

[13] J. Makhoul, "A fast cosine transform in one and two dimensions," *IEEE Trans. Acoust., Speech, Signal Processing*, vol. ASSP-28, pp. 27–34, Feb. 1980.

[14] S. Winograd, "On computing the discrete Fourier transform," *Math. Comput.*, vol. 32, pp. 175–199, Jan. 1978.

[15] C. S. Burrus and P. W. Eschenbacher, "An in-place in-order prime factor FFT algorithm," *IEEE Trans. Acoust., Speech, Signal Processing*, vol. ASSP-29, pp. 806–817, Aug. 1981.

[16] D. E. Knuth, *The Art of Computer Programming —Sorting and Searching*. Reading. MA: Addison-Wesley, 1973, vol. 3.

Hybrid vector quantization

Kuei-Ann Wen
Chung-Yen Lu
National Chiao Tung University
Institute of Electronics
1001 Ta Shieh Road
Hsinchu 300, Taiwan

Abstract. Vector quantization (VQ) is a powerful technique for low-bit-rate image coding. However, initial studies of image coding with VQ have revealed that VQ causes degradations, most notably around edges. Moreover, the computational complexity is high. Although a few algorithms have been developed to reduce edge degradation, such as block truncation coding (BTC) with VQ (BTC/VQ) or classified vector quantization, their compression ratios are not satisfactory. Discrete cosine transformation with VQ (DCT/VQ) has been applied to image compression, showing a high compression ratio, but the edge degradation problem still exists. We present an image compression algorithm that takes advantage of the merits of DCT/VQ and BTC/VQ to achieve a high-quality and low-bit-rate compression of images. High quality images can be achieved at rates of 0.34 to 0.46 bit/pixel.

Subject terms: visual communication; hybrid vector quantization; block truncation coding; discrete cosine transform.

Optical Engineering 32(7), 1496–1502 (July 1993).

1 Introduction

Natural images can be segmented into regions with widely varying perceptual importance. There are three types of regions in a typical image. The region in which the contrast between objects and background is high is categorized as the *edge*. Due to the high contrast, human eyes will naturally pay much attention to the edges. Thus, edge regions are very important for human perception. The second type of region is the *smooth* area, in which the brightness of neighboring pixels changes slowly. The third type of region is the *texture* part. Pixels in the texture region change slower than the edge region but faster than the smooth region. Typically, in a photograph such as "Lena" [see Fig. 5(a)], the boundary of the face is categorized as the edge part, the cheek is the smooth part, and the hair is viewed as the texture part. We propose a new and simple method for classifying the edge and smooth parts; and then we encode the image using block coding with discrete cosine transform/vector quantization (DCT/VQ)[1] and the modified block truncation coding/vector quantization (BTC/VQ) derived from BTC/VQ.[2]

In our coding algorithm, we use block coding and, according to the eye model, treat the texture part as a composition of some smooth blocks. We then devote our attention

to the coding of the edge part to maintain the high quality of the image. Thus, more bits are allocated for edge regions to reduce the edge degradation. On the other hand, the major compression of the image is dependent on coding the smooth part. Block coding algorithms are usually applied to one of three rudimentary coding techniques: transform coding (TC),[3] vector quantization (VQ),[4] and block truncation coding (BTC).[5] In each scheme, the block size is a parameter. The block size of TC and BTC are usually 8×8 and 4×4, respectively. The block sizes of VQ may vary for different applications. We chose a block size of 8×8 for the DCT and 4×4 for the BTC, and block sizes such as 3×1 and 4×4 were used for different applications. We proposed a hybrid VQ algorithm that combines DCT, BTC, and classified VQ (CVQ) to classify edges from smooth parts.

2 Hybrid VQ Algorithm

The hybrid VQ algorithm is illustrated in Fig. 1. The smooth part and the edge part are first distinguished and then coded with different approaches. Each 8×8 block is first transformed with a DCT to obtain important coefficients. Because we do not need all the coefficients in the DCT domain, we use a technique, called the partial discrete cosine transform (PDCT), to obtain four coefficients. These four coefficients represent the four lowest frequency coefficients, denoted as $d(0,0)$, $d(0,1)$, $d(1,0)$, and $d(1,1)$, respectively. Two of these four coefficients are used to classify each 8×8 block into either a smooth region or edge region. The decision is made

Paper VCI-20 received Oct. 15, 1992; revised manuscript received Feb. 18, 1993; accepted for publication March 11, 1993.
© 1993 Society of Photo-Optical Instrumentation Engineers. 0091-3286/93/$2.00.

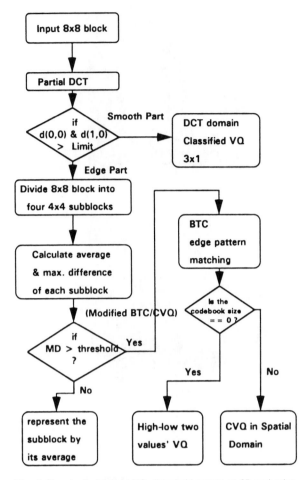

Fig. 1 Flowchart of hybrid VQ: threshold preset at 85 and edge region marked by the white line.

by comparing $d(0,1)$ and $d(1,0)$ with a threshold value. If both of them are less than the threshold value, the block is classified as a smooth block; otherwise, it is an edge block. Because these two coefficients represent the amount of brightness change in the horizontal and vertical direction, we choose the threshold experimentally. Typically, the threshold value is 85, which is determined by a set of training images shown in Fig. 2.

For smooth blocks, we use CVQ[6] to code three DCT coefficients, that is, $d(0,1)$, $d(1,0)$, and $d(1,1)$. For $d(0,0)$, 8 bits are allocated.

For edge blocks, we divide the 8×8 block into four 4×4 subblocks,[7] and process them sequentially. As illustrated in Fig. 1, the process for the 4×4 subblocks is denoted as modified BTC/VQ. The maximum difference, which is defined as the difference between the maximum and the minimum intensities in the subblock, is found first. Then, we compare the maximum difference with a preset threshold value, typically 18 (see Ref. 8), to determine whether or not the subblock is uniform (smooth). If the subblock is uniform, we use its average to represent all the intensities in the subblock; otherwise, we use the BTC technique to determine its edge pattern and compare the edge pattern with the edge pattern

table (shown in Table 1) to choose the nearest pattern. The edge pattern table represents normal edge patterns in normal images. Then, according to the index of its edge pattern, the VQ code book size is found by looking up a size table. The size table is obtained by calculating the frequency of the edge patterns in the training set images. The size is not fixed—its value may be 0, 16, 32, or 64. If the size is zero, it means that the edge pattern is seldom used. Thus, the 4×4 edge subblock is coded with VQ by using the two output values of BTC. Otherwise, we use VQ to code the subblock.

2.1 Smooth Area Processing

For processing the smooth region, we use the CVQ proposed in Ref. 6 to encode the three DCT coefficients. We classify the 8×8 block according to the sign of these three coefficients. In total, we have eight subcode books $(+ + +, + + -, + - +, + - -, - + +, - + -, - - +, - - -)$. Each code book size is 128 code words. We send the dc value, namely $d(0,0)$, with eight bits. Finally, we code the smooth block by 19 bits in total, which is the sum of the decision bit (1 bit), dc value (8 bits), classifying index (3 bits), and VQ index (7 bits) (e.g., $19 = 1 + 8 + 3 + 7$).

2.2 Edge Area Processing

The goal in processing the edge region is to obtain high-quality compressed images with edge preservation. Consider a 4×4 subblock of an image. It is desired that the 4×4 block be placed in one of two categories: either in the areas in which the intensities of the pixels in the block are relatively uniform or the block contains an edge.

Coding the image efficiently, without introducing unreasonable distortion, requires an auxiliary method for each case. For the first case, the block is represented by its average (mean), with 10 bits in total representing the sum of the decision bit (1 bit), decision bit (1 bit), and the bits representing the mean value (8 bits). For the second case, the block is coded with the modified BTC/VQ. The test to determine whether or not a block is relatively uniform (smooth) can be performed by using the mean (average) and the deviation, which is the difference between the maximum and the minimum intensities in the 4×4 block. This is compared to a preset threshold usually in the range of 13 to 50 (see Ref. 8). We set it to be 18. Higher threshold values result in more blockiness in the image. For blocks containing edges, we use look-up tables to represent cases of edges, in which the 16 binary bits of BTC are classified into 64 edge patterns. If the size is not equal to zero, we send the 4×4 block to the CVQ coder. The total number of bits for CVQ block coding is equal to the sum of the decision bit (1 bit), decision bit (1 bit), classification index (6 bits), and VQ index (4 to 6 bits). Note that only 32 cases are used for CVQ. The others are coded with high/low VQ that utilizes the high and low levels from the BTC method. In this case, the total bits for high/low block coding is equal to the sum of the decision bit (1 bit), decision bit (1 bit), classification index (6 bits), and high/low VQ index (8 bits). As a result, the total bits for an image = the number of smooth blocks (8×8) * bits of a smooth block coding + number of mean blocks (4×4) * bits of mean block coding + number of BTC/CVQ blocks * bits of a BTC/CVQ block coding + number of high/low blocks * bits of high/low block coding.

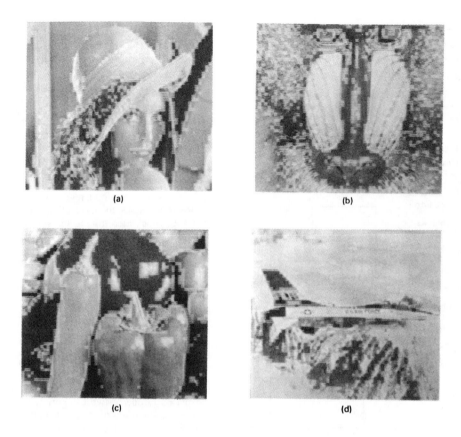

Fig. 2 Experimental images for the classification of the smooth and edge regions.

3 Elements of Hybrid VQ

Some key elements of the hybrid VQ, including PDCT, BTC, CVQ, and code-book training are described below.

3.1 *Partial Discrete Cosine Transform*

The partial discrete cosine transform (PDCT) is used to obtain the most important DCT coefficients. For 1-D PDCT, where $d0$ and $d1$ are the first two coefficients in the 1-D DCT domain:

$$d0 = \frac{\sqrt{2}}{4} * \sum_{k=0}^{7} I_k$$

$$d1 = \sum_{k=0}^{7} C_k * I_k \ ,$$

where I_k ($k = 0. . .7$) is the pixel intensity and $C_k(k = 0. . .7)$ is the 1-D DCT transform coefficient.

Each row of an 8×8 block is transformed with a 1-D PDCT. Then, the 1-D PDCT is applied to the first two columns. This procedure is called the 2-D PDCT, and is shown in Fig. 3.

3.2 *BTC and Edge Pattern Table*

BTC encodes every 4×4 block of the image by its average,

Table 1 Different edge patterns.

1110	1111	0011	0111	1111	1111	1100	0011
1100	1110	0001	0011	1111	1111	1100	0011
1000	1100	0000	0001	1100	0011	1111	1111
0000	1000	0000	0000	1100	0011	1111	1111
0011	0001	1100	1000	1111	0001	1000	1111
0110	0011	0110	1100	1000	0001	1000	0001
1100	0110	0011	0110	1000	0001	1000	0001
1000	1100	0001	0011	1000	1111	1111	0001
1111	1111	1111	0001	1111	1111	1111	1001
0000	1111	1111	0001	0011	1100	1111	1001
0000	0000	1111	0001	0011	1100	1001	1111
0000	0000	0000	0001	1111	1111	1001	1111
0011	0111	0110	0000	0010	0000	0100	0000
0011	0111	0110	1111	0100	0001	0010	1000
0011	0111	0110	1111	1000	0010	0001	0100
0011	0111	0110	0000	0000	0100	0000	0010

its variance, and by 16 binary bits. Each bit indicates whether or not the original intensity at a pixel is above the average intensity value. The two levels A and B are the averages of all the pixels whose intensities are above and below the mean, respectively. According to the 16 binary bits, appropriate VQ is found for each 4×4 block by matching the 16-bit pattern with an edge pattern table. The edge pattern table is shown in Table 1, which lists half of all the edge patterns. The other half is complementary to Table 1.

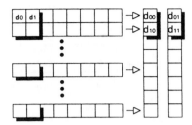

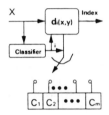

Fig. 3 Structure of the 2-D partial DCT.

Fig. 4 Classified VQ.

3.3 Classified VQ

The CVQ coder is depicted in Fig. 4. There are M classes. If the input X belongs to class i, the i'th subcode book Ci of size Ni is employed to encode X, by using the distortion measure $di(\ )$. In the hybrid VQ algorithm, we have two types of CVQ: one is 3×1 in the DCT domain and the other is 4×4 in the spatial domain. The classification for the former is decided by the signs of the three DCT coefficients. In this case, $M = 8$ and the size Ni of each subcode book Ci is 128. The latter is classified by the BTC 16 binary bits with an edge pattern table. There are 64 edge patterns, but $M = 32$ classes for this case. This is because some edge patterns are seldom used and are processed with block truncation coding with high/low VQ. The other patterns are fed to CVQ with the subcode book size varying from 16 to 64.

3.4 VQ Code-Book Training

The LBG algorithm[9] with least-squares-error measurement is used to train the VQ code book. The training image set is shown in Fig. 5.

(a)

(b)

(c)

(d)

Fig. 5 Training set images (512×512): (a) "Lena," (b) "baboon," (c) "peppers," and (d) "jet1."

Table 2 Results of training images coded by HVQ.

	PSNR	Compression rate	Total bits of encoded image	Amount of Smooth blocks (8x8)	Amount of edge subblocks (4x4 each)		
					Mean	High-Low	CVQ
Lena	29.52	20.10 (0.3979bpp)	104320	3196	506	116	2978
Baboon	21.74	17.69 (0.4523bpp)	118556	2756	101	512	4747
Peper	28.96	19.70 (0.4062bpp)	106476	3096	648	143	3209
Jet1	29.06	19.57 (0.4087bpp)	107138	3066	666	171	3283

Table 3 Results of nontraining images coded by HVQ.

	PSNR	Compression rate	Total bits of encoded image	Amount of Smooth blocks (8x8)	Amount of edge subblocks (4x4 each)		
					Mean	High-Low	CVQ
Rocket	33.05	23.39 (0.3421bpp)	89676	3667	462	86	1168
Bicycle	31.78	22.28 (0.3590bpp)	94116	3506	610	101	1649
Beach	29.89	20.99 (0.3811bpp)	99902	3327	455	165	2456
Vocano	29.24	23.73 (0.3371bpp)	88370	3739	170	107	1151
Model	28.56	20.56 (0.3891bpp)	102009	3287	244	218	2774
Girl	28.06	21.92 (0.3650bpp)	95682	3488	339	140	1953

4 Experimental Results

The peak signal-to-noise ratio (PSNR) and the compression rates are shown in Tables 2 and 3. The formula of PSNR is

$$PSNR = 10 \, \log_{10} \frac{255^2}{Mean \; Square \; Error} .$$

The original images are shown in Figs. 5 and 6 and the compressed images are shown in Figs. 7 and 8. These show that, without entropy coding and with purely hybrid VQ, the image quality at bit rates ranging from 0.34 to 0.46 bit/pixel is high.

5 Conclusion

The hybrid VQ algorithm is a technique combining DCT, BTC, and CVQ for image compression. This algorithm takes advantage of DCT/VQ and modified BTC/VQ to achieve a high compression ratio and images of high-quality. The key element is the classification of the edge and smooth parts. We use the characteristics of each part to obtain adequate compression so that there are more bits for the edge region and less bits for the smooth region. The results from the hybrid VQ are shown at bit rates ranging from 0.34 to 0.46 bit/pixel with high quality.

(a)   (b)   (c)

(d)   (e)   (f)

Fig. 6 Nontraining images (512×512): (a) "rocket," (b) "bicycle," (c) "beach," (d) "volcano," (e) "model," and (f) "girl."

Fig. 7 Compression images: (a) "Lena," (b) "baboon," (c) "peppers," and (d) "jet1."

Fig. 8 Compression images: (a) "rocket," (b) "bicycle," (c) "beach," (d) "volcano," (e) "model," and (f) "girl."

279

Acknowledgment

This work was sponsored by the National Science Council under the project "VLSI Design for HDTV Signal Processing."

References

1. T. Satio, H. Takeo, K. Aizawa, H. Harashima, and H. Miyakawa, "Adaptive discrete cosine transform image coding using gain/shape vector quantizers," in *Proc. ICASSP '86*, pp. 129–132 (1986).
2. N. Efrati, H. Licitin, and H. B. Mitchell, "Classified block truncation coding-vector quantization: an edge sensitive image compression algorithm," *Sig. Process. Image Commun.* **3**, 275–283 (1991).
3. R. Clarke, "Transform coding of images," Academic Press, New York (1985).
4. N. M. Nasrabadi and R. A. King, "Image coding using vector quantization: a review," *IEEE Trans. Commun.* **COM-27**, 957–971 (1979).
5. E. J. Delp and R. Mitchell, "Image compression using block truncation coding," *IEEE Trans. Commun.* **8**, 1245–1254 (Aug. 1991).
6. B. Ramamurthi and A. Gersho, "Classified vector quantization of images," *IEEE Trans. Commun.* **COM-34**(11), 1105–1115 (Nov. 1986).
7. J. Vaisey and A. Gersho, "Image compression with variable block size segmentation," *IEEE Trans. Sig. Process.* **8**, 2040–2060 (Aug. 1992).
8. P. Nasiopoulos, R. K. Ward, and D. J. Morse, "Adaptive compression coding," *IEEE Trans. Commun.* **8**, 1245–1254 (Aug. 1991).
9. Y. Linde, A. Buzo, and R. M. Gray, "An algorithm for vector quantizer design," *IEEE Trans. Commun.* **COM-28**(1), 84–95 (Jan. 1980).

Chapter 8
Desirable Developments

The future scope and potential of BTC in the data compression arena can be succinctly stated: Hybrids are the way to go! The merits of the BTC approach itself were summarized at the end of Chapter 1 and need not be repeated here, except to say that its ease of implementation relative to most other techniques is beyond question and, when combined with other techniques, BTC can meet desired compression and fidelity requirements without unduly adding to the complexity level. As the papers presented in the last chapter dramatically show, hybrids offer the most potential since they synergistically combine the advantages of different classes of techniques, such as transform techniques, with special schemes, such as BTC, and quantization tools, such as vector quantization. One of the virgin avenues in this arena is the hybridization of BTC with wavelet transforms. This is an area worthy of investigation along the lines of other BTC-based hybrids such as those of Wu and Coll [B54] and Wen and Lu [B73] presented in the previous chapter. This avenue is currently under investigation by the author, whose research is still in early stages and will be reported elsewhere in due course. Further evidence of the hybrid approach as the way of the future is the advent of patents in the area, an example of which is a recent one by Rodriguez, Hancock, and Pietras.[1] The patent is described as a set of processes built and integrated around BTC and VPIC. The impetus to these developments has been the exploding developments in the area of multi-media applications.

Hybrids are also highly appealing in the domain of color imagery data compression in view of the multidimensional structure of the data set—a natural field for transform approaches. One could also go through the list of potential avenues listed in these papers and offer a compilation of sorts on these topics for further research. It is also possible to add to such a list by examining the scope for cross-fertilization of ideas, which is but another boost to the hybrid concept. For example, vector quantization in the context of AMBTC instead of the classical BTC deserves attention. One might also mention in this context the desirability of investigating the relationship of VPIC/VQ/BTC hybrids and wavelet/subband/pyramid transform coding.

As can be gleaned by a careful scrutiny of the bibliography in Chapter 1, the two areas that have received the most attention in recent years in the data compression field are vector quantization and wavelet transforms. While a review of the vector quantization field appeared in 1988, a new detailed

---

[1]A.A. Rodriguez, S.M. Hancock, and M.A. Pietras, International Business Machines, Inc., Armonk, N.Y. "Hybrid Video Compression System and Method Capable of Software-Only Decompression in Selected Multimedia Systems," U.S. Patent Number 05392072, February 21, 1995.

review of the these two areas as applied to data compression (similar to the way BTC has been covered in this book) would be useful in identifying additional avenues for developing effective hybrids among these three approaches. To a certain extent these developments have gained prominence since the JPEG standards were first defined, and hence are not as effectively covered in the JPEG-related studies.

At a more detailed level, one could point out numerous specific investigations that would be helpful, such as a study of the effect of the number of SAR looks on BTC performance in the context of SAR imagery data compression problems. However, formulation of such an exhaustive list of desirable developments is beyond the scope of this book, as defined at the outset.

Learning Resources
Centre

About the Author

Belur V. Dasarathy is a senior principal engineer at Dynetics, Inc. in Huntsville, Alabama. He is currently engaged in research and development in the areas of sensor fusion, pattern recognition, image analysis, fuzzy logic, neural nets, data compression, machine intelligence, and related topics for the design and development of automated intelligent decision systems as applied to a broad spectrum of multispectral and multisensor environments arising in various strategic and tactical DoD applications. His more than two decades of experience include NASA and other civilian (commercial and biomedical) applications of these technologies as well. Previously, as senior technical manager at Intergraph Corporation, he was responsible for the design and development of their first commercial symbol/character recognition (SCR) and image processing (IDEALS) systems as well as a target recognition system (TARECS) for MICOM.

Dasarathy earned his PhD in engineering from the Indian Institute of Science, Bangalore, India, where he later served as a founding member of the faculty of the School of Automation. His other professional associations include Southern Methodist University in Dallas, Texas, and Computer Sciences Corporation in Huntsville, Alabama, where he worked on multispectral remote sensing applications. He has also served as an adjunct professor at the Department of Computer Sciences at the University of Alabama in Huntsville for several years. He was recognized and honored as a "Professional of the Year" in 1994 by the Huntsville Area Technical Societies (HATS) organization.

Dasarathy has previously authored two other IEEE Computer Society Press books, *Nearest Neighbor (NN) Norms: NN Pattern Classification Techniques* and *Decision Fusion*. He is now working on his fourth book with the IEEE Computer Society Press on "learning in IQ constrained environments." Dasarathy has published 140 technical papers in his various fields of interest and has been a reviewer for numerous international journals including several IEEE publications in these areas. He is a senior member of the IEEE and he chaired the IEEE Huntsville Section during 1992–1993. In previous years, he has served as the group's vice-chair and program chair, as well as the editor of the section newsletter, LIVEWIRE.

Earlier, Dasarathy was the chair of the Huntsville IEEE Computer Faire and the Rocket City seminars. His biographical listings include *Who's Who in Computer Graphics,* Marquis 1984; *Personalities of the South*, American Biographical Institute, 1986; *Who's Who in Technology Today*, Dick Publishing, 5th edition; *Who's Who in the*

South and Southwest, 22nd edition, 1991; and *The Official Registry of Who's Who of American Business Leaders,* 1991 edition.

Dasarathy has been invited to be a guest editor for a special issue on sensor fusion of the SPIE Journal *Optical Engineering,* scheduled for release in March of 1996.

IEEE COMPUTER SOCIETY
50 YEARS OF SERVICE • 1946-1996

http://www.computer.org

Press Activities Board

IEEE Computer Society Press Publications

The world-renowned Computer Society Press publishes, promotes, and distributes a wide variety of authoritative computer science and engineering texts. These books are available in two formats: 100 percent original material by authors preeminent in their field who focus on relevant topics and cutting-edge research, and reprint collections consisting of carefully selected groups of previously published papers with accompanying original introductory and explanatory text.

Submission of proposals: For guidelines and information on CS Press books, send e-mail to csbooks@computer.org or write to the Acquisitions Editor, IEEE Computer Society Press, P.O. Box 3014, 10662 Los Vaqueros Circle, Los Alamitos, CA 90720-1264. Telephone +1 714-821-8380. FAX +1 714-761-1784.

IEEE Computer Society Press Proceedings

The Computer Society Press also produces and actively promotes the proceedings of more than 130 acclaimed international conferences each year in multimedia formats that include hard and softcover books, CD-ROMs, videos, and on-line publications.

For information on CS Press proceedings, send e-mail to csbooks@computer.org or write to Proceedings, IEEE Computer Society Press, P.O. Box 3014, 10662 Los Vaqueros Circle, Los Alamitos, CA 90720-1264. Telephone +1 714-821-8380. FAX +1 714-761-1784.

Additional information regarding the Computer Society, conferences and proceedings, CD-ROMs, videos, and books can also be accessed from our web site at www.computer.org.

3/11/96